FOURTH EDITION

Henretta Brody Ware Johnson

Selected Historical Documents to Accompany

America's History

Volume 2 SINCE 1865

Samuel T. McSeveney

Vanderbilt University

Bedford/St. Martin's

Boston • New York

For information, write:
Bedford/St. Martin's, 75 Arlington Street, Boston, MA 02116   (617-399-4000)

ISBN: 0-312-19387-4

Preface

Volume 2 of the *Selected Historical Documents* brings together over 190 primary source documents to enrich the study of *America's History*. It is our goal that this reader enhance the educational experience of both students and instructors by adding breadth and depth to many facets of American history that deserve a closer look. In addition to key speeches, laws, contemporary accounts, letters, oral histories, autobiographies, and other written documents, the collection includes political cartoons, statistical tables, and figures that shed light on all aspects of political, social, economic, and cultural history.

Following the chapter organization of *America's History*, the documents in each chapter of this reader are grouped into three or four sets corresponding to the main headings of the textbook chapter. Each set begins with an introduction that places that group of documents in their wider historical context. The individual documents follow, each with its own headnote and questions, allowing instructors the flexibility to focus on an individual document or explore a particular section in depth. The wide array of readings enriches a student's learning experience, offering interesting comparisons and contrasts to specific features in the textbook itself. Many of the document sets also present pieces with opposing views meant to stimulate debate in the university classroom. The document set concludes with Questions for Further Thought designed to help students recognize connections among the documents and realize how the documents illustrate or exemplify larger themes.

Having incurred numerous debts during the preparation of this volume, I wish to express my gratitude to: Katherine Kurzman, Executive Editor, history and political science; Edith Trost Kirkland, sales representative; Emily Berleth, production editor; and, above all, Jennifer Rush, development editor, Bedford/St. Martin's; the editors of prior editions of the reader for providing the foundations on which this version rests; Dr. Craig Kaplowitz, now of Middle Tennessee State University, my indefatigable research assistant; my colleagues—David Carlton, Thomas Schwartz, Jimmie Franklin, Elizabeth Rose, Colin Talley, Matthew Ramsey, Arleen Tuchman, Jane Landers, and Marshall Eakin—for their suggestions; Vicki Crowthers, Lori Cohen, and Brenda Hummel in my department office for their labors; my survey course students, from whom I have learned much over the years.

Samuel T. McSeveney

Contents

PART 5

The Modern State and Society, 1914–1945

★   ★   ★

CHAPTER 15

Reconstruction, 1865–1877

★   ★   ★

Presidential Reconstruction

Planning for Reconstruction began to take shape in December 1863, when President Lincoln laid out his ideas in a presidential proclamation. His pronouncement opened a debate that became the central issue in American politics for more than a decade. The power struggle that followed led to a collision between the executive and legislative branches of government, the displacement of presidential Reconstruction by congressional Reconstruction, and the first impeachment of a president of the United States.

Reconstruction involved fundamental questions. To begin with, who had the primary responsibility for Reconstruction—the president or Congress? Believing that rebuilding the Union was simply a matter of suppressing "rebels" under presidential war powers, Lincoln's successor, Andrew Johnson, took the early initiative, establishing provisional governments that would purge secessionists from southern leadership, repudiate secession and Confederate debts, and recognize the end of slavery (Document 15-1). Beyond these measures Johnson was unwilling to go: a former southern slaveholder himself, he had no sympathy for blacks; in addition, as a southern Democrat he was firmly devoted to states' rights. Although Johnson was satisfied with these measures, northerners were hearing increasingly alarming reports that white southerners were refusing to recognize their defeat; engaging in brutal reprisals against blacks, northern whites, and southern unionists; and enacting "black codes" that appeared to be backdoor attempts to restore slavery (Documents 15-2 and 15-3). A rising tide of northern outrage pushed the Republican-dominated Congress toward the views of the Republicans' Radical wing; in 1866, over the violent opposition of President Johnson, Congress undertook an unprecedented extension of federal power. With the Civil Rights Act of 1866 (Document 15-4) and the Fourteenth Amendment, Congress declared for the first time that federal citizenship was not restricted by race, and guaranteeing to all citizens the "equal protection of the laws," even if it required federal intervention into the affairs of a state. The outcome of the Civil War was beginning to force fundamental changes in the constitutional character of the American political system, with profound consequences for subsequent American history.

15-1   Plan of Reconstruction (1865)

Andrew Johnson

As the Civil War came to an end, Lincoln's successor, Andrew Johnson, moved quickly to implement his plan for Reconstruction, which differed little from Lincoln's plan (see text pp. 478–479). Johnson acted largely on his own, without much consultation with Congress. In particular, he ignored Congress's demand for a harsher policy toward the former Confederate states.

On May 29, 1865, President Johnson set forth his plan in two presidential proclamations. In the first he promised amnesty to all rebels who would swear an oath of future loyalty, except for certain high-ranking officials and officers of the Confederacy, who had to petition for a presidential pardon.

In the second proclamation, which appears below, Johnson announced the creation of a provisional government for North Carolina. After appointing William W. Holden, a North Carolina Unionist who had opposed secession, as the provisional governor, Johnson described the means by which that state could be restored to the Union. Johnson intended this plan to serve as a model for the other seceded states, hoping that all could be restored before Congress reconvened in December.

Johnson's approach to Reconstruction was very different from that proposed by the Wade-Davis bill (see text p. 478), which stipulated that more than 50 percent of the voters who were qualified in 1860 in each southern state had to be able to prove their past loyalty and swear future loyalty to the Union. Johnson and Congress also differed about allowing former Confederate leaders to participate in Reconstruction and in government. Presidents Lincoln and Johnson envisioned temporary disqualification; Congress favored permanent exclusion.

Source: James D. Richardson, ed., *A Compilation of the Messages and Papers of the Presidents* (Washington, D.C.: U.S. Government Printing Office, 1896–1899), 6: 312–313.

Whereas the fourth section of the fourth article of the Constitution of the United States declares that the United States shall guarantee to every State in the Union a republican form of government and shall protect each of them against invasion and domestic violence; and

Whereas the President of the United States is by the Constitution made Commander in Chief of the Army and Navy, as well as chief civil executive officer of the United States, and is bound by solemn oath faithfully to execute the office of President of the United States and to take care that the laws be faithfully executed; and

Whereas the rebellion which has been waged by a portion of the people of the United States against the properly constituted authorities of the Government . . . and

Whereas it becomes necessary and proper to carry out and enforce the obligations of the United States to the people of North Carolina in securing them in the enjoyment of a republican form of government:

Now, therefore, in obedience to the high and solemn duties imposed upon me by the Constitution of the United States and for the purpose of enabling the loyal people of said State to organize a State government whereby justice may be established, domestic tranquillity insured, and loyal citizens protected in all their rights of life, liberty, and property, I, Andrew Johnson, President of the United States and Commander in Chief of the Army and Navy of the United States, do hereby appoint William W. Holden provisional governor of the State of North Carolina, whose duty it shall be, at the earliest practicable period, to prescribe such rules and regulations as may be necessary and proper for convening a convention composed of delegates to be chosen by that portion of the people of said State who are loyal to the United States, and no others, for the purpose of altering or amending the constitution thereof, and with authority to exercise within the limits of said State all the powers necessary and proper to enable such loyal people of the State of North Carolina to restore said State to its constitutional relations to the Federal Government and to present such a republican form of State government as will entitle the State to the guaranty of the United States therefor and its people to protection by the United States against invasion, insurrection, and domestic violence: *Provided*, That in any election that may be hereafter held for choosing delegates to any State convention as aforesaid no person shall be qualified as an elector or shall be eligible as a member of such convention unless he shall have previously taken and subscribed the oath of amnesty as set forth in the President's proclamation of May 29, A.D. 1865, and is a voter qualified as prescribed by the constitution and laws of the State of North Carolina in force immediately before the 20th day of May, A.D. 1861, the date of the so-called ordinance of secession; and the said convention, when convened, or the legislature that may be thereafter assembled, will prescribe the qualification of electors and the eligibility of persons to hold office under the constitution and laws of the State—a power the people of the several States composing the Federal Union have rightfully exercised from the origin of the Government to the present time.

And I do hereby direct—

. . . That the military commander of the department and all officers and persons in the military and naval service aid and assist the said provisional governor in carrying into effect this proclamation; and they are enjoined to abstain from in any way hindering, impeding, or discouraging the loyal people from the organization of a State government as herein authorized. . . .

Questions

1. According to President Johnson, what was his authority for this proclamation? Who was to be in charge of the process?
2. What steps did Johnson prescribe for restoring civil government in North Carolina?
3. Under Johnson's plan, would freedmen be able to vote? (*Hint*: See the section starting "*Provided*.")

15-2   Report on Conditions in the South (1865)

Carl Schurz

By December 1865, when Congress was gathering in Washington for a new session, Johnson had declared that all the Confederate states but Texas had met his requirements for restoration. Newly elected senators and congressmen from the former Confederacy had arrived to take seats in Congress.

Johnson's efforts to restore the South stalled. Congress exercised its constitutional authority to deny seats to delegations from the South and launched an investigation into conditions there. In response to a Senate resolution requesting "information in relation to the States of the Union lately in rebellion," Johnson painted a rosy picture: "In 'that portion of the Union lately in rebellion' the aspect of affairs is more promising than, in view of all the circumstances, could well have been expected. The people throughout the entire south evince a laudable desire to renew their allegiance to the government, and to repair the devastations of war by a prompt and cheerful return to peaceful pursuits. An abiding faith is entertained that their actions will conform to their professions, and that, in acknowledging the supremacy of the Constitution and the laws of the United States, their loyalty will be unreservedly given to the government, whose leniency they cannot fail to appreciate, and whose fostering care will soon restore them to a condition of prosperity. It is true, that in some of the States the demoralizing effects of war are to be seen in occasional disorders, but these are local in character, not frequent in occurrence, and are rapidly disappearing as the authority of civil law is extended and sustained."

Johnson's message to the Senate was accompanied by a report from Major General Carl Schurz. Among the subjects on which Schurz reported were whether southern whites had accepted defeat and emancipation, and whether ex-slaves and southern Unionists were safe in the South and were receiving fair treatment. Schurz's report was apparently largely ignored by President Johnson, who had assigned him to make the report but was not happy with what he said.

Schurz went to considerable lengths to get an accurate reading of attitudes in the South. He tried to get a representative sample of people to interview in his three-month tour of portions of South Carolina, Georgia, Alabama, Mississippi, and Louisiana and gathered documentary evidence as well as interviews. Then he tried to analyze his findings carefully and make recommendations on the basis of those findings. Clearly, he believed that Reconstruction in the South involved more than the restoration of civil government.

Source: U.S. Congress, Senate, 39th Cong., 1st sess., 1865, Ex. Doc. No. 2, 1–5, 8, 36–39, 41–44.

SIR: . . . You informed me that your "policy of reconstruction" was merely experimental, and that you would change it if the experiment did not lead to satisfactory results. To aid you in forming your conclusions upon this point I understood to be the object of my mission, . . .

CONDITION OF THINGS IMMEDIATELY AFTER THE CLOSE OF THE WAR

In the development of the popular spirit in the south since the close of the war two well-marked periods can be distinguished. The first commences with the sudden collapse of the confederacy and the dispersion of its armies, and the second with the first proclamation indicating the "reconstruction policy" of the government. . . . When the news of Lee's and Johnston's surrenders burst upon the southern country the general consternation was extreme. People held their breath, indulging in the wildest apprehensions as to what was now to come. . . . Prominent Unionists told me that persons who for four years had scorned to recognize them on the street approached them with smiling faces and both hands extended. Men of standing in the political world expressed serious doubts as to whether the rebel States would ever again occupy their position as States in the Union, or be governed as conquered provinces. The public mind was so despondent that if readmission at some future time under whatever conditions had been promised, it would then have been looked upon as a favor. The most uncompromising rebels prepared for leaving the country. The masses remained in a state of fearful expectancy. . . .

Such was, according to the accounts I received, the character of that first period. The worst apprehensions were gradually relieved as day after day went by without bringing the disasters and inflictions which had been vaguely anticipated, until at last the appearance of the North Carolina proclamation substituted new hopes for them. The development of this second period I was called

upon to observe on the spot, and it forms the main subject of this report.

RETURNING LOYALTY

. . . [T]he white people at large being, under certain conditions, charged with taking the preliminaries of "reconstruction" into their hands, the success of the experiment depends upon the spirit and attitude of those who either attached themselves to the secession cause from the beginning, or, entertaining originally opposite views, at least followed its fortunes from the time that their States had declared their separation from the Union. . . .

I may group the southern people into four classes, each of which exercises an influence upon the development of things in that section:

1. Those who, although having yielded submission to the national government only when obliged to do so, have a clear perception of the irreversible changes produced by the war, and honestly endeavor to accommodate themselves to the new order of things. Many of them are not free from traditional prejudice but open to conviction, and may be expected to act in good faith whatever they do. This class is composed, in its majority, of persons of mature age—planters, merchants, and professional men; some of them are active in the reconstruction movement, but boldness and energy are, with a few individual exceptions, not among their distinguishing qualities.

2. Those whose principal object is to have the States without delay restored to their position and influence in the Union and the people of the States to the absolute control of their home concerns. They are ready, in order to attain that object, to make any ostensible concession that will not prevent them from arranging things to suit their taste as soon as that object is attained. This class comprises a considerable number, probably a large majority, of the professional politicians who are extremely active in the reconstruction movement. They are loud in their praise of

the President's reconstruction policy, and clamorous for the withdrawal of the federal troops and the abolition of the Freedmen's Bureau.

3. The incorrigibles, who still indulge in the swagger which was so customary before and during the war, and still hope for a time when the southern confederacy will achieve its independence. This class consists mostly of young men, and comprises the loiterers of the towns and the idlers of the country. They persecute Union men and negroes whenever they can do so with impunity, insist clamorously upon their "rights," and are extremely impatient of the presence of the federal soldiers. A good many of them have taken the oaths of allegiance and amnesty, and associated themselves with the second class in their political operations. This element is by no means unimportant; it is strong in numbers, deals in brave talk, addresses itself directly and incessantly to the passions and prejudices of the masses, and commands the admiration of the women.

4. The multitude of people who have no definite ideas about the circumstances under which they live and about the course they have to follow; whose intellects are weak, but whose prejudices and impulses are strong, and who are apt to be carried along by those who know how to appeal to the latter. . . .

FEELING TOWARDS THE SOLDIERS AND THE PEOPLE OF THE NORTH

. . . [U]pon the whole, the soldier of the Union is still looked upon as a stranger, an intruder—as the "Yankee," "the enemy." . . .

It is by no means surprising that prejudices and resentments, which for years were so assiduously cultivated and so violently inflamed, should not have been turned into affection by a defeat; nor are they likely to disappear as long as the southern people continue to brood over their losses and misfortunes. They will gradually subside when those who entertain them cut resolutely loose from the past and embark in a career of new activity on a common field with those whom they have so long considered their enemies. . . . [A]s long as these feelings exist in their present strength, they will hinder the growth of that reliable kind of loyalty which springs from the heart and clings to the country in good and evil fortune.

SITUATION OF UNIONISTS

. . . It struck me soon after my arrival in the south that the known Unionists—I mean those who during the war had been to a certain extent identified with the national cause—were not in communion with the leading social and political circles; and the further my observations extended the clearer it became to me that their existence in the south was of a rather precarious nature. . . . Even Governor [William L.] Sharkey, in the course of a conversation I had with him in the presence of Major General Osterhaus, ad-

mitted that, if our troops were then withdrawn, the lives of northern men in Mississippi would not be safe. . . . [General Osterhaus said]: "There is no doubt whatever that the state of affairs would be intolerable for all Union men, all recent immigrants from the north, and all negroes, the moment the protection of the United States troops were withdrawn." . . .

NEGRO INSURRECTIONS AND ANARCHY

. . . [I do] not deem a negro insurrection probable as long as the freedmen were assured of the direct protection of the national government. Whenever they are in trouble, they raise their eyes up to that power, and although they may suffer, yet, as long as that power is visibly present, they continue to hope. But when State authority in the south is fully restored, the federal forces withdrawn, and the Freedmen's Bureau abolished, the colored man will find himself turned over to the mercies of those whom he does not trust. If then an attempt is made to strip him again of those rights which he justly thought he possessed, he will be apt to feel that he can hope for no redress unless he procure it himself. If ever the negro is capable of rising, he will rise then. . . .

There is probably at the present moment no country in the civilized world which contains such an accumulation of anarchical elements as the south. The strife of the antagonistic tendencies here described is aggravated by the passions inflamed and the general impoverishment brought about by a long and exhaustive war, and the south will have to suffer the evils of anarchical disorder until means are found to effect a final settlement of the labor question in accordance with the logic of the great revolution.

THE TRUE PROBLEM—DIFFICULTIES AND REMEDIES

In seeking remedies for such disorders, we ought to keep in view, above all, the nature of the problem which is to be solved. As to what is commonly termed "reconstruction," it is not only the political machinery of the States and their constitutional relations to the general government, but the whole organism of southern society that must be reconstructed, or rather constructed anew, so as to bring it in harmony with the rest of American society. The difficulties of this task are not to be considered overcome when the people of the south take the oath of allegiance and elect governors and legislatures and members of Congress, and militia captains. That this would be done had become certain as soon as the surrenders of the southern armies had made further resistance impossible, and nothing in the world was left, even to the most uncompromising rebel, but to submit or to emigrate. It was also natural that they should avail themselves of every chance offered them to resume control of their home affairs and to regain their influence in the Union. But this can hardly be called the first step towards the solution of the true problem, and it is a fair question to ask, whether the hasty gratification of their desire to resume such control would not create new embarrassments.

The true nature of the difficulties of the situation is this: The general government of the republic has, by proclaiming the emancipation of the slaves, commenced a great social revolution in the south, but has, as yet, not completed it. Only the negative part of it is accomplished. The slaves are emancipated in point of form, but free labor has not yet been put in the place of slavery in point of fact. And now, in the midst of this critical period of transition, the power which originated the revolution is expected to turn over its whole future development to another power which from the beginning was hostile to it and has never yet entered into its spirit, leaving the class in whose favor it was made completely without power to protect itself and to take an influential part in that development. The history of the world will be searched in vain for a proceeding similar to this which did not lead either to a rapid and violent reaction, or to the most serious trouble and civil disorder. It cannot be said that the conduct of the southern people since the close of the war has exhibited such extraordinary wisdom and self-abnegation as to make them an exception to the rule.

In my despatches from the south I repeatedly expressed the opinion that the people were not yet in a frame of mind to legislate calmly and understandingly upon the subject of free negro labor. And this I reported to be the opinion of some of our most prominent military commanders and other observing men. It is, indeed, difficult to imagine circumstances more unfavorable for the development of a calm and unprejudiced public opinion than those under which the southern people are at present laboring. The war has not only defeated their political aspirations, but it has broken up their whole social organization. . . .

In which direction will these people be most apt to turn their eyes? Leaving the prejudice of race out of the question, from early youth they have been acquainted with but one system of labor, and with that one system they have been in the habit of identifying all their interests. They know of no way to help themselves but the one they are accustomed to. . . .

It is certain that every success of free negro labor will augment the number of its friends, and disarm some of the prejudices and assumptions of its opponents. I am convinced one good harvest made by unadulterated free labor in the south would have a far better effect than all the oaths that have been taken, and all the ordinances that have as yet been passed by southern conventions. But how can such a result be attained? The facts enumerated in this report, as well as the news we receive from the south from day to day, must make it evident to every unbiased observer that unadulterated free labor cannot be had at present, unless the national government holds its protective and controlling hand over it. . . . One reason why the southern people are so slow in accommodating themselves to the new order of things is, that they confidently expect soon to be permit-

ted to regulate matters according to their own notions. Every concession made to them by the government has been taken as an encouragement to persevere in this hope, and, unfortunately for them, this hope is nourished by influences from other parts of the country. Hence their anxiety to have their State governments restored *at once,* to have the troops withdrawn, and the Freedmen's Bureau abolished, although a good many discerning men know well that, in view of the lawless spirit still prevailing, it would be far better for them to have the general order of society firmly maintained by the federal power until things have arrived at a final settlement. Had, from the beginning, the conviction been forced upon them that the adulteration of the new order of things by the admixture of elements belonging to the system of slavery would under no circumstances be permitted, a much larger number would have launched their energies into the new channel, and, seeing that they could do "no better," faithfully co-operated with the government. It is hope which fixes them in their perverse notions. That hope nourished or fully gratified, they will persevere in the same direction. That hope destroyed, a great many will, by the force of necessity, at once accommodate themselves to the logic of the change. If, therefore, the national government firmly and unequivocally announces its policy not to give up the control of the free-labor reform until it is finally accomplished, the progress of that reform will undoubtedly be far more rapid and far less difficult than it will be if the attitude of the government is such as to permit contrary hopes to be indulged in. . . .

IMMIGRATION [AND CAPITAL]

[The south would benefit] from immigration of northern people and Europeans. . . . The south needs capital. But capital is notoriously timid and averse to risk. . . . Capitalists will be apt to consider—and they are by no means wrong in doing so—that no safe investments can be made in the south as long as southern society is liable to be convulsed by anarchical disorders. No greater encouragement can, therefore, be given to capital to transfer itself to the south than the assurance that the government will continue to control the development of the new social system in the late rebel States until such dangers are averted by a final settlement of things upon a thorough free-labor basis.

How long the national government should continue that control depends upon contingencies. It ought to cease as soon as its objects are attained; and its objects will be attained sooner and with less difficulty if nobody is permitted to indulge in the delusion that it will cease *before* they are attained. This is one of the cases in which a determined policy can accomplish much, while a half-way policy is liable to spoil things already accomplished. . . .

NEGRO SUFFRAGE

It would seem that the interference of the national authority in the home concerns of the southern States would be rendered less necessary, and the whole problem of political and social reconstruction be much simplified, if, while the masses lately arrayed against the government are permitted to vote, the large majority of those who were always loyal, and are naturally anxious to see the free labor problem successfully solved, were not excluded from all influence upon legislation. In all questions concerning the Union, the national debt, and the future social organization of the south, the feelings of the colored man are naturally in sympathy with the views and aims of the national government. While the southern white fought against the Union, the negro did all he could to aid it; while the southern white sees in the national government his conqueror, the negro sees in it his protector; while the white owes to the national debt his defeat, the negro owes to it his deliverance; while the white considers himself robbed and ruined by the emancipation of the slaves, the negro finds in it the assurance of future prosperity and happiness. In all the important issues the negro would be led by natural impulse to forward the ends of the government, and by making his influence, as part of the voting body, tell upon the legislation of the States, render the interference of the national authority less necessary.

As the most difficult of the pending questions are intimately connected with the status of the negro in southern society, it is obvious that a correct solution can be more easily obtained if he has a voice in the matter. In the right to vote he would find the best permanent protection against oppressive class-legislation, as well as against individual persecution. The relations between the white and black races, even if improved by the gradual wearing off of the present animosities, are likely to remain long under the troubling influence of prejudice. It is a notorious fact that the rights of a man of some political power are far less exposed to violation than those of one who is, in matters of public interest, completely subject to the will of others. . . .

In discussing the matter of negro suffrage I deemed it my duty to confine myself strictly to the practical aspects of the subject. I have, therefore, not touched its moral merits nor discussed the question whether the national government is competent to enlarge the elective franchise in the States lately in rebellion by its own act; I deem it proper, however, to offer a few remarks on the assertion frequently put forth, that the franchise is likely to be extended to the colored man by the voluntary action of the southern whites themselves. My observation leads me to a contrary opinion. Aside from a very few enlightened men, I found but one class of people in favor of the enfranchisement of the blacks: it was the class of Unionists who found themselves politically ostracised and looked upon the enfranchisement of the loyal negroes as the salvation of the whole loyal element. But their numbers and influence are sadly insufficient to secure such a result. The masses are strongly opposed to colored suffrage; anybody that dares to advocate it is stigmatized as a dangerous fanatic; nor do I deem it probable that in the ordinary course of things prejudices will wear off to such an extent as to make it a popular measure. . . .

DEPORTATION OF THE FREEDMEN

. . . [T]he true problem remains, not how to remove the colored man from his present field of labor, but how to make him, where he is, a true freeman and an intelligent and useful citizen. The means are simple: protection by the government until his political and social status enables him to protect himself, offering to his legitimate ambition the stimulant of a perfectly fair chance in life, and granting to him the rights which in every just organization of society are coupled with corresponding duties.

CONCLUSION

I may sum up all I have said in a few words. If nothing were necessary but to restore the machinery of government in the States lately in rebellion in point of form, the movements made to that end by the people of the south might be considered satisfactory. But if it is required that the southern people should also accommodate themselves to the results of the war in point of spirit, those movements fall far short of what must be insisted upon. . . .

Questions

1. Why did Schurz recommend keeping the Freedmen's Bureau and the army in the South? How did that differ from what Johnson wanted?
2. Why did Schurz suggest that it might be wise to give African Americans in the South the vote?
3. What does Schurz say about the Unionists in the South? About the emergence of a free labor system?

15-3   The Mississippi Black Codes (1865)

As Carl Schurz reported, after the Civil War whites in the South sought a system of race relations in which African Americans would be clearly subordinate to whites and would constitute a readily accessible and controllable work force (see text p. 479).

Immediately after the Civil War southern whites wrote or revised vagrancy laws and the old slave codes as a means of establishing the system of race relations they wanted. Below is one of their most famous attempts to codify race relations, the Black Codes passed by the Mississippi legislature.

The Mississippi codes gave blacks rights they had not had before and clearly acknowledged that chattel slavery had ended. The codes recognized the right of African Americans to own property, though not in incorporated towns or cities. (Before the Civil War there were black property owners in Mississippi and even a few black slaveholders, but their legal standing was not clear.) The 1865 codes also recognized marriages among blacks as legal.

Not all the southern states passed comprehensive Black Codes, and some codes were much less stringent than those of Mississippi. South Carolina's codes differed in that they restricted blacks to buying property in cities or towns.

The creators of the codes drew their ideas from the world in which they lived. Slavery had just ended very abruptly, and the ravages of war were ever present. The men who drafted these codes used the old slave codes from the South, vagrancy laws from the North and the South, laws for former slaves in the British West Indies, and antebellum laws for free blacks. They were also aware that most northern states had laws that discriminated against African Americans and that very few northern states allowed African Americans to vote.

Most of these codes and similar measures were declared void by the Union army officials who were stationed in the former Confederate states. Subsequently, during Reconstruction, the rights of African Americans were greatly expanded (see text pp. 484–485).

Source: Laws of Mississippi, 1865, pp. 82ff.

---

1. CIVIL RIGHTS OF FREEDMEN IN MISSISSIPPI

. . . That all freedmen, free negroes, and mulattoes may sue and be sued . . . may acquire personal property . . . and may dispose of the same in the same manner and to the same extent that white persons may: [but no] freedman, free negro, or mulatto . . . [shall] rent or lease any lands or tenements except in incorporated cities or towns, in which places the corporate authorities shall control the same. . . .

All freedmen, free negroes, or mulattoes who do now and have herebefore lived and cohabited together as husband and wife shall be taken and held in law as legally married, and the issue shall be taken and held as legitimate for all purposes; that it shall not be lawful for any freedman, free negro, or mulatto to intermarry with any white person; nor for any white person to intermarry with any freedman, free negro, or mulatto; and any person who shall so intermarry, shall be deemed guilty of felony, and on conviction thereof shall be confined in the State penitentiary for life; and those shall be deemed freedmen, free negroes, and mulattoes who are of pure negro blood, and those descended from a negro to the third generation, inclusive, though one ancestor in each generation may have been a white person. . . .

[F]reedmen, free negroes, and mulattoes are now by law competent witnesses . . . in civil cases [and in criminal cases where they are the victims]. . . .

All contracts for labor made with freedmen, free negroes, and mulattoes for a longer period than one month shall be in writing, and in duplicate. . . . and said contracts shall be taken and held as entire contracts, and if the laborer shall quit the service of the employer before the expiration of his term of service, without good cause, he shall forfeit his wages for that year up to the time of quitting.

. . . Every civil officer shall, and every person may, arrest and carry back to his or her legal employer any freedman, free negro, or mulatto who shall have quit the service of his or her employer before the expiration of his or her term of service without good cause; and said officer and person shall be entitled to receive for arresting and carrying back every deserting employee aforesaid the sum of five dollars. . . .

. . . If any person shall persuade or attempt to persuade, entice, or cause any freedman, free negro, or mulatto to desert from the legal employment of any person before the expiration of his or her term of service, or shall knowingly employ any such deserting freedman, free negro, or mulatto, or shall knowingly give or sell to any such deserting freedman, free negro, or mulatto, any food, raiment, or other thing, he or she shall be guilty of a misdemeanor. . . .

2. MISSISSIPPI APPRENTICE LAW

. . . It shall be the duty of all sheriffs, justices of the peace, and other civil officers of the several counties in this State, to report to the probate courts of their respective counties semi-annually, at the January and July terms of said courts, all freedmen, free negroes, and mulattoes, under the age of eighteen, in their respective counties, beats or districts, who are orphans, or whose parent or parents have not the means or who refuse to provide for and support said minors; . . . the clerk of said court to apprentice said minors to some competent and suitable person, on such terms as the court may direct, having a particular care to the interest of said minor: *Provided,* that the former owner of said minors shall have the preference when, in the opinion of the court, he or she shall be a suitable person for that purpose. . . .

. . . In the management and control of said apprentice, said master or mistress shall have the power to inflict such moderate corporal chastisement as a father or guardian is allowed to inflict on his or her child or ward at common law: *Provided,* that in no case shall cruel or inhuman punishment be inflicted. . . .

3. MISSISSIPPI VAGRANT LAW

. . . That all rogues and vagabonds, idle and dissipated persons, beggars, jugglers, or persons practicing unlawful games or plays, runaways, common drunkards, common night-walkers, pilferers, lewd, wanton, or lascivious persons, in speech or behavior, common railers and brawlers, persons who neglect their calling or employment, misspend what they earn, or do not provide for the support of themselves or their families, or dependents, and all other idle and disorderly persons, including all who neglect all lawful business, habitually misspend their time by fre-

quenting houses of ill-fame, gaming-houses, or tippling shops, shall be deemed and considered vagrants, under the provisions of this act, and upon conviction thereof shall be fined not exceeding one hundred dollars . . . and be imprisoned at the discretion of the court, not exceeding ten days.

. . . All freedmen, free negroes and mulattoes in this State, over the age of eighteen years, found on the second Monday in January, 1866, or thereafter, with no lawful employment or business, or found unlawfully assembling themselves together, either in the day or night time, and all white persons so assembling themselves with freedmen, free negroes or mulattoes, or usually associating with freedmen, free negroes or mulattoes, on terms of equality, or living in adultery or fornication with a freed woman, free negro or mulatto, shall be deemed vagrants, and on conviction thereof shall be fined in a sum not exceeding, in the case of a freedman, free negro or mulatto, fifty dollars, and a white man two hundred dollars, and imprisoned at the discretion of the court, the free negro not exceeding ten days, and the white man not exceeding six months. . . .

4. PENAL LAWS OF MISSISSIPPI

. . . That no freedman, free negro or mulatto, not in the military service of the United States government, and not licensed so to do by the board of police of his or her county, shall keep or carry fire-arms of any kind, or any ammunition, dirk or bowie knife. . . .

. . . Any freedman, free negro, or mulatto committing riots, routs, affrays, trespasses, malicious mischief, cruel treatment to animals, seditious speeches, insulting gestures, language, or acts, or assaults on any person, disturbance of the peace, exercising the function of a minister of the Gospel without a license from some regularly organized church, vending spirituous or intoxicating liquors, or committing any other misdemeanor, the punishment of which is not specifically provided for by law, shall, upon conviction thereof in the county court, be fined not less than ten dollars, and not more than one hundred dollars, and may be imprisoned at the discretion of the court, not exceeding thirty days. . . .

. . . If any freedman, free negro, or mulatto, convicted of any of the misdemeanors provided against in this act, shall fail or refuse for the space of five days, after conviction, to pay the fine and costs imposed, such person shall be hired out by the sheriff or other officer, at public outcry, to any white person who will pay said fine and all costs, and take said convict for the shortest time.

Questions

1. What was the intent of these laws?
2. Who was charged with enforcing them? ("Every civil officer shall, and every person may, arrest and carry back to his or her legal employer. . . .") Who was considered a "person"? Who was not a "person"?
3. How were vagrants defined? Were these laws based on the assumption that the only vagrants were African Americans? What restrictions were placed on the freedom of expression of African Americans? What restrictions were placed on their freedom of association? On whites in Mississippi?

15-4   The Civil Rights Act of 1866

When Congress reconvened in December 1865, it blocked President Johnson's attempts to restore the South quickly. It extended the life of the Freedmen's Bureau over the president's veto and passed another landmark law, the Civil Rights Act of 1866, again over the president's veto (see text p. 484). This act made African Americans citizens and countered the 1857 *Dred Scott* decision, in which the Supreme Court had declared that no African American who was descended from a slave was or could ever be a citizen.

Doubts about the constitutionality and permanence of the Civil Rights Act of 1866 prompted Congress to pass the Fourteenth Amendment (see text pp. 484–485 and D-17). Ratified in 1868, this amendment for the first time constitutionally defined citizenship and some of the basic rights of citizenship; it also embraced the Republican program for Reconstruction.

Source: U.S. Statutes at Large, 14 (1868?), 27ff.

An Act to protect all Persons in the United States in their Civil Rights, and furnish the Means of their Vindication.

Be it enacted, That all persons born in the United States and not subject to any foreign power, excluding Indians not taxed, are hereby declared to be citizens of the United States; and such citizens, of every race and color, without regard to any previous condition of slavery or involuntary servitude, except as a punishment for crime whereof the party shall have been duly convicted, shall have the same right, in every State and Territory in the United States, to make and enforce contracts, to sue, be parties, and give evidence, to inherit, purchase, lease, sell, hold, and convey real and personal property, and to full and equal benefit of all laws and proceedings for the security of person and property, as is enjoyed by white citizens, and shall be subject to like punishment, pains, and penalties, and to none other, any law, statute, ordinance, regulation, or custom, to the contrary notwithstanding.

SEC. 2. *And be it further enacted,* That any person who, under color of any law, statute, ordinance, regulation, or custom, shall subject, or cause to be subjected, any inhabitant of any State or Territory to the deprivation of any right secured or protected by this act, or to different punishment, pains, or penalties on account of such person having at any time been held in a condition of slavery or involuntary servitude, except as a punishment for crime whereof the party shall have been duly convicted, or by reason of his color or race, than is prescribed for the punishment of white persons, shall be deemed guilty of a misdemeanor, and, on conviction, shall be punished by fine not exceeding one thousand dollars, or imprisonment not exceeding one year, or both, in the discretion of the court.

SEC. 3. *And be it further enacted,* That the district courts of the United States, . . . shall have, exclusively of the courts of the several States, cognizance of all crimes and offences committed against the provisions of this act, and also, concurrently with the circuit courts of the United States, of all causes, civil and criminal, affecting persons who are denied or cannot enforce in the courts or judicial tribunals of the State or locality where they may be any of the rights secured to them by the first section of this act. . . .

SEC. 4. *And be it further enacted,* That the district attorneys, marshals, and deputy marshals of the United States, the commissioners appointed by the circuit and territorial courts of the United States, with powers of arresting, imprisoning, or bailing offenders against the laws of the United States, the officers and agents of the Freedmen's Bureau, and every other officer who may be specially empowered by the President of the United States, shall be, and they are hereby, specially authorized and required, at the expense of the United States, to institute proceedings against all and every person who shall violate the provisions of this act, and cause him or them to be arrested and imprisoned, or bailed, as the case may be, for trial before such court of the United States or territorial court as by this act has cognizance of the offence. . . .

SEC. 8. *And be it further enacted,* That whenever the President of the United States shall have reason to believe that offences have been or are likely to be committed against the provisions of this act within any judicial district, it shall be lawful for him, in his discretion, to direct the judge, marshal, and district attorney of such district to attend at such place within the district, and for such time as he may designate, for the purpose of the more speedy arrest and trial of persons charged with a violation of this act; and it shall be the duty of every judge or other officer, when any such requisition shall be received by him, to attend at the place and for the time therein designated.

SEC. 9. *And be it further enacted,* That it shall be lawful for the President of the United States, or such person as he may empower for that purpose, to employ such part of the land or naval forces of the United States, or of the militia, as shall be necessary to prevent the violation and enforce the due execution of this act.

SEC. 10. *And be it further enacted,* That upon all questions of law arising in any cause under the provisions of this act a final appeal may be taken to the Supreme Court of the United States.

Questions

1. What was the intent of the Civil Rights Act?
2. Who was responsible for enforcing this law, and what powers might they use? Was it necessary to wait until the law was violated before officers of the law could act?
3. According to the Fourteenth Amendment, who is a citizen of the United States? What rights does the amendment say citizens have? What does "equal protection of the laws" mean?

Questions for Further Thought

1. Compare and contrast President Johnson's description of conditions in the South (Document 15-1) with that of General Schurz (Document 15-2). Which do you find to be more accurate? Why?
2. What did Johnson and Schurz say about relations between blacks and whites?
3. Compare the Mississippi Black Codes (Document 15-3) with the Civil Rights Act of 1866 (Document 15-4). Why do you think Congress believed that it had to pass the Civil Rights Act and then adopt the Fourteenth Amendment?

Radical Reconstruction

When only Tennessee ratified the Fourteenth Amendment (and was readmitted to the Union), Congressional Republicans, strengthened by their victories in the 1866 congressional elections, passed the Reconstruction Acts. These laws forced unreconstructed former Confederate states to meet Republican conditions for readmission, including granting African American men the vote. While these measures were called radical by their detractors (and this phase of Reconstruction referred to as "radical Reconstruction"), these measures actually fell far short of what some in Congress desired

(Document 15-5). They fell even further short of the hopes of women's rights advocates that the vote might be extended to them as well as blacks—a frustration that seriously split the movement, but led ultimately to the creation of a new, and ultimately successful, woman suffrage movement (Document 15-6).

During Reconstruction African Americans obtained a number of civil and political rights, most especially in the realm of politics. While no former Confederate state was controlled by blacks, a large group of African American politicians surged into prominence, seeking to use government power to help constituents who previously had not even been regarded as citizens (Document 15-7). While many of these new political rights were lost in the years following Reconstruction, other gains, especially in social and economic realms, were more enduring. At the insistence of the freed slaves, planters dismantled much of the old slave regime, replacing gang labor and the old slave quarters with a new system of individual plots worked by families for shares of the crops. Black marriages were formalized, and African Americans gained control over their family lives. They pursued education, built new institutions such as the black church, and began to acquire property. While white racism and white landlord power raised enormous barriers to black advancement, through the years increasing (though still small) numbers of African Americans became property holders (Document 15-8).

15-5   Black Suffrage and Land Redistribution (1867)

Thaddeus Stevens

The Radical Republicans, including Congressman Thaddeus Stevens of Pennsylvania, believed that besides the vote, freedmen would need an economic basis for controlling their lives (see text pp. 485–486). Below are excerpts from the remarks of Thaddeus Stevens and from a bill in which he proposed to alter the South drastically.

Source: Congressional Globe, 3 January 1867, 252; 19 March 1867, 203.

ON BLACK SUFFRAGE

Unless the rebel States, before admission, should be made republican in spirit, and placed under the guardianship of loyal men, all our blood and treasure will have been spent in vain. I waive now the question of punishment which, if we are wise, will still be inflicted by moderate confiscations. . . . Impartial suffrage, both in electing the delegates and ratifying their proceedings, is now the fixed rule. There is more reason why colored voters should be admitted in the rebel States than in the Territories. In the States they form the great mass of the loyal men. Possibly with their aid loyal governments may be established in most of those States. Without it all are sure to be ruled by traitors; and loyal men, black and white, will be oppressed, exiled, or murdered. There are several good reasons for the passage of this bill. In the first place, it is just. I am now confining my argument to negro suffrage in the rebel States. Have not loyal blacks quite as good a right to choose rulers and make laws as rebel whites? In the second place,

it is a necessity in order to protect the loyal white men in the seceded States. The white Union men are in a great minority in each of those States. With them the blacks would act in a body; and it is believed that in each of said States, except one, the two united would form a majority, control the States, and protect themselves. Now they are the victims of daily murder. . . .

Another good reason is, it would insure the ascendency of the Union party. . . . I believe . . . that on the continued ascendency of that party depends the safety of this great nation. If impartial suffrage is excluded in the rebel States, then every one of them is sure to send a solid rebel representative delegation to Congress, and cast a solid rebel electoral vote. They, with their kindred Copperheads of the North, would always elect the President and control Congress. While slavery sat upon her defiant throne, and insulted and intimidated the trembling North, the South frequently divided on questions of policy between Whigs and Democrats, and gave victory alternately to the sections. Now, you must divide them between loyalists, without regard to color, and disloyalists, or you will be the perpetual vassals of the free-trade, irritated, revengeful South. . . . I am for negro suffrage in every rebel State. If it be just, it should not be denied; if it be necessary, it should be adopted; if it be a punishment to traitors, they deserve it.

BILL ON LAND REDISTRIBUTION

Whereas it is due to justice, as an example to future times, that some proper punishment should be inflicted on the people who constituted the "confederate States of America," both because they, declaring an unjust war against the United States for the purpose of destroying republican liberty and permanently establishing slavery, as well as for the cruel and barbarous manner in which they conducted said war, in violation of all the laws of civilized warfare, and also to compel them to make some compensation for the damages and expenditures caused by said war: Therefore,

Be it enacted by the Senate and House of Representatives of the United States of America in Congress assembled, That all the public lands belonging to the ten States that formed the government of the so-called "confederate States of America" shall be forfeited by said States and become forthwith vested in the United States. . . .

That out of the lands thus seized and confiscated the slaves who have been liberated by the operations of the war and the amendment to the Constitution or otherwise, who resided in said "confederate States" on the 4th day of March, A.D. 1861, or since, shall have distributed to them as follows, namely: to each male person who is the head of a family, forty acres; to each adult male, whether the head of a family or not, forty acres; to each widow who is the head of a family, forty acres—to be held by them in fee-simple, but to be inalienable for the next ten years after they become seized thereof. . . .

That out of the balance of the property thus seized and confiscated there shall be raised, in the manner hereinafter provided, a sum equal to fifty dollars, for each homestead, to be applied by the trustees hereinafter mentioned toward the erection of buildings on the said homesteads for the use of said slaves; and the further sum of $500,000,000, which shall be appropriated as follows, to wit: $200,000,000 shall be invested in United States six per cent securities; and the interest thereof shall be semi-annually added to the pensions allowed by law to pensioners who have become so by reason of the late war; $300,000,000, or so much thereof as may be needed, shall be appropriated to pay damages done to loyal citizens by the civil or military operations of the government lately called the "confederate States of America." . . .

That in order that just discrimination may be made, the property of no one shall be seized whose whole estate on the 4th day of March, A.D. 1865, was not worth more than $5,000, to be valued by the said commission, unless he shall have voluntarily become an officer or employé in the military or civil service of the "confederate States of America," or in the civil or military service of some one of said States. . . .

Questions

1. On what grounds did Stevens justify granting African American men the vote?
2. What did Stevens want to do with land confiscated in the South?
3. Why do you think Congress rejected Stevens's land confiscation and redistribution proposal? Do you think that if Congress had adopted the proposal, it would have made a difference in the history of the South or the United States? Why or why not?

15-6   The Fourteenth Amendment and Woman Suffrage (1873, 1875)

As noted in the text (p. 488), not only did the Fourteenth and Fifteenth amendments ignore the demands of the women's rights movement for equal access to the ballot box, but the Fourteenth Amendment introduced the word "male" for the first time into the U.S. Constitution. Nonetheless, many suffragists continued to believe that the newly formalized and broadened definition of American citizenship established by the Fourteenth Amendment could be used to gain women the vote through a judicial ruling. In 1872 a number of suffragists, including Susan B. Anthony, voted in the presidential election; Anthony was indicted and brought to trial, providing her the opportunity she sought to make her case (Document 15-6a). Anthony was blocked from making her appeal, but another suffragist, Virginia Minor of Missouri, sued the official who blocked her from the ballot box and saw her case reach the Supreme Court. The Court's decision (Document 15-6b), handed down in 1875, effectively ended all hopes that gender relations as well as race relations had been "reconstructed" by the Fourteenth Amendment, and strengthened the movement for a constitutional woman suffrage amendment. Furthermore, by effectively separating the right to vote from fundamental citizenship rights, the Court also helped set the stage for the later movement to use "color-blind" laws to disfranchise African Americans.

Sources: Ruth Barnes Moynihan, Cynthia Russett, and Laurie Crumpacker, eds., *Second to None: A Documentary History of American Women* (Lincoln: University of Nebraska Press, 1993), 2: 16–19; *Minor v. Happersett*, 88 U.S. 162, in Linda Kerber and Jane Sherron DeHart, eds., *Women's America: Refocusing the Past*, 5th ed. (New York: Oxford University Press, 2000), 245–246.

(a) I Stand Before You Under Indictment (1873)

Friends and Fellow-Citizens:—I stand before you under indictment for the alleged crime of having voted at the last presidential election, without having a lawful right to vote. It shall be my work this evening to prove to you that in thus doing, I not only committed no crime, but instead simply exercised my citizen's right, guaranteed to me and all United States citizens by the National Constitution beyond the power of any State to deny.

Our democratic-republican government is based on the idea of the natural right of every individual member thereof to a voice and a vote in making and executing the laws. We assert the province of government to be to secure the people in the enjoyment of their inalienable rights. We throw to the winds the old dogma that government can give rights. No one denies that before governments were organized each individual possessed the right to protect his own life, liberty and property. When 100 or 1,000,000 people enter into a free government, they do not barter away their natural rights; they simply pledge themselves to protect each other in the enjoyment of them through prescribed judicial and legislative tribunals. They agree to abandon the methods of brute force in the adjustment of their differences and adopt those of civilization. Nor can you find a word in any of the grand documents left us by the fathers which assumes for government the power to create or to confer rights. The Declaration of Independence, the United States Constitution, the constitutions of the several States and the organic laws of the Territories, all alike propose to *protect* the people in the exercise of their God-given rights. Not one of them pretends to bestow rights.

All men are created equal, and endowed by their Creator with certain inalienable rights. Among these are life, liberty and the pursuit of happiness. To secure these, governments are instituted among men, deriving their just powers from the consent of the governed.

Here is no shadow of government authority over rights, or exclusion of any class from their full and equal enjoyment. Here is pronounced the right of all men, and "consequently," as the Quaker preacher said, "of all women," to a voice in the government. And here, in this first paragraph of the Declaration, is the assertion of the natural right of all to the ballot; for how can "the consent of the governed" be given, if the right to vote be denied? Again:

Whenever any form of government becomes destructive of these ends, it is the right of the people to alter or abolish it, and to institute a new government, laying its foundations on such principles, and organizing its powers in such form, as to them shall seem most likely to effect their safety and happiness.

Surely the right of the whole people to vote is here clearly implied; for however destructive to their happiness this government might become, a disfranchised class could neither alter nor abolish it, nor institute a new one, except by the old brute force method of insurrection and rebellion. One-half of the people of this nation today are utterly powerless to blot from the statute books an unjust law, or to write there a new and just one. The women, dissatisfied as they are with this form of government, that enforces taxation without representation—that compels them to obey laws to which they never have given their consent—that imprisons and hangs them without a trial by a jury of their peers—that robs them, in marriage, of the custody of their own persons, wages and children—are this half of the people who are left wholly at the mercy of the other half, in direct violation of the spirit and letter of the declarations of the framers of this government, every one of which was based on the immutable principle of equal rights to all. By these declarations, kings, popes, priests, aristocrats, all were alike dethroned and placed on a common level, politically, with the lowliest born subject or serf. By them, too, men, as such, were deprived of their divine right to rule and placed on a political level with women. By the practice of these declarations all class and caste distinctions would be abolished, and slave, serf, plebeian, wife, woman, all alike rise from their subject position to the broader platform of equality.

The preamble of the Federal Constitution says:

We, the people of the United States, in order to form a more perfect union, establish justice, insure domestic tranquillity, provide for the common defence, promote the general welfare and secure the blessings of liberty to ourselves and our posterity, do ordain and establish this Constitution for the United States of America.

It was we, the people, not we, the white male citizens, nor we, the male citizens; but we, the whole people, who formed this Union. We formed it not to give the blessings of liberty but to secure them; not to the half of ourselves and the half of our posterity, but to the whole people—women as well as men. It is downright mockery to talk to women of their enjoyment of the blessings of liberty while they are denied the only means of securing them provided by this democratic-republican government—the ballot. . . .

For any State to make sex a qualification, which must ever result in the disfranchisement of one entire half of the people, is to pass a bill of attainder, an ex post facto law, and is therefore a violation of the supreme law of the land. By it the blessings of liberty are forever withheld from women and their female posterity. For them, this government has no just powers derived from the consent of the governed. For them this government is not a democracy; it is not a republic. It is the most odious aristocracy ever established on the face of the globe. An oligarchy of wealth, where the rich govern the poor; an oligarchy of learning, where the educated govern the ignorant; or even an oligarchy of race, where the Saxon rules the African, might be endured; but this oligarchy of sex which makes father, brothers, husband, sons, the oligarchs over the mother and sisters, the wife and daughters of every household; which ordains all men sovereigns, all women subjects—carries discord and rebellion into every home of the nation. . . . The moment you deprive a person of his right to a voice in the government, you degrade him from the status of a citizen of the republic to that of a subject. It matters very little to him whether his monarch be an individual tyrant, as is the Czar of Russia, or a 15,000,000 headed monster, as here in the United States; he is a powerless subject, serf or slave; not in any sense a free and independent citizen. . . .

Though the words persons, people, inhabitants, electors, citizens, are all used indiscriminately in the national and State constitutions, there was always a conflict of opinion, prior to the war, as to whether they were synonymous terms, but whatever room there was for doubt, under the old regime, the adoption of the Fourteenth Amendment settled that question forever in its first sentence:

All persons born or naturalized in the United States, and subject to the jurisdiction thereof, are citizens of the United States, and of the State wherein they reside.

The second settles the equal status of all citizens:

No State shall make or enforce any law which shall abridge the privileges or immunities of citizens of the United States; nor shall any State deprive any person of life, liberty or property without due process of law, or deny to any person within its jurisdiction the equal protection of the laws.

The only question left to be settled now is: Are women persons? I scarcely believe any of our opponents will have the hardihood to say they are not. Being persons, then, women are citizens, and no State has a right to make any new law, or to enforce any old law, which shall abridge their privileges or immunities. Hence, every discrimination against women in the constitutions and laws of the several States is today null and void, precisely as is every one against negroes.

Is the right to vote one of the privileges or immunities of citizens? I think the disfranchised ex-rebels and ex-State prisoners all will agree that it is not only one of them, but the one without which all the others are nothing. Seek first the kingdom of the ballot and all things else shall be added, is the political injunction. . . .

If once we establish the false principle that United States citizenship does not carry with it the right to vote in every State in this Union, there is no end to the petty tricks and cunning devices which will be attempted to exclude one and another class of citizens from the right of suffrage. It will not always be the men combining to disfranchise all women; native born men combining to abridge the rights of all naturalized citizens, as in Rhode Island. It will not always be the rich and educated who may combine to cut off the poor and ignorant; but we may live to see the hardworking, uncultivated day laborers, foreign and native born, learning the power of the ballot and their vast majority of numbers, combine and amend State constitutions so as to disfranchise the Vanderbilts, the Stewarts, the Conklings and the Fentons. It is a poor rule that won't work more ways than one. Establish this precedent, admit the State's right to deny suffrage, and there is no limit to the confusion, discord, and disruption that may await us. There is and can be but one safe principle of government—equal rights to all. Discrimination against any class on account of color, race, nativity, sex, property, culture, can but embitter and disaffect that class, and thereby endanger the safety of the whole people. Clearly, then, the national government not only must define the rights of citizens, but must stretch out its powerful hand and protect them in every State of this Union.

(b) *Minor v. Happersett* (1875)

Mr. Chief Justice Morrison R. Waite Delivered The Opinion Of The Court:

The question is presented in this case, whether, since the adoption of the fourteenth amendment, a woman, who is a citizen of the United States and of the State of Missouri, is a voter in that State, notwithstanding the provision of the constitution and laws of the State, which confine the right of suffrage to men alone. . . . The argument is, that as a woman, born or naturalized in the United States and subject to the jurisdiction thereof, is a citizen of the United States and of the State in which she resides, she has the right of suffrage as one of the privileges and immunities of her citizenship, which the State cannot by its laws or constitution abridge.

There is no doubt that women may be citizens. They are persons, and by the fourteenth amendment "all persons born or naturalized in the United States and subject to the jurisdiction thereof" are expressly declared to be "citizens of the United States and of the State wherein they reside." But, in our opinion, it did not need this amendment to give them that position . . . sex has never been made one of the elements of citizenship in the United States. In this respect men have never had an advantage over women. The same laws precisely apply to both. The fourteenth amendment did not affect the citizenship of women any more than it did of men . . . Mrs. Minor . . . has always been a citizen from her birth, and entitled to all the privileges and immunities of citizenship.

If the right of suffrage is one of the necessary privileges of a citizen of the United States, then the constitution and laws of Missouri confining it to men are in violation of the Constitution of the United States, as amended, and conse-

quently void. The direction question is, therefore, presented whether all citizens are necessarily voters.

The Constitution does not define the privileges and immunities of citizens. For that definition we must look elsewhere. In this case we need not determine what they are, but only whether suffrage is necessarily one of them.

It certainly is nowhere made so in express terms. The United States has no voters in the States of its own creation. The elective officers of the United States are all elected directly or indirectly by state voters. . . . it cannot for a moment be doubted that if it had been intended to make all citizens of the United States voters, the framers of the Constitution would not have left it to implication. . . .

It is true that the United States guarantees to every State a republican form of government. . . . No particular government is designated as republican, neither is the exact form to be guaranteed, in any manner especially designated. . . . When the Constitution was adopted . . . all the citizens of the States were not invested with the right of suffrage. In all, save perhaps New Jersey, this right was only bestowed upon men and not upon all of them. . . . Under these circumstances it is certainly now too late to contend that a government is not republican, within the meaning of this guaranty in the Constitution, because women are not made voters. . . . If suffrage was intended to be included within its obligations, language better adapted to express that intent would most certainly have been employed. . . .

. . . For nearly ninety years the people have acted upon the idea that the Constitution, when it conferred citizenship, did not necessarily confer the right of suffrage. If uniform practice long continued can settle the construction of so important an instrument as the Constitution of the United States confessedly is, most certainly it has been done here. Our province is to decide what the law is, not to declare what it should be.

We have given this case the careful consideration its importance demands. If the law is wrong, it ought to be changed; but the power for that is not with us. . . . No argument as to woman's need of suffrage can be considered. We can only act upon her rights as they exist. . . .

Questions

1. What case does Anthony make for treating voting as an "inalienable right"?
2. What does Anthony see as the consequence of denying that the right to vote is intrinsic to citizenship? Is her view prophetic?
3. Compare the reasoning of Anthony and of Chief Justice Waite on the question of whether the right to vote is one of the "privileges and immunities" of citizenship. What sorts of evidence do they cite?

15-7 An Advocate of Federal Aid for Land Purchase (1868)

Richard H. Cain

With the enactment of the Reconstruction Act of 1867, the cast of political leadership in the South dramatically changed. One good example of the new men rising to prominence was Richard H. Cain (1825–1887). Born in Virginia of African American and Cherokee parents, Cain was raised in Ohio, attending Wilberforce University and becoming a minister in the African Methodist Episcopal (A.M.E.) Church. After spending the Civil War as pastor of a Brooklyn church, he went south in 1865 as a missionary; reorganizing the Emmanuel A.M.E. Church of Charleston, South Carolina, Cain built it into the largest A.M.E. congregation in the state and used it as a political base. He was a delegate to the South Carolina constitutional convention of 1868; served as a state senator from 1868 to 1870; unsuccessfully sought the Republican nomination for lieutenant governor in 1872; and served in the U.S. House of Representatives from 1873 to 1875 and again from 1877 to 1879. Cain left South Carolina in 1880 and spent the remainder of his life as a bishop and college president in the A.M.E. Church.

Like many successful African American preachers, Cain was an astute businessman, eager to lend his services to build up the black community. Like many other black politicians, he saw the issue of land for the freedmen as paramount. An early advocate of redistribution of confiscated lands à la Thaddeus Stevens (Document 15-5), at the constitutional convention Cain advocated petitioning the federal government to appropriate $1 million to finance land purchases by the freedmen. When his proposal was attacked by C. P. Leslie, a white Republican delegate, Cain defended it with the following remarks.

Source: Proceedings of the Constitutional Convention of South Carolina (Charleston: Denny and Perry, 1868), 378–382.

... Mr. CAIN. I offer this resolution with good intentions. I believe there is need of immediate relief to the poor people of the State. I know from my experience among the people, there is pressing need of some measures to meet the wants of the utterly destitute. The gentleman says it will only take money out of the Treasury. Well that is the intention. I do not expect to get it anywhere else. I expect to get the money, if at all, through the Treasury of the United States, or some other department. It certainly must come out of the Government. I believe such an appropriation would remove a great many of the difficulties now in the State and do a vast amount of good to poor people. It may be that we will not get it, but that will not debar us from asking. It is our privilege and right. Other Conventions have asked from Congress appropriations. Georgia and other States have sent in their petitions. One has asked for $30,000,000 to be appropriated to the Southern States. I do not see any inconsistency in the proposition presented by myself.

Mr. C. P. LESLIE. Suppose I should button up my coat and march up to your house and ask you for money or provisions, when you had none to give, what would you think of me?

Mr. CAIN. You would do perfectly right to run the chance of getting something to eat. This is a measure of relief to those thousands of freed people who now have no lands of their own. I believe the possession of lands and homesteads is one of the best means by which a people is made industrious, honest and advantageous to the State. I believe it is a fact well known, that over three hundred thousand men, women and children are homeless, landless. The abolition of slavery has thrown these people upon their own resources. How are they to live? I know the philosopher of the New York *Tribune* says, "root hog or die;" but in the meantime we ought to have some place to root. My proposition is simply to give the hog some place to root. I believe if the proposition is sent to Congress, it will certainly receive the attention of our friends. I believe the whole country is desirous to see that this State shall return to the Union in peace and quiet, and that every inhabitant of the State shall be made industrious and profitable to the State. I am opposed to this Bureau system. I want a system adopted that will do away with the Bureau, but I cannot see how it can be done unless the people have homes. As long as people are working on shares and contracts, and at the end of every year are in debt, so long will they and the country suffer. But give them a chance to buy lands, and they become steady, industrious men. That is the reason I desire to bring this money here and to assist them to buy lands. It will be the means of encouraging them to industry if the petition be granted by Congress. It will be the means of meeting one of the great wants of the present among the poor. It will lay the foundation for the future prosperity of the country as no other measure will at this time, because it will bring about a reconciliation in the minds of thousands of these helpless people, which nothing else can. This measure, if carried out, will bring capital to the State and stimulate the poor to renewed efforts in life, such as they never had before. Such a measure will give to the landholders relief from their embarrassments financially, and enable them to get fair compensation for their lands. It will relieve the Government of the responsibility of taking care of the thousands who now are fed at the Commissaries and fostered in laziness. I have gone through the country and on every side I was besieged with questions: How are we to get homesteads, to get lands? I desire to devise some plan, or adopt some measure by which we can dissipate one of the arguments used against us, that the African race will not work. I do not believe the black man hates work any more than the white man does. Give these men a place to work, and I will guarantee before one year passes, there will be no necessity for the Freedman's Bureau, or any measure aside from those measures which a people may make in protecting themselves.

But a people without homes become wanderers. If they possess lands they have an interest in the soil, in the State, in its commerce, its agriculture, and in everything pertaining to the wealth and welfare of the State. If these people had homes along the lines of railroads, and the lands were divided and sold in small farms, I will guarantee our railroads will make fifty times as much money, banking systems will be advanced by virtue of the settlement of the people throughout the whole State. We want these large tracts of land cut up. The land is productive, and there is nothing to prevent the greatest and highest prosperity. What we need is a system of small farms. Every farmer owning his own land will feel he is in possession of something. It will have a tendency to settle the minds of the people in the State and settle many difficulties. In the rural districts now there is constant discontent, constant misapprehension between the parties, a constant disregard for each other. One man won't make an engagement to work, because he fears if he makes a contract this year, he will be cheated again as he thinks he was last year. We have had petitions from planters asking the Convention to disabuse the minds of the freedmen of the thought that this Convention has any lands at its disposal, but I do desire this Convention to do something at least to relieve the wants of these poor suffering people. I believe this measure, if adopted and sent to Congress, will indicate to the people that this Convention does desire they shall possess homes and have relief.

Some of my friends say that the sum is too small, and ask why I do not make it more. I made it a million, because I thought there would be more probability of getting one

million than five. It might be put into the hands of the Bureau, and I am willing to trust the Bureau. . . .

I do not desire to have a foot of land in this State confiscated. I want every man to stand upon his own character. I want these lands purchased by the government, and the people afforded an opportunity to buy from the government. I believe every man ought to carve out for himself a character and position in this life. I believe every man ought to be made to work by some means or other, and if he does not, he must go down. I believe if the same amount of money that has been employed by the Bureau in feeding lazy, worthless men and women, had been expended in purchasing lands, we would to-day have no need of the Bureau. Millions upon millions have been expended, and it is still going on *ad infinitum*. I propose to let the poor people buy these lands, the government to be paid back in five years time. It is one of the great cries of the enemies of reconstruction, that Congress has constantly fostered laziness. I want to have the satisfaction of showing that the freedmen are as capable and willing to work as any men on the face of the earth. This measure will save the State untold expenses. I believe there are hundreds of persons in the jail and penitentiary cracking rock to-day who have all the instincts of honesty, and who, had they an opportunity of making a living, would never have been found in such a place. I think if Congress will accede to our request, we shall be benefited beyond measure, and save the State from taking charge of paupers, made such by not having the means to earn a living for themselves.

I can look to a part of my constituency, men in this hall, mechanics, plasterers, carpenters, engineers, men capable of doing all kind of work, now idle because they cannot find any work in the city. Poverty stares them in the face, and their children are in want. They go to the cotton houses, but can find no labor. They are men whose honesty and integrity has never been called in question. They are suffering in consequence of the poverty-stricken condition of the city and State. I believe the best measure is to open a field where they can labor, where they can take the hoe and the axe, cut down the forest, and make the whole land blossom as the Garden of Eden, and prosperity pervade the whole land.

Now, the report of Major General Howard gives a surplus of over seven millions in the Freedman's Bureau last year. Out of that seven millions I propose we ask Congress to make an appropriation of one million, which will be properly distributed and then leave several millions in that Department, my friend from Barnwell notwithstanding.

I think there could be no better measure for this Convention to urge upon Congress. If that body should listen to our appeal, I have no doubt we shall be benefited. This measure of relief, it seems to me, would come swiftly. It is a swift messenger that comes in a week's time after it is passed; so that in the month of February or March the people may be enabled to go to planting and raising crops for the ensuing year. One gentleman says it will take six months or a year, but I hope, with the assistance of the Government, we could accomplish it in less time.

Mr. C. P. LESLIE. Did you ever see the Government do anything quick?

Mr. R. H. CAIN. They make taxes come quick. If this measure is carried out, the results will be that we will see all along our lines of railroad and State roads little farms, log cabins filled with happy families, and thousands of families coming on the railroads with their products. There will also spring up depots for the reception of cotton, corn and all other cereals. Prosperity will return to the State, by virtue of the people being happy, bound to the Govern-ment by a tie that cannot be broken. The taxes, that are so heavy now that men are compelled to sell their horses, will be lightened. I want to see the State alive, to hear the hum of the spindle and the mills! I want to see cattle and horses, and fowls, and everything that makes up a happy home and family. I want to see the people shout with joy and gladness. There shall then be no antagonism between white men and black men, but we shall all realize the end of our being, and realize that we are all made to dwell upon the earth in peace and happiness. The white man and the black man may then work in harmony, and secure prosperity to all coming generations. . . .

Questions

1. What arguments does Cain make in favor of his proposal? To what present poli-cies, especially of the Freedmen's Bureau, does he object?
2. In certain respects, Cain's proposal can be characterized as *conservative*. How? Would you agree, or not?
3. How would you characterize Cain's intentions toward the *whites* of South Carolina?

15-8   Statistics on Black Ownership (1870–1910)

During Reconstruction the lives of African Americans improved significantly, largely as a result of their own efforts. When Reconstruction ended, many of those gains were lost, particularly in the areas of civil and political rights. Still, African Americans con-tinued to improve themselves. As the statistics below indicate, African Americans after 1870 increasingly joined the ranks of farm owners and homeowners.

Source: Loren Schweninger, *Black Property Owners in the South, 1790–1915,* 164, 170, 174, 180. Copyright 1990 by the Board of Trustees of the University of Illinois. Used with permis-sion of the University of Illinois Press.

(a) Black Farm Owners in the South, 1870–1910: Total Number and Percentage of Owners (Black and White)

State	1870 Total	1870 Percentage	1890 Total	1890 Percentage	Percentage of increase, 1870–1890	1900 Total	1900 Percentage	Percentage of increase, 1890–1900	1910 Total	1910 Percentage	Percentage of increase, 1900–1910
Alabama	1,152	1.3	8,847	13	668	14,110	15	59	17,047	15	21
Arkansas	1,203	5.2	8,004	24	565	11,941	25	49	14,660	23	23
Florida	596	3.5	4,940	38	729	6,551	48	33	7,286	50	11
Georgia	1,367	1.4	8,131	13	495	11,375	14	40	15,698	13	38
Louisiana	1,107	1.8	6,685	18	504	9,378	16	40	10,681	19	14
Mississippi	1,600	1.9	11,526	13	620	20,973	16	82	24,949	15	19
North Carolina	1,628	2.2	10,494	26	545	16,834	31	60	20,707	32	23
South Carolina	3,062	4.0	13,075	21	327	18,970	22	45	20,356	21	7
Tennessee	1,301	2.2	6,378	23	390	9,414	28	48	10,698	28	14
Texas	839	1.8	12,513	26	1,391	20,139	31	61	21,182	30	5
Virginia	860	1.0	13,678	43	1,490	26,527	59	94	32,168	67	21

(b) Black Homeowners* in the South, 1870–1910: Total Number and Percentage of Owners (Black and White)

State	1870 Total	1870 Percentage	1890 Total	1890 Percentage	1910 Total	1910 Percentage
Alabama	215	4.3	6,898	11	16,714	17
Arkansas	56	5.3	3,840	17	9,802	27
Florida	46	3.7	5,709	28	13,581	22
Georgia	232	2.9	11,874	12	22,544	16
Louisiana	639	5.7	7,917	11	16,160	16
Mississippi	138	4.5	5,430	11	13,783	20
North Carolina	199	5.6	9,516	15	19,627	26
South Carolina	312	4.8	8,026	11	12,730	15
Tennessee	187	3.0	8,285	16	16,070	23
Texas	27	1.0	8,367	22	20,443	26
Virginia	409	3.3	16,210	20	24,405	27

*Excludes farm homes

Questions

1. Which state(s) had the greatest increase in black farm owners? In black homeowners?
2. What do the tables reveal about African Americans in the South in an era when they were systematically oppressed by whites?
3. How can you explain this evidence of the success of African Americans in the South in the late nineteenth century?

Questions for Further Thought

1. Compare Cain's argument on land reform (Document 15-7) to that of Thaddeus Stevens (Document 15-5). To what degree does Cain, like Stevens, see land redistribution as a means of punishing "rebels"? What does each man see as the proper role of the federal government in "reconstructing" the South?
2. Susan B. Anthony's argument (Document 15-6a) rests on an analogy between the status of women in the pre-Reconstruction United States and the status of African Americans. How well does that analogy work?
3. In view of the preceding documents, just how "radical" would you say radical Reconstruction really was? Bear in mind the meaning of the word *radical*—to desire change not on the surface of society, but *at its roots*.

The Undoing of Reconstruction

Northern support for Reconstruction was never reliable. Because most white northerners feared that President Johnson's program threatened to undo the Union victory and place Confederates back in the saddle (Document 15-9a), they preferred the program of congressional Republicans. However, they were at best only slightly more liberal in their racial views than were southerners, and over time northerners were increasingly receptive to southern white arguments that blacks were not to be trusted to govern (Document 15-9b).

Most southern whites, of course, opposed congressional Reconstruction from the outset, though the vehemence of the opposition fluctuated. The animosity of southern whites toward Reconstruction, Republicans, and African Americans intensified when elections were contested or when sensitive issues were placed before the public. The Ku Klux Klan was especially active during such times (Document 15-10), despite legislation passed against it.

The final undoing of Reconstruction came in the mid-1870s. A serious economic crisis struck the nation in 1873, plunging it into depression. New, economic issues, such as unemployment, labor conflict, and monetary policy, increasingly took precedence over the aging agenda of the sectional conflict, while northern lack of sympathy for blacks became increasingly important in shaping federal policy toward the South (Document 15-11). At the same time, southern whites got bolder, organizing paramilitary organizations to carry elections by whatever means were necessary. In such states as Mississippi and South Carolina, the end of Reconstruction resulted not so much from an election as from a white counterrevolution (Document 15-12).

15-9   The Rise and Fall of Northern Support for Reconstruction (1868, 1874)

Thomas Nast

Evidence of broad northern support for the Republican program could be found in many places other than the ballot box. Illustrations from *Harper's Weekly,* such as the one in the text (p. 485) and the one here from 1868 titled "This Is a White Man's Government," reflected popular attitudes in the North in the 1860s. However, northern support for Reconstruction began to erode as early as 1868 and was exhausted by

1874 (see text pp. 495–499), the year the second *Harper's Weekly* illustration presented here appeared. Both cartoons shown here on pages 23 and 24 are by Thomas Nast.

The first cartoon satirizes the Democratic Party in 1868, with its platform rejecting the Congressional Reconstruction Acts as "unconstitutional, null, and void." Nathan Bedford Forrest—the Confederate general who became the first Grand Wizard of the Ku Klux Klan—is represented in the center, while to his right stands an Irish immigrant, depicted (as was common in Nast cartoons) as a barbaric hoodlum. The third figure (to Forrest's left) is the Democratic candidate for President in 1868, Governor Horatio Seymour—depicted here as the prosperous associate of New York financiers. This unholy alliance unites in what to Nast were the characteristic Democratic Party activities of racial oppression and treason, illustrated by scenes from the New York Draft riots (see Document 14-7) and the postwar South, and by their trampling on the prostrate form of a black Union soldier.

The second cartoon shows a sharp shift in opinion on the part of both Nast and his audience. The cartoon illustrates a derisive news account of the black-majority South Carolina House of Representatives, reprinted from the white conservative *Charleston News.* In 1868 the views of the *News* would have been dismissed as "disloyal" by Nast's employer, *Harper's Weekly;* by 1874 the magazine was allowing those views a respectful hearing, and its famous cartoonist was giving them his stamp of approval. Why?

Sources: Thomas Nast, "This Is a White Man's Government," *Harper's Weekly,* 5 September 1868; Thomas Nast, "Colored Rule in a Reconstructed State," *Harper's Weekly,* 14 March 1874. Art courtesy the Research Libraries, New York Public Library.

Questions

1. Note the picture of African Americans presented here and in the illustration on text page 485. Contrast that with the portrayal of government by southern whites.
2. Compare the portrayal of African Americans in the last illustration with that in the earlier illustrations.
3. What do you think accounts for the change?

(a) This Is a White Man's Government (1868)

(b) Colored Rule in a Reconstructed State (1874)

COLORED RULE IN A RECONSTRUCTED (?) STATE.—[See Page 242.]

(THE MEMBERS CALL EACH OTHER THIEVES, LIARS, RASCALS, AND COWARDS.)

COLUMBIA. "You are Aping the lowest Whites. If you disgrace your Race in this way you had better take Back Seats."

15-10   A Fool's Errand. By One of the Fools (1879)

Albion W. Tourgee

A native of Ohio, Albion Winegar Tourgee (1838–1905) was working as a school-teacher in New York when the Civil War began. In April 1861 he joined the 27th New York Regiment and was wounded at the first battle of Bull Run. He returned to the army in July 1862 as a lieutenant in the 105th Ohio Regiment. Captured in 1863 at Murfreesboro, he returned to Ohio through a prisoner exchange and then rejoined his regiment to fight at Chickamauga, Lookout Mountain, and Missionary Ridge. Twice charged with insubordination, Tourgee resigned his commission in December 1863 and returned to Ohio to study law. By the fall of 1865 he had relocated, as a "carpet-bagger" (see text p. 489), in Greensboro, North Carolina. In 1868, under the electoral rule imposed under radical Reconstruction (see text pp. 490–491), Tourgee won election as a judge on the state superior court. He served there for six years, finding ample opportunity to defend the rights of freedmen and denounce the atrocities of the Ku Klux Klan. When his tenure on the court ended, President Grant appointed him pension agent at Raleigh, from which office he continued his battle with the Klan and with redeemer Democrats (see text pp. 494–495). By the summer of 1879 he had had enough and moved north with his family, making Mayville, New York, his home by 1881. In the novel *A Fool's Errand,* published in the year of his departure from North Carolina, Tourgee described his experiences during Reconstruction through the character Colonel Comfort Servosse, whom he depicted as "the Fool."

Source: [Albion W. Tourgee], *A Fool's Errand. By One of the Fools* (New York: Fords, Howard, & Hulbert, 1878), 182–192.

It was in the winter of 1868–69 . . . when it was said that already Reconstruction had been an approved success, [and] the traces of the war been blotted out . . . a little company of colored men came to the Fool one day; and one of them, who acted as spokesman said,—

"What's dis we hear, Mars Kunnel [Master Colonel], bout de Klux?"

"The what?" he asked.

"De Klux—de Ku-Kluckers dey calls demselves."

"Oh! The Ku-Klux, Ku-Klux-Klan . . . you mean."

"Yes: dem folks what rides about at night a-pesterin' pore colored people, an' pretendin' tu be jes from hell, or some of de battle-fields ob ole Virginny."

"Oh, that's all gammon [humbug]! There is nothing in the world in it,—nothing at all. . . ."

"You don't think dey's ghostses, nor nothing' ob dat sort?" asked another.

"Think! I know they are not."

"So do I," growled one of their number who had not spoken before, in a tone . . . that . . . drew the eyes of the Fool upon him at once.

"So your mind's made up on that point too, is it Bob?" he asked laughingly.

"I know dey's not ghosts, Kunnel. I wish ter God dey was!" was the reply.

"Why, what do you mean, Bob?" asked the colonel in surprise.

"Will you jes help me take off my shirt, Jim?" said Bob . . . as he turned to one of those with him. . . .

"What d'ye tink ob dat, Kunnel?"

"My God!" exclaimed the Fool, starting back in surprise and horror. "What does this mean, Bob?"

"Seen de Kluckers, sah," was the grimly-laconic answer.

The sight which presented itself to the Fool's eyes was truly terrible. . . . The whole back was livid and swollen, bruised as if it had been brayed in a mortar. Apparently, after having cut the flesh with closely-laid welts and furrows, sloping downward from the left side towards the right, with the peculiar skill . . . which could only be obtained through the abundant opportunity for severe . . . flagellation which prevailed under . . . slavery, the operator had changed his position, and scientifically cross-checked the whole. . . . "Nobody but an ole oberseer ebber dun dat, Kunnel." . . . When his clothing had been resumed, he sat down and poured into the wondering ears of the Fool this story:—

BOB'S EXPERIENCE.

"Yer see, I'se a blacksmith at Burke's Cross-Roads. I've been thar ever sence a few days arter I heer ob de surrender. I rented an ole house dar, an' put up a sort of shop . . . an' went to work. . . .

"Long a while back—p'raps five er six month—I refused ter du some work fer Michael Anson or his boy, 'cause they'd run up quite a score at de shop, an' allers put me off when I wanted pay. . . . Folks said I waz gettin' too smart fer a nigger, an' sech like; but I kep right on; tole em I waz a free man . . . an' I didn't propose ter do any man's work fer noffin'. Most everybody hed somefin' ter say about it; but it didn't seem ter hurt my trade very much. . . . When ther come an election, I sed my say, did my own votin', an' tole de other colored people dey waz free, an' hed a right ter du de same. Thet's bad doctrine up in our country. . . . Dey don't mind 'bout . . . our votin', so long ez we votes ez day tell us. Dat' dare idea uv liberty fer a nigger.

"Well, here a few weeks ago, I foun' a board stuck up on my shop one mornin', wid dese words on it:—

"'BOB MARTIN,—You're gettin' too dam smart! The white folks round Burke's Cross-Roads don't want any sech smart niggers round thar. You'd better git, er you'll hev a call from the

"'K.K.K.'

. . . [Y]esterday . . . my ole 'ooman . . . tuk part ob de chillen into bed wid her; an' de rest crawled in wid me. . . . I kinder remember hearin' de dog bark, but I didn't mind it; an', de fust ting I knew, de do' was bust in. . . . Dar was 'bout tirty of 'em standin' dar in de moonlight, all dressed in black gowns thet come down to ther boots, an' some sort of high hat on, dat come down ober der faces. . . . Den dey tied me tu a tree, an' done what you've seen. Dey tuk my wife an' oldes' gal out of de house, tore de close right about off 'em, an' abused 'em shockin' afore my eyes. After tarin' tings up a heap in de house, dey rode off, tellin' me dey reckoned I's larn to be 'spectful to white folks hereafter. . . .

"Why have you not complained of this outrage to the authorities?" . . . asked [the Fool] after a moment.

"I tole Squire Haskins an' Judge Thompson what I hev tole you," answered Bob.

"And what did they say?"

"Dat dey couldn't do noffin' unless I could sw'ar to the parties." . . .

There was a moment's silence. Then the colored man asked,—

"Isn't dere no one else, Kunnel, dat could do any ting? Can't de President or Congress do somefin'? De gov'ment sot us free, an' it 'pears like it oughtn't to let our old masters impose on us in no sech way now. . . . We ain't cowards. We showed dat in de wah. I'se seen darkeys go whar de white troops wa'n't anxious to foller 'em, mor'n once."

"Where was that, Bob?"

"Wal, at Fo't Wagner, for one."

"How did you know about that?"

"How did I know 'bout dat? Bress yer soul, Kunnel, I was dar!"

Questions

1. Tourgee, thinly disguised as Servosse, depicts himself as "the Fool." Why?
2. Could the president or Congress have acted in ways that they did not to suppress the Ku Klux Klan? Describe the measures you think would have been necessary.
3. Were equal rights for blacks and the restoration of civil government in the South compatible? Explain why or why not.

15-11   President Grant Refuses to Aid Republicans in Mississippi (1875)

As one of three southern states with a black-majority population, one whose black voters were well organized, Mississippi should logically have remained secure for the Republicans. However, in the state election year of 1875, white Democrats launched a campaign of systematic violent intimidation of black and Republican voters. Against the massive mobilization of white "Rifle Clubs," the state government of Governor Adelbert Ames was helpless, and in September Ames sent President Grant a desperate plea for federal troops. Grant and his attorney general, Edwards Pierrepont, turned down Ames's request; Pierrepont's letter to Ames of September 14, quoting Grant, was subsequently released to the press (Document 15-11a). Thanks to a catastrophic decline in Republican votes and blatant ballot-box stuffing, Democrats "redeemed" the state in a landslide. One of the few survivors of the Democratic onslaught, African American Congressman John R. Lynch, wrote some years later of a postelection encounter with President Grant, who explained to him the political considerations behind his abandonment of Mississippi Republicans (Document 15-11b).

Sources: New York Times, 17 September 1875, 1; John Roy Lynch, *The Facts of Reconstruction* (New York: Neale Publishing Co, 1913), 150–153.

(a) Pierrepont's Letter of Refusal

DEPARTMENT OF JUSTICE,
WASHINGTON, Sept. 14, 1875.

To Gov. Ames, Jackson, Miss.:

This hour I have had dispatches from the President. I can best convey to you his ideas by extracts from his dispatch: "The whole public are tired out with these annual Autumnal outbreaks in the South, and the great majority are ready now to condemn any interference on the part of the Government. I heartily wish that peace and good order may be restored without issuing the proclamation; but if it is not the proclamation must be issued, and if it is I shall instruct the commander of the forces to have *no child's play.* If there is a necessity for military interference, there is justice in such interference as shall deter evil-doers. . . . I would suggest the sending of a dispatch (or better, a private messenger,) to Gov. Ames, urging him to strengthen his own position by exhausting his own resources in restoring order before he receives Government aid. He might accept the assistance offered by the citizens of Jackson and elsewhere. . . . Gov. Ames and his advisors can be made perfectly secure. As many of the troops in Mississippi as he deems necessary may be sent to Jackson. If he is betrayed by those who offer assistance, he will be in a position to defeat their ends and punish them."

You see by this the mind of the President, with which I and every member of the Cabinet who has been consulted are in full accord. You see the difficulties—you see the responsibilities which you assume. We cannot understand why you do not strengthen yourself in the way the President suggests, nor do we see why you do not call the Legislature together, and obtain from them whatever powers, money, and arms you need. The Constitution is explicit that the Executive of the State can call upon the President for aid in suppressing "domestic violence" only "when the Legislature cannot be convened," and the law expressly says: "In case of an insurrection in any State against the Government thereof, it shall be lawful for the President, on application of the Legislature of such State, or of the Executive, when the Legislature cannot be convened, to call," &c. It is the plain meaning of the Constitution and laws when taken together that the Executive of the State may call upon the President for military aid to quell "domestic violence" only in case of an insurrection in any State against the Government thereof when the Legislature can-

not be called together. You make no suggestions even that there is any insurrection against the Government of the State, or that the Legislature would not support you in any measures you might propose to preserve the public order. I suggest that you take all lawful means and all needed measures to preserve the peace by the forces in your own State, and let the country see that the citizens of Mississippi, who are largely favorable to good order, and who are largely Republican, have the courage and the manhood to fight for their rights and to destroy the bloody ruffians who murder the innocent and inoffending freedmen. Everything is in readiness. Be careful to bring yourself strictly within the Constitution and the laws, and if there is such resistance to your State authorities as you cannot, by all the means at your command, suppress, the President will swiftly aid you in crushing those lawless traitors to human rights.

Telegraph me on receipt of this, and state explicitly what you need. Very respectfully yours,
EDWARDS PIERREPONT, Attorney General.

(b) Grant's Subsequent Explanation

. . . I then informed the President that there was another matter about which I desired to have a short talk with him, that was the recent election in Mississippi. After calling his attention to the sanguinary struggle through which we had passed, and the great disadvantages under which we labored, I reminded him of the fact that the Governor, when he saw that he could not put down without the assistance of the National Administration what was practically an insurrection against the State Government, made application for assistance in the manner and form prescribed by the Constitution, with the confident belief that it would be forthcoming. But in this we were, for some reason, seriously disappointed and sadly surprised. The reason for this action, or rather non-action, was still an unexplained mystery to us. For my own satisfaction and information I should be pleased to have the President enlighten me on the subject.

The President said that he was glad I had asked him the question, and that he would take pleasure in giving me a frank reply. He said he had sent Governor Ames' requisition to the War Department with his approval and with instructions to have the necessary assistance furnished without delay. He had also given instructions to the Attorney-General to use the marshals and the machinery of the Federal judiciary as far as possible in coöperation with the War Department in an effort to maintain order and to bring about a condition which would insure a peaceable and fair election. But before the orders were put into execution a committee of prominent Republicans from Ohio had called on him. (Ohio was then an October State,—that is, her elections took place in October instead of November.) An important election was then pending in that State. This committee, the President stated, protested against having the requisition of Governor Ames honored. The committee, the President said, informed him in a most emphatic way that if the requisition of Governor Ames were honored, the Democrats would not only carry Mississippi,—a State which would be lost to the Republicans in any event,—but that Democratic success in Ohio would be an assured fact. If the requisition were not honored it would make no change in the result in Mississippi, but that Ohio would be saved to the Republicans. The President assured me that it was with great reluctance that he yielded,—against his own judgment and sense of official duty,—to the arguments of this committee, and directed the withdrawal of the orders which had been given the Secretary of War and the Attorney-General in that matter.

This statement, I confess, surprised me very much.

"Can it be possible," I asked, "that there is such a prevailing sentiment in any State in the North, East or West as renders it necessary for a Republican President to virtually give his sanction to what is equivalent to a suspension of the Constitution and laws of the land to insure Republican success in such a State? I cannot believe this to be true, the opinion of the Republican committee from Ohio to the contrary notwithstanding. What surprises me more, Mr. President, is that you yielded and granted this remarkable request. That is not like you. It is the first time I have ever known you to show the white feather. Instead of granting the request of that committee, you should have rebuked the men,—told them that it is your duty as chief magistrate of the country to enforce the Constitution and laws of the land, and to protect American citizens in the exercise and enjoyment of their rights, let the consequences be what they may; and that if by doing this Ohio should be lost to the Republicans it ought to be lost. In other words, no victory is worth having if it is to be brought about upon such conditions as those,—if it is to be purchased at such a fearful cost as was paid in this case."

"Yes," said the President, "I admit that you are right. I should not have yielded. I believed at the time that I was making a grave mistake. But as presented, it was duty on one side, and party obligation on the other. Between the two I hesitated, but finally yielded to what was believed to be party obligation. If a mistake was made, it was one of the head and not of the heart. That my heart was right and my intentions good, no one who knows me will question. If I had believed that any effort on my part would have saved Mississippi I would have made it, even if I had been convinced that it would have resulted in the loss of Ohio to the Republicans. But I was satisfied then, as I am now, that Mississippi could not have been saved to the party in any event and I wanted to avoid the responsibility of the loss of Ohio, in addition. This was the turning-point in the case. . . ."

Questions

1. Do you think that Grant was correct in his argument against federal intervention? Was there really nothing that the federal government and the national Republican Party could have done to "save" Mississippi?
2. Had Governor Ames convened the Mississippi legislature to deal with "the bloody ruffians," how successful do you think he would have been?
3. What does Grant's decision illuminate about how Republicans, and many people in the North, had come to view the South and the progress of Reconstruction—especially in the Deep South—by the mid-1870s?

15-12   Plan of the Campaign (1876)

Martin W. Gary

The Mississippi Plan of 1875 proved so successful in "redeeming" that state in 1875 that it attracted attention from white Democrats in the other southern states still under Republican rule. In South Carolina—like Mississippi a black-majority state—white "Conservatives" created a paramilitary organization called the Red Shirts. The chief organizer of the campaign to overthrow the Republicans, an upcountry lawyer and politician named Martin W. Gary, prepared the following "Plan of the Campaign," which in revised form was sent out to all county Conservative organizations. The "rules" in italics were omitted in the printed version. Like the "Mississippi Plan," Gary's plan was successful in ousting the Republican regime in the state, although the Conservative victory was only ratified when President Hayes withdrew federal troops from the state as part of the Compromise of 1877.

Source: Francis Butler Simkins and Robert Hilliard Woody, *South Carolina during Reconstruction* (Chapel Hill: University of North Carolina Press, 1932), 564–569.

1. That every Democrat in the Townships must be put upon the Roll of the Democratic Clubs. Nolens volens.

2. That a Roster must be made of every *white* and of *every negro* voter in the Townships and *returned immediately* to the Country Executive Committee.

3. *That the Democratic Military Clubs are to be armed with rifles and pistols and such other arms as they may command. They are to be divided into two companies, one of the old men the other of the young; an experienced captain or commander to be placed over each of them. That each Company is to have a 1st and 2nd Lieutenant. That the number of ten privates is to be the unit of organization. That each Captain is to see that his men are well armed and provided with at least thirty rounds of ammunition. That the Captain of the young men is to provide a Baggage wagon, in which three days rations for the horses and three days rations for the men are to be stored on the day before the election in order that they may be prepared at a moments notice to move to any point in the County when ordered by the Chairman of the Executive Committee.*

ELECTION

4. We must get the three Commissioners of Election, who are appointed by the Governor, as favorable to us as possible, and we must demand that at least one reliable Democrat is on the Commission and he must endeavor to get to be Chairman of the Commission, and the clerk that is allowed them must be a Democrat if we can possibly bring it about.

5. We must have at least one half of the managers of Election Democrats and as many more as we can get. We must have the Chairman of the Board of Managers a Democrat by all means. Also all the clerks to the managers of Precincts must be Democrats.

6. We must have a duplicate of the result of the Election made out for the benefit of the Executive Committee so soon as the ballots are counted and forwarded at once by a courier, on the night of the Election. There must be a Committee who shall keep watch and guard over the ballot boxes to prevent the Radicals from tampering with them in any way.

7. We must send a committee with a duplicate of the Election to Columbia in order to see to it that the State Canvassers do not perpetrate any fraud upon us after the Election is held, and . . . that the Clerk of the Court files a copy of the returns of Election in accordance with Law.

8. *There must be at least two hundred select men, chosen from the different Clubs, to go to Columbia in the event of a refusal to seat the Democratic members elected, to compel and enforce their rights to be seated at all hazards.*

9. Every Democrat must be at the polls by five o'clock in the morning of the election, carry his dinner with him and stay there until the votes are counted, unless the exigencies require him elsewhere.

10. It shall be the duty of each club to provide transportation to old and helpless voters and assist them to the Polls, and at the same time see to it that all Democrats turn out and vote.

11. Every Democrat must be on the alert on the day of Election to see that negroes under age do not vote and that those who are properly entitled to vote do not repeat, and if they should discover that squads should leave the precincts and go in the direction of another precinct, they must follow them and challenge their vote at the next precinct.

12. Every Democrat must feel honor bound to control the vote of at least one negro, by intimidation, purchase, keeping him away or as each individual may determine, how he may best accomplish it.

13. We must attend every Radical meeting that we hear of whether they meet at night or in the day time. Democrats must go in as large numbers as they can get together, and well armed, behave at *first* with great courtesy and assure the ignorant negroes that you mean them no harm and so soon as their *leaders* or speakers begin to speak and make false statements of facts, tell them *then* and *there* to their faces, that they are liars, thieves and rascals, and are only trying to mislead the ignorant negroes and if you get a chance get upon the platform and address the negroes.

14. In speeches to negroes you must remember that *argument* has no effect upon them: They can only be influenced by their *fears,* superstition and cupidity. Do not attempt to flatter and persuade them. Tell them plainly of our wrongs and grievances, perpetrated upon us, by their rascally leaders. Prove to them that we can carry the election without them and if they coöperate with us, it will benefit them more than it will us. Treat them so as to show

them, you are the superior race, and that their natural position is that of subordination to the white man.

15. Let it be generally known that if any blood is shed, houses burnt, votes repeated, ballot boxes stuffed, false counting of votes, or any acts on their part that are in violation of *Law* and *Order!* that we will hold the leaders of the *Radical Party personally responsible,* whether they were present at the time of the commission of the offense or crime or not; beginning *first* with the white men, second the mulatto men and third with the black leaders. This should be proclaimed from one end of the country to the other, so that *every Radical* may know it, as the *certain, fixed* and *unalterable determination* of every Democrat in this county.

16. *"Never threaten a man individually if he deserves to be threatened, the necessities of the times require that he should die. A dead Radical is very harmless—a threatened Radical or one driven off by threats from the scene of his operations is often very troublesome, sometimes dangerous, always vindictive."* . . .

21. *In the month of September we ought to begin to organize negro clubs, or pretend that we have organized them and write letters from different parts of the County giving the facts of organization out from prudential reasons, the names of the negroes are to be withheld. Those who join are to be taken on probation and are not to be taken into full fellowship, until they have proven their sincerity by voting our ticket.*

22. In the nomination of candidates we should nominate those who will give their time, their money, their brains, their energies and if necessary lay down their lives to carry this election. Any attempt to run independent candidates must be prevented at any risk.

23. There should not be any assessment for money to carry on the campaign, before the month of October, when the cotton crop begins to mature and our people have an opportunity of raising money by its sale.

24. In voting for or nominating candidates for County, State or Federal offices, we must give the preference to native born *white South Carolinians* over Carpet baggers.

25. The watch word of our Campaign should be "fight the Devil with fire." That we are in favor of local self government, home rule by home folks and that we are determined to drive the carpet baggers from this State at all hazards. . . .

28. In all processions the clubs must parade with banners, mottoes, etc. and keep together so as to make an imposing spectacle.

29. Every club must be uniformed in a red shirt and they must be sure and wear it upon all public meetings and particularly on the day of election. . . .

30. Secrecy should shroud all of transactions. Let not your left hand know what your right does. . . .

33. Any member of the Party who fails to vote the ticket must be read out of the Party.

Questions

1. Is this a plan for a political or a military campaign? Explain the difference.
2. What distinguishes the provisions in italics from those in regular typeface?
3. What are Gary's attitudes toward blacks? Does he regard them as citizens to be persuaded of the justice of his cause?

Questions for Further Thought

1. Compare and contrast northern and southern views of blacks (Documents 15-9a, 15-9b, and 15-10). How are they the same? How are they different? What impact did the northern view of blacks have on the progress of Reconstruction?
2. Why did the Radical Republican program (Document 15-5) for reconstruction fail? After years of promises, why did the Republican Party in particular, and northerners in general, turn their backs on the freedmen and leave them to the mercy of their former masters in the South (Documents 15-11 and 15-12)?
3. If the Republican Party had pressed ahead with Reconstruction, do you think that it could have achieved its goals? Or was Albion Tourgee correct in calling the effort to reform the post–Civil War South "a fool's errand" (Document 15-10)?

CHAPTER **16**

The American West

★   ★   ★

The Great Plains

Before the Civil War, eastern and midwestern farmers might well have agreed with Horace Greeley's depiction of the Great Plains (see Map 16.1, p. 508) as a "treeless desert" with a "terrible" climate. After the war, however, despite climatic and environmental problems, a combination of factors made the Plains attractive to settlers. Primary among these factors was cheap land, secured directly from the federal government or indirectly from railroads, which sold off their federal land grants to generate business along their lines. Through other promotions and advertising, state and territorial governments and private interests promoted western settlement and development, too. Thus between 1870 and 1890, Kansas, Nebraska, and the Dakotas, which straddled the line between the humid, tall-grass prairies and the subhumid, short-grass plains, jumped in population from 500,000 to 3 million.

Technology contributed to the opening and development of the West. Railroads brought in settlers and materials, transforming a raw frontier into a settled area, and they carried crops, livestock, and meat to market. Mechanization made possible the cultivation of extensive acreage, an imperative on the Plains, where grains were the foundation of agriculture. Throughout this period of development and mechanization in agriculture, family operators continued to predominate among farmers (see text pp. 508–518).

With overwhelming numbers of farmers and ranchers pouring onto the Plains (and smaller numbers of miners into hilly and mountainous areas), conflict between the settlers and the greatly outnumbered native Americans, whose nations had settled in the West long before or had been forced to relocate there by treaties with the U.S. government, was virtually inevitable. Warfare flared across the West from the 1860s until the Wounded Knee Massacre of 1890 (see text pp. 509–510, 518–521, including Map 16.3).

Hamlin Garland (Document 16-1) deals with western farm life. In Document 16-2, Helen Hunt Jackson criticizes the failure of the U.S. government to keep its promises to native Americans. In 1887, Congress tried to deal with the plight of native Americans through the Dawes Severalty Act (Document 16-3). Document 16-4 sheds light on native Americans on the eve of the Wounded Knee Massacre of 1890.

16-1   Our First Winter on the Prairie (c. 1870)

Hamlin Garland

During his childhood and youth, Hamlin Garland (1860–1940) lived in Wisconsin, Minnesota, Iowa, and the Dakota Territory. As an adult, he lived in Boston, Chicago, New York City, and the Los Angeles area. A writer of essays, short stories, novels, and autobiography, Garland was realistic in his depiction of farm life and sympathetic toward women's rights, native Americans' rights, and farmers' political movements. Although this piece depicts life on the Iowa prairie, homesteaders on the Great Plains faced similar hardships and pleasures.

Source: Hamlin Garland, *A Son of the Middle Border* (New York: Macmillan, 1920), 85–98.

For a few days my brother and I had little to do other than to keep the cattle from straying, and we used our leisure in becoming acquainted with the region round about.

It burned deep into our memories, this wide, sunny, windy country. The sky so big, and the horizon line so low and so far away, made this new world of the plain more majestic than the world of the Coulee.—The grasses and many of the flowers were also new to us. On the uplands the herbage was short and dry and the plants stiff and woody, but in the swales the wild oat shook its quivers of barbed and twisted arrows, and the crow's foot, tall and sere, bowed softly under the feet of the wind, while everywhere, in the lowlands as well as on the ridges, the bleaching white antlers of by-gone herbivora lay scattered, testifying to "the herds of deer and buffalo" which once fed there. We were just a few years too late to see them.

To the south the sections were nearly all settled upon, for in that direction lay the county town, but to the north and on into Minnesota rolled the unplowed sod, the feeding ground of the cattle, the home of foxes and wolves, and to the west, just beyond the highest ridges, we loved to think the bison might still be seen.

The cabin on this rented farm was a mere shanty, a shell of pine boards, which needed re-enforcing to make it habitable and one day my father said, "Well, Hamlin, I guess you'll have to run the plow-team this fall. I must help neighbor Button wall up the house and I can't afford to hire another man."

This seemed a fine commission for a lad of ten, and I drove my horses into the field that first morning with a manly pride which added an inch to my stature. I took my initial "round" at a "land" which stretched from one side of the quarter section to the other, in confident mood. I was grown up!

But alas! my sense of elation did not last long. To guide a team for a few minutes as an experiment was one thing—to plow all day like a hired hand was another. It was not a chore, it was a job. It meant moving to and fro hour after hour, day after day, with no one to talk to but the horses. It meant trudging eight or nine miles in the forenoon and as many more in the afternoon, with less than an hour off at noon. It meant dragging the heavy implement around the corners, and it meant also many shipwrecks, for the thick, wet stubble matted with wild buckwheat often rolled up between the coulter and the standard and threw the share completely out of the ground, making it necessary for me to halt the team and jerk the heavy plow backward for a new start.

Although strong and active I was rather short, even for a ten-year-old, and to reach the plow handles I was obliged to lift my hands above my shoulders; and so with the guiding lines crossed over my back and my worn straw hat bobbing just above the cross-brace I must have made a comical figure. At any rate nothing like it had been seen in the neighborhood and the people on the road to town looking across the field, laughed and called to me, and neighbor Button said to my father in my hearing, "That chap's too young to run a plow," a judgment which pleased and flattered me greatly. . . .

The flies were savage, especially in the middle of the day, and the horses, tortured by their lances, drove badly, twisting and turning in their despairing rage. Their tails were continually getting over the lines, and in stopping to kick their tormentors from their bellies they often got astride the traces, and in other ways made trouble for me. Only in the early morning or when the sun sank low at night were they able to move quietly along their ways.

The soil was the kind my father had been seeking, a smooth dark sandy loam, which made it possible for a lad to do the work of a man. Often the share would go the entire "round" without striking a root or a pebble as big as a walnut, the steel running steadily with a crisp crunching ripping sound which I rather liked to hear. In truth work would have been quite tolerable had it not been so long drawn out. Ten hours of it even on a fine day made about twice too many for a boy.

Meanwhile I cheered myself in every imaginable way. I whistled. I sang. I studied the clouds. I gnawed the beautiful red skin from the seed vessels which hung upon the wild rose bushes, and I counted the prairie chickens as they began to come together in winter flocks running through the stubble in search of food. I stopped now and again to examine the lizards unhoused by the share, tormenting them to make them sweat their milky drops (they were curiously repulsive to me), and I measured the little granaries of wheat which the mice and gophers had deposited deep under the ground, storehouses which the plow had violated. My eyes dwelt enviously upon the sailing hawk, and on the passing of ducks. The occasional shadowy figure of a prairie wolf made me wish for Uncle David and his rifle.

On certain days nothing could cheer me. When the bitter wind blew from the north, and the sky was filled with wild geese racing southward, with swiftly-hurrying clouds, winter seemed about to spring upon me. The horses' tails streamed in the wind. Flurries of snow covered me with clinging flakes, and the mud "gummed" my boots and trouser legs, clogging my steps. At such times I suffered from cold and loneliness—all sense of being a man evaporated. I was just a little boy, longing for the leisure of boyhood.

Day after day, through the month of October and deep into November, I followed that team, turning over two acres of stubble each day. I would not believe this without proof, but it is true! At last it grew so cold that in the early morning everything was white with frost and I was obliged to put one hand in my pocket to keep it warm, while holding the plow with the other, but I didn't mind this so much, for it hinted at the close of autumn. I've no doubt facing the wind in this way was excellent discipline, but I didn't think it necessary then and my heart was sometimes bitter and rebellious.

The soldier did not intend to be severe. As he had always been an early riser and a busy toiler it seemed perfectly natural and good discipline, that his sons should also plow and husk corn at ten years of age. He often told of beginning life as a "bound boy" at nine, and these stories helped me to perform my own tasks without whining. I feared to voice my weakness.

At last there came a morning when by striking my heel upon the ground I convinced the boss that the soil was frozen too deep for the mold-board to break. "All right," he said, "you may lay off this afternoon."

Oh, those beautiful hours of respite! With time to play or read I usually read, devouring anything I could lay my hands upon. Newspapers, whether old or new, or pasted on the wall or piled up in the attic,—anything in print was wonderful to me. One enthralling book, borrowed from neighbor Button, was *The Female Spy*, a Tale of the Rebellion. Another treasure was a story called *Cast Ashore*, but this volume unfortunately was badly torn and fifty pages were missing so that I never knew, and do not know to this day, how those indomitable shipwrecked seamen reached their English homes. I dimly recall that one man carried a pet monkey on his back and that they all lived on "Bustards."

Finally the day came when the ground rang like iron under the feet of the horses, and a bitter wind, raw and gusty, swept out of the northwest, bearing gray veils of sleet. Winter had come! Work in the furrow had ended. The plow was brought in, cleaned and greased to prevent its rusting, and while the horses munched their hay in well-earned holiday, father and I helped farmer Button husk the last of his corn. . . .

The school-house which was to be the center of our social life stood on the bare prairie about a mile to the southwest and like thousands of other similar buildings in the west, had not a leaf to shade it in summer nor a branch to break the winds of savage winter. "There's been a good deal of talk about setting out a wind-break," neighbor Button explained to us, "but nothing has as yet been done." It was merely a square pine box painted a glaring white on the outside and a desolate drab within; at least drab was the original color, but the benches were mainly so greasy and hacked that original intentions were obscured. It had two doors on the eastern end and three windows on each side.

A long square stove (standing on slender legs in a puddle of bricks), a wooden chair, and a rude table in one corner, for the use of the teacher, completed the movable furniture. The walls were roughly plastered and the windows had no curtains.

It was a barren temple of the arts even to the residents of Dry Run, and Harriet and I, stealing across the prairie one Sunday morning to look in, came away vaguely depressed. We were fond of school and never missed a day if we could help it, but this neighborhood center seemed so small and bleak and poor.

With what fear, what excitement we approached the door on that first day, I can only faintly indicate. All the scholars were strange to me except Albert and Cyrus Button, and I was prepared for rough treatment. However, the experience was not so harsh as I had feared. True, Rangely Field did throw me down and wash my face in snow, and Jack Sweet tripped me up once or twice, but I bore these indignities with such grace [as I] could command, and soon made a place for myself among the boys. . . .

I cannot recover much of that first winter of school. It was not an experience to remember for its charm. Not one line of grace, not one touch of color relieved the room's bare walls or softened its harsh windows. Perhaps this very barrenness gave to the poetry in our readers an appeal that seems magical. . . .

This winter was made memorable also by a "revival" which came over the district with sudden fury. It began late in the winter—fortunately, for it ended all dancing and merry-making for the time. It silenced Daddy Fairbanks' fiddle and subdued my mother's glorious voice to a wail. A cloud of puritanical gloom settled upon almost every household. Youth and love became furtive and hypocritic.

The evangelist, one of the old-fashioned shouting, hysterical, ungrammatical, gasping sort, took charge of the services, and in his exhortations phrases descriptive of lakes of burning brimstone and ages of endless torment abounded. Some of the figures of speech and violent gestures of the man still linger in my mind, but I will not set them down on paper. They are too dreadful to perpetuate.

At times he roared with such power that he could have been heard for half a mile.

And yet we went, night by night, mother, father, Jessie, all of us. It was our theater. Some of the roughest characters in the neighborhood rose and professed repentance, for a season, even old Barton, the profanest man in the township, experienced a "change of heart."

We all enjoyed the singing, and joined most lustily in the tunes. Even little Jessie learned to sing *Heavenly Wings, There is a Fountain filled with Blood,* and *Old Hundred.*

As I peer back into that crowded little school-room, smothering hot and reeking with lamp smoke, and recall the half-lit, familiar faces of the congregation, it all has the quality of a vision, something experienced in another world. The preacher, leaping, sweating, roaring till the windows rattle, the mothers with sleeping babes in their arms, the sweet, strained faces of the girls, the immobile wondering men, are spectral shadows, figures encountered in the phantasmagoria of disordered sleep.

Questions

1. What did Garland's life as a ten-year-old entail? What are his pleasures and his hardships?
2. When speaking of his father, Garland reveals both fear and pride in "the soldier" who demanded "good discipline" and had high expectations. How might Garland have been influenced by a father who was a "bound boy" at age nine and a Union soldier later in life?
3. What roles did the schoolhouse play in the lives of local children and families? What does this reveal about life in a farming area?

16-2   A Century of Dishonor (1881)

Helen Hunt Jackson

Born in Amherst, Massachusetts, Helen Hunt Jackson (1830–1885) was raised in the New England moral climate that nurtured the abolitionist and women's movements of the mid-nineteenth century. However, this childhood friend of Emily Dickinson showed no interest in reform causes until her second marriage and her move to Colorado in 1875. Ironically, it was during a trip to Boston in 1879 that Jackson heard the Ponca chief Standing Bear speak on the plight of the Plains Indians.

The incident served as a conversion experience, and Jackson began making herself an expert on the history of relations between the government and native Americans. Within two years she published *A Century of Dishonor*. Not all readers were pleased with Jackson's condemnation of the government for its mistreatment of native Americans. Because the book was "written in good English" by an author "intensely in earnest," Theodore Roosevelt feared that it was "capable of doing great harm."

Source: Helen Hunt Jackson, *A Century of Dishonor* (New York: Harper and Brothers, 1881; reprint, New York: Harper and Row, 1965), 338–342.

In 1869 President Grant appointed a commission of nine men, representing the influence and philanthropy of six leading States, to visit the different Indian reservations, and to "examine all matters appertaining to Indian affairs."

In the report of this commission are such paragraphs as the following: "To assert that 'the Indian will not work' is as true as it would be to say that the white man will not work.

"Why should the Indian be expected to plant corn, fence lands, build houses, or do anything but get food from day to day, when experience has taught him that the product of his labor will be seized by the white man to-morrow? The most industrious white man would become a drone under similar circumstances. Nevertheless, many of the Indians" (the commissioners might more forcibly have said 130,000 of the Indians) "are already at work, and furnish ample refutation of the assertion that 'the Indian will not work.' There is no escape from the inexorable logic of facts.

"The history of the Government connections with the Indians is a shameful record of broken treaties and unfulfilled promises. The history of the border white man's connection with the Indians is a sickening record of murder, outrage, robbery, and wrongs committed by the former, as the rule, and occasional savage outbreaks and unspeakably barbarous deeds of retaliation by the latter, as the exception.

"Taught by the Government that they had rights entitled to respect, when those rights have been assailed by the rapacity of the white man, the arm which should have been raised to protect them has ever been ready to sustain the aggressor.

"The testimony of some of the highest military officers of the United States is on record to the effect that, in our Indian wars, almost without exception, the first aggressions have been made by the white man; and the assertion is supported by every civilian of reputation who has studied the subject. In addition to the class of robbers and outlaws who find impunity in their nefarious pursuits on the frontiers, there is a large class of professedly reputable men who use every means in their power to bring on Indian wars for the sake of the profit to be realized from the presence of troops and the expenditure of Government funds in their midst. They proclaim death to the Indians at all times in words and publications, making no distinction between the innocent and the guilty. They irate the lowest class of men to the perpetration of the darkest deeds against their victims, and as judges and jurymen shield them from the justice due to their crimes. Every crime committed by a white man against an Indian is concealed or palliated. Every offence committed by an Indian against a white man is borne on the wings of the post or the telegraph to the remotest corner of the land, clothed with all the horrors which the reality or imagination can throw around it. Against such influences as these the people of the United States need to be warned."

To assume that it would be easy, or by any one sudden stroke of legislative policy possible, to undo the mischief and hurt of the long past, set the Indian policy of the country right for the future, and make the Indians at once safe and happy, is the blunder of a hasty and uninformed judgment. The notion which seems to be growing more prevalent, that simply to make all Indians at once citizens of the United States would be a sovereign and instantaneous panacea for all their ills and all the Government's perplexities, is a very inconsiderate one. To administer complete citizenship of a sudden, all round, to all Indians, barbarous and civilized alike, would be as grotesque a blunder as to dose them all round with any one medicine, irrespective of the symptoms and needs of their diseases. It would kill more than it would cure. Nevertheless, it is true, as was well stated by one of the superintendents of Indian Affairs in 1857, that, "so long as they are not citizens of the United States, their rights of property must remain insecure against invasion. The doors of the federal tribunals being barred against them while wards and dependents, they can only partially exercise the rights of free government, or give to those who make, execute, and construe the few laws they are allowed to enact, dignity sufficient to make them respectable. While they continue individually to gather the crumbs that fall from the table of the United States, idleness, improvidence, and indebtedness will be the rule, and industry, thrift, and freedom from debt the exception. The utter absence of individual title to particular lands deprives every one among them of the chief incentive to labor and exertion—the very mainspring on which the prosperity of a people depends."

All judicious plans and measures for their safety and salvation must embody provisions for their becoming citizens as fast as they are fit, and must protect them till then in every right and particular in which our laws protect other "persons" who are not citizens.

There is a disposition in a certain class of minds to be impatient with any protestation against wrong which is unaccompanied or unprepared with a quick and exact scheme of remedy. This is illogical. When pioneers in a new country find a tract of poisonous and swampy wilderness to be reclaimed, they do not withhold their hands from fire and axe till they see clearly which way roads should run, where good water will spring, and what crops will best grow on the redeemed land. They first clear the swamp. So with this poisonous and baffling part of the domain of our national affairs—let us first "clear the swamp."

However great perplexity and difficulty there may be in the details of any and every plan possible for doing at this late day anything like justice to the Indian, however hard it may be for good statesmen and good men to agree upon the things that ought to be done, there certainly is, or ought to be, no perplexity whatever, no difficulty whatever, in agreeing upon certain things that ought not to be done, and which must cease to be done before the first steps can be taken toward righting the wrongs, curing the ills, and wiping out the disgrace to us of the present condition of our Indians.

Cheating, robbing, breaking promises—these three are clearly things which must cease to be done. One more thing, also, and that is the refusal of the protection of the law to the Indian's rights of property, "of life, liberty, and the pursuit of happiness."

When these four things have ceased to be done, time, statesmanship, philanthropy, and Christianity can slowly and surely do the rest. Till these four things have ceased to be done, statesmanship and philanthropy alike must work in vain, and even Christianity can reap but small harvest.

Questions

1. Why didn't official reports critical of U.S. government policy toward native Americans have a greater effect on the American public?
2. What was the importance of granting citizenship to native Americans? What problems with granting citizenship does Jackson see?
3. What was Jackson's prescription for improved relations with native Americans?

16-3   The Dawes Severalty Act (1887)

Congress responded to Helen Hunt Jackson and other critics of its native American policy with the Dawes Severalty Act of 1887. The act attempted to "mainstream" Indians into American society: reservations were to be abolished, and native Americans were to be given land. The act accomplished little beyond reducing the amount of land under native American control, and the reservation policy was revived in the 1930s.

Source: United States, *Statutes at Large,* 24: 388ff.

Be it enacted by the Senate and House of Representatives of the United States of America in Congress assembled, That in all cases where any tribe or band of Indians has been, or shall hereafter be, located upon any reservation created for their use, either by treaty stipulation or by virtue of an act of Congress or executive order setting apart the same for their use, the President of the United States be, and he hereby is, authorized, whenever in his opinion any reservation or any part thereof of such Indians is advantageous for agricultural and grazing purposes, to cause said reservation, or any part thereof, to be surveyed, or resurveyed if necessary, and to allot the lands in said reservation in severalty to any Indian located thereon in quantities as follows:

To each head of a family, one-quarter of a section;

To each single person over eighteen years of age, one-eighth of a section;

To each orphan child under eighteen years of age, one-eighth of a section; and

To each other single person under eighteen years now living, or who may be born prior to the date of the order of the President directing an allotment of the lands embraced

in any reservation, one-sixteenth of a section: *Provided,* That in case there is not sufficient land in any of said reservations to allot lands to each individual of the classes above named in quantities as above provided, the lands embraced in such reservation or reservations shall be allotted to each individual of each of said classes pro rata in accordance with the provisions of this act: *And provided further,* That where the treaty or act of Congress setting apart such reservation provides for the allotment of lands in severalty in quantities in excess of those herein provided, the President, in making allotments upon such reservation, shall allot the lands to each individual Indian belonging thereon in quantity as specified in such treaty or act: *And provided further,* That when the lands allotted are only valuable for grazing purposes, an additional allotment of such grazing lands, in quantities as above provided, shall be made to each individual. . . .

And provided further, That at any time after lands have been allotted to all the Indians of any tribe as herein provided, or sooner if in the opinion of the President it shall be for the best interests of said tribe, it shall be lawful for the Secretary of the Interior to negotiate with such Indian tribe for the purchase and release by said tribe, in conformity with the treaty or statute under which such reservation is held, of such portions of its reservation not allotted as such tribe shall, from time to time, consent to sell, on such terms and conditions as shall be considered just and equitable between the United States and said tribe of Indians, which purchase shall not be complete until ratified by Congress, and the form and manner of executing such release shall also be prescribed by Congress: *Provided however,* That all lands adapted to agriculture, with or without irrigation so sold or released to the United States by any Indian tribe shall be held by the United States for the sole purpose of securing homes to actual settlers and shall be disposed of by the United States to actual and bona fide settlers only in tracts not exceeding one hundred and sixty acres to any one person, on such terms as Congress shall prescribe, subject to grants which Congress may make in aid of education: *And provided further,* That no patents shall issue therefor except to the person so taking the same as and for a homestead, or his heirs, and after the expiration of five years occupancy thereof as such homestead; and any conveyance of said lands so taken as a homestead, or any contract touching the same, or lien thereon, created prior to the date of such patent, shall be null and void. And the sums agreed to be paid by the United States as purchase money for any portion of any such reservation shall be held in the Treasury of the United States for the sole use of the tribe or tribes of Indians; to whom such reservations belonged; and the same, with interest thereon at three per cent per annum, shall be at all times subject to appropriation by Congress for the educa-

tion and civilization of such tribe or tribes of Indians or the members thereof. . . . And hereafter in the employment of Indian police, or any other employees in the public service among any of the Indian tribes or bands affected by this act, and where Indians can perform the duties required, those Indians who have availed themselves of the provisions of this act and become citizens of the United States shall be preferred.

SEC. 6. That upon the completion of said allotments and the patenting of the lands to said allottees, each and every member of the respective bands or tribes of Indians to whom allotments have been made shall have the benefit of and be subject to the laws, both civil and criminal, of the State or Territory in which they may reside; and no Territory shall pass or enforce any law denying any such Indian within its jurisdiction the equal protection of the law. And every Indian born within the territorial limits of the United States to whom allotments shall have been made under the provisions of this act, or under any law or treaty, and every Indian born within the territorial limits of the United States who has voluntarily taken up, within said limits, his residence separate and apart from any tribe of Indians therein, and has adopted the habits of civilized life, is hereby declared to be a citizen of the United States, and is entitled to all the rights, privileges, and immunities of such citizens, whether said Indian has been or not, by birth or otherwise, a member of any tribe of Indians within the territorial limits of the United States without in any manner impairing or otherwise affecting the right of any such Indian to tribal or other property.

Questions

1. What was the stated purpose of this act?
2. Why did Congress offer citizenship to native Americans?
3. To what extent was the Dawes Act coercive?

16-4   Interview of Kuwapi (1890)

Selwyn

With the Great Sioux Reservation being divided into individual parcels by the terms of the Dawes Severalty Act of 1887, with portions of the reservation being turned over for settlement by whites, and with a drought destroying crops during the summer of 1890, the Sioux faced interrelated crises, including one of the spirit. Around this time, they and other native Americans responded to a new faith that had originated on a Paiute reservation in Nevada: the Ghost Dance, or (as whites called it) the Messiah Craze.

The following exchange comes from the interview of Kuwapi, a Rosebud Reservation Indian arrested for leading the Ghost Dance at Yankton Reservation. Selwyn, who arrested and interviewed Kuwapi, was a Sioux federal policeman at Yankton (see text pp. 520–521).

Source: James Mooney, *The Ghost Dance Religion and the Sioux Outbreak,* Fourteenth Annual Report of the Bureau of Ethnology (Washington, D.C.: Government Printing Office, 1896), 2: 798–801, excerpted in Elliott J. Gorn, Randy Roberts, and Terry Bilhartz, eds., *Constructing the American Past: A Source Book of a People's History,* 3rd ed. (New York: Addison Wesley Longman, 1999), 2: 48–49.

Q. Do you believe in the new messiah?—*A.* I somewhat believe it.

Q. What made you believe it?—*A.* Because I ate some of the buffalo meat that he (the new messiah) sent to the Rosebud Indians through Short Bull.

Q. Did Short Bull say that he saw the living herd of roaming buffaloes while he was with the son of the Great Spirit?—*A.* Short Bull told the Indians at Rosebud that the buffalo and other wild game will be restored to the Indians at the same time when the general resurrection in favor of the Indians takes place.

Q. You said a "general resurrection in favor of the Indians takes place"; when or how soon will this be?—*A.* The father sends word to us that he will have all these caused to be so in the spring, when the grass is knee high.

Q. You said "father"; who is this father?—*A.* It is the new messiah. He has ordered his children (Indians) to call him "father."

Q. You said the father is not going to send the buffalo until the resurrection takes place. Would he be able to send a few buffaloes over this way for a sort of a sample, so as to have his children (Indians) to have a taste of the meat?—*A.* The father wishes to do things all at once, even in destroying the white race. . . .

Q. What other object could you come to by which you are led to believe that there is such a new messiah on earth at present?—*A.* The ghost dancers are fainted whenever the dance goes on.

Q. Do you believe that they are really fainted?—*A.* Yes.

Q. What makes you believe that the dancers have really fainted?—*A.* Because when they wake or come back to their senses they sometimes bring back some news from the unknown world, and some little trinkets, such as buffalo tail, buffalo meat, etc.

Q. What did the fainted ones see when they get fainted?—*A.* They visited the happy hunting ground, the camps, multitudes of people, and a great many strange people.

Q. What did the ghost or the strange people tell the fainted one or ones?—*A.* When the fainted one goes to the camp, he is welcomed by the relatives of the visitor (the fainted one), and he is also invited to several feasts.

Q. Were the people at Rosebud agency anxiously waiting or expecting to see all of their dead relatives who have died several years ago?—*A.* Yes.

Q. We will have a great many older folks when all the dead people come back, would we not?—*A.* The visitors all say that there is not a single old man nor woman in the other world—all changed to young.

Q. Are we going to die when the dead ones come back?—*A.* No; we will be just the same as we are today.

Q. Did the visitor say that there is any white men in the other world?—*A.* No; no white people.

Q. If there is no white people in the other world, where did they get their provisions and clothing?—*A.* In the other world, the messenger tells us that they have depended altogether for their food on the flesh of buffalo and other wild game; also, they were all clad in skins of wild animals.

Q. Did the Rosebud agency Indians believe the new messiah, or the son of the Great Spirit?—*A.* Yes.

Q. How do they show that they . . . believe in the new messiah?—*A.* They show themselves by praying to the father by looking up to heaven, and call him "father," just the same as you would in a church.

Q. Have you ever been in a church?—*A.* No.

Q. Do you faithfully believe in the new messiah?—*A.* I did not in the first place, but as I became more acquainted with the doctrines of the new messiah . . . I really believe in him.

Q. How many people at Rosebud, in your opinion, believe this new messiah?—*A.* Nearly every one.

Q. Did not the Rosebud people prepare to attack the white people this summer? While I was at Pine Ridge agency this summer the Oglalla Sioux Indians say they will resist against the government if the latter should try to put a stop to the messiah question. Did your folks at Rosebud say the same thing?—*A.* Yes. . . .

Q. You do not mean to say that the Rosebud Indians will try and cause an outbreak?—*A.* That seems to be the case. . . .

Questions

1. What light does Kuwapi's testimony shed on the plight of the Sioux and other native American nations around 1890?
2. What vision of the future did "the son of the Great Spirit" offer?

Question for Further Thought

1. Drawing on the text and Documents 16-2, 16-3, and 16-4, consider whether "the fate of the Indians" was inevitable.

The Far West

The Rockies, the Columbia and Colorado plateaus, the Great Basin, the Sierra Nevada and the Cascades, the Pacific Coast (from Mexico to Canada)—these formed the Far West. In this vast and varied region, Anglos (white Americans) interacted not only with native Americans, but also with Chinese immigrants and Hispanics (both immigrants and natives of a Southwest that had once been Spanish and, later, Mexican).

As settlers moved onto the Great Plains, others sought to "strike it rich" by prospecting for precious metals in the hilly and mountainous areas of the Far West, the "mining frontier" (Map 16.5, p. 524). Prospectors eventually gave way to large-scale, heavily capitalized enterprises as mining for precious and industrial metals developed.

Among immigrant groups in the United States, none was subjected to greater hostility than the Chinese, who remained concentrated in the Far West, California in particular, though smaller numbers made it to the Northeast and the South. During the 1870s and 1880s, anti-Chinese prejudice, rooted in racism, became widespread across the nation; agitation and violence were most intense in the Far West.

Document 16-5 (a) spells out the positions of the national political parties on Chinese immigration. Document 16-5 (b) reveals Congress's subsequent action relative to the immigration of Chinese laborers.

16-5 On Chinese Immigration (1876, 1882)

In 1874 and 1875, President Grant criticized aspects of Chinese immigration in his State of the Union Addresses, emphasizing the involuntary nature of contract immigration and the importation of women for "shameful purposes." Both major political parties addressed the issue of Chinese ("Mongolian") immigration in their national platforms for 1876.

Immigration has always made Americans uneasy, in part because of the fear that newcomers would not be assimilated. Chinese immigrants provoked extreme anxiety on the West Coast with their different language, customs, and dress. Congress responded to the pleas of nativists by passing the Chinese Exclusion Act in 1882 (see text p. 531).

The revision in 1880 of the Burlingame Treaty paved the way for the enactment of this law, which suspended the immigration of Chinese laborers for ten years. Representatives from the East and Midwest supported the measure by 112-37, those from the West and South by 89-0. The law was subsequently renewed and tightened.

Sources: Donald Bruce Johnson, comp., *National Party Platforms*, 2 vols. (rev. ed., Urbana: University of Illinois Press, 1978), 1: 1840–1956, 50, 54. United States, *Statutes at Large*, 22: 58ff.

(a) Republican and Democratic National Platforms on Chinese Immigration (1876)

REPUBLICAN

11. It is the immediate duty of congress fully to investigate the effects of the immigration and importation of Mongolians on the moral and material interests of the country.

DEMOCRATIC

Reform is necessary to correct the omissions of a Republican Congress and the errors of our treaties and our diplomacy, which . . . [have] exposed our brethren of the Pacific coast to the incursions of a race not sprung from the same great parent stock, and in fact now by law denied citizenship through naturalization as being unaccustomed to the traditions of a progressive civilization, one exercised in liberty under equal laws; and we denounce the policy which . . . tolerates the revival of the coolie-trade in Mongolian women for immoral purposes, and Mongolian men held to perform servile labor contracts, and demand such modification of the treaty with the Chinese Empire, or such legislation within constitutional limitations, as shall prevent further importation or immigration of the Mongolian race.

(b) The Chinese Exclusion Act (1882)

Whereas, in the opinion of the Government of the United States the coming of Chinese laborers to this country endangers the good order of certain localities within the territory thereof: Therefore,

Be it enacted by the Senate and House of Representatives of the United States of America in Congress assembled, That from and after the expiration of ninety days next after the passage of this act, and until the expiration of ten years next after the passage of this act, the coming of Chinese laborers to the United States be, and the same is hereby, suspended; and during such suspension it shall not be lawful for any Chinese laborer to come, or, having so come after the expiration of said ninety days, to remain within the United States. . . .

SEC. 4. That for the purpose of properly identifying Chinese laborers who were in the United States on the seventeenth day of November, eighteen hundred and eighty, or who shall have come into the same before the expiration of ninety days next after the passage of this act, and in order to furnish them with the proper evidence of their right to go from and come to the United States of their free will and accord, as provided by the treaty between the United States and China dated November seventeenth, eighteen hundred and eighty, the collector of customs of the district from which any such Chinese laborer shall

depart from the United States shall, in person or by deputy, go on board each vessel having on board any such Chinese laborer and cleared or about to sail from his district for a foreign port, and on such vessel make a list of all such Chinese laborers, which shall be entered in registry-books to be kept for that purpose, in which shall be stated the name, age, occupation, last place of residence, physical marks or peculiarities, and all facts necessary for the identification of each of such Chinese laborers, which books shall be safely kept in the custom-house; and every such Chinese laborer so departing from the United States shall be entitled to, and shall receive, free of any charge or cost upon application therefor, from the collector or his deputy, at the time such list is taken, a certificate, signed by the collector or his deputy and attested by his seal of office, in such form as the Secretary of the Treasury shall prescribe, which certificate shall contain a statement of the name, age, occupation, last place of residence, personal description, and facts of identification of the Chinese laborer to whom the certificate is issued, corresponding with the said list and registry in all particulars. . . .

SEC. 14. That hereafter no State court or court of the United States shall admit Chinese to citizenship; and all laws in conflict with this act are hereby repealed.

Questions

1. Why might the Democrats have been more outspoken than the Republicans in the parties' 1876 platforms regarding Chinese immigration?
2. How did sections 4 and 14 of the Chinese Exclusion Act affect Chinese immigrants?

Question for Further Thought

1. Drawing on the text and documents for Chapters 15 and 16, compare and contrast the lot of African Americans, native Americans, Hispanics, and Chinese immigrants between 1865 and 1890.

The Farmers' World

Farming was a way of life in which families generally lived and operated businesses in the same location. Agriculturalists were at the mercy of both nature (in a frightening range of manifestations) and an impersonal, far-flung market. Most farmers might consider themselves independent, small-scale entrepreneurs, but they were involved in complex regional, national, and international markets of great size.

A remarkable array of businesses was essential to the functioning of commercial agriculture: banks and land-mortgage companies; commodity exchanges; suppliers of equipment, seed, and fertilizer; processors (flour millers, meat packers, canneries, dairies); transportation lines (railroads, ships, barges); and storage facilities (elevators, warehouses). All were involved. Farmers and their organizations and supporters, believing themselves to be virtuous and embattled producers, were given to exaggerating the power of the businesses on which they depended, seeing them as exploitative, manipulative, and politically influential monopolies (see text pp. 533–537).

Document 16-6 provides a farmers' movement view of farmers' achievement and peril. Document 16-7 illuminates farm life and problems from the perspective of a farm woman who became politically active.

16-6   Farmer Green's Reaper (1874)

The loneliness and rigors of farm life led agriculturists to value social organizations—churches, one-room schools (at least for children), and farm organizations. The last of these sought to advance the economic interests of farmers. Thus the National Grange of the Patrons of Husbandry, founded in 1867, and its network of local granges not only offered members opportunities for social interaction, but also established cooperatives to compete with better organized suppliers, financiers, and middlemen and entered the political arena to secure railroad rate regulation and to support independent candidates. Successor groups, such as the farmer's alliances and the People's (Populist)

Party, continued the farmers' movement to the end of the nineteenth century (see text pp. 535–537). The narrative relates the cautionary tale of Farmer Green, calling for reform in the face of modernization.

Source: Edward Winslow Martin, *History of the Grange Movement; or, The Farmer's War against Monopolies* (Chicago: National Publishing Company, 1874), 339–346.

The sad history of Farmer Green (a veritable character, although we introduce him here by a fictitious name) should be a lesson and a warning to all his brethren.

Farmer Green was a resident of Iowa, and was reputed to be a sensible and prosperous man. He was far on in life, and had cleared his farm of debt, had stocked it with many things needful to his business, and was generally counted a prosperous man. His snug farm was his pride and boast, and he looked forward to the time when he should be able to add to it by the purchase of a desirable section of land adjoining it.

It was the early summer, and Farmer Green was rejoicing in the magnificent crop of wheat that was springing up on his land, and giving the promise of a handsome return for his care and labor. Day after day he watched the superb growth, and counted over in his mind the number of bushels of golden grain it would yield when the summer sun had warmed it into maturity. Many were the plans he laid for the use of the proceeds of that glorious crop. The goodwife's wants should be all supplied this year, and none of the children should be forced to put up with the deprivations that had fallen to their lot when he was still struggling to clear the farm from its encumbrance of debt.

One day, as he stood watching the bright field of green that spread out before him, and imagining what he would do when the grain was harvested and the money received for it, he was accosted by a stranger who came driving down the road from the village.

"A beautiful crop of wheat you've got there," said the stranger, as he drew rein before the farm gate.

"Yes," said Farmer Green, "I reckon it will turn out pretty well."

"A fine farm you have, too," said the stranger, glancing admiringly around him.

"Yes," said the farmer, pleased with the compliment to his place. "There's none better in the neighborhood."

"Paid for yet?" asked the stranger.

"Every dollar, thank God," said the owner, heartily. "It's clear at last, and I hope to keep it so."

"That's right," said the stranger. "Never contract a debt you're not sure of paying, and the farm will remain yours. That's a mighty nice crop of wheat," he added, as if speaking to himself. "I never saw anything look prettier. It will be ready for cutting soon. How do you cut it? By hand?"

"Yes," replied the farmer. "We've no reapers in this part of the country, and we farm in the oldfashioned way."

"That's a pity," said the stranger. "A reaper would work beautifully on this land. Why it would be no trouble at all to get your wheat in with a good reaper."

"That's true," said Farmer Green.

"You ought to have a reaper to cut it with," said the stranger.

"Can't afford it; haven't got the money to spare," said the farmer.

"See here, now," said the stranger, in a more confidential tone. "I'm selling a patent reaper—a first-class machine, and dirt-cheap at the money asked for it. You'd better let me sell you one."

"It's no use to talk about it, my friend. I haven't the money to spare."

"I don't want your money now," said the man, temptingly. "I'll sell you one at a bargain, and wait till it has paid for itself."

And with that the agent produced pencil and paper, and went into a calculation, showing the farmer how much it would cost him to cut his crop that year, and how much the reaper would save him, as well as a calculation of the amount of grain he could cut for other farmers in the vicinity.

"So you see," added the agent, persuasively, "before the time of payment comes around you will have saved and earned enough to pay for the reaper, and will still have a fine machine capable of doing more work, equally profitable, next season."

Farmer Green's better judgment bade him refuse the terms thus offered, liberal as they seemed. He knew the evil consequences of running into debt, and his conscience bade him put the temptation behind him. He wanted a reaper, however; he had always wanted one; and here was an opportunity of purchasing one upon terms which would enable him to pay for it out of its actual earnings. There was not a reaper in the county, and he felt confident that he would be able to keep it busy on his neighbors' farms, all through the season, after he had cut his own crop.

The agent was a smooth tongued, plausible fellow, and he plied the farmer with every argument he was master of. The result was that the farmer bought the reaper. He had not the money to pay for it, but he gave what is called in Iowa "an iron-clad note" for it. In plainer English, he gave his note accompanied with a statement of property. By the laws of Iowa such a note is equivalent to a mortgage. And so, in order to purchase the reaper, the farmer had imperilled his property, and had placed the safety of his home upon the turn of a chance.

The machine arrived in due time, and was found to be all the agent had claimed for it. It was a capital reaper, and a very handsome machine withal. Farmer Green could not help feeling a little downhearted as he remembered the risk he had incurred in order to obtain it; but he consoled himself with the hope that he would be able to make it pay for itself. When the harvest came around, the machine proved itself a good worker. Farmer Green soon had his crop cut and stacked, and then began to look about him for engagements for cutting his neighbors' grain. Some were willing to make the trial, and a few jobs of this kind enabled him to earn something with his reaper. But the work was less in amount than he had looked forward to, for the agent who had sold him the reaper had found other customers in the vicinity, and the demand for Farmer Green's machine was very much less than he had anticipated. The reaper stood idle under its shed during the better portion of the harvest season, and the farmer was doomed to a severe disappointment.

When the crop was sold there was another disappointment. There had been a heavy decline in the price of wheat, and the farmer did not receive as much as he had expected for his grain. All this while the day upon which the note must be paid was drawing near, and the farmer's chances of meeting it were rapidly diminishing. And still another blow fell upon him. Just after the harvest his wife fell sick, and her illness was long and expensive.

Upon the appointed day, the agent of the Reaper Company presented the note of Farmer Green, and demanded its payment. With a sad heart the farmer related his troubles to him, and told him he was unable to meet his note. He had not the money. The agent's face grew very long as he listened to the woeful tale, and after considerable hesitation, he said he was very sorry; that Farmer Green should have made allowance for all these risks, in making the purchase. However, the mischief was done, and there was nothing but to accept the situation. If the farmer could not pay, he supposed the time would have to be extended, but it would be necessary to charge him a fair rate of interest. Farmer Green said that that was only just. He had done his best to meet the note, but failing to do so, he was willing to pay for his failure. What, he inquired, would be a fair rate of interest?

"Twenty per cent. per annum," replied the agent, gravely.

Farmer Green's heart sank, and he said in a despairing tone, that the rate was too high.

"For ordinary interest, perhaps," replied the agent; "but, you see, we assume a serious risk in this case. I'd rather have the money down than one hundred per cent.

interest. But you haven't got it. We take the risk of your failing entirely to pay us, and it is only fair that we should be paid for this risk as well as for the delay we are put to."

There was no help for it, and Farmer Green was obliged to pay the extortionate demand. He had placed himself at the mercy of the Reaper Company, and he must do their bidding. He hoped that a succession of good crops would enable him to pay the interest and take up the note; but, alas for him, this hope was destined to disappointment also. He paid the interest once or twice, but the burden was too heavy for him, and at last, in sheer despair, he mortgaged the farm, paid the note, and got rid of the Reaper Company. But he had only shifted his burdens. The mortgage proved as troublesome as the note had been, and instead of being able to decrease it, he was obliged to increase it as time passed on. By the first false step he had placed the farm of which he was so proud in danger. He had voluntarily incurred a useless debt, and the rest of his bad luck was simply the logical consequence of a reckless and foolish act. He ran behind steadily, and at length his difficulties increased to such an extent that in order to rid himself of the debts he had no hope of paying in any other way, he sold his farm, discharged the mortgage, and bidding adieu to his old home and friends, went farther West, to a section where lands were cheaper, and there began life anew at the time he had once hoped to enjoy some rest from his labors.

And yet, Farmer Green, with all his shrewdness, never attributed his misfortunes to their true cause. He never admitted, even to himself, that his great error had been in contracting a useless debt, and assuming an obligation he had no certainty of meeting. He never believed that it was the reaper that ruined him, yet such was the case. Had he put by the temptation held out to him by the Reaper agent, there would have been no burden resting upon him, and his short crop, and other misfortunes, would not have driven him to the expedients he was obliged to resort to. "Out of debt, out of danger" is a true maxim; the wisdom and force of which only those who have passed through the agony and humiliation of such a slavery can appreciate.

There are debts enough that the farmer cannot help assuming; burdens that fall upon him through no fault of his. They are heavy enough, God knows, and they should teach him to assume none from which he can possibly escape.

Improved machinery is useful where it is honestly made, but even the best is worth less than the farmer ordinarily pays for it. He is charged too high, and his hard earnings, instead of constituting a fund for the rearing of his children and the protection of his old age, go to make up the colossal fortunes of the manufacturers and dealers in such machinery. A reform is needed, and it is near at hand.

Questions

1. How does this story convey the defensiveness of midwestern farmers in the 1870s?
2. How sound was the Grange's advice about debt and the use of farm machinery?

16-7 Personal Memoir (c. 1925)

Luna Kellie

Luna (Sanford) Kellie wrote her memoirs during the mid-1920s, nearly seventy years after her birth, a half century after her arrival in Nebraska. Only in 1992 were they published. Kellie's account of rural life and political involvement in Nebraska provides a woman's perspective on family, farming, and public affairs over the final quarter of the nineteenth century. This section deals with her early years in Nebraska, where she and her husband, James Thompson (J. T.) Kellie, later became politically active.

Source: Luna Kellie, "Personal Memoir," in Jane Taylor Nelson, ed., *A Prairie Populist: The Memoirs of Luna Kellie* (Iowa City: University of Iowa Press, 1992), 6–14, 21–24, 33–34, 63–64.

. . . So when the train started my German friends carried my valise and basket and Willie onto the train and the girl sat by me to help hold the baby. The man had been out near Kearney and taken a homestead and built a house and gone back for his family. There were several children, and their kindness made the rest of the journey endurable. How often I wished I could meet them again. I hope they found friends in their time of need which comes to all.

That afternoon it was so hot we had to have some windows open and as the prairie had been burnt over and was all black ashes with a little grass starting we got our clothing and all the car filled with the black soot and it was very very bad. Everyone was warm and sweaty and the black stuck all over us and we all looked terrible. A prim old maid over 40 I am sure sat opposite and she got to looking so funny we could not help laughing. . . .

It was nearly sundown when we reached Grand Island and I bade farewell to my kind friends. I was real excited as I was sure my father would be waiting for me and I was so proud to show him my baby. Cab drivers and hotel runners crowded around so I could not see but I told them all no I was waited for. The train pulled out everyone departed and I was alone on the platform where I stayed some time and could not see anyone coming or looking for anyone.

Such an appalling catastrophe had never occurred to me and I did not know what to do. If I went away from the depot I feared my father would come and not find me so I sat around till dark and then asked the agent where

was a good cheap hotel. He finally sent a man to me who had a hotel nearby, another German. He took me over to their hotel and said he would keep watch and if anyone came looking for me [he] would call me. His wife was a good motherly woman and took me up to a small but very clean room, the only one left, and told me the town was so full of people crowding in because of the Indian uprising that it had been and was very hard to get a place to stay. I could see the town was crowded and lots camping around. It seemed that all the north part of the state was greatly excited and rushing into the railroad towns. Of course that made me quite uneasy and I wished Father was there. After thinking things over awhile I concluded nothing but severe sickness or death had prevented my father from meeting me. Perhaps he had been waylaid by Indians. I went down to the good landlady and told her I must get someone to take me in the morning on somewhere between there and Hastings to my father's and she had word sent and a man came to see me and agreed to start early in the morning if my father had not arrived and to take me and my trunk as far as Hastings (about 25 miles) for four (4) dollars, if he had to go farther it would be more.

So eating some more cold lunch in the morning we started early [and] went across the river and along a lot of low land willows etc. out 4 or 5 miles I think when we saw a team and lumber wagon coming the horses old and poor but good travellers and the man so haggard and poor we almost passed him but he pulled up and it was Father. He had been breaking prairie on the Blue River fully 70 miles from Grand Island. . . .

It almost broke my heart to see my father look so old and poor and worried besides being so poorly clad and when we got to Hastings which had only 3 or 4 stores I think and only one with dry goods I bought some shirting to make shirts for him and the boys who had been batching. There had been some rain and Hastings seemed to be in a mudhole no sidewalks and altogether the worst looking little town I had ever seen. We got a little lunch to put with mine and jogged on.

The sun was very hot and bright. The prairie had all been burnt and grass just starting [and] not one spear seemed to dare to grow an inch higher than another. Not a tree a shrub or even a gooseberry bush to be seen all the way and not many houses and most of them sod. The first one I saw I said "But it is most black." Pa said "What color did you think a sod house would be?" "Oh nice and green and grassy" I said "not such a dirty looking thing." "Well" he said "it is dirty looking because it is made of dirt." Really I had thought a sod house would be kind of nice but the sight of the first one sickened me. The bright sun in our faces soon gave me a terrific headache which is the most I remember of the ride except there was hardly anything to call a road. We went down all the little ditches and up again, no culverts or anything. I was so frighted I thought I would stay still when I got there.

Just before dark we got to Aunt Hattie's where Sister Susie was staying and of course I was delighted to see her and her to see the baby. I should have said his Grandpa was so delighted with him he would not let me hold him but gave him the end of the line to drive with. . . .

A word as to how Father came to Nebraska. In the summer of 1871 Father was working on the Northern Pacific R.R. and we were living in a rented house in the village of Lansing, Minnesota. Mother got hold of some literature sent out by the B. & M. R.R. telling of the glories of Nebraska and how there were homesteads to be taken within 4 miles of the State Capitol and the University. She was greatly enthused and as Father came home that fall she read it all to him and urged him to go and as we say now and "get in the ground floor." He very sensibly told her he had absolutely nothing to start on except one team and wagon but she still urged him to put our household goods in the wagon and start out before all the homesteads close to the Capitol were taken.

This was a very odd thing as she always was opposed to moving and would rather stay most anyplace than to have to move. But Father had taken her to one new country when they were first married (Minnesota where I was born) and he knew she was not built for a pioneer and how she nearly died with homesickness, and winter coming on and all he stood firm not to go. His brother Joseph was visiting us then and he sided with Mother and said he would buy another team so they could take more stuff and he would go with us and together they would find something to do and get along. But one day Father came in and said he had rented a farm near there and was going to move onto it and start plowing right away.

As most young folk would be I was greatly disappointed. It seemed to me a great chance to see a beautiful country like the pictures showed and have a lot of thrilling adventures. Besides I hoped in a few years to go to a University and it would be so nice to have it near home.

Well 2 years of farming bankrupted Father so we moved off the farm without even a team. Spent the hard winter of '72 and '73 in Austin where Father worked in a roundhouse and developed a bad cough from his old army wound and in February or March he went South to St. Louis and went to work on a R.R. bridge gang of which Mr. Kellie was foreman. He sent for us in April and we spent the summer on the east bank of the Mississippi nearly opposite the old Jefferson Barracks. It was very unhealthy and very hot and misty. Everyone around us had the ague and expected to have it. Mother held off until fall [and] then got the malarial Typhoid and died.

Father had such bitter regrets that he had not come to Nebraska when she wanted to where whatever hardships she might have to have undergone the climate was so healthy she would likely have lived to raise the family. [It] made him take the first opportunity to move there.

The glowing accounts of the golden west sent out by the R.R. company remained in my mind and I had a vague idea being only 14 years old that they were doing a noble work to let poor people know there was such a grand haven they could reach. It was quite a number of years afterwards that I saw a statement in a Boston paper from one of the R.R. officials saying how profitable the advertising had been and that they estimated that they had cleared $1500 from each emigrant they had obtained. Well that was a low estimate I know now though I did not see it even at the time, for the minute you crossed the Missouri River your fate both soul and body was in their hands. What you should eat and drink, what you should wear, everything was in their hands and they robbed us of all we produced except enough to keep body and soul together and many many times not that as too many of the early settlers filled early graves on account of being ill nourished and ill clad while the wealth they produced was being coldly calculated as paying so much per head. But more of that later as it was many years before the situation became clear to us and I am glad of it for during those years we had youth and *hope* which means happiness and we worked ourselves harder than slaves were ever worked to be able to fulfill our hopes.

When I think back now to the little girl I really was when I came to Nebraska not quite 19 years old with a dearly loved husband left behind and a bright healthy baby boy who lived entirely on his mother's milk, it does not seem strange that I was unnaturally homesick and nothing around seemed good to me. Of course I was very glad to see my father and brothers and sister again but to see them in such wretched circumstances made me heartsick indeed and I would not go to any of the neighbors' for some time and felt most wretched when any of them came there as I could not realize that they were no better off and indeed many of them not nearly so well off as we were. For instance our dugout had two rooms and I had the inner one which was as private as need be while many perhaps most of the sod houses only had one room. Then we had a very good cave by the house and many things were kept in it that others had to crowd in their one room. Then our roof did not leak and most of them did but Father had used large logs in the roof so he was able to pile on enough dirt to keep it from leaking which most of them could not do, but I did not realize any of these blessings until time had gone on and I was deprived of them.

The dugout was made by digging out the ground the same as for a cellar. Ours was down about 3 feet in the ground, then sod [was] laid in a wall about 2 feet thick and 3 1/2 feet high and it was plastered with mud on the inside walls and the dirt floor was levelled down pretty good and pounded down quite hard. But oh what a place, I thought, for a baby just beginning to creep and no dresses but white ones. . . .

It was not hard to get ventilation those days. It seemed to be always blowing some way. I had kept close in the house all winter and now the awful wind made me feel I never wanted to go out of doors. It seemed to blow from the north until it was blown out and then turn around and blow it all back again. The others did not seem to mind it but it was a real misery to me and I hardly seemed that first summer to get the real charm of the Prairie at all. . . .

The days seemed very long with just Susie 5 years old and baby and I. There was nothing to read. There were few weeds in the garden on the new sod and no material to sew, only some patching. When it began to get dark we used to go and sit on the cave where we could see all around and the little owls used to hoot so lonesome and sometime the coyotes would howl, and I used to be sure at times it was Indians signalling to one another off in the sand hills south and west of us for there were no houses in sight and it seemed like the end of the world. But most every night when we sat alone some little antelopes would come and look at us with great curiosity and come a little nearer and nearer till sometimes they got real close just a few rods but they always went away before Pa and the boys came. They were pretty and graceful little things and they seemed to want to know us but as soon as the wagon rattled in the distance, a flash, and they were gone. I never can hear a coyote or hoot owl now without seeming to see a picture of us there grouped on top of the cave because we were afraid to stay in the house as it had only one outside door and if Indians or anything came in that door we could not get away. So though sometimes the nights were chilly we wrapped something around us and cuddled close

together and I kept close watch and listened for the least noise, for I had the idea that out there if Indians came we might run and hide out in the corn or grass and not be caught in a trap.

Well there were no Indians anywhere around and I did not see one for 20 years when I saw one at the depot in Omaha but the fear was as dreadful to me as if they were really there and I guess no one knew for sure but they might be. For that was the summer of the Custer massacre and the plains Indians were all off their regular hunting grounds. . . .

Although only one year from sod the garden spot where the fruit trees and bushes were planted had by repeated plowing and harrowing been so pulverized that we had a really fine garden with very few weeds. We all took a great interest and pride in it and very soon it made a lot of difference in our table. I then learned as I had not realized before what a difference a few fresh vegetables can make in the appearance of the table as well as the satisfaction of the appetite; and I resolved always to have abundance of them in season and a cellar full for winter, which resolve has been pretty fully carried out to a great advantage both to pocket book and health. I am convinced that nothing else equals an early hour or two in the garden with hoe and rake to keep an *overworked* housewife equal to her duties. She comes back to the dishes and cooking with lungs full of fresh air which could not be got by simply walking or riding around, and the outdoor interest brightens the day, and makes the indoor work more pleasing. I always began to feel more fit in the spring as soon as I could get out to work in the dirt.

While Father and the boys had been off harvesting the year before, the grasshoppers had "lit" where they were at work, and ending all need of work had harvested everything themselves, even the grain already shocked. So the boys were often talking about it and wishing I could have seen them and wondering when they would come again. I had seen a few hoppers I thought all my life and could not realize how they could do all the damage they did in so short a time but one clear afternoon about 3 o'clock Johnny came to the dugout door and hollered "Luna come out here and see the grasshoppers flying over."

I came out and looked around but did not see any hoppers. Looked up and did not see any.

"Why there are no hoppers" I said.

"Yes that cloud is hoppers" said John.

"No that is just a cloud" I said. "See, it is going to rain."

"Yes I am afraid it will rain hoppers" said John. "Can't you see them?"

"No."

"Come here" he said. "Now get the edge of the roof between you and the sun and look."

As I did so I exclaimed "Oh John it is going to snow. The air up there is full of snow, big white flakes of snow. Lots of it is beginning to come down."

"Yes" said John "they are starting to light. What can we do, what can we save? Let us go to the garden and get what we can. We can put some things in the cellar."

And off he ran for [a] box or sack to gather something in. I was slower as I did not see the need to gather green and perishable garden stuff until something was destroying it but by the time I could get out the things were already gray with locusts and the air full of more coming down. They lit on me my head my dress my hands and no place to put my feet except as they hopped up probably onto me. John was frantically pulling young beets and carrots and onions but he shouted to me to go back and try and keep them out of the house. He could save what we could use of the green stuff before it spoiled.

The sweet corn was just getting big enough to begin using but now no corn could be seen. The green was all covered with gray hoppers and where the ears were was simply a large cluster of hoppers while between the rows they were several hoppers deep waiting for a chance to feed. And the noise. Who could believe a grasshopper feeding made a noise but the whole army of them made a noise as of a bunch of hogs chanking. I was glad to get back in the house but found the entry way well stacked with hoppers so it was hard to shake them off my clothes and get in without a lot of them going in also and I had no desire to go out among them again. They still kept slowly coming down, coming down looking like snow till nearly down they changed to gray. Finally John gave up and came in and we sure felt pretty blue.

"That is the end of all our fruit trees and berries" said John "as well as the corn and potatoes."

"Oh surely they can't eat the potatoes John."

"Well they will eat all the tops and all that are near the top and they are so green they will rot in the ground." John had brought the shovel in the house when he came and I now saw why as he opened the door and went out and shovelled the hoppers out of the entry way to the dugout. This he did every little while and between times he chased and threw out those that had got in the house so he kept pretty busy and when he went after a bucket of water he took a big cloth to tie over the pail so he could get it home without half hoppers as he said. Night came. Father and Fred came home and we went to bed but could still hear the hoppers chanking chanking.

The next morning the hoppers were still there though the chanking was not so loud as most of the green stuff was eaten. I think that towards night they rose up and left as suddenly as they came though it may have been the morning after.

Anyway when they said they were gone I went out of the house and to the garden to see what was left. Desolation only. Where the onions carrots beets and sweet potatoes had been was not a single thing, no sign of leaf or stem, only holes in the ground where they had eaten down and eaten out every bit of vegetable fiber. The fruit trees had all the small limbs completely eaten away and all the

bark from the entire tree and if they had stayed a few hours longer I suppose there would have been only holes in the ground where roots were eaten out. The corn was eaten off completely, nothing to tell there had been a corn field there. Also, on going out to the road and onto the prairie [I saw] all the grass was eaten down into the roots. . . .

Well we [my husband and I] knew of course one of the first things to do was to raise our own meat and we must get started in hogs. John Ellis had an old chicken-eating razor back sow he had brought from Illinois and she pestered me to distraction by coming up and catching my chickens. She would come on a lope as far as I could see her and spite of all I could do to head her off would run around and around the house till [she] tired out when I would chase her home. She seemed fairly crazy to catch chickens. Well she had a litter of pigs and John sold one to J.T. for $2.00 as soon as it was two weeks old. I did not like the breed [and] feared it would be like its mother but J.T. said he did not know where we could get another and it would probably be all right if we did not let it get a taste of chicken. But no sir, no sooner had it come than it began to chase chickens and it kept me busy watching it. It was rather a cute little pig for that and we gave it a good deal of our milk but nothing would satisfy it but to smell chickens and run after them and in spite of me it got one occasionally. We had no pen for it and nothing to make one of but shut it in a little box at night. It soon became the pest of my life and when we had had it about 4 weeks I went to the garden one day. At such times I would get Willie to play with it or shut it in the box but this time I was coming right back so put it and Willie in the house. Some way I felt very uneasy and ran back as fast as I could and on opening the door got an awful shock. There lay Willie flat on his back, the pig standing on his chest with its snout in his mouth and the blood running freely down both sides of Willie's face. He could not make a noise as his mouth was full of pig's snout. Of course I grabbed the pig but it was fairly crazed to get back for more blood but I finally threw it out the door.

Willie had found his voice by that time and was so covered with blood it took some time washing him to see how bad he was hurt. Finally found big gashes inside of his lip and in his tongue on the underside mostly. I was terribly frightened but there was no one near so after a while it stopped bleeding and while he had a very sore mouth for some time no great harm was done. . . .

This spring an election was held (I suppose by petition from Hastings people) to try to move the County Seat from Juniata to Hastings. Juniata was much nearer the center of the county and was filled with a better class of business people as Hastings was located by the R.R. interest and was filled with boomers and swindlers of all kinds. Rotten horse traders who shipped old worthless horses they picked up for almost nothing to this country where work horses were greatly needed and sold them at fabulous prices as in the prime of life, sound etc. etc. while I doubt if they ever shipped a reasonable sound animal in.

But if anyone needed money to buy seed or grains or anything which was needed to farm with the town was full of money lenders the most of whom took 10 times the needful security and as a great favor procured your money "from a friend in the east" at never less than 2 come 10 and I have known the Updike Brothers to charge 7 come 10 interest. Three per cent come was the usual charge if you were not too hard up and it meant that to borrow a hundred dollars for seed or harvest hands or anything you gave a mortgage on everything you had and all your future prospects for $100 at 10% interest. Then if it was to run 6 months 3% a month or $18 was kept back. The note was made for 100 and 10% interest but you only got 82 dollars. This was the business that started a number of soon wealthy families and they were known as 3 come 10ers. At the time the Updikes tried to charge us 7 come 10 they assured us there was more demand for their money at that rate than they could supply. As this was needed to farm with and in the spring we could have afforded to pay any reasonable interest but for 6 months we would only have received 58 dollars and given note for 100 and 10% interest, no wonder the Updikes soon became millionaires and great ones on the Chicago board of trade. . . .

There was a good deal of sickness among the babies in the neighborhood but we stayed at home. Fred came to help harvest and though we knew Jimmie [the baby] was not well we did not think it anything serious till one day all of a sudden we got scared and sent to Juniata for Dr. Ackley and when he came and looked him over baby looked up at him and smiled and I thought he would say we did not need to call him but he said "I am sorry but it is too late to do anything now."

We were dumbfounded stupefied and as he was a young doctor then we thought he did not know. He left us something of course and said something about while there was life there was always a little hope and went away. But alas he knew too well. Old Lady Strohl, Jim's mother, came up to stay with us. I suppose Fred went home and told them on the way how sick the baby was. I could not let him out of my arms all night and in the morning with a look of love and [a] bright smile he was gone. He looked in my eyes and smiled and looked up over my head and smiled as if he saw something fine and I felt that he went from my arms to my mother's. I told Mrs. Strohl and she said "Might be, might be." She wanted to wash and dress him but I could not allow anyone else to touch my baby and so washed dressed him for the last time putting on him a little embroidered dress and skirt my mother made for me. Without my knowing it Aunt Hattie, I suppose, cut a piece out of the back of each and gave me afterwards which I still have.

We buried him in the yard. We could not take our baby away too far and a great many came to the burial that I never saw before or since. It seemed to me many thought it a holiday of some sort and the women acted very curious regarding everything in the house. I had a fine bedspread my mother had made on the bed and everything fixed up as good as possible and I guess they meant all right but to me nothing mattered but that the baby was gone from our lives and I could not bear to see folks act so concerned with every little thing. I soon found I could not stand up. My limbs would not support me and I had to spend several days in bed while the men folks got along with the harvest and cows and made out the best they could.

They got Vernie Barnhart to come and do some cooking but I got around in a few days though nothing seemed to matter much. J.T. was as heartbroken as I was but someone had to look after things and as I failed to rally he had to keep things going. All he could say was "We have each other and one boy left." But we knew then as always that if we had a thousand babies no one would or could take Jimmie's place. . . .

Questions

1. What most strikes you about Luna Kellie's "Personal Memoir"?
2. Which of her reflections had political implications?

Questions for Further Thought

1. How might you integrate personal, economic, and political factors to better understand farmers in the Midwest and West during the 1870s and 1880s?
2. Compare and contrast the autobiographical accounts of Hamlin Garland and Luna Kellie.

CHAPTER 17

Capital and Labor in the Age of Enterprise, 1877–1900

★   ★   ★

Industrial Capitalism Triumphant

Late-nineteenth-century America underwent a remarkable economic transformation. Many manufacturers still worked agricultural products into *consumer goods*—footwear, textiles, furniture, paper, and the like—to be purchased by individuals. But other manufacturers, increasingly important, produced iron and steel and related equipment: locomotives, rolling stock, and rails for railroads; machinery for factories, mines, and oil fields; and various forms for construction. These *capital goods,* purchased by businesses, added to economic growth. By century's end, the United States stood as the world's ranking industrial nation.

Steel and railroads defined the new economic order. The former were essential to a broad range of private enterprises and public undertakings; the latter were crucial to cheap, reliable overland transportation and the creation of a national economy. In the process of developing an integrated national economy, railroads standardized both track gauge (width) and time (dividing the nation into four time zones.)

Economic growth brought with it declining prices, increasing real incomes, and widening economic inequality. The period also witnessed recurring economic depressions, especially those of 1873 and 1893, and social conflict arose out of hard times and labor-management confrontations.

Contemporary participants and observers reflected on the transformation of America's economy and society—some to question, others to celebrate. Among the most famous of these commentators were Henry George (Document 17-1) and Andrew Carnegie (Document 17-2).

17-1   Progress and Poverty (1879)

Henry George

Written during the later stages of the depression of 1873, *Progress and Poverty* made Henry George (1839–1897) a major reform figure in the United States and Great Britain (see text p. 641). George insisted on the need for reform; he espoused a single tax on land that would throw it on the market for productive use by industry and agriculture and would eliminate the need for taxes that burdened entrepreneurs and workers. George ran twice for mayor of New York City as a labor-reform candidate.

Source: Henry George, *Progress and Poverty: An Inquiry into the Cause of Industrial Depressions and of Increase of Want with Increase of Wealth: The Remedy* (New York: Random House, 1929), 3–8, 10, 528–529, 534–535.

The present century has been marked by a prodigious increase in wealth-producing power. The utilization of steam and electricity, the introduction of improved processes and labor-saving machinery, the greater subdivision and grander scale of production, the wonderful facilitation of exchanges, have multiplied enormously the effectiveness of labor.

At the beginning of this marvelous era it was natural to expect, and it was expected, that labor-saving inventions would lighten the toil and improve the condition of the laborer; that the enormous increase in the power of producing wealth would make real poverty a thing of the past. Could a man of the last century—a Franklin or a Priestley—have seen, in a vision of the future, the steamship taking the place of the sailing vessel, the railroad train of the wagon, the reaping machine of the scythe, the threshing machine of the flail; could he have heard the throb of the engines that in obedience to human will, and for the satisfaction of human desire, exert a power greater than that of all the men and all the beasts of burden of the earth combined; . . . could he have conceived of the hundred thousand improvements which these only suggest, what would he have inferred as to the social condition of mankind? . . .

Plainly, in the sight of the imagination, he would have beheld these new forces elevating society from its very foundations, lifting the very poorest above the possibility of want, exempting the very lowest from anxiety for the material needs of life; he would have seen these slaves of the lamp of knowledge taking on themselves the traditional curse, these muscles of iron and sinews of steel making the poorest laborer's life a holiday, in which every high quality and noble impulse could have scope to grow.

And out of these bounteous material conditions he would have seen arising, as necessary sequences, moral conditions realizing the golden age of which mankind have always dreamed. Youth no longer stunted and starved; age no longer harried by avarice; the child at play with the tiger; the man with the muck-rake drinking in the glory of the stars. Foul things fled, fierce things tame; discord turned to harmony! For how could there be greed where all had enough? How could the vice, the crime, the ignorance, the brutality, that spring from poverty and the fear of poverty, exist where poverty had vanished? Who should crouch where all were freemen; who oppress where all were peers? . . .

Now, however, we are coming into collision with facts which there can be no mistaking. From all parts of the civilized world come complaints of industrial depression; of labor condemned to involuntary idleness; of capital massed and wasting; of pecuniary distress among business men; of want and suffering and anxiety among the working classes. All the dull, deadening pain, all the keen, maddening anguish, that to great masses of men are involved in the words "hard times," afflict the world to-day. This state of things, common to communities differing so widely in situation, in political institutions, in fiscal and financial systems, in density of population and in social organization, can hardly be accounted for by local causes. There is distress where large standing armies are maintained, but there is also distress where the standing armies are nominal; there is distress where protective tariffs stupidly and wastefully hamper trade, but there is also distress where trade is nearly free; there is distress where autocratic government yet prevails, but there is also distress where political power is wholly in the hands of the people; in countries where paper is money, and in countries where gold and silver are the only currency. Evidently, beneath all such things as these, we must infer a common cause. . . .

. . . Where the conditions to which material progress everywhere tends are most fully realized—that is to say, where population is densest, wealth greatest, and the machinery of production and exchange most highly developed—we find the deepest poverty, the sharpest struggle for existence, and the most of enforced idleness.

It is to the newer countries—that is, to the countries where material progress is yet in its earlier stages—that laborers emigrate in search of higher wages, and capital flows in search of higher interest. It is in the older countries—that is to say, the countries where material progress has reached later stages—that widespread destitution is found in the midst of the greatest abundance. . . .

. . . [J]ust as such a community realizes the conditions which all civilized communities are striving for, and advances in the scale of material progress—just as closer settlement and a more intimate connection with the rest of the world, and greater utilization of labor-saving machinery, make possible greater economies in production and exchange, and wealth in consequence increases, not merely in the aggregate, but in proportion to population—so does poverty take a darker aspect. Some get an infinitely better and easier living, but others find it hard to get a living at all. The "tramp" comes with the locomotive, and almshouses and prisons are as surely the marks of "material progress" as are costly dwellings, rich warehouses, and magnificent churches. Upon streets lighted with gas and patrolled by uniformed policemen, beggars wait for the passer-by, and in the shadow of college, and library, and museum, are gathering the more hideous Huns and fiercer Vandals of whom Macaulay prophesied. . . .

And, unpleasant as it may be to admit it, it is at last becoming evident that the enormous increase in productive power which has marked the present century and is still going on with accelerating ratio, has no tendency to extirpate poverty or to lighten the burdens of those compelled to toil. It simply widens the gulf between Dives and Lazarus, and makes the struggle for existence more intense. . . .

This association of poverty with progress is the great enigma of our times. It is the central fact from which spring industrial, social, and political difficulties that perplex the world, and with which statesmanship and philanthropy and education grapple in vain. From it come the clouds that overhang the future of the most progressive and self-reliant nations. It is the riddle which the Sphinx of Fate puts to our civilization, and which not to answer is to be destroyed. So long as all the increased wealth which modern progress brings goes but to build up great fortunes, to increase luxury and make sharper the contrast between the House of Have and the House of Want, progress is not real and cannot be permanent. The reaction must come. The tower leans from its foundations, and every new story but hastens the final catastrophe. To educate men who must be condemned to poverty, is but to make them restive; to base on a state of most glaring social inequality political institutions under which men are theoretically equal, is to stand a pyramid on its apex. . . .

What has destroyed every previous civilization has been the tendency to the unequal distribution of wealth and power. This same tendency, operating with increasing force, is observable in our civilization to-day, showing itself in every progressive community, and with greater intensity the more progressive the community. Wages and interest tend constantly to fall, rent to rise, the rich to become very much richer, the poor to become more helpless and hopeless, and the middle class to be swept away. . . .

. . . The history of modern civilization is the history of advances in this direction—of the struggles and triumphs of personal, political, and religious freedom. And the general law is shown by the fact that just as this tendency has asserted itself civilization has advanced, while just as it has been repressed or forced back civilization has been checked.

This tendency has reached its full expression in the American Republic, where political and legal rights are absolutely equal, and, owing to the system of rotation in office, even the growth of a bureaucracy is prevented; where every religious belief or non-belief stands on the same footing; where every boy may hope to be President, every man has an equal voice in public affairs, and every official is mediately or immediately dependent for the short lease of his place upon a popular vote. This tendency has yet some triumphs to win in England, in extending the suffrage, and sweeping away the vestiges of monarchy, aristocracy, and prelacy. . . .

In theory we are intense democrats. The proposal to sacrifice swine in the temple would hardly have excited greater horror and indignation in Jerusalem of old than would among us that of conferring a distinction of rank upon our most eminent citizen. But is there not growing up among us a class who have all the power without any of the virtues of aristocracy? We have simple citizens who control thousands of miles of railroad, millions of acres of land, the means of livelihood of great numbers of men; who name the Governors of sovereign States as they name their clerks, choose Senators as they choose attorneys, and whose will is as supreme with Legislatures as that of a French King sitting in bed of justice. . . .

There is no mistaking it—the very foundations of society are being sapped before our eyes, while we ask, *how* is it possible that such a civilization as this, with its railroads, and daily newspapers, and electric telegraphs, should ever be destroyed? . . .

Questions

1. What was the significance of George's choice of a title for his book?
2. What, according to George, were the implications of economic development for American democracy?

17-2   Triumphant Democracy (1885)

Andrew Carnegie   Andrew Carnegie (1835–1919) was unusual among America's business leaders in that he was an immigrant of humble origins and an entrepreneur who sought to give larger meaning to his personal success in "the beloved republic" (see text pp. 542–543, 578).

Source: Andrew Carnegie, *Triumphant Democracy or Fifty Years' March of the Republic* (Garden City, N.Y.: Doubleday, Doran, 1993), vii–viii (Preface), 1–3, 5, 8–10, 13–16 ("The Republic").

PREFACE

BORN a subject of the Monarchy, adopted a citizen of the Republic, how could it be otherwise than that I should love both lands and long to do whatever in me lay to bring their people to a like affection for each other! The lamentable ignorance concerning the new land which I have found even in the highest political circles of the old first suggested to me how delightful the task would be to endeavor to show something of what the Republic really is, and thus remove, at least in part, the misconceptions which still linger in the minds of many good people of Britain. I believed, also, that my attempt would give to Americans a better idea of the great work their country had done and is still doing in the world. Probably few Americans will read this book without being astonished at some of the facts elicited. During its progress I have been deeply interested in it, and it may truly be regarded as a labor of love—the tribute of a very dutiful and grateful adopted son to the country which has removed the stigma of inferiority which his native land saw proper to impress upon him at birth, and has made him, in the estimation of its great laws as well as in his own estimation (much the more important consideration), the peer of any human being who draws the breath of life, be he pope, kaiser, priest or king—henceforth the subject of no man, but a free man, a citizen!

It is to the people, the plain, common folk, the Democracy of Britain, that I seek to show the progress, prosperity, and happiness of their child, the Republic, that they may still more deeply love it and learn that the government of the people through the republican form and not the government of a class through the monarchical form is the surest foundation of individual growth and of national greatness. . . .

CHAPTER I

The Republic

The old nations of the earth creep on at a snail's pace; the Republic thunders past with the rush of the express. The United States, the growth of a single century, has already reached the foremost rank among nations, and is destined soon to out-distance all others in the race. In population, in wealth, in annual savings, and in public credit; in freedom from debt, in agriculture, and in manufactures, America already leads the civilized world. . . .

Truly the Republic is the Minerva of nations; full-armed has she sprung from the brow of Jupiter Britain. The thirteen millions of Americans of 1830 have now increased to fifty-six millions—more English-speaking people than exist in all the world besides; more than in the United Kingdom and all her colonies, even were the latter doubled in population!

Startling as is this statement, it is tame in comparison with that which is to follow. In 1850 the total wealth of the United States was but $8,430,000,000 (£1,686,000,000), while that of the United Kingdom exceeded $22,500,000,000 (£4,500,000,000), or nearly three times that sum. Thirty short years sufficed to reverse the positions of the respective countries. . . . Let him try to "know" the import of this—$43,600,000,000 (£8,720,000,000)! It is impossible. But stupendous as this seems, it is exceeded by the wealth of the Republic, which in 1880, two years before, amounted to $48,950,000,000 (£9,790,000,000). What a mercy we write for 1880; for had we to give the wealth of one year later another figure would have to be found, and added to the interminable row. America's wealth to-day greatly exceeds ten thousand millions sterling. Nor is this altogether due to her enormous agricultural resources, as may at first glance be thought; for all the world knows she is first among nations in agriculture. It is largely attributable to her manufacturing industries, for, as all the world does not know, she, and not Great Britain, is also the greatest manufacturing country. . . .

In military and naval power the Republic is at once the weakest and the strongest of nations. Her regular army consists of but twenty-five thousand men scattered all over the continent in companies of fifty or a hundred. Her navy, thank God! is as nothing. But twenty years ago, as at the blast of a trumpet, she called into action two millions of armed men, and floated six hundred and twenty-six warships. . . .

Of more importance even than commercial or military strength is the Republic's commanding position among nations in intellectual activity; for she excels in the number of schools and colleges, in the number and extent of her libraries, and in the number of newspapers and other periodicals published.

In the application of science to social and industrial uses, she is far in advance of other nations. Many of the most important practical inventions which have contributed to the progress of the world during the past century originated with Americans. No other people have devised so many labor-saving machines and appliances. . . .

. . . What has brought about such stupendous results—so unparalleled a development of a nation within so brief a period! The most important factors in this problem are three: the ethnic character of the people, the topographical and climatic conditions under which they developed, and the influence of political institutions founded upon the equality of the citizen.

Certain writers in the past have maintained that the ethnic type of a people has less influence upon its growth as a nation than the conditions of life under which it is developing. The modern ethnologist knows better. We have only to imagine what America would be to-day if she had fallen, in the beginning, into the hands of any other people than the colonizing British, to see how vitally important is this question of race. America was indeed fortunate in the seed planted upon her soil. With the exception of a few Dutch and French it was wholly British; and, as will be shown in the next chapter, the American of to-day remains true to this noble strain and is four-fifths British. The special aptitude of this race for colonization, its vigor and enterprise, and its capacity for governing, although brilliantly manifested in all parts of the world, have never been shown to such advantage as in America. Freed here from the pressure of feudal institutions no longer fitted to their present development, and freed also from the dominion of the upper classes, which have kept the people at home from effective management of affairs and sacrificed the nation's interest for their own, as is the nature of classes, these masses of the lower ranks of Britons, called upon to found a new state, have proved themselves possessors of a positive genius for political administration.

The second, and perhaps equally important factor in the problem of the rapid advancement of this branch of the British race, is the superiority of the conditions under which it has developed. The home which has fallen to its lot, a domain more magnificent than has cradled any other race in the history of the world, presents no obstructions to unity—to the thorough amalgamation of its dwellers, North, South, East, and West, into one homogeneous mass—for the conformation of the American continent differs in important respects from that of every other great division of the globe. . . .

In the course of her short career the Republic has had to face and overcome two sources of great danger, either of which might have overtaxed the powers and stability of any political fabric, resting upon a less wide and indestructible base than the perfect equality of the citizen. The infant state was left with the viper, human slavery, gnawing at its vitals, and it grew and strengthened with the growth and strength of the Republic until sufficiently powerful to threaten its very life. . . .

The second source of danger lay in the millions of foreigners who came from all lands to the hospitable shores of the nation, many of them ignorant of the English language, and all unaccustomed to the exercise of political duties. If so great a number stood aloof from the national life and formed circles of their own, or if they sought America for a period only, to earn money with which to return to their original homes, the injury to the State must inevitably be serious.

The generosity, shall I not say the incredible generosity, with which the Republic has dealt with these people met its reward. They are won to her side by being offered for their *subject*ship the boon of citizenship. For denial of equal privileges at home, the new land meets them with perfect equality, saying, be not only with us, but be of us. They reach the shores of the Republic *subjects* (insulting word), and she makes them citizens; serfs, and she makes them men, and their children she takes gently by the hand and leads to the public schools which she has founded for her own children, and gives them, without money and without price, a good primary education as the most precious gift which even she has, in her bountiful hand, to bestow upon human beings. This is Democracy's "gift of welcome" to the new comer. The poor immigrant cannot help growing up passionately fond of his new home and, alas, with many bitter thoughts of the old land which has defrauded him of the rights of man, and thus the threatened danger is averted—the homogeneity of the people secured.

The unity of the American people is further powerfully promoted by the foundation upon which the political structure rests, the equality of the citizen. There is not one shred of privilege to be met with anywhere in all the laws. One man's right is every man's right. The flag is the guarantor and symbol of equality. The people are not emasculated by being made to feel that their own country decrees their inferiority, and holds them unworthy of privileges accorded to others. No ranks, no titles, no hereditary dignities, and therefore no classes. Suffrage is universal, and votes are of equal weight. Representatives are paid, and political life and usefulness thereby thrown open to all. Thus there is brought about a community of interests and aims which a Briton, accustomed to monarchical and aristocratic institutions, dividing the people into classes with separate interests, aims, thoughts, and feelings, can only with difficulty understand.

The free common school system of the land is probably, after all, the greatest single power in the unifying process which is producing the new American race. Through the crucible of a good common English education, furnished free by the State, pass the various racial elements—children of Irishmen, Germans, Italians, Spaniards, and Swedes, side by side with the native American, all to be fused into one, in language, in thought, in feeling, and in patriotism. The Irish boy loses his brogue, and the German child learns English. The sympathies suited to the feudal systems of Europe, which they inherit from their fathers, pass off as dross, leaving behind the pure gold of the only noble political creed: "All men are created free and equal." Taught now to live and work for the common weal, and not for the maintenance of a royal family or an overbearing aristocracy, not for the continuance of a social system which ranks them beneath an arrogant class of drones, children of Russian and German serfs, of Irish evicted tenants, Scotch crofters, and other victims of feudal tyranny, are transmuted into republican Americans, and are made one in love for a country which provides equal rights and privileges for all her children. . . .

Questions

1. What was the significance of Carnegie's choice of a title for his book?
2. What standards did Carnegie employ to judge that the United States was triumphant? Did Carnegie's depiction of the "triumphant democracy" of the United States correspond with American realities during the period about which he wrote?
3. What were Carnegie's feelings about Great Britain and the British people?

Questions for Further Thought

1. Were there points of agreement between Henry George and Andrew Carnegie?
2. What were the main points of disagreement between the two men?
3. What do you find most persuasive in George's argument? In Carnegie's?

The World of Work

"Free labor" ideology, which extolled the value of men rising from wage-earning laborers to become land-owning farmers or craftsmen, was important to the early Republican Party. But from mid-century on, "the world of work" was becoming increasingly stratified; entrepreneurs did indeed employ wage earners, but relatively few of these laborers would become independent farmers or craftsmen.

Women were an important element in the growing labor force, constituting about 25 percent thereof in 1900, about one-third each in industry, domestic service, and those white-collar fields in which women were concentrated. Before the end of the nineteenth century, few *married* white women—but a considerable number of *married* African American women—worked outside the home. As northern industrial states prohibited child labor and limited the working hours of adolescents, thereby reducing working-class family income, more married women felt the need to take jobs outside the home.

Documents 17-3 and 17-4 illuminate aspects of the lives and labors of women in very different settings. Meanwhile, Frederick W. Taylor (Document 17-5), who had trained as an engineer, was gaining on-the-job experience of a very different nature, experience that would make him the high priest of "scientific management" in industry (see text pp. 558–560, 563–564).

17-3   Studies of Factory Life: Among the Women (1888)

Lillie B. Chase Wyman   Lillie B. Chase Wyman wrote her article on factory workers in Rhode Island in response to a statement that it was "very much needed . . . for rich men to find out how poor men live." Poor women and children needed a voice, too, as this excerpt makes clear.

Source: Lillie B. Chase Wyman, "Studies of Factory Life: Among the Women," *Atlantic Monthly* 62 (September 1888), 320–321.

Two years ago, a ten-hour law was enacted in Rhode Island. Philanthropists and workmen urged the passage of the bill. They were concerned about the health of the workwomen, the undermining of whose strength involved not only suffering, but the weakness of the next generation. The manufacturers, so far as they took any action, opposed the law. Some of them were sure their business would be ruined, if it went on to the statute book. Others were merely afraid that financial disasters would be the result. The women themselves were not consulted, and, according to the fashion of the republic, had no part nor lot in deciding their own destiny. Various sorts of men, workmen, manufacturers, and legislators deliberated together about woman's flesh and blood, considered her maternal capacities and her muscular strength, and compared them with the exactions of business and of machinery. She stood and waited—or rather she worked and waited—their decision that sixty hours a week in a factory was enough for her and for her little children. The bill passed, and there was no financial collapse.

There is a young girl working in a thread factory in the State who was much pleased to have some more leisure time. She was taking a Chautauqua course of reading with her mother. She lives some distance from the mill, and so does not go home to dinner. Under the new arrangement she had an hour's recess at noon. She carried her book as well as her lunch, and employed the extra moments in reading. She was anxious to obtain a complete copy of the Iliad, having read some portions of it in the prescribed course, which made her desire to know the whole poem. She read translations of some of the Greek plays, and was glad to have the opportunity to borrow a version of the Electra of Sophocles; and when she returned it, she said she liked it better than any of the others she had read. This girl is, however, unique in my experience. She is a Protestant, of English parentage. From childhood on she has shown an earnest nature. She always tried to do what seemed right to her, or what might help some one else. It was a terrible cross to her to be obliged to leave school when she was about fourteen, and go into the mill, but she did it; and her character shows its fine fibre now, in that she does her duty simply, trying constantly to improve herself, but not trying to get into any place which she is not fitted to fill thoroughly. She is not a sham lady nor a sham worker because she has a desire for something besides spindles and a taste for something other than clothes. She dresses simply, and is very willing to use her Saturday half-holidays visiting in behalf of the Associated Charities.

Homely but pathetic was the rejoicing of a hard-worked Irish widow over the ten-hour law. She had been the mother of thirteen or fourteen children, but most of them died; and last of all, her husband, a handsome man, whom she seemed to consider a being quite superior to herself, died, after a protracted illness. He did the housework long after he could not do other labor, so that she might be the chief wage-earner of the family. After his death, she said: "I fretted a deal for him,—I could n't help it. I know he had been sick a long time, but you miss a person just the same if they have been sick; an' he was such a clean man about the house, an' kept it so neat when he was able to be about."

In a worldly way she manages very well without him. She and a grown girl and two young lads work in the mill. Two younger children profess to guard the house, and sometimes go to school. The daughter takes books occasionally from the village library, and she has read The Scarlet Letter and even the Blithedale Romance. She said she liked these stories about as well as she did Marion Harland's novels. The mother found the ten-hour law a great help. "Why," said she, "the extra quarter of an hour at noon gives me time to mix my bread; an' then when I comes home at night, at six o'clock, it is ready to put in the pans, an' I can do that while Katie sets the table; an' after supper, an' the dishes are washed, I can bake; an' then I am through, an' ready to go to bed, mebbe afore it's quite nine o'clock. Oh, it's splendid, the best thing as ever 'appened. I used to be up till 'way into the night, bakin', after my day's work in the mill was done."

She probably was glad of the Saturday half-holiday, because it gave her a good chance to do her washing. Holidays, to women like her, mean little but the time to do some different kind of work from that by which they earn their living. Her boy rejoiced in healthy fashion. "Saturdays," says he, "when you are let out at one o'clock, you don't feel as if you'd been at work at all."

Questions

1. What might an advocate of woman suffrage make of Wyman's account?
2. What significance did the people that Wyman interviewed attach to the state's ten-hour law?

17-4   More Slavery at the South (c. 1912)

**Anonymous
(A Black Domestic)**

As the textbook notes, more than one-fourth of the nonfarm work force in 1900 consisted of women, most of whom worked out of necessity. Outside of teaching, social work, and nursing, women did not expect to enjoy a professional career (or equal pay), and a majority worked in factories or as domestics. This reading details the work of an African American woman. Although caring for white children gave her a degree of social status, she found her life "just as bad as, if not worse than, it was during the days of slavery."

Source: Anonymous (A Negro Nurse), "More Slavery at the South," *The Independent* 72 (January 25, 1912), 196–200. In W. Elliot Brownlee and Mary M. Brownlee, *Women in the American Economy: A Documentary History, 1675 to 1929* (New Haven, Conn.: Yale University Press, 1976), 244–249.

I am a negro woman, and I was born and reared in the South. I am now past forty years of age and am the mother of three children. My husband died nearly fifteen years ago, after we had been married about five years. For more than thirty years—or since I was ten years old—I have been a servant in one capacity or another in white families in a thriving Southern city, which has at present a population of more than 50,000. In my early years I was at first what might be called a "house-girl," or better, a "house-boy." I used to answer the doorbell, sweep the yard, go on errands, and do odd jobs. Later on I became a chambermaid. . . . Still later I was graduated into a cook, in which position I served at different times for nearly eight years in all. During the last ten years I have been a nurse. I have worked for only four different families during all these thirty years. But, belonging to the servant class, which is the majority class among my race at the South, and associating only with servants, I have been able to become intimately acquainted not only with the lives of hundreds of household servants, but also with the lives of their employers. I can, therefore, speak with authority on the so-called servant question; and what I say is said out of an experience which covers many years.

To begin with, then, I should say that more than two-thirds of the negroes of the town where I live are menial servants of one kind or another, and besides that more than two-thirds of the negro women here, whether married or single, are compelled to work for a living,—as nurses, cooks, washerwomen, chambermaids, seamstresses, hucksters [peddlers], janitresses, and the like. I will say, also, that the condition of this vast host of poor colored people is just as bad as, if not worse than, it was during the days of slavery. Though today we are enjoying nominal freedom, we are literally slaves. And, not to generalize, I will give you a sketch of the work I have to do—and I'm only one of many.

I frequently work from fourteen to sixteen hours a day. I am compelled by my contract, which is oral only, to sleep in the house. I am allowed to go home to my own children, the oldest of whom is a girl of 18 years, only once in two weeks, every other Sunday afternoon—even then I'm not permitted to stay all night. I not only have to nurse a little white child, now eleven months old, but I have to act as playmate or "handy-andy," not say governess, to three other children in the home, the oldest of whom is only nine years of age. I wash and dress the baby two or three times each day; I give it its meals, mainly from a bottle; I have to put it to bed each night; and, in addition, I have to get up and attend to its every call between midnight and morning. If the baby falls to sleep during the day, as it has been trained to do every day about eleven o'clock, I am not permitted to rest. It's "Mammy, do this," or "Mammy, do that," or "Mammy, do the other," from my mistress, all the time. So it is not strange to see "Mammy" watering the lawn in front with the garden hose, sweeping the sidewalk, mopping the porch and halls, dusting around the house, helping the cook, or darning stockings. Not only so, but I have to put the other three children to bed each night as well as the baby, and I have to wash them and dress them each morning. I don't know what it is to go to church; I don't know what it is to go to a lecture or entertainment or anything of the kind; I live a treadmill life; and I see my own children only when they happen to see me on the streets when I am out with the children, or when my children come to the "yard" to see me, which isn't often, because my white folks don't like to see their servants' children hanging around their premises. You might as well say that I'm on duty all the time—from sunrise to sunrise, every day in the week. I am the slave, body and soul, of this family. And what do I get for this work—this lifetime bondage? The pitiful sum of ten dollars a month! And what am I expected to do with these ten dollars? With this money I'm expected to pay my house rent, which is four dollars per month, for a little house of two rooms, just big enough to turn round in; and I'm expected, also to feed and clothe myself and three children. For two years my oldest child, it is true, has helped a little toward our support by taking in a little washing at home. She does the washing and ironing of two white families, with a total of five persons; one of these families pays her $1.00 per week, and the other 75 cents per week, and my daughter has to furnish her own soap and starch and wood. For six months my youngest child, a girl about thirteen years old, has been nursing, and she receives $1.50 per week but has no night work. When I think of the low rate of wages we poor colored people receive, and when I hear so much said about our unreliability, our untrustworthiness, and even our vices, I recall the story of the private soldier in a certain army who, once upon a time, being upbraided by the commanding officer because the heels of his shoes were not polished, is said to have replied: "Captain, do you expect all the virtues for $13 per month?"

Of course, nothing is being done to increase our wages, and the way things are going at present it would seem that nothing could be done to cause an increase in wages. We have no labor unions or organizations of any kind that could demand for us a uniform scale of wages for cooks, washerwomen, nurses, and the like; and, for another thing, if some negroes did here and there refuse to work for seven and eight and ten dollars a month, there would be hundreds of other negroes right on the spot ready to take their places and do the same work, or more, for the low wages that had been refused. So that, the truth is, we have to work for little or nothing or become vagrants! And that, of course, in this State would mean that we would be arrested, tried, and despatched to the "State Farm," where we would surely have to work for nothing or be beaten with many stripes!

Nor does this low rate of pay tend to make us efficient servants. The most that can be said of us negro household servants in the South—and I speak as one of them—is that we are to the extent of our ability willing and faithful

slaves. We do not cook according to scientific principles because we do not know anything about scientific principles. Most of our cooking is done by guesswork or by memory. We cook well when our "hand" is in, as we say, and when anything about the dinner goes wrong, we simply say, "I lost my hand today!" We don't know anything about scientific food for babies, nor anything about what science says must be done for infants at certain periods of their growth or when certain symptoms of disease appear; but somehow we "raise" more of the children than we kill, and, for the most part, they are lusty chaps—all of them. But the point is, we do not go to cooking-schools nor to nurse-training schools, and so it cannot be expected that we should make as efficient servants without such training as we should make were such training provided. And yet with our cooking and nursing, such as it is, the white folks seem to be satisfied—perfectly satisfied. I sometimes wonder if this satisfaction is the outgrowth of the knowledge that more highly trained servants would be able to demand better pay! . . .

Another thing—it's a small indignity, it may be, but an indignity just the same. No white person, not even the little children just learning to talk, no white person at the South ever thinks of addressing any negro man or woman as Mr., or Mrs., or Miss. The women are called, "Cook," or "Nurse," or "Mammy," or "Mary Jane," or "Lou," or "Dilcey," as the case might be, and the men are called "Bob," or "Boy," or "Old Man," or "Uncle Bill," or "Pate." In many cases our white employers refer to us, and in our presence, too, as their "niggers." No matter what they call us—no matter what they teach their children to call us—we must tamely submit, and answer when we are called; we must enter no protest; if we did object, we should be driven out without the least ceremony, and, in applying for work at other places, we should find it very hard to procure another situation. In almost every case, when our intending employers would be looking up our record, the information would be given by telephone or otherwise that we were "impudent," "saucy," "dishonest," and "generally unreliable." In our town we have no such thing as an employment agency or intelligence bureau, and, therefore, when we want work, we have to get out on the street and go from place to place, always with hat in hand, hunting for it. . . .

You hear a good deal nowadays about the "service pan." The "service pan" is the general term applied to "left-over" food, which in many a Southern home is freely placed at the disposal of the cook, or, whether so placed or not, it is usually disposed of by the cook. In my town, I know, and I guess in many other towns also, every night when the cook starts for her home she takes with her a pan or a plate of cold victuals. The same thing is true on Sunday afternoon after dinner—and most cooks have nearly every Sunday afternoon off. Well, I'll be frank with you, if it were not for the service pan, I don't know what the majority of our Southern colored families would do. The service pan is the mainstay in many a home. Good cooks in the South receive on an average $8 per month. Porters, butlers, coachmen, janitors, "office boys" and the like, receive on an average $16 per month. Few and far between are the colored men in the South who receive $1 or more per day. Some mechanics do; as, for example, carpenters, brick masons, wheelwrights, blacksmiths, and the like. The vast majority of negroes in my town are serving in menial capacities in homes, stores and offices. Now taking it for granted, for the sake of illustration, that the husband receives $16 per month and the wife $8. That would be $24 between the two. The chances are that they will have anywhere from five to thirteen children between them. Now, how far will $24 go toward housing and feeding and clothing ten or twelve persons for thirty days? And, I tell you, with all of us poor people the service pan is a great institu-

tion; it is a great help to us, as we wag along the weary way of life. And then most of the white folks expect their cooks to avail themselves of these perquisites; they allow it; they expect it. I do not deny that the cooks find opportunity to hide away at times, along with the cold "grub," a little sugar, a little flour, a little meal, or a little piece of soap; but I indignantly deny that we are thieves. We don't steal; we just "take" things—they are a part of the oral contract, expressed or implied. We understand it, and most of the white folks understand it. Others may denounce the service pan, and say that it is used only to support idle negroes, but many a time, when I was a cook, and had the responsibility of rearing my three children upon my lone shoulders, many a time I have had occasion to bless the Lord for the service pan! . . .

Questions

1. How did domestic work humiliate women like the narrator?
2. What is the paradox that the narrator experiences in working for white families?
3. What was the service pan? What was its significance to African American workers?

17-5   The Principles of Scientific Management (1911)

Frederick Winslow Taylor

Frederick Winslow Taylor (1856–1915) combined the American love of machines with a passion for improving production systems. Taylor believed so deeply in the ideal of efficiency that he designed his own tennis racquet and golf putter. Trained as an engineer, he began to implement his notion of "scientific management" in the 1890s. Taylor argued that productivity could be improved through better-designed machines and work habits as well as a pay formula based on piecework. This selection is taken from his *Principles of Scientific Management,* published in 1911.

There were skeptics, and in 1912 Taylor went before a special committee of the House of Representatives to defend what he called "this great mental revolution." However, critics persisted in charging that scientific management dehumanized work by emphasizing machines and productivity.

Source: Frederick Winslow Taylor, "The Principles of Scientific Management" (1911), in Frederick Winslow Taylor, *Scientific Management* (New York: Harper and Brothers, 1947; reprint, Westport, Conn.: Greenwood Press, 1972), 58–67.

To return now to our pig-iron handlers at the Bethlehem Steel Company. If Schmidt had been allowed to attack the pile of 47 tons of pig iron without the guidance or direction of a man who understood the art, or science, of handling pig iron, in his desire to earn his high wages he would probably have tired himself out by 11 or 12 o'clock in the day. He would have kept so steadily at work that his mus-

cles would not have the proper periods of rest absolutely needed for recuperation, and he would have been completely exhausted early in the day. By having a man, however, who understood this law, stand over him and direct his work, day after day, until he acquired the habit of resting at proper intervals, he was able to work at an even gait all day long without unduly tiring himself.

Now one of the very first requirements for a man who is fit to handle pig iron as a regular occupation is that he shall be so stupid and so phlegmatic that he more nearly resembles in his mental make-up the ox than any other type. The man who is mentally alert and intelligent is for this very reason entirely unsuited to what would, for him, be the grinding monotony of work of this character. Therefore the workman who is best suited to handling pig iron is unable to understand the real science of doing this class of work. He is so stupid that the word "percentage" has no meaning to him, and he must consequently be trained by a man more intelligent than himself into the habit of working in accordance with the laws of this science before he can be successful.

The writer trusts that it is now clear that even in the case of the most elementary form of labor that is known, there is a science, and that when the man best suited to this class of work has been carefully selected, when the science of doing the work has been developed, and when the carefully selected man has been trained to work in accordance with this science, the results obtained must of necessity be overwhelmingly greater than those which are possible under the plan of "initiative and incentive."

Let us, however, again turn to the case of these pig-iron handlers, and see whether, under the ordinary type of management, it would not have been possible to obtain practically the same results.

The writer has put the problem before many good managers, and asked them whether, under premium work, piece work, or any of the ordinary plans of management, they would be likely even to approximate 47 tons per man per day, and not a man has suggested that an output of over 18 to 25 tons could be attained by any of the ordinary expedients. It will be remembered that the Bethlehem men were loading only 12½ tons per man.

To go into the matter in more detail, however: As to the scientific selection of the men, it is a fact that in this gang of 75 pig-iron handlers only about one man in eight was physically capable of handling 47½ tons per day. With the very best of intentions, the other seven out of eight men were physically unable to work at this pace. Now the one man in eight who was able to do this work was in no sense superior to the other men who were working on the gang. He merely happened to be a man of the type of the ox,—no rare specimen of humanity, difficult to find and therefore very highly prized. On the contrary, he was a man so stupid that he was unfitted to do most kinds of laboring work, even. The selection of the man, then, does not involve finding some extraordinary individual, but merely picking out from among very ordinary men the few who are especially suited to this type of work. Although in this particular gang only one man in eight was suited to doing the work, we had not the slightest difficulty in getting all the men who were needed—some of them from inside of the works and others from the neighboring country—who were exactly suited to the job.

Under the management of "initiative and incentive" the attitude of the management is that of "putting the work up to the workmen." What likelihood would there be, then, under the old type of management, of these men properly selecting themselves for pig-iron handling? Would they be likely to get rid of seven men out of eight from their own gang and retain only the eighth man? No! And no expedient could be devised which would make these men properly select themselves. Even if they fully realized the necessity of doing so in order to obtain high wages (and they are not sufficiently intelligent properly to grasp this necessity), the fact that their friends or their brothers who were working right alongside of them would temporarily be thrown out of a job because they were not suited to this kind of work would entirely prevent them from properly selecting themselves, that is, from removing the seven out of eight men on the gang who were unsuited to pig-iron handling.

As to the possibility, under the old type of management, of inducing these pig-iron handlers (after they had been properly selected) to work in accordance with the science of doing heavy laboring, namely, having proper scientifically determined periods of rest in close sequence to periods of work. As has been indicated before, the essential idea of the ordinary types of management is that each workman has become more skilled in his own trade than it is possible for any one in the management to be, and that, therefore, the details of how the work shall best be done must be left to him. The idea, then, of taking one man after another and training him under a competent teacher into new working habits until he continually and habitually works in accordance with scientific laws, which have been developed by some one else, is directly antagonistic to the old idea that each workman can best regulate his own way of doing the work. And besides this, the man suited to handling pig iron is too stupid properly to train himself. Thus it will be seen that with the ordinary types of management the development of scientific knowledge to replace rule of thumb, the scientific selection of the men, and inducing the men to work in accordance with these scientific principles are entirely out of the question. And this because the philosophy of the old management puts the entire responsibility upon the workmen, while the philosophy of the new places a great part of it upon the management.

With most readers great sympathy will be aroused because seven out of eight of these pig-iron handlers were thrown out of a job. This sympathy is entirely wasted, because almost all of them were immediately given other jobs with the Bethlehem Steel Company. And indeed it should be understood that the removal of these men from pig-iron handling, for which they were unfit, was really a kindness to themselves, because it was the first step toward finding them work for which they were peculiarly fitted, and at which, after receiving proper training, they could permanently and legitimately earn higher wages.

Although the reader may be convinced that there is a certain science back of the handling of pig iron, still it is more than likely that he is still skeptical as to the existence of a science for doing other kinds of laboring. One of the important objects of this paper is to convince its readers that every single act of every workman can be reduced to a science. With the hope of fully convincing the reader of this fact, therefore, the writer proposes to give several more simple illustrations from among the thousands which are at hand.

For example, the average man would question whether there is much of any science in the work of shoveling. Yet there is but little doubt, if any intelligent reader of this paper were deliberately to set out to find what may be called the foundation of the science of shoveling, that with perhaps 15 to 20 hours of thought and analysis he would be almost sure to have arrived at the essence of this science. On the other hand, so completely are the rule-of-thumb ideas still dominant that the writer has never met a single shovel contractor to whom it had ever even occurred that there was such a thing as the science of shoveling. This science is so elementary as to be almost self-evident.

For a first class shoveler there is a given shovel load at which he will do his biggest day's work. What is this shovel load? Will a first-class man do more work per day with a shovel load of 5 pounds, 10 pounds, 15 pounds, 20, 25, 30, or 40 pounds? Now this is a question which can be answered only through carefully made experiments. By first selecting two or three first-class shovelers, and paying them extra wages for doing trustworthy work, and then gradually varying the shovel load and having all the conditions accompanying the work carefully observed for several weeks by men who were used to experimenting, it was found that a first-class man would do his biggest day's work with a shovel load of about 21 pounds. For instance, that this man would shovel a larger tonnage per day with a 21-pound load than with a 24-pound load or than with an 18-pound load on his shovel. It is, of course, evident that no shoveler can always take a load of exactly 21 pounds on his shovel, but nevertheless, although his load may vary 3 or 4 pounds one way or the other, either below or above the 21 pounds, he will do his biggest day's work when his average for the day is about 21 pounds.

The writer does not wish it to be understood that this is the whole of the art or science of shoveling. There are many other elements, which together go to make up this science. But he wishes to indicate the important effect which this one piece of scientific knowledge has upon the work of shoveling.

At the works of the Bethlehem Steel Company, for example, as a result of this law, instead of allowing each shoveler to select and own his own shovel, it became necessary to provide some 8 to 10 different kinds of shovels, etc., each one appropriate to handling a given type of material; not only so as to enable the men to handle an average load of 21 pounds, but also to adapt the shovel to several other requirements which become perfectly evident when this work is studied as a science. A large shovel tool room was built, in which were stored not only shovels but carefully designed and standardized labor implements of all kinds, such as picks, crowbars, etc. This made it possible to issue to each workman a shovel which would hold a load of 21 pounds of whatever class of material they were to handle: a small shovel for ore, say, or a large one for ashes. Iron ore is one of the heavy materials which are handled in a works of this kind, and rice coal, owing to the fact that it is so slippery on the shovel, is one of the lightest materials. And it found on studying the rule-of-thumb plan at the Bethlehem Steel Company, where each shoveler owned his own shovel, that he would frequently go from shoveling ore, with a load of about 30 pounds per shovel, to handling rice coal, with a load on the same shovel of less than 4 pounds. In the one case, he was so overloaded that it was impossible for him to do a full day's work, and in the other case he was so ridiculously underloaded that it was manifestly impossible to even approximate a day's work.

Briefly to illustrate some of the other elements which go to make up the science of shoveling, thousands of stop-watch observations were made to study just how quickly a laborer, provided in each case with the proper type of shovel, can push his shovel into the pile of materials and then draw it out properly loaded. These observations were made first when pushing the shovel into the body of the pile. Next when shoveling on a dirt bottom, that is, at the outside edge of the pile, and next with a wooden bottom, and finally with an iron bottom. Again a similar accurate time study was made of the time required to swing the shovel backward and then throw the load for a given horizontal distance, accompanied by a given height. This time study was made for various combinations of distance and height. With data of this sort before him, coupled with the law of endurance described in the case of the pig-iron handlers, it is evident that the man who is directing shovelers can first teach them the exact methods which should be employed. . . .

Questions

1. In what ways does Taylor exhibit a bias against workers? How does he cloak that bias in a mantle of objective science?
2. Who was likely to benefit from and who was likely to be hurt by scientific management?

Questions for Further Thought

1. Compare and contrast the lives, on the job and off, of the Rhode Island factory workers and the African American domestic.
2. What do the accounts of female workers' lives (Documents 17-3 and17-4) reveal about the lives of their children?
3. Frederick Winslow Taylor appeared to sense that Americans deferred to the power of "science." Why might they have done so? In what ways would scientific management discourage innovation on the work floor?

The Labor Movement

When Thomas B. McGuire, a wagon driver, told a Senate committee in 1883 that he had once hoped to "become something of a capitalist eventually," he gave plaintive voice to an aspiration of many working-class Americans (see text p. 564). McGuire had found it impossible to succeed as an independent cabdriver. Economic change had reduced opportunities among those who viewed themselves as the heirs of the self-employed of an earlier America.

Labor unrest grew during the 1870s and 1880s, and the Knights of Labor were the initial beneficiary (see text pp. 564–568). Under the leadership of Terence V. Powderly, the Knights were an urban version of the Grange, combining social activities with group action (Document 17-6). Beset by various problems, the group was in fatal decline by the 1890s. In its place, the American Federation of Labor (AFL), which brought together "pure and simple" trade unions, emerged as the nation's preeminent labor organization. Meanwhile, some workers turned to more radical movements, socialism or anarchism, the latter a factor in the Haymarket Square Riot in Chicago during 1886 (see text pp. 564–571).

Trade unionism accepted capitalism; socialism did not. The defeat of the American Railway Union in the Pullman strike and boycott helped turn the union's leader, Eugene V. Debs, into a socialist (Document 17-7). Document 17-8 provides insight into management's position leading to the Pullman crisis.

17-6   The Army of Unemployed (1887)

Terence V. Powderly

The growth of the factory system left the working class unsettled. Periodically, as with the Haymarket Square riot and the Pullman boycott, discontent led to violence. But overall, workers were more concerned with finding a way to protect their interests.

The Knights of Labor, founded in 1869, offered some promise in that regard. The group's use of ritual and ceremony cloaked it in nineteenth-century respectability: the Knights could claim that they were little different from the Masons. The Knights were not a union in the modern sense; they focused on education rather than organization. Although membership reached 700,000 by 1885, the Knights did not win any significant victories.

In the following selection, Terence V. Powderly, the Knights' Grand Master Workman, struggles to offer a solution to the labor problems of the 1880s.

Source: Terence V. Powderly, "The Army of Unemployed," in George E. McNeill, ed., *The Labor Movement: The Problem of Today* (Boston: A. M. Bridgeman, and New York: M. W. Hazen, 1887; reprint, New York: Augustus M. Kelley, 1971), 577–584.

The Cincinnati riots, that occurred less than one year ago, were not brought about through the agitation of the labor-leader. If the demand for "the removal of unjust technicalities, delays and discriminations in the administration of justice," had been listened to when first made by the Knights of Labor, Cincinnati would have been spared sorrow and disgrace, and her "prominent citizens" would not have had to lead a mob, in order to open the eyes of the country to the manner in which her courts were throttled, and virtue and truth were trampled upon in her temples of justice. That the army of the discontented is gathering fresh recruits day by day, is true; and if this army should become so large, that, driven to desperation, it should one day arise in its wrath, and grapple with its real or fancied enemy, the responsibility for that act must fall upon the heads of those who could have averted the blow, but who turned a deaf ear to the supplication of suffering humanity, and gave the screw of oppression an extra turn, because they had the power. Workingmen's organizations are doing all they can to avert the blow; but if that day dawns upon us, it will be chargeable directly to men who taunt others with unequal earnings, and distort the truth, as was done in an interview recently had with Mr. William H. Vanderbilt:—

> One of the troubles in this country, just now, is the relation of wages to the cost of production. A skilled workman, in almost every branch of business, gets every day money enough to buy a barrel of flour. I don't refer to ordinary laborers, but to men skilled at their trades. The man who makes the article receives as much wages, in many instances, as the article is worth when it is finished. This is not exactly fair, in my opinion, and must be adjusted. Until wages bear a truer relation to production, there can be no real prosperity in the country.

I have seen no denial of the above, and take it for granted that it is a correct report. Mr. Vanderbilt starts out well enough; but he is in error when he says that "a skilled workman, in almost every branch of business, gets money enough every day to buy a barrel of flour." I know of no business in the United States, in which a skilled mechanic, working regularly at his trade day by day, gets money enough for his day's labor to buy a barrel of flour. That they earn the price of a barrel of flour, I do not deny; but that they get it, is not true. It may be that Mr. Vanderbilt refers to superintendents, foremen or contractors; for they are the only ones that receive such wages. The average wages paid to the skilled mechanic will not exceed $2.50 a day. I know of but few branches of business in which men can command that price. The wages of skilled mechanics are on the decline, while the price of flour remains unchanged, from $5.75 to $8.50 a barrel. If Mr. Vanderbilt will demonstrate how one can purchase a six-dollar barrel of flour for two dollars and a half, he will have solved a very difficult problem for the workingman. . . .

It may be said that many of the employees of the manufacturing establishments are minors, and consequently cannot perform as great an amount of labor as a corresponding number of adults. That argument might have had some weight years ago, but now it is fruitless. The age and strength of the workman are no longer regarded as factors in the field of production; it is the skill of the operator in managing a labor-saving machine that is held to be the most essential. It is true that a child can operate a machine as successfully as a man, and that muscle is no longer a requisite in accomplishing results. It is also true that less time is required to perform a given amount of labor than heretofore. This being the case, the plea for shorter hours is not unreasonable. Benjamin Franklin said, one hundred years ago, that "if the workers of the world would labor but four hours each day, they could produce enough in that length of time to supply the wants of mankind." While it is true that the means of supplying the wants of man have increased as if by magic, yet man has acquired no new wants; he is merely enabled to gratify his needs more fully. If it were true in Franklin's time that four hours of toil each day would prove sufficient to minister to the necessities of the world's inhabitants, the argument certainly has lost none of its force since then. At that time, it took the sailing-vessel three months to cross the ocean; the stage-coach made its thirty or forty miles a day; the electric wire was not dreamed of; and the letter that traveled but little faster than the stage-coach was the quickest medium of communication.

It required six days' labor at the hands of the machinist, with hammer, chisel and file to perfect a certain piece of machinery at the beginning of this century. The machinist of the present day can finish a better job in six hours, with the aid of a labor-saving machine. In a yarn-mill in Philadelphia, the proprietor says that improved machinery has caused a displacement of fifty per cent. of the former employees within five years, and that one person, with the aid of improved machinery, can perform the work that it took upward of one hundred carders and spinners to do with the tools and implements in use at the beginning of this century. In Massachusetts, it has been estimated that 318,768 men, women and children do, with improved machinery, the work that it would require 1,912,468 men to perform, if improved machinery were not in use. To insure safety on a passenger-train, it is no longer necessary to have a brakeman at each end of the car; the automatic air-brake does the work, while one brakeman can shout, "All right here!" for the whole train. The employee that has had a limb cut off in a collision, must beg for bread or turn the crank of a hand-organ, and gather his pennies under the legend, "Please assist a poor soldier, who lost his leg at Gettysburg." He is no longer stationed, flag in hand, at the switch; the automatic lever directs the course of the train, and renders the one-legged switchman unnecessary. It is said that the iron-moulder recently invented is capable of performing as much labor as three skilled workmen; while the following dispatch to a Philadelphia paper, from Mahanoy City, shows what is being done in the mines.—

For the past three years the reduction in wages has been systematic and steady. When one of the officials of one of the great companies was interviewed on the matter, he replied that the advance in labor-saving machinery had lightened the labor of the men. A miner at one of the Reading collieries says that some months ago he expended a large sum for a patent drill, which enabled him to do five times the usual amount of work. He was employed in driving a gangway, the price paid being $10 a yard; but at the end of the week, when the officials saw the amount of work he had done, the rate was reduced to $4.50 a yard. . . .

A great many remedies are recommended for the ills that I speak of. Let me deal with what seems to be the most unimportant,—the reduction of the hours of labor to eight a day. Men, women and children are working from ten to eighteen hours a day, and two million men have nothing to do. If four men, following a given occupation, at which they work ten hours a day, would rest from their labors two hours each day, the two hours taken from the labor of each, if added together, would give the tramp that stands looking on, an opportunity of stepping into a position at eight hours a day. It is said that a vast majority of those who are idle would not work, if they had work to do. That statement is untrue; but let us admit that five hundred thousand of the two million idle men would not work, and we still have a million and a half who are anxious and willing to work. If but six million of the seventeen million producers will abstain from working ten, fifteen, and eighteen hours a day, and work but eight, the one million and a half of idle men that are willing to work, can again take their places in the ranks of the world's producers. Need it be said, that a million and a half of new hats will be needed;

that a corresponding number of pairs of shoes, suits of clothing, and a hundred other things will be required; that the wants of these men and their families will be supplied; that shelves will be emptied of their goods, and that the money expended will again go into circulation. It would entail hardship on some branches of business, to require men employed in them to work eight hours a day. Miners and those working by contract could not very well adopt the eight-hour plan, without lengthening their hours of labor. Before giving the matter a second thought, many of these men look upon the eight-hour agitation as of no consequence to them. If a mechanic is thrown out of employment, and cannot find anything to do at his trade, he turns toward the first place where an opportunity for work is presented. If he is re-enforced by two million idle men, the number that apply at the mouth of the mine, or seek to secure contracts at lower figures, becomes quite large; and the miner and contract-man grumble, because so many men are crowding in upon them in quest of work. Every new applicant for work in the mine makes it possible for the boss to let his contract to a lower bidder; therefore, it is clearly to the interest of the miner to assist in reducing the hours of labor in the shop, mill and factory, to the end that the idle millions may be gathered in from the streets to self-sustaining positions.

The eight-hour system, to be of value to the masses, must be put in operation all over the country; for the manufacturers of one State cannot successfully compete with those of other States, if they run their establishments but eight hours, while others operate theirs ten or twelve hours a day. The movement should be national, and should have the hearty co-operation of all men. . . .

When the President of the United States issued his Thanksgiving proclamation, in 1884, there were millions of men and women in want of bread, notwithstanding "the abundant harvests and continued prosperity which God hath vouchsafed to this nation;" and the cry, not of thanksgiving, went up from millions of farmers, of "Too much wheat!" Doubting as to the exact meaning of the Creator in growing so much wheat, they invoked the aid of such institutions as the Chicago Board of Trade, in the hope of thwarting the will of God, by cornering wheat. These men invoked blessings on their Thanksgiving dinners, and thanked God for the turkey, while they hoarded the wheat away from those who asked for bread.

Give men shorter hours in which to labor, and you give them more time to study, and learn why bread is so scarce, while wheat is so plenty. You give them more time in which to learn that millions of acres of American soil are controlled by alien landlords, that have no interest in America but to draw a revenue from it. You give them time to learn that America belongs to Americans, native and naturalized, and that the landlord who drives his tenant from the Old World must not be permitted to exact tribute from him when he settles in our country.

Questions

1. How does Powderly's use of the term *mechanic* suggest that the Knights were a backward-looking movement?
2. What does Powderly suggest as a remedy for the workers' situation?
3. How does Powderly characterize businessmen?

17-7   How I Became a Socialist (1902)

Eugene V. Debs

For some people, the goals of organized labor were too limited. Even if the AFL won some victories, the economy would remain firmly under the control of a capitalist elite. Rather than accept that prospect, some workers turned to socialism.

The movement had a deep if limited appeal. Socialism promised to address inequality in industrial America by giving workers—the great majority of the population—control over the economy and the government. This was not Jeffersonian or Jacksonian democracy, and socialism remained a marginal idea as long as it appeared to be a Marxist import from Europe.

Eugene V. Debs (1855–1926) helped make socialism respectable, even mainstream, in the first decades of the twentieth century (see text pp. 569–571). Debs came from a middle-class family in Terre Haute, Indiana, and at one time had been a conventional Democrat and trade unionist. In this essay, Debs explains the reasons for his change of philosophy. The "anarchists" he mentions were the four Chicago labor figures who were hanged for their role in the Haymarket Square riot of 1886 (see text pp. 567–568).

Source: Eugene V. Debs, "How I Became a Socialist," *The Comrade* (April 1902).

As I have some doubt about the readers of *The Comrade* having any curiosity as to "how I became a socialist" it may be in order to say that the subject is the editor's, not my own; and that what is here offered is at his bidding—my only concern being that he shall not have cause to wish that I had remained what I was instead of becoming a socialist.

On the evening of February 27, 1875, the local lodge of the Brotherhood of Locomotive Firemen was organized at Terre Haute, Indiana, by Joshua A. Leach, then grand master, and I was admitted as a charter member and at once chosen secretary. "Old Josh Leach," as he was affectionately called, a typical locomotive fireman of his day, was the founder of the brotherhood, and I was instantly attracted by his rugged honesty, simple manner and homely speech. How well I remember feeling his large, rough hand on my shoulder, the kindly eye of an elder brother searching my own as he gently said: "My boy, you're a little young, but I believe you're in earnest and will make your mark in the brotherhood." Of course, I assured him that I would do my best. What he really thought at the time flat-

tered my boyish vanity not a little when I heard of it. He was attending a meeting at St. Louis some months later, and in the course of his remarks said: "I put a tow-headed boy in the brotherhood at Terre Haute not long ago, and some day he will be at the head of it." . . .

My first step was thus taken in organized labor and a new influence fired my ambition and changed the whole current of my career. I was filled with enthusiasm and my blood fairly leaped in my veins. Day and night I worked for the brotherhood. To see its watchfires glow and observe the increase of its sturdy members were the sunshine and shower of my life. To attend the "meeting" was my supreme joy, and for ten years I was not once absent when the faithful assembled.

At the convention held in Buffalo in 1878 I was chosen associate editor of the magazine, and in 1880 I became grand secretary and treasurer. With all the fire of youth I entered upon the crusade which seemed to fairly glitter with possibilities. For eighteen hours at a stretch I was glued to my desk reeling off the answers to my many correspondents. Day and night were one. Sleep was time wasted and often, when all oblivious of her presence in the still small hours my mother's hand turned off the light, I went to bed under protest. Oh, what days! And what quenchless zeal and consuming vanity! . . .

My grip was always packed; and I was darting in all directions. To tramp through a railroad yard in the rain, snow or sleet half the night, or till daybreak, to be ordered out of the roundhouse for being an "agitator," or put off a train, sometimes passenger, more often freight, while attempting to deadhead over the division, were all in the program, and served to whet the appetite to conquer. One night in midwinter at Elmira, New York, a conductor on the Erie kindly dropped me off in a snowbank, and as I clambered to the top I ran into the arms of a policeman, who heard my story and on the spot became my friend.

I rode on the engines over mountain and plain, slept in the cabooses and bunks, and was fed from their pails by the swarthy stokers who still nestle close to my heart, and will until it is cold and still.

Through all these years I was nourished at Fountain Proletaire. I drank deeply of its waters and every particle of my tissue became saturated with the spirit of the working class. I had fired an engine and been stung by the exposure and hardship of the rail. I was with the boys in their weary watches, at the broken engine's side and often helped to bear their bruised and bleeding bodies back to wife and child again. How could I but feel the burden of their wrongs? How could the seed of agitation fail to take deep root in my heart?

And so I was spurred on in the work of organizing, not the firemen merely, but the brakemen, switchmen, telegraphers, shopmen, trackhands, all of them in fact, and as I had now become known as an organizer, the calls came from all sides and there are but few trades I have not helped to organize and less still in whose strikes I have not at some time had a hand.

In 1894 the American Railway Union was organized and a braver body of men never fought the battle of the working class.

Up to this time I had heard but little of socialism, knew practically nothing about the movement, and what little I did know was not calculated to impress me in its favor. I was bent on thorough and complete organization of the railroad men and ultimately the whole working class, and all my time and energy were given to that end. My supreme conviction was that if they were only organized in every branch of the service and all acted together in concert they could redress their wrongs and regulate the conditions of their employment. The stockholders of the corporation acted as one, why not the men? It was such a plain proposition—simply to follow the example set before their eyes by their masters—surely they could not fail to see it, act as one, and solve the problem.

It is useless to say that I had yet to learn the working of the capitalist system, the resources of its masters and the weakness of its slaves. Indeed, no shadow of a "system"

fell athwart my pathway; no thought of ending wage misery marred my plans. I was too deeply absorbed in perfecting wage servitude and making it a "thing of beauty and a joy forever."

It all seems very strange to me now, taking a backward look, that my vision was so focalized on a single objective point that I utterly failed to see what now appears as clear as the noonday sun—so clear that I marvel that any workingman, however dull, uncomprehending, can resist it.

But perhaps it was better so. I was to be baptized in socialism in the road of conflict and I thank the gods for reserving to this fitful occasion the fiat, "Let there be light!"—the light that streams in steady radiance upon the broad way to the socialist republic.

The skirmish lines of the A.R.U. were well advanced. A series of small battles was fought and won without the loss of a man. A number of concessions was made by the corporations rather than risk an encounter. Then came the fight on the Great Northern, short, sharp, and decisive. The victory was complete—the only railroad strike of magnitude ever won by an organization in America.

Next followed the final shock—the Pullman strike— and the American Railway Union again won, clear and complete. The combined corporations were paralyzed and helpless. At this juncture there was delivered, from wholly unexpected quarters, a swift succession of blows that blinded me for an instant and then opened wide my eyes— and in the gleam of every bayonet and the flash of every rifle *the class struggle was revealed*. This was my first practical lesson in socialism, though wholly unaware that it was called by that name.

An army of detectives, thugs and murderers was equipped with badge and beer and bludgeon and turned loose; old hulks of cars were fired; the alarm bells tolled; the people were terrified; the most startling rumors were set afloat; the press volleyed and thundered, and over all the wires sped the news that Chicago's white throat was in the clutch of a red mob; injunctions flew thick and fast, arrests followed, and our office and headquarters, the heart of the strike, was sacked, torn out and nailed up by the "lawful" authorities of the federal government; and when in company with my loyal comrades I found myself in Cook County Jail at Chicago, with the whole press screaming conspiracy, treason and murder, and by some fateful coincidence I was given the cell occupied just previous to his execution by the assassin of Mayor Carter Harrison, Sr., overlooking the spot, a few feet distant, where the anarchists were hanged a few years before, I had another exceedingly practical and impressive lesson in socialism.

Acting upon the advice of friends we sought to employ John Harlan, son of the Supreme Justice, to assist in our defense—a defense memorable to me chiefly because of the skill and fidelity of our lawyers, among whom were the brilliant Clarence Darrow and the venerable Judge Lyman Trumbull, author of the thirteenth amendment to the Constitution, abolishing slavery in the United States.

Mr. Harlan wanted to think of the matter overnight; and the next morning gravely informed us that he could not afford to be identified with the case, "for," said he, "you will be tried upon the same theory as were the anarchists, with probably the same result." That day, I remember, the jailer, by way of consolation, I suppose, showed us the bloodstained rope used at the last execution and explained in minutest detail, as he exhibited the gruesome relic, just how the monstrous crime of lawful murder is committed.

But the tempest gradually subsided and with it the bloodthirstiness of the press and "public sentiment." We were not sentenced to the gallows, nor even to the penitentiary—though put on trial for conspiracy—for reasons that will make another story.

The Chicago jail sentences were followed by six months at Woodstock and it was here that socialism gradually laid hold of me in its own irresistible fashion. Books and pamphlets and letters from socialists came by every mail and I began to read and think and dissect the anatomy of the system in which workingmen, however organized, could be shattered and battered and splintered at a single stroke. . . .

It was at this time, when the first glimmerings of socialism were beginning to penetrate, that Victor L. Berger—and I have loved him ever since—came to Woodstock, as if a providential instrument, and delivered the first impassioned message of socialism I had ever heard—the very first to set the "wires humming in my system." As a souvenir of that visit there is in my library a volume of *Capital*, by Karl Marx, inscribed with the compliments of Victor L. Berger, which I cherish as a token of priceless value.

The American Railway Union was defeated but not conquered—overwhelmed but not destroyed. It lives and pulsates in the socialist movement, and its defeat but blazed the way to economic freedom and hastened the dawn of human brotherhood.

Questions

1. What makes Debs's story persuasive?
2. To what extent was Debs a romantic?
3. How did the Pullman boycott affect Debs's thinking?

17-8   Testimony before the U.S. Strike Commission on the Pullman Strike (1894)

Andrew Carnegie's practice regarding labor unions differed from his rhetoric, as was revealed during the Homestead strike (1892), but rhetoric and policy were as one at the Pullman Palace Car Company, prompting a strike and boycott that created a national crisis two years later (see text pp. 569–570).

In this document, Thomas H. Wickes, second vice-president of the Pullman Company, responded to the questions of John D. Kernan, a member of the U.S. Strike Commission. That body was formed under the terms of the Arbitration Act of 1888, which provided for voluntary arbitration and temporary investigatory commissions (comprising the U.S. commissioner of labor and two presidential appointees) in labor-management disputes involving interstate railways. President Grover Cleveland initiated the commission investigation of 1894 at the request of labor. The commission conducted hearings during August and September and reported to the president that November.

Source: U.S. Strike Commission, *Report on the Chicago Strike of June–July, 1894.* . . . Senate. Executive Document No. 7, 53rd Congress, 3rd Session (Washington D.C.: Government Printing Office, 1895), 621–622.

222 (Commissioner KERNAN). Has the company had any policy with reference to labor unions among its help?—Ans. No; we have never objected to unions except in one instance. I presume that there are quite a number of unions in our shops now.

223 (Commissioner KERNAN). What are they?—Ans. I couldn't tell you, but I have heard of some of them. I suppose the cabinetmakers have a union, and I suppose the car builders have a union, and the carvers and the painters and other classes of men. We do not inquire into that at all.

224 (Commissioner KERNAN). That is, unions among themselves in the works?—Ans. Members of the craft, belonging to other unions; that is, the cabinet union might have its headquarters in Chicago and our men would be members of it; but we did not object to anything of that kind.

225 (Commissioner KERNAN). The only objection you ever made was to the American Railway Union, wasn't it?—Ans. Yes, sir.

226 (Commissioner KERNAN). What is the basis of your objection to that union?—Ans. Our objection to that was that we would not treat with our men as members of the American Railway Union, and we would not treat with them as members of any union. We treat with them as individuals and as men.

227 (Commissioner KERNAN). That is, each man as an individual, do you mean that?—Ans. Yes, sir.

228 (Commissioner KERNAN). Don't you think, Mr. Wickes, that would give the corporation a very great advantage over those men if it could take them up one at a time and discuss the question with him. With the ability that you have got, for instance, where do you think the man would stand in such a discussion?—Ans. The man has got probably more ability than I have.

229 (Commissioner KERNAN). You think that it would be fair to your men for each of one of them to come before you and take up the question of his grievances and attempt to maintain his end of the discussion, do you?—Ans. I think so, yes. If he is not able to do that that is his misfortune.

230 (Commissioner KERNAN). Don't you think that the fact that you represent a vast concentration of capital, and are selected for that because of your ability to repre-

sent it, entitles him if he pleases to unite with all of the men of his craft and select the ablest one they have got to represent the cause?—Ans. As a union?

231 (Commissioner KERNAN). As a union.—Ans. They have the right; yes, sir. We have the right to say whether we will receive them or not.

232 (Commissioner KERNAN). Do you think you have any right to refuse to recognize that right in treating with the men?—Ans. Yes, sir; if we chose to.

233 (Commissioner KERNAN). If you chose to. Is it your policy to do that?—Ans. Yes, sir.

234 (Commissioner KERNAN). Then you think that you have the right to refuse to recognize a union of the men designed for the purpose of presenting, through the ablest of their members, to your company the grievances which all complain of or which any complain of?—Ans. That is the policy of the company; yes, sir. If we were to receive these men as representatives of the unions they could probably force us to pay any wages which they saw fit, and get the Pullman company in the same shape that some of the railroads are by making concessions which ought not to be made.

235 (Commissioner KERNAN). Don't you think that the opposite policy, to wit, that all your dealings with the men, as individuals, in case you were one who sought to abuse your power, might enable you to pay to the men, on the other hand, just what you saw fit?—Ans. Well, of course a man in an official position, if he is arbitrary and unfair, could work a great deal of injustice to the men; no doubt about that. But then it is a man's privilege to go to work somewhere else.

236 (Commissioner KERNAN). Don't you recognize as to many men, after they had become settled in a place at work of that kind, that really that privilege does not amount to much?—Ans. We find that the best men usually come to the front; the best of our men don't give us any trouble with unions or anything else. It is only the inferior men—that is, the least competent—that give us the trouble as a general thing.

237 (Commissioner KERNAN). As a rule, then, the least competent men make the most trouble, do they?—Ans. Yes, sir; if these gentlemen allow themselves to be led by the incompetent men that is their misfortune.

Question

1. What light do the exchanges between Kernan and Wickes shed on labor-management relations at Pullman? Does any particular question and answer strike you as especially illuminating?

Questions for Further Thought

1. Drawing on Documents 17-2, 17-5, and 17-8 and the text, come to an understanding of businessmen's reading of "capital and labor in the age of enterprise."

2. Drawing on Documents 17-3, 17-4, 17-6, and 17-7 and "American Voices" (John Brophy and Abraham Bisno), come to an understanding of workers' reading of "capital and labor in the age of enterprise."

CHAPTER 18

The Politics of Late Nineteenth-Century America

★ ★ ★

The Politics of the Status Quo, 1877–1893

"The Undoing of Reconstruction" (see text pp. 494–502) involved not only the defeat of Republican governments in the former Confederate states, but also a retreat from the activism of the federal and state governments, North as well as South, that had characterized the Republican Party during the Civil War and the early postwar years. The economic depression that followed the Panic of 1873 led businessmen to oppose public spending, borrowing, and taxes; hard times contributed to the Democrats' recapture of the House of Representatives in 1874. This midterm victory of the Democrats, who held a narrower view of government than the Republicans, ushered in a period of generally divided government in Washington, D.C. From the late 1870s into the 1890s, national politics remained intensely partisan and highly competitive, but it no longer involved sustained debate over national issues of fundamental importance (see text pp. 575–580).

James Bryce, a Briton, offered the most celebrated reading of American politics during the late nineteenth century: *The American Commonwealth* (Document 18-1). The relative inactivity of national government during much of this period reflected in part the pervasiveness of "the ideology of individualism" (see text pp. 578–580), the most famous social Darwinist exponent of which was William Graham Sumner (Document 18-2).

18-1   The American Commonwealth (1888)

James Bryce

James Bryce (1838–1922), a Scot, taught law at Oxford University in England and sat in the House of Commons and later (as Viscount Bryce of Dechmont) in the House of Lords. When he wrote *The American Commonwealth*, he had traveled in the United

States three times for a total of nine months. A number of like-minded Americans assisted in writing the book and in later revisions. Bryce served as British ambassador to the United States between 1906 and 1913.

Source: James Bryce, *The American Commonwealth,* 2 vols. (London and New York: Macmillan, 1888); rev. ed., with an introduction by Gary L. McDowell, 2 vols. (Indianapolis: Liberty Fund, 1995), 2: 731–740.

THE POLITICIANS

Institutions are said to form men, but it is no less true that men give to institutions their colour and tendency. It profits little to know the legal rules and methods and observances of government, unless one also knows something of the human beings who tend and direct this machinery, and who, by the spirit in which they work it, may render it the potent instrument of good or evil to the people. These men are the politicians.

What is one to include under this term? In England it usually denotes those who are actively occupied in administering or legislating, or discussing administration and legislation. That is to say, it includes ministers of the Crown, members of Parliament (though some in the House of Commons and the majority in the House of Lords care little about politics), a few leading journalists, and a small number of miscellaneous persons, writers, lecturers, organizers, agitators, who occupy themselves with trying to influence the public. Sometimes the term is given a wider sweep, being taken to include all who labour for their political party in the constituencies, as, e.g., the chairmen and secretaries of local party associations, and the more active committeemen of the same bodies. The former, whom we may call the inner-circle men, are professional politicians in this sense, and in this sense only, that politics is the main though seldom the sole business of their lives. But at present extremely few of them make anything by it in the way of money. A handful hope to get some post; a somewhat larger number find that a seat in Parliament enables them to push their financial undertakings or make them at least more conspicuous in the commercial world. But the gaining of a livelihood does not come into the view of the great majority at all. The other class, who may be called the outer circle, are not professionals in any sense, being primarily occupied with their own avocations; and none of them, except here and there an organizing secretary, or registration, agent, and here and there a paid lecturer, makes any profit out of the work. . . .

To see why things are different in the United States, why the inner circle is much larger both absolutely and relatively to the outer circle than in Europe, let us go back a little and ask what are the conditions which develop a political class. The point has so important a bearing on the

characteristics of American politicians that I do not fear to dwell somewhat fully upon it.

In self-governing communities of the simpler kind—for one may leave absolute monarchies and feudal monarchies on one side—the common affairs are everybody's business and nobody's special business. Some few men by their personal qualities get a larger share of authority, and are repeatedly chosen to be archons, or generals, or consuls, or burgomasters, or landammans, but even these rarely give their whole time to the state, and make little or nothing in money out of it. This was the condition of the Greek republics, of early Rome, of the cities of mediæval Germany and Italy, of the cantons of Switzerland till very recent times.

When in a large country public affairs become more engrossing to those who are occupied in them, when the sphere of government widens, when administration is more complex and more closely interlaced with the industrial interests of the community and of the world at large, so that there is more to be known and to be considered, the business of a nation falls into the hands of the men eminent by rank, wealth, and ability, who form a sort of governing class, largely hereditary. The higher civil administration of the state is in their hands; they fill the chief council or legislative chamber and conduct its debates. They have residences in the capital, and though they receive salaries when actually filling an office, and have opportunities for enriching themselves, the majority possess independent means, and pursue politics for the sake of fame, power, or excitement. Those few who have not independent means can follow their business or profession in the capital, or can frequently visit the place where their business is carried on. This was the condition of Rome under the later republic, and of England and France till quite lately—indeed it is largely the case in England still—as well as of Prussia and Sweden.

Let us see what are the conditions of the United States.

There is a relatively small leisured class of persons engaged in no occupation and of wealth sufficient to leave them free for public affairs. So far as such persons are to be found in the country, for some are to be sought abroad, they are to be found in a few great cities.

There is no class with a sort of hereditary prescriptive right to public office, no great families whose names are known to the people, and who, bound together by class sympathy and ties of relationship, help one another by keeping offices in the hands of their own members.

The country is a very large one, and has its political capital in a city without trade, without manufactures, without professional careers. Even the seats of state governments are often placed in comparatively small towns. Hence a man cannot carry on his gainful occupation at the same time that he attends to "inner-circle" politics.

Members of Congress and of state legislatures are invariably chosen from the places where they reside. Hence a person belonging to the leisured class of a great city cannot get into the House of Representatives or the legislature of his state except as member for a district of his own city.

The shortness of terms of office, and the large number of offices filled by election, make elections very frequent. All these elections, with trifling exceptions, are fought on party lines, and the result of a minor one for some petty local office, such as county treasurer, affects one for a more important post, e.g., that of member of Congress. Hence constant vigilance, constant exertions on the spot, are needed. The list of voters must be incessantly looked after, newly admitted or newly settled citizens enrolled, the active local men frequently consulted and kept in good humour, meetings arranged for, tickets (i.e., lists of candidates) for all vacant offices agreed upon. One election is no sooner over than another approaches and has to be provided for, as the English sporting man reckons his year by "events," and thinks of Newmarket after Ascot, and of Goodwood after Newmarket.

Now what do these conditions amount to? To this—a great deal of hard and dull election and other local political work to be done. Few men of leisure to do it, and still fewer men of leisure likely to care for it. Nobody able to do it in addition to his regular business or profession. Little motive for anybody, whether leisured or not, to do the humbler and local parts of it (i.e., so much as concerns the minor elections), the parts which bring neither fame nor power.

If the work is to be done at all, some inducement, other than fame or power, must clearly be found. Why not, someone will say, the sense of public duty? I will speak of public duty presently; meantime let it suffice to remark that to rely on public duty as the main motive power in politics is to assume a commonwealth of angels. Men such as we know them must have some other inducement. Even in the Christian church there are other than spiritual motives to lead its pastors to spiritual work; nor do all poets write because they seek to express the passion of their souls. In America we discover a palpable inducement to undertake the dull and toilsome work of election politics. It is the inducement of places in the public service. To make them attractive they must be paid. They are paid, nearly all of them, memberships of Congress and other federal places, state places (including memberships of state legislatures), city and county places. Here then—and to some extent even in humbler forms, such as the getting of

small contracts or even employment as labourers—is the inducement, the remuneration for political work performed in the way of organizing and electioneering. Now add that besides the paid administrative and legislative places which a democracy bestows by election, judicial places are also in most of the states elective, and held for terms of years only; and add further, that the holders of nearly all those administrative places, federal, state, and municipal, which are not held for a fixed term, are liable to be dismissed, as indeed many still are so liable and are in practice dismissed, whenever power changes from one party to another, so that those who belong to the party out of office have a direct chance of office when their party comes in. The inducement to undertake political work we have been searching for is at once seen to be adequate, and only too adequate. The men needed for the work are certain to appear because remuneration is provided. Politics has now become a gainful profession, like advocacy, stockbroking, the dry goods trade, or the getting up of companies. People go into it to live by it, primarily for the sake of the salaries attached to the places they count on getting, secondarily in view of the opportunities it affords of making incidental and sometimes illegitimate gains. Every person in a high administrative post, whether federal, state, or municipal, and, above all, every member of Congress, has opportunities of rendering services to wealthy individuals and companies for which they are willing to pay secretly in money or in money's worth. The better officials and legislators—they are the great majority, except in large cities—resist the temptation. The worst succumb to it, and the prospect of these illicit profits renders a political career distinctly more attractive to an unscrupulous man.

We find therefore that in America all the conditions exist for producing a class of men specially devoted to political work and making a livelihood by it. It is work much of which cannot be done in combination with any other kind of regular work, whether professional or commercial. Even if the man who unites wealth and leisure to high intellectual attainments were a frequent figure in America, he would not take to this work; he would rather be a philanthropist or cultivate arts and letters. It is work which, steadily pursued by an active man, offers an income. Hence a large number of persons are drawn into it, and make it the business of their life; and the fact that they are there as professionals has tended to keep amateurs out of it.

There are, however, two qualifications which must be added to this statement of the facts, and which it is best to add at once. One is that the mere pleasure of politics counts for something. Many people in America as well as in England undertake even the commonplace work of local canvassing and organizing for the sake of a little excitement, a little of the agreeable sense of self-importance, or from that fondness for doing something in association with others which makes a man become secretary to a cricket club or treasurer of a fund raised by subscription for some purpose he may not really care for. And the second qualification is that pecuniary motives operate with less force in rural districts than in cities, because in the former the income obtainable by public office is too small to induce men to work long in the hope of getting it. Let it therefore be understood that what is said in this chapter refers primarily to cities, and of course also to persons aiming at the higher federal and state offices; and that I do not mean to deny that there is plenty of work done by amateurs as well as by professionals.

Having thus seen what are the causes which produce professional politicians, we may return to inquire how large this class is, compared with the corresponding class in the free countries of Europe, whom we have called the inner circle.

In America the inner circle, that is to say, the persons who make political work the chief business of life, for the time being, includes:

Firstly. All members of both houses of Congress.

Secondly. All federal officeholders except the judges, who are irremovable, and who have sometimes taken no prominent part in politics.

Thirdly. A large part of the members of state legislatures. How large a part, it is impossible to determine, for it varies greatly from state to state. . . . But the line between a professional and nonprofessional politician is too indefinite to make any satisfactory estimate possible.

Fourthly. Nearly all state officeholders, excluding all judges in a very few states, and many of the judges in the rest.

Fifthly. Nearly all holders of paid offices in the greater and in many of the smaller cities, and many holders of paid offices in the counties. There are, however, great differences in this respect between different states, the New England states and the newer states of the Northwest, as well as some Southern states, choosing many of their county officials from men who are not regularly employed on politics, although members of the dominant party.

Sixthly. A large number of people who hold no office but want to get one, or perhaps even who desire work under a municipality. This category includes, of course, many of the "workers" of the party which does not command the majority for the time being, in state and municipal affairs, and which has not, through the president, the patronage of federal posts. It also includes many expectants belonging to the party for the time being dominant, who are earning their future places by serving the party in the meantime.

All the above may fairly be called professional or inner-circle politicians, but of their number I can form no estimate, save that it must be counted by hundreds of thousands, inasmuch as it practically includes nearly all state and local and most federal officeholders as well as most expectants of public office.

It must be remembered that the "work" of politics means in America the business of winning nominations (of which more anon) and elections, and that this work is incomparably heavier and more complex than in England, because:

(1) The voters are a larger proportion of the population; (2) the government is more complex (federal, state, and local) and the places filled by election are therefore far more numerous; (3) elections come at shorter intervals; (4) the machinery of nominating candidates is far more complete and intricate; (5) the methods of fighting elections require more technical knowledge and skill; (6) ordinary private citizens do less election work, seeing that they are busier than in England, and the professionals exist to do it for them.

I have observed that there are also plenty of men engaged in some trade or profession who interest themselves in politics and work for their party without any definite hope of office or other pecuniary aim. They correspond to what we have called the outer-circle politicians of Europe. It is hard to draw a line between the two classes, because they shade off into one another, there being many farmers or lawyers or saloonkeepers, for instance, who, while pursuing their regular calling, bear a hand in politics, and look to be some time or other rewarded for doing so. When this expectation becomes a considerable part of the motive for exertion, such an one may fairly be called a professional, at least for the time being, for although he has other means of livelihood, he is apt to be impregnated with the habits and sentiments of the professional class.

The proportion between outer-circle and inner-circle men is in the United States a sort of ozonometer by which the purity and healthiness of the political atmosphere may be tested. Looking at the North only, for I have no tolerable data as to the South, and excluding congressmen, the proportion of men who exert themselves in politics without pecuniary motive is largest in New England, in the country parts of New York, in northern Ohio, and the Northwestern states, while the professional politicians most abound in the great cities—New York, Philadelphia, Brooklyn, Boston, Baltimore, Buffalo, Cincinnati, Louisville, Chicago, St. Louis, New Orleans, San Francisco. This is because these cities have the largest masses of ignorant voters, and also because their municipal governments, handling large revenues, offer the largest facilities for illicit gains.

I shall presently return to the outer-circle men. Meantime let us examine the professionals somewhat more closely; and begin with those of the humbler type, whose eye is fixed on a municipal or other local office, and seldom ranges so high as a seat in Congress.

As there are weeds that follow human dwellings, so this species thrives best in cities, and even in the most crowded parts of cities. It is known to the Americans as the "ward politician," because the city ward is the chief sphere of its activity, and the ward meeting the first scene of its exploits. A statesman of this type usually begins as a saloon- or barkeeper, an occupation which enables him to form a large circle of acquaintances, especially among the "loafer" class who have votes but no reason for using them one way more than another, and whose interest in political issues is therefore as limited as their stock of political knowledge. But he may have started as a lawyer of the lowest kind, or lodginghouse keeper, or have taken to politics after failure in storekeeping. The education of this class is only that of the elementary schools. If they have come after boyhood from Europe, it is not even that. They have of course no comprehension of political questions or zeal for political principles; politics mean to them merely a scramble for places or jobs. They are usually vulgar, sometimes brutal, not so often criminal, or at least the associates of criminals. It is they who move about the populous quarters of the great cities, form groups through whom they can reach and control the ignorant voter, pack meetings with their creatures.

Their methods and their triumphs must be reserved for a later chapter. Those of them who are Irish, an appreciable though diminishing proportion in a few cities, have seldom Irish patriotism to redeem the mercenary quality of their politics. They are too strictly practical for that, being regardful of the wrongs of Ireland only so far as these furnish capital to be used with Irish voters. Their most conspicuous virtues are shrewdness, a sort of rough good-fellowship with one another, and loyalty to their chiefs, from whom they expect promotion in the ranks of the service. The plant thrives in the soil of any party, but its growth is more vigorous in whichever party is for the time dominant in a given city.

English critics, taking their cue from American pessimists, have often described these men as specimens of the whole class of politicians. This is misleading. The men are bad enough both as an actual force and as a symptom. But they are confined to a few great cities, those eleven or twelve I have already mentioned; it is their achievements there, and particularly in New York, where the mass of ignorant immigrants is largest, that have made them famous.

In the smaller cities, and in the country generally, the minor politicians are mostly native Americans, less ignorant and more respectable than these last-mentioned street vultures. The barkeeping element is represented among them, but the bulk are petty lawyers, officials, federal as well as state and county, and people who for want of a better occupation have turned office seekers, with a fair sprinkling of storekeepers, farmers, and newspaper men. The great majority have some regular avocation, so that they are by no means wholly professionals. Law is of course the business which best fits in with politics. They are only a little below the level of the class to which they belong, which is what would be called in England the lower middle, or in France the *petite bourgeoisie,* and they often suppose themselves to be fighting for Republican or Democratic principles, even though in fact concerned chiefly with place hunting. It is not so much positive moral defects that are to be charged on them as a slightly sordid and selfish view of politics and a laxity in the use of electioneering methods.

These two classes do the local work and dirty work of politics. They are the rank and file. Above them stand the officers in the political army, the party managers, including the members of Congress and chief men in the state legislatures, and the editors of influential newspapers. Some of these have pushed their way up from the humbler ranks. Others are men of superior ability and education, often college graduates, lawyers who have had practice, less frequently merchants or manufacturers who have slipped into politics from business. There are all sorts among them, creatures clean and unclean, as in the sheet of St. Peter's vision, but that one may say of politicians in all countries. What characterizes them as compared with the corresponding class in Europe is that their whole time is more frequently given to political work, that most of them draw an income from politics and the rest hope to do so, that they come more largely from the poorer and less cultivated than from the higher ranks of society, and that they include but few men who have pursued any of those economical, social, or constitutional studies which form the basis of politics and legislation, although many are proficients in the arts of popular oratory, of electioneering, and of party management. . . .

Questions

1. What is Bryce's view of politics in the United States?
2. How does Bryce's familiarity with politics in Great Britain influence his view of politics in the United States?
3. How does Bryce see politics in America's larger cities? What factors does Bryce deem significant to understanding city politics?

18-2   The Forgotten Man (1883)

William Graham Sumner
Social Darwinism invoked science to argue that society should not go out of its way to help the poor or to check the abuses of the robber barons. Its proponents tried to apply Charles Darwin's theory of natural selection to society, not just to plants and animals (see text pp. 578–579). The most prominent American social Darwinist was Yale professor William Graham Sumner (1840–1910), who warned, "If we do not like the survival of the fittest, we have only one possible alternative, and that is the survival of the unfittest."

Source: William Graham Sumner, "The Forgotten Man," an address to the Brooklyn Historical Society in 1883, in Albert Galloway Keller, ed., *The Forgotten Man and Other Essays* (New Haven, Conn.: Yale University Press, 1919).

Now you know that "the poor and the weak" are continually put forward as objects of public interest and public obligation. In the appeals which are made, the terms "the poor" and "the weak" are used as if they were terms of exact definition. Except the pauper, that is to say, the man who cannot earn his living or pay his way, there is no possible definition of a poor man. Except a man who is incapacitated by vice or by physical infirmity, there is no definition of a weak man. The paupers and the physically incapacitated are an inevitable charge on society. About them no more need be said. But the weak who constantly arouse the pity of humanitarians and philanthropists are the shiftless, the imprudent, the negligent, the impractical, and the inefficient, or they are the idle, the intemperate, the extravagant, and the vicious. Now the troubles of these persons are constantly forced upon public attention, as if they and their interests deserved especial consideration, and a great portion of all organized and unorganized effort for the common welfare consists in attempts to relieve these classes of people. I do not wish to be understood now as saying that nothing ought to be done for these people by those who are stronger and wiser. That is not my point. What I want to do is to point out the thing which is overlooked and the error which is made in all these charitable efforts. The notion is accepted as if it were not open to any question that if you help the inefficient and vicious you may gain something for society or you may not, but that you lose nothing. This is a complete mistake. Whatever capital you divert to the support of a shiftless and good-for-nothing person is so much diverted from some other employment, and that means from somebody else. I would spend any conceivable amount of zeal and eloquence if I possessed it to try to make people grasp this idea. Capital is force. If it goes one way it cannot go another. If you give a loaf to a pauper you cannot give the same loaf to a laborer. Now this other man who would have got it but for the charitable sentiment which bestowed it on a worthless member of society is the Forgotten Man. The philanthropists and humanitarians have their minds all full of the wretched and miserable whose case appeals to compassion, attacks the sympathies, takes possession of the imagination, and excites the emotions. They push on towards the quickest and easiest remedies and they forget the real victim.

Now who is the Forgotten Man? He is the simple, honest laborer, ready to earn his living by productive work. We pass him by because he is independent, self-supporting, and asks no favors. He does not appeal to the emotions or excite the sentiments. He only wants to make a contract and fulfill it, with respect on both sides and favor on neither side. He must get his living out of the capital of the country. The larger the capital is, the better living he can get. Every particle of capital which is wasted on the vicious, the idle, and the shiftless is so much taken from the capital available to reward the independent and productive laborer. But we stand with our backs to the independent and productive laborer all the time. We do not remember him because he makes no clamor; but I appeal to you whether he is not the man who ought to be remembered first of all, and whether, on any sound social theory, we ought not to protect him against the burdens of the good-for-nothing. In these last years I have read hundreds of articles and heard scores of sermons and speeches which were really glorifications of the good-for-nothing, as if these were the charge of society, recommended by right reason to its care and protection. We are addressed all the time as if those who are respectable were to blame because some are not so, and as if there were an obligation on the part of those who have done their duty towards those who have not done their duty. Every man is bound to take care of himself and his family and to do his share in the work of society. It is totally false that one who has done so is bound to bear the care and charge of those who are wretched because they have not done so. The silly popular notion is that the beggars live at the expense of the rich, but the truth is that those who eat and produce not, live at the expense of those who labor and produce. The next time that you are tempted to subscribe a dollar to a charity, I do not tell you not to do it, because after you have fairly considered the matter, you may think it right to do it, but I ask you to stop and remember the Forgotten Man and understand that if you put your dollar in the savings bank it will go to swell the capital of the country which is available for division amongst those who, while they earn it, will reproduce it with increase.

Let us now go on to another class of cases. There are a great many schemes brought forward for "improving the condition of the working classes." I have shown already that a free man cannot take a favor. One who takes a favor or submits to patronage demeans himself. He falls under obligation. He cannot be free and he cannot assert a station of equality with the man who confers the favor on him. The only exception is where there are exceptional bonds of affection or friendship, that is, where the sentimental relation supersedes the free relation. Therefore, in a country which is a free democracy, all propositions to do something for the working classes have an air of patronage and superiority which is impertinent and out of place. No one can do anything for anybody else unless he has a surplus of energy to dispose of after taking care of himself. In the United States, the working classes, technically so called, are the strongest classes. It is they who have a surplus to dispose of if anybody has. Why should anybody else offer to take care of them or to serve them? They can get whatever they think worth having and, at any rate, if they are free men in a free state, it is ignominious and unbecoming to introduce fashions of patronage and favoritism here. A man who, by superior education and experience of business, is in a position to advise a struggling man of the wages class, is certainly held to do so and will, I believe, always be willing and glad to do so; but this sort of activity lies in the range of private and personal relations.

I now, however, desire to direct attention to the public, general, and impersonal schemes, and I point out the fact that, if you undertake to lift anybody, you must have a fulcrum or point of resistance. All the elevation you give to one must be gained by an equivalent depression on someone else. The question of gain to society depends upon the balance of the account, as regards the position of the persons who undergo the respective operations. But nearly all the schemes for "improving the condition of the working man" involve an elevation of some working men at the expense of other working men. When you expend capital or labor to elevate some persons who come within the sphere of your influence, you interfere in the conditions of competition. The advantage of some is won by an equivalent loss of others. The difference is not brought about by the energy and effort of the persons themselves. If it were, there would be nothing to be said about it, for we constantly see people surpass others in the rivalry of life and carry off the prizes which the others must do without. In the cases I am discussing, the difference is brought about by an interference which must be partial, arbitrary, accidental, controlled by favoritism and personal preference. I do not say, in this case, either, that we ought to do no work of this kind. On the contrary, I believe that the arguments for it quite outweigh, in many cases, the arguments against it.

What I desire, again, is to bring out the forgotten element which we always need to remember in order to make a wise decision as to any scheme of this kind. I want to call to mind the Forgotten Man, because, in this case also, if we recall him and go to look for him, we shall find him patiently and perseveringly, manfully and independently struggling against adverse circumstances without complaining or begging. If, then, we are led to heed the groaning and complaining of others and to take measures for helping these others, we shall, before we know it, push down this man who is trying to help himself.

Let us take another class of cases. So far we have said nothing about the abuse of legislation. We all seem to be under the delusion that the rich pay the taxes. Taxes are not thrown upon the consumers with any such directness and completeness as is sometimes assumed; but that, in ordinary states of the market, taxes on houses fall, for the most part, on the tenants and that taxes on commodities fall, for the most part, on the consumers, is beyond question. Now the state and municipality go to great expense to support policemen and sheriffs and judicial officers, to protect people against themselves, that is, against the results of their own folly, vice, and recklessness. Who pays for it? Undoubtedly the people who have not been guilty of folly, vice, or recklessness. Out of nothing comes nothing. We cannot collect taxes from people who produce nothing and save nothing. The people who have something to tax must be those who have produced and saved.

When you see a drunkard in the gutter, you are disgusted, but you pity him. When a policeman comes and picks him up you are satisfied. You say that "society" has interfered to save the drunkard from perishing. Society is a fine word, and it saves us the trouble of thinking to say that society acts. The truth is that the policeman is paid by somebody, and when we talk about society we forget who it is that pays. It is the Forgotten Man again. It is the industrious workman going home from a hard day's work, whom you pass without noticing, who is mulcted of a percentage of his day's earnings to hire a policeman to save the drunkard from himself. All the public expenditure to prevent vice has the same effect. Vice is its own curse. If we let nature alone, she cures vice by the most frightful penalties. It may shock you to hear me say it, but when you get over the shock, it will do you good to think of it: a drunkard in the gutter is just where he ought to be. Nature is working away at him to get him out of the way, just as she sets up her processes of dissolution to remove whatever is a failure in its line. Gambling and less mentionable vices all cure themselves by the ruin and dissolution of their victims. Nine-tenths of our measures for preventing vice are really protective towards it, because they ward off the penalty. "Ward off," I say, and that is the usual way of looking at it; but is the penalty really annihilated? By no means. It is turned into police and court expenses and spread over those who have resisted vice. It is the Forgotten Man again who has been subjected to the penalty while our minds were full of the drunkards, spendthrifts, gamblers, and other victims of dissipation. Who is, then, the Forgotten Man? He is the clean, quiet, virtuous, domestic citizen, who pays his debts and his taxes and is never heard of out of his little circle. Yet who is there in the society of a civilized state who deserves to be remembered and considered by the legislator and statesman before this man?

Another class of cases is closely connected with this last. There is an apparently invincible prejudice in people's minds in favor of state regulation. All experience is against state regulation and in favor of liberty. The freer the civil institutions are, the more weak or mischievous state regulation is. The Prussian bureaucracy can do a score of things for the citizen which no governmental organ in the United States can do; and, conversely, if we want to be taken care of as Prussians and Frenchmen are, we must give up something of our personal liberty.

Questions

1. Why does Sumner oppose all attempts to help the weak?
2. To what extent is Sumner a true friend of the "Forgotten Man," especially if that man found himself unemployed in the Panic of 1893?
3. What would be the ultimate cost to a society that allowed nature to eliminate vice through people's destruction, as Sumner proposes?

Question for Further Thought

1. How do James Bryce and William Graham Sumner contribute to the late-nineteenth-century view that government should play a limited role?

Sources of Popular Participation

However unimaginative and limited national government appeared during the late nineteenth century, politics engaged not only party leaders and workers, but also the citizenry; the rank and file frequently attended political gatherings and, of greater significance, regularly voted in impressively large numbers. The political parties' coalitions were primarily based on cultural identities—religious, ethnic, racial, and regional—rather than on economic class or occupation. Once formed, political party identifications proved to be enduring, even across generational lines. Thus voters who became disaffected with their party in particular situations were more likely to abstain on Election Day than to vote for the opposing party (see text pp. 580–583).

Late-nineteenth-century partisan political culture was aggressively masculine—in political offices and party conventions and on Election Day, when men voted in male surroundings: barbershops, cigar stores, and the like. Women were permitted to vote in government elections only in four states, three of them admitted to the Union during the 1890s. Women did vote in school board and tax-related elections in some states. In one religiously divisive Boston School Board election, an outpouring of female voters testified to the motivational power of Protestant-Catholic conflict among women, as well as men. During the period, women worked to create a political culture of their own, some claiming political rights for women as for all citizens, others arguing in terms of advancing causes of concern to women (see text pp. 584–585).

A series of documents illuminates political issues central to politics from the mid-1870s into the 1890s. Document 18-3 provides highlights from an address of President Ulysses S. Grant regarding "the School Question." Document 18-4 is a political cartoon grounded in that address. Document 18-5 reports Republican and Democratic state platform planks from Wisconsin in 1890 and Iowa in 1889; Document 18-6 presents planks from the two parties' national platforms of 1892. Documents 18-7 and 18-8 offer arguments for the vote for women; Document 18-9 is a woman's case against the vote.

18-3   Address, Des Moines, Iowa (1875)

Ulysses S. Grant

Speaking before Union veterans of the Army of the Tennessee on September 29, 1875, President Ulysses S. Grant (1822–1885) stressed the centrality of "the School Question" to Protestant-Catholic controversy (see text p. 580–581). The schools had for some time been a primary battleground in recurring Protestant-Catholic conflicts, but with the Democrats gaining ground during the mid-1870s, the Republicans believed the religious issue was important to Protestants and advantageous to the GOP, unlike issues relating to Reconstruction and the Depression of 1873, which benefited the Democrats.

In his annual message to Congress later in 1875, President Grant proposed a constitutional amendment to forbid "the teaching . . . of religious, atheistic, or pagan tenets" in public schools and to deny school funds or taxes in aid of any religion. Representative James G. Blaine, a Republican from Maine, soon proposed a constitutional amendment to achieve the second objective. Passage failed, but the amendment provided the Republicans with a campaign issue.

Source: Harper's Weekly, 19 (October 23, 1875), 860.

"COMRADES,—It always affords me much gratification to meet my comrades in arms of ten or fourteen years ago, and to tell over again from memory the trials and hardships of those days of hardships imposed for the preservation and perpetuation of our free institutions. We believed then and we believe now that we have a government worth fighting for, and, if need be, dying for. How many of our comrades paid the latter price for our preserved Union! Let their heroism and sacrifice be ever green in our memory. Let not the result of their sacrifices be destroyed. The Union and the free institutions for which they died should be held more dear for their sacrifices. We will not deny to any of those who fought against us any privilege under the government which we claim for ourselves. On the contrary, we welcome all such who come forward in good faith to help build up the waste places and to perpetuate our institutions against all enemies as brothers in full interest with us in a common heritage; but we are not prepared to apologize for the part we took in the war. It is to be hoped that like trials will never again befall our country. In this sentiment no class of people can more heartily join than the soldier who submitted to the dangers, trials, and hardships of the camp and the battle-field, on whichever side he fought. No class of people are more interested in guarding against a recurrence of those days. Let us, then, begin by guarding against every enemy threatening the prosperity of free republican institutions. I do not bring into this assemblage politics, certainly not partisan politics; but it is a fair subject for the soldiers in their deliberations to consider what may be necessary to secure the prize for which they battled. In a republic like ours, where the citizen is the sovereign and the official the servant, where no power is exercised except by the will of the people, it is important that the sovereign, the people, should foster intelligence—that intelligence which is to preserve us as a free nation. If we are to have another contest in the near future of our national existence, I predict that the dividing line will not be Mason and Dixon's, but between patriotism and intelligence on the one side, and superstition, ambition, and ignorance on the other. Now the centennial year of our national existence, I believe, is a good time to begin the work of strengthening the foundations of the structure commenced by our patriotic forefathers one hundred years ago at Lexington. Let us all labor to aid all needful guarantees for the security of free thought, free speech, a free press, pure morals, unfettered religious sentiments, and of equal rights and privileges to all men, irrespective of nationality, color, or religion. Encourage free schools, and resolve that not one dollar appropriated for their support shall be appropriated to the support of any sectarian schools. Resolve that neither the state nor the nation, nor both combined, shall support institutions of learning other than those sufficient to afford to every child growing up in the land the opportunity of a good common-school education, unmixed with sectarian, pagan, or atheistical dogmas. Leave the matter of religion to the family altar, the church, and the private school supported entirely by private contributions. Keep the church and the state forever separate. With these safeguards, I believe the battles which created the Army of the Tennessee will not have been fought in vain."

Questions

1. Why might President Grant have chosen this particular audience for his address?
2. What political considerations might have influenced the timing of the speech, which was delivered in September 1875?
3. What is the meaning of Grant's reference to "superstition, ambition, and ignorance"?

18-4   The Plank—Hitting the Nail on the Head (1875)

Thomas Nast

Thomas Nast (1840–1902), the great Bavarian-born cartoonist, based "The Plank" on President Grant's address (Document 18-3). Indeed, that speech forms part of the cartoon. (Grant's and Nast's references to "free thought, free speech, a free press" echo the pre–Civil War Republican slogan, "Free Soil, Free Labor, Free Men.")

In 1876, the Republican national platform endorsed a constitutional amendment to bar the use of public money or property for sectarian schools or institutions. The Democratic national platform declared the party's support for public schools and its opposition to the diversion of public funds for sectarian purposes; it accused the Republicans of raising a false issue to create religious strife.

Source: Harper's Weekly, 19 (October 23, 1875), 860–861.

Questions

1. Why does Nast portray the serpent's head as he does?
2. Why does Nast refer to the centennial in identifying the national platform of 1876?

18-5   Republican and Democratic State Platforms on the Bennett English-Language School Law (Wisconsin, 1890) and the Liquor Question (Iowa, 1889)

Unlike political campaigns marked by Protestant-Catholic conflict, which usually worked to the Republicans' advantage by costing the Democrats Protestant support, other cultural controversies threatened the Republicans. Thus state laws in Wisconsin and Illinois that required public and private schools (Protestant, especially Lutheran, as well as Catholic) to employ English as the language of instruction angered German-Americans, contributing to unusual Democratic gubernatorial and presidential election victories in both states between 1890 and 1892. Campaigns involving the liquor question also threatened the Republicans. If they took a prohibitionist position, they risked losing German supporters to the Democrats; if they moved too far from that position, they risked losing prohibitionist adherents to the Prohibition Party. In Iowa, the issue contributed to Democratic gubernational election victories in 1889 and 1891, the party's first there since 1850 (see text pp. 580–581).

Source: The Tribune Almanac and Political Register (New York: Tribune Association, 1890, 1891): *1890,* 21–22; *1891,* 84–86.

(a) Wisconsin (1890)

Republican

THE SCHOOL QUESTION.

The Republican party, in convention assembled, declares its devotion to the common school as the chief factor in the education of the people, and pledges itself to support, strengthen and defend it.

It recognizes as valuable auxiliaries in the work of popular education the private and parochial schools supported without aid from public funds, and disclaims absolutely any purpose whatever to interfere in any manner with such schools, either as to their terms, government or branches to be taught therein.

We affirm the right and duty of the State to enact laws that will guarantee all children sufficient instruction in the legal language of the State to enable them to read and write the same. We believe that the compulsory education law passed by the last Legislature is wise and humane in all its essential purposes, and we are opposed to its repeal,[1] but

---

[1]The act of April 18, 1890 (popularly known as the Bennett law), requires that every child between seven and fourteen years shall attend some public or private day school in the city, town or district in which the child resides, for a period not less than twelve weeks nor more than twenty-four weeks in each year, the periods to be fixed and announced by the respective school boards. Penalties are provided.

Section 5 provides that "No school shall be regarded as a school under this act, unless there shall be taught therein, as part of the elementary education of children, reading, writing, arithmetic and United States history in the English language."

Democratic

DENUNCIATION OF THE REPUBLICAN PARTY

We, the Democrats of Wisconsin, in convention assembled, declare our continued opposition to all forms of paternalism and centralization. The Republican party is the exponent of these dangerous principles. . . .

THE SCHOOL QUESTION.

We oppose any division or diversion of public school funds to sectarian uses. The Democratic party created the public school system of this State, and will always jealously guard and maintain it. The Bennett law is a local manifestation of the settled Republican policy of paternalism.

Favoring laws providing for the compulsory attendance at school of all children, we believe that the school law in force prior to the passage of the Bennett law guaranteed to all children of the State opportunity for education, and in this essential feature was stronger than the Bennett law. The underlying principle of the Bennett law is needless interference with parental rights and liberty of conscience, and the provisions for its enforcement place the accused at the mercy of the School Directors and deny his right to trial by jury and according to the law of the land. To mask this tyrannical invasion of individual and constitutional rights the shallow plea of defence of the English language is advanced.

The history of this State, largely peopled with foreign citizens, demonstrates the fact that natural causes and the

Republican (continued)

at the same time we assert that the parent or guardian has the right to select the time of the year and the place, whether public or private, and wherever situated, in which his child or ward shall receive instruction, and we pledge ourselves to modify the existing law so that it shall conform to the foregoing declarations.

We are unalterably opposed to any union of Church and State, and will resist any attempt upon the part of either to invade the domain of the other. We repudiate as a gross misrepresentation of our purposes the suggestion, come whence it may, that we will in any manner invade the domain of conscience, trample upon parental rights or religious liberty. Our only purpose in respect to the educational policy of the State is to secure to all children within its borders at the earliest practicable age proper equipment for the discharge of the ordinary duties of citizenship, and to this end, alike important to the State, to the children and to the parents of the children, we invite the co-operation and aid of all broad-minded and patriotic people. . . .

Democratic (continued)

necessity of the situation are advancing the growth of the English language to the greatest possible extent. We therefore denounce the law as unnecessary, unwise, unconstitutional, un-American, and undemocratic, and demand its repeal. . . .

(b) Iowa (1889)

Republican

. . . That we reaffirm the past utterances of the Republican party of Iowa upon prohibition, which has become the settled policy of the State and upon which there should be no backward step. We stand for the complete enforcement of the law. . . .

Democratic

. . . In the interest of true temperance we demand the passage of a carefully guarded license tax law which shall provide for the issuance of licenses in towns, townships and municipal corporations of the State by vote of the people of such corporations, and which shall provide that for each license an annual tax of $500 be paid into the county treasury, and such further tax as the town, township or municipal corporation shall prescribe, the proceeds thereof to go to the use of such municipalities.

We also arraign the Republican party for changing the pharmacy laws of the State, by which a great hardship and gross indignity has been imposed on honorable pharmacists and upon all the people requiring liquor for the actual necessities of medicine. . . .

Questions

1. What is the thrust of the Wisconsin Republicans' argument in favor of the Bennett Law?
2. What is the thrust of the Wisconsin Democrats' argument against the law?
3. What is the meaning of the Iowa Democrats' advocacy of "true temperance"? How does their position differ from that of the Republicans?

18-6   Democratic and Republican National Platforms on the Currency, the Tariff, and Federal Elections (1892)

By the standards of the time, political conflict was sharp between 1888 and 1892 (see text pp. 585, 589–591). Republican successes in 1888 gave the party control of the presidency and both houses of Congress, an unusual development during the period, enabling the GOP to seek enactment of an ambitious agenda to achieve the party's major goals. In 1890, the Republicans won passage of the Sherman Silver Purchase Act to mollify western inflationists without embracing Free Silver, which was opposed in the East, and the McKinley Tariff Act, proof of the party's continued commitment to the protective tariff. However, they failed to secure enactment of the Lodge Federal Elections Bill, demonized by the Democrats as "the Force Bill." The Bill proposed federal judicial supervision of federal elections upon the petition of one hundred voters within a congressional district or city of twenty thousand, a measure aimed at curbing Democratic election fraud in the South and urban North. Meanwhile, the Democrats scored widespread gains in the midterm elections of 1890, recapturing the House of Representatives, and mounting discontent in the South and West, especially among farmers, led eventually to the creation of a national People's (Populist) Party during 1892.

In their national platforms of 1892, the Democrats and the Republicans dealt with the monetary, tariff, and federal election issues; they also referred to cultural issues prominent in state politics. (For the 1892 national platform of the People's Party, see Document 18-10).

Source: Donald Bruce Johnson, comp., *National Party Platforms,* rev. ed., 2 vols. (Urbana: University of Illinois Press, 1978), 1: *1840–1956,* 86–89, 93–95.

PARTY PLATFORMS OF 1892

Democratic

. . . we solemnly declare that the need of a return to these fundamental principles of free popular government, based on home rule and individual liberty, was never more urgent than now, when the tendency to centralize all power at the Federal capital has become a menace to the reserved rights of the States that strikes at the very roots of our Government under the Constitution as framed by the fathers of the Republic.

We warn the people of our common country, jealous for the preservation of their free institutions, that the policy of Federal control of elections, to which the Republican party has committed itself, is fraught with the gravest dangers, scarcely less momentous than would result from a revolution practically establishing monarchy on the ruins of the Republic. It strikes at the North as well as at the South, and injures the colored citizen even more than the white; it means a horde of deputy marshals at every polling place, armed with Federal power; returning boards appointed and controlled by Federal authority, the outrage of the electoral rights of the people in the several States, the subjugation of the colored people to the control of the

party in power, and the reviving of race antagonisms, now happily abated, of the utmost peril to the safety and happiness of all; a measure deliberately and justly described by a leading Republican Senator as "the most infamous bill that ever crossed the threshold of the Senate." Such a policy, if sanctioned by law, would mean the dominance of a self-perpetuating obligarchy of office-holders, and the party first intrusted with its machinery could be dislodged from power only by an appeal to the reserved right of the people to resist oppression, which is inherent in all self-governing communities. Two years ago this revolutionary policy was emphatically condemned by the people at the polls, but in contempt of that verdict the Republican party has defiantly declared in its latest authoritative utterance that its success in the coming elections will mean the enactment of the Force Bill and the usurpation of despotic control over elections in all the States.

Believing that the preservation of Republican government in the United States is dependent upon the defeat of this policy of legalized force and fraud, we invite the support of all citizens who desire to see the Constitution maintained in its integrity with the laws pursuant thereto, which have given our country a hundred years of unexampled prosperity; and we pledge the Democratic party, if it be intrusted with power, not only to the defeat of the Force Bill, but also to relentless opposition to the Republican policy of profligate expenditure, which, in the short space of two years, has squandered an enormous surplus and emptied an overflowing Treasury, after piling new burdens of taxation upon the already overtaxed labor of the country.

We denounce Republican protection as a fraud, a robbery of the great majority of the American people for the benefit of the few. We declare it to be a fundamental principle of the Democratic party that the Federal Government has no constitutional power to impose and collect tariff duties, except for the purpose of revenue only, and we demand that the collection of such taxes shall be limited to the necessities of the Government when honestly and economically administered.

We denounce the McKinley tariff law enacted by the Fifty-first Congress as the culminating atrocity of class legislation; we indorse the efforts made by the Democrats of the present Congress to modify its most oppressive features in the direction of free raw materials and cheaper manufactured goods that enter into general consumption; and we promise its repeal as one of the beneficent results that will follow the action of the people in intrusting power to the Democratic party. Since the McKinley tariff went into operation there have been ten reductions of the wages of the laboring man to one increase. We deny that there has been any increase of prosperity to the country since that tariff went into operation, and we point to the fullness and distress, the wage reductions and strikes in the iron trade, as the best possible evidence that no such prosperity has resulted from the McKinley Act.

We call the attention of thoughtful Americans to the fact that, after thirty years of restrictive taxes against the importation of foreign wealth, in exchange for our agricultural surplus, the homes and farms of the country have become burdened with a real estate mortgage debt of over $2,500,000,000, exclusive of all other forms of indebtedness; that in one of the chief agricultural States of the West there appears a real estate mortgage debt averaging $165 per capita of the total population, and that similar conditions and tendencies are shown to exist in other agricultural-exporting States. We denounce a policy which fosters no industry so much as it does that of the Sheriff.

Trade interchange, on the basis of reciprocal advantages to the countries participating, is a time-honored doctrine of the Democratic faith, but we denounce the sham reciprocity which juggles with the people's desire for enlarged foreign markets and freer exchanges by pretending to establish closer trade relations for a country whose articles of export are almost exclusively agricultural products with other countries that are also agricultural, while erecting a custom-house barrier of prohibitive tariff taxes against the richest countries of the world, that stand ready to take our entire surplus of products, and to exchange

therefor commodities which are necessaries and comforts of life among our own people. . . .

We denounce the Republican legislation known as the Sherman Act of 1890 as a cowardly make-shift, fraught with possibilities of danger in the future, which should make all of its supporters, as well as its author, anxious for its speedy repeal. We hold to the use of both gold and silver as the standard money of the country, and to the coinage of both gold and silver without discriminating against either metal or charge for mintage, but the dollar unit of coinage of both metals must be of equal intrinsic and exchangeable value, or be adjusted through international agreement or by such safeguards of legislation as shall insure the maintenance of the parity of the two metals and the equal power of every dollar at all times in the markets and in the payment of debts; and we demand that all paper currency shall be kept at par with and redeemable in such coin. We insist upon this policy as especially necessary for the protection of the farmers and laboring classes, the first and most defenseless victims of unstable money and a fluctuating currency. . . .

Popular education being the only safe basis of popular suffrage, we recommend to the several States most liberal appropriations for the public schools. Free common schools are the nursery of good government, and they have always received the fostering case of the Democratic party, which favors every means of increasing intelligence. Freedom of education, being an essential of civil and religious liberty, as well as a necessity for the development of intelligence, must not be interfered with under any pretext whatever. We are opposed to State interference with parental rights and rights of conscience in the education of children as an infringement of the fundamental Democratic doctrine that the largest individual liberty consistent with the rights of others insures the highest type of American citizenship and the best government. . . .

We are opposed to all sumptuary laws,[1] as an interference with the individual rights of the citizen. . . .

Republican

. . . We reaffirm the American doctrine of protection. We call attention to its growth abroad. We maintain that the prosperous condition of our country is largely due to the wise revenue legislation of the Republican congress.

We believe that all articles which cannot be produced in the United States, except luxuries, should be admitted free of duty, and that on all imports coming into competition with the products of American labor, there should be levied duties equal to the difference between wages abroad and at home. We assert that the prices of manufactured articles of general consumption have been reduced under the operations of the tariff act of 1890. . . .

---

[1]Sumptuary laws regulated personal behavior on moral grounds—for example, Prohibition.

We point to the success of the Republican policy of reciprocity,[2] under which our export trade has vastly increased and new and enlarged markets have been opened for the products of our farms and workshops. We remind the people of the bitter opposition of the Democratic party to this practical business measure, and claim that, executed by a Republican administration, our present laws will eventually give us control of the trade of the world.

The American people, from tradition and interest, favor bi-metallism, and the Republican party demands the use of both gold and silver as standard money, with such restrictions and under such provisions, to be determined by legislation, as will secure the maintenance of the parity of values of the two metals so that the purchasing and debt-paying power of the dollar, whether of silver, gold, or paper, shall be at all times equal. The interests of the producers of the country, its farmers and its workingmen, demand that every dollar, paper or coin, issued by the government, shall be as good as any other.

We commend the wise and patriotic steps already taken by our government to secure an international conference, to adopt such measures as will insure a parity of value between gold and silver for use as money throughout the world.

We demand that every citizen of the United States shall be allowed to cast one free and unrestricted ballot in all public elections, and that such ballot shall be counted and returned as cast; that such laws shall be enacted and enforced as will secure to every citizen, be he rich or poor, native or foreign-born, white or black, this sovereign right, guaranteed by the Constitution. The free and honest popular ballot, the just and equal representation of all the people, as well as their just and equal protection under the laws, are the foundation of our Republican institutions, and the party will never relax its efforts until the integrity of the ballot and the purity of elections shall be fully guaranteed and protected in every State.

SOUTHERN OUTRAGES

We denounce the continued inhuman outrages perpetrated upon American citizens for political reasons in certain Southern States of the Union. . . .

The ultimate reliance of free popular government is the intelligence of the people, and the maintenance of freedom among men. We therefore declare anew our devotion to liberty of thought and conscience, of speech and press, and approve all agencies and instrumentalities which contribute to the education of the children of the land, but while insisting upon the fullest measure of religious liberty, we are opposed to any union of Church and State. . . .

INTEMPERANCE

We sympathize with all wise and legitimate efforts to lessen and prevent the evils of intemperance and promote morality. . . .

---

[2]Reciprocity, introduced in 1890, allowed for the tariff-free importation of specified products from Western Hemisphere nations in return for their admitting American exports on the same terms.

Questions

1. What major differences between the Democratic and Republican platform positions can you identify?
2. A platform not only states the party's positions on the issues, but it also employs language, about the party and its opponents, designed to elicit emotional responses from supporters. Do these platforms contain terms and characterizations that strike you?
3. Do the parties' state and national platforms (Documents 18-5 and 18-6) resemble each other in significant ways?

18-7   Woman and Temperance (1876)

Frances E. Willard

The reform movements of the nineteenth century brought women out of the home and into the larger community. Abolition and temperance touched on politics, which in turn led to the call for suffrage and women's right to shape responses to the issues that affected them (see text pp. 584–585). Frances E. Willard (1839–1898), a founder of the Woman's Christian Temperance Union, emerged as a leader of the suffrage movement. The following selection is excerpted from Willard's first major temperance speech, delivered in 1876. Willard likens the alcohol interests to Chimborazo, the highest peak in Ecuador.

Source: Frances E. Willard, "Woman and Temperance," a speech delivered in 1876, in Frances E. Willard, *Woman and Temperance or, The Work and Workers of the Woman's Christian Temperance Union* (1883; reprint, New York: Arno Press, 1972), 452–457.

The rum power looms like a Chimborazo among the mountains of difficulty over which our native land must climb to reach the future of our dreams. The problem of the rum power's overthrow may well engage our thoughts as women and as patriots. To-night I ask you to consider it in the light of a truth which Frederick Douglass has embodied in these words: "We can in the long run trust all the knowledge in the community to take care of all the ignorance of the community, and all of its virtue to take care of all of its vice." The difficulty in the application of this principle lies in the fact that vice is always in the active, virtue often in the passive. Vice is aggressive. It deals swift, sure blows, delights in keen-edged weapons, and prefers a hand-to-hand conflict, while virtue instinctively fights its unsavory antagonist at arm's length; its great guns are unwieldy and slow to swing into range.

Vice is the tiger, with keen eyes, alert ears, and cat-like tread, while virtue is the slow-paced, complacent, easy-going elephant, whose greatest danger lies in its ponderous weight and consciousness of power. So the great question narrows down to one of two(?) methods. It is not, when we look carefully into the conditions of the problem, How shall we develop more virtue in the community to offset the tropical growth of vice by which we find ourselves environed? but rather, How the tremendous force we have may best be brought to bear, how we may unlimber the huge cannon now pointing into vacancy, and direct their full charge at short range upon our nimble, wily, vigilant foe?

As bearing upon a consideration of that question, I lay down this proposition: All pure and Christian sentiment concerning any line of conduct which vitally affects humanity will, sooner or later, crystallize into law. But the keystone of law can only be firm and secure when it is held in place by the arch of that keystone, which is public sentiment. . . .

There is a class whose instinct of self-preservation must forever be opposed to a stimulant which nerves, with dangerous strength, arms already so much stronger than their own, and so maddens the brain God meant to guide those arms, that they strike down the wives men love, and the little children for whom, when sober, they would die. The wife, largely dependent for the support of herself and little ones upon the brain which strong drink paralyzes, the arm it masters, and the skill it renders futile, will, in the nature of the case, prove herself unfriendly to the actual or potential source of so much misery. But besides this primal instinct of self-preservation, we have, in the same class of which I speak, another far more high and sacred—I mean the instinct of a mother's love, a wife's devotion, a sister's faithfulness, a daughter's loyalty. And now I ask you to consider earnestly the fact that none of these blessed rays of light and power from woman's heart, are as yet brought to bear upon the rum-shop at the focus of power. They are, I know, the sweet and pleasant sunshine of our homes; they are the beams which light the larger home of social life and send their gentle radiance out even into the great and busy world. But I know, and as the knowledge has grown clearer, my heart was thrilled with gratitude and hope too deep for words, that in a republic all these now divergent beams of light can, through that magic lens, that powerful sun-glass which we name the ballot, be made to converge upon the rum-shop in a blaze of light that shall reveal its full abominations, and a white flame of heat which, . . . shall burn this cancerous excrescence from America's fair form. Yes, for there is nothing in the universe so sure, so strong, as love; and love shall do all this—the love of maid for sweetheart, wife for husband, of a sister for her brother, of a mother for her son. And I call upon you who are here to-day, good men and brave—you who have welcomed us to other fields in the great fight of the angel against the dragon in society—I call upon you thus to match force with force, to set over against the liquor-dealer's avarice our instinct of self-preservation; and to match the drinker's love of liquor with our love of him! When you can centre all this power in that small bit of paper which falls

"As silently as snow-flakes fall upon the sod,
But executes a freeman's will as lightnings do the will of God,"

the rum power will be as much doomed as was the slave power when you gave the ballot to the slaves.

In our argument it has been claimed that by the changeless instincts of her nature and through the most sacred relationships of which that nature has been rendered capable, God has indicated woman, who is the born conservator of home, to be the Nemesis of home's arch enemy, King Alcohol. And further, that in a republic, this power of hers may be most effectively exercised by giving her a voice in the decision by which the rum-shop door shall be opened or closed beside her home.

This position is strongly supported by evidence. About the year 1850 petitions were extensively circulated in Cincinnati (later the fiercest battle ground of the woman's crusade), asking that the liquor traffic be put under the ban of law. Bishop Simpson—one of the noblest and most discerning minds of his century—was deeply interested in this movement. It was decided to ask for the names of women as well as those of men, and it was found that the former signed the petition more readily and in much larger numbers than the latter. Another fact was ascertained which rebuts the hackneyed assertion that women of the lower class will not be on the temperance side in this great war. For it was found—as might, indeed, have been most reasonably predicted—that the ignorant, the poor (many of them wives, mothers, and daughters of intemperate men), were among the most eager to sign the petition.

MANY A HAND WAS TAKEN FROM THE WASH-TUB
to hold the pencil and affix the signature of women of this class, and many another, which could only make the sign of the cross, did that with tears, and a hearty "God bless you." "That was a wonderful lesson to me," said the good Bishop, and he has always believed since then that God will give our enemy into our hands by giving to us an ally still more powerful, woman with the ballot against rum-shops in our land. It has been said so often that the very frequency of reiteration has in some minds induced belief that women of the better class will never consent to declare themselves at the polls. But tens of thousands from the most tenderly-sheltered homes have gone day after day to the saloons, and have spent hour after hour upon their sanded floors, and in their reeking air—places in which not the worst politician would dare to locate the ballot box of freemen—though they but stay a moment at the window, slip in their votes, and go their way.

Nothing worse can ever happen to women at the polls than has been endured by the hour on the part of conservative women of the churches in this land, as they, in scores of towns, have plead with rough, half-drunken men to vote the temperance tickets they have handed them, and which, with vastly more of propriety and fitness they might have dropped into the box themselves. They could have done this in a moment, and returned to their homes, instead of spending the whole day in the often futile endeavor to beg from men like these the votes which should preserve their homes from the whisky serpent's breath for one uncertain year. I spent last May in Ohio, traveling constantly, and seeking on every side to learn the views of the noble women of the Crusade. They put their opinions in words like these: "We believe that as God led us into this work by way of the saloons,

HE WILL LEAD US OUT BY WAY OF THE BALLOT.
We have never prayed more earnestly over the one than we will over the other. One was the Wilderness, the other is the Promised Land."

A Presbyterian lady, rigidly conservative, said: "For my part, I never wanted to vote until our gentlemen passed a prohibition ordinance so as to get us to stop visiting saloons, and a month later repealed it and chose a saloon-keeper for mayor."

Said a grand-daughter of Jonathan Edwards, a woman with no toleration toward the Suffrage Movement, a woman crowned with the glory of gray hairs—a central figure in her native town—

AND AS SHE SPOKE THE COURAGE AND FAITH OF THE PURITANS THRILLED HER VOICE—
"If, with the ballot in our hands, we can, as I firmly believe, put down this awful traffic, I am ready to lead the women of my town to the polls, as I have often led them to the rum shops."

We must not forget that for every woman who joins the Temperance Unions now springing up all through the land, there are at least a score who sympathize but do not join. Home influence and cares prevent them, ignorance of our aims and methods, lack of consecration to Christian work—a thousand reasons, sufficient in their estimation, though not in ours, hold them away from us. And yet they have this Temperance cause warmly at heart; the logic of events has shown them that there is but one side on which a woman may safely stand in this great battle, and on that side they would indubitably range themselves in the quick, decisive battle of election day, nor would they give their voice a second time in favor of the man who had once betrayed his pledge to enforce the most stringent law for the protection of their homes. There are many noble women, too, who, though they do not think as do the Temperance Unions about the deep things of religion, and are not as yet decided in their total abstinence sentiments, nor ready for the blessed work of prayer, are nevertheless decided in their views of Woman Suffrage, and ready to vote a Temperance ticket side by side with us. And there are the drunkard's wife and daughters, who from very shame will not come with us, or who dare not, yet who could freely vote with us upon this question; for the folded ballot tells no tales.

Among other cumulative proofs in this argument from experience, let us consider, briefly, the attitude of the Catholic Church toward the Temperance Reform. It is friendly, at least. Father Matthew's spirit lives to-day in many a faithful parish priest. In our procession on the Centennial Fourth of July, the banners of Catholic Total Abstinence Societies were often the only reminders that the Republic has any temperance people within its borders, as they were the only offset to brewers' wagons and distillers' casks, while among the monuments of our cause, by which this memorable year is signalized, their fountain in Fairmount Park—standing in the midst of eighty drinking places licensed by our Government—is chief. Catholic women would vote with Protestant women upon this issue for the protection of their homes.

Again, among the sixty thousand churches of America, with their eight million members, two-thirds are women. Thus, only one-third of this trustworthy and thoughtful class has any voice in the laws by which, between the church and the public school, the rum shop nestles in this Christian land. Surely all this must change before the Government shall be upon His shoulders "Who shall one day reign King of nations as He now reigns King of saints."

Furthermore, four-fifths of the teachers in this land are women, whose thoughtful judgment, expressed with the authority of which I speak, would greatly help forward the victory of our cause. And, finally, by those who fear the effect of the foreign element in our country, let it be remembered that we have sixty native for every one woman who is foreign born, for it is men who emigrate in largest number to our shores.

When all these facts (and many more that might be added) are marshaled into line, how illogical it seems for good men to harangue us as they do about our "duty to educate public sentiment to the level of better law," and their exhortations to American mothers to "train their sons to vote aright." As said Mrs. Governor Wallace, of Indiana—until the Crusade an opponent of the franchise—"What a bitter sarcasm you utter, gentlemen, to us who have the public sentiment of which you speak, all burning in our hearts, and yet are not permitted to turn it to account."

Let us, then, each one of us, offer our earnest prayer to God, and speak our honest word to man in favor of this added weapon in woman's hands, remembering that every petition in the ear of God, and every utterance in the ears of men, swells the dimensions of that resistless tide of influence which shall yet float within our reach all that we ask or need. Dear Christian women who have crusaded in the rum shops, I urge that you begin crusading in halls of legislation, in primary meetings, and the offices of excise commissioners. Roll in your petitions, burnish your arguments, multiply your prayers. Go to the voters in your town—procure the official list and see them one by one—and get them pledged to a local ordinance requiring the votes of men and women before a license can be issued to open rum-shop doors beside your homes; go to the Legislature with the same; remember this may be just as really Christian work as praying in saloons was in those other glorious days. Let us not limit God, whose modes of operation are so infinitely varied in nature and in grace. I believe in the correlation of spiritual forces, and that the heat which melted hearts to tenderness in the Crusade is soon to be the light which shall reveal our opportunity and duty as the Republic's daughters.

Questions

1. Why does Willard invoke the name of the abolitionist Frederick Douglass in her speech on temperance?
2. To what extent is her argument based on a kind of political feminism?
3. How do Catholics, usually viewed as unsympathetic to the temperance movement, fare with Willard as compared with their treatment by her contemporaries, Ulysses Grant and Thomas Nast (Documents 18-3 and 18-4)?

18-8   The Solitude of Self (1892)

Elizabeth Cady Stanton

Elizabeth Cady Stanton (1815–1902) became involved in the antislavery and women's rights causes as early as 1840. With Lucretia Mott, Stanton led in the calling of the Seneca Falls Women's Rights Convention in 1848; she drafted the Declaration of Sentiments adopted there. During Reconstruction, Stanton and Susan B. Anthony opposed subordinating women's suffrage to the cause of winning the vote for black men. She subsequently campaigned for a women's suffrage amendment to the Constitution and, still later, stressed the need for federal action in behalf of universal suffrage, which would protect the vote of blacks, increasingly threatened in southern states, and extend the vote to women (see text pp. 392, 393, 396, 397, 488). Stanton delivered her speech on "The Solitude of Self" at a meeting of the National American Woman Suffrage Association (NAWSA), at which she stepped down as the group's president.

Source: Susan B. Anthony, "The Solitude of Self," in *The Woman's Column* (January 1892), pp. 2–3, excerpted in Ellen Carol DuBois, ed., *The Elizabeth Cady Stanton–Susan B. Anthony Reader: Correspondence, Writings, Speeches,* rev. ed. (Boston: Northeastern University Press, 1992), 246–254.

The point I wish plainly to bring before you on this occasion is the individuality of each human soul; our Protestant idea, the right of individual conscience and judgement; our republican idea, individual citizenship. In discussing the rights of woman, we are to consider, first, what belongs to her as an individual, in a world of her own, the arbiter of her own destiny, an imaginary Robinson Crusoe, with her woman, Friday, on a solitary island. Her rights under such circumstances are to use all her faculties for her own safety and happiness.

Secondly, if we consider her as a citizen, as a member of a great nation, she must have the same rights as all other members, according to the fundamental principles of our Government.

Thirdly, viewed as a woman, an equal factor in civilization, her rights and duties are still the same—individual happiness and development.

Fourthly, it is only the incidental relations of life, such as mother, wife, sister, daughter, which may involve some special duties and training. . . .

The strongest reason for giving woman all the opportunities for higher education, for the full development of her faculties, her forces of mind and body; for giving her the most enlarged freedom of thought and action; a complete emancipation from all forms of bondage, of custom, dependence, superstition; from all the crippling influences of fear—is the solitude and personal responsibility of her own individual life. The strongest reason why we ask for woman a voice in the government under which she lives; in the religion she is asked to believe; equality in social life, where she is the chief factor; a place in the trades and professions, where she may earn her bread, is because of her birthright to self-sovereignty; because, as an individual, she must rely on herself. No matter how much women prefer to lean, to be protected and supported, nor how much men desire to have them do so, they must make the voyage of life alone, and for safety in an emergency, they must know something of the laws of navigation. To guide our own craft, we must be captain, pilot, engineer; with chart and compass to stand at the wheel; to watch the winds and waves, and know when to take in the sail, and to read the signs in the firmament over all. It matters not whether the solitary voyager is man or woman; nature, having endowed them equally, leaves them to their own skill and judgment in the hour of danger, and, if not equal to the occasion, alike they perish.

To appreciate the importance of fitting every human soul for independent action, think for a moment of the immeasurable solitude of self. We come into the world alone, unlike all who have gone before us, we leave it alone, under circumstances peculiar to ourselves. No mortal ever has been, no mortal ever will be like the soul just launched on the sea of life. There can never again be just such a combination of prenatal influences; never again just such environments as make up the infancy, youth and manhood of this one. Nature never repeats herself, and the possibilities

of one human soul will never be found in another. No one has ever found two blades of ribbon grass alike, and no one will ever find two human beings alike. Seeing, then, what must be the infinite diversity in human character, we can in a measure appreciate the loss to a nation when any large class of the people is uneducated and unrepresented in the government.

We ask for the complete development of every individual, first, for his own benefit and happiness. In fitting out an army, we give each soldier his own knapsack, arms, powder, his blanket, cup, knife, fork and spoon. We provide alike for all their individual necessities; then each man bears his own burden.

Again, we ask complete individual development for the general good; for the consensus of the competent on the whole round of human interests, on all questions of national life; and here each man must bear his share of the general burden. It is sad to see how soon friendless children are left to bear their own burdens, before they can analyze their feelings; before they can even tell their joys and sorrows, they are thrown on their own resources. The great lesson that nature seems to teach us at all ages is self-dependence, self-protection, self-support. . . .

We ask no sympathy from others in the anxiety and agony of a broken friendship or shattered love. When death sunders our nearest ties, alone we sit in the shadow of our affliction. Alike amid the greatest triumphs and darkest tragedies of life, we walk alone. On the divine heights of human attainment, eulogized and worshipped as a hero or saint, we stand alone. In ignorance, poverty and vice, as a pauper or criminal, alone we starve or steal; alone we suffer the sneers and rebuffs of our fellows; alone we are hunted and hounded through dark courts and alleys, in by-ways and high-ways; alone we stand in the judgment seat; alone in the prison cell we lament our crimes and misfortunes; alone we expiate them on the gallows. In hours like these we realize the awful solitude of individual life, its pains, its penalties, its responsibilities; hours in which the youngest and most helpless are thrown on their own resources for guidance and consolation. Seeing, then, that life must ever be a march and a battle, that each soldier must be equipped for his own protection, it is the height of cruelty to rob the individual of a single natural right.

To throw obstacles in the way of a complete education is like putting out the eyes; to deny the rights of property is like cutting off the hands. To refuse political equality is to rob the ostracized of all self-respect; of credit in the market place; of recompense in the world of work, of a voice in choosing those who make and administer the law, a choice in the jury before whom they are tried, and in the judge who decides their punishment. [Think of] . . . woman's position! Robbed of her natural rights, handicapped by law and custom at every turn, yet compelled to fight her own battles, and in the emergencies of life to fall back on herself for protection. . . .

. . . An uneducated woman trained to dependence, with no resources in herself, must make a failure of any position in life. But society says women do not need a knowledge of the world, the liberal training that experience in public life must give, all the advantages of collegiate education; but when for the lack of all this, the woman's happiness is wrecked, alone she bears her humiliation; and the solitude of the weak and the ignorant is indeed pitiable. In the wild chase for the prizes of life, they are ground to powder.

In age, when the pleasures of youth are passed, children grown up, married and gone, the hurry and bustle of life in a measure over, when the hands are weary of active service, when the old arm chair and the fireside are the chosen resorts, then men and women alike must fall back on their own resources. . . . If, from a life-long participation in public affairs, a woman feels responsible for the laws regulating our system of education, the discipline of our jails and prisons, the sanitary condition of our private homes, public buildings and thoroughfares, an interest in commerce, finance, our foreign relations, in any or all these questions, her solitude will at least be respectable, and she will not be driven to gossip or scandal for entertainment.

The chief reason for opening to every soul the doors to the whole round of human duties and pleasures is the individual development thus attained, the resources thus provided under all circumstances to mitigate the solitude that at times must come to everyone.

Inasmuch, then, as woman shares equally the joys and sorrows of time and eternity, is it not the height of presumption in man to propose to represent her at the ballot box and the throne of grace, to do her voting in the state, her praying in the church, and to assume the position of high priest at the family altar?

Nothing strengthens the judgment and quickens the conscience like individual responsibility. Nothing adds such dignity to character as the recognition of one's self-sovereignty; the right to an equal place, everywhere conceded—a place earned by personal merit, not an artificial attainment by inheritance, wealth, family and position. Conceding, then, that the responsibilities of life rest equally on man and woman, that their destiny is the same, they need the same preparation for time and eternity. The talk of sheltering woman from the fierce storms of life is the sheerest mockery, for they beat on her from every point of the compass, just as they do on man, and with more fatal results, for he has been trained to protect himself, to resist, and to conquer. Such are the facts in human experience, the responsibilities of individual sovereignty. Rich and poor, intelligent and ignorant, wise and foolish, virtuous and vicious, man and woman; it is ever the same, each soul must depend wholly on itself. . . .

Women are already the equals of men in the whole realm of thought, in art, science, literature and government. . . . The poetry and novels of the century are theirs, and they have touched the keynote of reform, in religion, politics and social life. They fill the editor's and professor's chair, plead at the bar of justice, walk the wards of the hospital, speak from the pulpit and the platform. Such is the type of womanhood that an enlightened public sentiment welcomes to-day, and such the triumph of the facts of life over the false theories of the past.

Is it, then, consistent to hold the developed woman of this day within the same narrow political limits as the dame with the spinning wheel and knitting needle occupied in the past? No, no! Machinery has taken the labors of woman as well as man on its tireless shoulders; the loom and the spinning wheel are but dreams of the past; the pen, the brush, the easel, the chisel, have taken their places, while the hopes and ambitions of women are essentially change. . . .

And yet, there is a solitude which each and every one of us has always carried with him, more inaccessible than the ice-cold mountains, more profound than the midnight sea; the solitude of self. Our inner being which we call ourself, no eye nor touch of man or angel has ever pierced. It is more hidden than the caves of the gnome; the sacred adytum of the oracle; the hidden chamber of Eleusinian mystery, for to it only omniscience is permitted to enter.

Such is individual life. Who, I ask you, can take, dare take on himself the rights, the duties, the responsibilities of another human soul?

Questions

1. What is the significance of the title of Stanton's address?
2. What are her arguments in favor of women's rights, including the vote?

18-9   Discontented Women (1896)

Amelia Barr

The cause of woman suffrage did not enjoy universal support among women. Indeed, organized opposition groups were usually led by women. (By way of contrast, movements to expand the suffrage to include those without property, African Americans, and eighteen-year-olds met with no such organized opposition within the affected groups.) Amelia Barr (1831–1919), born in England, immigrated with her husband to the United States in 1853. Widowed, the mother of three children (her ten other children had died), she turned to writing in 1869. Over a lengthy career, she produced numerous articles, short stories, poems, and novels.

Source: Amelia Barr, "Discontented Women," *North American Review,* 162 (February 1896): 201, 205–207, 209, excerpted in Ellen Skinner, ed., *Women and the National Experience: Primary Sources in American History* (Reading, Mass.: Addison-Wesley Educational, 1996), 105–106.

Discontent is a vice six thousand years old, and it will be eternal; because it is in the race. Every human being has a complaining side, but discontent is bound up in the heart of woman; it is her original sin. For if the first woman had been satisfied with her conditions, if she had not aspired to be "as gods," and hankered after unlawful knowledge, Satan would hardly have thought it worth his while to discuss her rights and wrongs with her. That unhappy controversy has never ceased; and, without reason, woman has been perpetually subject to discontent with her conditions and, according to her nature, has been moved by its influence. Some, it has made peevish, some plaintive, some ambitious, some reckless, while a noble majority have found in its very control that serene composure and cheerfulness which is granted to those who conquer, rather than to those who inherit.

Finally, women cannot get behind or beyond their nature, and their nature is to substitute sentiment for reason—a sweet and not unlovely characteristic in womanly ways and places; yet reason, on the whole, is considered a desirable necessity in politics. . . . Women may cease to be women, but they can never learn to be men and feminine softness and grace can never do the work of the virile virtues of men. Very fortunately this class of discontented women have not yet been able to endanger existing conditions by combinations analogous to trades unions; nor is it likely they ever will; because it is doubtful if women, under any circumstances, could combine at all. Certain qualities are necessary for combination, and these qualities are represented in women by their opposites. . . .

The one unanswerable excuse for woman's entrance into active public life of any kind, is *need* and alas! need is growing daily, as marriage becomes continually rare, and more women are left adrift in the world without helpers and protectors. But this is a subject too large to enter on here, though in the beginning it sprung from discontented women, preferring the work and duties of men to their own work and duties. Have they found the battle of life any more ennobling in masculine professions, than in their old feminine household ways? Is work done in the world for strangers, any less tiresome and monotonous, than work done in the house for father and mother, husband and children? If they answer truly, they will reply "the home duties were the easiest, the safest and the happiest."

Of course all discontented women will be indignant at any criticism of their conduct. They expect every one to consider their feelings without examining their motives. Paddling in the turbid maelstrom of life, and dabbling in politics and the most unsavory social questions, they still think men, at least, ought to regard them as the Sacred Sex. But women are not sacred by grace of sex, if they voluntarily abdicate its limitations and its modesties, and make a public display of unsexed sensibilities, an unabashed familiarity with subjects they have nothing to do with. If men criticize such women with asperity it is not to be wondered at; they have so long idealized women, that they find it hard to speak moderately. They excuse them too much, or else they are too indignant at their follies, and unjust and angry in their denunciation. Women must be criticized by women; then they will hear the bare uncompromising truth, and be the better for it.

Questions

1. What is the significance of the title of Barr's article?
2. What arguments does she advance in opposition to women's rights, including the vote?

Questions for Further Thought

1. Compare and contrast the views of Frances Willard and William Graham Sumner relative to society's proper response to the damages of alcohol.
2. Compare and contrast Willard, Elizabeth Cady Stanton, Helen Potter (see "American Voices," text p. 586), and Amelia Barr regarding women's suffrage.
3. How might Willard have reacted to the Prohibition planks of the Republican and Democratic Iowa and national platforms (Documents 18-5 and 18-6)?

The Crisis of American Politics: The 1890s

From time to time, American politics enters periods of crisis, during which "politics as usual" gives way to intense controversy over issues of national significance. Thus deepening sectional conflict during the 1850s gave birth to the Republican Party, which went on to win the presidency in 1860, with momentous consequences. Similarly, during the 1890s, issues arising out of economic hard times further defined politics, again to the advantage of the GOP.

Storm signals were already apparent when Grover Cleveland, a Democrat, became president in March 1893. The previous year had witnessed a classic labor-management clash at Homestead, Pennsylvania, while agrarian discontent in the South and West had led to the creation of the national People's (Populist) Party. Then, in 1893, business failures led to a panic, following which the nation slid into a serious economic depression, adding urban unrest to rural protest (see text pp. 569, 585–591).

Against this backdrop, President Cleveland sought to stem the decline of Treasury gold reserves by ending monthly government purchases of silver under the Sherman Silver-Purchase Act. He succeeded in doing so in 1893, but he alienated western and southern inflationists in the process. Next, Congress enacted the Wilson-Gorman Tariff Act of 1894, which superseded the McKinley Tariff, disappointing ardent tariff reformers (including the president) but enabling the Republicans to excoriate the Democrats for failing to appreciate the need for tariff protection, especially during hard times. The Republicans went on to score widespread victories in the midterm elections that year. During 1895 and 1896, southern and western Democrats came to dominate their party, which at its 1896 national convention declared itself for free silver, refused to endorse the administration of President Cleveland, and nominated William Jennings Bryan for president. Many Gold Democrats deserted the party. Despite their own Silverite defections, the Republicans, defending gold as the nation's monetary standard, defeated the Free-Silver Democrats and their Populist allies in the climactic presidential election of 1896 (see text pp. 589–593).

Document 18-10 is the 1892 national platform of the People's Party; William Jennings Bryan's "Cross of Gold" speech, which electrified the Democratic National Convention of 1896, appears in Document 18-11.

18-10   People's (Populist) Party National Platform (1892)

Responding to the worsening economic situation and building on earlier organizational and political experience (the Patrons of Husbandry or Grange, the farmers' alliances), agrarians and other protesters, already active on the state level, formed a national party, framed a national platform, and ran a national ticket in 1892 (see text pp. 535–537, 585–594, and Map 18–1, text p. 587).

As the text notes (pp. 587–588), women played roles in the farmers' alliances and in the Populist Party that were closed to them in the two major parties. Mary Elizabeth Lease was one such woman, Luna Kellie another. Kellie served as secretary of the Nebraska Alliance and edited and wrote for an Alliance newspaper there. Kellie's "Personal Memoir" (Document 16-7) contains political observations within its personal reminiscences.

Source: Donald Bruce Johnson, comp., *National Party Platforms*, rev. ed., 2 vols. (Urbana: University of Illinois Press, 1978), vol. 1, *1840–1956*, 89–91.

Assembled upon the 116th anniversary of the Declaration of Independence, the People's Party of America in their first national convention, invoking upon their action the blessing of Almighty God, put forth in the name and on behalf of the people of this country, the following preamble and declaration of principles:

PREAMBLE

The conditions which surround us best justify our co-operation; we meet in the midst of a nation brought to the verge of moral, political, and material ruin. Corruption dominates the ballot-box, the Legislatures, the Congress, and touches even the ermine of the bench. The people are demoralized; most of the States have been compelled to isolate the voters at the polling places to prevent universal intimidation and bribery. The newspapers are largely subsidized or muzzled, public opinion silenced, business prostrated, homes covered with mortgages, labor impoverished, and the land concentrating in the hands of capitalists. The urban workmen are denied the right to organize for self-protection; imported pauperized labor beats down their wages, a hireling standing army, unrecognized by our laws, is established to shoot them down, and they are rapidly degenerating into European conditions. The fruits of the toil of millions are boldly stolen to build up colossal fortunes for a few, unprecedented in the history of mankind; and the possessors of these, in turn despise the Republic and endanger liberty. From the same prolific womb of governmental injustice we breed the two great classes—tramps and millionaires.

The national power to create money is appropriated to enrich bond-holders; a vast public debt payable in legal tender currency has been funded into gold-bearing bonds, thereby adding millions to the burdens of the people.

Silver, which has been accepted as coin since the dawn of history, has been demonetized to add to the purchasing power of gold by decreasing the value of all forms of property as well as human labor, and the supply of currency is purposely abridged to fatten usurers, bankrupt enterprise, and enslave industry. A vast conspiracy against mankind has been organized on two continents, and it is rapidly taking possession of the world. If not met and overthrown at once, it forebodes terrible social convulsions, the destruction of civilization, or the establishment of an absolute despotism.

We have witnessed for more than a quarter of a century the struggles of the two great political parties for power and plunder, while grievous wrongs have been inflicted upon the suffering people. We charge that the controlling influence dominating both these parties have permitted the existing dreadful conditions to develop without serious effort to prevent or restrain them. Neither do they now promise us any substantial reform. They have agreed together to ignore, in the coming campaign, every issue but one. They propose to drown the outcries of a plundered people with the uproar of a sham battle over the tariff, so that capitalists, corporations, national banks, rings, trusts, watered stock, the demonetization of silver and the oppressions of the usurers may all be lost sight of. They propose to sacrifice our homes, lives, and children on the altar of mammon; to destroy the multitude in order to secure corruption funds from the millionaires.

Assembled on the anniversary of the birthday of the nation, and filled with the spirit of the grand general and chief who established our independence, we seek to restore the government of the Republic to the hands of "the plain people," with which class it originated. We assert our purposes to be identical with the purposes of the National

Constitution, to form a more perfect union and establish justice, insure domestic tranquillity, provide for the common defense, promote the general welfare, and secure the blessings of liberty for ourselves and our posterity.

We declare that this Republic can only endure as a free government while built upon the love of the whole people for each other and for the nation; that it cannot be pinned together by bayonets; that the civil war is over and that every passion and resentment which grew out of it must die with it, and that we must be in fact, as we are in name, one united brotherhood of freemen.

Our country finds itself confronted by conditions for which there is no precedent in the history of the world; our annual agricultural productions amount to billions of dollars in value, which must, within a few weeks or months be exchanged for billions of dollars' worth of commodities consumed in their production; the existing currency supply is wholly inadequate to make this exchange; the results are falling prices, the formation of combines and rings, the impoverishment of the producing class. We pledge ourselves that, if given power, we will labor to correct these evils by wise and reasonable legislation, in accordance with the terms of our platform.

We believe that the power of government—in other words, of the people—should be expanded (as in the case of the postal service) as rapidly and as far as the good sense of an intelligent people and the teachings of experience shall justify, to the end that oppression, injustice and poverty, shall eventually cease in the land.

While our sympathies as a party of reform are naturally upon the side of every proposition which will tend to make men intelligent, virtuous and temperate, we nevertheless regard these questions, important as they are, as secondary to the great issues now pressing for solution, and upon which not only our individual prosperity, but the very existence of free institutions depend; and we ask all men to first help us to determine whether we are to have a republic to administer, before we differ as to the conditions upon which it is to be administered, believing that the forces of reform this day organized will never cease to move forward, until every wrong is remedied, and equal rights and equal privileges securely established for all the men and women of this country.

PLATFORM

We declare, therefore,

First—That the union of the labor forces of the United States this day consummated shall be permanent and perpetual; may its spirit enter into all hearts for the salvation of the Republic and the uplifting of mankind.

Second—Wealth belongs to him who creates it, and every dollar taken from industry without an equivalent is robbery. "If any will not work, neither shall he eat." The interests of rural and civic labor are the same; their enemies are identical.

Third—We believe that the time has come when the railroad corporations will either own the people or the people must own the railroads, and should the government enter upon the work of owning and managing all railroads, we should favor an amendment to the Constitution by which all persons engaged in the government service shall be placed under a civil service regulation of the most rigid character, so as to prevent the increase of the power of the national administration by the use of such additional government employees.

Finance—We demand a national currency, safe, sound, and flexible, issued by the general government only, a full legal tender for all debts, public and private, and that without the use of banking corporations, a just, equitable and efficient means of distribution direct to the people, at a tax not to exceed 2 per cent per annum, to be provided as set forth by the sub-treasury plan of the Farmers' Alliance, or a better system; also by payments in discharge of its obligations for public improvements.

1. We demand free and unlimited coinage of silver and gold at the present legal ratio of 16 to 1.

2. We demand that the amount of circulating medium be speedily increased to not less than $50 per capita.

3. We demand a graduated income tax.

4. We believe that the money of the country should be kept as much as possible in the hands of the people, and hence we demand that all State and national revenues shall be limited to the necessary expenses of the government, economically and honestly administered.

5. We demand that postal savings banks be established by the government for the safe deposit of the earnings of the people and to facilitate exchange.

Transportation—Transportation being a means of exchange and a public necessity, the government should own and operate the railroads in the interest of the people. The telegraph and telephone, like the post office system, being a necessity for the transmission of news, should be owned and operated by the government in the interest of the people.

Land—The land, including all the natural sources of wealth, is the heritage of the people, and should not be monopolized for speculative purposes, and alien ownership of land should be prohibited. All land now held by railroads and other corporations in excess of their actual needs, and all lands now owned by aliens, should be reclaimed by the government and held for actual settlers only.

Questions

1. What are the main points of the preamble to the Populists' platform?
2. What are the key planks of the platform? Which depart most from major party positions at the time (1892)?
3. Referring to the text, appropriate "American Voices," and the documents in Chapters 16–18, explain the place of the Populists in late-nineteenth-century protest and reform politics.

18-11   Cross of Gold Speech (1896)

William Jennings Bryan

A former two-term congressman and unsuccessful senatorial aspirant from Nebraska, the youthful William Jennings Bryan (1860–1925) made his debut as a prime player on the national political stage at the contentious Democratic national convention of 1896. He delivered his "Cross of Gold" speech during the debate over the platform, then went on to win the party's presidential nomination on the fifth roll-call ballot. Bryan also became the nominee of the People's and National Silver parties. He went down to defeat in the presidential election that November. He later lost presidential elections in 1900 and 1908.

The Mr. Carlisle to whom Bryan refers in the speech is John G. Carlisle, a representative from Kentucky in 1878 who had taken an inflationist position.

Source: William Jennings Bryan, *The First Battle: A Story of the Campaign of 1896* (Chicago: W. B. Conkey, 1896), 199–206.

Mr. Chairman and Gentlemen of the Convention: I would be presumptuous, indeed, to present myself against the distinguished gentlemen to whom you have listened if this were a mere measuring of abilities; but this is not a contest between persons. The humblest citizen in all the land, when clad in the armor of a righteous cause, is stronger than all the hosts of error. I come to speak to you in defense of a cause as holy as the cause of liberty—the cause of humanity.

When this debate is concluded, a motion will be made to lay upon the table the resolution offered in commendation of the administration. We object to bringing this question down to the level of persons. The individual is but an atom; he is born, he acts, he dies; but principles are eternal; and this has been a contest over a principle.

Never before in the history of this country has there been witnessed such a contest as that through which we have just passed. Never before in the history of American politics has a great issue been fought out as this issue has been, by the voters of a great party. On the fourth of March, 1895, a few Democrats, most of them members of Congress, issued an address to the Democrats of the nation, asserting that the money question was the paramount issue of the hour; declaring that a majority of the Democratic party had the right to control the action of the party on this paramount issue; and concluding with the request that the believers in the free coinage of silver in the Democratic party should organize, take charge of, and control the policy of the Democratic party. Three months later, at Memphis, an organization was perfected, and the silver Democrats went forth openly and courageously proclaiming their belief, and declaring that, if successful, they would crystallize into a platform the declaration which they had made. Then began the conflict. With a zeal approaching the zeal which inspired the crusaders . . . our silver Democrats went forth from victory unto victory until they are now assembled, not to discuss, not to debate, but to enter up the judgment already rendered by the plain people of this country. In this contest brother has been arrayed against brother, father against son. The warmest ties of love, acquaintance and association have been disregarded; old leaders have been cast aside when they have refused to give expression to the sentiments of those whom they would lead, and new leaders have sprung up to give direction to this cause of truth. Thus has the contest been waged, and we have assembled here under as binding and solemn instructions as were ever imposed upon representatives of the people. . . .

When you (turning to the gold delegates) come before us and tell us that we are about to disturb your business interests, we reply that you have disturbed our business interests by your course.

We say to you that you have made the definition of a business man too limited in its application. The man who is employed for wages is as much a business man as his employer; the attorney in a country town is as much a business man as the corporation counsel in a great metropolis; the merchant at the cross-roads store is as much a business man as the merchant of New York; the farmer who goes forth in the morning and toils all day—who begins in the spring and toils all summer—and who by the application of brain and muscle to the natural resources of the country creates wealth, is as much a business man as the man who goes upon the board of trade and bets upon the price of grain; the miners who go down a thousand feet into the earth, or climb two thousand feet upon the cliffs, and bring forth from their hiding places the precious metals to be poured into the channels of trade are as much business men as the few financial magnates who, in a back room, corner the money of the world. We come to speak for this broader class of business men.

Ah, my friends, we say not one word against those who live upon the Atlantic coast, but the hardy pioneers who have braved all the dangers of the wilderness, who have made the desert to blossom as the rose—the pioneers out there (pointing to the West), who rear their children near to Nature's heart, where they can mingle their voices with the voices of the birds—out there where they have erected schoolhouses for the education of their young, churches where they praise their Creator, and cemeteries where rest the ashes of their dead—these people, we say, are as deserving of the consideration of our party as any people in this country. It is for these that we speak. We do not come as aggressors. Our war is not a war of conquest; we are fighting in the defense of our homes, our families, and posterity. We have petitioned, and our petitions have been scorned; we have entreated, and our entreaties have been disregarded; we have begged, and they have mocked when our calamity came. We beg no longer; we entreat no more; we petition no more. We defy them.

The gentleman from Wisconsin has said that he fears a Robespierre. My friends, in this land of the free you need not fear that a tyrant will spring up from among the people. What we need is an Andrew Jackson to stand, as Jackson stood, against the encroachments of organized wealth.

They tell us that this platform was made to catch votes. We reply to them that changing conditions make new issues; that the principles upon which Democracy rests are as everlasting as the hills, but that they must be applied to new conditions as they arise. Conditions have arisen, and we are here to meet those conditions. They tell us that the income tax ought not to be brought in here; that it is a new idea. They criticise us for our criticism of the Supreme Court of the United States. My friends, we have not criticised; we have simply called attention to what you already know. If you want criticisms, read the dissenting opinions of the court. There you will find criticisms. They say that we passed an unconstitutional law; we deny it. The income tax law was not unconstitutional when it was passed; it was not unconstitutional when it went before the Supreme Court for the first time; it did not become unconstitutional until one of the judges changed his mind, and we cannot be expected to know when a judge will change his mind. The income tax is just. It simply intends to put the burdens of government justly upon the backs of the people. I am in favor of an income tax. When I find a man who is not willing to bear his share of the burdens of the government which protects him, I find a man who is unworthy to enjoy the blessings of a government like ours.

They say that we are opposing national bank currency; it is true. . . . We say in our platform that we believe that the right to coin and issue money is a function of government. We believe it. We believe that it is a part of sovereignty, and can no more with safety be delegated to private individuals than we could afford to delegate to private individuals the power to make penal statutes or levy taxes. Mr. [Thomas] Jefferson, who was once regarded as good Democratic authority, seems to have differed in opinion from the gentleman who has addressed us on the part of the minority. Those who are opposed to this proposition tell us that the issue of paper money is a function of the bank, and that the Government ought to go out of the banking business. I stand with Jefferson rather than with them, and tell them, as he did, that the issue of money is a function of government, and that the banks ought to go out of the governing business.

They complain about the plank which declares against life tenure in office. They have tried to strain it to mean that which it does not mean. What we oppose by that plank is the life tenure which is being built up in Washington, and which excludes from participation in official benefits the humbler members of society.

Let me call your attention to two or three important things. The gentleman from New York says that he will propose an amendment to the platform providing that the proposed change in our monetary system shall not affect contracts already made. Let me remind you that there is no intention of affecting those contracts which according to present laws are made payable in gold; but if he means to say that we cannot change our monetary system without protecting those who have loaned money before the change was made, I desire to ask him where, in law or in morals, he can find justification for not protecting the debtors when the act of 1873 [dropping silver as a medium of exchange] was passed, if he now insists that we must protect the creditors.

He says he will also propose an amendment which will provide for the suspension of free coinage if we fail to maintain the parity within a year. We reply that when we advocate a policy which we believe will be successful, we are not compelled to raise a doubt as to our own sincerity by suggesting what we shall do if we fail. I ask him, if he would apply his logic to us, why he does not apply it to himself. He says he wants this country to try to secure an international agreement. Why does he not tell us what he is going to do if he fails to secure an international agreement? There is more reason for him to do that than there is for us to provide against the failure to maintain the parity. Our opponents have tried for twenty years to secure an international agreement, and those are waiting for it most patiently who do not want it at all.

And now, my friends, let me come to the paramount issue. If they ask us why it is that we say more on the money question than we say upon the tariff question, I reply that, if protection has slain its thousands, the gold standard has slain its tens of thousands. If they ask us why we do not employ in our platform all the things that we believe in, we reply that when we have restored the money of the Constitution all other necessary reforms will be possible; but that until this is done there is no other reform that can be accomplished.

Why is it that within three months such a change has come over the country? Three months ago, when it was confidently asserted that those who believe in the gold standard would frame our platform and nominate our candidates, even the advocates of the gold standard did not think that we could elect a president. And they had good reason for their doubt, because there is scarcely a State here today asking for the gold standard which is not in the absolute control of the Republican party. But note the change. Mr. McKinley was nominated at St. Louis upon a platform which declared for the maintenance of the gold standard until it can be changed into bimetallism by international agreement. Mr. McKinley was the most popular man among the Republicans, and three months ago everybody in the Republican party prophesied his election. How is today? Why, the man who was once pleased to think that he looked like Napoleon—that man shudders today when he remembers that he was nominated on the anniversary of the battle of Waterloo. Not only that, but as he listens he can hear with ever-increasing distinctness the sound of the waves as they beat upon the lonely shores of St. Helena.

Why this change? Ah, my friends, is not the reason for the change evident to any one who will look at the matter? No private character, however pure, no personal popularity, however great, can protect from the avenging wrath of an indignant people a man who will declare that he is in favor of fastening the gold standard upon this country, or who is willing to surrender the right of self-government and place the legislative control of our affairs in the hands of foreign potentates and powers.

We go forth confident that we shall win. Why? Because upon the paramount issue of this campaign there is not a spot of ground upon which the enemy will dare to challenge battle. If they tell us that the gold standard is a good thing, we shall point to their platform and tell them that their platform pledges the party to get rid of the gold standard and substitute bimetallism. If the gold standard is a good thing, why try to get rid of it? I call your attention to the fact that some of the very people who are in this convention today and who tell us that we ought to declare in favor of international bimetallism—thereby declaring that the gold standard is wrong and the principle of bimetallism is better—these very people four months ago were open and avowed advocates of the gold standard, and were then telling us that we could not legislate two metals together, even with the aid of all the world. If the gold standard is a good thing, we ought to declare in favor of its retention and not in favor of abandoning it; and if the gold standard is a bad thing why should we wait until other nations are willing to help us to let go? Here is the line of battle, and we care not upon which issue they force the fight; we are prepared to meet them on either issue or on both. If they tell us that the gold standard is the standard of civilization, we reply to them that this, the most enlightened of all the nations of the earth, has never declared for a gold standard and that both the great parties this year are declaring against it. If the gold standard is the standard of civilization, why, my friends, should we not have it? If they come to meet us on that issue we can present the history of our nation. More than that; we can tell them that they will search the pages of history in vain to find a single instance where the common people of any land have ever declared themselves in favor of the gold standard. They can find where the holders of fixed investments have declared for a gold standard, but not where the masses have.

Mr. Carlisle said in 1878 that this was a struggle between "the idle holders of idle capital" and "the struggling masses, who produce the wealth and pay the taxes of the country;" and, my friends, the question we are to decide is: Upon which side will the Democratic party fight; upon the side of "the idle holders of idle capital" or upon the side of "the struggling masses?" That is the question which the party must answer first, and then it must be answered by each individual hereafter. The sympathies of the Democratic party, as shown by the platform, are on the side of the struggling masses who have ever been the foundation of the Democratic party. There are two ideas of government. There are those who believe that, if you will only legislate to make the well-to-do prosperous, their prosperity will leak through on those below. The Democratic idea, however, has been that if you legislate to make the masses prosperous, their prosperity will find its way up through every class which rests upon them.

You come to us and tell us that the great cities are in favor of the gold standard; we reply that the great cities rest upon our broad and fertile prairies. Burn down your cities and leave our farms, and your cities will spring up again as if by magic; but destroy our farms and the grass will grow in the streets of every city in the country.

My friends, we declare that this nation is able to legislate for its own people on every question, without waiting for the aid or consent of any other nation on earth; and upon that issue we expect to carry every State in the Union. . . . It is the issue of 1776 over again. Our ancestors, when but three millions in number, had the courage to declare their political independence of every other nation; shall we, their descendants, when we have grown to seventy millions, declare that we are less independent than our forefathers? No, my friends, that will never be the verdict of our people. Therefore, we care not upon what lines the battle is fought. If they say bimetallism is good, but that we cannot have it until other nations help us, we reply that, instead of having a gold standard because England has, we will restore bimetallism, and then let England have bimetallism because the United States has it. If they dare to come out in the open field and defend the gold standard as a good thing, we will fight them to the uttermost. Having behind us the producing masses of this nation and the world, supported by the commercial interests, the laboring interests, and the toilers everywhere, we will answer their demand for a gold standard by saying to them: You shall not press down upon the brow of labor this crown of thorns, you shall not crucify mankind upon a cross of gold.

Questions

1. What reforms did Bryan propose in this speech?
2. Cite some of the more powerful examples of Bryan's use of imagery.
3. How might that imagery have alienated the urban residents whose votes Bryan needed to be elected president?

Questions for Further Thought

1. Compare and contrast politics between 1889 and 1892 with politics between 1893 and 1896. The politics of which period more closely resembled the politics of the dozen or so years before 1889?
2. Relate the "Cross of Gold" speech to the People's Party platform of 1892 and to earlier farmer and labor protests (see text and documents, Chapters 16–18).

Race and Politics in the South

For a number of years after the end of Reconstruction in 1877, southern race relations and politics retained some measure of fluidity. Blacks were still subordinated and segregation was widespread, but not until the late 1880s and especially the 1890s did de jure segregation, segregation in law, become the rule. Meanwhile, through the 1880s, the Republicans managed to remain competitive in a few former Confederate states and a number of congressional districts. It was this surviving competitiveness, and the closeness of the national political balance, that prompted congressional Republicans to seek a federal elections law in 1890 to protect southern supporters and the GOP from Democratic fraud. African Americans, though badly weakened by the collapse of Republican state governments as Reconstruction waned, still won a few victories within largely black districts. Independents (such as Virginia's Readjusters) challenged the Democrats during the 1880s, likewise the Populists during the 1890s, both sometimes with success, especially where they gained biracial support and cooperated with the Republicans (see text pp. 594–597).

At best, though, the Democrats' opponents were only temporarily successful. Within Congress, the Democrats sidetracked the federal elections bill. Within the southern states, they employed whatever means necessary to defeat their foes. To maintain dominance without fraud, intimidation, and violence, which might have revived support for a federal elections law, the Democrats drafted state constitutions and laws to restrict the suffrage, especially of African Americans and poor, ill-educated whites, thereby breaking the backs of the Republicans and the Populists (see text pp. 594–599).

Document 18-12 presents the suffrage provisions of the Mississippi State Constitution of 1890. Violence, lynchings, and riots played a role in the imposition of the drastic racial order. Lynchings of African Americans numbered one hundred or more per year in all but two years (1891 and 1901), reaching a peak in 1892. Document 18-13 reports a triple lynching in Tennessee. For the reactions to these developments by two African American leaders, Booker T. Washington and W. E. B. Du Bois, see Documents 18-14 and 18-15. (Also consider "American Lives: Robert Charles," text pp. 599–604.)

As the text makes clear, the U.S. Supreme Court played an important part in the emergence of the new southern political and social order. For majority and minority opinions in *Plessy v. Ferguson* (1896), see *Instructor's Resource Manual*, vol. 2: *Since 1865*, 4th ed., Document 6a, pp. 441–443.

18-12   The 1890 Mississippi Constitution

Long before George Orwell conceived of doublespeak, there was the 1890 Mississippi Constitution. It had the veneer of a liberal document, complete with a lengthy bill of rights, but the text also included a section that detailed how voting rights could be denied (see text pp. 594–599). Such disfranchisement schemes persisted in the South into the 1960s.

Source: Francis N. Thorpe, ed., *The Federal and State Constitutions . . . of the United States* (Washington, D.C.: U.S. Government Printing Office, 1909), 4: 2120–2121.

We, the people of Mississippi, in Convention assembled, grateful to Almighty God, and invoking His blessing on our work, do ordain and establish this Constitution. . . .

ARTICLE 12

Franchise

SEC. 240. All elections by the people shall be by ballot.

SEC. 241. Every male inhabitant of this State, except idiots, insane persons and Indians not taxed, who is a citizen of the United States, twenty-one years old and upwards, who has resided in this State two years, and one year in the election district, or in the incorporated city or town, in which he offers to vote, and who is duly registered as provided in this article, and who has never been convicted of bribery, burglary, theft, arson, obtaining money or goods under false pretenses, perjury, forgery, im-

bezzlement or bigamy, and who has paid, on or before the first day of February of the year in which he shall offer to vote, all taxes which may have been legally required of him, and which he has had an opportunity of paying according to law, for the two preceding years, and who shall produce to the officers holding the election satisfactory evidence that he has paid said taxes, is declared to be a qualified elector; but any minister of the gospel in charge of an organized church shall be entitled to vote after six months residence in the election district, if otherwise qualified.

SEC. 242. The legislature shall provide by law for the registration of all persons entitled to vote at any election, and all persons offering to register shall take the following oath or affirmation: "I —————— ——————, do solemnly swear (or affirm) that I am twenty-one years old, (or I will be before the next election in this county) and that I will have resided in this State two years, and ——————election district of —————— county one year next preceding the ensuing election [or if it be stated in the oath that the person proposing to register is a minister of the gospel in charge of an organized church, then it will be sufficient to aver therein, two years residence in the State and six months in said election district], and am now in good faith a resident of the same, and that I am not disqualified from voting by reason of having been convicted of any crime named in the constitution of this State as a disqualification to be an elector; that I will truly answer all questions propounded to me concerning my antecedents so far as they relate to my right to vote, and also as to my residence before my citizenship in this district; that I will faithfully support the constitution of the United States and of the State of Mississippi, and will bear true faith and allegiance to the same. So help me God." In registering voters in cities and towns, not wholly in one election district, the name of such city or town may be substituted in the oath for the election district. Any willful and corrupt false statement in said affidavit, or in answer to any material question propounded as herein authorized, shall be perjury.

SEC. 243. A uniform poll tax of two dollars, to be used in aid of the common schools, and for no other purpose, is hereby imposed on every male inhabitant of this State between the ages of twenty-one and sixty years, except persons who are deaf and dumb or blind, or who are maimed by loss of hand or foot; said tax to be a lien only upon taxable property. The board of supervisors of any county may, for the purpose of aiding the common schools in that county, increase the poll tax in said county, but in no case shall the entire poll tax exceed in any one year three dollars on each poll. No criminal proceedings shall be allowed to enforce the collection of the poll tax.

SEC. 244. On and after the first day of January, A. D., 1892, every elector shall, in addition to the foregoing qualifications, be able to read any section of the constitution of this State; or he shall be able to understand the same when read to him, or give a reasonable interpretation thereof. A new registration shall be made before the next ensuing election after January the first, A. D., 1892.

Questions

1. What methods of disfranchisement does this constitution allow?
2. What purpose was served by Sec. 244 of Article 12?

18-13 Lynching at the Curve (1892)

Ida B. Wells

Violence was not an abstract concept for an African American like Ida B. Wells, who was born a slave in 1862. She worked as a teacher before becoming the part owner of a Memphis newspaper in 1889 (see text pp. 599–602). The lynching Wells describes here persuaded her to leave Memphis. Wells eventually settled in Chicago, where she took part in suffrage and other reform activities until her death in 1931.

Source: Ida B. Wells, *Crusade for Justice: The Autobiography of Ida B. Wells,* ed. Alfreda M. Duster, 47–51. Copyright 1970 by the University of Chicago Press. Reprinted by permission.

While I was thus carrying on the work of my newspaper, happy in the thought that our influence was helpful and that I was doing the work I loved and had proved that I could make a living out of it, there came the lynching in Memphis which changed the whole course of my life. I was on one of my trips away from home. I was busily engaged in Natchez when word came of the lynching of three men in Memphis. It came just as I had demonstrated that I could make a living by my newspaper and need never tie myself down to school teaching.

Thomas Moss, Calvin McDowell, and Henry Stewart owned and operated a grocery story in a thickly populated suburb. Moss was a letter carrier and could only be at the store at night. Everybody in town knew and loved Tommie. An exemplary young man, he was married and the father of one little girl, Maurine, whose godmother I was. He and his wife Betty were the best friends I had in town. And he believed, with me, that we should defend the cause of right and fight wrong wherever we saw it.

He delivered mail at the office of the *Free Speech,* and whatever Tommie knew in the way of news we got first. He owned his little home, and having saved his money he went into the grocery business with the same ambition that a young white man would have had. He was the president of the company. His partners ran the business in the day-time.

They had located their grocery in the district known as the "Curve" because the streetcar line curved sharply at that point. There was already a grocery owned and operated by a white man who hitherto had had a monopoly on the trade of this thickly populated colored suburb. Thomas's grocery changed all that, and he and his associates were made to feel that they were not welcome by the white grocer. The district being mostly colored and many of the residents belonging either to Thomas's church or to his lodge, he was not worried by the white grocer's hostility.

One day some colored and white boys quarreled over a game of marbles and the colored boys got the better of the fight which followed. The father of the white boys whipped the victorious colored boy, whose father and friends pitched in to avenge the grown white man's flogging of a colored boy. The colored men won the fight, whereupon the white father and grocery keeper swore out a warrant for the arrest of the colored victors. Of course the colored grocery keepers had been drawn into the dispute. But the case was dismissed with nominal fines. Then the challenge was issued that the vanquished whites were coming on Saturday night to clean out the People's Grocery Company.

Knowing this, the owners of the company consulted a lawyer and were told that as they were outside the city limits and beyond police protection, they would be justified in protecting themselves if attacked. Accordingly the grocery company armed several men and stationed them in the rear of the store on that fatal Saturday night, not to attack but to repel a threatened attack. And Saturday night was the time when men of both races congregated in their respective groceries.

About ten o'clock that night, when Thomas was posting his books for the week and Calvin McDowell and his clerk were waiting on customers preparatory to closing, shots rang out in the back room of the store. The men stationed there had seen several white men stealing through the rear door and fired on them without a moment's pause. Three of these men were wounded, and others fled and gave the alarm.

Sunday morning's paper came out with lurid headlines telling how officers of the law had been wounded while in the discharge of their duties, hunting up criminals whom they had been told were harbored in the People's Grocery Company, this being "a low dive in which drinking and gambling were carried on: a resort of thieves and thugs." So ran the description in the leading white journals of Memphis of this successful effort of decent black men to carry on a legitimate business. The same newspaper told of the arrest and jailing of the proprietor of the store and many of the colored people. They predicted that it would go hard with the ringleaders if these "officers" should die. The tale of how the peaceful homes of that suburb were raided on that quiet Sunday morning by police pretending to be looking for others who were implicated in what the papers had called a conspiracy, has been often told. Over a hundred colored men were dragged from their homes and put in jail on suspicion.

All day long on that fateful Sunday white men were permitted in the jail to look over the imprisoned black men. Frenzied descriptions and hearsays were detailed in the papers, which fed the fires of sensationalism. Groups of white men gathered on the street corners and meeting places to discuss the awful crime of Negroes shooting white men.

There had been no lynchings in Memphis since the Civil War, but the colored people felt that anything might happen during the excitement. Many of them were in business there. Several times they had elected a member of their race to represent them in the legislature in Nashville. And a Negro, Lymus Wallace, had been elected several times as a member of the city council and we had had representation on the school board several times. Mr. Fred Savage was then our representative on the board of education.

The manhood which these Negroes represented went to the county jail and kept watch Sunday night. This they did also on Monday night, guarding the jail to see that nothing happened to the colored men during this time of race prejudice, while it was thought that the wounded white men would die. On Tuesday following, the newspapers which had fanned the flame of race prejudice announced that the wounded men were out of danger and would recover. The colored men who had guarded the jail for two nights felt that the crisis was past and that they need not guard the jail the third night.

While they slept a body of picked men was admitted to the jail, which was a modern Bastille. This mob took out of their cells Thomas Moss, Calvin McDowell, and Henry Stewart, the three officials of the People's Grocery Company. They were loaded on a switch engine of the railroad which ran back of the jail, carried a mile north of the city limits, and horribly shot to death. One of the morning papers held back its edition in order to supply its readers with the details of that lynching.

From its columns was gleaned the above information, together with details which told that "It is said that Tom Moss begged for his life for the sake of his wife and child and his unborn baby"; that when asked if he had anything to say, told them to "tell my people to go West—there is no justice for them here"; that Calvin McDowell got hold of one of the guns of the lynchers and because they could not loosen his grip a shot was fired into his closed fist. When the three bodies were found, the fingers of McDowell's right hand had been shot to pieces and his eyes were gouged out. This proved that the one who wrote that news report was either an eyewitness or got the facts from someone who was.

Questions

1. How and why did the lynching take place?
2. Why would public officials allow a lynching, which by its very nature represents a challenge to authority?
3. For the supporters of Jim Crow in Memphis, the lynching served one purpose. How did it affect the black community?

18-14   Atlanta Exposition Address (1895)

Booker T. Washington

During his lifetime, Booker T. Washington (1856–1915) was hailed as an African American hero: he was a former slave who went on to found the Tuskegee Institute (see text pp. 599–603). His accommodationist approach did not win support for long. Washington's reputation suffered after his death, especially during the civil rights movement of the 1960s, when he was criticized as an apologist for segregation. More recently, however, some black leaders have revived his concept of self-help. Both ideas—segregation and group autonomy—appear in Washington's Atlanta Exposition Address of 1895.

Source: Booker T. Washington, *Up from Slavery: An Autobiography* (1900; reprint, Williamstown, Mass.: Corner House, 1978), 218–225.

Mr. President and Gentlemen of the Board of Directors and Citizens.

One-third of the population of the South is of the Negro race. No enterprise seeking the material, civil, or moral welfare of this section can disregard this element of our population and reach the highest success. I but convey to you, Mr. President and Directors, the sentiment of the masses of my race when I say that in no way have the value and manhood of the American Negro been more fittingly and generously recognized than by the managers of this magnificent Exposition at every stage of its progress. It is a recognition that will do more to cement the friendship of the two races than any occurrence since the dawn of our freedom.

Not only this, but the opportunity here afforded will awaken among us a new era of industrial progress. Ignorant and inexperienced, it is not strange that in the first years of our new life we began at the top instead of at the bottom; that a seat in Congress or the state legislature was more sought than real estate or industrial skill; that the political convention of stump speaking had more attractions than starting a dairy farm or truck garden.

A ship lost at sea for many days suddenly sighted a friendly vessel. From the mast of the unfortunate vessel was seen a signal, "Water, water; we die of thirst!" The an-swer from the friendly vessel at once came back, "Cast down your bucket where you are." A second time the signal, "Water, water; send us water!" ran up from the distressed vessel, and was answered, "Cast down your bucket where you are." The captain of the distressed vessel, at last heeding the injunction, cast down his bucket, and it came up full of fresh, sparkling water from the mouth of the Amazon River. To those of my race who depend on bettering their condition in a foreign land or who underestimate the importance of cultivating friendly relations with the Southern white man, who is their next-door neighbour, I would say: "Cast down your bucket where you are"—cast it down in making friends in every manly way of the people of all races by whom we are surrounded.

Cast it down in agriculture, mechanics, in commerce, in domestic service, and in the professions. And in this connection it is well to bear in mind that whatever other sins the South may be called to bear, when it comes to business, pure and simple, it is in the South that the Negro is given a man's chance in the commercial world, and in nothing is this Exposition more eloquent than in emphasizing this chance. Our greatest danger is that in the great leap of slavery to freedom we may overlook the fact that the masses of us are to live by the productions of our hands, and fail to keep in mind that we shall prosper in proportion as we learn to dignify and glorify common labour and put brains and skill into the common occupations of life; shall prosper in proportion as we learn to draw the line between the superficial and the substantial, the ornamental gewgaws of life and the useful. No race can prosper till it learns that there is as much dignity in tilling a field as in writing a poem. It is at the bottom of life we must begin, and not at the top. Nor should we permit our grievances to overshadow our opportunities.

To those of the white race who look to the incoming of those of foreign birth and strange tongue and habits for the prosperity of the South, were I permitted I would repeat what I say to my own race, "Cast down your bucket where you are." Cast it down among the eight millions of Negroes whose habits you know, whose fidelity and love you have tested in days when to have proved treacherous meant the ruin of your firesides. Cast down your bucket among these people who have, without strikes and labour wars, tilled your fields, cleared your forests, builded your railroads and cities, and brought forth treasures from the bowels of the earth, and helped make possible this magnificent representation of the progress of the South. Casting down your bucket among my people, helping and encouraging them as you are doing on these grounds, and to education of head, hand, and heart, you will find that they will buy your surplus land, make blossom the waste places in your fields, and run your factories. While doing this, you can be sure in the future, as in the past, that you and your families will be surrounded by the most patient, faithful, law-abiding, and unresentful people that the world has seen. As we have proved our loyalty to you in the past, in nursing your children, watching by the sick-bed of your mothers and fathers, and often following them with tear-dimmed eyes to their graves, so in the future, in our humble way, we shall stand by you with a devotion that no foreigner can approach, ready to lay down our lives, if need be, in defence of yours, interlacing our industrial, commercial, civil, and religious life with yours in a way that shall make the interests of both races one. In all things that are purely social we can be as separate as the fingers, yet one as the hand in all things essential to mutual progress.

There is no defence or security for any of us except in the highest intelligence and development of all. If anywhere there are efforts tending to curtail the fullest growth of the Negro, let these efforts be turned into stimulating, encouraging, and making him the most useful and intelligent citizen. Effort or means so invested will pay a thousand per cent. interest. These efforts will be twice blessed—"blessing him that gives and him that takes."

There is no escape through law of man or God from the inevitable:—

The laws of changeless justice bind
  Oppressor with oppressed;
And close as sin and suffering joined
  We march to fate abreast.

Nearly sixteen millions of hands will aid you in pulling the load upward, or they will pull against you the load downward. We shall constitute one-third and more of the ignorance and crime of the South, or one-third its intelligence and progress; we shall contribute one-third to the business and industrial prosperity of the South, or we shall prove a veritable body of death, stagnating, depressing, retarding every effort to advance the body politic.

Gentlemen of the Exposition, as we present to you our humble effort at an exhibition of our progress, you must not expect overmuch. Starting thirty years ago with ownership here and there in a few quilts and pumpkins and chickens (gathered from miscellaneous sources), remember the path that has led from these to the inventions and production of agricultural implements, buggies, steam-engines, newspapers, books, statuary, carving, paintings, the management of drug-stores and banks, has not been trodden without contact with thorns and thistles. While we take pride in what we exhibit as a result of our independent efforts, we do not for a moment forget that our part in this exhibition would fall far short of your expectations but for the constant help that has come to our educational life, not only from the Southern states, but especially from Northern philanthropists, who have made their gifts a constant stream of blessing and encouragement.

The wisest among my race understand that the agitation of questions of social equality is the extremest folly, and that progress in the enjoyment of all the privileges that will come to us must be the result of severe and constant struggle rather than of artificial forcing. No race that has anything to contribute to the markets of the world is long in any degree ostracized. It is important and right that all privileges of the law be ours, but it is vastly more important that we be prepared for the exercises of these privileges. The opportunity to earn a dollar in a factory just now is worth infinitely more than the opportunity to spend a dollar in an opera-house.

In conclusion, may I repeat that nothing in thirty years has given us more hope and encouragement, and drawn us so near to you of the white race, as this opportunity offered by the Exposition; and here bending, as it were, over the altar that represents the results of the struggles of your race and mine, both starting practically empty-handed three decades ago, I pledge that in your effort to work out the great and intricate problem which God had laid at the doors of the South, you shall have at all times the patient, sympathetic help of my race; only let this be constantly in mind, that, while from representations in these buildings of the product of field, of forest, of mine, of factory, letters, and art, much good will come, yet far above and beyond material benefits will be that higher good, that, let us pray God, will come, in a blotting out of sectional differences and racial animosities and suspicions, in a determination to administer absolute justice, in a willing obedience among all classes to the mandates of law. This, this, coupled with our material prosperity, will bring into our beloved South a new heaven and a new earth.

Questions

1. What is Washington's message to blacks? To whites?
2. Why does Washington mention immigrants?
3. What does he mean in saying, "In all things that are purely social we can be as separate as the fingers, yet one as the hand in all things essential to mutual progress"?

18-15   Of Mr. Booker T. Washington and Others (1903)

W. E. B. Du Bois

Unlike Booker T. Washington, W. E. B. Du Bois never experienced slavery. Du Bois was born in Barrington, Massachusetts, in 1868 and was educated at Fisk and Harvard, where he earned a Ph.D. As the selection here indicates, Du Bois could not accept Washington's toleration of segregation (see text p. 603). His call for social equality led him to participate in the founding of the NAACP. Du Bois spent his last years in Ghana, where he died in 1963. Du Bois's critique of Washington appears in *The Souls of Black Folk,* first published in 1903.

Source: W. E. B. Du Bois, *The Souls of Black Folk* (A. C. McClurg, 1903; reprint, New York: Penguin, 1989), 36–50.

Easily the most striking thing in the history of the American Negro since 1876 is the ascendancy of Mr. Booker T. Washington. It began at the time when war memories and ideals were rapidly passing; a day of astonishing commercial development was dawning; a sense of doubt and hesitation overtook the freedmen's sons,—then it was that his leading began. Mr. Washington came, with a simple definite programme, at the psychological moment when the nation was a little ashamed of having bestowed so much sentiment on Negroes, and was concentrating its energies on Dollars. His programme of industrial education, conciliation of the South, and submission and silence as to civil and political rights, was not wholly original; the Free Negroes from 1830 up to wartime had striven to build industrial schools, and the American Missionary Association had from the first taught various trades; and Price and others had sought a way of honorable alliance with the best of the Southerners. But Mr. Washington first indissolubly linked these things; he put enthusiasm, unlimited energy, and perfect faith into this programme, and changed it from a by-path into a veritable Way of Life. And the tale of the methods by which he did this is a fascinating study of human life.

It startled the nation to hear a Negro advocating such a programme after many decades of bitter complaint; it startled and won the applause of the South, it interested and won the admiration of the North; and after a confused murmur of protest, it silenced if it did not convert the Negroes themselves.

To gain the sympathy and coöperation of the various elements comprising the white South was Mr. Washington's first task; and this, at the time Tuskegee was founded, seemed, for a black man, well-nigh impossible. And yet ten years later it was done in the word spoken at Atlanta: "In all things purely social we can be as separate as the five fingers, and yet one as the hand in all things essential to mutual progress." This "Atlanta Compromise" is by all odds the most notable thing in Mr. Washington's career. The South interpreted it in different ways: The radicals received it as a complete surrender of the demand for civil and political equality; the conservatives, as a generously conceived working basis for mutual understanding. So both approved it, and to-day its author is certainly the most distinguished Southerner since Jefferson Davis, and the one with the largest personal following.

Next to this achievement comes Mr. Washington's work in gaining place and consideration in the North. Others less shrewd and tactful had formerly essayed to sit on these two stools and had fallen between them; but as Mr. Washington knew the heart of the South from birth and training, so by singular insight he intuitively grasped the spirit of the age which was dominating the North. And so thoroughly did he learn the speech and thought of triumphant commercialism, and the ideals of material prosperity, that the picture of a lone black boy poring over a French grammar amid the weeds and dirt of a neglected home soon seemed to him the acme of absurdities. One wonders what Socrates and St. Francis of Assisi would say to this.

And yet this very singleness of vision and thorough oneness with his age is a mark of the successful man. It is as though Nature must needs make men narrow in order to give them force. So Mr. Washington's cult has gained unquestioning followers, his work has wonderfully prospered, his friends are legion, and his enemies are confounded. To-day he stands as the one recognized spokesman of his ten million fellows, and one of the most notable figures in a nation of seventy millions. One hesitates, therefore, to criticise a life which, beginning with so little, has done so much. And yet the time is come when one may speak in all sincerity and utter courtesy of the mistakes and shortcomings of Mr. Washington's career, as well as of his triumphs, without being thought captious or envious, and without forgetting that it is easier to do ill than well in the world.

The criticism that has hitherto met Mr. Washington has not always been of this broad character. In the South especially has he had to walk warily to avoid the harshest judgments,—and naturally so, for he is dealing with the one subject of deepest sensitiveness to that section. Twice—once when at the Chicago celebration of the Spanish-American War he alluded to the color-prejudice that is "eating away the vitals of the South," and once when he dined with President Roosevelt—has the resulting Southern criticism been violent enough to threaten seriously his popularity. In the North the feeling has several times forced itself into words, that Mr. Washington's counsels of submission overlooked certain elements of true manhood, and that his educational programme was unnecessarily narrow. Usually, however, such criticism has not found open expression, although, too, the spiritual sons of the Abolitionists have not been prepared to acknowledge that the schools founded before Tuskegee, by men of broad ideals and self-sacrificing spirit, were wholly failures or worthy of ridicule. While, then, criticism has not failed to follow Mr. Washington, yet the prevailing public opinion of the land has been but too willing to deliver the solution of a wearisome problem into his hands, and say, "If that is all you and your race ask, take it."

Among his own people, however, Mr. Washington has encountered the strongest and most lasting opposition, amounting at times to bitterness, and even to-day continuing strong and insistent even though largely silenced in outward expression by the public opinion of the nation. Some of this opposition is, of course, mere envy; the disappointment of displaced demagogues and the spite of narrow minds. But aside from this, there is among educated and thoughtful colored men in all parts of the land a feeling of deep regret, sorrow, and apprehension at the wide currency and ascendancy which some of Mr Washington's

theories have gained. These same men admire his sincerity of purpose, and are willing to forgive much to honest endeavor which is doing something worth the doing. They coöperate with Mr. Washington as far as they conscientiously can; and, indeed, it is no ordinary tribute to this man's tact and power that, steering as he must between so many diverse interests and opinions, he so largely retains the respect of all.

But the hushing of the criticism of honest opponents is a dangerous thing. It leads some of the best of the critics to unfortunate silence and paralysis of effort, and others to burst into speech so passionately and intemperately as to lose listeners. Honest and earnest criticism from those whose interests are most nearly touched,—criticism of writers by readers, of government by those governed, of leaders by those led,—this is the soul of democracy and the safeguard of modern society. If the best of the American Negroes receive by outer pressure a leader whom they had not recognized before, manifestly there is here a certain palpable gain. Yet there is also irreparable loss,—a loss of that peculiarly valuable education which a group receives when by search and criticism it finds and commissions its own leaders. The way in which this is done is at once the most elementary and the nicest problem of social growth. History is but the record of such group-leadership; and yet how infinitely changeful is its type and character! And of all types and kinds, what can be more instructive than the leadership of a group within a group?—that curious double movement where real progress may be negative and actual advance be relative retrogression. All this is the social student's inspiration and despair. . . .

Mr. Washington represents in Negro thought the old attitude of adjustment and submission; but adjustment at such a peculiar time as to make his programme unique. This is an age of unusual economic development, and Mr Washington's programme naturally takes an economic cast, becoming a gospel of Work and Money to such an extent as apparently almost completely to overshadow the higher aims of life. Moreover, this is an age when the more advanced races are coming in closer contact with the less developed races, and the race-feeling is therefore intensified; and Mr. Washington's programme practically accepts the alleged inferiority of the Negro races. Again, in our own land, the reaction from the sentiment of war time has given impetus to race-prejudice against Negroes, and Mr. Washington withdraws many of the high demands of Negroes as men and American citizens. In other periods of intensified prejudice all the Negro's tendency to self-assertion has been called forth; at this period a policy of submission is advocated. In the history of nearly all other races and peoples the doctrine preached at such crises has been that manly self-respect is worth more than lands and houses, and that a people who voluntarily surrender such respect, or cease striving for it, are not worth civilizing.

In answer to this, it has been claimed that the Negro can survive only through submission. Mr. Washington distinctly asks that black people give up, at least for the present, three things,—

First, political power,

Second, insistence on civil rights,

Third, higher education of Negro youth,—

and concentrate all their energies on industrial education, the accumulation of wealth, and the conciliation of the South. This policy has been courageously and insistently advocated for over fifteen years, and has been triumphant for perhaps ten years. As a result of this tender of the palm-branch, what has been the return? In these years there have occurred:

1. The disfranchisement of the Negro.

2. The legal creation of a distinct status of civil inferiority for the Negro.

3. The steady withdrawal of aid from institutions for the higher training of the Negro.

These movements are not, to be sure, direct results of Mr. Washington's teachings; but his propaganda has, without a shadow of doubt, helped their speedier accomplishment. The question then comes: Is it possible, and probable, that nine millions of men can make effective progress in economic lines if they are deprived of political rights, made a servile caste, and allowed only the most meagre chance for developing their exceptional men? If history and reason give any distinct answer to these questions, it is an emphatic *No*. And Mr. Washington thus faces the triple paradox of his career:

1. He is striving nobly to make Negro artisans business men and property-owners; but it is utterly impossible, under modern competitive methods, for workingmen and property-owners to defend their rights and exist without the right of suffrage.

2. He insists on thrift and self-respect, but at the same time counsels a silent submission to civic inferiority such as is bound to sap the manhood of any race in the long run.

3. He advocates common-school and industrial training, and depreciates institutions of higher learning; but neither the Negro common-schools, nor Tuskegee itself, could remain open a day were it not for teachers trained in Negro colleges, or trained by their graduates.

This triple paradox in Mr. Washington's position is the object of criticism by two classes of colored Americans. One class is spiritually descended from Toussaint the Savior, through Gabriel, Vesey, and Turner, and they represent the attitude of revolt and revenge; they hate the white South blindly and distrust the white race generally, and so far as they agree on definite action, think that the Negro's only hope lies in emigration beyond the borders of the United States. And yet, by the irony of fate, nothing has more effectually made this programme seem hopeless than the recent course of the United States toward weaker and darker peoples in the West Indies, Hawaii, and the Philippines,—for where in the world may we go and be safe from lying and brute force?

The other class of Negroes who cannot agree with Mr. Washington has hitherto said little aloud. They deprecate the sight of scattered counsels, of internal disagreement; and especially they dislike making their just criticism of a useful and earnest man an excuse for a general discharge of venom from small-minded opponents. Nevertheless, the questions involved are so fundamental and serious that it is difficult to see how men like the Grimkes, Kelly Miller, J. W. E. Bowen, and other representatives of this group, can much longer be silent. Such men feel in conscience bound to ask of this nation three things:

1. The right to vote.

2. Civic equality.

3. The education of youth according to ability.

They acknowledge Mr. Washington's invaluable service in counselling patience and courtesy in such demands; they do not ask that ignorant black men vote when ignorant whites are debarred, or that any reasonable restrictions in the suffrage should not be applied; they know that the low social level of the mass of the race is responsible for much discrimination against it, but they also know, and the nation knows, that relentless color-prejudice is more often a cause than a result of the Negro's degradation; they seek the abatement of this relic of barbarism, and not its systematic encouragement and pampering by all agencies of social power from the Associated Press to the Church of Christ. They advocate, with Mr. Washington, a broad system of Negro common schools supplemented by thorough industrial training; but they are surprised that a man of Mr. Washington's insight cannot see that no such educational system ever has rested or can rest on any other basis than that of the well-equipped college and university, and they insist that there is a demand for a few such institutions throughout the South to train the best of the Negro youth as teachers, professional men, and leaders.

This group of men honor Mr. Washington for his attitude of conciliation toward the white South; they accept the "Atlanta Compromise" in its broadest interpretation; they recognize, with him, many signs of promise, many men of high purpose and fair judgment, in this section; they know that no easy task has been laid upon a region already tottering under heavy burdens. But, nevertheless, they insist that the way to truth and right lies in straightforward honesty, not in indiscriminate flattery; in praising those of the South who do well and criticising uncompromisingly those who do ill; in taking advantage of the opportunities at hand and urging their fellows to do the same, but at the same time in remembering that only a firm adherence to their higher ideals and aspirations will ever keep those ideals within the realm of possibility. They do not expect that the free right to vote, to enjoy civic rights, and to be educated, will come in a moment; they do not expect to see the bias and prejudices of years disappear at the blast of a trumpet; but they are absolutely certain that the way for a people to gain their reasonable rights is not by voluntarily throwing them away and insisting that they do not want them; that the way for a people to gain respect is not by continually belittling and ridiculing themselves; that, on the contrary, Negroes must insist continually, in season and out of season, that voting is necessary to modern manhood, that color discrimination is barbarism, and that black boys need education as well as white boys.

In failing thus to state plainly and unequivocally the legitimate demands of their people, even at the cost of opposing an honored leader, the thinking classes of American Negroes would shirk a heavy responsibility,—a responsibility to themselves, a responsibility to the struggling masses, a responsibility to the darker races of men whose future depends so largely on this American experiment, but especially a responsibility to this nation,—this common Fatherland. It is wrong to aid and abet a national crime simply because it is unpopular not to do so. The growing spirit of kindliness and reconciliation between the North and South after the frightful differences of a generation ago ought to be a source of deep congratulation to all, and especially to those whose mistreatment caused the war; but if that reconciliation is to be marked by the industrial slavery and civic death of those same black men, with permanent legislation into a position of inferiority, then those black men, if they are really men, are called upon by every consideration of patriotism and loyalty to oppose such a course by all civilized methods, even though such opposition involves disagreement with Mr. Booker T. Washington. We have no right to sit silently by while the inevitable seeds are sown for a harvest of disaster to our children, black and white. . . .

The South ought to be led, by candid and honest criticism, to assert her better self and do her full duty to the race she has cruelly wronged and is still wronging. The North—her co-partner in guilt—cannot salve her conscience by plastering it with gold. We cannot settle this problem by diplomacy and suaveness, by "policy" alone. If worse come to worst, can the moral fibre of this country survive the slow throttling and murder of nine millions of men?

The black men of America have a duty to perform, a duty stern and delicate,—a forward movement to oppose a part of the work of their greatest leader. So far as Mr. Washington preaches Thrift, Patience, and Industrial Training for the masses, we must hold up his hands and strive with him, rejoicing in his honors and glorying in the strength of this Joshua called of God and of man to lead the headless host. But so far as Mr. Washington apologizes for injustice, North or South, does not rightly value the privilege and duty of voting, belittles the emasculating effects of caste distinctions, and opposes the higher training and ambition of our brighter minds,—so far as he, the South, or the Nation, does this,—we must unceasingly and firmly oppose them. By every civilized and peaceful method we must strive for the rights which the world accords to men, clinging unwaveringly to those great words which the sons of the Fathers would fain forget: "We hold these truths to be self-evident: That all men are created equal; that they are endowed by their Creator with certain unalienable rights; that among these are life, liberty, and the pursuit of happiness."

Questions

1. Which aspects of Washington's philosophy does Du Bois criticize?
2. Who does Du Bois expect to lead in the criticism of Washington?
3. What role does Du Bois envision for blacks in American society?
4. In this essay, does Du Bois appear to consider himself an American or an African American? Why would that matter in regard to his view of Washington?

Questions for Further Thought

1. Which philosophy was better suited to the Jim Crow world of Mississippi: Booker T. Washington's (Document 18-14) or W. E. B. Du Bois's (Document 18-15)? Why?
2. How did the Mississippi Constitution (Document 18-12) encourage the kind of violence described by Ida B. Wells in Document 18-13?
3. How does Du Bois explain Washington's success? What criticisms of Washington does Du Bois voice?
4. Which aspects of Washington's speech have enjoyed a resurgence in popularity among African Americans? Why?

CHAPTER 19

The Rise of the City

★   ★   ★

Urbanization

In a sense, Americans have never been comfortable with or in cities. "The yellow fever will discourage the growth of great cities in our nation, and I view great cities as pestilential to the morals, the health, and the liberties of man," Thomas Jefferson wrote to Benjamin Rush in 1800. "True, they nourish some of the elegant arts, but the useful ones can thrive elsewhere, and less perfection in the others, with more health, virtue and freedom, would be my choice." Rush responded: "I consider them [cities] in the same light that I do abscesses on the human body, viz., as reservoirs of all the impurities of a community."

Jefferson envisioned a nation of yeomen farmers, but the Industrial Revolution impelled those farmers to leave the countryside for urban factory work. With the advent of steam power, factories increasingly were located in cities during the nineteenth century. The labor, transportation, and markets needed for success were tied in with ever-growing cities. There was unimagined wealth in urban America, together with problems that could not be solved by individuals working alone.

In Document 19-1, the progressive reformer Frederic C. Howe offers a strong defense of the city, or at least of its potential. The Italian visitor Giuseppe Giacosa (Document 19-2) provides an eyewitness account of an industrial city and one of its byproducts, smoke.

19-1 The City Beautiful (1905)

Frederic C. Howe

Like many other Americans, Frederic C. Howe (1867–1940) moved from a small town to a city. Howe was born in Meadville, Pennsylvania. He attended Johns Hopkins University and eventually (and, he says in his autobiography, reluctantly) became a lawyer.

Rather than practice in a small town, Howe moved to Cleveland, where he served as an advisor to Mayor Tom Johnson (1901–1909). That experience helped convince Howe that city life was filled with promise. In the following selection from *The City: The Hope of Democracy* (1905), Howe considers the importance of the "City Beautiful" movement (see text p. 614).

Source: Frederic C. Howe, *The City: The Hope of Democracy* (New York: Charles Scribner's Sons, 1905; reprint, Seattle: University of Washington Press, 1967), 239–245.

One of the most significant evidences of the gain we are making appears in the beautification of our cities. This interest is general. In Washington, New York, Boston, Cleveland, San Francisco, and Chicago public and private movements have been organized for the unified treatment of the city's architecture, while hundreds of other communities are aiming to make their cities more presentable through parks, cleaner streets and higher ideas of municipal art.

This indicates that the public is learning to act in an organized way. Heretofore we have lacked a city sense. In consequence, collective action has been impossible. It also indicates a new attitude towards the city, a belief in its life, outward form and appearance, its architectural expression, its parks, schools, and playgrounds. A determination has come to make the city a more beautiful as well as a more wholesome place of living. All this is foreign to the business man's ideal of merely getting his money's worth out of government. The belief in the city as a home, as an object of public-spirited endeavor, has superseded the earlier commercial ideals that characterized our thought.

The great cities of every age have probably passed through a similar evolution. First business, commerce, and wealth, then culture, beauty, and civic activity. It was so with Athens, which became great as a commercial centre before it was adorned by the hands of Pericles and Phidias. Rome became mistress of the Mediterranean before she enriched her streets and public places with the spoils of foreign conquest. The mediæval Italian cities of Florence, Venice, and Milan were the creations of organized democracy, as well as the centres of the world's trade with the East. In these cities it was freedom that gave birth to a local patriotism that inspired democracy to its highest achievements in the realm of art, literature, and architecture. And it is probable that, next to religion, democracy and the sense of a free city have been the greatest inspirations to art in the history of mankind. . . .

The splendid projects now on foot in America are an evidence that modern democracy is not satisfied with the commonplace. Just as the monumental cathedrals which everywhere dot Europe are the expression of the ideals and aspirations of mankind, so in America, democracy is coming to demand and appreciate fitting monuments for the realization of its life, and splendid parks and structures as the embodiment of its ideals. The twentieth century offers high promise of the ultimate possibilities of democracy in generous expenditure for public purposes. . . .

Probably no other city in America has projected as well as assured the carrying out of the systematic beautification of the city on so splendid a scale as has the city of Cleveland. This is the more remarkable inasmuch as no American city, with the possible exception of Chicago, is so essentially democratic in its instincts. Nowhere have the movements centring about municipal ownership, taxation, and the great industrial issues found more ready response at the hands of the voters than in this great industrial centre on the southern shore of Lake Erie. Cleveland is a commercial city *par excellence*. It has been termed the Sheffield of America. It is a centre second only to Pittsburg[h] in the iron, steel, coal, and coke trade. One-third of its population is foreign-born. But despite this fact, as well as the newness of its life, it has shown a willingness to expend many millions of dollars in the development of the artistic side of its existence.

The city is fortunate in the fact that all its public buildings are to be constructed at the same time. A uniform plan of procedure was thus possible. The Federal Building, County Courthouse, City Hall, and Public Library, as well as several other semi-public structures, are all to be built. Under ordinary circumstances and with the subterranean political and commercial forces at work in a city, isolated construction would doubtless have been the result. But public-spirited men have brought about a harmony of action among the many political agencies which had to be satisfied, and achieved a result not far from ideal in its possibilities. Through the aid of state legislation a Board of Supervising Architects was appointed, endowed with a final veto upon the location, plans, and style of architecture of all the public buildings. Despite some local jealousies, the city called to its aid Daniel H. Burnham, of Chicago, the supervising architect of the Chicago Exposition; John M. Carrere, supervising architect of the Pan-American Exposition of Buffalo, and Arnold W. Brunner, of New York, the architect of the new Federal Building in Cleveland. The members of this commission were employed by the city at generous salaries and given absolute freedom in the working out of a ground plan for the arrangement and development of the scheme. The commission is also entrusted with the problem of improving the public square, the approaches to the sites of the public buildings, and the development of the lake front.

This is the most significant forward step taken in America in the matter of municipal art. It is comparable to the designs of Napoleon III., who remade Paris, with the aid of Baron Haussmann, or to the prescience of Jefferson, who called a distinguished architect to the aid of the new government in the laying out of the national capital on its present scale.

The commission thus appointed was at work for more than two years, and has presented the results of its labors in a completed plan for the arrangement of the public buildings. The design has met with such enthusiastic ap-proval that its consummation is now assured. The total ex-penditure involved approximates $14,000,000 for public purposes, with from three to five millions more for a termi-nal railway station, music-hall, museum, and the like. It in-volves the clearing of a large area of land laying between the business portion of the city and Lake Erie, and the uti-lization of this space as a site for the public buildings, parkage, a splendid mall, and the development of a lake-front park sixty acres in extent into a splendid terminal railway station, which is to be the gateway to the city. . . .

Questions

1. For Howe, the city has a symbolic function "foreign to the business man's ideal of merely getting his money's worth out of government." What is that function?
2. How did the people of Cleveland create a "City Beautiful"?
3. Why should museums and lakefront parks matter to the urban poor and working classes?

19-2   A Visitor in Chicago (1892)

Giuseppe Giacosa

Rudyard Kipling said of Chicago, "Having seen it, I urgently desire never to see it again. It is inhabited by savages." Kipling might have added that the residents were smoke-eating savages, at that. Coal, used for residential heating and industrial power, led to what now would be recognized as a serious air pollution problem. Giuseppe Gi-acosa (1847–1906) encountered that problem during a visit from Italy in 1892.

Source: Giuseppe Giacosa, "Chicago and Her Italian Colony," *Nuova Antologia (*March 1893), 16–28, trans. L. B. Davis, in Bessie Louise Pierce, ed., *As Others See Chicago: Impressions of Visitors, 1673–1933,* 276–278. Copyright © 1933 by the University of Chicago Press. Reprinted by permission.

I had two different impressions of Chicago, one sensual and immediate, which comes from seeing persons and things. The other, intellectual and gradual, born from intel-ligence, induction and comparisons. To the eye, the city ap-pears abominable. . . . I would not want to live there for anything in the world. I think that whoever ignores it is not entirely acquainted with our century and of what is its ultimate expression.

During my stay of one week, I did not see in Chicago anything but darkness: smoke, clouds, dirt and an extraor-dinary number of sad and grieved persons. Certain remote quarters are the exception, in which there breathes from little houses and tiny gardens a tranquil air of rustic habi-tation where a curious architecture with diverting and im-mature whims makes a pleasant appearance, where the houses seem to be toys for the use of the hilarious people who live there in complete repose, eating candy, swinging in their faithful little rocking chairs, and contemplating oleographs.[1]

But with the exception of these rare cases, the rich me-tropolis gave me a sense of oppression so grave that I still doubt whether, beyond their factories, there exist celestial spaces. Was it a storm-cloud? I cannot say, because the covered sky spreads a light equal and diffused, which makes no shade; while here, depending on the time of day, a few thick shadows line the houses. And I can not even say that a ghost of the sun shines, because the appearance of things close up makes me always uncertain and con-fused. I am inclined to believe that that spacious plain, *café*

---

[1]An oleograph is a chromolithograph printed with oil paint on canvas in imitation of an oil painting.

au lait in colour, which stretches along the edge of the city, which appears to the eye three hundred paces wide, and which disappears in gray space, might be the lake; but I could not press close to it with security. Certainly the ships plow through a dense atmosphere rather than a watery plain.

I recall one morning when I happened to be on a high railroad viaduct. From it the city seemed to smolder a vast unyielding conflagration, so much was it wrapped in smoke. . . . Perhaps, in Chicago, I was influenced by bad weather, by which incentive I do not affirm how things may be, but that I saw them thus, and hence was born the ill-tempered, pouting expression which I read on almost every face. It made me feel, in noting it, how I interpose in such a crowd; a few might show a little courtesy, I do not mean with hats off, but by a nod or glance of recognition. They all were running about desperately. In New York there are more people than in Chicago, and none idle; nevertheless I observe on their streets our same quick friendliness. Here, it seems to me, all might be lost, as I, without company in the formidable tumult. Or if two persons should discourse together, their speech would be in a whining tone, low and nasal, without the least variance of accent. . . . They say that all Americans have nasal voices. That does not seem to me true of New Yorkers, or only slightly; but it could be said of Chicagoans that their voices come out of their nostrils, and that articulation is made in the pharynx. It is a positive fact that a great many noses in Chicago are in a continuous pathological condition. I have seen in many shop windows certain apparatus for covering the nose, a kind of nasal protector, or false nostrils—but

without intent to deceive. I did not see any in operation, however; October, as it seems, still yields to the most delicate the use of the natural nose, but the kingdom of the artificial must be nearby, and I cannot forgive myself for having missed seeing it.

Furthermore, the mass of factories is overpowering without being imposing. That immense building, the Auditorium, where there is a hotel for more than 1,000 guests, an abundance of seats and writing desks of every kind, a conservatory of music, and on the sixth or seventh floor, I don't recall which, a theatre seating 8,000 persons; is this not marvelous to think upon? Its vastness lacks ostentation; it is a vastness of the whole, ostentation means a co-ordination of parts. All the immense factories of Chicago have low, squatty doors and suffocating stories which the menacing building crushes ridiculously. The two floors of the Tolomei Palace at Siena would be, in Chicago, divided into eight compartments. Certain important houses of twenty stories do not measure one and half voltas, the height of the Stozzi Palace. Surely they take care to mask the frequency of compartments by means of openings which reach from the first floor to the fourth, but to see this from the street, in the height of a single window, three men seated at three writing desks, people and furniture almost suspended in the air, and leaning against a transparent wall, gives one a feeling of irritating unrest. . . .

The dominant characteristic of the exterior life of Chicago is violence. Everything leads you to extreme expressions: dimensions, movements, noises, rumors, window displays, spectacles, ostentation, misery, activity, and alcoholic degradation.

Questions

1. Giacosa, familiar with historic Italian cities, might have had set notions about what a city should be. Does he betray any prejudices in describing Chicago?
2. What sources of pollution do you imagine Giacosa encountered?
3. Why might many Americans of the period have celebrated the smokiness of their cities?

Questions for Further Thought

1. Why have Americans tended to view cities from the perspective of Giuseppe Giacosa (Document 19-2) and not that of Frederic Howe (Document 19-1)?
2. Using Giacosa as an example, discuss the advantages and problems facing a historian who uses eyewitness accounts.
3. Technology allowed city dwellers to build skyscrapers, design reliable mass-transit systems, and safeguard water supplies. In light of those successes, how do you explain the persistence of problems like inadequate education and housing?

City People

Unlike most Europeans, who tend to think of themselves as part of a national community, Americans have always celebrated their individuality. The man or woman alone on the frontier became a powerful myth, but city life did not make for individualism. Success in business was a product of chain of command and interdependence. Even going from one end of a city to the other meant depending on strangers such as street-car conductors and bridge tenders, and directions could come in Polish, Yiddish, or Italian (see Table 19-2, text p. 616). To their credit, Americans adapted, some more quickly than others.

For Mark Twain, New York was "too large," an inconvenience; for immigrants, it was dangerously crowded. The journalist Jacob Riis, a Danish immigrant, noted that New York's Thirteenth Ward had a population density of 274,432 people *per square mile* in 1890. In that setting, diseases like smallpox, diphtheria, cholera, typhoid fever, typhus, and tuberculosis became all too familiar to the residents.

When it became obvious by the turn of the century that change was necessary, the urban middle class formed numerous reform groups for public health, decent housing, and better schools and playgrounds. Some reformers argued the cause of good government, whereas others demanded change in the name of Christianity. However, large segments of the urban population were not interested in reform. Their needs were satisfied by machine politics (see text pp. 618–620), with perhaps some public entertainment on the side (see text pp. 624–627, and "Voices from Abroad: José Martí, Coney Island, 1881," text p. 625). The Reverend Josiah Strong (Document 19-3) plays on the fears and prejudices of the middle class as he warns of the dangers of cities. The letters that make up Document 19-4 show how a Polish family dealt with the uncertainties of the immigration experience. (Compare these letters with those presented in "American Voices: *Bintel Brief,*" text p. 619). In Document 19-5 James Michael Curley reflects on his remarkable political career in Boston.

19-3   The Dangers of Cities (1886)

Josiah Strong

Americans accepted the city, among other reasons, because it generated prosperity. By the second half of the nineteenth century, there was a large urban middle class, confident in its success but worried about the future of city life. The Reverend Josiah Strong (1847–1916), a Congregationalist pastor, addressed some of those concerns in *Our Country,* first published in 1886. Strong did not want simply to sit by as nature ran its course in the American city, as social Darwinists recommended. However, Strong's call to action reflected the prejudices of his day.

Source: Josiah Strong, *Our Country* (1886; reprint, edited by Jurgen Herbst, Cambridge, Mass.: Harvard University Press, 1963), 171–174, 176, 183–185. Copyright 1963 by the President and Fellows of Harvard College. Reprinted by permission of the publisher.

The city is the nerve center of our civilization. It is also the storm center. The fact, therefore, that it is growing much more rapidly than the whole population is full of significance. . . .

The city has become a serious menace to our civilization, because in it, excepting Mormonism, each of the dangers we have discussed is enhanced, and all are focalized. It has a peculiar attraction for the immigrant. Our fifty principal cities in 1880 contained 39.3 per cent of our entire German population, and 45.8 per cent of the Irish. Our ten larger cities at that time contained only nine per cent of the entire population, but 23 per cent of the foreign. While a little less than one-third of the population of the United States was foreign by birth or parentage, sixty-two per cent of the population of Cincinnati was foreign, eighty-three per cent of Cleveland, sixty-three per cent of Boston, eighty per cent of New York, and ninety-one per cent of Chicago. A census of Massachusetts, taken in 1885, showed that in 65 towns and cities of the state 65.1 per cent of the population was foreign by birth or parentage.

Because our cities are so largely foreign, Romanism finds in them its chief strength.

For the same reason the saloon, together with the intemperance and the liquor power which it represents, is multiplied in the city. East of the Mississippi there was, in 1880, one saloon to every 438 of the population; in Boston, one to every 329; in Cleveland, one to every 192; in Chicago, one to every 179; in New York, one to every 171; in Cincinnati, one to every 124. Of course the demoralizing and pauperizing power of the saloons and their debauching influence in politics increase with their numerical strength.

It is the city where wealth is massed; and here are the tangible evidences of it piled many stories high. Here the sway of Mammon is widest, and his worship the most constant and eager. Here are luxuries gathered—everything that dazzles the eye, or tempts the appetite; here is the most extravagant expenditure. Here, also, is the *congestion* of wealth the severest. Dives and Lazarus are brought face to face; here, in sharp contrast, are the *ennui* of surfeit and the desperation of starvation. The rich are richer, and the poor are poorer, in the city than elsewhere; and, as a rule, the greater the city, the greater are the riches of the rich and the poverty of the poor. Not only does the proportion of the poor increase with the growth of the city, but their condition becomes more wretched. The poor of a city of 8,000 inhabitants are well off compared with many in New York; and there are hardly such depths of woe, such utter and heart-wringing wretchedness in New York as in London. . . .

Socialism centers in the city, and the materials of its growth are multiplied with the growth of the city. Here is heaped the social dynamite; here roughs, gamblers, thieves, robbers, lawless and desperate men of all sorts, congregate; men who are ready on any pretext to raise riots for the purpose of destruction and plunder; here gather foreigners and wage-workers who are especially susceptible to social arguments; here skepticism and irreligion abound; here inequality is the greatest and most obvious, and the contrast between opulence and penury the most striking; here is suffering the sorest. As the greatest wickedness in the world is to be found not among the cannibals of some far-off coast, but in Christian lands where the light of truth is diffused and rejected, so the utmost depth of wretchedness exists not among savages who have few wants, but in great cities, where, in the presence of plenty and of every luxury men starve. Let a man become the owner of a home, and he is much less susceptible to socialistic propagandism. But real estate is so high in the city that it is almost impossible for a wage-worker to become a householder. . . .

1. In gathering up the results of the foregoing discussion of these several perils, it should be remarked that to preserve republican institutions requires a *higher average* intelligence and virtue among large populations than among small. The government of 5,000,000 people was a simple thing compared with the government of 50,000,000; and the government of 50,000,000 is a simple thing compared with that of 500,000,000. There are many men who can conduct a small business successfully, who are utterly incapable of managing large interests. In the latter there are multiplied relations whose harmony must be preserved. A mistake is farther reaching. It has, as it were, a longer leverage. This is equally true of the business of government. The man of only average ability and intelligence discharges creditably the duties of mayor in his little town; but he would fail utterly at the head of the state or the nation. If the people are to govern, they must grow more intelligent as the population and the complications of government increase. And a higher morality is even more essential. As civilization increases, as society becomes more complex, as labor-saving machinery is multiplied and the division of labor becomes more minute, the individual becomes more fractional and dependent. Every savage possesses all the knowledge of the tribe. Throw him upon his own resources, and he is self-sufficient. A civilized man in like circumstances would perish. The savage is independent. Civilize him, and he becomes dependent; the more civilized, the more dependent. And, as men become more dependent on each other, they should be able to rely more implicitly on each other. More complicated and multiplied relations require a more delicate conscience and a stronger sense of justice. And any failure in character or conduct under such conditions is farther reaching and more disastrous in its results.

Is our progress in morals and intelligence at all comparable to the growth of population? The nation's illiteracy has not been discussed, because it is not one of the perils which peculiarly threaten the West; but any one who would calculate our political horoscope must allow it great influence in connection with the baleful stars which are in the ascendant. But the danger which arises from the corruption of popular morals is much greater. The republics of Greece and Rome, and if I mistake not, all the republics that have ever lived and died, were more intelligent at the end than at the beginning; but growing intelligence could not compensate decaying morals. What, then, is our moral progress? Are popular morals as sound as they were twenty years ago? There is, perhaps, no better index of general morality than Sabbath observance; and everybody knows there has been a great increase of Sabbath desecration in twenty years. We have seen that we are now using as a beverage 29 per cent more of alcohol per caput [per head] than we were fifty years ago. Says Dr. S. W. Dike: "It is safe to say that divorce has been doubled, in proportion to marriages or population, in most of the Northern States within thirty years. Present figures indicate a still greater increase." And President Woolsey,[1] speaking of the United States, said in 1883: "On the whole, there can be little, if any, question that the ratio of divorces to marriages or to population exceeds that of any country in the Christian world." While the population increased thirty per cent from 1870 to 1880, the number of criminals in the United States increased 82.33 per cent. It looks very much as if existing tendencies were in the direction of the deadline of vice. Excepting Mormonism, all the perils which have been discussed seem to be increasing more rapidly than the population. *Are popular morals likely to improve under their increasing influence?*

2. The fundamental idea of popular government is the distribution of power. It has been the struggle of liberty for ages to wrest power from the hands of one or the few, and lodge it in the hands of the many. We have seen, in the foregoing discussion, that centralized power is rapidly growing. The "boss" makes his bargain, and sells his ten thousand or fifty thousand voters as if they were so many cattle. Centralized wealth is centralized power; and the capitalist and corporation find many ways to control votes. The liquor power controls thousands of votes in every considerable city. The president of the Mormon Church casts, say, sixty thousand votes. The Jesuits, it is said, are all under the command of one man in Washington. The Roman Catholic vote is more or less perfectly controlled by the priests. That means that the Pope can

[1]Theodore Dwight Woolsey (1801–1889) was the president of Yale College from 1846 to 1871.

dictate some hundreds of thousands of votes in the United States. Is there anything unrepublican in all this? And we must remember that, if present tendencies continue, these figures will be greatly multiplied in the future. And not only is this immense power lodged in the hand of one man, which in itself is perilous, but it is wielded without the slightest reference to any policy or principle of government, solely in the interests of a church or a business, or for personal ends.

The result of a national election may depend on a single state; the vote of that state may depend on a single city; the vote of that city may depend on a "boss," or a capitalist, or a corporation; or the election may be decided, and the policy of the government may be reversed, by the socialist, or liquor, or Roman Catholic or immigrant vote.

It matters not by what name we call the man who wields this centralized power—whether king, czar, pope, president, capitalist, or boss. Just so far as it is absolute and irresponsible, it is dangerous.

3. These several dangerous elements are singularly netted together, and serve to strengthen each other. It is not necessary to prove that any *one* of them is likely to destroy our national life, in order to show that it is imperiled. A man may die of wounds no one of which is fatal. No sober-minded man can look fairly at the facts, and doubt that *together* these perils constitute an array which will seriously endanger our free institutions, if the tendencies which have been pointed out continue; and especially is this true in view of the fact that these perils peculiarly confront the West, where our defense is weakest.

Questions

1. What problems does Strong associate with immigrants and "the liquor power"?
2. Why does he fear the growth of socialism in the cities?
3. How does Strong stereotype Mormon and Catholic voters? Why does he assume that Protestant voters would act differently?

19-4   The Immigrant Experience: Letters Home (1901–1903)

The American city could be a forbidding place for newcomers. To gauge the extent of immigrants' experiences, sociologists William I. Thomas (1863–1947) and Florian Znaniecki (1882–1958) undertook a massive research project that led to the publication of *The Polish Peasant in Europe and America* (1918). Their work focused on letters exchanged between immigrants in the United States and their families and friends in the old country. Thomas and Znaniecki hoped to demonstrate how city life overwhelmed rural immigrants and led to their "social disorganization."

Source: Letters from Konstanty and Antoni Butkowski to their parents, December 6, 1901–April 21, 1903, in William I. Thomas and Florian Znaniecki, *The Polish Peasant in Europe and America*, 2nd ed. (New York: Knopf, 1927; reprint, New York: Dover, 1958), 782–789.

SOUTH CHICAGO, December 6, 1901
DEAR PARENTS: I send you my lowest bow, as to a father and mother, and I greet you and my brothers with these words: "Praised be Jesus Christus," and I hope in God that you will answer me, "For centuries of centuries. Amen."

And now I wish you, dearest parents, and you also, dearest brother, to meet the Christmas eve and merry holidays in good health and happiness. May God help you in your intentions. Be merry, all of you together. [Health and success; letter received.] I could not answer you at once, for you know that when one comes from work he has no wish to occupy himself with writing [particularly] as I work always at night. . . . I sent you money, 100 roubles, on November 30. I could not send more now, for you know that winter is coming and I must buy clothes. I inform you that Marta has no work yet. She will get work after the holidays, and it may happen that she will marry. . . . I inform you about Jasiek, my brother, that he wrote me a letter from Prussia asking me to take him to America, but he is still too young. Inform me about Antoni, how his health is, for in the spring I will bring him to me. I will send him a ship-ticket, if God grants me health. [Greetings for family and relatives.]

[KONSTANTY BUTKOWSKI]

February 17, 1902
DEAREST PARENTS: . . . I inform you that I have sent a ship-ticket for Antoni. . . . Expect to receive it soon. . . . And remember, Antoni, don't show your papers to anybody, except in places where you must show them. . . . And if you receive the ticket soon, don't wait, but come at once. And if you receive it a week or so before Easter, then don't leave until after the holidays. But after the holidays don't wait; come at once. . . . And send me a telegram from the Castle Garden. You won't pay much and I shall know and will go to the railway-station. Take 15 roubles with you, it will be enough, and change them at once for Prussian money. As to the clothes, take the worst which you have, some three old shirts, that you may have a change on the water. And when you come across the water happily, then throw away all these rags. Bring nothing with you except what you have upon yourself. And don't bring any good shoes either, but everything the worst. As to living, take some dry bread and much sugar, and about half a quart of spirits, and some dry meat. You may take some onions, but don't take any cheese. . . . And be careful in every place about money. Don't talk to any girls on the water. . . . Learn in Bzory when Wojtek will come, for he comes to the same place where I am, so you would have a companion. And about Jan Plonka, if he wants to come, he is not to complain about [reproach] me for in America there are neither Sundays nor holidays; he must go and work. I inform [him] that I shall receive him as my brother. If he wishes he may come. . . .

[KONSTANTY BUTKOWSKI]

June 13 [1902]
DEAREST PARENTS: . . . Konstanty works in the same factory as before and earns $2 a day. I have yet no work, but don't be anxious about me, dear parents . . . for I came to a brother and uncle, not to strangers. If our Lord God gives me health, I shall work enough in America. [News about friends and relatives.] Now I inform you, dear parents, about Wladyslawa Butkowska [cousin]. She lives near us, we see each other every day. She is a doctor's servant. And this doctor has left his wife in Chicago and came [*sic*] to South Chicago. She cooks for him, and she is alone in his house, so people talk about her, that she does not behave well. He pays her $5 a week. I don't know whether it is true or not, but people talk thus because he has left his wife. . . .

[ANTONI BUTKOWSKI[

November 11 [1902]
DEAREST PARENTS: . . . Now I inform you about Antoni, that he is working in Chicago; it costs 15 cents to go to him. He is boarding, as well as Marta, with acquaintances, with Malewski. He has an easy and clean work, but he earns only enough to live, for he is unable to do heavy work. I see them almost every evening. I go to them. And Marta works in a tailor-shop, but she refuses to listen to me, else she would have been married long ago. So I inform you that I loved her as my own sister, but now I won't talk to her any more, for she refuses to listen. Family remains family only in the first time after coming from home, and later they forget and don't wish any more to acknowledge the familial relations; the American meat inflates them.

I have nothing more to write, except that we are all in good health. Moreover, I declare about your letters, give them to somebody else to write, for neither wise nor fool can read such writing. If such writers are to write you may as well not send letters, for I won't read them, only I will throw them into the fire, for I cannot understand. I beg you, describe to me about our country, how things are going on there. And please don't be angry with me for this which I shall write. I write you that it is hard to live alone, so please find some girl for me, but an orderly [honest] one, for in America there is not even one single orderly girl. . . .

KONSTANTY BUTKOWSKI

December 21 [1902]
I, your son, Konstanty Butkowski, inform you, dear parents, about my health. . . . I thank you kindly for your letter, for it was happy. As to the girl, although I don't know her, my companion, who knows her, says that she is stately and pretty. I believe him, as well as you, my parents. For although I don't know her, I ask you, my dear parents, and as you will write me so it will be well. Shall I send her a ship-ticket, or how else shall I do? Ask Mr. and Mrs. Sad-

owski [her parents], what they will say. And I beg you, dear parents, give them my address and let them write a letter to me, then I shall know with certainty. And write me, please, about her age and about everything which concerns her. I don't need to enumerate; you know yourselves, dear parents. For to send a ship-ticket it is not the same as to send a letter which costs a nickel; what is done cannot be undone. So I beg you once more, as my loving parents, go into this matter and do it well, that there may be no cheating. . . . I shall wait for your letter with great impatience, that I may know what to do. . . .

KONSTANTY BUTKOWSKI

Please inform me, which one is to come, whether the older or the younger one, whether Aleksandra or Stanislawa. Inform me exactly.

CHICAGO, December 31, 1902

DEAR PARENTS: . . . If Konstanty wrote you to send him a girl answer him that he may send a ship-ticket either to the one from Popów or to the one from Grajewo. Let the one come which is smarter, for he does not know either of them, so send the one which pleases you better. For in America it is so: Let her only know how to prepare for the table, and be beautiful. For in America there is no need of a girl who knows how to spin and to weave. If she knows how to sew, it is well. For if he does not marry he will never make a fortune and will never have anything; he wastes his work and has nothing. And if he marries he will sooner put something aside. For he won't come back any more. In America it is so: Whoever does not intend to return to his country, it is best for him to marry young; then he will sooner have something, for a bachelor in America will never have anything, unless he is particularly self-controlled. [Greetings, wishes, etc.]

ANTONI BUTKOWSKI

SOUTH CHICAGO, April 21, 1903

Now I, Antoni, your son, my dearest parents, and my uncle and the whole family, we inform you that your son Konstanty is no longer alive. He was killed in the foundry [steel-mills]. Now I inform you, dear parents, that he was insured in an association for $1,000. His funeral will cost $300. And the rest which remains, we have the right to receive this money. So now I beg you, dear parents, send an authorization and his birth-certificate to my uncle, Piotr Z., for I am still a minor and cannot appear in an American lawsuit. When he joined his association he insured himself for $1,000 . . . . and made a will in your favor, dear parents. But you cannot get it unless you send an authorization to our uncle, for the lawsuit will be here, and it would be difficult for you to get the money [while remaining] in our country, while we shall get it soon and we will send it to you, dear parents. So now, when you receive this letter, send us the papers soon. Only don't listen to stupid people, but ask wise people. . . .

Now I inform you, dear parents, that strange people will write to you letters. Answer each letter, and answer thus, that you commit everything to Piotr Z. For they will try to deceive you, asking to send the authorization to them. But don't listen to anybody . . . only listen to me, as your son; then you will receive money paid for your son and my brother. [Repeats the advice; wishes from the whole family.]

Now I beg you, dear parents, don't grieve. For he is no more, and you won't raise him, and I cannot either. For if you had looked at him, I think your heart would have burst open with sorrow [he was so mutilated]. But in this letter I won't describe anything, how it was with him. It killed him on April 20. In the next letter I shall describe to you everything about the funeral. . . . Well, it is God's will; God has wished thus, and has done it. Only I beg you, dear parents, give for a holy mass, for the sake of his soul. And he will be buried beautifully, on April 22.

[ANTONI BUTKOWSKI]

Questions

1. What are the everyday concerns of Konstanty and his brother Antoni?
2. How does the relationship between Konstanty and his parents change over time? How do his letters show this?
3. Does the correspondence reveal more than the sociologists intended? If so, what?

19-5 I'd Do It Again (1930s)

James Michael Curley The son of Irish immigrants, James Michael Curley (1874–1958) served as the model for Boss Skeffington in Edwin O'Connor's novel *The Last Hurrah*. Curley was an unabashed Democrat and a machine politician (see text pp. 618–620). As four-time mayor of Boston, Curley depended on public works. Every new school and park benefited his

Irish Catholic working-class constituency and guaranteed its vote in the next election. And every vote for Curley infuriated Boston's Brahmins, the wealthy descendants of its seventeenth-century (Protestant) founders. As his autobiography shows, Curley was not above the grand gesture and self-promotion: they were good politics.

Source: Reprinted with the permission of Simon & Schuster from *I'd Do It Again: A Record of All My Uproarious Years* by James Michael Curley, 36, 125–127. Copyright © 1957 by Samuel Nesson, renewed 1985 by Samuel Nesson.

My father was earning less than two dollars a day in the city's paving division when he died three days after one of the other members of the construction gang challenged him to lift onto a wagon an edgestone that weighed over four hundred pounds. Father lifted it, all right, but then dropped it and collapsed, and was never to recover from the strain. Since he left no insurance money, my mother was obliged to work as a cleaning-woman, and as a scrub-woman toiling nights in office buildings downtown. I thought of her one night while leaving City Hall during my first term as Mayor. I told the scrubwomen cleaning the corridors to get up: "The only time a woman should go down on her knees is when she is praying to Almighty God," I said. Next morning I ordered long-handled mops and issued an order that scrubwomen were never again to get down on their knees in City Hall. . . .

My long-range program for civic beautification, which was to encompass my four terms as mayor, would have been effected far sooner but for the Machiavellian tactics of the very persons who had been swindling the city, while blubbering about the high cost of government.

As Al Smith used to say, let's look at the record. In 1890, the Boston tax rate was $12.60. During my first mayoralty term (1914–17) the average rate was $17.75. The increase during that administration was a mere $1.15. It was when I was out of office that the Boston tax rate shot up. Maladministration is intolerable when there are no civic improvements to show for a drained treasury.

From the moment I assumed office, my enemies campaigned against me day and night. Bankers, editors and empire-builders attacked me in language no less colorful than had been used by some of the tin-pot ward boss Achilles whom I had sent to their tents to sulk. These unfortunate persons of limited perspective changed their tune later. In 1930, John F. Fitzgerald called me "the greatest fighter known in Boston politics," and also late in 1915 he had assured everyone what a splendid gentleman I was; but only a short time before he had spoken of me as a despised enemy. One of my worst critics at this time was Robert Washburn, the most vitriolic writer on the *Boston Transcript,* that "Sturdy Old Lady of Milk Street" as she was known to her Brahmin readers. In a 1933 editorial, Washburn mentioned the changed attitude toward me:

"Some who have been the first to berate him now assert that Boston is the best governed city in the country.

They endorse him, from Alpha to Omega, without limitation of qualification." He was referring to the purified Beaconese[1] who gather at shrines like the Odd Volume Club and the Boston Athenauem. He went on to say that I had made myself "a master of literature and of diction, on whom Harvard has 'nuthin.' He has a modulation of voice unsurpassed. He can purr like a pussycat, fight like a tiger-cat. He touches his hat to some obscure and too much forgotten woman with a gallantry which would discount even the South. He dynamites an adversary so that the fragments cannot be gathered together in as few as twelve baskets."

It was an agonizing reappraisal, indeed, for the burghers of Louisburg Square[2] and their brethren and sistren, although there is still remained the incorrigible who loathed me because I did not subscribe to the doctrine, "to him that hath shall be given." One Brahmin, commenting on the legislation that succored the poor, said, "God help the rich now that Curley's Mayor. The poor, after all, can beg."

My enemies screamed that Curley was out to ruin Boston, and the *Boston Herald* and its sister sheet, the *Boston Evening Traveler,* bitterly assailed my program of reform and civic improvement, but when they saw the results, they also saw the light.

In August of 1930, I received the Mayor of Waltham, England. After listening while I read to the press a list of awards of contracts for building and road construction, he remarked:

"You are spending a lot of money on building and roads."

"I think it is better to spend public money in improvements of this kind," I answered, "than to spend it on the dole system[3] that obtains in England."

He agreed.

There was a dole system in Boston, so to speak, when I became Mayor in 1914. I took people off welfare rolls and restored their self-respect by providing them with jobs, and while reducing the ranks of the unemployed, launched

---

[1] A Beaconese is one who belongs to Beacon Hill, an elite residential area of Boston.

[2] Louisburg Square is a prestigious location in Beacon Hill.

[3] The dole system is the British system of distributing governmental relief payments.

a program of public works that had so shamefully been neglected by my predecessors in office. I extended tunnel and transit systems, expanded hospital facilities, replaced slum sections with parks and playgrounds and filled in swampy lowlands to provide beaches for the poor who had previously had little if any opportunity to enjoy bathing or swimming in the ocean, even though they lived on the Atlantic seaboard. Even a Republican legislature honored my request for funds to assist with these projects. I persuaded Boston businessmen to donate $82,000 to develop the Port of Boston. Meanwhile, I saw that there was no unnecessary hardship when the impact of World War I was felt in Boston. I arranged for food and shelter for thousands of people thrown out of work, housing them in schoolhouses and other city-owned buildings.

Boston survived the depression occasioned by that war, and even the sharpest critics will concede that before my first term as Mayor had ended, fewer persons were out of work or on welfare rolls than at any other time during the history of Boston. . . .

Questions

1. What is the political significance of symbolic gestures like issuing long-handled mops to the scrubwomen at City Hall?
2. What is Curley's alternative to welfare?
3. Curley tended to blame his failures on his Protestant critics. How might this us-versus-them stance have both helped and hurt him politically?
4. What do the careers of Curley and New York's Big Tim Sullivan (see "American Lives," text pp. 622–623) suggest about urban conditions and politics early in the twentieth century?

Questions for Further Thought

1. How did James Michael Curley (Document 19-5) help his constituents? In what ways might his style of politics have complicated their lives?
2. Josiah Strong (Document 19-3) and Frederic Howe (Document 19-1) spoke out about the need for a common or civic culture in the American city. How did the idea of the "private city" (see text pp. 612–615) frustrate such hopes?

The World of the Urban Elite and *The Urban Middle Class*

"To clear, cultivate and transform the huge uninhabited continent which is their domain, the Americans need the everyday support of an energetic passion; that passion can only be the love of wealth," Alexis de Tocqueville wrote. That same passion carried over into urban life.

The wealthy were the most obvious beneficiaries of urbanism, although daily newspapers gave millions the vicarious thrill of reading about the Astors and the Vanderbilts. Some members of the elite collected art, others collected European nobility (as in-laws), and nearly every rich person seemed to build an incredibly expensive mansion or summer home. However, not all millionaires spent their money exclusively on themselves. John Rockefeller and Andrew Carnegie, among others, took seriously the Christian obligation of stewardship. Rockefeller financed the University of Chicago, and Carnegie took a particular interest in funding public libraries.

The Industrial Revolution produced wealth for more than the fortunate few. The manufacturing economy also created a sizable, largely urban middle class (see text pp. 631–632). Its members fought to reform the cities and, when that failed, began to move to the suburbs. With husbands out of the house, middle-class housewives took charge of family and household matters (see text pp. 632–635). In the process, they grew interested in political issues and women's rights. The middle class also provided an audience for both high and popular culture.

The following selections give a sense of the emotional and intellectual ferment of American cities. Catharine Beecher (Document 19-6) offers her view on how women could create the ideal middle-class household. In Document 19-7, social critic Thorstein Veblen argues that "conspicuous consumption" by the wealthy had a definite purpose. Theodore Dreiser's *Sister Carrie* (Document 19-8) succeeds both as fiction and as social history, while Henry Adams (Document 19-9) broods over the meaning of the Machine Age.

19-6   The Christian Family (1869)

Catharine E. Beecher

Like her sister, Harriet Beecher Stowe, the author of *Uncle Tom's Cabin,* Catharine E. Beecher (1800–1878) hoped to reach a wide audience through her writings. *The American Woman's Home* was subtitled in part "a guide to the formation and maintenance of economical, healthful, beautiful and Christian homes" (see text p. 632) and was dedicated "to THE WOMEN OF AMERICA, in whose hands rest the real destinies of the republic, as moulded by the early training and preserved amid the maturer influences of home." Beecher's more famous sister was listed as a coauthor to increase the book's popularity; Catharine did most of the writing.

Source: Catharine E. Beecher, "The Christian Family," in Catharine E. Beecher and Harriet Beecher Stowe, *The American Woman's Home or, Principles of Domestic Science* (J. B. Ford, 1869; reprint, Watkins Glen, N.Y.: Library of Victorian Culture, American Life Foundation, 1979), 17–22.

It is the aim of this volume to elevate the honor and the remuneration of all employments that sustain the many difficult and varied duties of the family state, and thus to render each department of woman's profession as much desired and respected as are the most honored professions of men.

What, then, is the end designed by the family state which Jesus Christ came into this world to secure?

It is to provide for the training of our race to the highest possible intelligence, virtue, and happiness, by means of the self-sacrificing labors of the wise and good, and this with chief reference to a future immortal existence.

The distinctive feature of the family is self-sacrificing labor of the stronger and wiser members to raise the weaker and more ignorant to equal advantages. The father undergoes toil and self-denial to provide a home, and then the mother becomes a self-sacrificing laborer to train its inmates. The useless, troublesome infant is served in the humblest offices; while both parents unite in training it to an equality with themselves in every advantage. Soon the older children become helpers to raise the younger to a level with their own. When any are sick, those who are well become self-sacrificing ministers. When the parents

are old and useless, the children become their self-sacrificing servants.

Thus the discipline of the family state is one of daily self-devotion of the stronger and wiser to elevate and support the weaker members. Nothing could be more contrary to its first principles than for the older and more capable children to combine to secure to themselves the highest advantages, enforcing the drudgeries on the younger, at the sacrifice of their equal culture.

Jesus Christ came to teach the fatherhood of God and consequent brotherhood of man. He came as the "firstborn Son" of God and the Elder Brother of man, to teach by example the self-sacrifice by which the great family of man is to be raised to equality of advantages as children of God. For this end, he "humbled himself" from the highest to the lowest place. He chose for his birthplace the most despised village; for his parents the lowest in rank; for his trade, to labor with his hands as a carpenter, being "subject to his parents" thirty years. And, what is very significant, his trade was that which prepares the family home, as if he would teach that the great duty of man is labor—to provide for and train weak and ignorant creatures. Jesus Christ worked with his hands nearly thirty years, and preached less than three. And he taught that his kingdom is exactly opposite to that of the world, where all are striving for the highest positions. "Whoso will be great shall be your minister, and whoso will be chiefest shall be servant of all."

The family state then, is the aptest earthly illustration of the heavenly kingdom, and in it woman is its chief minister. Her great mission is self-denial, in training its members to self-sacrificing labors for the ignorant and weak: if not her own children, then the neglected children of her Father in heaven. She is to rear all under her care to lay up treasures, not on earth, but in heaven. All the pleasures of this life end here; but those who train immortal minds are to reap the fruit of their labor through eternal ages.

To man is appointed the out-door labor—to till the earth, dig the mines, toil in the foundries, traverse the ocean, transport merchandise, labor in manufactories, construct houses, conduct civil, municipal, and state affairs, and all the heavy work, which, most of the day, excludes him from the comforts of a home. But the great stimulus to all these toils, implanted in the heart of every true man, is the desire for a home of his own, and the hopes of paternity. Every man who truly lives for immortality responds to the beatitude, "Children are a heritage from the Lord: blessed is the man that hath his quiver full of them!" The more a father and mother live under the influence of that "immortality which Christ hath brought to light," the more is the blessedness of rearing a family understood and appreciated. Every child trained aright is to dwell forever in exalted bliss with those that gave it life and trained it for heaven.

The blessed privileges of the family state are not confined to those who rear children of their own. Any woman who can earn a livelihood, as every woman should be trained to do, can take a properly qualified female associate, and institute a family of her own, receiving to its heavenly influences the orphan, the sick, the homeless, and the sinful, and by motherly devotion train them to follow the self-denying example of Christ, in educating his earthly children for true happiness in this life and for his eternal home.

And such is the blessedness of aiding to sustain a truly Christian home, that no one comes so near the pattern of the All-perfect One as those who might hold what men call a higher place, and yet humble themselves to the lowest in order to aid in training the young, "not as men-pleasers, but as servants to Christ, with good-will doing service as to the Lord, and not to men." Such are preparing for high places in the kingdom of heaven. "Whosoever will be chiefest among you, let him be your servant."

It is often the case that the true humility of Christ is not understood. It was not in having a low opinion of his own character and claims, but it was in taking a low place in order to raise others to a higher. The worldling seeks to raise himself and family to an equality with others, or, if possible, a superiority to them. The true follower of Christ comes down in order to elevate others.

The maxims and institutions of this world have ever been antagonistic to the teachings and example of Jesus Christ. Men toil for wealth, honor, and power, not as means for raising others to an equality with themselves, but mainly for earthly, selfish advantages. Although the experience of this life shows that children brought up to labor have the fairest chance for a virtuous and prosperous life, and for hope of future eternal blessedness, yet it is the aim of most parents who can do so, to lay up wealth that their children need not labor with the hands as Christ did. And although exhorted by our Lord not to lay up treasure on earth, but rather the imperishable riches which are gained in toiling to train the ignorant and reform the sinful, as yet a large portion of the professed followers of Christ, like his first disciples, are "slow of heart to believe."

Not less have the sacred ministries of the family state been undervalued and warred upon in other directions; for example, the Romish Church has made celibacy a prime virtue, and given its highest honors to those who forsake the family state as ordained by God. Thus came great communities of monks and nuns, shut out from the love and labors of a Christian home; thus, also, came the monkish systems of education, collecting the young in great establishments away from the watch and care of parents, and the healthful and self-sacrificing labors of a home. Thus both religion and education have conspired to degrade the family state.

Still more have civil laws and social customs been opposed to the principles of Jesus Christ. It has ever been assumed that the learned, the rich, and the powerful are not to labor with the hands, as Christ did, and as Paul did when he would "not eat any man's bread for naught, but wrought with labor, not because we have not power" [to live without hand-work,] "but to make ourselves an example." (2 Thess. 3.)

Instead of this, manual labor has been made dishonorable and unrefined by being forced on the ignorant and poor. Especially has the most important of all hand-labor, that which sustains the family, been thus disgraced; so that to nurse young children, and provide the food of a family by labor, is deemed the lowest of all positions in honor and profit, and the last resort of poverty. And so our Lord, who himself took the form of a servant, teaches, "How hardly shall they that have riches enter the kingdom of heaven!" —that kingdom in which all are toiling to raise the weak, ignorant, and sinful to such equality with themselves as the children of a loving family enjoy. One mode in which riches have led to antagonism with the true end of the family state is in the style of living, by which the hand-labor, most important to health, comfort, and beauty, is confined to the most ignorant and neglected members of society, without any effort being made to raise them to equal advantages with the wise and cultivated.

And, the higher civilization has advanced, the more have children been trained to feel that to labor, as did Christ and Paul, is disgraceful, and to be made the portion of a degraded class. Children of the rich grow up with the feeling that servants are to work for them, and they themselves are not to work. To the minds of most children and servants, "to be a lady," is almost synonymous with "to be waited on, and do no work." It is the earnest desire of the authors of this volume to make plain the falsity of this growing popular feeling, and to show how much happier and more efficient family life will become when it is strengthened, sustained, and adorned by family work.

Questions

1. To what extent does Beecher offer a traditional view of women?
2. In what way does she broaden or modernize women's role in society?
3. What prejudice does she reveal?

19-7   Conspicuous Consumption (1899)

Thorstein Veblen

Thorstein Veblen (1857–1929) published *The Theory of the Leisure Class* in 1899. Veblen's thesis centered on the idea of conspicuous consumption. In his view, the purchases and interests of the wealthy were intended to demonstrate their superiority. The theory proved more popular than its author. Something of an iconoclast, Veblen failed to capitalize on the critical success of his work. He held a series of teaching jobs before his death.

Source: Thorstein Veblen, *The Theory of the Leisure Class: An Economic Study of Institutions* (1899; reprint, New York: Modern Library, 1934), 73–75, 140–143.

During the earlier stages of economic development, consumption of goods without stint, especially consumption of the better grades of goods—ideally all consumption in excess of the subsistence minimum,—pertains normally to the leisure class. This restriction tends to disappear, at least formally, after the later peaceable stage has been reached, with private ownership of goods and an industrial system based on wage labour or on the petty household economy. But during the earlier quasi-peaceable stage, when so many of the traditions through which the institution of a leisure class has affected the economic life of later times were taking form and consistency, this principle has had the force of a conventional law. It has served as the norm to which consumption has tended to conform, and any appreciable departure from it is to be regarded as an aberrant form, sure to be eliminated sooner or later in the further course of development.

The quasi-peaceable gentleman of leisure, then, not only consumes of the staff of life beyond the minimum required for subsistence and physical efficiency, but his consumption also undergoes a specialisation as regards the quality of the goods consumed. He consumes freely and of the best, in food, drink, narcotics, shelter, services, ornaments, apparel, weapons and accoutrements, amusements, amulets, and idols or divinities. In the process of gradual amelioration which takes place in the articles of his consumption, the motive principle and the proximate aim of innovation is no doubt the higher efficiency of the improved and more elaborate products for personal comfort and well-being. But that does not remain the sole purpose of their consumption. The canon of reputability is at hand and seizes upon such innovations as are, according to its standard, fit to survive. Since the consumption of these more excellent goods is an evidence of wealth, it becomes honorific; and conversely, the failure to consume in due quantity and quality becomes a mark of inferiority and demerit.

This growth of punctilious discrimination as to qualitative excellence in eating, drinking, etc., presently affects not only the manner of life, but also the training and intellectual activity of the gentleman of leisure. He is no longer simply the successful, aggressive male,—the man of strength, resource, and intrepidity. In order to avoid stultification he must also cultivate his tastes, for it now becomes incumbent on him to discriminate with some nicety between the noble and the ignoble in consumable goods. He becomes a connoisseur in creditable viands of various degrees of merit, in manly beverages and trinkets, in seemly apparel and architecture, in weapons, games, dancers, and the narcotics. This cultivation of the æsthetic faculty requires time and application, and the demands made upon the gentleman in this direction therefore tend to change his life of leisure into a more or less arduous application to the business of learning how to live a life of ostensible leisure in a becoming way. Closely related to the requirement that the gentleman must consume freely and of the right kind of goods, there is the requirement that he must know how to consume them in a seemly manner. His life of leisure must be conducted in due form. Hence arise good manners in the way pointed out in an earlier chapter. High-bred manners and ways of living are items of conformity to the norm of conspicuous leisure and conspicuous consumption.

Conspicuous consumption of valuable goods is a means of reputability to the gentleman of leisure. As wealth accumulates on his hands, his own unaided effort will not avail to sufficiently put his opulence in evidence by this method. The aid of friends and competitors is therefore brought in by resorting to the giving of valuable presents and expensive feasts and entertainments. Presents and feasts had probably another origin than that of naïve ostentation, but they acquired their utility for this purpose very early, and they have retained that character to the present; so that their utility in this respect has now long been the substantial ground on which these usages rest. Costly entertainments, such as the potlatch or the ball, are peculiarly adapted to serve this end. The competitor with whom the entertainer wishes to institute a comparison is, by this method, made to serve as a means to the end. He consumes vicariously for his host at the same time that he is a witness to the consumption of that excess of good things which his host is unable to dispose of single-handed, and he is also made to witness his host's facility in etiquette. . . .

In the case of those domestic animals which are honorific and are reputed beautiful, there is a subsidiary basis of merit that should be spoken of. Apart from the birds which belong in the honorific class of domestic animals, and which owe their place in this class to their non-lucrative character alone, the animals which merit particular attention are cats, dogs, and fast horses. The cat is less reputable than the other two just named, because she is less wasteful; she may even serve a useful end. At the same time the cat's temperament does not fit her for the honorific purpose. She lives with man on terms of equality, knows nothing of that relation of status which is the ancient basis of all distinctions of worth, honour, and repute, and she does not lend herself with facility to an invidious comparison between her owner and his neighbours. The exception to this last rule occurs in the case of such scarce and fanciful products as the Angora cat, which have some slight honorific value on the ground of expensiveness, and have, therefore, some special claim to beauty on pecuniary grounds.

The dog has advantages in the way of uselessness as well as in special gifts of temperament. He is often spoken of, in an eminent sense, as the friend of man, and his intelligence and fidelity are praised. The meaning of this is that the dog is man's servant and that he has the gift of an unquestioning subservience and a slave's quickness in guessing his master's mood. Coupled with these traits, which fit him well for the relation of status—and which must for the present purpose be set down as serviceable traits—the dog has some characteristics which are of a more equivocal æsthetic value. He is the filthiest of the domestic animals in his person and the nastiest in his habits. For this he makes up in a servile, fawning attitude towards his master, and a readiness to inflict damage and discomfort on all else. The dog, then, commends himself to our favour by affording play to our propensity for mastery, and as he is also an item of expense, and commonly serves no industrial purpose, he holds a well-assured place in men's regard as a thing of good repute. The dog is at the same time associated in our imaginations with the chase—a meritorious employment and an expression of the honourable predatory impulse.

Standing on this vantage ground, whatever beauty of form and motion and whatever commendable mental traits he may possess are conventionally acknowledged and magnified. And even those varieties of the dog which have been bred into grotesque deformity by the dog-fancier are in good faith accounted beautiful by many. These varieties of dogs—and the like is true of other fancy-bred animals—are rated and graded in æsthetic value somewhat in proportion to the degree of grotesqueness and instability of the particular fashion which the deformity takes in the given case. For the purpose in hand, this differential utility on the ground of grotesqueness and instability of structure is reducible to terms of a great scarcity and consequent expense. The commercial value of canine monstrosities, such as the prevailing styles of pet dogs both for men's and women's use, rests on their high cost of production, and their value to their owners lies chiefly in their utility as items of conspicuous consumption. Indirectly, through reflection upon their honorific expensiveness, a social worth is imputed to them; and so, by an easy substitution of words and ideas, they come to be admired and reputed beautiful. Since any attention bestowed upon these animals is in no sense gainful or useful, it is also reputable; and since the habit of giving them attention is consequently not deprecated, it may grow into an habitual attachment of great tenacity and of a most benevolent character. So that in the affection bestowed on pet animals the canon of expensiveness is present more or less remotely as a norm which guides and shapes the sentiment and the selection of its object. The like is true, as will be noticed presently, with respect to affection for persons also; although the manner in which the norm acts in that case is somewhat different.

The case of the fast horse is much like that of the dog. He is on the whole expensive, or wasteful and useless—for the industrial purpose. What productive use he may possess, in the way of enhancing the well-being of the community or making the way of life easier for men, takes the form of exhibitions of force and facility of motion that gratify the popular æsthetic sense. This is of course a substantial serviceability. The horse is not endowed with the spiritual aptitude for servile dependence in the same measure as the dog; but he ministers effectually to his master's impulse to convert the "animate" forces of the environment to his own use and discretion and so express his own dominating individuality through them. The fast horse is at least potentially a race-horse, of high or low degree; and it is as such that he is peculiarly serviceable to his owner.

The utility of the fast horse lies largely in his efficiency as a means of emulation; it gratifies the owner's sense of aggression and dominance to have his own horse outstrip his neighbour's. This use being not lucrative, but on the whole pretty consistently wasteful, and quite conspicuously so, it is honorific, and therefore gives the fast horse a strong presumptive position of reputability. Beyond this, the race horse proper has also a similarly non-industrial but honorific use as a gambling instrument. . . .

Questions

1. How does conspicuous consumption work?
2. Where do dogs and racehorses fit into Veblen's thesis?
3. Was Veblen's theory applicable only to the rich in the nineteenth century?

19-8   Sister Carrie (1900)

Theodore Dreiser

In 1900, Theodore Dreiser (1871–1945) published *Sister Carrie,* the story of a small-town Wisconsin girl. Carrie Meeber leaves Columbia City for a factory job in Chicago. She hates the work and eventually becomes a successful (though unhappy) actress in New York. This story of an independent woman—and one who lived out of wedlock with men—shocked its turn-of-the-century audience. Worried that the public would reject such a non-Victorian work, the publisher printed only a thousand copies of *Sister Carrie* and virtually ignored it. The book finally received greater acceptance when it was reissued in 1912.

Source: Theodore Dreiser, *Sister Carrie* (New York: Doubleday, Page, 1900; reprint, New York: Bantam Books, 1958), 28–33.

It was with weak knees and a slight catch in her breathing that she came up to the great shoe company at Adams and Fifth Avenue and entered the elevator. When she stepped out on the fourth floor there was no one at hand, only great aisles of boxes piled to the ceiling. She stood, very much frightened, awaiting some one.

Presently Mr. Brown came up. He did not seem to recognise her.

"What is it you want?" he inquired.

Carrie's heart sank.

"You said I should come this morning to see about work—"

"Oh," he interrupted. "Um—yes. What is your name?"

"Carrie Meeber."

"Yes," said he. "You come with me."

He led the way through dark, box-lined aisles which had the smell of new shoes, until they came to an iron door which opened into the factory proper. There was a large, low-ceiled room, with clacking, rattling machines at which men in white shirt sleeves and blue gingham aprons were working. She followed him diffidently through the clattering automatons, keeping her eyes straight before her, and flushing slightly. They crossed to a far corner and took an elevator to the sixth floor. Out of the array of machines and benches, Mr. Brown signalled a foreman.

"This is the girl," he said, and turning to Carrie[,] "You go with him." He then returned, and Carrie followed her new superior to a little desk in a corner, which he used as a kind of official centre.

"You've never worked at anything like this before, have you?" he questioned, rather sternly.

"No, sir," she answered.

He seemed rather annoyed at having to bother with such help, but put down her name and then led her across to where a line of girls occupied stools in front of clacking machines. On the shoulder of one of the girls who was punching eye-holes in one piece of the upper, by the aid of the machine, he put his hand.

"You," he said, "show this girl how to do what you're doing. When you get through, come to me."

The girl so addressed rose promptly and gave Carrie her place.

"It isn't hard to do," she said, bending over. "You just take this so, fasten it with this clamp, and start the machine."

She suited action to word, fastened the piece of leather, which was eventually to form the right half of the upper of a man's shoe, by little adjustable clamps, and pushed a small steel rod at the side of the machine. The latter jumped to the task of punching, with sharp, snapping clicks, cutting circular bits of leather out of the side of the upper, leaving the holes which were to hold the laces. After observing a few times, the girl let her work at it alone. Seeing that it was fairly well done, she went away.

The pieces of leather came from the girl at the machine to her right, and were passed to the girl at her left. Carrie saw at once that an average speed was necessary or the work would pile up on her and all those below would be delayed. She had no time to look about, and bent anxiously to her task. The girls at her left and right realised her predicament and feelings, and, in a way, tried to aid her, as much as they dared, by working slower.

At this task she laboured incessantly for some time, finding relief from her own nervous fears and imaginings in the humdrum, mechanical movement of the machine. She felt, as the minutes passed, that the room was not very light. It had a thick odour of fresh leather, but that did not worry her. She felt the eyes of the other help upon her, and troubled lest she was not working fast enough.

Once, when she was fumbling at the little clamp, having made a slight error in setting in the leather, a great hand appeared before her eyes and fastened the clamp for her. It was the foreman. Her heart thumped so that she could scarcely see to go on.

"Start your machine," he said, "start your machine. Don't keep the line waiting."

This recovered her sufficiently and she went excitedly on, hardly breathing until the shadow moved away from behind her. Then she heaved a great breath.

As the morning wore on the room became hotter. She felt the need of a breath of fresh air and a drink of water but did not venture to stir. The stool she sat on was without a back or foot-rest, and she began to feel uncomfortable. She found, after a time, that her back was beginning to ache. She twisted and turned from one position to another slightly different, but it did not ease her for long. She was beginning to weary.

"Stand up, why don't you?" said the girl at her right, without any form of introduction. "They won't care."

Carrie looked at her gratefully. "I guess I will," she said.

She stood up from her stool and worked that way for a while, but it was a more difficult position. Her neck and shoulders ached in bending over.

The spirit of the place impressed itself on her in a rough way. She did not venture to look around, but above the clack of the machine she could hear an occasional remark. She could also note a thing or two out of the side of her eye.

"Did you see Harry last night?" said the girl at her left, addressing her neighbour.

"No."

"You ought to have seen the tie he had on. Gee, but he was a mark."

"S-s-t," said the other girl, bending over her work. The first, silenced, instantly assumed a solemn face. The foreman passed slowly along, eyeing each worker distinctly. The moment he was gone, the conversation was resumed again.

"Say," began the girl at her left, "what jeh think he said?"

"I don't know."

"He said he saw us with Eddie Harris at Martin's last night."

"No!" They both giggled.

A youth with tan-coloured hair, that needed clipping very badly, came shuffling along between the machines, bearing a basket of leather findings under his left arm, and pressed against his stomach. When near Carrie, he stretched out his right hand and gripped one girl under the arm.

"Aw, let me go," she exclaimed angrily. "Duffer."

He only grinned broadly in return.

"Rubber!" he called back as she looked after him. There was nothing of the gallant in him.

Carrie at last could scarcely sit still. Her legs began to tire and she wanted to get up and stretch. Would noon never come? It seemed as if she had worked an entire day. She was not hungry at all, but weak, and her eyes were tired, straining at the one point where the eye-punch came down. The girl at the right noticed her squirmings and felt sorry for her. She was concentrating herself too thoroughly—what she did really required less mental and physical strain. There was nothing to be done, however. The halves of the uppers came piling steadily down. Her hands began to ache at the wrists and then in the fingers, and towards the last she seemed one mass of dull, complaining muscles, fixed in an eternal position and performing a single mechanical movement which became more and more distasteful, until at last it was absolutely nauseating. When she was wondering whether the strain would ever cease, a dull-sounding bell clanged somewhere down an elevator shaft, and the end came. In an instant there was a buzz of action and conversation. All the girls instantly left their stools and hurried away; in an adjoining room, men passed through, coming from some department which opened on the right. The whirling wheels began to sing in a steadily modifying key, until at last they died away in a low buzz. There was an audible stillness, in which the common voice sounded strange.

Carrie got up and sought her lunch box. She was stiff, a little dizzy, and very thirsty. On the way to the small space portioned off by wood, where all the wraps and lunches were kept, she encountered the foreman, who stared at her hard.

"Well," he said, "did you get along all right?"

"I think so," she replied, very respectfully.

"Um," he replied, for want of something better, and walked on.

Under better material conditions, this kind of work would not have been so bad, but the new socialism which involves pleasant working conditions for employees had not then taken hold upon manufacturing companies.

The place smelled of the oil of the machines and the new leather—a combination which, added to the stale odours of the building, was not pleasant even in cold weather. The floor, though regularly swept every evening, presented a littered surface. Not the slightest provision had been made for the comfort of the employees, the idea being that something was gained by giving them as little and making the work as hard and unremunerative as possible. What we know of foot-rests, swivel-back chairs, dining-rooms for the girls, clean aprons and curling irons supplied free, and a decent cloak room, were unthought of. The washrooms were disagreeable, crude, if not foul places, and the whole atmosphere was sordid.

Carrie looked about her, after she had drunk a tinful of water from a bucket in one corner, for a place to sit and eat. The other girls had ranged themselves about the windows or the work-benches of those of the men who had gone out. She saw no place which did not hold a couple or a group of girls, and being too timid to think of introducing herself, she sought out her machine and, seated upon her stool, opened her lunch on her lap. There she sat listening to the chatter and comment about her. It was, for the most part, silly and graced by the current slang. Several of the men in the room exchanged compliments with the girls at long range.

"Say, Kitty," called one to a girl who was doing a waltz step in a few feet of space near one of the windows, "are you going to the ball with me?"

"Look out, Kitty," called another, "you'll jar your back hair."

"Go on, Rubber," was her only comment.

As Carrie listened to this and much more of similar familiar badinage among the men and girls, she instinctively withdrew into herself. She was not used to this type, and felt that there was something hard and low about it all. She feared that the young boys about would address such remarks to her—boys who . . . seemed uncouth and ridiculous. She made the average feminine distinction between clothes, putting worth, goodness, and distinction in a dress

suit, and leaving all the unlovely qualities and those beneath notice in overalls and jumper.

She was glad when the short half hour was over and the wheels began to whirr again. Though wearied, she would be inconspicuous. This illusion ended when another young man passed along the aisle and poked her indifferently in the ribs with his thumb. She turned about, indignation leaping to her eyes, but he had gone on and only once turned to grin. She found it difficult to conquer an inclination to cry.

The girl next to her noticed her state of mind. "Don't you mind," she said. "He's too fresh."

Carrie said nothing, but bent over her work. She felt as though she could hardly endure such a life. Her idea of work had been so entirely different. All during the long afternoon she thought of the city outside and its imposing show, crowds, and fine buildings. Columbia City and the better side of her home life came back. By three o'clock she was sure it must be six, and by four it seemed as if they had forgotten to note the hour and were letting all work overtime. The foreman became a true ogre, prowling constantly about, keeping her tied down to her miserable task. What she heard of the conversation about her only made her feel sure that she did not want to make friends with any of these. When six o'clock came she hurried eagerly away, her arms aching and her limbs stiff from sitting in one position.

As she passed out along the hall after getting her hat, a young machine hand, attracted by her looks, made bold to jest with her.

"Say, Maggie," he called, "if you wait, I'll walk with you."

It was thrown so straight in her direction that she knew who was meant, but never turned to look.

In the crowded elevator, another dusty, toil-stained youth tried to make an impression on her by leering in her face.

One young man, waiting on the walk outside for the appearance of another, grinned at her as she passed.

"Ain't going my way, are you?" he called jocosely.

Carrie turned her face to the west with a subdued heart. As she turned the corner, she saw through the great shiny window the small desk at which she had applied. There were the crowds, hurrying with the same buzz and energy-yielding enthusiasm. She felt a slight relief, but it was only at her escape. She felt ashamed in the face of better dressed girls who went by. She felt as though she should be better served, and her heart revolted.

Questions

1. According to Dreiser, why did so many women work in such difficult conditions?
2. What does the banter between workers accomplish?
3. How does *Sister Carrie* succeed as social history in ways that a factory-inspection report from that era could not?

19-9 The Columbian Exposition of 1893

Henry Adams

Henry Adams (1838–1918) could be forgiven for his air of self-importance. He was, after all, the great-grandson and grandson of presidents. A historian and social critic, Adams dissented from the popular view that progress and the Industrial Age were one. In this passage from his autobiography, *The Education of Henry Adams* (1918), Adams relates his experience with modern technology at the Columbian Exposition of 1893. (Like the rest of the book, this passage was written in the third person.)

Source: Henry Adams, *The Education of Henry Adams* (Boston: Massachusetts Historical Society, 1918; reprint, New York: Modern Library, 1931), 340–343.

The first astonishment became greater every day. That the Exposition should be a natural growth and product of the Northwest offered a step in evolution to startle Darwin; but that it should be anything else seemed an idea more startling still; and even granting it were not—admitting it to be a sort of industrial, speculative growth and product of the Beaux Arts artistically induced to pass the summer on the shore of Lake Michigan—could it be made to seem at home there? Was the American made to seem at home in it? Honestly, he had the air of enjoying it as though it were all his own; he felt it was good; he was proud of it; for the most part, he acted as though he had passed his life in landscape gardening and architectural decoration. If he had not done it himself, he had known how to get it done to suit him, as he knew how to get his wives and daughters dressed at Worth's or Paquin's [designers of the finest women's clothes]. Perhaps he could not do it again; the next time he would want to do it himself and would show his own faults; but for the moment he seemed to have leaped directly from Corinth and Syracuse and Venice, over the heads of London and New York, to impose classical standards on plastic Chicago. Critics had no trouble in criticising the classicism, but all trading cities had always shown traders' taste, and, to the stern purist of religious faith, no art was thinner than Venetian Gothic. All trader's taste smelt of bric-à-brac; Chicago tried at least to give her taste a look of unity.

One sat down to ponder on the steps beneath Richard Hunt's dome almost as deeply as on the steps of Ara Cœli, and much to the same purpose. Here was a breach of continuity—a rupture in historical sequence! Was it real, or only apparent? One's personal universe hung on the answer, for, if the rupture was real and the new American world could take this sharp and conscious twist towards ideals, one's personal friends would come in, at last, as winners in the great American chariot-race for fame. If the people of the Northwest actually knew what was good when they saw it, they would some day talk about Hunt and Richardson [architects], La Farge and St. Gaudens [sculptors], Burnham and McKim, and Stanford White [architects] when their politicians and millionaires were otherwise forgotten. The artists and architects who had done the work offered little encouragement to hope it; they talked freely enough, but not in terms that one cared to quote; and to them the Northwest refused to look artistic. They talked as though they worked only for themselves; as though art, to the Western people, was a stage decoration; a diamond shirt-stud; a paper collar; but possibly the architects of Pæstum and Girgenti [ancient Italian cities] had talked in the same way, and the Greek had said the same thing of Semitic Carthage two thousand years ago.

Jostled by these hopes and doubts, one turned to the exhibits for help, and found it. The industrial schools tried to teach so much and so quickly that the instruction ran to waste. Some millions of other people felt the same helplessness, but few of them were seeking education, and to them helplessness seemed natural and normal, for they had grown up in the habit of thinking a steam-engine or a dynamo as natural as the sun, and expected to understand one as little as the other. For the historian alone the Exposition made a serious effort. Historical exhibits were common, but they never went far enough; none were thoroughly worked out. One of the best was that of the Cunard steamers, but still a student hungry for results found himself obliged to waste a pencil and several sheets of paper trying to calculate exactly when, according to the given increase of power, tonnage, and speed, the growth of the ocean steamer would reach its limits. His figures brought him, he thought, to the year 1927; another generation to spare before force, space, and time should meet. The ocean steamer ran the surest line of triangulation into the future, because it was the nearest of man's products to a unity; railroads taught less because they seemed already finished except for mere increase in number; explosives taught most, but needed a tribe of chemists, physicists, and mathematicians to explain; the dynamo taught least because it had barely reached infancy, and, if its progress was to be constant at the rate of the last ten years, it would result in infinite costly energy within a generation. One lingered long among the dynamos, for they were new, and they gave to history a new phase. Men of science could never understand the ignorance and naïveté of the historian, who, when he came suddenly on a new power, asked naturally what it was; did it pull or did it push? Was it a screw or thrust? Did it flow or vibrate? Was it a wire or a mathematical line? And a score of such questions to which he expected answers and was astonished to get none.

Education ran riot at Chicago, at least for retarded minds which had never faced in concrete form so many matters of which they were ignorant. Men who knew nothing whatever—who had never run a steam-engine, the simplest of forces—who had never put their hands on a lever—had never touched an electric battery—never talked through a telephone, and had not the shadow of a notion what amount of force was meant by a *watt* or an *ampère* or an *erg,* or any other term of measurement introduced within a hundred years—had no choice but to sit down on the steps and brood as they had never brooded on the benches of Harvard College, either as student or professor, aghast at what they had said and done in all these years, and still more ashamed of the childlike ignorance and babbling futility of the society that let them say and do it. The historical mind can think only in historical processes, and probably this was the first time since historians existed, that any of them had sat down helpless before a mechanical sequence. Before a metaphysical or a theological or a political sequence, most historians had felt helpless, but the single clue to which they had hitherto trusted was the unity of natural force.

Did he himself quite know what he meant? Certainly not! If he had known enough to state his problem, his education would have been complete at once. Chicago asked in 1893 for the first time the question whether the American people knew where they were driving. Adams answered, for one, that he did not know, but would try to find out. On reflecting sufficiently deeply, under the shadow of Richard Hunt's architecture, he decided that the American people probably knew no more than he did; but that they might still be driving or drifting unconsciously to some point in thought, as their solar system was said to be drifting towards some point in space; and that, possibly, if relations enough could be observed, this point might be fixed. Chicago was the first expression of American thought as a unity; one must start there. . . .

Questions

1. Why did the fair's architecture confuse Adams?
2. In what ways did the technology on display overwhelm him?
3. Have subsequent generations experienced this kind of unsettling encounter with modernity? Explain.

Questions for Further Thought

1. Compare the ways in which Catharine Beecher (Document 19-6) and Theodore Dreiser (Document 19-8) portray American women. Is one portrait more realistic than the other? Why or why not?
2. Thorstein Veblen (Document 19-7) thought he could expose the vanity and purposeful extravagance of the rich. The term *conspicuous consumption* has become part of our vocabulary, but our fascination with the rich and famous has not abated. Why?

3. Which is a more important gauge of American society in 1900, that Theodore Dreiser could publish *Sister Carrie* (Document 19-8) or that his publisher abandoned the novel in fear of protests? Why?

4. Henry Adams (Document 19-9) wanted to find out "whether the American people knew where they were driving." Where has technology taken us in the last century?

CHAPTER 20

The Progressive Era

★   ★   ★

The Intellectual Roots of Progressivism

The Progressive period was marked by diverse, indeed sometimes contradictory, reform impulses. It should come as no surprise, then, that the period's reformers and reform movements were influenced by differing figures and ideas. Among the influences of the period were Henry George, who had sought to explain the paradox of *Poverty and Progress,* and his Single Tax movement; Thorstein Veblen, who sought to explain economic behavior in terms different from those of classical economists; Eugene V. Debs, who gave voice to American radicalism through the Socialist Party; and, in a very different vein, Frederick W. Taylor, who practiced and preached the promise of Scientific Management (see text, chaps. 17 and 19, and pp. 640–642; also Documents 17-1, 17-5, and 17-7, and 19-7). All of these figures except George were active during the Progressive Era; Debs and Veblen lived beyond it.

Among those central to Progressive Era thought were three men who were at one and the same time tough-minded and idealistic: Walter Lippmann, who expressed progressivism's confidence in his aptly titled *Drift and Mastery* (Document 20-1); Walter Rauschenbusch, who had ministered in a New York City slum neighborhood and who preached the Social Gospel (Document 20-2); and Supreme Court Justice Oliver Wendell Holmes Jr., who challenged orthodox economic and legal thinking (Document 20-3).

20-1   Drift and Mastery (1914)

Walter Lippmann

Walter Lippmann's career spanned much of the twentieth century, from the Progressive Era to the Great Society of the 1960s. Both a gifted critic and a journalist, Lippmann (1889–1974) was fascinated by the workings of American society. In the introduction to *Drift and Mastery* (1914), Lippmann discusses how the success of American democracy led to a new set of problems.

Source: Walter Lippmann, *Drift and Mastery: An Attempt to Diagnose the Current Unrest* (Mitchell Kennerley, 1914; reprint, Madison: University of Wisconsin Press, 1985), 15–19.

In the early months of 1914 widespread unemployment gave the anarchists in New York City an unusual opportunity for agitation. The newspapers and the police became hysterical, men were clubbed and arrested on the slightest provocation, meetings were dispersed. The issue was shifted, of course, from unemployment to the elementary rights of free speech and assemblage. Then suddenly, the city administration, acting through a new police commissioner, took the matter in hand, suppressed official lawlessness, and guaranteed the men who were conducting the agitation their full rights. This had a most disconcerting effect on the anarchists. They were suddenly stripped of all the dramatic effect that belongs to a clash with the police. They had to go back to the real issue of unemployment, and give some message to the men who had been following them. But they had no message to give: they knew what they were against but not what they were for, and their intellectual situation was as uncomfortable as one of those bad dreams in which you find yourself half-clothed in a public place.

Without a tyrant to attack an immature democracy is always somewhat bewildered. Yet we have to face the fact in America that what thwarts the growth of our civilization is not the uncanny, malicious contrivance of the plutocracy, but the faltering method, the distracted soul, and the murky vision of what we call grandiloquently the will of the people. If we flounder, it is not because the old order is strong, but because the new one is weak. Democracy is more than the absence of czars, more than freedom, more than equal opportunity. It is a way of life, a use of freedom, an embrace of opportunity. For republics do not come in when kings go out, the defeat of a propertied class is not followed by a coöperative commonwealth, the emancipation of woman is more than a struggle for rights. A servile community will have a master, if not a monarch, then a landlord or a boss, and no legal device will save it. A nation of uncritical drifters can change only the form of tyranny, for like Christian's sword, democracy is a weapon in the hands of those who have the courage and the skill to wield it; in all others it is a rusty piece of junk.

The issues that we face are very different from those of the last century and a half. The difference, I think, might be summed up roughly this way: those who went before inherited a conservatism and overthrew it; we inherit freedom, and have to use it. The sanctity of property, the patriarchal family, hereditary caste, the dogma of sin, obedience to authority,—the rock of ages, in brief, has been blasted for us. Those who are young to-day are born into a world

in which the foundations of the older order survive only as habits or by default. So Americans can carry through their purposes when they have them. If the standpatter is still powerful amongst us it is because we have not learned to use our power, and direct it to fruitful ends. The American conservative, it seems to me, fills the vacuum where democratic purpose should be.

So far as we are concerned, then, the case is made against absolutism, commercial oligarchy, and unquestioned creeds. *The rebel program is stated.* Scientific invention and blind social currents have made the old authority impossible in fact, the artillery fire of the iconoclasts has shattered its prestige. We inherit a rebel tradition. The dominant forces in our world are not the sacredness of property, nor the intellectual leadership of the priest; they are not the divinity of the constitution, the glory of industrial push, Victorian sentiment, New England respectability, the Republican Party, or John D. Rockefeller. Our time, of course, believes in change. The adjective "progressive" is what we like, and the word "new," be it the New Nationalism of Roosevelt, the New Freedom of Wilson, or the New Socialism of the syndicalists. The conservatives are more lonely than the pioneers, for almost any prophet to-day can have disciples. The leading thought of our world has ceased to regard commercialism either as permanent or desirable, and the only real question among intelligent people is how business methods are to be altered, not whether they are to be altered. For no one, unafflicted with invincible ignorance, desires to preserve our economic system in its existing form.

The business man has stepped down from his shrine; he is no longer an oracle whose opinion on religion, science, and education is listened to dumbly as the valuable by-product of a paying business. We have scotched the romance of success. In the emerging morality the husband is not regarded as the proprietor of his wife, nor the parents as autocrats over the children. We are met by women who are "emancipated"; for what we hardly know. We are not stifled by a classical tradition in art: in fact artists to-day are somewhat stunned by the rarefied atmosphere of their freedom. There is a wide agreement among thinking people that the body is not a filthy thing, and that to implant in a child the sense of sin is a poor preparation for a temperate life.

The battle for us, in short, does not lie against crusted prejudice, but against the chaos of a new freedom.

This chaos is our real problem. So if the younger critics are to meet the issues of their generation they must give their attention, not so much to the evils of authority, as to the weaknesses of democracy. But how is a man to go about doing such a task? He faces an enormously complicated world, full of stirring and confusion and ferment. He hears of movements and agitations, criticisms and reforms, knows people who are devoted to "causes," feels angry or hopeful at different times, goes to meetings, reads radical books, and accumulates a sense of uneasiness and pending change.

He can't, however, live with any meaning unless he formulates for himself a vision of what is to come out of the unrest. I have tried in this book to sketch such a vision for myself. At first thought it must seem an absurdly presumptuous task. But it is a task that everyone has to attempt if he is to take part in the work of his time. For in so far as we can direct the future at all, we shall do it by laying what we see against what other people see.

This doesn't mean the constructing of utopias. The kind of vision which will be fruitful to democratic life is one that is made out of latent promise in the actual world. There is a future contained in the trust and the union, the new status of women, and the moral texture of democracy. It is a future that can in a measure be foreseen and bent somewhat nearer to our hopes. A knowledge of it gives a sanction to our efforts, a part in a larger career, and an invaluable sense of our direction. We make our vision, and hold it ready for any amendment that experience suggests. It is not a fixed picture, a row of shiny ideals which we can exhibit to mankind, and say: Achieve these or be damned. All we can do is to search the world as we find it, extricate the forces that seem to move it, and surround them with criticism and suggestion. Such a vision will inevitably reveal the bias of its author; that is to say it will be a human hypothesis, not an oracular revelation. But if the hypothesis is honest and alive it should cast a little light upon our chaos. It should help us to cease revolving in the mere routine of the present or floating in a private utopia. For a vision of latent hope would be woven of vigorous strands; it would be concentrated on the crucial points of contemporary life, on that living zone where the present is passing into the future. It is the region where thought and action count. Too far ahead there is nothing but your dream; just behind, there is nothing but your memory. But in the unfolding present, man can be creative if his vision is gathered from the promise of actual things.

The day is past, I believe, when anybody can pretend to have laid down an inclusive or a final analysis of the de-

mocratic problem. Everyone is compelled to omit infinitely more than he can deal with; everyone is compelled to meet the fact that a democratic vision must be made by the progressive collaboration of many people. Thus I have touched upon the industrial problem at certain points that seem to me of outstanding importance, but there are vast sections and phases of industrial enterprise that pass unnoticed. The points I have raised are big in the world I happen to live in, but obviously they are not the whole world.

It is necessary, also, to inquire how "practical" you can be in a book of generalizations. That amounts to asking how detailed you can be. Well, it is impossible when you mention a minimum wage law, for example, to append a draft of the bill and a concrete set of rules for its administration. In human problems especially there is a vagueness which no one can escape entirely. Even the most voluminous study in three volumes of some legal question does not meet at every point the actual difficulties of the lawyer in a particular case. But it can be useful if it is made with a sense of responsibility to action. I have tried, therefore, to avoid gratuitously fine sentiments; I have tried to suggest nothing that with the information at my command doesn't seem at least probable.

This book, then, is an attempt to diagnose the current unrest and to arrive at some sense of what democracy implies. It begins with the obvious drift of our time and gropes for the conditions of mastery. I have tried in the essays that follow to enter the American problem at a few significant points in order to trace a little of the immense suggestion that radiates from them. I hope the book will leave the reader, as it does me, with a sense of the varied talents and opportunities, powers and organizations that may contribute to a conscious revolution. I have not been able to convince myself that one policy, one party, one class, or one set of tactics, is as fertile as human need.

It would be very easy if such a belief were possible. It would save time and energy and no end of grubbing: just to keep on repeating what you've learnt, eloquent, supremely confident, with the issues clean, a good fight and an inevitable triumph: Marx, or Lincoln, or Jefferson with you always as guide, counsellor and friend. All the thinking done by troubled dead men for the cocksure living; no class to consider but your own; no work that counts but yours; every party but your party composed of fools and rascals; only a formula to accept and a specific fight to win,—it would be easy. It might work on the moon.

Questions

1. What does Lippmann think is threatening American civilization?
2. How does he distinguish between his proposals and a utopia?
3. Why does Lippmann not offer a single comprehensive answer to the social conditions he has studied?

20-2   The Church and the Social Movement (1907)

Walter Rauschenbusch   While serving as the pastor of a Baptist church in New York's Hell's Kitchen, Walter Rauschenbusch learned firsthand that the poor could not be satisfied merely by exhortations to faith. Rauschenbusch set out to apply the teachings of the Gospels to contemporary urban life. His writings on the Social Gospel, like the following selection from *Christianity and the Social Crisis* (1907), were those of a Christian socialist.

Source: Walter Rauschenbusch, *Christianity and the Social Crisis* (New York: Macmillan, 1907), 304–305, 328–331. Courtesy of Carl Rauschenbusch, age ninety-five (Walter's last surviving child).

Other organizations may conceivably be indifferent when confronted with the chronic or acute poverty of our cities. The Christian Church cannot. The very name of "Christian" would turn into an indictment if it did not concern itself in the situation in some way.

One answer to the challenge of the Christian spirit has been the organization of institutional church work. A church perhaps organizes a day-nursery or kindergarten; a playground for the children; a meeting-place for young people, or educational facilities for those who are ambitious. It tries to do for people who are living under abnormal conditions what these people under normal conditions ought to do for themselves. This saving helpfulness toward the poor must be distinguished sharply from the money-making efforts of some churches called institutional, which simply run a continuous sacred variety performance.

Confront the Church of Christ with a homeless, play-less, joyless, proletarian population, and that is the kind of work to which some Christian spirits will inevitably feel impelled. All honor to me! But it puts a terrible burden on the Church. Institutional work is hard work and costly work. It requires a large plant and an expensive staff. It puts such a strain on the organizing ability and the sympathies of the workers that few can stand it long. The Church by the voluntary gifts and labors of a few here tries to furnish what the entire coöperative community ought to furnish.

Few churches have the resources and leadership to undertake institutional work on a large scale, but most churches in large cities have some institutional features, and all pastors who are at all willing to do it, have institutional work thrust on them. They have to care for the poor. Those of us who passed through the last great industrial depression will never forget the procession of men out of work, out of clothes, out of shoes, and out of hope. They wore down our threshold, and they wore away our hearts. This is the stake of the churches in modern poverty. They are buried at times under a stream of human wreckage. They are turned aside constantly from their more spiritual functions to "serve tables." They have a right, therefore, to inquire who is unloading this burden of poverty and suffering upon them by underpaying, exhausting, and maiming the people. The good Samaritan did not go after the robbers with a shot-gun, but looked after the wounded and helpless man by the wayside. But if hundreds of good Samaritans travelling the same road should find thousands of bruised men groaning to them, they would not be such very good Samaritans if they did not organize a vigilance committee to stop the manufacturing of wounded men. If they did not, presumably the asses who had to lug the wounded to the tavern would have the wisdom to inquire into the causes of their extra work. . . .

In its struggle the working class becomes keenly conscious of the obstacles put in its way by the great institutions of society, the courts, the press, or the Church. It demands not only impartiality, but the kind of sympathy which will condone its mistakes and discern the justice of its cause in spite of the excesses of its followers. When our sympathies are enlisted, we develop a vast faculty for making excuses. If two dogs fight, our own dog is rarely the aggressor. Stealing peaches is a boyish prank when our boy does it, but petty larceny when that dratted boy of our neighbor does it. If the other political party grafts, it is a flagrant shame; if our own party does it, we regret it politely or deny the fact. If Germany annexes a part of Africa, it is brutal aggression; if England does it, she "fulfils her mission of civilization." If the business interests exclude the competition of foreign merchants by a protective tariff, it is a grand national policy; if the trades-unions try to exclude the competition of non-union labor, it is a denial of the right to work and an outrage.

The working class likes to get that kind of sympathy which will take a favorable view of its efforts and its mistakes, and a comprehension of the wrongs under which it suffers. Instead of that the pulpit of late has given its most vigorous interest to the wrongs of those whom militant labor regards as traitors to its cause. It has been more concerned with the fact that some individuals were barred from a job by the unions, than with the fact that the entire wage-working class is debarred from the land, from the tools of production, and from their fair share in the proceeds of production.

It cannot well be denied that there is an increasing alienation between the working class and the churches. That alienation is most complete wherever our industrial development has advanced farthest and has created a distinct class of wage-workers. Several causes have contributed. Many have dropped away because they cannot afford to take their share in the expensive maintenance of a church in a large city. Others because the tone, the spirit, the point of view in the churches, is that of another social class. The commercial and professional classes dominate the spiritual atmosphere in the large city churches. As the workingmen grow more class-conscious, they come to regard the business men as their antagonists and the possessing classes as exploiters who live on their labor, and they resent it when persons belonging to these classes address them with the tone of moral superiority. When ministers handle the labor question, they often seem to the working class partial against them even when the ministers think they are most impartial. Foreign workingmen bring with them the long-standing distrust for the clergy and the Church as tools of oppression which they have learned abroad, and they perpetuate that attitude here. The churches of America suffer for the sins of the churches abroad. The "scientific socialism" imported from older countries through its literature and its advocates is saturated with materialistic philosophy and is apt to create dislike and antagonism for the ideas and institutions of religion.

Thus in spite of the favorable equipment of the Church in America there is imminent danger that the working people will pass from indifference to hostility, from religious enthusiasm to anti-religious bitterness. That would be one of the most unspeakable calamities that could come upon the Church. If we would only take warning by the fate of the churches in Europe, we might avert the desolation that threatens us. We may well be glad that in nearly every city there are a few ministers who are known as the outspoken friends of labor. Their fellow-ministers may regard them as radicals, lacking in balance, and very likely they are; but in the present situation they are among the most valuable servants of the Church. The workingmen see that there is at least a minority in the Church that champions their cause, and that fact helps to keep their judgment in hopeful suspense about the Church at large. Men who are just as one-sided in favor of capitalism pass as sane and conservative men. If the capitalist class have their court-chaplains, it is only fair that the army of labor should have its army-chaplains who administer the consolations of religion to militant labor.

Thus the Church has a tremendous stake in the social crisis. It may try to maintain an attitude of neutrality, but neither side will permit it. If it is quiescent, it thereby throws its influence on the side of things as they are, and the class which aspires to a fitter place in the organization of society will feel the great spiritual force of the Church as a dead weight against it. If it loses the loyalty and trust of the working class, it loses the very class in which it originated, to which its founders belonged, and which has lifted it to power. If it becomes a religion of the upper classes, it condemns itself to a slow and comfortable death. Protestantism from the outset entered into an intimate alliance with the intelligence and wealth of the city population. As the cities grew in importance since the Reformation, as commerce overshadowed agriculture, and as the business class crowded the feudal aristocracy out of its leading position since the French Revolution, Protestantism throve with the class which had espoused it. It lifted its class, and its class lifted it. . . .

Questions

1. In Rauschenbusch's opinion, why are churches supposed to help the poor?
2. What consequences does Rauschenbusch fear if churches fail to act?
3. Would (and should) the First Amendment interfere with Rauschenbusch's call for an activist faith? Why or why not?
4. How do the religious faith of the Butkowski family (see Document 19-4) and that of Rauschenbusch differ?

20-3 Dissenting Opinion, *Lochner v. New York* (1905)

Oliver Wendell Holmes Jr.   Before serving on the U.S. Supreme Court (1902–1932), Oliver Wendell Holmes Jr. (1841–1935), thrice wounded in the Civil War and a graduate of Harvard's college and law school, had written a legal classic, *The Common Law*, and had sat on the Supreme Judicial Court of Massachusetts for twenty years.

Although the Supreme Court had earlier upheld another state's law limiting miners and smelter workers to an eight-hour workday, in *Lochner* a 5-4 majority held that the state's police powers did not include limiting bakers' right to contract for a ten-hour, six-day workweek (see text pp. 640–641).

Herbert Spencer (1820–1903), of whom Holmes writes, was the most famous British social Darwinist. *Social Statics* (1851) was his first major work. Spencer introduced the phrase "survival of the fittest" (see text pp. 579, 640).

Source: Lochner v. New York, 198 U.S. 45 (1905), excerpted in Donald O. Dewey, ed., Union and Liberty: A Documentary History of American Constitutionalism (New York: McGraw-Hill, 1969), 185.

This case is decided upon an economic theory which a large part of the country does not entertain. If it were a question whether I agreed with that theory, I should desire to study it further and long before making up my mind. But I do not conceive that to be my duty, because I strongly believe that my agreement or disagreement has nothing to do with the right of a majority to embody their opinions in law. It is settled by various decisions of this court that state constitutions and state laws may regulate life in many ways which we as legislators might think as injudicious or if you like as tyrannical as this, and which equally with this interfere with the liberty to contract. The Fourteenth Amendment does not enact Mr. Herbert Spencer's Social Statics. . . . But a constitution is not intended to embody a particular economic theory, whether of paternalism and the organic relation of the citizen to the State or of *laissez faire*. It is made for people of fundamentally differing views, and the accident of our finding certain opinions nat-ural and familiar or novel and even shocking ought not to conclude our judgment upon the question whether statutes embodying them conflict with the Constitution of the United States.

. . . I think that the word liberty in the Fourteenth Amendment is perverted when it is held to prevent the natural outcome of a dominant opinion, unless it can be said that a rational and fair man necessarily would admit that the statute proposed would infringe fundamental principles as they have been understood by the traditions of our people and our law. It does not need research to show that no such sweeping condemnation can be passed upon the statute before us. A reasonable man might think it a proper measure on the score of health. Men whom I certainly could not pronounce unreasonable would uphold it as a first instalment of a general regulation of the hours of work. Whether in the latter aspect it would be open to the charge of inequality I think it unnecessary to discuss.

Questions

1. What is the essence of Holmes's dissent from "nineteenth-century formalism"?
2. At one point, Holmes qualifies an argument as follows: "unless it can be said that a rational and fair man necessarily would admit. . . ." What significance attaches to the word *necessarily*?

Questions for Further Thought

1. Compare and contrast the arguments of Walter Lippmann (Document 20-1) and Walter Rauschenbusch (Document 20-2). How did each influence progressive reform?
2. With which of the following would Rauschenbusch have had the most in common: Eugene V. Debs, Frederick W. Taylor, or Henry George? The least?
3. Can you identify any theme or way of thinking common to Justice Oliver Wendell Holmes Jr. (Document 20-3) and Walter Lippmann?

The Many Faces of Reform

As the text puts it, "Progressivism was not a movement in any meaningful sense," but rather "a widespread, many-sided effort after 1900 to build a better society" (see text p. 643). This meant, for example, that reformers interested in measures to improve the lot of industrial workers did not necessarily involve themselves in other reformers' campaigns to curb prostitution. In fact, pro-labor reformers might very well have found themselves at odds with reform advocates of scientific management and their efforts to improve the productivity of industry.

Among the many faces of reform was political reform—at the local (especially city), state, and national levels of government. As usual, the motives of those who sought to modernize, democratize, or purify political institutions and practices were mixed: power, as well as "reform," was at issue. Among state-based Progressive Era reformers, none was more famous than Governor Robert M. La Follette of Wisconsin, who deals with economic and political issues—and their interconnection—in Document 20-4. Political reform, and indeed a number of reform causes, involved investigative journalists who, writing for popular magazines, exposed corruption and wrongdoing. One such muckraker—the term, from John Bunyan's *Pilgrim's Progress,* was applied to such writers by Theodore Roosevelt—was Edward Charles Russell ("American Voices," text p. 643). Ida Tarbell was another (see text pp. 640–643, 650).

Meanwhile, women organized to play important roles in various reform causes, especially those touching the lives of women and children, at first privately, but increasingly through government action. Women were also central to the settlement-house movement, which took middle-class adherents into slum neighborhoods, where they learned about slum life and politics. In Documents 20-5, Jane Addams reports on life at Hull-House in Chicago. Progressive Era women mounted a drive, ultimately successful, to achieve women's suffrage. Many went beyond the vote to espouse *feminism,* "freedom for full personal development," including, for some, birth control by means of contraception. Margaret Sanger (Document 20-6) spearheaded the birth control movement (see text pp. 645–650).

Drawing on scientific expertise and acting through public agencies and private organizations, reformers sought to address a range of social and medical issues, among them alcohol and drugs, prostitution, venereal diseases, other communicable diseases, and various "inferiors"—immigrants, African Americans, and those deemed hereditarily unfit to reproduce. Document 20-7 deals with New York City's organized campaign against tuberculosis. Document 20-8 is Indiana's pioneering compulsory sterilization law (see text pp. 655–657).

20-4 Autobiography (1913)

Robert M. La Follette

Although he spent some thirty years in public office, Robert M. La Follette (1855–1925) was anything but a professional politician in the conventional sense. As a Wisconsin congressman, governor, and senator, La Follette left no doubt that he stood on the side of reform. His emphasis on social reform and expert administration during his governorship (1901–1905) became known nationally as the Wisconsin Idea. In this excerpt from his autobiography, La Follette recalls his attempts to pass legislation involving direct primary elections and railroad taxation. Although both measures were defeated in the 1901 legislative session, La Follette ultimately succeeded in having them passed.

Source: Robert M. La Follette, *La Follette's Autobiography: A Personal Narrative of Political Experiences* (Madison, Wis.: Robert M. La Follette, 1913; reprint, Madison: University of Wisconsin Press, 1960), 105–108, 111.

All the governors before me, so far as I know, had sent in their messages to the legislature to be mumbled over by a reading clerk. I know that I could make a very much stronger impression with my recommendations if I could present my message in person to the legislature in joint session. I felt that it would invest the whole matter with a new seriousness and dignity that would not only affect the legislators themselves, but react upon the public mind. This I did: and in consequence awakened a wide interest in my recommendations throughout the state.

The predominant notes in the message were direct primaries and railroad taxation—one political and one economic reform.

The railroads at that time paid taxes in the form of a license fee upon their gross earnings. The report of the Tax Commission showed that while real property in Wisconsin paid 1.19 per cent. of its market value in taxes, the railroads paid only .53 per cent. of their market value (based on the average value of stocks and bonds) or less than one half the rate paid by farmers, manufacturers, home owners and others. Upon this showing we contended that the railroads were not bearing their fair share of the burdens of the state. The Tax Commission suggested two measures of reform. One of their bills provided for a simple increase in the license tax, the other provided for a physical valuation of the railroads and a wholly new system of taxation upon an ad valorem basis, measures which I had earnestly advocated in my campaign speeches, and recommended in my message. I regarded this latter as the more scientific method of taxation. The Commission stated that while they had so framed the bills as to err on the side of injustice to the people rather than to the railroads, the passage of either of them would mean an increase of taxes paid by railroads and other public service corporations of more than three quarters of a million dollars annually.

No sooner had the taxation and direct primary bills been introduced than the lobby gathered in Madison in full force. Lobbyists had been there before, but never in such numbers or with such an organization. I never saw anything like it. The railroads, threatened with the taxation bills, and the bosses, threatened by the direct primary, evidently regarded it as the death struggle. Not only were the regular lobbyists in attendance but they made a practice during the entire winter of bringing in delegations of more or less influential men from all parts of the state, some of whom often remained two or three weeks and brought every sort of pressure to bear on the members of the legislature. The whole fight was centred upon me personally. They thought that if they could crush me, that would stop the movement. How little they understood! Even if they had succeeded in eliminating me, the movement, which is fundamental, would still have swept on! They sought to build up in the minds of the people the fear that the executive was controlling the legislative branch of the government. They deliberately organized a campaign of abuse and misrepresentation. Their stories were minutely detailed and spread about among the hotels and on railroad trains. They said that I had completely lost my head. They endeavored to give me a reputation for discourtesy and browbeating; stories were told of my shameless treatment of members, of my backing them up against the wall of the executive office, shaking my fist in their faces and warning them if they did not pass our bills I would use all my power to crush them. In so far as anything was said in disparagement of the administration members of the legislature it was that they were sycophants who took their orders every morning from the executive office. The newspapers, controlled by the machine interests, began to print these abusive statements and sent them broadcast. At first we took no notice of their campaign of misrepresentation, but it grew and grew until it got on the nerves of all of us. It came to be a common thing to have one after another of my friends drop in and say: "Governor, is it true that you have had a row with——? Is it true that you ordered—— out of the executive office?"

It seems incredible, as I look back upon it now, that it could be humanly possible to create such an atmosphere of distrust. We felt that we were fighting something in the dark all the while; there was nothing we could get hold of.

In spite of it all, however, we drove straight ahead. After the bills prepared by the Tax Commission were in, the primary election bill was drafted and redrafted and introduced by E. Ray Stevens of Madison, one of the ablest men ever in public life in Wisconsin, and now a judge of the circuit court of the state. The committee having it in charge at once began a series of open meetings, and the lobby brought to Madison people from every part of the state to attend the hearings and to protest. Extended speeches were made against it, and these were promptly printed and sent broadcast. The most preposterous arguments were advanced. They argued that the proposed law was unconstitutional because it interfered with the "right of the people to assemble!" They tried to rouse the country people by arguing that it favored the cities; they said that city people could get out more readily to primaries than country people. It did not seem to occur to them that practically every argument they made against the direct primary applied far more strongly to the old caucus and convention system.

But we fought as vigorously as they, and presently it began to appear that we might get some of our measures through. It evidently made an impression on the lobby. One night, after the legislature had been in session about two months, Emanuel Phillipp came to my office. He moved his chair up close to mine.

"Now, look here," he said, "you want to pass the primary election bill, don't you? I will help you put it through."

"Phillipp," I said, "there is no use in you and me trying to mislead each other. I understand and you understand that the senate is organized against both the direct primary and taxation bills. You know that better than I do."

"Well," he said, "now look here. This railroad taxation matter—wouldn't you be willing to let that go if you could get your primary bill through? What good will it do you, anyhow, to increase railroad taxation? We can meet that all right just by raising rates or by changing a classification here and there. No one will know it and we can take back every cent of increased taxes in rates from the people."

"Phillipp," I said, "you have just driven in and clinched the argument for regulating your rates. And that is the next thing we are going to do. No," I said, "these pledges are straight promises."

"But," he argued, "if you can get this primary election bill through you will have done a great thing. And I will pass it for you, if you will let up on railroad taxation."

"Just how will you pass it?" I asked.

"How will I pass it?" he repeated. "How will I pass it? Why, I'll take those fellows over to a room in the Park Hotel, close the door and stand them up against the wall. And I'll say to them, 'You vote for the primary election bill!' And they'll vote for it, because I own them, they're mine!" And this was Phillipp's last interview with me. . . .

When we continued to make progress in spite of all this opposition the lobby made another move against us. It brought to bear all the great influence of the federal office-holders who were especially disturbed over the possible effect of a direct primary upon their control of the state. United States District Attorney Wheeler, an appointee of Spooner, and the United States District Attorney of the Eastern District, an appointee of Quarles, were much on the ground; so were United States Marshal Monahan and Collector of Internal Revenue Fink.

Finally, before the vote on the direct primary was taken in the senate, Senator Spooner, who rarely came to Wisconsin while Congress was in session, appeared in Madison. He was there only a few days, but he was visited by members of the senate, and we felt his influence strongly against us.

All the efforts of the lobby, combined with the opposition of the newspapers and the federal office-holders, was not without its effect upon our forces. Every moment from the time the senate convened down to the final vote on the railroad taxation bills they were weakening us, wearing us down, getting some men one way, some another, until finally before the close of the session they had not only the senate but a majority of the Republicans in the assembly. It was a pathetic and tragic thing to see honest men falling before these insidious forces. For many of them it meant plain ruin from which they never afterward recovered.

In order to make very clear the methods employed I shall here relate in detail the stories of several of the cases which came directly under my own observation. I shall withhold the real names of the Senators and Assemblymen concerned, because many of them were the victims of forces and temptations far greater than they could resist. If I could also give the names of the men really responsible for the corruption, bribery and debauchery—the men higher up, the men behind the lobbyists—I would do it without hesitation.

Questions

1. How does La Follette signal that he is different from previous governors?
2. What are the elements of his railroad tax proposal?
3. According to La Follette, how did the opposition counterattack?

20-5   Twenty Years at Hull-House (1910)

Jane Addams

The text makes clear that settlement houses not only did "modest good" in poor neighborhoods, but also gave meaning to the lives of those who served in them, providing these settlement-house workers with an understanding of both social reform and the class, ethnic, and political realities of city life (see text pp. 645–648). In this selection, Jane Addams (1860–1935), of Hull-House in Chicago, recounts part of her education in social work.

Source: Jane Addams, *Twenty Years at Hull-House: With Autobiographical Notes* (Phillips, 1910; reprint, New York: New American Library, n.d.), 200–204.

One of the striking features of our neighborhood twenty years ago, and one to which we never became reconciled, was the presence of huge wooden garbage boxes fastened to the street pavement in which the undisturbed refuse accumulated day by day. The system of garbage collecting was inadequate throughout the city but it became the greatest menace in a ward such as ours, where the normal amount of waste was much increased by the decayed fruit and vegetables discarded by the Italian and Greek fruit peddlers, and by the residuum left over from the piles of filthy rags which were fished out of the city dumps and brought to the homes of the rag pickers for further sorting and washing.

The children of our neighborhood twenty years ago played their games in and around these huge garbage boxes. They were the first objects that the toddling child learned to climb; their bulk afforded a barricade and their contents provided missiles in all the battles of the older boys; and finally they became the seats upon which absorbed lovers held enchanted converse. We are obliged to remember that all children eat everything which they find and that odors have a curious and intimate power of entwining themselves into our tenderest memories, before even the residents of Hull-House can understand their own early enthusiasm for the removal of these boxes and the establishment of a better system of refuse collection.

It is easy for even the most conscientious citizen of Chicago to forget the foul smells of the stockyards and the garbage dumps, when he is living so far from them that he is only occasionally made conscious of their existence, but the residents of a Settlement are perforce constantly surrounded by them. During our first three years on Halsted Street, we had established a small incinerator at Hull-House and we had many times reported the untoward conditions of the ward to the city hall. We had also arranged many talks for the immigrants, pointing out that although a woman may sweep her own doorway in her native village and allow the refuse to innocently decay in the open air and sunshine, in a crowded city quarter, if the garbage is not properly collected and destroyed, a tenement-house mother may see her children sicken and die, and that the immigrants must therefore not only keep their own houses clean, but must also help the authorities to keep the city clean.

Possibly our efforts slightly modified the worst conditions, but they still remained intolerable, and the fourth summer the situation became for me absolutely desperate when I realized in a moment of panic that my delicate little nephew for whom I was guardian could not be with me at Hull-House at all unless the sickening odors were reduced. I may well be ashamed that other delicate children who were torn from their families, not into boarding school but into eternity, had not long before driven me into effective action. Under the direction of the first man who came as a resident to Hull-House we began a systematic investigation of the city system of garbage collection, both as to its efficiency in other wards and its possible connection with the death rate in the various wards of the city.

The Hull-House Woman's Club had been organized the year before by the resident kindergartner who had first inaugurated a mothers' meeting. The members came together, however, in quite a new way that summer when we discussed with them the high death rate so persistent in our ward. After several club meetings devoted to the subject, despite the fact that the death rate rose highest in the congested foreign colonies and not in the streets in which most of the Irish American club women lived, twelve of their number undertook in connection with the residents, to carefully investigate the condition of the alleys. During August and September the substantiated reports of violations of the law sent in from Hull-House to the health department were one thousand and thirty-seven. For the club woman who had finished a long day's work of washing or ironing followed by the cooking of a hot supper, it would have been much easier to sit on her doorstep during a summer evening than to go up and down ill-kept alleys and get into trouble with her neighbors over the condition of their garbage boxes. It required both civic enterprise and moral conviction to be willing to do this three evenings a week during the hottest and most uncomfortable months of the year. Nevertheless, a certain number of women persisted, as did the residents, and three city inspectors in succession were transferred from the ward because of unsatisfactory services. Still the death rate remained high and the condition seemed little improved throughout the next winter. In sheer desperation, the following spring when the city contracts were awarded for the removal of garbage, with the backing of two well-known business men, I put in a bid for the garbage removal of the nineteenth ward. My paper was thrown out on a technicality but the incident induced the mayor to appoint me the garbage inspector of the ward.

The salary was a thousand dollars a year, and the loss of that political "plum" made a great stir among the politicians. The position was no sinecure whether regarded from the point of view of getting up at six in the morning to see that the men were early at work; or of following the loaded wagons, uneasily dropping their contents at intervals, to their dreary destination at the dump; or of insisting that the contractor must increase the number of his wagons from nine to thirteen and from thirteen to seventeen, although he assured me that he lost money on every one and that the former inspector had let him off with seven; or of taking careless landlords into court because they would not provide the proper garbage receptacles; or of arresting the tenant who tried to make the garbage wagons carry away the contents of his stable.

With the two or three residents who nobly stood by, we set up six of those doleful incinerators which are supposed to burn garbage with the fuel collected in the alley itself. The one factory in town which could utilize old tin cans was a window weight factory, and we deluged that with ten times as many tin cans as it could use—much less would pay for. We made desperate attempts to have the dead animals removed by the contractor who was paid most liberally by the city for that purpose but who, we slowly discovered, always made the police ambulances do the work, delivering the carcasses upon freight cars for shipment to a soap factory in Indiana where they were sold for a good price although the contractor himself was the largest stockholder in the concern. Perhaps our greatest achievement was the discovery of a pavement eighteen inches under the surface in a narrow street, although after it was found we triumphantly discovered a record of its existence in the city archives. The Italians living on the street were much interested but displayed little astonishment, perhaps because they were accustomed to see buried cities exhumed. This pavement became the *casus belli* [cause of war] between myself and the street commissioner when I insisted that its restoration belonged to him, after I had removed the first eight inches of garbage. The matter was finally settled by the mayor himself, who permitted me to drive him to the entrance of the street in what the children called my "garbage phaëton" and who took my side of the controversy.

Questions

1. How was garbage collected in Chicago?
2. Why were conditions so bad in the area around Hull-House?
3. What did Addams accomplish as a garbage collector?

20-6   The Case for Birth Control (1917)

Margaret Sanger

Margaret Sanger (1883–1966), born to a free-thinking Irish father and a religious Irish-American Catholic mother, championed the cause of birth control in the United States. She encountered opposition not only from traditionalists, but also from progressives like Theodore Roosevelt who were fearful of "race suicide" among "the better element," even as "the lower classes" grew in numbers (see text p. 650). Since 1873, the federal "Comstock law" had proscribed as "obscene" the mailing of birth-control devices and information; state laws also provided obstacles to the birth-control movement (see text pp. 633–635).

Source: Margaret Sanger, *The Case for Birth Control* (New York: Modern Art, 1917), 5–7, 8–11, in Elliott J. Gorn, Randy Roberts, and Terry D. Bilhartz, eds., *Constructing the American Past: A Source Book of a People's History* (New York: HarperCollins, 1991), 2: 205–210.

(The following is the case for birth control, as I found it during my fourteen years' experience as a trained nurse in New York City and vicinity. It appeared as a special article in "Physical Culture," April 1917, and has been delivered by me as a lecture throughout the United States. It is a brief summary of facts and conditions, as they exist in this country.)

For centuries woman has gone forth with man to till the fields, to feed and clothe the nations. She has sacrificed her life to populate the earth. She has overdone her labors. She now steps forth and demands that women shall cease producing in ignorance. To do this she must have knowledge to control birth. This is the first immediate step she must take toward the goal of her freedom.

Those who are opposed to this are simply those who do not know. Any one who like myself has worked among the people and found on one hand an ever-increasing population with its ever-increasing misery, poverty and ignorance, and on the other hand a stationary or decreasing population with its increasing wealth and higher standards of living, greater freedom, joy and happiness, cannot doubt that birth control is the livest issue of the day and one on which depends the future welfare of the race.

Before I attempt to refute the arguments against birth control, I should like to tell you something of the conditions I met with as a trained nurse and of the experience that convinced me of its necessity and led me to jeopardize my liberty in order to place this information in the hands of the women who need it.

My first clear impression of life was that large families and poverty went hand in hand. I was born and brought up in a glass factory town in the western part of New York State. I was one of eleven children—so I had some personal experience of the struggles and hardships a large family endures.

When I was seventeen years old my mother died from overwork and the strain of too frequent child bearing. I was left to care for the younger children and share the burdens of all. When I was old enough I entered a hospital to take up the profession of nursing.

In the hospital I found that seventy-five percent of the diseases of men and women are the result of ignorance of their sex functions. I found that every department of life was open to investigation and discussion except that shaded valley of sex. The explorer, scientist, inventor, may go forth in their various fields for investigation and return to lay the fruits of their discoveries at the feet of society. But woe to him who dares explore that forbidden realm of sex. No matter how pure the motive, no matter what miseries he sought to remove, slanders, persecutions and jail await him who dares bear the light of knowledge into that cave of darkness.

So great was the ignorance of the women and girls I met concerning their own bodies that I decided to specialize in woman's diseases and took up gynecological and obstetrical nursing.

A few years of this work brought me to a shocking discovery—that knowledge of the methods of controlling birth was accessible to the women of wealth while the working women were deliberately kept in ignorance of this knowledge!

I found that the women of the working class were as anxious to obtain this knowledge as their sisters of wealth, but that they were told that there are laws on the statute books against imparting it to them. And the medical profession was most religious in obeying these laws when the patient was a poor woman.

I found that the women of the working class had emphatic views on the crime of bringing children into the world to die of hunger. They would rather risk their lives through abortion than give birth to little ones they could not feed and care for.

For the laws against imparting this knowledge force these women into the hands of the filthiest midwives and the quack abortionists—unless they bear unwanted children—with the consequence that the deaths from abortions are almost wholly among the working-class women.

No other country in the world has so large a number of abortions nor so large a number of deaths of women resulting therefrom as the United States of America. Our law makers close their virtuous eyes. A most conservative estimate is that there are 250,000 abortions performed in this country every year.

How often have I stood at the bedside of a woman in childbirth and seen the tears flowing in gladness and heard the sigh of "Thank God" when told that her child was born dead! What can man know of the fear and dread of unwanted pregnancy? What can man know of the agony of carrying beneath one's heart a little life which tells the mother every instant that it cannot survive? Even were it born alive the chances are that it would perish within a year.

Do you know that three hundred thousand babies under one year of age die in the United States every year from poverty and neglect, while six hundred thousand parents remain in ignorance of how to prevent three hundred thousand more babies from coming into the world the next year to die of poverty and neglect?

I found from records concerning women of the underworld that eighty-five per cent of them come from parents averaging nine living children. And that fifty percent of these are mentally defective.

We know, too, that among mentally defective parents the birth rate is four times as great as that of the normal parent. Is this not cause for alarm? Is it not time for our physicians, social workers and scientists to face this array of facts and stop quibbling about woman's morality? I say this because it is these same people who raise objection to birth control on the ground that it *may* cause women to be immoral.

Solicitude for woman's morals has ever been the cloak Authority has worn in its age-long conspiracy to keep women in bondage. . . .

Is woman's health not to be considered? Is she to remain a producing machine? Is she to have time to think, to study, to care for herself? Man cannot travel to his goal alone. And until woman has knowledge to control birth she cannot get the time to think and develop. Until she has the time to think, neither the suffrage question nor the social question nor the labor question will interest her, and she will remain the drudge that she is and her husband the slave that he is just as long as they continue to supply the market with cheap labor.

Let me ask you: Has the State any more right to ravish a woman against her will by keeping her in ignorance than a man has through brute force? Has the State a better right to decide when she shall bear offspring?

Picture a woman with five or six little ones living on the average working man's wage of ten dollars a week. The mother is broken in health and spirit, a worn out shadow of the woman she once was. Where is the man or woman who would reproach me for trying to put into this woman's hands knowledge that will save her from giving birth to any more babies doomed to certain poverty and misery and perhaps to disease and death.

Am I to be classed as immoral because I advocate small families for the working class while Mr. Roosevelt can go up and down the length of the land shouting and urging these women to have large families and is neither arrested nor molested but considered by all society as highly moral?

But I ask you which is the more moral—to urge this class of women to have only those children she desires and can care for, or to delude her into breeding thoughtlessly. Which is America's definition of morality?

You will agree with me that a woman should be free.

Yet no adult woman who is ignorant of the means to prevent conception can call herself free.

No woman can call herself free who cannot choose the time to be a mother or not as she sees fit. This should be woman's first demand.

Our present laws force women into one of two ways: Celibacy, with its nervous results, or abortion. All modern physicians testify that both these conditions are harmful; that celibacy is the cause of many nervous complaints, while abortion is a disgrace to a civilized community. Physicians claim that early marriage with knowledge to control birth would do away with both. For this would enable two young people to live and work together until such time as they could care for a family. I found that young people desire early marriage, and would marry early were it not for the dread of a large family to support. Why will not society countenance and advance this idea? Because it is still afraid of the untried and the unknown.

I saw that fortunes were being spent in establishing baby nurseries, where new babies are brought and cared for while the mothers toil in sweatshops during the day. I saw that society with its well-intentioned palliatives was in this respect like the quack, who cures a cancer by burning off the top while the deadly disease continues to spread underneath. I never felt this more strongly than I did three years ago, after the death of the patient in my last nursing case.

This patient was the wife of a struggling working man—the mother of three children—who was suffering from the results of a self-attempted abortion. I found her in a very serious condition, and for three weeks both the attending physician and myself labored night and day to bring her out of the Valley of the Shadow of Death. We finally succeeded in restoring her to her family.

I remember well the day I was leaving. The physician, too, was making his last call. As the doctor put out his hand to say "Good-bye," I saw the patient had something to say to him, but was shy and timid about saying it. I started to leave the room, but she called me back and said:

"Please don't go. How can both of you leave me without telling me what I can do to avoid another illness such as I have just passed through?"

I was interested to hear what the answer of the physician would be, and I went back and sat down beside her in expectation of hearing a sympathetic reply. To my amazement, he answered her with a joking sneer. We came away.

Three months later, I was aroused from my sleep one midnight. A telephone call from the husband of the same woman requested me to come immediately as she was dangerously ill. I arrived to find her beyond relief. Another conception had forced her into the hands of a cheap abortionist, and she died at four o'clock the same morning, leaving behind her three small children and a frantic husband.

I returned home as the sun was coming over the roofs of the Human Bee-Hive, and I realized how futile my efforts and my work had been. I, too, like the philanthropists and social workers, had been dealing with the symptoms rather than the disease. I threw my nursing bag into the corner and announced to my family that I would never take another case until I had made it possible for working women in America to have knowledge of birth control.

I found, to my utter surprise, that there was very little scientific information on the question available in America. Although nearly every country in Europe had this knowledge, we were the only civilized people in the world whose postal laws forbade it.

The tyranny of the censorship of the post office is the greatest menace to liberty in the United States to-day. The post office was never intended to be a moral or ethical institution. It was intended to be mechanically efficient; certainly not to pass upon the opinions in the matter it conveys. If we concede this power to this institution, which is only a public service, we might just as well give to the streetcar companies and railroads the right to refuse to carry passengers whose ideas they do not like.

I will not take up the story of the publication of "The Woman Rebel." You know how I began to publish it, how it was confiscated and suppressed by the post office authorities, how I was indicted and arrested for bringing it out, and how the case was postponed time and time again and finally dismissed by Judge Clayton in the Federal Court.

These, and many more obstacles and difficulties were put in the path of this philosophy and this work to suppress it if possible and discredit it in any case.

My work has been to arouse interest in the subject of birth control in America, and in this, I feel that I have been successful. The work now before us is to crystallize and to organize this interest into action, not only for the repeal of the laws but for the establishment of free clinics in every large center of population in the country where scientific, individual information may be given every adult person who comes to ask it. . . .

The free clinic is the solution for our problem. It will enable women to help themselves, and will have much to do with disposing of this soul-crushing charity which is at best a mere temporary relief.

Woman must be protected from incessant childbearing before she can actively participate in the social life. She must triumph over Nature's and Man's laws which have kept her in bondage. Just as man has triumphed over Nature by the use of electricity, shipbuilding, bridges, etc., so must woman triumph over the laws which have made her a childbearing machine.

Questions

1. What is Sanger's position regarding marriage? Regarding abortion? Regarding celibacy?
2. What, according to Sanger, would knowledge and the practice of birth control offer women?
3. What does the excerpt reveal about Sanger's attitudes toward social classes?

20-7   The Administrative Control of Tuberculosis in New York City (1909)

Hermann M. Biggs

The Progressive Era witnessed the development of public health programs to deal with a range of social and medical problems. Among the targeted infectious diseases, none were more dangerous than tuberculosis, the nation's third biggest cause of death at the turn of the century. Tuberculosis, a contagious bacterial disease, is usually transmitted by inhalation and is characterized by toxic symptoms primarily affecting the lungs. It is particularly dangerous to people in poor living conditions.

In this selection, Dr. Hermann M. Biggs, a pioneering bacteriologist and General Medical Officer of the New York City Department of Health, describes how far municipal government and cooperating private agencies were prepared to go to prevent a disease that medicine could not yet cure. (It should be noted that New York City, struggling today with an epidemic of drug-resistant tuberculosis, has again isolated uncooperative patients on an East River island.)

Source: Hermann M. Biggs, *The Administrative Control of Tuberculosis in New York City* (New York: Department of Health, 1909), 4–23, 27, 30–32.

. . . [E]arly in 1894 an ordinance was enacted by the Board of Health declaring tuberculosis to be an infectious and communicable disease dangerous to the public health. This ordinance *required* the notification of all cases coming under the care of public or semi-public institutions of all kinds—dispensaries, clinics, homes, hospitals, asylums, etc., but only *requested* private physicians to report cases. It provided for the free examination of sputum, for the disinfection of premises vacated by death or removal of tuberculous persons, for the visitation of such cases in their homes, for conducting an extensive educational campaign and for several other measures of less importance.

Work was continued under this ordinance with marked success until 1897, when the scope of the work was extended, and notification of *all* cases was made obligatory. . . .

This action of the Board, requiring the notification of all cases of tuberculosis, aroused bitter opposition in the medical profession and much hostile criticism both in the medical and lay press, but the Board of Health had, in the course adopted, the hearty support of the Advisory Board of the Department of Health, composed of nine of the most distinguished medical men in the city. The work was therefore continued, notwithstanding the active and determined hostility of a large section of the medical profession, and notwithstanding the strenuous but unsuccessful efforts which were made in the New York State Legislature to obtain an amendment of the general law under which the Board of Health derived its power to deal with this disease. . . .

It is not quite easy for us in New York, who have had to do with the development of the present comprehensive scheme of control of tuberculosis, now in force for more than ten years, to understand the hesitation and reluctance shown by most sanitary authorities in assuming responsibility for the surveillance of the tuberculous diseases. Even in this country, where the influence of the Department of Health of New York City is considerable in determining the policy adopted by other authorities, only a very small percentage of municipal and state authorities have adopted and *enforced* provisions, which can be regarded as in any way comprehensive or effective in dealing with this disease. The authorities in many states and cities have *enacted* ordinances declaring tuberculosis to be a communicable disease, requiring notification, forbidding spitting in public places, etc., but for the most part, the necessary facilities for dealing with this disease have been lacking, or no determined effort has been made to enforce the ordinances after their adoption.

If we seek for an adequate explanation for this attitude, it is, perhaps after all, not difficult to find. In speaking of this matter more than ten years ago, Professor Robert Koch said in substance to the writer: "The adoption in Germany of such measures as are in force in New York City will be possible only when the present older generation of physicians has gone, and a younger generation has come which has had a different scientific training and holds views more in harmony with the known facts regarding the etiology of tuberculosis. Then it will be possible to bring about an intelligent supervision of this disease."

A great obstacle to the sanitary surveillance of tuberculosis has been the idea firmly fixed in the mind of the sanitary authorities and the medical profession, that administrative control properly applies only to the more readily communicable acute diseases, like smallpox, scarlet fever, diphtheria, etc., and the inclusion of tuberculosis with these diseases has seemed to them unwarranted. The enactment of suitable legislation conferring on the sanitary authorities power to deal with this disease in another way has either not been considered or has been regarded as impracticable.

On the Continent of Europe the sanitary authorities generally have no power in themselves to adopt comprehensive plans for dealing with this disease, except as it is conferred by legislation. Then, too, strange as it may seem, the procedures which are readily accepted under popular government in the United States are regarded as too radical, and too autocratic there. To forcibly remove from their homes cases of scarlet fever, diphtheria or smallpox, and to retain them in a hospital until convalescence is complete would not be attempted by most authorities on the Continent, much less would they think of forcibly removing and retaining a person suffering from such a slow chronic disease as pulmonary tuberculosis. Still, in New York, the Board of Health has for many years followed this procedure with reference to the acute diseases without causing any serious protest, and has followed the same course with reference to tuberculosis for the past six or seven years. . . .

THE CAMPAIGN IN NEW YORK.

The following procedures are now followed in New York: They have existed largely in their present form since 1897, but have been from time to time perfected in detail and amplified. Previous to 1897 the supervision of the disease was somewhat less complete.

I. The Notification and Registration of All Cases of Tuberculosis of All Varieties Is Required.

The fundamental importance of this measure in any plan for the administrative control of tuberculosis is so evident that its consideration seems hardly necessary. It must, of course, at once be apparent that unless there is a complete system of notification and registration, the enforcement of any uniform measures for prevention is impossible. Practical experience with this procedure for a period of more than ten years has made it perfectly clear that the objections which have been and are still urged against it are without force or foundation. . . .

The notification of a case of tuberculosis does not require any action on the part of the authorities, if it seems reasonable to assume that such action is unnecessary because proper precautions are already being observed. The very fact that a case of tuberculosis is notified by the attending physician as a communicable disease has great educational value, and justifies the assumption in those instances in which the case is regularly under the supervision of a private physician, that the reasonable precautions necessary for the protection of others will be taken. If, however, the tuberculous person is without a home, or is living in a lodging house, or in a poorly furnished room, or in a family in a tenement house, or is receiving charitable medical advice through a clinic or dispensary, or some public institution, *then all objection to the visitation and the supervision by sanitary inspectors or trained nurses is removed, and in the interests of the public such supervision becomes necessary.* . . .

II. The Provision of Suitable Relief of Various Kinds as May Be Required Is Extremely Important, and Constitutes a Very Difficult Part of the Tuberculosis Problem.

. . . Very difficult economic problems are presented in some of these cases. For example, a family consists of a mother with moderately advanced consumption and four or five small children, the father is dead, the income of the family from all sources is insufficient to maintain it properly and furnish the mother with suitable food; but the apartments are well ventilated and sufficiently commodious, they are clean and neat, and the mother makes every effort to obey instructions and heed every suggestion. She insists on remaining with her children, and her presence is necessary to keep the family together. Undoubtedly the mother would be better off in an institution, and then the children, too, would probably be removed to an institution for children, and would be better protected from the danger of tuberculous infection, but the children would grow up as institutional children, which is most unfortunate, and, furthermore, there is no sufficient sanitary ground for the forcible removal of the mother. . . .

If, however, the apartments are dirty and not well kept, or are small, dark and badly ventilated, or the instructions are not followed and proper precautions are not taken, then it is better that the family be broken up. The mother should be removed to an institution, if necessary, by force, and the children should be otherwise provided for. . . .

III. Facilities Are Furnished for the Free Bacteriological Examination of the Sputum in All Instances of Suspected Disease to Aid in the Early and Definite Diagnosis of Pulmonary Tuberculosis.

. . . At the present time there are over 300 depots in New York City where the outfits, blanks, etc., for the collection of specimens of sputum may be obtained and where the specimens may be left. They are collected daily by the regular collectors of the Department, examined the following morning, and a report of the result is immediately forwarded to the attending physician.

IV. The Disinfection or Renovation Is Required of Rooms or Apartments Which Have Been Vacated by Consumptives Either by Death or Removal.

. . . Disinfection of all kinds is performed by the Department of Health without cost to the owner or occupant. Renovation and cleaning, as required and when required, is ordered by the Department, and the owner or occupant of the premises must bear the expense. . . .

V. Persons Suffering from Pulmonary Tuberculosis Are Visited in Their Homes.

. . . Where the conditions are such that it seems desirable to send the patient to a hospital, efforts are made to accomplish this by persuasion. When, however, the patient refuses to go and there is serious danger to the other occupants of the apartment, either because of overcrowding, or because of the excessive prostration of the patient and the consequent inability to observe proper precaution, or because of the unwillingness to do so, then forcible removal is resorted to, the patient being removed to an institution and retained there.

New York City institutions will have nearly 5,000 beds devoted solely to the care of tuberculous persons when the plans already adopted are completed.

VI. Provision Has Been Made for Making Repeated Visits to Cases in Tenement Houses,

when for any reason it is undesirable or impossible to remove the patient to an institution. . . .

VII. The Sanitary Authorities in New York City Have Provided Three Classes of Institutions for the Care of Tuberculous Persons as Follows:

1. CLINICS.

The first free clinic (dispensary) designed for the observation and treatment of ambulatory cases was authorized by the Board of Health in 1902, and was opened in 1904 in a building especially constructed for the purpose in the Borough of Manhattan. Since that time the Department of Health has established similar clinics in the Borough of Brooklyn and in the Borough of The Bronx, while other tuberculosis clinics have been opened in connection with different hospitals and dispensaries in various parts of the city. Under the patronage of the Tuberculosis Committee of the Charity Organization Society, an Association of Tuberculosis Clinics has been formed with Dr. James Alexander Miller as President. Only such clinics are admitted to membership in this association as comply with certain requirements, such as providing trained nurses to visit in their homes the cases which are under the care of the clinic.

The Borough of Manhattan is divided into seventeen districts, each clinic supervising the care of all home cases in its district. . . .

The clinics also act as clearing houses for tuberculous persons, and suitable cases are referred to the various institutions, hospitals or sanatoria having facilities for their care. This is chiefly done through the clinics of the Department of Health. All tuberculous cases discharged from institutions are referred to the clinic having supervision over the district in which the patient lives, and as far as possible continuous supervision is subsequently exercised over them. Cases are constantly referred to the clinics for diagnosis or medical care by private physicians, by other city departments and by various charitable organizations. The clinics also serve as places for the examination of other members of the family of tuberculous patients for the detection of unrecognized tuberculous disease. In this their work is very similar to that of the Auskunfts-und Fürsorgestellen, established by Pütter in Germany.

2. HOSPITALS FOR THE CARE OF ADVANCED CASES.

It is not necessary that all the hospitals for the care of advanced cases should be directly under the control of the sanitary authorities, although the latter should exercise a general supervision over these institutions. . . . It is necessary, at least in a very large city like New York, that the health authorities should have the direct control of at least one institution with adequate facilities for the care of such advanced cases of the disease, as it becomes necessary to forcibly remove to a hospital and to involuntarily retain. These are likely to be of several types, as follows:

(A) Those which are discharged from other institutions, because from the institutional standpoint they are undesirable patients, or, because they have violated the regulations of the institution. A moment's consideration will show that the point of view of the sanitary authorities and that of the managers of an institution widely differ. In order to maintain the discipline of an institution, patients who persistently violate its regulations must be dismissed. From the sanitary standpoint these are of all cases those which it is especially important should be provided with institutional care.

Homeless, friendless, dependent, dissolute, dissipated and vicious consumptives are those which are likely to be most dangerous to the community. If not cared for in an institution, they wander from place to place, frequenting saloons, lodging houses, sleeping in hallways or wherever cover can be found. Negligent as to the disposal of their expectoration, they disseminate infection in every place which they visit. Such cases must be provided for by the sanitary authorities at any cost, and if necessary they must be forcibly removed to proper institutions and there detained.

(B) Consumptives living in lodging houses, or consumptive inmates of public institutions, not having facilities for their care, who are unwilling to enter any of the institutions which are available, must be provided for and must also be forcibly removed, if necessary, and detained.

(C) It infrequently becomes necessary in a large city to remove from their homes patients who are almost necessarily sources of danger to the other members of their family, viz., in those instances in which the sanitary conditions are very unfavorable, when there is great poverty, destitution or overcrowding, and when the patients themselves are unwilling to enter an institution. Then the health authorities must intervene and remove such patients by force and retain them.

(D) There are numerous cases in which patients who have already been under the care of an institution, for some reason become dissatisfied with their care and are determined to return to their homes. They demand their discharge. In such instances when their families are unwilling or unable to provide properly for them, they should be removed by the authorities and retained under supervision. . . .

The Department of Health of New York City established an institution of this kind in 1902, or rather it set aside for cases of this sort two pavilions in one of its hospitals for infectious diseases. Accommodations were thus provided for about forty patients; the number of beds at present available for advanced cases is more than two hundred and fifty.

3. SANATORIUM.

The City of New York has established a free municipal sanatorium for the care of early cases of pulmonary tuberculosis, located in the country at Otisville, about seventy-five miles from New York. . . .

The necessity for the establishment of sanatoria under the care of the health authorities requires no comment, as the authorities must deal with both prevention and treatment of tuberculosis. Such institutions, therefore, are imperatively demanded. As has often been pointed out, every early case admitted to a sanatorium not only removes the individual, who would probably otherwise become for a long period a source of danger to others and eventually a public charge, but also affords the best opportunity for arresting the disease, and for thus restoring his permanent usefulness to the community. . . .

VIII. Educational Measures.

It is difficult to overestimate the importance of the duties of the sanitary authorities in the education of the medical profession and of the people on the subject of tuberculosis. Circulars designed to reach different classes of the community and covering different phases of the subject have been widely distributed in New York year after year, and the public press has been utilized to a large extent in the diffusion of information.

Exhibitions, consisting of charts, maps, models, etc., illustrating the tuberculosis work, have been prepared and shown in many parts of the city in conjunction with the work of the Tuberculosis Committee of the Charity Organization Society. Efforts were made in each instance to enlist the co-operation of the various charitable organizations working in the locality to assist in stimulating attendance on the exhibits. . . .

The Board of Health has enacted and partially enforced regulations prohibiting spitting in all public conveyances, such as street cars, steam railroad cars, ferryboats, etc., and on the floors of public buildings and places of public assembly, such as ferry-houses, depots, etc., and in the halls of tenement houses, theatres, in factories, etc. Spitting on the sidewalks is also prohibited.

The fundamental importance of the careless disposal of sputum in the causation both of pulmonary tuberculosis and the acute respiratory disease is often not fully recognized. . . . We should gradually inculcate the idea that the habit of coughing and spitting carelessly anywhere is not only filthy and indecent, but is to be regarded as showing an almost criminal disregard for the safety and welfare of others. When we have educated the mass of the people up to this view so that coughing without covering the mouth and the habit of spitting will no longer be tolerated, an important factor in the solution of the problem of the prevention of tuberculosis will have been overcome.

IX. The Inspection of the Inmates of Lodging Houses, and House to House Visitation in the Poorest Tenement House Districts.

. . . What may reasonably be expected from the enforcement of such measures? we again find an answer, in part at least, in the experience in New York. There has been a rapid fall in the tuberculosis death rate in New York City, notwithstanding the fact that the conditions in many respects are most unfavorable because of the very dense population in the great tenement house districts of the city, and the large element of foreign-born population. It should be remembered that no such density of population as exists in many of the wards of the Borough of Manhattan is found in any other city of the world. In many of the districts on the East Side the population varies from 600 to 1,000 persons to the acre, whereas the most densely populated districts of Paris, London, Vienna and Prague have less than four hundred persons to the acre. With this great density of population the difficulties are still further increased be-

cause of the large foreign-born element, composed of nearly every nationality in the world. . . .

So far as I know there is no city on the Continent of Europe in which such extensive and determined efforts have been made to control the prevalence of the infectious diseases as has been the case in New York City. European sanitary authorities will realize more fully what is meant by this when it is remembered that the Department of Health of New York City regularly employs nearly four hundred physicians and more than one thousand other employees. . . .

If we accept at all the necessary deductions of our scientific convictions in relation to tuberculosis, there can be no escape from the conclusion that tuberculosis is, of all the important infectious diseases with which we have to deal, certainly the most preventable. . . .

The suppression of tuberculosis is coming more and more to be recognized as the great urgent social and sanitary problem of the time. In no other direction can such large results be achieved so certainly and at such relatively small cost. The time is not far distant when those states and municipalities which have not adopted a comprehensive plan for dealing with tuberculosis will be regarded as negligent in their sanitary administration and inexcusably blind to their own best economic interests.

Questions

1. In what ways does the tuberculosis-control campaign involve cooperation between public and private agencies and individuals?
2. Which municipal government policies reported here strike you as the most drastic?
3. What are Biggs's attitudes toward the program he administered, toward others involved in the campaign, and toward the citizenry he served?

20-8   Progressivism and Compulsory Sterilization (1907)

Progressive Era debates over immigration and birth control included frequent references to the threat to American society posed by "inferior" people or groups. Eugenics, which sought to improve human heredity by selective breeding, influenced the policy of states regarding categories of people deemed hereditarily unfit to reproduce—for example, by prohibiting them from marrying or by sterilizing such men and women in state facilities, thus reducing the risks to society of their release. Indiana enacted the first such law in 1907 (reproduced in this selection); over the next thirty years, a number of other states followed suit.

In *Buck v. Bell* (1927), the Supreme Court upheld, 8-1, the constitutionality of Virginia's compulsory sterilization law, viewing it as protective of individuals and society, analogous to the compulsory vaccination of children in public schools, even though others were not required to undergo vaccination. Of Carrie Buck, allegedly feeble-minded, the child of a feeble-minded mother and the mother of a feeble-minded child, Justice Oliver Wendell Holmes Jr. declared that rather than "waiting to execute degenerate offspring . . . or to let them starve for their imbecility, society can prevent those who are manifestly unfit from continuing their kind. . . . Three generations of imbeciles are enough."

Source: Laws of the State of Indiana, 1907, 377–378.

PREAMBLE.

Whereas, Heredity plays a most important part in the transmission of crime, idiocy and imbecility;

PENAL INSTITUTIONS—SURGICAL OPERATIONS.

Therefore, *Be it enacted by the general assembly of the State of Indiana,* That on and after the passage of this act it shall be compulsory for each and every institution in the state, entrusted with the care of confirmed criminals, idiots, rapists and imbeciles, to appoint upon its staff, in addition to the regular institutional physician, two (2) skilled surgeons of recognized ability, whose duty it shall be, in conjunction with the chief physician of the insti-

tution, to examine the mental and physical condition of such inmates as are recommended by the institutional physician and board of managers. If, in the judgment of this committee of experts and the board of managers, procreation is inadvisable and there is no probability of improvement of the mental condition of the inmate, it shall be lawful for the surgeons to perform such operation for the prevention of procreation as shall be decided safest and most effective. But this operation shall not be performed except in cases that have been pronounced unimprovable: *Provided,* That in no case shall the consultation fee be more than three ($3.00) dollars to each expert, to be paid out of the funds appropriated for the maintenance of such institution.

Questions

1. What assumption is made in the statute's preamble?
2. Which types of inmates are considered to be eligible for sterilization?
3. Does the screening process respect an inmate's human rights?
4. Besides procreation, what does the legislation seem to be intended to control?

Questions for Further Thought

1. What intellectual and emotional traits appear to have been shared by two or more of the following: Walter Rauschenbusch (Document 20-2), Robert La Follette (Document 20-4), Jane Addams (Document 20-5), and Margaret Sanger (Document 20-6)?
2. Who would have been more offended by the Indiana sterilization law, Rauschenbusch or Walter Lippmann (Document 20-1)?
3. Are there any points of similarity in Hermann Biggs's *Administrative Control of Tuberculosis in New York City* (Document 20-7), Indiana's compulsory sterilization law (Document 20-8), and Oliver Wendell Holmes Jr.'s opinion in *Buck v. Bell* (headnote for Document 20-8)?

Progressivism and National Politics

Politics in the Progressive Era never lacked excitement. Tom Johnson, the mayor of Cleveland from 1901 to 1909, used circus tents to house his political rallies; an advocate of the single tax (on real estate, especially land held for speculation) and municipal ownership of public utilities, Johnson raced from rally to rally in his car, the Red Devil. Wisconsin governor and U.S. senator Robert La Follette was so combative that he earned the nickname Fighting Bob. And then there was Theodore Roosevelt. . . .

Roosevelt drove conservative Republicans to despair. "Don't any of you realize there's only one life between this madman and the White House?" Republican boss Mark Hanna asked after Roosevelt's nomination as vice-president in 1900. Hanna's fears were realized when President William McKinley was assassinated in 1901. Roosevelt virtually redefined the presidency and, in so doing, modernized the office. His progressivism drew heavily on the ideas of Alexander Hamilton and the leadership qualities of Abraham Lincoln. Roosevelt believed that government should foster social and economic progress, as outlined in Hamilton's "Report on Manufactures" (1791). In this view, government was best run by men who could demonstrate a combination of energy and wisdom, as Lincoln had during the Civil War and as Teddy Roosevelt thought he would do in the first decade of the new century. As president, Roosevelt put his ideas to work in his Square Deal with legislation aimed at the conservation of natural resources, railroad regulation, and consumer protection (see text pp. 658–663).

In keeping with his reputation as a trust-buster, Roosevelt thought that a modern economy could thrive under a system of regulation, not laissez-faire competition. That belief, coupled with a commitment to social justice, formed the basis of Roosevelt's New Nationalism in 1912. Woodrow Wilson disagreed with Roosevelt's theories, offering in their place an updated version of Jacksonian democracy (see text pp. 664–667). "What this country needs above all else," Wilson said during the 1912 presidential campaign, "is a body of laws which will look after the men who are on the make rather than the men who are already made." The Democrat and his New Freedom triumphed, but in his presidency Wilson borrowed much from the New Nationalism.

Document 20-9 offers a taste of Roosevelt's third-party rhetoric. The Progressive Party platform (Document 20-10) is exceptionally comprehensive in its social welfare proposals. Progressive lawyer Louis Brandeis's faith in competition, as shown in Document 20-11, greatly influenced Woodrow Wilson.

20-9   The Struggle for Social Justice (1912)

Theodore Roosevelt

When Theodore Roosevelt (1858–1919) left the White House in 1908 and went on safari in Africa, a wag commented, "I hope some lion will do his duty." Roosevelt returned home safely only to be disappointed by the conservative politics of his successor, William Howard Taft (see text pp. 663–664). Roosevelt challenged Taft for the Republican presidential nomination in 1912 and, when that failed, formed his own Progressive Party. During the campaign, Roosevelt often spoke about issues of social justice.

Source: Theodore Roosevelt, *Progressive Principles: Selections from Addresses Made during the Presidential Campaign of 1912*, ed. Elmer H. Youngman (New York: Progressive National Service, 1913), 199–207.

Lincoln made his fight on the two great fundamental issues of the right of the people to rule themselves, and not to be ruled by any mere part of the people, and of the vital need that this rule of the people should be exercised for social and industrial justice in a spirit of broad charity and kindliness to all, but with stern insistence that privilege should be eliminated from our industrial life and should be shorn of its power in our political life.

In describing his actions I am using the words which we use at the present day; but they exactly and precisely set forth his position fifty years ago. This position is ours at the present day.

The very rich men whom we mean when we speak of Wall Street have at this crisis shown that they are not loyal to the cause of human rights, human justice, human liberty. The rich man who is a good citizen first of all and a rich man only next, stands on a level with all other good citizens, and the rich man of this type is with us in this contest just as other good citizens, who happen to be wage-workers or retail traders or professional men, are with us. But the rich man who trusts in his riches, the rich man who feels that his wealth entitles him to more than his share of political, social and industrial power, is naturally against us. So likewise the men of little faith, the timid men who fear the people and do not dare trust them, the men who at the bottom of their hearts disbelieve in our whole principle of democratic governmental rule, are also against us. . . .

The representatives of privilege, the men who stand for the special interests and against the rule of the plain people and who distrust the people, care very little for party names.

They oppose us who stand for the cause of progress and of justice. They were accurately described by Lincoln . . . when he said that there had been nothing in politics since the Revolution so congenial to their nature as the position taken by his opponents.

The same thing is true now. Those people are against me because they are against the cause I represent.

These men against whom we stand include the men who desire to exploit the people for their own purposes and to profit financially by the wicked alliance between crooked business and crooked politics. Of course, they include also a large number of worthy and respectable men, who have no improper purpose to serve but who either do not see far into the future, or who are misled as to the facts of the case. Finally, they include those who at this moment represent what Lincoln described as the "old exclusive silk-stocking Whigs—nearly all the Whigs of the nice exclusive sort." . . .

The boss system is based on and thrives by injustice. Wherever you get the boss, wherever you get a Legislature controlled by mercenary politicians, there you will always find that privilege flourishes; there you will always find the great special interests striking hands with the crooked politicians and helping them plunder the people in the interest of both wings of the corrupt alliance.

It is to the interest of every honest man, and perhaps most especially to the interest of the honest big business man, that this alliance shall be broken up, and that we shall have a genuine rule of the people in a spirit of honesty and fair play toward all.

There is far more in this contest than is involved in the momentary victory of any man or any faction.

We are now fighting one phase of the eternal struggle for right and for justice. . . .

As far as we are concerned, the battle is just begun, and we shall go on with it to the end. We hail as our brothers all who contend in any way for the great cause of human rights, for the realization in measurable degree of the doctrines of the brotherhood of man.

We do not for a moment believe that any system of laws, no matter how good, or that any governmental action, can ever take the place of the individual character of the average man and the average woman, which must always in the last analysis be the chief factor in that man's or that woman's success.

But we insist that without just laws and just governmental action the high standard of character of the average American will not suffice to get all that as a Nation we are entitled to.

We must, through the law, make conditions of life more fair, make equality of opportunity more real. We must strive for industrial as well as political democracy.

Every man who fights for the protection of children from excessive toil, for the protection of women from working in factories for too long hours, for the protection, in short, of the workingman and his family so that he may live decently and bring up his children honorably and well—every man who works for any such cause is our fellow worker and we hail him as such.

Remember, that when we work to make this country a better place to live in for those who have been harshly treated by fate, we are also at the same time making it a better place to live in for those who have been well treated by fate.

The great representatives and beneficiaries of privilege, nineteen-twentieths of whom are opposing us with intense animosity, are acting with the utmost short-sightedness from the standpoint of the welfare of their children and their children's children.

We who stand for justice wish to make this country a better place to live in for the man who actually toils, for the wage-worker, for the farmer, for the small business man; and in so striving, we are really defending the cause of the children of those beneficiaries of privilege against what would be fatal action by their fathers. . . .

None of us can really prosper permanently if there are masses among us who are debased and degraded.

The sons of the millionaires will find this a very poor country to live in if men and women who make up the bulk of our ordinary citizenship do not have conditions so shaped that they can lead self-respecting lives on a basis which will permit them to retain their own sense of dignity, to treat their children aright, and to take their part in the life of the community as good citizens.

Exactly as each of us in his private life must stand up for his own rights and yet must respect the rights of others and acknowledge in practical fashion that he is indeed his brother's keeper, so all of us taken collectively, the people as a whole, must feel our obligation to work by governmental action, and in all other ways possible, to make the conditions better for those who are unfairly pressed down in the fierce competition of modern industrial life.

I ask justice for those who in actual life meet with most injustice—and I ask this not only for their sakes but for our own sakes, for the sake of the children and the children's children who are to come after us.

The children of all of us will pay in the future if we do not do justice in the present.

This country will not be a good place for any of us to live in if we do not strive with zeal and efficiency to make it a reasonably good place for all of us to live in.

Nor can our object be obtained save through the genuine control of the people themselves. The people must rule or gradually they will lose all power of being good citizens. The people must control their own destinies or the power of such control will atrophy.

Our cause is the cause of the plain people. It is the cause of social and industrial justice to be achieved by the plain people through the resolute and conscientious use of all the machinery, public and private, State and National, governmental and individual, which is at their command.

This is a great fight in which we are engaged, for it is a fight for human rights, and we who are making it are really making it for every good citizen of this Republic, no matter to what party he may belong.

Questions

1. By Roosevelt's standards, what constitutes a moral rich man?
2. Why does Roosevelt invoke Abraham Lincoln in this speech?
3. How does Roosevelt define social justice?

20-10   The Progressive Party Platform of 1912

There was nothing ordinary about the Progressive Party's presidential convention, held in Chicago in August 1912. The delegates sang "Onward Christian Soldiers" from the convention floor, Jane Addams seconded the nomination of the candidate, and Theodore Roosevelt delivered an acceptance speech titled "A Confession of Faith." The party platform was no less remarkable, as it blended Roosevelt's view of the future with a deeply ingrained religious passion.

Source: Kirk H. Porter and Donald Bruce Johnson, comps., *National Party Platforms, 1840–1964* (Urbana: University of Illinois Press, 1966), 175–178.

The conscience of the people, in a time of grave national problems, has called into being a new party, born of the nation's sense of justice. We of the Progressive party here dedicate ourselves to the fulfillment of the duty laid upon us by our fathers to maintain the government of the people, by the people and for the people whose foundations they laid.

We hold with Thomas Jefferson and Abraham Lincoln that the people are the masters of their Constitution, to fulfill its purposes and to safeguard it from those who, by perversion of its intent, would convert it into an instrument of injustice. In accordance with the needs of each generation the people must use their sovereign powers to establish and maintain equal opportunity and industrial justice, to secure which this Government was founded and without which no republic can endure.

This country belongs to the people who inhabit it. Its resources, its business, its institutions and its laws should be utilized, maintained or altered in whatever manner will best promote the general interest.

It is time to set the public welfare in the first place.

THE OLD PARTIES

Political parties exist to secure responsible government and to execute the will of the people.

From these great tasks both of the old parties have turned aside. Instead of instruments to promote the general welfare, they have become the tools of corrupt interests which use them impartially to serve their selfish purposes. Behind the ostensible government sits enthroned an invisible government owing no allegiance and acknowledging no responsibility to the people.

To destroy this invisible government, to dissolve the unholy alliance between corrupt business and corrupt politics is the first task of the statesmanship of the day.

The deliberate betrayal of its trust by the Republican party, the fatal incapacity of the Democratic party to deal with the new issues of the new time, have compelled the people to forge a new instrument of government through which to give effect to their will in laws and institutions.

Unhampered by tradition, uncorrupted by power, undismayed by the magnitude of the task, the new party offers itself as the instrument of the people to sweep away old abuses, to build a new and nobler commonwealth.

A COVENANT WITH THE PEOPLE

This declaration is our covenant with the people, and we hereby bind the party and its candidates in State and Nation to the pledges made herein.

THE RULE OF THE PEOPLE

The National Progressive party, committed to the principles of government by a self-controlled democracy expressing its will through representatives of the people, pledges itself to secure such alterations in the fundamental law of the several States and the United States as shall insure the representative character of the government.

In particular, the party declares for direct primaries for the nomination of State and National officers, for nationwide preferential primaries for candidates for the presidency; for the direct election of United States Senators by the people; and we urge on the States the policy of the short ballot, with responsibility to the people secured by the initiative, referendum and recall.

AMENDMENT OF CONSTITUTION

The Progressive party, believing that a free people should have the power from time to time to amend their fundamental law so as to adapt it progressively to the changing needs of the people, pledges itself to provide a more easy and expeditious method of amending the Federal Constitution.

NATION AND STATE

Up to the limit of the Constitution, and later by amendment of the Constitution, if found necessary, we advocate bringing under effective national jurisdiction those problems which have expanded beyond reach of the individual States.

It is as grotesque as it is intolerable that the several States should by unequal laws in matter of common concern become competing commercial agencies, barter the lives of their children, the health of their women and the safety and well being of their working people for the benefit of their financial interests.

The extreme insistence on States' rights by the Democratic party in the Baltimore platform demonstrates anew its inability to understand the world into which it has survived or to administer the affairs of a union of States which have in all essential respects become one people.

EQUAL SUFFRAGE

The Progressive party, believing that no people can justly claim to be a true democracy which denies political rights on account of sex, pledges itself to the task of securing equal suffrage to men and women alike.

CORRUPT PRACTICES

We pledge our party to legislation that will compel strict limitation of all campaign contributions and expenditures, and detailed publicity of both before as well as after primaries and elections.

PUBLICITY AND PUBLIC SERVICE

We pledge our party to legislation compelling the registration of lobbyists; publicity of committee hearings except on foreign affairs, and recording of all votes in committee; and forbidding federal appointees from holding office in State or National political organizations, or taking part as officers or delegates in political conventions for the nomination of elective State or National officials.

THE COURTS

The Progressive party demands such restriction of the power of the courts as shall leave to the people the ultimate authority to determine fundamental questions of social welfare and public policy. To secure this end, it pledges itself to provide:

1. That when an Act, passed under the police power of the State, is held unconstitutional under the State Constitution, by the courts, the people, after an ample interval for deliberation, shall have an opportunity to vote on the question whether they desire the Act to become law, notwithstanding such decision.

2. That every decision of the highest appellate court of a State declaring an Act of the Legislature unconstitutional on the ground of its violation of the Federal Constitution shall be subject to the same review by the Supreme Court of the United States as is now accorded to decisions sustaining such legislation.

ADMINISTRATION OF JUSTICE

The Progressive party, in order to secure to the people a better administration of justice and by that means to bring about a more general respect for the law and the courts, pledges itself to work unceasingly for the reform of legal procedures and judicial methods.

We believe that the issuance of injunctions in cases arising out of labor disputes should be prohibited when such injunctions would not apply when no labor disputes existed.

We also believe that a person cited for contempt in labor disputes, except when such contempt was committed in the actual presence of the court or so near thereto as to interfere with the proper administration of justice, should have a right to trial by jury.

SOCIAL AND INDUSTRIAL JUSTICE

The supreme duty of the Nation is the conservation of human resources through an enlightened measure of social and industrial justice. We pledge ourselves to work unceasingly in State and Nation for:

Effective legislation looking to the prevention of industrial accidents, occupational diseases, overwork, involuntary unemployment, and other injurious effects incident to modern industry;

The fixing of minimum safety and health standards for the various occupations, and the exercise of the public authority of State and Nation, including the Federal Control over interstate commerce, and the taxing power, to maintain such standards;

The prohibition of child labor;

Minimum wage standards for working women, to provide a "living wage" in all industrial occupations;

The general prohibition of night work for women and the establishment of an eight hour day for women and young persons;

One day's rest in seven for all wage workers;

The eight hour day in continuous twenty-four-hour industries;

The abolition of the convict contract labor system; substituting a system of prison production for governmental consumption only; and the application of prisoners' earnings to the support of their dependent families;

Publicity as to wages, hours and conditions of labor; full reports upon industrial accidents and diseases, and the opening to public inspection of all tallies, weights, measures and check systems on labor products;

Standards of compensation for death by industrial accident and injury and trade disease which will transfer the burden of lost earnings from the families of working people to the industry, and thus to the community;

The protection of home life against the hazards of sickness, irregular employment and old age through the adoption of a system of social insurance adapted to American use;

The development of the creative labor power of America by lifting the last load of illiteracy from American youth and establishing continuation schools for industrial education under public control and encouraging agricultural education and demonstration in rural schools;

The establishment of industrial research laboratories to put the methods and discoveries of science at the service of American producers;

We favor the organization of the workers, men and women, as a means of protecting their interests and of promoting their progress. . . .

BUSINESS

We believe that true popular government, justice and prosperity go hand in hand, and, so believing, it is our purpose to secure that large measure of general prosperity which is the fruit of legitimate and honest business, fostered by equal justice and by sound progressive laws.

We demand that the test of true prosperity shall be the benefits conferred thereby on all the citizens, not confined to individuals or classes, and that the test of corporate efficiency shall be the ability better to serve the public; that those who profit by control of business affairs shall justify that profit and that control by sharing with the public the fruits thereof.

We therefore demand a strong National regulation of inter-State corporations. The corporation is an essential part of modern business. The concentration of modern business, in some degree, is both inevitable and necessary for national and international business efficiency. But the existing concentration of vast wealth under a corporate system, unguarded and uncontrolled by the Nation, has placed in the hands of a few men enormous, secret, irresponsible power over the daily life of the citizen—a power insufferable in a free Government and certain of abuse.

This power has been abused, in monopoly of National resources, in stock watering, in unfair competition and unfair privileges, and finally in sinister influences on the public agencies of State and Nation. We do not fear commercial power, but we insist that it shall be exercised openly, under publicity, supervision and regulation of the most efficient sort, which will preserve its good while eradicating and preventing its ill.

To that end we urge the establishment of a strong Federal administrative commission of high standing, which shall maintain permanent active supervision over industrial corporations engaged in inter-State commerce, or such of them as are of public importance, doing for them what the Government now does for the National banks, and what is now done for the railroads by the Inter-State Commerce Commission.

Such a commission must enforce the complete publicity of those corporation transactions which are of public interest; must attack unfair competition, false capitalization and special privilege, and by continuous trained watchfulness guard and keep open equally all the highways of American commerce.

Thus the business man will have certain knowledge of the law, and will be able to conduct his business easily in conformity therewith; the investor will find security for his capital; dividends will be rendered more certain, and the savings of the people will be drawn naturally and safely into the channels of trade.

Under such a system of constructive regulation, legitimate business, freed from confusion, uncertainty and fruitless litigation, will develop normally in response to the energy and enterprise of the American business man.

We favor strengthening the Sherman Law by prohibiting agreement to divide territory or limit output; refusing to sell to customers who buy from business rivals; to sell below cost in certain areas while maintaining higher prices in other places; using the power of transportation to aid or injure special business concerns; and other unfair trade practices.

Questions

1. Why would a political party insist on making a "covenant" with voters? What does this "covenant" suggest about the way progressives viewed themselves and politics?
2. How does this platform propose to change the courts?
3. What does the section on social and industrial justice indicate about the United States in 1912?

20-11 In Defense of Competition (1912)

Louis D. Brandeis

Born in Virginia and raised in the South, Woodrow Wilson came naturally to a Democratic ideology that stressed the virtues of the common people and the free market (see text pp. 664–667). Both ideas thrived below the Mason-Dixon Line. Those beliefs were reinforced by Louis D. Brandeis (1856–1941), a famous lawyer and reformer who served as a Wilson campaign advisor. Brandeis authored his defense of competition in 1912.

Brandeis's comment on the "crimes of trade-union leaders" refers to a 1911 bombing of the offices of the *Los Angeles Times* that left twenty dead. Two labor activists, brothers James and John McNamara, were convicted for their roles in the explosion.

Source: "Shall We Abandon the Policy of Competition?" from *The Curse of Bigness: Miscellaneous Papers* by Louis D. Brandeis; Osmond K. Fraenkel, editor. Copyright 1934 by Louis D. Brandeis; renewed © 1962 by Susan Brandeis Gilbert and Elizabeth Brandeis Raushenbush. Used by permission of Viking Penguin, a division of Penguin Books USA Inc. (In reprint edition, Port Washington, N.Y.: Kennikat Press, 1965, 104–108.)

Shall we abandon as obsolete the long-cherished policy of competition, and accept in its place the long-detested policy of monopoly? The issue is not (as it is usually stated by advocates of monopoly), "Shall we have unrestricted competition or regulated monopoly?" It is, "Shall we have regulated competition or regulated monopoly?"

Regulation is essential to the preservation and development of competition, just as it is necessary to the preservation and best development of liberty. We have long curbed physically the strong, to protect those physically weaker. More recently we have extended such prohibitions to business. We have restricted theoretical freedom of contract by factory laws. The liberty of the merchant and manufacturer to lie in trade, expressed in the fine phrase of *caveat emptor* [let the buyer beware], is yielding to the better conceptions of business ethics, before pure-food laws and postal-fraud prosecutions. Similarly, the right to competition must be limited in order to preserve it. For excesses of competition lead to monopoly, as excesses of liberty lead to absolutism. The extremes meet.

The issue, therefore, is: Regulated competition *versus* regulated monopoly. The policy of regulated competition is distinctly a constructive policy. It is the policy of development as distinguished from the destructive policy of private monopoly.

It is asserted that to persist in the disintegration of existing unlawful trusts is to pursue a policy of destruction. No statement could be more misleading. Progress demands that we remove the obstacles in the path of progress; and private monopoly is the most serious obstacle.

One has heard of late the phrases: "You can't make people compete by law." "Artificial competition is undesirable."

These are truisms, but their implication is false. The suggestion is not that traders be compelled to compete, but that they be prevented from killing competition. Equally misleading is the phrase, "Natural monopolies should not be interfered with." There are no natural monopolies today in the industrial world. The Oil Trust and the Steel Trust have been referred to as natural monopolies, but they are both most unnatural. The Oil Trust acquired its control of the market by conduct which involved flagrant violations of law. Without the aid of criminal rebating, of bribery and corruption, the Standard Oil would never have acquired the vast wealth and power which enabled it to destroy its small competitors by price-cutting and similar practices.

The Steel Trust acquired control not through greater efficiency, but by buying up existing plants and ore supplies at fabulous prices. It is believed that not a single industrial monopoly exists today which is the result of natural growth. Competition has been suppressed either by ruthless practices or by an improper use of inordinate wealth and power. . . .

The only argument that has been seriously advanced in favor of private monopoly is that competition involves waste, while the monopoly prevents waste and leads to efficiency. This argument is essentially unsound. The wastes of competition are negligible. The economies of monopoly are superficial and delusive. The efficiency of monopoly is at the best temporary.

Undoubtedly competition involves waste. What human activity does not? The wastes of democracy are among the greatest obvious wastes, but we have compensations in democracy which far outweigh that waste and make it more efficient than absolutism. So it is with competition. The waste is relatively insignificant. There are wastes of competition which do not develop, but kill. These the law can and should eliminate, by regulating competition.

It is true that the unit in business may be too small to be efficient. It is also true that the unit may be too large

to be efficient, and this is no uncommon incident of monopoly.

Whenever trusts have developed efficiency, their fruits have been absorbed almost wholly by the trusts themselves. From such efficiency as they have developed, the community has gained substantially nothing.

The proposed Government commission to fix prices would not greatly relieve the evils attendant upon monopoly. It might reduce a trust's profits, but it would fail to reduce the trust's prices; because the limitation of the monopoly's profits would, by lessening this incentive, surely reduce the monopoly's efficiency.

To secure successful management of any private business, reward must be proportionate to success. The establishment of any rule fixing a maximum return on capital would, by placing a limit upon the fruits of achievement, tend to lessen efficiency.

No selling price for monopoly products could be set constitutionally at a point lower than that which would allow a reasonable return on capital. And in the absence of comparative data from any competing businesses producing the same article at less cost, it would be virtually impossible to determine that the cost should be lower.

The success of the Interstate Commerce Commission has been invoked as an argument in favor of licensing and regulating monopoly.

But the Interstate Commerce Commission has been effective principally in preventing rate increases and in stopping discrimination. In those instances where the Commission has reduced rates (as distinguished from preventing increases) the Commission rested its decisions largely on the ground that existing rates amount to discriminations against particular places or articles, or the lower rates were justified by a comparison with other rates of the same or other companies. Price-fixing of that nature applied to industrial thrusts would afford little protection to the public.

In the second place, there is a radical difference between attempts to fix rates for transportation and similar public services, and fixing prices in industrial businesses. Problems of transportation, while varying infinitely in detail, are largely the same throughout the whole country, and they are largely the same yesterday, today, and tomorrow. In industry we have, instead of uniformity, infinite variety; instead of stability, constant change.

In the third place, the problems of the Interstate Commerce Commission, relatively simple as they are, already far exceed the capacity of that or any single board. Think of the infinite questions which would come before an industrial commission seeking to fix rates, and the suffering of the community from the inability of that body promptly and efficiently to dispose of them.

Every business requires for its business health the *memento mori* [reminder of mortality] of competition from without. It requires likewise a certain competition from within, which can exist only where the ownership and management, on the one hand, and the employees, on the other, shall each be alert, hopeful, self-respecting, and free to work out for themselves the best conceivable conditions.

The successful, the powerful trusts, have created conditions absolutely inconsistent with these—America's—industrial and social needs. It may be true that as a legal proposition mere size is not a crime, but mere size may become an industrial and social menace, because it frequently creates as against possible competitors and as against the employees conditions of such gross inequality, as to imperil the welfare of the employees and of the industry.

In the midst of our indignation over the unpardonable crimes of trade-union leaders, disclosed at Los Angeles, would not our statesmen and thinkers seek to ascertain the underlying cause of this widespread, deliberate outburst of crimes of violence? What was it that led men like the McNamaras to believe really that the only recourse they had for improving the condition of the wage-earner was to use dynamite against property and life?

Certainly it was not individual depravity. Was it not because they, and men like them, believed that the wage-earner, acting singly, or collectively, is not strong enough to secure substantial justice? Is there not a causal connection between the development of these huge indomitable trusts and the horrible crimes now under investigation? Are not these irresistible trusts important contributing causes of these crimes—these unintelligent expressions of despairing social unrest? Is it not irony to speak of the equality of opportunity, in a country cursed with their bigness?

The right of labor to organize and to deal collectively with its employers should not be curtailed.

There is not the slightest danger that labor will assume control of industry. It has become exceedingly difficult for the unions to maintain themselves because of the constant inflow of foreign labor and the great number of non-union men. This maintains a state of competition, which, did it exist in the industrial and financial business of the country, would make unnecessary any change in existing laws.

The only right claimed by the labor unions is that of collective bargaining, and this right employers also should have and exercise. It would be perfectly proper for independent competing employers to form employers' organizations, and to deal with the labor unions upon exactly the same footing as is the case with unions—that is, collectively.

Nothing has been done to improve the conditions under which men labor, that has not increased their efficiency. Shorter hours often lead to greater production; and there is economy in high wages.

Questions

1. How does Brandeis counter the argument that some monopolies are inevitable or natural?
2. Why does he support competition instead of monopoly?
3. What are his views on organized labor?

Questions for Further Thought

1. What would Jane Addams (Document 20-5) find appealing in Theodore Roosevelt's speech on social justice (Document 20-9) and in the Progressive Party platform (Document 20-10)?
2. Drawing on the text and Documents 20-10 and 20-11, clarify similarities and differences between the positions of the Progressive Party and Louis D. Brandeis relative to competition and regulation.

CHAPTER 21

An Emerging World Power, 1877–1914

★   ★   ★

The Roots of Expansionism

Many aspects of nineteenth-century American foreign policy were isolationist. Between 1814 and 1898, the United States avoided war with European nations, and American secretaries of state heeded George Washington's warning against entangling alliances. However, an active foreign policy did exist: the Louisiana and Alaska purchases, relations with Mexico, and the status of native American tribes were important issues.

By the 1890s, a far more ambitious American foreign policy was evolving. The change reflected the status of the United States as an emerging economic power. By the turn of the century, American factory, oil, and steel products were competing for a share of the world market. The republic whose citizens had once made clothes at home was selling sewing machines worldwide. The republic that under Thomas Jefferson had all but abandoned its navy had begun an ambitious naval buildup by the century's end.

However, economic strength brought its own set of problems. Americans soon discovered that the modern world did not respond well to the counsel of eighteenth-century leaders, especially if the United States wanted to be a world power. Stepping onto the world stage meant answering a series of difficult questions: How was a democracy to act as a world power? What was the proper mix of self-interest and principle in foreign policy? Should the United States control overseas possessions, and what if the native peoples resisted? Both the American public and its leaders struggled over the answers in relation to Latin America, the Philippines, Cuba, Puerto Rico, and Hawaii.

Alfred Thayer Mahan's treatise on sea power (Document 21-1) challenges the assumptions of a society long suspicious of the military. Document 21-2 presents the Reverend Josiah Strong's argument for the justness—and inevitability—of an American empire. In Document 21-3, Grace Service recounts her life as an American missionary in China.

21-1   The Influence of Sea Power upon History (1890)

Alfred Thayer Mahan   Except in times of war, Americans have never favored the establishment of a large, standing military force. The navy, for example, was greatly expanded during the Civil War, only to deteriorate over the next twenty-five years. To naval officer Alfred Thayer Mahan (1840–1914), the situation had to be reversed if the United States was to become a true world power. Mahan's *The Influence of Sea Power upon History, 1660–1783* appeared in 1890 and had an enormous influence on U.S. foreign policy (see text pp. 675–679). Before the end of the decade, the U.S. Navy had modernized to the point where it easily defeated its Spanish counterpart.

Source: Alfred Thayer Mahan, *The Influence of Sea Power upon History, 1660–1783* (Boston: Little, Brown, 1890), 83–89.

As the practical object of this inquiry is to draw from the lessons of history inferences applicable to one's own country and service, it is proper now to ask how far the conditions of the United States involve serious danger, and call for action on the part of the government, in order to build again her sea power. It will not be too much to say that the action of the government since the Civil War, and up to this day, has been effectively directed solely to what has been called the first link in the chain which makes sea power. Internal development, great production, with the accompanying aim and boast of self-sufficingness, such has been the object, such to some extent the result. In this the government has faithfully reflected the bent of the controlling elements of the country, though it is not always easy to feel that such controlling elements are truly representative, even in a free country. However that may be, there is no doubt that, besides having no colonies, the intermediate link of a peaceful shipping, and the interests involved in it, are now likewise lacking. In short, the United States has only one link of the three.

The circumstances of naval war have changed so much within the last hundred years, that it may be doubted whether such disastrous effects on the one hand, or such brilliant prosperity on the other, as were seen in the wars between England and France, could now recur. In her secure and haughty sway of the seas England imposed a yoke on neutrals which will never again be borne; and the principle that the flag covers the goods is forever secured. The commerce of a belligerent can therefore now be safely carried on in neutral ships, except when contraband of war or to blockaded ports; and as regards the latter, it is also certain that there will be no more paper blockades. Putting aside therefore the question of defending her seaports from capture or contribution, as to which there is practical unanimity in theory and entire indifference in practice, what need has the United States of sea power? Her commerce is even now carried on by others; why should her people desire that which, if possessed, must be defended at great cost? So far as this question is economical, it is outside the scope of this work; but conditions which may entail suffering and loss on the country by war are directly pertinent to it. Granting therefore that the foreign trade of the United States, going and coming, is on board ships which an enemy cannot touch except when bound to a blockaded port, what will constitute an efficient blockade? The present definition is, that it is such as to constitute a manifest danger to a vessel seeking to enter or leave the port. This is evidently very elastic. Many can remember that during the Civil War, after a night attack on the United States fleet off Charleston, the Confederates next morning sent out a steamer with some foreign consuls on board, who so far satisfied themselves that no blockading vessel was in sight that they issued a declaration to that effect. On the strength of this declaration some Southern authorities claimed that the blockade was technically broken, and could not be technically re-established without a new notification. Is it necessary, to constitute a real danger to blockade runners, that the blockading fleet should be in sight? Half a dozen fast steamers, cruising twenty miles off-shore between the New Jersey and Long Island coast, would be a very real danger to ships seeking to go in or out by the principal entrance to New York; and similar positions might effectively blockade Boston, the Delaware, and the Chesapeake. The main body of the blockading fleet, prepared not only to capture merchant-ships but to resist military attempts to break the blockade, need not be within sight, nor in a position known to the shore. The bulk of Nelson's fleet was fifty miles from Cadiz two days before Trafalgar, with a small detachment watching close to the harbor. The allied fleet began to get under way at 7 A.M., and Nelson, even under the conditions of those days, knew it by 9.30. The English fleet at that distance was a very real danger to its enemy. It seems possible, in these days of submarine telegraphs, that the blockading forces in-shore and off-shore, and from one port to another, might be in telegraphic communication with one another along the whole coast of the United States, readily giving mutual support; and if, by some fortunate military combination, one detachment were attacked in force, it could warn the others and retreat upon them. Granting that such a blockade off one port were broken on one day, by fairly driving away the ships maintaining it, the notification of its being re-established could be cabled all over the world the next. To avoid such blockades there must be a military force afloat that will at all times so endanger a blockading fleet that it can by no means keep its place. Then neutral ships, except those laden with contraband of war, can come and go freely, and maintain the commercial relations of the country with the world outside.

It may be urged that, with the extensive sea-coast of the United States, a blockade of the whole line cannot be effectively kept up. No one will more readily concede this than officers who remember how the blockade of the Southern coast alone was maintained. But in the present condition of the navy, and, it may be added, with any additions not exceeding those so far proposed by the government, the attempt to blockade Boston, New York, the Delaware, the Chesapeake, and the Mississippi, in other words, the great centres of export and import, would not entail upon one of the large maritime nations efforts greater than have been made before. England has at the same time blockaded Brest, the Biscay coast, Toulon, and Cadiz, when there were powerful squadrons lying within the harbors. It is true that commerce in neutral ships can then enter other ports of the United States than those named; but what a dislocation of the carrying traffic of the country, what failure of supplies at times, what inadequate means of transport by rail or water, of dockage, of lighterage, of warehousing, will be involved in such an enforced change of the ports of entry! Will there be no money loss, no suffering, consequent upon this? And when with much pain and expense these evils have been partially remedied, the enemy may be led to stop the new inlets as he did the old. The people of the United States will certainly not starve, but they may suffer grievously. As for supplies which are contraband of war, is there not reason to fear that the United States is not now able to go alone if an emergency should arise?

The question is eminently one in which the influence of the government should make itself felt, to build up for the nation a navy which, if not capable of reaching distant countries, shall at least be able to keep clear the chief approaches to its own. The eyes of the country have for a quarter of a century been turned from the sea; the results of such a policy and of its opposite will be shown in the instance of France and of England. Without asserting a narrow parallelism between the case of the United States and either of these, it may safely be said that it is essential to the welfare of the whole country that the conditions of trade and commerce should remain, as far as possible, unaffected by an external war. In order to do this, the enemy must be kept not only out of our ports, but far away from our coasts.[1]

Can this navy be had without restoring the merchant shipping? It is doubtful. History has proved that such a purely military sea power can be built up by a despot, as was done by Louis XIV.; but though so fair seeming, experience showed that his navy was like a growth which having no root soon withers away. But in a representative government any military expenditure must have a strongly represented interest behind it, convinced of its necessity. Such an interest in sea power does not exist, cannot exist here without action by the government. How such a merchant shipping should be built up, whether by subsidies or by free trade, by constant administration of tonics or by free movement in the open air, is not a military but an economical question. Even had the United States a great national shipping, it may be doubted whether a sufficient navy would follow; the distance which separates her from other great powers, in one way a protection, is also a snare. The motive, if any there be, which will give the United States a navy, is probably now quickening in the Central American Isthmus. Let us hope it will not come to the birth too late.

Here concludes the general discussion of the principal elements which affect, favorably or unfavorably, the growth of sea power in nations. The aim has been, first to consider those elements in their natural tendency for or against, and then to illustrate by particular examples and by the experience of the past. Such discussions, while undoubtedly embracing a wider field, yet fall mainly within the province of strategy, as distinguished from tactics. The

---

[1]The word "defence" in war involves two ideas, which for the sake of precision in thought should be kept separated in the mind. There is defence pure and simple, which strengthens itself and awaits attack. This may be called passive defence. On the other hand, there is a view of defence which asserts that safety for one's self, the real object of defensive preparation, is best secured by attacking the enemy. In the matter of sea-coast defence, the former method is exemplified by stationary fortifications, submarine mines, and generally all immobile works destined simply to stop an enemy if he tries to enter. The second method comprises all those means and weapons which do not wait for attack, but go to meet the enemy's fleet, whether it be but for a few miles, or whether to his own shores. Such a defence may seem to be really offensive war, but it is not; it becomes offensive only when its object of attack is changed from the enemy's fleet to the enemy's country. England defended her own coasts and colonies by stationing her fleets off the French ports, to fight the French fleet if it came out. The United States in the Civil War stationed her fleets off the Southern ports, not because she feared for her own, but to break down the Confederacy by isolation from the rest of the world, and ultimately by attacking the ports. The methods were the same; but the purpose in one case was defensive, in the other offensive.

The confusion of the two ideas leads to much unnecessary wrangling as to the proper sphere of army and navy in coast-defence. Passive defences belong to the army; everything that moves in the water to the navy, which has the prerogative of the offensive defence. If seamen are used to garrison forts, they become part of the land forces, as surely as troops, when embarked as part of the complement, become part of the sea forces.

considerations and principles which enter into them belong to the unchangeable, or unchanging, order of things, remaining the same, in cause and effect, from age to age. They belong, as it were, to the Order of Nature, of whose stability so much is heard in our day; whereas tactics, using as its instruments the weapons made by man, shares in the change and progress of the race from generation to generation. From time to time the superstructure of tactics has to be altered or wholly torn down; but the old foundations of strategy so far remain, as though laid upon a rock. There will next be examined the general history of Europe and America, with particular reference to the effect exercised upon that history, and upon the welfare of the people, by sea power in its broad sense. From time to time, as occasion offers, the aim will be to recall and reinforce the general teaching, already elicited, by particular illustrations. The general tenor of the study will therefore be strategical, in that broad definition of naval strategy which has before been quoted and accepted: "Naval strategy has for its end to found, support, and increase, as well in peace as in war, the sea power of a country." In the matter of particular battles, while freely admitting that the change of details has made obsolete much of their teaching, the attempt will be made to point out where the application or neglect of true general principles has produced decisive effects; and, other things being equal, those actions will be preferred which, from their association with the names of the most distinguished officers, may be presumed to show how far just tactical ideas obtained in a particular age or a particular service. It will also be desirable, where analogies between ancient and modern weapons appear on the surface, to derive such probable lessons as they offer, without laying undue stress upon the points of resemblance. Finally, it must be remembered that, among all changes, the nature of man remains much the same; the personal equation, though uncertain in quantity and quality in the particular instance, is sure always to be found.

Questions

1. According to Mahan, how could an enemy cripple American trade and commerce?
2. Why does he see this country's geographic isolation from other powerful nations as both a strength and a weakness?
3. In general, what is Mahan's view of history?

21-2   America in the World's Future (1886)

Josiah Strong

The interests of the Reverend Josiah Strong ranged from the cities (see Document 19-3) to foreign policy. In this excerpt from *Our Country*, Strong blends religion with a sense of Anglo-Saxon superiority to portray America's coming greatness. Like other observers of his time, Strong invoked Social Darwinism. He was not alone in arguing that nations, too, evolve through a process of natural selection. Others making that case included Brooks Adams and John Fiske (see text p. 680).

Source: Josiah Strong, *Our Country* (1886; reprint, ed. Jurgen Herbst, Cambridge, Mass.: Harvard University Press, 1963), 210, 212–216.

Mr. Darwin is not only disposed to see, in the superior vigor of our people, an illustration of his favorite theory of natural selection, but even intimates that the world's history thus far has been simply preparatory for our future, and tributary to it. He says: "There is apparently much truth in the belief that the wonderful progress of the United States, as well as the character of the people, are the results of natural selection; for the most energetic, restless, and courageous men from all parts of Europe have emigrated during the last ten or twelve generations to that great country, and have there succeeded best. Looking at the distant future, I do not think that the Rev. Mr. Zincke takes an exaggerated view when he says: 'All other series of events—as that which resulted in the culture of mind in Greece, and that which resulted in the Empire of Rome—only appear to have purpose and value when viewed in connection with, or rather as subsidiary to, the great stream of Anglo-Saxon emigration to the West.'" . . .

Again, another marked characteristic of the Anglo-Saxon is what may be called an instinct or genius for colonizing. His unequaled energy, his indomitable perseverance, and his personal independence, made him a pioneer. He excels all others in pushing his way into new countries. It was those in whom this tendency was strongest that came to America, and this inherited tendency has been further developed by the westward sweep of successive generations across the continent. So noticeable has this characteristic become that English visitors remark it. Charles Dickens once said that the typical American would hesitate to enter heaven unless assured that he could go farther west.

Again, nothing more manifestly distinguished the Anglo-Saxon than his intense and persistent energy, and he is developing in the United States an energy which, in eager activity and effectiveness, is peculiarly American.

This is due partly to the fact that Americans are much better fed than Europeans, and partly to the undeveloped resources of a new country, but more largely to our climate, which acts as a constant stimulus. Ten years after the landing of the Pilgrims, the Rev. Francis Higginson, a good observer, wrote: "A sup of New England air is better than a whole flagon of English ale." Thus early had the stimulating effect of our climate been noted. Moreover, our social institutions are stimulating. In Europe the various ranks of society are, like the strata of the earth, fixed and fossilized. There can be no great change without a terrible upheaval, a social earthquake. Here society is like the waters of the sea, mobile . . . that which is at the bottom today may one day flash on the crest of the highest wave. Every one is free to become whatever he can make of himself; free to transform himself from a rail-splitter or a tanner or a canal-boy, into the nation's President. Our aristocracy, unlike that of Europe, is open to all comers. Wealth, position, influence, are prizes offered for energy; and every farmer's boy, every apprentice and clerk, every friendless and penniless immigrant, is free to enter the list. Thus many causes co-operate to produce here the most forceful and tremendous energy in the world.

What is the significance of such facts? These tendencies infold the future; they are the mighty alphabet with which God writes his prophecies. May we not, by a careful laying together of the letters, spell out something of his meaning? It seems to me that God, with infinite wisdom and skill, is training the Anglo-Saxon race for an hour sure to come in the world's future. Heretofore there has always been in the history of the world a comparatively unoccupied land westward, into which the crowded countries of the East have poured their surplus populations. But the widening waves of migration, which millenniums ago rolled east and west from the valley of the Euphrates,[1] meet to-day on our Pacific coast. There are no more new

worlds. The unoccupied arable lands of the earth are limited, and will soon be taken. The time is coming when the pressure of population on the means of subsistence will be felt here as it is now felt in Europe and Asia. Then will the world enter upon a new stage of its history—*the final competition of races, for which the Anglo-Saxon is being schooled.* Long before the thousand millions are here, the mighty *centrifugal* tendency, inherent in this stock and strengthened in the United States, will assert itself. Then the race of unequaled energy, with all the majesty of numbers and the might of wealth behind it—the representative, let us hope, of the largest liberty, the purest Christianity, the highest civilization—having developed peculiarly aggressive traits calculated to impress its institutions upon mankind, will spread itself over the earth. If I read not amiss, this powerful race will move down upon Mexico, down upon Central and South America, out upon the islands of the sea, over upon Africa and beyond. And can any one doubt that the result of this competition of races will be the "survival of the fittest"? "Any people," says Dr. Bushnell,[2] "that is physiologically advanced in culture, though it be only in a degree beyond another which is mingled with it on strictly equal terms, is sure to live down and finally live out its inferior. Nothing can save the inferior race but a ready and pliant assimilation. Whether the feebler and more abject races are going to be regenerated and raised up, is already very much of a question. What if it should be God's plan to people the world with better and finer material?

"Certain it is, whatever expectations we may indulge, that there is a tremendous overbearing surge of power in the Christian nations, which, if the others are not speedily raised to some vastly higher capacity, will inevitably submerge and bury them forever. These great populations of Christendom—what are they doing, but throwing out their colonies on every side, and populating themselves, if I may so speak, into the possession of all countries and climes?" To this result no war of extermination is needful; the contest is not one of arms, but of vitality and of civilization. "At the present day," says Mr. Darwin, "civilized nations are everywhere supplanting barbarous nations, excepting where the climate opposes a deadly barrier; and they succeed mainly, though not exclusively, through their arts, which are the products of the intellect." Thus the Finns were supplanted by the Aryan races in Europe and Asia, the Tartars by the Russians, and thus the aborigines of North America, Australia and New Zealand are now disappearing before the all-conquering Anglo-Saxons. It seems as if these inferior tribes were only precursors of a superior race, voices in the wilderness crying: "Prepare ye the way of the Lord!" The savage is a hunter; by the incoming of civilization the game is driven away and disappears before the hunter becomes a herder or an agricul-

---

[1]*Valley of the Euphrates:* Mesopotamia, between the Euphrates and Tigris Rivers, was an area of ancient settlement.

[2]*Dr. Horace Bushnell* (1802–1876) was a Congregational minister and theologian.

turist. The savage is ignorant of many diseases of civilization which, when he is exposed to them, attack him before he learns how to treat them. Civilization also has its vices, of which the uninitiated savage is innocent. He proves an apt learner of vice, but dull enough in the school of morals.

Every civilization has its destructive and preservative elements. The Anglo-Saxon race would speedily decay but for the salt of Christianity. Bring savages into contact with our civilization, and its destructive forces become operative at once, while years are necessary to render effective the saving influences of Christian instruction. Moreover, the pioneer wave of our civilization carries with it more scum than salt. Where there is one missionary, there are hundreds of miners or traders or adventurers ready to debauch the native.

Whether the extinction of inferior races before the advancing Anglo-Saxon seems to the reader sad or otherwise, it certainly appears probable. I know of nothing except climatic conditions to prevent this race from populating Africa as it has peopled North America. And those portions of Africa which are unfavorable to Anglo-Saxon life are less extensive than was once supposed. The Dutch Boers, after two centuries of life there, are as hardy as any race on earth. The Anglo-Saxon has established himself in climates totally diverse—Canada, South Africa, and India—and, through several generations, has preserved his essential race characteristics. He is not, of course, superior to climatic influences; but even in warm climates, he is likely to retain his aggressive vigor long enough to supplant races already enfeebled. Thus, in what Dr. Bushnell calls "the out-populating power of the Christian stock," may be found God's final and complete solution of the dark problem of heathenism among many inferior peoples.

Some of the stronger races, doubtless, may be able to preserve their integrity; but, in order to compete with the Anglo-Saxon, they will probably be forced to adopt his methods and instruments, his civilization and his religion. Significant movements are now in progress among them. While the Christian religion was never more vital, or its hold upon the Anglo-Saxon mind stronger, there is taking place among the nations a widespread intellectual revolt against traditional beliefs. "In every corner of the world," says Mr. Froude,[3] "there is the same phenomenon of the decay of established religions. . . . Among the Mohammedans, Jews, Buddhists, Brahmins, traditionary creeds are losing their hold. An intellectual revolution is sweeping over the world, breaking down established opinions, dissolving foundations on which historical faiths have been built up." The contact of Christian with heathen nations is awakening the latter to new life. Old superstitions are loosening their grasp. The dead crust of fossil faiths is being shattered by the movements of life underneath. In Catholic countries, Catholicism is losing its influence over educated minds, and in some cases the masses have already lost all faith in it. Thus, while on this continent God is training the Anglo-Saxon race for its mission, a complemental work has been in progress in the great world beyond. God has two hands. Not only is he preparing in our civilization the die with which to stamp the nations, but, by what Southey[4] called the "timing of Providence," he is preparing mankind to receive our impress.

---

[3]*James A. Froude (1818–1894) was an English historian.*
[4]*Robert Southey (1774–1843) was an English author.*

Questions

1. How would you characterize Strong's version of Social Darwinism?
2. What kind of Christianity is he talking about?
3. What does Strong predict about the fate of peoples that encounter the United States as it expands?

21-3   Open House Days for a China Missionary (1900s)

Grace Service

China has long fascinated American missionaries as well as businessmen as a market for either souls or products. Grace Service (1879–1954) and Robert Service (1879–1935) devoted themselves to the former. The Services were a college-educated couple who in 1905 volunteered to work in China for the Young Men's Christian Association. They spent the rest of their lives in China. It would be the land that welcomed their three sons just as it claimed the life of their infant daughter.

Grace Service's memoirs were edited by her son John, whose career as a China specialist for the State Department became a victim of the witch-hunts of Senator Joseph McCarthy (see Document 27-9).

Source: John S. Service, ed., *Golden Inches: The China Memoir of Grace Service*, 67–75. Copyright © 1989 by the Regents of the University of California. Reprinted by permission of the University of California Press.

When we left Kiating that September we hired a cargo boat with a high *peng* (a rounded mat roof) and a good wooden floor. The Boy had gone with us as cook to Golden Summit and did so well that we now discharged the dirty cook at Kiating, giving him travel money. The hold of our boat was loaded with loose dried beans which looked to be a clean and non-odorous cargo. We put all our things on the floor level, and the boat was large enough to give plenty of room and, best of all, good head space. Our teacher was with us on the boat and we studied as we traveled. We could even sit at our new desk to study and write. The trip to Chengtu was expected to take about a week.

The floods that summer had caused damage along the river and we saw signs on every hand. Once, walking on the bank, we noticed tangled vines above our heads in tree branches. These were peanut vines that had been washed out of the fields and lodged in the trees. Even at Chengtu the river had covered the big stone bridge outside the South Gate. Close to this place, a big section of the city wall had been undermined (and took many months to repair). But, despite the summer flood, the river was now rather low for that time of the year—and our boat was large.

Life was very pleasant for the first two or three days, and we congratulated ourselves on the size and comfort of our craft. Then trouble began. At first we found only a few tiny white worms. In a few hours they had multiplied and were into everything: food boxes, beds, clothing, even into our ears when we took refuge tucked tightly inside a bed net. The little worms were everywhere. Complaints to the captain were useless; worms meant nothing to him. We then tried to hurry the boat, but its draft was considerable and the river seemed to be falling. We could only proceed by the main channel and frequently had to wait for other boats to negotiate narrow spots. After a couple of days of worms, we began to have a pest of little white moths. The worms were busying themselves in their life cycle under our very eyes. These tiny blundering creatures flew everywhere, and our tempers were decidedly on edge.

I began to feel that we would never reach Chengtu, and the eternal singsong of Bob repeating Chinese phrases after his teacher's intoned speech made me weary beyond words. To be honest, I was probably as much of a trial to live with as the worms and moths! Bob suggested that from a village about a hundred *li* from Chengtu, I could reach the city in a day in my chair, the Boy escorting me. But when we reached the village that evening, it was im-possible to find chair men. Next morning it was raining, which ruled out the possibility of making the trip in one day even if bearers could be found. So I settled down to sticking it out on the bean boat. We had still more trouble, having to lighten cargo at one place where the channel was shallow and the current swift. We did not reach Chengtu until the next Tuesday. Then there was a joyous farewell to that nice, clean boat full of its worms and moths with whom we had spent eleven unforgettable days.

We were delighted to reach our Chinese home again. A quick check showed that the robbers had taken practically all my table linen as well as some other things. Otherwise all was in good order. A few days of scrubbing, washing windows, hanging clean curtains, and changing shelf and drawer papers made us as clean and fresh as could be. I liked the new desk very much and had it set up in our living room, where it became my special possession and delight. Bob had a large Chinese desk of red bean wood in his study, so he did not need it. My new desk was of what was called "buried nanmu." It had a large flat top. On each side above the table top were six small drawers. Between these stacks an open space was just right for a row of books. Below on either side were tiers of large drawers. Many and many a letter I wrote on that desk, and many that I received were stowed inside.

That fall we studied, and continued to widen our acquaintances among Chinese. Bob spent much time and thought making plans and establishing contacts with people. An advisory committee was formed as a preliminary step toward the organization of a full-fledged YMCA. Sunday afternoon meetings were held, sometimes at our house, sometimes at the Hodgkins'.

I was still miserable with my severe pain and suffered exceedingly with backaches which wore me out. My cook could not make good bread, and there were no bakeries whatsoever. The bread, rolls, cakes, and cookies all had to come from my hands. For ourselves alone, this was not much; but we entertained Chinese constantly, and they were all pleased to have foreign-style refreshments. Late that year I finally got our new cook, who had been our Boy at Omei, trained to make acceptable cookies and cupcakes. This was a great help. Tea had always to be served to our guests. If they did not eat the cakes served with it, these were gladly pocketed to be taken home to a small brother or sister, to children, or even to a mother interested in sampling the odd things served by the Westerners.

About that time we rented a piece of land at the rear of the Methodist school adjacent to us on the west. It belonged to the mission but was then not needed. It gave us space for two tennis courts with a tea pavilion west of them in the shadow of a high wall. There was also some ground left over for raising vegetables. Eventually we enjoyed many products of our own garden.

Our young friends among Chinese students began to ask if I would call on their families or be at home to receive calls from them. Doors thus opened in both directions, and we became deeply involved in our surroundings. I began to teach English to a few young men. At first my work was individual instruction in conversation and composition. Our careful attention was given to the young man who was later to become the first Chinese YMCA secretary in Chengtu. In 1907 I did not keep a careful record of the guests at special teas we had for Chinese students, but I know the total ran into 600 or 700. For 1908 I did keep a weekly record. It gives a total of 967 as counted. However, on numerous occasions we were not able to count late comers, so our figures would read "42 plus" and so on. Also these records showed only those who came to our regular, announced teas. Bob had many individual callers in both those years; in 1908 he doubtless entertained well over 1,200. These contacts were valuable to him and gave me considerable to oversee and manage.

When Chinese women called, I had to drop everything. They often came at inopportune times for us, as Chinese meal hours were not the same as ours, and they would stay and stay and stay. To come at ten in the forenoon, or even around noon, and then sit until three in the afternoon was asking a good deal of a hostess, but we had to conform to the habits of the country. A lady often brought a whole train of attendants: perhaps a sister or two, several grown daughters or younger children, and often four or five amahs. The guests sat down to visit, and the servants stood around gazing at everything and being what one might call movable fixtures in the room. It took me a long time to accustom myself to these calls. Gradually I learned the technique, and despite my lack of adequate language could carry them off with some sort of aplomb. I learned the polite phrases, and could fall back on the children and stock questions. Eventually, some of the women became my real friends, so that barriers no longer made such a chasm between us.

All women guests wanted to see our entire house. Most of them, if they expressed any opinion, thought we wasted too much time trying to be clean: clean kitchens and clean floors were no necessity to them. When I visited their homes, I was impressed by the dirty kitchens and their lack of any adequate attention to the floors. Their kitchens were in what we would call sheds. Most of their floors were dingy brick or grimy wood. Frequent expectoration, together with the habit of allowing babies to urinate freely on the floor anywhere and everywhere, made

for unhygienic conditions and offensive odors. Cobwebs never seemed to bother Chinese; to this day I have to call servants' attention to them. Upper walls and ceiling spaces seem never to come within range of the Chinese eye; special orders must be given if you want to be sure that high corners will be cleaned. On the other hand, Chinese take great care in polishing the flat top and side surfaces of furniture such as cupboards and sideboards; and a Boy will carefully dust framed pictures every day, sometimes even dusting behind them.

Another of my household duties at this time was my husband's collars. Men were still wearing stiff collars every day. It seemed impossible for the Chinese to get them stiff enough, or to keep from scorching them during the ironing. And there were no tailors in these early years who knew anything about "foreign-style" sewing. So what sewing I needed, I also did myself, by hand and machine. I sent for American patterns and made clothes as I could, studying the illustrations of magazines and inspecting the clothes of new arrivals from home. It was my boast that I could cut out a man's shirt one evening and have it finished, save buttonholes, by the next afternoon. I learned to stitch such pieces without any basting and thus could save time. I taught my amah to do buttonholes. Her first attempts were what my New England grandmother would have called "pigs' eyes," but Amah improved and became a fine buttonholer.

I was busy during these early Chengtu days. Often I rose at 6:30 in the morning to work down my bread. Then there was study, sewing, and general housekeeping. This could include a lot of mold prevention, and packing away all woolens and winter things at the approach of hot weather. Dry cleaners were unheard of, and laundry work demanded much attention and training of servants. It is quite a task to do up men's white summer suits, be they duck, silk, serge, or flannel. I found the Szechwanese to be good washers but poor rinsers. It was my rule to demand ample water for that use. By this means I kept our clothes from taking on that dull, muddy tinge which many housewives regard as one of the prices of living in the Orient.

Late in 1907 the West China Missionary Conference was impending, and I was determined to find a Boy who could be wide-awake and efficient. I interviewed several prospects without success. At last a young fellow named Liu Pei-yun appeared. I had never wanted a country boy, because it seemed to me that some education, however little, would hold more potential for training. This boy was the son of a buyer of silk yarn. He could read and write and was an apt pupil in learning the work expected from him. On arrival he knew nothing whatsoever of any foreign furnishings or usages. When I first showed him how to set the table, he asked what the forks were and how they were used! He became a trusted servant, was married in our home, and worked for us from the fall of 1907 until that of 1920. Bob then helped him set up a business for himself in Chengtu. In later years he visited us several times in Shanghai and has always kept up connection with our family. . . .

The American community grew slowly. Late in 1907 another young Californian, C. W. Batdorf [UC 1906], had come to teach in the government university near us. He and Mr. Bullock [also UC 1906] kept bachelor's hall together. We were always glad to help them when we could; I made curtains, sheets, and such items for them. Early in 1908, Chee Soo Lowe, a California-born Chinese who had graduated in mining from the University of California [still another member of 1906], came to investigate the mineral resources of Szechwan under employment by the viceroy. He was often in our home and we greatly enjoyed him.

As the Chinese ladies became less bashful I began to have more callers. Many of them besought me to start some sort of classes for them. They wanted to "learn foreign ways," to knit, crochet, and even to bake the light cakes which they ate in our homes. We were constantly invited to Chinese feasts. Here the procedure is the reverse of our custom. Chinese socializing is done before the meal, and the guests leave directly from the table. This meant that we often sat talking while the very food we were to eat was in preparation. We might hear the fowls squawking as they were chased and killed to be served to us later. The men and women always ate in separate rooms: the men in the main hall or some such public apartment, while we women were relegated to women's bedrooms. I was teaching a few pupils and kept busy in spite of not being well. I still had my attacks of severe pain now and then and was forced to spend a good many days in bed.

Questions

1. What conditions did the Services encounter in China?
2. How does Service characterize the Chinese people?
3. Why would a westerner tend to feel superior to the Chinese people in the period about which Service wrote?

Questions for Further Thought

1. Compare and contrast the arguments in support of expansionism advanced by Alfred Thayer Mahan (Document 21-1) and Josiah Strong (Document 21-2). Does expansionism mean the same thing to both?
2. Do common themes run through Strong's "The Dangers of Cities" (Document 19-3) and his "America in the World's Future" (Document 21-2)?
3. In what ways does Grace Service (Document 21-3) embody the principles of Josiah Strong?

An American Empire

Throughout the nineteenth century Americans argued about the direction of foreign policy. Some people thought it should be guided by Manifest Destiny, or the belief that the United States was destined for greatness in an imperial sense (see text p. 684). Others insisted on a foreign policy based on mission, with the United States leading the rest of the world by setting a selfless example. Presidential administrations over the past century have occasionally embraced one of these extremes, but for the most part American foreign policy has been a not always successful mixture of the two.

Thus, in empowering President William McKinley (see *Instructor's Resource Manual*, vol. 2: *Since 1865*, 4th ed., 464–465) to intervene to end the fighting in Cuba in April 1898, Congress passed the Teller Amendment, which proclaimed the American intention to "leave the government and control of the Island to its people." Three years later, however, the Cuban Constitution included the American-authored Platt Amendment, which made Cuba an American protectorate. Also, in peace negotiations with Spain, the United States annexed the Philippine Islands, another Spanish colony that was seeking independence. The platform of the American Anti-Imperialist League might have condemned acquisition of the Philippines, but other Americans saw the islands, Manila Bay in particular, as a stepping-stone to the China market, real and imagined.

Document 21-4 presents Senator Albert J. Beveridge's defense of the Philippines annexation, and Document 21-5 reproduces Mark Twain's denunciation thereof. Document 21-6 offers a cartoonist's view of Cuban and Filipino conduct and American policy.

21-4   American Imperialism in the Pacific (1902)

Albert J. Beveridge

Republican Senator Albert J. Beveridge (1862–1927) of Indiana strongly advocated annexation of the Philippines. Here, in a speech delivered to a San Francisco audience, he stresses economic opportunities in Asia, but he also justifies colonialism. In a Senate speech two years earlier, he had even more pointedly made clear his racism and Anglo-Saxonism, heaping scorn on both Filipinos and Spaniards. The Filipinos, he declared, "are a barbarous race, modified by three centuries of contact with a decadent race. . . three hundred years of superstition in religion, dishonesty in dealing, disorder in habits of industry, and cruelty, caprice, and corruption in government."

Source: Albert J. Beveridge, "The Command of the Pacific," in *The Meaning of the Times and Other Speeches* (Indianapolis: Bobbs-Merrill, 1908; reprint, Freeport, N.Y.: Books for Libraries Press, 1968), 188, 190–197.

Fellow Americans of California and the Pacific Slope:
The Pacific is the ocean of the future; and the Pacific is yours. The markets of the Orient are the Republic's future commercial salvation; and the Orient's commercial future is yours. Important as other questions are, the one great question that covers seas, and islands, and continents; that will last when other questions have been answered and forgotten; that will determine your present prosperity and the greatness of your children's children in their day, is the mastery of the Pacific and the commercial conquest of the eastern world.

That question is peculiarly your question, people of the Pacific slope. If your wealth is to increase you must produce a surplus; and if you produce a surplus, you must sell it. And where will you sell it, people of the Pacific slope, save over the seas of sunset? If your laboring-men are to be employed, you must have commerce; and where will commerce great enough for your ever increasing population be found, save in your supply of the ever increasing demands of the millions of the Orient? . . .

Mark now the historic conjunction of the elements of national growth, national duty and national necessity. First, the time had come when the Republic was prepared to do its part in governing peoples and lands not ready to govern themselves. Second, at this hour of our preparation for this duty, war gave us the Philippines and our possessions in the Gulf [of Mexico]. And, third, at that very time our commerce was crying aloud for new markets where we

might sell the surplus products of our factories and farms—and the only remaining markets on the globe were those surrounding the lands which war had given us. American duty, American preparedness, American commercial necessity came in the same great hour of fate.

Let us consider the argument of advantage to ourselves, flowing from the Philippines, the Orient and from American mastery of the Pacific. What is the great commercial necessity of the Republic? It is markets—foreign markets. At one time we needed to build up our industries here and for that purpose to save for them our home markets. Protection did that; and to-day our home market is supplied. Now we have invaded the markets of Europe and filled them almost to their capacity with American goods. Our great combinations of capital devoted to manufacturing and transportation compete successfully with foreign manufacturers in their own countries.

But still we have a surplus; and an unsold surplus is commercial peril. Every unsold bushel of wheat reduces the pride of every other one of the millions of bushels of wheat produced. If our manufacturers produce more than they can sell, that surplus product causes the mills to shut down until they produce no more than they can sell. And after we supply our own market, after we sell all we can to the markets of Europe, we still have an unsold surplus. If our prosperity continues this must be sold.

Where shall the Republic sell its surplus? Where shall the Pacific coast sell its surplus? And your surplus unsold means your commerce paralyzed, your laboring-men starving. Expansion answers that question. . . .

If it is not true that her possessions help England's commerce, why does not England give them up? Why does not Germany give up her possession in Northern China? Why is she spending tens of millions of dollars there, building German railways, German docks and vast plants for future German commerce? Why does Russia spend a hundred million dollars of Russian gold building Russian railways through Manchuria[1] and binding that territory, vast in extent as all the states of the Pacific slope combined, to the Russian empire with bands of steel? Why is Japan now preparing to take Manchuria from Russia as she has already taken Formosa[2] from China?

The Philippines do not help us in Oriental commerce! They have helped us even now by making the American name known throughout the East, and our commerce with the islands and countries influenced by the Philippines has in two short years leaped from $43,000,000 to $120,000,000.

If an American manufacturer established a great storehouse in London believing that it would help his business and then found his sales in London increasing 300 per cent, in less than three years, would he give away that branch establishment because some theorist told him that branch houses did not help trade and that he could sell as much and more if he shipped direct from his factory to the English purchaser?

And yet this practically is what the Opposition asks the American people to believe about and do with the Philippines. From every English and German possession in the East English and German goods are shipped in bulk and then reshipped as quick orders near at hand call for them. And these possessions influence the entire population of the countries where they are located.

If this is true of English and German possessions, will it not be true of America's possessions at the very door of this mighty market? If it is not true, it will be because American energy, American sagacity, American enterprise are not equal to the commercial opportunity which the Philippines give us in the Orient. Americans never yet found an obstacle which they did not overcome, an opportunity they did not make their own.

Has the decay of American energy begun with you, men of the West? Who says so is infidel to American character. Answer these slanders of your energy and power, people of the Pacific states—answer them with our ballots! Tell the world that, of all this masterful Nation, none more vital than the men and women who hold aloft the Republic's flag on our Pacific shores!

If we need this Oriental market—and we can not dispose of our surplus without it—what American farmer is willing for us to give the Philippines to America's competitors? What American manufacturer is willing to surrender this permanent commercial advantage to the nations who are striving for those very markets? Yet, that is what the Opposition asks you to do. For if we quit them certainly Germany or England or Japan will take them.

And these markets, great as they are, are hardly yet opened to the modern world. They are like a gold mine worked by ancient methods and yielding only a fraction of its wealth. Apply to that gold mine modern machinery, modern science, modern methods and its stream of gold swells in volume. This illustration applies to Oriental markets. For example, China buys from all the world at the present time $250,000,000 worth of foreign products. These are consumed by less than 75,000,000 of the Chinese people. The reason of this is that foreign goods can not penetrate the interior. There are no railways, no roads; merchandise must be transported on human backs, and corrupt officials lay heavy transportation taxes at every stage. But now all this begins to change. All over China railroads are projected, surveyed and even now are building.

And wherever they have gone Chinese commerce has increased, just as our own commerce increases here wherever a railroad goes. And wherever railways go wagon roads branch from them. Thus the methods of modern civilization are weaving a network of modern conditions among this most ancient of peoples. And if China now buys $250,000,000 worth of products from the rest of the world, what will she buy when all this change that is now taking place brings her 400,000,000 as purchasers to the markets of the world? The most conservative experts estimate that China alone will buy at least one thousand million dollars worth of the products of other countries every year. . . .

The Philippines and the Orient are your commercial opportunity. Does our duty as a Nation forbid you to accept it? Does our fitness for the work prevent us from doing it? Or does the Nation's preparedness, the Republic's duty and the commercial necessity of the American people unite in demanding of American statesmanship the holding of the Philippines and the commercial conquest of the Oriental world?

Do they say that it is a wrong to any people to govern them without their consent? Consider Hayti [*sic*] and read in her awful decline since French government there was overthrown the answer to that theory. Remember that English administration in Egypt has in less than twenty years made fertile her fields and redeemed her people, debased by a thousand years of decline, and read in that miracle the answer to that theory.

Examine every example of administration of government in the Orient or Africa by a superior power and find the answer to that theory. Come nearer home. Analyze the three years of American administration in Porto [*sic*] Rico—American schools for the humblest, just laws, honest government, prosperous commerce. Now sail for less than a day to the sister island of San [*sic*] Domingo and behold commerce

---

[1]*Manchuria* was an economically important region of northeastern China, at times dominated or occupied by Russia or Japan.

[2]*Formosa* (now Taiwan) is an island off southeast China that was seized by Japan after war with China during the 1890s.

extinguished, justice unknown, government and law a whim, religion degenerated to voodoo rites, and answer whether American administration in Porto Rico, even if it had been without the consent of the governed, is not better for that people than San Domingo's independent savagery.

Let us trust the American people! The most fervent belief in their purity, their power and their destiny is feeble, after all, compared with the reality on which that faith is founded. Great as our fathers were, the citizens of this Republic, on the whole, are greater still to-day, with broader education, loftier outlook. And if this were not so, we should not be worthy of our fathers; for, to do as well as they we must do better. Over the entire Republic the people's common schools increase, churches multiply, culture spreads, the poorest have privileges impossible to the wealthiest fifty years ago.

When any man fears the decay of American institutions, he ignores the elemental forces around him which are building future generations of Americans, stronger, nobler than ourselves. And those who ask you to believe that administration of orderly government in the Philippines will poison the fountain of Americanism here at home, ask you to believe that your children are a mockery, your schools a myth, your churches a dream.

American soldiers, American teachers, American administrators—all are the instruments of the Nation in discharging the Nation's high duty to the ancient and yet infant people which circumstance has placed in our keeping. If it is said that our duty is to teach the world by example, I ask if our duty ends with that? Does any man's duty to his children end with mere example? Does organized society owe no duty to the orphan and the abandoned save that of example? Why, then, are our schools, our asylums, our benevolent institutions, which force physical and mental training upon the neglected youth of the Republic? And does the parent or does organized society refrain from discharging this duty if the child resists?

And just so nations can not escape the larger duties to senile or infant peoples. Nations can not escape the charge laid upon them to develop the world's neglected resources, to make the wilderness, the fields, the mines and countries inhabited by barbarous peoples useful to civilized man. No nation lives to itself alone. It can not if it would. Even the great powers influence one another, not only by example, but by tariffs, by trade arrangements, by armies, by navies. How much greater should be this influence when circumstance gives to the keeping of a great power the destiny of an undeveloped race and the fortunes of an undeveloped country?

Questions

1. What are some of Beveridge's justifications for American imperialism in the Pacific?
2. What assumption does he make concerning Asian markets and the American surplus?
3. How does Beveridge believe that Puerto Rico—and, by implication, the Philippines—would benefit from American control?

21-5   To the Person Sitting in Darkness (1901)

Mark Twain

Although Secretary of State John Hay called the fight with Spain "a splendid little war," not everyone viewed it that way. A group of prominent Americans who opposed the acquisition of colonies founded the American Anti-Imperialist League. Among their number was famed author Mark Twain (1835–1910). He ostensibly addressed part of the following essay to "the person sitting in darkness," that is, to a person in what would today be called the Third World.

Twain refers to Joseph Chamberlain, who as colonial secretary for the British government refused to consider South African independence. Chamberlain's policies helped cause the Boer War, which was being fought when Twain wrote this essay. The Mr. Croker to whom Twain refers later in the essay is Richard Croker, notorious "boss" of Tammany Hall, New York City's corrupt Democratic machine.

Source: Excerpted from Mark Twain, "To the Person Sitting in Darkness" (1901), in *Mark Twain: Collected Tales, Sketches, Speeches, and Essays, 1891–1910* (New York: Library of America, 1992), 465–473.

And by and by comes America, and our Master of the Game plays it badly—plays it as Mr. Chamberlain was playing it in South Africa. It was a mistake to do that; also, it was one which was quite unlooked for in a Master who was playing it so well in Cuba. In Cuba, he was playing the usual and regular *American* game, and it was winning, for there is no way to beat it. The Master, contemplating Cuba, said: "Here is an oppressed and friendless little nation which is willing to fight to be free; we go partners, and put up the strength of seventy million sympathizers and the resources of the United States: play!" Nothing but Europe combined could call that hand: and Europe cannot combine on anything. There, in Cuba, he was following our great tradition in a way which made us very proud of him, and proud of the deep dissatisfaction which his play was provoking in continental Europe. Moved by a high inspiration, he threw out those stirring words which proclaimed that forcible annexation would be "criminal aggression"; and in that utterance fired another "shot heard round the world." The memory of that fine saying will be outlived by the remembrance of no act of his but one—that he forgot it within the twelvemonth, and its honorable gospel along with it.

For, presently, came the Philippine temptation. It was strong; it was too strong, and he made that bad mistake: he played the European game, the Chamberlain game. It was a pity; it was a great pity, that error; that one grievous error, that irrevocable error. For it was the very place and time to play the American game again. And at no cost. Rich winnings to be gathered in, too; rich and permanent; indestructible; a fortune transmissible forever to the children of the flag. Not land, not money, not dominion—no, something worth many times more than that dross: our share, the spectacle of a nation of long harrassed and persecuted slaves set free through our influence; our posterity's share, the golden memory of that fair deed. The game was in our hands. If it had been played according to the American rules, Dewey would have sailed away from Manila as soon as he had destroyed the Spanish fleet—after putting up a sign on shore guaranteeing foreign property and life against damage by the Filipinos, and warning the Powers that interference with the emancipated patriots would be regarded as an act unfriendly to the United States. The Powers cannot combine, in even a bad cause, and the sign would not have been molested.

Dewey could have gone about his affairs elsewhere, and left the competent Filipino army to starve out the little Spanish garrison and send it home, and the Filipino citizens to set up the form of government they might prefer, and deal with the friars and their doubtful acquisitions according to Filipino ideas of fairness and justice—ideas which have since been tested and found to be as high an order as any that prevail in Europe or America.

But we played the Chamberlain game, and lost the chance to add another Cuba and another honorable deed to our good record.

The more we examine the mistake, the more clearly we perceive that it is going to be bad for the Business. The Person Sitting in Darkness is almost sure to say: "There is something curious about this—curious and unaccountable. There must be two Americans; one that sets the captive free, and one that takes a once-captive's new freedom away from him, and picks a quarrel with him with nothing to found it on; then kills him to get his land."

The truth is, the Person Sitting in Darkness *is* saying things like that; and for the sake of the Business we must persuade him to look at the Philippine matter in another and healthier way. We must arrange his opinions for him. I believe it can be done; for Mr. Chamberlain has arranged England's opinion of the South African matter, and done it most cleverly and successfully. He presented the facts—some of the facts—and showed those confiding people what the facts meant. He did it statistically, which is a good way. He used the formula: "Twice 2 are 14, and 2 from 9 leaves 35." Figures are effective; figures will convince the elect.

Now, my plan is a still bolder one than Mr. Chamberlain's, though apparently a copy of it. Let us be franker than Mr. Chamberlain; let us audaciously present the whole of the facts, shirking none, then explain them according to Mr. Chamberlain's formula. This daring truthfulness will astonish and dazzle the Person Sitting in the Darkness, and he will take the Explanation down before his mental vision has had time to get back into focus. Let us say to him:

"Our case is simple. On the 1st of May, Dewey destroyed the Spanish fleet. This left the Archipelago in the hands of its proper and rightful owners, the Filipino nation. Their army numbered 30,000 men, and they were competent to whip out or starve out the little Spanish garrison; then the people could set up a government of their own devising. Our traditions required that Dewey should now set up his warning sign, and go away. But the Master of the Game happened to think of another plan—the European plan. He acted upon it. This was, to send out an army—ostensibly to help the native patriots put the finishing touch upon their long and plucky struggle for independence, but really to take their land away from them and keep it. That is, in the interest of Progress and Civilization. The plan developed, stage by stage, and quite satisfactorily. We entered into a military alliance with the trusting Filipinos, and they hemmed in Manila on the land side, and by their valuable help the place, with its garrison of 8,000 or 10,000 Spaniards, was captured—a thing which we could not have accomplished unaided at that time. We got their help by—by ingenuity. We knew they were fighting for their independence, and that they had been at it for two years. We knew they supposed that we also were fighting in their worthy cause—just as we had helped the Cubans fight for Cuban independence—and we allowed them to go on thinking so. *Until Manila was ours and we could get along without them.* Then we showed our hand. Of course, they were surprised—that was natural; surprised and disappointed; disappointed and grieved. To them it looked un-American; uncharacteristic; foreign to our established traditions. And this was natural, too; for we were only playing the American Game in public—in private it was the European. It was neatly done, very neatly, and it bewildered them. They could not understand it; for we had been so friendly—so affectionate, even—with those simple-minded patriots! We, our own selves, had brought back out of exile their leader, their hero, their hope, their Washington—Aguinaldo; brought him in a warship, in high honor, under the sacred shelter and hospitality of the flag; brought him back and restored him to his people, and got their moving and eloquent gratitude for it. Yes, we had been so friendly to them, and had heartened them up in so many ways! We had lent them guns and ammunition; advised with them; exchanged pleasant courtesies with them; placed our sick and wounded in their kindly care; intrusted our Spanish prisoners to their humane and honest hands; fought shoulder to shoulder with them against "the common enemy" (our own phrase); praised their mercifulness, praised their fine and honorable conduct; borrowed their trenches, borrowed strong positions which they had previously captured from the Spaniards; petted them, lied to them—officially proclaiming that our land and naval forces came to give them their freedom and displace the bad Spanish Government—fooled them, used them until we needed them no longer; then derided the sucked orange and threw it away. We kept the positions which we had beguiled them of; by and by, we moved a force forward and overlapped patriot ground—a clever thought, for we needed trouble, and this would produce it. A Filipino soldier, crossing the ground, where no one had a right to forbid him, was shot by our sentry. The badgered patriots resented this with arms, without waiting to know whether Aguinaldo, who was absent, would approve or not. Aguinaldo did not approve; but that availed nothing. What we wanted, in the interest of Progress and Civilization, was the Archipelago, unencumbered by patriots struggling for independence; and War was what we needed. We clinched our opportunity. It is Mr. Chamberlain's case over again—at least in its motive and intention; and we played the game as adroitly as he played it himself."

At this point in our frank statement of fact to the Person Sitting in Darkness, we should throw in a little trade taffy about the Blessings of Civilization—for a change and for the refreshment of his spirit—then go on with our tale:

We and the patriots having captured Manila, Spain's ownership of the Archipelago and her sovereignty over it were at an end—obliterated—annihilated—not a rag or shred of either remaining behind. It was then that we conceived the divinely humorous idea of *buying* both of these specters from Spain! [It is quite safe to confess this to the Person Sitting in Darkness, since neither he nor any other sane person will believe it.] In buying those ghosts for twenty millions, we also contracted to take care of the friars and their accumulations. [I think we also agreed to

propagate leprosy and smallpox, but as to this there is doubt. But it is not important; persons afflicted with the friars do not mind other diseases.]

"With our Treaty ratified, Manila subdued, and our Ghosts secured, we had no further use for Aguinaldo and the owners of the Archipelago. We forced a war, and we have been hunting America's guest and ally through the woods and swamps ever since."

At this point in the tale, it will be well to boast a little of our war work and our heroisms in the field, so as to make our performance look as fine as England's in South Africa; but I believe it will not be best to emphasize this too much. We must be cautious. Of course, we must read the war telegrams to the Person, in order to keep up our frankness; but we can throw an air of humorousness over them, and that will modify their grim eloquence a little, and their rather indiscret [sic] exhibitions of gory exultation. Before reading to him the following display heads of the dispatches of November 18, 1900, it will be well to practice on them in private first, so as to get the right tang of lightness and gayety into them:

"ADMINISTRATION WEARY OF PROTRACTED HOSTILITIES!"

"REAL WAR AHEAD FOR FILIPINO REBELS"[1]

"WILL SHOW NO MERCY!" . . .

Of course, we must not venture to ignore our General MacArthur's reports—oh, why do they keep on printing those embarrassing things?—we must drop them trippingly from the tongue and take the chances:

During the last ten months our losses have been 268 killed and 750 wounded; Filipino loss, *three thousand two hundred and twenty-seven killed,* and 694 wounded.

We must stand ready to grab the Person Sitting in Darkness, for he will swoon away at this confession, saying: "Good God! those 'niggers' spare their wounded, and the Americans massacre theirs!"

We must bring him to, and coax him and coddle him, and assure him that the ways of Providence are best, and that it would not become us to find fault with them; and then, to show him that we are only imitators, not originators, we must read the following passage from the letter of an American soldier lad in the Philippines to his mother, published in *Public Opinion,* of Decorah, Iowa, describing the finish of a victorious battle:

"WE NEVER LEFT ONE ALIVE. IF ONE WAS WOUNDED, WE WOULD RUN OUR BAYONETS THROUGH HIM."

---

[1]"Rebels!" Mumble that funny word—don't let the Person catch it distinctly.—M.T.

Having now laid all the historical facts before the Person Sitting in Darkness, we should bring him to again, and explain them to him. We should say to him:

"They look doubtful, but in reality they are not. There have been lies; yes, but they were told in a good cause. We have been treacherous; but that was only in order that real good might come out of apparent evil. True, we have crushed a deceived and confiding people; we have turned against the weak and the friendless who trusted us; we have stamped out a just and intelligent and well-ordered republic; we have stabbed an ally in the back and slapped the face of a guest; we have bought a Shadow from an enemy that hadn't it to sell; we have robbed a trusting friend of his land and his liberty; we have invited our clean young men to shoulder a discredited musket and do bandits' work under a flag which bandits have been accustomed to fear, not to follow; we have debauched America's honor and blackened her face before the world; but each detail was for the best. We know this. The Head of every State and Sovereignty in Christendom and 90 per cent. of every legislative body in Christendom, including our Congress and our fifty state legislatures, are members not only of the church, but also of the Blessings-of-Civilization Trust. This world-girdling accumulation of trained morals, high principles, and justice cannot do an unright thing, an unfair thing, an ungenerous thing, an unclean thing. It knows what it is about. Give yourself no uneasiness; it is all right."

Now then, that will convince the Person. You will see. It will restore the Business. Also, it will elect the Master of the Game to the vacant place in the Trinity of our national gods; and there on their high thrones the Three will sit, age after age, in the people's sight, each bearing the Emblem of his service: Washington, the Sword of the Liberator; Lincoln, the Slave's Broken Chains; the Master, the Chains Repaired.

It will give the Business a splendid new start. You will see.

Everything is prosperous, now; everything is just as we should wish it. We have got the Archipelago, and we shall never give it up. Also, we have every reason to hope that we shall have an opportunity before very long to slip out of our congressional contract with Cuba and give her something better in the place of it. It is a rich country, and many of us are already beginning to see that the contract was a sentimental mistake. But now—right now—is the best time to do some profitable rehabilitating work—work that will set us up and make us comfortable, and discourage gossip. We cannot conceal from ourselves that, privately, we are a little troubled about our uniform. It is one of our prides; it is acquainted with honor; it is familiar with great deeds and noble; we love it, we revere it; and so this errand it is on makes us uneasy. And our flag—another pride of ours, our chiefest! We have worshipped it so; and when we have seen it in far lands—glimpsing it unexpectedly in that strange sky, waving its welcome and benediction to us—we have caught our breaths, and uncovered our heads, and couldn't speak, for a moment, for the thought of what it was to us and the great ideals it stood for. Indeed, we *must* do something about these things; it is easily managed. We can have a special one—our states do it: we can have just our usual flag, with the white stripes painted black and the stars replaced by the skull and crossbones.

And we do not need that Civil Commission out there. Having no powers, it has to invent them, and that kind of work cannot be effectively done by just anybody; an expert is required. Mr. Croker can be spared. We do not want the United States represented there, but only the Game.

By help of these suggested amendments, Progress and Civilization in that country can have a boom, and it will take in the Persons who are Sitting in Darkness, and we can resume Business at the old stand.

Questions

1. How does Twain say he will argue the cause of empire?
2. What is his real purpose in recounting recent events?
3. Why is Twain so cynical?

21-6 Cartoon on the Philippines and Cuba (1901)

R. C. Bowman

R. C. Bowman, a cartoonist for the *Minneapolis Tribune,* here relates American policy toward the Philippines and Cuba to the conduct of Filipinos and Cubans.

Source: Minneapolis Tribune (1901), reprinted by permission in John J. Johnson, *Latin America in Caricature* (Austin and London: University of Texas Press, 1980), 209.

THE PHILIPPINES: "What yer got?"
CUBA: "Pie."
THE PHILIPPINES: "Where'd yer git it?"
CUBA: "Mah Uncle Sam gin it to me; any maybe ef
you was half way decent he' gin you some."

Question

1. Does the cartoonist's depiction of Cuba and the Philippines involve racial stereo-typing?
2. What importance do you attach to the gender, age, and clothing Bowman selected for the characters in his cartoon?

Questions for Further Thought

1. What do "Voices from Abroad" and "American Voices" (pp. 688–692) contribute to your thinking about America, the Spanish-American War, and the Philippine insurrection?
2. Drawing on the text and documents for Chapters 18 and 21, reflect on the role of race in both domestic and foreign affairs in turn-of-the-century America.
3. How does the tone of Mark Twain's essay (Document 21-5) differ from that of Josiah Strong's essay (Document 21-2) and Albert J. Beveridge's essay (Document 21-4)?

Onto the World Stage

American foreign policy focused on two areas: the Caribbean and the Pacific. Beginning in the 1890s, European nations exhibited what the United States feared was an imperial interest in the Caribbean. For example, in 1895 Great Britain pressed a border claim for British Guiana against Venezuela. Grover Cleveland responded by invoking the Monroe Doctrine (see text p. 677).

Seven years after the Venezuela crisis, Venezuela defaulted on some loans. Great Britain, Germany, and Italy then sent a naval force that fired on Venezuelan installations. This time Theodore Roosevelt mounted a diplomatic counteroffensive with the so-called Roosevelt Corollary to the Monroe Doctrine. Roosevelt warned that governmental incompetence by Caribbean nations would "force the United States, however reluctantly, in flagrant cases . . . of wrong doing or impotence, to the exercise of an international police power."

Although Europe heeded the warning, the United States was only partially successful as the dominant Caribbean power. Policy makers found that it was easier to build the Panama Canal (see text pp. 693–694) than to avoid invoking the Roosevelt Corollary. By 1917, American troops had landed at various times in Cuba, the Dominican Republic, Haiti, Mexico, and Nicaragua. Although the intent was to create order out of chaos, the policy resulted in anti-Americanism throughout the region.

In Asia, the United States spent two years breaking the insurrection of Philippine nationalists; these military operations cost some 4,300 American lives and as many as 300,000 Filipino lives. Once pacified, the islands were supposed to serve as a springboard for American business interests in China. However, China proved to be a difficult market to enter. Europeans were long established there, and in 1900 the Chinese attempted to end all foreign domination. Although the Boxer Rebellion (see text pp. 695–697) failed, it allowed Secretary of State John Hay to insist that all the powers recognize the independence of China, along with the legitimacy of American interests there.

John Hay's Open-Door Notes are reprinted in Document 21-7; they should be read as a contrast to Document 21-8, the Roosevelt Corollary.

21-7   Open-Door Notes (1899, 1900)

John Hay

Unwilling to make a military commitment to China, the United States pressed its interests through diplomacy. The following notes from Secretary of State John Hay (1838–1905) made up the open-door policy, which remained in force until the triumph of Mao Ze-dong (Mao Tse-tung) in 1949. Hay's first communication is to Andrew D. White, the American ambassador to Germany. His second is a telegram sent to the American embassies and missions in all the countries that wanted to trade with China.

Source: John Hay to Andrew D. White, September 6, 1899; and John Hay's circular letter to the powers cooperating in China, July 3, 1900. In Henry Steele Commager and Milton Cantor, eds., *Documents of American History,* 10th ed. (Englewood Cliffs, N.J.: Prentice Hall, 1988), 2: 9–11.

JOHN HAY TO ANDREW D. WHITE

Department of State, Washington, September 6, 1899

At the time when the Government of the United States was informed by that of Germany that it had leased from His Majesty the Emperor of China the port of Kiao-chao and the adjacent territory in the province of Shantung, assurance were given to the ambassador of the United States at Berlin by the Imperial German minister for foreign affairs that the rights and privileges insured by treaties with China to citizens of the United States would not thereby suffer or be in anywise impaired within the area over which Germany had thus obtained control.

More recently, however, the British Government recognized by a formal agreement with Germany the exclusive right of the latter country to enjoy in said leased area and the contiguous "sphere of influence or interest" certain privileges, more especially those relating to railroads and mining enterprises; but as the exact nature and extent of the rights thus recognized have not been clearly defined, it is possible that serious conflicts of interest may at any time arise not only between British and German subjects within said area, but that the interests of our citizens may also be jeopardized thereby.

Earnestly desirous to remove any cause of irritation and to insure at the same time to the commerce of all nations in China the undoubted benefits which should accrue from a formal recognition by the various powers claiming "spheres of interest" that they shall enjoy perfect equality of treatment for their commerce and navigation within such "spheres," the Government of the United States would be pleased to see His German Majesty's Government give formal assurance, and lend its cooperation in securing like assurances from the other interested powers, that each, within its respective sphere of whatever influence—

First. Will in no way interfere with any treaty port or any vested interest within any so-called "sphere of interest" or leased territory it may have in China.

Second. That the Chinese treaty tariff of the time being shall apply to all merchandise landed or shipped to all such ports as are within said "sphere of interest" (unless they be "free ports"), no matter to what nationality it may belong, and that duties so leviable shall be collected by the Chinese Government.

Third. That it will levy no higher harbor dues on vessels of another nationality frequenting any port in such "sphere" than shall be levied on vessels of its own nationality, and no higher railroad charges over lines built, controlled, or operated within its "sphere" on merchandise belonging to citizens or subjects of other nationality transported through such "sphere" than shall be levied on similar merchandise belonging to its own nationals transported over equal distances.

The liberal policy pursued by His Imperial German Majesty in declaring Kiao-chao a free port and in aiding the Chinese Government in the establishment there of a customhouse are so clearly in line with the proposition which this Government is anxious to see recognized that it entertains the strongest hope that Germany will give its acceptance and hearty support.

The recent ukase of His Majesty the Emperor of Russia declaring the port of Ta-lien-wan open during the whole of the lease under which it is held from China to the merchant ships of all nations, coupled with the categorical assurances made to this Government by His Imperial Majesty's representative at this capital at the same time and since repeated to me by the present Russian ambassador, seem to insure the support of the Emperor to the proposed measure. Our ambassador at the Court of St. Petersburg has in consequence, been instructed to submit it to the Russian Government and to request their early consideration of it. A copy of my instruction on the subject to Mr. Tower[1] is herewith inclosed for your confidential information.

The commercial interests of Great Britain and Japan will be so clearly served by the desired declaration of intentions, and the views of the Governments of these countries as to the desirability of the adopting of measures insuring the benefits of equality of treatment of all foreign trade throughout China are so similar to those entertained by the United States, that their acceptance of the propositions herein outlined and their cooperation in advocating their adoption by the other powers can be confidently expected. I enclosed herewith copy of the instruction which I have sent to Mr. Choate[2] on the subject.

In view of the present favorable conditions, you are instructed to submit the above considerations to His Imperial German Majesty's Minister for Foreign Affairs, and to request his early consideration of the subject.

CIRCULAR TELEGRAM TO THE POWERS COOPERATING IN CHINA

Department of State, Washington, July 3, 1900

In this critical posture of affairs in China it is deemed appropriate to define the attitude of the United States as far as present circumstances permit this to be done. We adhere to the policy initiated by us in 1857 of peace with the Chinese nation, of furtherance of lawful commerce, and of protection of lives and property of our citizens by all means guaranteed under extraterritorial treaty rights and by the law of nations. If wrong be done to our citizens we propose to hold the responsible authors to the uttermost accountability. We regard the condition at Pekin as one of virtual anarchy, whereby power and responsibility are practically devolved upon the local provincial authorities.

[1]*Charlemagne Tower* (1848–1923) was the ambassador to Russia from 1899 to 1902.

[2]*Joseph H. Choate* (1832–1917), an attorney and diplomat, was ambassador to Great Britain from 1899–1905.

So long as they are not in overt collusion with rebellion and use their power to protect foreign life and property, we regard them as representing the Chinese people, with whom we seek to remain in peace and friendship. The purpose of the President is, as it has been heretofore, to act concurrently with the other powers; first, in opening up communication with Pekin and rescuing the American officials, missionaries, and other Americans who are in danger; secondly, in affording all possible protection everywhere in China to American life and property; thirdly, in guarding and protecting all legitimate American interests; and fourthly, in aiding to prevent a spread of the disorders to the other provinces of the Empire and a recurrence of such disasters. It is of course too early to forecast the means of attaining this last result; but the policy of the Government of the United States is to seek a solution which may bring about permanent safety and peace to China, preserve Chinese territorial and administrative entity, protect all rights guaranteed to friendly powers by treaty and international law, and safeguard for the world the principle of equal and impartial trade with all parts of the Chinese Empire. . . .

Questions

1. What was the purpose of Hay's first Open-Door Note?
2. In what ways does the second note differ from the first?
3. Taken together, what do the notes say about the American attitude toward China?

21-8 The Roosevelt Corollary to the Monroe Doctrine (1904, 1905)

Theodore Roosevelt

After advising that it was wisdom to "speak softly and carry a big stick," President Theodore Roosevelt proceeded to speak and act as policeman of the Western Hemisphere, at least in areas of strategic importance to the United States—the Caribbean, Central America, and the northernmost nations of South America. The following excerpt offers his corollary to the Monroe Doctrine, which Roosevelt proclaimed in successive annual messages to Congress.

Source: Theodore Roosevelt, fourth annual message to Congress, December 6, 1904; and Theodore Roosevelt, fifth annual message to Congress, December 5, 1905. in James D. Richardson, ed., *A Compilation of the Messages and Papers of the Presidents* (Washington, D.C.: U.S. Printing Office, n.d.), 10: 831–832; 14: 6944ff.

ROOSEVELT'S ANNUAL MESSAGE TO CONGRESS, DECEMBER 6, 1904

. . . It is not true that the United States feels any land hunger or entertains any project as regards the other nations of the Western Hemisphere save such as are for their welfare. All that this country desires is to see the neighboring countries stable, orderly, and prosperous. Any country whose people conduct themselves well can count upon our hearty friendship. If a nation shows that it knows how to act with reasonable efficiency and decency in social and political matters, if it keeps order and pays its obligations, it need fear no interference from the United States. Chronic wrong doing, or an impotence which results in a general loosening of the ties of civilized society, may in America, as elsewhere, ultimately require intervention by some civilized nation, and in the Western Hemisphere the adherence of the United States to the Monroe Doctrine may force the United States, however reluctantly, in flagrant cases of such wrong doing or impotence, to the exercise of an international police power. If every country washed by the Caribbean Sea would show the progress in stable and just civilization which with the aid of the Platt amendment Cuba has shown since our troops left the island, and which so many of the republics in both Americas are constantly and brilliantly showing, all question of interference by this Nation with their affairs would be at an end. Our interests and those of our southern neighbors are in reality identical. They have great natural riches, and if within their borders the reign of law and justice obtains, prosperity is sure to come to them. While they thus obey the primary laws of civilized society they may rest assured that they will be treated by us in a spirit of cordial and helpful sympathy. We would interfere with them only in the last resort, and then only if it became evident that their inability or unwillingness to do justice at home and abroad had violated the rights of the United States or had invited foreign aggression to the detriment of the entire body of American nations. It is a mere truism to say that every nation . . . which desires to maintain its freedom, its independence, must ultimately realize that the right of such independence can not be separated from the responsibility of making good use of it.

ROOSEVELT'S ANNUAL MESSAGE TO CONGRESS, DECEMBER 5, 1905

. . . It must be understood that under no circumstances will the United States use the Monroe Doctrine as a cloak for territorial aggression. We desire peace with all the world, but perhaps most of all with the other peoples of the American Continent. There are, of course, limits to the wrongs which any self-respecting nation can endure. It is always possible that wrong actions toward this Nation, or toward citizens of this Nation, in some State unable to keep order among its own people, unable to secure justice from outsiders, and unwilling to do justice to those outsiders who treat it well, may result in our having to take action to protect our rights; but such action will not be taken with a view to territorial aggression, and it will be taken at all only with extreme reluctance and when it has become evident that every other resource has been exhausted.

Moreover, we must make it evident that we do not intend to permit the Monroe Doctrine to be used by any nation on this Continent as a shield to protect it from the consequences of its own misdeeds against foreign nations. If a republic to the south of us commits a tort against a foreign nation, such as an outrage against a citizen of that na-

tion, then the Monroe Doctrine does not force us to interfere to prevent punishment of the tort, save to see that the punishment does not assume the form of territorial occupation. . . . The case is more difficult when it refers to a contractual obligation. Our own Government has always refused to enforce such contractual obligations on behalf of its citizens by an appeal to arms. It is much to be wished that all foreign governments would take the same view. But they do not; and in consequence we are liable at any time to be brought face to face with disagreeable alternatives. On the one hand, this country would certainly decline to go to war to prevent a foreign government from collecting a just debt; on the other hand, it is very inadvisable to permit any foreign power to take possession, even temporarily, of the custom houses of an American Republic in order to enforce the payment of its obligations; for such temporary occupation might turn into a permanent occupation. The only escape from these alternatives may at any time be that we must ourselves undertake to bring about some arrangement by which so much as possible of a just obligation shall be paid. It is far better that this country should put through such an arrangement, rather than allow any foreign country to undertake it. To do so insures the defaulting republic from having to pay debt of an improper character under duress, while it also insures honest creditors of the republic from being passed by in the interest of dishonest or grasping creditors. Moreover, for the United States to take such a position offers the only possible way of insuring us against a clash with some foreign power. The position is, therefore, in the interest of peace as well as in the interest of justice. It is of benefit to our people; it is of benefit to foreign peoples; and most of all it is really of benefit to the people of the country concerned. . . .

Questions

1. Under what circumstances does Roosevelt propose to intervene in the affairs of Caribbean nations? Why would he abstain from intervention?
2. What is Roosevelt's view of Caribbean nations? Of the United States in relation to those nations?
3. What kind of precedent is involved in this proclamation of "an international police power"?

Questions for Further Thought

1. In what ways could John Hay's open-door notes (Document 21-7) and the Roosevelt Corollary (Document 21-8) antagonize the very people they ostensibly sought to protect? How might such feelings reveal themselves?
2. A number of factors, among them economic and strategic considerations and the presence or absence of other regional or outside powers, influence a nation's foreign policy. What factors influenced American foreign policy in the Far East? In the Caribbean?

In addition to reviewing the text and documents for Chapter 21, you might wish to consult the Platt Amendment (1901), *Instructor's Resource Manual,* vol. 2: *Since 1865,* 3rd ed., p. D-226. A seventh article required Cuba to sell or lease to the United States "coaling or naval stations" for the protection of Cuba and the defense of the United States. The U.S. naval base at Guantánamo Bay has its origin in this provision. That the United States required Cuba to incorporate the Platt Amendment in its 1903 constitution deeply angered Cuban nationalists.

CHAPTER **22**

War and the American State, 1914–1920

★   ★   ★

The Great War, 1914–1918

When the Great War began in August 1914, both the Allies and the Central Powers expected victory within a matter of weeks. No one anticipated a war that would last four years and take 14.5 million lives.

In the Napoleonic Wars a century before, opposing armies had fired at one another with muskets across an open field. In 1914, the tactics remained largely the same, but the weapons had changed profoundly. With the use of machine guns and high-powered rifles, frontal assaults caused ruinous casualties. Combat on the Western Front quickly evolved into trench warfare. Opposing armies again faced one another, but this time it was from the confines of a 25,000-mile network of trenches protected by barbed wire, running across Belgium and France. Periodically, an army would mount an offensive, with soldiers pouring into the disputed no-man's-land in an attempt to break through the enemy's lines. Casualties in a single battle often numbered in the hundreds of thousands on each side. Poison gas and artillery barrages added to the horror of a soldier's existence.

The war did not directly affect the United States at first, as President Woodrow Wilson tried to maintain a policy of neutrality. Although cultural ties and aggressive British propaganda generated sympathy for the Allies, such support was not universal. German Americans tended to support the old country, and Irish Americans were cool to the English, who appeared to be more interested in liberating Belgium than in freeing Ireland. Leading progressives, socialists, and pacifists all argued against war, and Henry Ford financed the voyage of a "peace ship," the passengers on which hoped to negotiate an end to the conflict. But circumstances conspired against Wilson. Even as the British navy swept the German merchant marine from the Atlantic, American trade with the allies grew.

The Germans attempted to neutralize this trade advantage through U-boat, or submarine, warfare, and American lives were lost in unannounced attacks, such as that on the *Lusitania*. On different occasions in 1915 and 1916, President Wilson forced the

Germans to abandon unrestricted submarine warfare, but in January 1917, Germany resumed its attacks. A month later, Americans learned that Germany had offered Mexico a chance to recover Texas, New Mexico, and Arizona if—in the event of war between the United States and Germany—Mexico declared war on the United States. In April, Congress voted for war.

Document 22-1 is drawn from a speech of Senator Robert M. La Follette opposing the declaration of war. Document 22-2 contains the heart of President Woodrow Wilson's "Fourteen Points" speech dealing with war aims in January 1918. The next three documents relate to American servicemen in the war: Document 22-3 describes their combat on the Western Front, Document 22-4 shows a sample of the mental tests administered to them, and Document 22-5 reproduces propaganda aimed at protecting them from venereal disease.

22-1   Anti-War Speech (1917)

Robert M. La Follette

President Woodrow Wilson, who as leader of the most powerful neutral nation had sought to mediate a negotiated end to the World War, came to feel in February and March 1917 that the Germans' ruthless new strategy (submarine warfare) might enable them to impose a victor's peace on the Allies, not a "peace without victory" influenced by the United States (see text pp. 708–710, 727). Hence his reluctant decision for war. However, in declaring America's war aims to be idealistic, not selfish, Wilson sought to distinguish between Germany's leaders and the German people, "with whom we have no quarrel," for whom we feel only "sympathy and friendship" (see text pp. 708–710). Among the six senators and fifty representatives who would have nothing of Wilson's case for war, none was more sharply critical than Senator Robert M. La Follette (1855–1925). In the following speech, given on April 4, La Follette rebuts the president point by point (see text p. 708).

Source: Congressional Record, Senate, 65th Congress, 1st Session (April 4, 1917), 227–229, 233, 234.

In his message of April 2 the President says:

> I was for a little while unable to believe that such things [referring to German submarine methods of warfare] would in fact be done by any Government that had heretofore subscribed to the humane practices of civilized nations. International law had its origin in the attempt to set up some law which would be respected and observed upon the sea, where no nation had right of dominion and where lay the free highways of the world. By painful stage after stage has that law been built up with meager enough results indeed, after all was accomplished that could be accomplished, but always with a clear view at least of what the heart and conscience of mankind demanded.

The recognition by the President that Germany had always heretofore subscribed to the humane practices of civilized nations is a most important statement. Does it not suggest a question as to why it is that Germany has departed from those practices in the present war? What the President had so admirably stated about international law and the painful stage by which it has been builded up is absolutely true. But in this connection would it not be well to say also that it was England, not Germany, who refused to obey the declaration of London, which represented the most humane ideas and was the best statement of the rules of international law as applied to naval warfare? Keep that in mind. Would it not have been fair to say, and to keep in mind, that Germany offered to abide by those principles and England refused; that in response to our request Germany offered to cease absolutely from the use of submarines in what we characterized an unlawful manner if England would cease from equally palpable and cruel violations of international law in her conduct of naval warfare?

The President in his message of April 2 says:

> The present German warfare against commerce is a warfare against mankind. It is a war against all nations.

Again referring to Germany's warfare he says:

> There has been no discrimination. The challenge is to all mankind.

Is it not a little peculiar that if Germany's warfare is against all nations the United States is the only nation that regards it necessary to declare war on that account? If it is true, as the President says, that "there has been no discrimination," that Germany has treated every neutral as she has treated us, is it not peculiar that no other of the great nations of the earth seem to regard Germany's conduct in this war as a cause for entering into it? Are we the only nation jealous of our rights? Are we the only nation insisting upon the protection of our citizens? Does not the strict neutrality maintained on the part of all the other nations of the earth suggest that possibly there is a reason for their action, and that that reason is that Germany's conduct under the circumstances does not merit from any nation which is determined to preserve its neutrality a declaration of war?

Norway, Sweden, the Netherlands, Switzerland, Denmark, Spain, and all the great Republics of South America are quite as interested in this subject as we are, and yet they have refused to join with us in a combination against Germany. I venture to suggest also that the nations named, and probably others, have a somewhat better right to be heard than we, for by refusing to sell war-material and munitions to any of the belligerents they have placed themselves in a position where the suspicion which attaches to us of a desire for war profits can not attach to them.

On August 4, 1914, the Republic of Brazil declared the exportation of war material from Brazilian ports to any of these powers at war to be strictly forbidden, whether such exports be under the Brazilian flag or that of any other country.

In that connection I note the following dispatch from Buenos Aires, appearing in the Washington papers of yesterday:

> President Wilson's war address was received here with interest, but no particular enthusiasm. . . . Government officials and politicians have adopted a cold shoulder toward the United States policy—an attitude apparently based on apprehension lest South American interests suffer.

The newspaper Razon's view was illustrative of this. "Does not the United States consider this an opportune time to consolidate the imperialistic policy everywhere north of Panama?" it said.

This is the question that neutral nations the world over are asking. Are we seizing upon this war to consolidate and extend an imperialistic policy? We complain also because Mexico has turned the cold shoulder to us, and are wont to look for sinister reasons for her attitude. Is it any wonder that she should also turn the cold shoulder when she sees us unite with Great Britain, an empire founded upon her conquests and subjugation of weaker nations. There is no doubt that the sympathy of Norway, Sweden, and other countries close to the scene of war is already with Germany. It is apparent that they view with alarm the entrance into the European struggle of the stranger from across the sea. It is suggested by some that our entrance into the war will shorten it. It is my firm belief, based upon such information as I have, that our entrance into the war will not only prolong it, but that it will vastly extend its area by drawing in other nations.

In his message of April 2, the President said:

> We have no quarrel with the German people—it was not upon their impulse that their Government acted in entering this war; it was not with their previous knowledge or approval.

Again he says:

> We are, let me say again, sincere friends of the German people and shall desire nothing so much as the early reestablishment of intimate relations of mutual advantage between us.

At least, the German people, then, are not outlaws. What is the thing the President asks us to do to these German people of whom he speaks so highly and whose sincere friend he declares us to be?

Here is what he declares we shall do in this war. We shall undertake, he says—

> The utmost practicable cooperation in council and action with the Governments now at war with Germany, and as an incident to that, the extension to those Governments of the most liberal financial credits in order that our resources may, so far as possible, be added to theirs.

"Practicable cooperation!" Practicable cooperation with England and her allies in starving to death the old men and women, the children, the sick and the maimed of Germany. The thing we are asked to do is the thing I have stated. It is idle to talk of a war upon a government only. We are leagued in this war, or it is the President's proposition that we shall be so leagued, with the hereditary enemies of Germany. Any war with Germany, or any other country for that matter, would be bad enough, but there are not words strong enough to voice my protest against the proposed combination with the entente allies. When we cooperate with those Governments we indorse their methods, we indorse the violations of international law by Great Britain, we indorse the shameful methods of warfare against which we have again and again protested in this war; we indorse her purpose to wreak upon the German people the animosities which for years her people have been taught to cherish against Germany; finally when the end comes, whatever it may be, we find ourselves in cooperation with our ally, Great Britain, and if we can not resist now the pressure she is exerting to carry us into the war, how can we hope to resist, then, the thousandfold greater pressure she will exert to bend us to her purposes and compel compliance with her demands?

We do not know what they are. We do not know what is in the minds of those who have made the compact, but we are to subscribe to it. We are irrevocably, by our votes here, to marry ourselves to a nondivorceable proposition veiled from us now. Once enlisted, once in the copartnership, we will be carried through with the purposes, whatever they may be, of which we now know nothing.

Sir, if we are to enter upon this war in the manner the President demands, let us throw pretense to the winds, let us be honest, let us admit that this is a ruthless war against not only Germany's army and her navy but against her civilian population as well, and frankly state that the purpose of Germany's hereditary European enemies has become our purpose. . . .

Just a word of comment more upon one of the points in the President's address. He says that this is a war "for the things which we have always carried nearest to our hearts—for democracy, for the right of those who submit to authority to have a voice in their own government." In many places throughout the address is this exalted sentiment given expression.

It is a sentiment peculiarly calculated to appeal to American hearts and, when accompanied by acts consistent with it, is certain to receive our support; but in this same connection, and strangely enough, the President says that we have become convinced that the German Government as it now exists—"Prussian autocracy" he calls it—can never again maintain friendly relations with us. His expression is that "Prussian autocracy was not and could never be our friend," and repeatedly throughout the address the suggestion is made that if the German people would overturn their Government it would probably be the way to peace. So true is this that the dispatches from London all hailed the message of the President as sounding the death knell of Germany's Government.

But the President proposes alliance with Great Britain, which, however liberty-loving its people, is a hereditary monarchy, with a hereditary ruler, with a hereditary House of Lords, with a hereditary landed system, with a limited and restricted suffrage for one class and a multiplied suffrage power for another, and with grinding industrial conditions for all the wageworkers. The President has not suggested that we make our support of Great Britain conditional to her granting home rule to Ireland, or Egypt, or India. We rejoice in the establishment of a democracy in Russia, but it will hardly be contended that if Russia was still an autocratic Government, we would not be asked to enter this alliance with her just the same. Italy and the

lesser powers of Europe, Japan in the Orient; in fact, all of the countries with whom we are to enter into alliance, except France and newly revolutionized Russia, are still of the old order—and it will be generally conceded that no one of them has done as much for its people in the solution of municipal problems and in securing social and industrial reforms as Germany.

Is it not a remarkable democracy which leagues itself with allies already far overmatching in strength the German nation and holds out to such beleaguered nation the hope of peace only at the price of giving up their Government? I am not talking now of the merits or demerits of any government, but I am speaking of a profession of democracy that is linked in action with the most brutal and domineering use of autocratic power. Are the people of this country being so well represented in this war movement that we need to go abroad to give other people control of their governments? Will the President and the supporters of this war bill submit it to a vote of the people before the declaration of war goes into effect? Until we are willing to do that, it illy becomes us to offer as an excuse for our entry into the war the unsupported claim that this war was forced upon the German people by their Government "without their previous knowledge or approval." . . .

With Germany likewise our relations were friendly. Many hundreds of thousands of the subjects of Germany had emigrated to this country, and they and their descendants had shown themselves to be in every way most worthy and desirable citizens. The great Civil War which saved the Union was successful largely through the services rendered by Germans, both as officers and as men serving in the ranks. B. A. Gould, in a work dealing with some of the phases of the Civil War, and prepared soon after its close, among other things, presented a table of the relative number of foreign-born soldiers in the Union Army. I quote from that table as follows:

English	45,508
Canadian	52,532
Irish	144,221
German	187,858
All other foreign born	48,410

Later and more careful investigation of the statistics show that there were in reality 216,000 native Germans in the Union Army, and, besides this, more than 300,000 Union soldiers who were born of German parents.

More than one-half a million of the men who carried the musket to keep this Government of ours undivided upon the map of the world were men who are now having their patriotism and loyalty to this country questioned, with secret-service men dogging their footsteps.

Who does not remember, among the most gallant and distinguished officers in the Union Army, Schurz, Sigel, Rosecrans, and scores of others? It is well to recall also that when President Lincoln issued his call for volunteers they volunteered much more largely from the German-settled States of the Middle West than from the war-mad States of the East. Is history to repeat itself?

The German people, either in this country or in the fatherland, need no tribute from me or from anyone else. In whatever land they have lived they have left a record of courage, loyalty, honesty, and high ideals second to no people which have ever inhabited this earth since the dawn of history. If the German people are less likely to be swept off their feet in the present crisis than some other nationalities, it is due to two facts. In the first place, they have a livelier appreciation of what war means than has the average American, and, in the second place, German speaking and reading people have had an opportunity to get both sides of the present controversy, which no one could possibly have, who has depended for his information solely on papers printed in English and English publications.

I have said that with the causes of the present war we have nothing to do. That is true. We certainly are not responsible for it. It originated from causes beyond the sphere of our influence and outside the realm of our responsibility. It is not inadmissible, however, to say that no responsible narrator of the events which have led up to this greatest of all wars has failed to hold that the Government of each country engaged in it is at fault for it. For my own part, I believe that this war, like nearly all others, originated in the selfish ambition and cruel greed of a comparatively few men in each Government who saw in war an opportunity for profit and power for themselves, and who were wholly indifferent to the awful suffering they knew that war would bring to the masses. The German people had been taught to believe that sooner or later war was inevitable with England and France and probably Russia allied against her. It is unfortunately true that there was much in the secret diplomacy of the years immediately preceding the breaking out of the war in 1914 to afford foundation for such belief. The secret treaty between France and England for the partition of Morocco, while making a public treaty with Germany, the terms of which were diametrically opposite to those of the secret treaty, did much to arouse the suspicion and hostility of the German people toward both France and England. . . .

At this point, sir, I say, with all deference but with the absolute certainty of conviction, that the present administration made a fatal mistake, and if war comes to this country with Germany for the present causes it will be due wholly to that mistake. The present administration has assumed and acted upon the policy that it could enforce to the very letter of the law the principles of international law against one belligerent and relax them as to the other. That thing no nation can do without losing its character as a neutral nation and without losing the rights that go with strict and absolute neutrality. . . .

Jefferson asserted that we could not permit one warring nation to curtail our neutral rights if we were not ready to allow her enemy the same privileges, and that any other course entailed the sacrifice of our neutrality.

That is the sensible, that is the logical position. No neutrality could ever have commanded respect if it was not based on that equitable and just proposition; and we from early in the war threw our neutrality to the winds by permitting England to make a mockery of it to her advantage against her chief enemy. Then we expect to say to that enemy, "You have got to respect my rights as a neutral." What is the answer? I say Germany has been patient with us. Standing strictly on her rights, her answer would be, "Maintain your neutrality; treat these other Governments warring against me as you treat me if you want your neutral rights respected." . . .

Questions

1. What do you consider to be the strongest and weakest points of La Follette's argument against President Wilson's war message?
2. Why do La Follette and the president refer to the German people in positive terms? Might they have done so for somewhat different reasons?

22-2   Fourteen Points (1918)

Woodrow Wilson

President Wilson (1856–1924) set out his Fourteen Points as the basis for a lasting peace in an address before Congress on January 8, 1918 (see text pp. 711–712, 727–728). The timing of his speech reflected his concern that V. I. Lenin's Bolsheviks, who had seized power in Russia late in the previous year, were propagandizing a revolutionary ending of the war even as they were negotiating with the Germans to extricate Russia from that war, however harsh Germany's terms. Such a peace would free German forces to concentrate on the Western Front. Addressing war-weary Europe, Wilson sought to deal with the Bolsheviks, rally the Allies, and appeal to elements within the Central Powers.

Source: Woodrow Wilson, address to Congress, January 8, 1918; reprinted in Arthur S. Link et al., eds., *Papers of Woodrow Wilson* (Princeton, N.J.: Princeton University Press, 1984), 45: 536–538.

I. Open covenants of peace, openly arrived at, after which there shall be no private international understandings of any kind but diplomacy shall proceed always frankly and in the public view.

II. Absolute freedom of navigation upon the seas, outside territorial waters, alike in peace and in war, except as the seas may be closed in whole or in part by international action for the enforcement of international covenants.

III. The removal, so far as possible, of all economic barriers and the establishment of an equality of trade conditions among all the nations consenting to the peace and associating themselves for its maintenance.

IV. Adequate guarantees given and taken that national armaments will be reduced to the lowest point consistent with domestic safety.

V. A free, open-minded, and absolutely impartial adjustment of all colonial claims, based upon a strict observance of the principle that in determining all such questions of sovereignty the interests of the populations concerned must have equal weight with the equitable claims of the government whose title is to be determined.

VI. The evacuation of all Russian territory and such a settlement of all questions affecting Russia as will secure the best and freest cooperation of the other nations of the world in obtaining for her an unhampered and unembarrassed opportunity for the independent determination of her own political development and national policy and assure her of a sincere welcome into the society of free nations under institutions of her own choosing; and, more than a welcome, assistance also of every kind that she may need and may herself desire. The treatment accorded Russia by her sister nations in the months to come will be the acid test of their good will, of their comprehension of her needs as distinguished from their own interests, and of their intelligent and unselfish sympathy.

VII. Belgium, the whole world will agree, must be evacuated and restored, without any attempt to limit the sovereignty which she enjoys in common with all other free nations. No other single act will serve as this will serve to restore confidence among the nations in the laws which they have themselves set and determined for the government of their relations with one another. Without this healing act the whole structure and validity of international laws is forever impaired.

VIII. All French territory should be freed and the invaded portions restored, and the wrong done to France by Prussia in 1871 in the matter of Alsace-Lorraine, which has unsettled the peace of the world for nearly fifty years, should be righted, in order that peace may once more be made secure in the interest of all.

IX. A readjustment of the frontiers of Italy should be effected along clearly recognizable lines of nationality.

X. The peoples of Austria-Hungary, whose place among the nations we wish to see safeguarded and assured, should be accorded the freest opportunity of autonomous development.

XI. Rumania, Serbia, and Montenegro should be evacuated; occupied territories restored; Serbia accorded free and secure access to the sea; and the relations of the several Balkan states to one another determined by friendly counsel along historically established lines of allegiance and nationality; and international guarantees of the political and economic independence and territorial integrity of the several Balkan states should be entered into.

XII. The Turkish portions of the present Ottoman Empire should be assured a secure sovereignty, but the other nationalities which are now under Turkish rule should be assured an undoubted security of life and an absolutely unmolested opportunity of autonomous development, and the Dardanelles should be permanently opened as a free passage to the ships and commerce of all nations under international guarantees.

XIII. An independent Polish state should be erected which should include the territories inhabited by indisputably Polish populations, which should be assured a free and secure access to the sea, and whose political and economic independence and territorial integrity should be guaranteed by international covenant.

XIV. A general association of nations must be formed under specific covenants for the purpose of affording mutual guarantees of political independence and territorial integrity to great and small states alike.

Questions

1. Which of the Fourteen Points concern specific nations or peoples? What guiding principle does Wilson advocate in determining their futures?
2. Of points I through V, which do you think was most important? Why?
3. What was the immediate importance of point VI and the symbolic importance of point VII?

22-3   German Dugouts (1918)

Hervey Allen

Poet and novelist Hervey Allen (1888–1949) joined the National Guard after his graduation from the University of Pittsburgh in 1915. Before going to France, Allen served with the expeditionary force that pursued Pancho Villa in Mexico (see text p. 714). The following excerpt from Allen's wartime diary, *Toward the Flame,* offers a firsthand account of soldiering on the Western Front (see text p. 713).

Source: Excerpted from Hervey Allen, "German Dugouts" (1918), in *Toward the Flame: A War Diary* by Hervey Allen. Copyright 1926, 1934 by Hervey Allen. Copyright 1954, © 1962 by Ann Andrews Allen. Reprinted by permission of Henry Holt and Co., Inc. (In reprint edition, Pittsburgh: University of Pittsburgh Press, 1968, 111–119.)

I awoke to hear the pleasant clinking of mess pans. The rain had stopped, but the forest was still dripping, and the mud was deep and peculiarly slippery. The captain and I crawled out, both about the same time, and made our way to the kitchen where a savory mess was being dished out, smoking hot gobs of bread and canned sweet potato, a favorite and frequent delicacy at the front. Paul and some of the other French soldiers were helping. By this time the men were happy again. A little rest and something to eat were doing wonders. The captain and I were not much behind the rest of the company as trenchermen, although I avoided eating much meat at the front.

We were issued beef in immense quantities, sometimes having to bury a whole quarter of it. It became tainted very easily, where of course there was no possible means of refrigeration. This meat ration came wrapped in burlap, generally reasonably fresh; but once open, it had to be carried around in the ration carts, and unless quickly cooked, it spoiled very rapidly, especially in those summer days along the Marne when the sun was hot.

Another thing which hastened the destruction of perishable food was the immense amount of decay all along the front. All those rotten woods were filled with dead horses, dead men, the refuse, excrement and the garbage of armies. The ground must have been literally alive with pus and decay germs. Scratch your hand, cut yourself in shaving, or get a little abrasion on your foot, and almost anything could happen. Bichloride tablets were invaluable; I always threw one into my canvas basin for good luck.

During the meal, Lieutenant Scott, who had been assistant division gas officer for a while, but who had now returned to the company, joined us, and mentioned that he was making all arrangements for a new gas alarm, having found some empty brass shells used for that purpose "over there"—and he pointed to a cape of trees that ran out from a wood-island into the surrounding fields.

That part of the world consisted of a great level plateau, prairie-like fields interspersed with woods, the "bois" of the French maps, like islands of all sizes and shapes. We were then camped in one of these wood "islands," and across "there," where the lieutenant had pointed, was another "island" in which were the remnants of a German battery. The captain and I strolled across after dinner, letting the warm sun dry us off.

The guns were still in their pits, as "Fritz" had left very suddenly here. The guns pointed their noses up at a high angle like hounds baying the moon, but they were silent now. The wood was full of little dugouts, walks, and houses. The Germans had evidently stayed here a long time. Out in the field were a large number of big shell craters in a line, *one, two, three* . . . where our 220's had evidently been ranging on the battery. They had come quite near, within fifty yards or so.

Along the edge of these thickets were a number of graves. I was greatly impressed by them. The crosses were well carved out of new wood, and the grave mounds carefully spaded. Here were wreaths of wax flowers, evidently sent from home, and a board giving the epitaph of the deceased, with his rank and honors: "He was a good Christian and fell in France fighting for the Fatherland, *Hier ruht in Gott* [Here he rests in God]." Verily, these seemed to be the same Goths and Vandals who left their graves even in Egypt; unchanged since the days of Rome, and still fighting her civilization, the woods-people against the Latins. Only the illuminating literary curiosity of a Tacitus was lacking to make the inward state of man visible by the delineation of the images of outer things.

We entered some of the dugouts, small, mound-like structures with straw inside. Some of the officers' were larger. There was a little beer garden in the middle of the wood with a chapel and a wreathed cross near by, white stones and twisting "rustic" paths. The railings and booths along these paths were made from roots and branches cleverly bent and woven, and sometimes carved. It reminded me of American "porch furniture" of a certain type. All quite German. Cast-off boots, shell-timers, one or two coats, and shrapnel-bitten helmets lay about with round Boche [an insulting nickname for "German"] hats, "the little round button on top." Picture post-cards and magazines, pistol holsters, and one or two broken rifles completed this cartoon of invasion.

All the litter of material thus left behind was useless. I noticed the pictures of some fat, and rather jolly-looking German girls, and piles of a vast quantity of shells. We looked around thoroughly, but were very wary of traps. I remember making up my mind to make for one of these dugouts in case we were shelled. One always kept a weather eye open.

About all this stuff there was at that time the dire taint of danger. Somehow everything German gave one the creeps. It was connected so intimately with all that was unpleasant, and associated so inevitably with organized fear, that one scarce regarded its owners as men. It seemed *then* as if we were fighting some strange, ruthless, insect-beings from another planet; that we had stumbled upon their nests after smoking them out. One had the same feeling as when waking up at night and realizing that there are rats under the bed.

The captain and I walked along the edge of the wood, encountering our French contingent on the way. They were "at home" in an old German dugout, happily squatted around several small fires, preparing their meal as *they* liked it. After a good deal of difficulty, they had prevailed on our mess sergeant to issue them their rations in bulk so that they could do their own cooking. Such little differences of customs are in reality most profound. Our physical habits were more like the Germans'!

The non-commissioned gas officer picked us up here. He was carrying back the big brass shell for a gas alarm. It gave forth a mellow musical note when touched with a bar of iron or a bayonet. The Germans had used this one themselves for that purpose, so it already had the holes and wire for suspending it. . . .

We moved before it was light, which is very early in summer time in France. The dim columns of men coming out of the woods, the lines of carts and kitchens assembling in the early, gray dawn, all without a light, and generally pretty silently, was always impressive.

In a few minutes we were headed back in the direction from which we had come. There was a full moon, or one nearly so, hanging low in the west. As I jolted along, on legs that seemed more like stilts than limbs with knees, the heavy equipment sagged at every step, and seemed to clink one's teeth together weakly. At last the weariness and the jangle took on a fagged rhythm that for me fell into the comfort of rhyme.

We were beginning to be pretty tired by now and even here needed relief. One no longer got up in the morning full of energy. Hunger, dirt, and strain were telling, and we felt more or less "all in" that day in particular. One was consciously weak.

Nevertheless the country was beautiful; the full moon just sinking in the west looked across the smoking, misty valleys at the rising sun. There was a gorgeous bloody-gold color in the sky, and the woods and fields sparkled deliciously green, looking at a little distance fresh and untouched. But that was only a distant appearance, for this was the country over which two days before the Americans had driven the Germans from one machine gun nest to another, and on from crest to crest. A nearer approach showed the snapped tree-trunks, the tossed branches and shell-pitted ground, and at one halt that we made, Nick called me down a little slope to see something.

There was a small spring in a draw beside the road, where two Germans were lying. One was a big, brawny fellow with a brown beard, and the other a mere lad. He looked to be about 14 or 15 with a pathetically childish chin, but he carried potatomasher bombs.[1] They had evidently stopped here to try to fill their canteens, probably both desperate with thirst, when they were overtaken by our men. The young boy must have sheltered himself behind the man while the latter held our fellows back a little. There was a scorched place up the side of the ravine where a hand grenade had exploded, but the big German had been surrounded, and killed by the bayonet right through his chest. His hands were still clutching at the place where the steel had gone through. He was one of the few I ever saw who had been killed by the bayonet. The boy was lying just behind him. His back appeared to have been broken, probably by a blow with the butt of a rifle, and he was contorted into a kind of arch, only his feet and shoulders resting on the ground. It was he who had probably thrown the grenade that had exploded near by. The little spring had evidently been visited by the wounded, as there were blood and first-aid wrappings about. I refused to have the company water tank filled there. . . .

---

[1] *Potatomasher bombs* were German hand grenades, so named for their mallet-like shape. Allied hand grenades were baseball-shaped with notched indentations so that they scattered fragments; they became known as "pineapples."

Questions

1. Describe conditions at the front.
2. How does Allen regard the enemy?
3. What did he find at the small spring? What does that scene indicate about the unpredictability of combat?

22-4   U.S. Army Mental Tests (1917)

War presented the U.S. Army with the immense challenge of classifying millions of men for military service. Intelligence testing appeared to be the key to that undertaking (see text p. 716). The tests excerpted below were reprinted in book form in 1920, and for some Americans measuring intelligence became more than a tool: xenophobes and racists now had a "scientific" argument to back their views.

Source: Tests 2 and 3 in Clarence S. Yoakum and Robert M. Yerkes, comps. and eds., *Army Mental Tests,* published with the authorization of the War Department (New York: Henry Holt, 1920), 206–209.

TEST 2
Get the answers to these examples as quickly as you can.
Use the side of this page to figure on if you need to.

SAMPLES
1 How many are 5 men and 10 men? ....Answer (**15**)
2 If you walk 4 miles an hour for 3 hours, how far do you walk? ....Answer (**12**)

1   How many are 30 men and 7 men? ....Answer (   )
2   If you save $7 a month for 4 months, how much will you save? ....Answer (   )
3   If 24 men are divided into squads of 8, how many squads will there be?.......Answer (   )
4   Mike had 12 cigars. He bought 3 more, and then smoked 6. How many cigars
    did he have left? ....Answer (   )
5   A company advanced 5 miles and retreated 3 miles. How far was it then from
    its first position? ....Answer (   )
6   How many hours will it take a truck to go 66 miles at the rate of 6 miles an hour? ....Answer (   )
7   How many cigars can you buy for 50 cents at the rate of 2 for 5 cents? ....Answer (   )
8   A regiment marched 40 miles in five days. The first day they marched 9 miles,
    the second day 6 miles, the third 10 miles, the fourth 8 miles. How many miles did
    they march the last day? ....Answer (   )
9   If you buy two packages of tobacco at 7 cents each and a pipe for 65 cents, how
    much change should you get from a two-dollar bill? ....Answer (   )
10 If it takes 6 men 3 days to dig a 180-foot drain, how many men are needed to dig it
    in half a day? ....Answer (   )
11 A dealer bought some mules for $800. He sold them for $1,000, making $40 on
    each mule. How many mules were there?..Answer (   )
12 A rectangular bin holds 400 cubic feet of lime. If the bin is 10 feet long and
    5 feet wide, how deep is it? ....Answer (   )
13 A recruit spent one-eighth of his spare change for post cards and four times as much for a
    box of letter paper, and then had 90 cents left. How much money did he have at first?............Answer (   )
14 If $3^{1}/_{2}$ tons of coal cost $21, what will $5^{1}/_{2}$ tons cost? ....Answer (   )
15 A ship has provisions to last her crew of 500 men 6 months. How long would it last
    1,200 men? ....Answer (   )
16 If a man runs a hundred yards in 10 seconds, how many feet does he run in
    a fifth of a second?...Answer (   )
17 A U-boat makes 8 miles an hour under water and 15 miles on the surface. How long
    will it take to cross a 100-mile channel, if it has to go two-fifths of the way under water? ....Answer (   )
18 If 241 squads of men are to dig 4,097 yards of trench, how many yards must be dug
    by each squad? ....Answer (   )
19 A certain division contains 3,000 artillery, 15,000 infantry and 1,000 cavalry. If
    each branch is expanded proportionately until there are in all 20,900 men, how
    many will be added to the artillery? ....Answer (   )

20   A commission house which had already supplied 1,897 barrels of apples to a
     cantonment delivered the remainder of its stock to 29 mess halls. Of this remainder
     each mess hall received 54 barrels. What was the total number of barrels supplied? ....Answer (   )

TEST 3

This is a test of common sense. Below are sixteen questions.
Three answers are given to each question. You are to look at
the answers carefully; then make a cross in the square before
the best answer to each question, as in the sample:

SAMPLE
{
Why do we use stoves? Because
☐ they look well
☒ they keep us warm
☐ they are black
}

Here the second answer is the best one and is marked with
a cross. Begin with No. 1 and keep on until time is called.

---

1 Cats are useful animals, because
   ☐ they catch mice
   ☐ they are gentle
   ☐ they are afraid of dogs
2 Why are pencils more commonly carried than fountain pens? Because
   ☐ they are brightly colored
   ☐ they are cheaper
   ☐ they are not so heavy
3 Why is leather used for shoes? Because
   ☐ it is produced in all countries
   ☐ it wears well
   ☐ it is an animal product
4 Why judge a man by what he does rather than what he
   says? Because
   ☐ what a man does shows what he really is
   ☐ it is wrong to tell a lie
   ☐ a deaf man cannot hear what is said
5 If you were asked what you thought of a person whom
   you didn't know, what should you say?
   ☐ I will go and get acquainted
   ☐ I think he is all right
   ☐ I don't know him and can't say
6 Streets are sprinkled in summer
   ☐ to make the air cooler
   ☐ to keep automobiles from skidding
   ☐ to keep down dust
7 Why is wheat better for food than corn? Because
   ☐ it is more nutritious
   ☐ it is more expensive
   ☐ it can be ground finer
8 If a man made a million dollars, he ought to
   ☐ pay off the national debt
   ☐ contribute to various worthy charities
   ☐ give it all to some poor man

9 Why do many persons prefer automobiles to street
   cars? Because
   ☐ an auto is made of higher grade materials
   ☐ an automobile is more convenient
   ☐ street cars are not as safe
10 The feathers on a bird's wings help him to fly because
   they
   ☐ make a wide, light surface
   ☐ keep the air off his body
   ☐ keep the wings from cooling off too fast
11 All traffic going one way keeps to the same side of the
   street because
   ☐ most people are right handed
   ☐ the traffic policeman insists on it
   ☐ it avoids confusion and collisions
12 Why do inventors patent their inventions? Because
   ☐ it gives them control of their inventions
   ☐ it creates a greater demand
   ☐ it is the custom to get patents
13 Freezing water bursts pipes because
   ☐ cold makes the pipes weaker
   ☐ water expands when it freezes
   ☐ the ice stops the flow of water
14 Why are high mountains covered with snow? Because
   ☐ they are near the clouds
   ☐ the sun seldom shines on them
   ☐ the air is cold there
15 If the earth were nearer the sun
   ☐ the stars would disappear
   ☐ our months would be longer
   ☐ the earth would be warmer
16 Why is it colder nearer the poles than nearer the equa-
   tor? Because
   ☐ the poles are always farther from the sun
   ☐ the sunshine falls obliquely at the poles
   ☐ there is more ice at the poles

Questions

1. What factors might affect test performance?
2. Who was most likely to test well? Poorly?
3. Is it possible that the tests, though not accurate indicators of intelligence, say something about the state of American education at that time? How so?

22-5 Posters from the Anti–Venereal Disease Campaign (1917–1918)

As the text points out, the war witnessed an intensification of progressive campaigns against venereal disease and alcohol (see text pp. 713–715). Homosexuals in cosmopolitan seaports, as well as prostitutes in various settings, were of particular concern to authorities. Various means were employed by government and private agencies to ensure that America's citizen army was "fit to fight" and "the cleanest army in the world." Among the efforts were these propagandistic posters of the Social Hygiene Division of the Army Educational Commission.

Source: Posters, the American Social Hygiene Association Papers, Social Welfare History Archives Center, University of Minnesota, Minneapolis, reproduced by permission in Allan M. Brandt, *No Magic Bullet: A Social History of Venereal Disease in the United States,* expanded ed. (New York: Oxford University Press, 1987), 110ff.

Question

1. Compare and contrast the views of women in the two posters.

Questions for Further Thought

1. What is the lasting significance of President Woodrow Wilson's Fourteen Points (Document 22-2)?
2. Compare and contrast the light shed on wartime America by Documents 22-3 and 22-4. Draw on the text as you consider the documents.
3. How do Documents 22-4 and 22-5 relate to Progressive Era America? Draw on the text as you consider the relationship.

War on the Home Front

The war transformed American society, at least for its duration, and government grew in response to the demands of a worldwide conflict. Major agencies were created to channel the activities of government officials, civilian and military, and the business, agriculture, and labor sectors. Among these agencies were the War Industries Board, which coordinated the wartime mobilization of industry; the National War Labor Board; the Food Administration; the Fuel Administration; and the Railroad War Board (see text pp. 717–720). Business was the best organized of the private interest groups, but the labor movement benefited from wartime prosperity and from favorable decisions of the War Labor Board relative to union organization, working hours, overtime pay, and equal pay for women. The wartime labor shortage increased opportunities for African Americans, Mexican Americans, and women (see text pp. 720–722).

Enthusiasm for the war was widespread, but opposition was considerable: feelings both ways frequently ran high. Propaganda sought to mobilize support for and marginalize opposition to the war. Under the circumstances, civil liberties became an early casualty of the war: federal, state, and local authorities and private groups suppressed dissent, legally, extra legally, and sometimes illegally (by violence) (see text pp. 722–727).

Document 22-6 excerpts the report of Bernard M. Baruch, chairman of the War Industries Board, on the board's activities. Documents 22-7 and 22-8 deal with the wartime contributions of an established women's organization, the Young Women's Christian Association, and of the Committee on Public Information, an agency formed to propagandize the war. Document 22-9 illustrates anti-German propaganda. In Document 22-10, thirty-one African American editors state the case for African American support for the war.

22-6   The War Industries Board (1917–1918)

Bernard M. Baruch

Central to the management of industry during wartime was the War Industries Board (see text pp. 719–720). Bernard M. Baruch (1870–1965), who became chairman of the WIB in 1918, here reports on its activities and suggests a peacetime role for such an organization based on wartime experience.

Source: Bernard M. Baruch, *American Industry in the War: A Report of the War Industries Board* (Washington, D.C.: U.S. Government Printing Office, 1921), 65–67, 69, 100; excerpted in Donald O. Dewey, ed., *Union and Liberty: A Documentary History of American Constitutionalism* (New York: McGraw-Hill, 1969), 220.

. . . Curtailment plans were carried out not by agreement among the concerns of an industry but by agreement between the industry as a group, on the one hand, and the Government, on the other. Many new trade practices were inaugurated in the same way. In many instances curtailment was the negative result of positive action in some other direction. This problem has already been considered at some length in the chapter on priorities. The plans and results of the Board's activities in carrying forward the conservation program are explained at some length in Part II of this book, in connection with the work of the various commodity sections dealing with the particular industries affected. Reference, by way of illustration, to some of these will be of general interest.

The conservation schedules for makers of men's and youth's clothing limited the length of sack coats and the length and sweep of overcoats, reduced the size of samples, and restricted each manufacturer to not more than 10 models of suits per season, resulting in a saving of 12 to 15 per cent in yardage. The number of trunks carried by traveling salesmen of dry goods houses underwent an average reduction of 44 per cent. The schedule for the women's garment industry was calculated as capable of saving 20 to 25 per cent in yardage.

The standardization of colors together with certain restrictions in styles of sweaters and analogous knitted articles released 33 per cent of the wool ordinarily used in that industry. A schedule providing that hosiery, underwear, and other knit goods, with certain small exceptions, should be packed for shipment in paper covered bales instead of pasteboard boxes resulted in a large saving in shipping space, while at the same time it released pasteboard to be used as a substitute for tin plate in the manufacture of containers for articles for which tin plate had been forbidden. It was estimated that this schedule would have effected an annual saving of 17,312 carloads of freight space, 141,000,000 cartons, and nearly a half million wooden packing cases. . . .

The manufacturers of automobile tires agreed to a reduction from 287 styles and sizes of tires to 32, with a further reduction to 9 within two years. This had a tendency to release a large amount of rubber and capital tied up in stocks everywhere. A schedule was issued also to the rubber clothing and the rubber footwear industries, the former eliminating 272 styles and types and agreeing to bale their product instead of shipping it in cartons. Even bathing caps were restricted to one style and one color for each manufacturer.

Savings in the agricultural implement industry are among the most important effected. Implement manufacturers were able to simplify manufacturing operations and reduce their stocks of raw materials; manufacturers, dealers. and jobbers found it possible to do business with smaller stocks of finished products; the steel mills saved, because every variation in size or shape had required a different set of rolls, and so on. Schedules were issued to manufacturers of portable grain elevators, plows and tillage implements, grain drills and seeders, harvesters, mowers, hay rakes, ensilage machinery, spring-tooth harrows, farm wagons and trucks, land rollers and pulverizers, and cream separators. The number of sizes and types of steel plows was reduced from 312 to 76; planters and drills from 784 to 29; disk harrows from 589 to 38; buggy wheels from 232 to 4; spring-wagon wheels from 32 to 4; buggy axles from over 100 to 1; buggy springs from over 120 to 1; spring wagons from over 25 to 2; buggy shafts from 36 to 1; buggy bodies from over 20 to 1 style, two widths; spring-wagon bodies from 6 to 2. . . .

The experience of the Conservation Division has clearly demonstrated that there are many practices in American industry which cost the ultimate consumers in the aggregate enormous sums without enriching the producers. These are often due to competitive demands, real or assumed. Many salesmen, in order to please the whims of particular customers, will insist upon the manufacture of new styles or new shapes of articles, requiring increased expense to the manufacturers and increased expense to both wholesalers and retailers in carrying more lines of stock; these in turn causing increased expense in maintaining salesmen and providing them with samples as well as in advertising. The consumer, the general public, is no better served by the satisfaction of these unreasonable demands, but the public ultimately pays the bill. We may well draw from this war experience a lesson to be applied to peace, by providing some simple machinery for eliminating wasteful trade practices which increase prices without in the remotest degree contributing to the well-being of the people. There is enough natural wealth in this country, and there is enough labor and technical skill for converting that wealth into objects of human satisfaction to provide abundantly for the elemental comforts of every person in the land. The problem before our Nation to-day is to bring about such adjustments of the industrial processes as lead toward that long-sought condition of life. . . .

The question, then, is what kind of Government organization can be devised to safeguard the public interest while these associations are preserved to carry on the good work of which they are capable. The country will quite properly demand the vigorous enforcement of all proper measures for the suppression of unfair competition and unreasonable restraint of trade. But this essentially negative policy of curbing vicious practices should, in the public interest, be supplemented by a positive program, and to this end the experience of the War Industries Board points to the desirability of investing some Government agency, perhaps the Department of Commerce or the Federal Trade Commission, with constructive as well as inquisitor-

ial powers—an agency whose duty it should be to encourage, under strict Government supervision, such cooperation and coordination in industry as should tend to increase production, eliminate waste, conserve natural resources, improve the quality of products, promote efficiency in operation, and thus reduce costs to the ultimate consumer.

Such a plan should provide a way of approaching industry, or rather of inviting industry to approach the Government, in a friendly spirit, with a view to help and not to hinder. The purpose contemplated is not that the Government should undertake any such far-reaching control over industry as was practiced during the war emergency by the War Industries Board; but that the experiences of the war should be capitalized; its heritage of dangerous practices should be fully realized that they might be avoided; and its heritage of wholesome and useful practices should be accepted and studied with a view to adapting them to the problems of peace. It is recommended that such practices of cooperation and coordination in industry as have been found to be clearly of public benefit should be stimulated and encouraged by a Government agency, which at the same time would be clothed with the power and charged with the responsibility of standing watch against and preventing abuses.

Questions

1. What most strikes you about the wartime operations of the War Industries Board, as described by Baruch?
2. What lessons for postwar America does Baruch see in the operations of the WIB?

22-7   The Home Front: The Young Women's Christian Association (1920)

Marcus L. Hansen

Not only were women able to take jobs in industry and government during wartime, but many (especially women from the middle class) also assumed leadership roles in women's organizations, which became increasingly involved in supporting the war effort on the home front (as this document reveals) and overseas.

Source: Excerpted from Marcus L. Hansen, "The Campaign of the Young Women's Christian Association," in *Welfare Campaigns in Iowa* (Iowa City: State Historical Society of Iowa, 1920), 100–103, 105–106, 108, 111–112.

In the recent struggle there were many active participants who did not shoulder a rifle. A year after the declaration of a state of war a million and a half men were in military service: at that time a million and a half women were engaged in the manufacture of war materials: and as the number in the one class increased, the other force expanded corre-

spondingly. Most of these women were living a life just as novel, just as separated from their previous existence as were the soldiers: and the woman worker was as prone to homesickness and loneliness as was the recruit in the camp. If he needed welfare work and the people furnished it, should she not also be remembered?

The inspector general of the Iowa militia had reported in 1901, on the presence of women in the militia camps, that they were "a nuisance, underfoot, and a detriment to the good work and benefits expected of camp". But, whether a nuisance or not, women were bound to come to the places where the soldiers were—to enjoy a family picnic, to visit the sick in the hospital, or to say a final goodbye before the departure over-seas. Cast alone into a city of barracks, the mother, the sister, or the friend was just as bewildered as was the recruit on his first visit to the neighboring city. If the War Camp Community Service provided for him, should not someone think of her?

Welfare work among soldiers had as one object the preservation of their efficiency by removing the incentives to immorality. But who would guide past temptation in the vicinity of the military camp the girl now suddenly brought into contact with thousands of fighting men?

It was to the Young Women's Christian Association that the welfare of the industrial workers, the women in the camps, and the girls in the cantonment cities was entrusted. The Women's Branch of the Industrial Service Section of the Ordnance Department invited the Association to supervise the recreational activities in these industries. Upon the request of a camp commander the Association was ready to construct a Hostess House for the convenience of women visitors, and safeguards were thrown around the girls by the organization of Patriotic Leagues—an outgrowth of work which had already been done under the Social Morality Committee of this society.

The Young Women's Christian Association was not without experience in tasks of this nature. For fifty years there had existed local groups of young women, some associated with the International Board of Women's and Young Women's Christian Associations and some with the American committee. In December, 1906, a National Board of the Young Women's Christian Association was created by these local groups, and by the constitution adopted in 1909 general supervision over all the work was delegated to this board which consisted of fifty-six members and fifteen auxiliary members. The country was divided into eleven fields, each of which was represented on the National Board by one delegate. The North Central Field included Iowa, Minnesota, Nebraska, North Dakota, and South Dakota, and had its headquarters at Minneapolis, Minnesota. Each field had an executive secretary who was aided by industrial, extension, county, student, and office secretaries.

Following the precedent of the Young Men's Christian Association, the women organized a special War Work Council to which was delegated all activities which arose in connection with the war. The first problem was the financing of these various tasks, and it was with this subject that the War Work Council dealt at their first meeting held in New York City on June 7, 1917. It was there resolved that the country should be appealed to for $1,000,000 of which $50,000 would be expended in work abroad.

Although an active campaign was started to obtain $1,000,000, it did not remain the goal. So great was the demand for hostess houses, so insistent the appeal from abroad, that on October 9th decision was made to place the sum at $4,000,000 of which $1,000,000 would be expended in France and Russia. . . .

How a rural county was organized is illustrated in a report written by Miss Caroline W. Daniels of Independence. "On Nov. 20, 1917, District Y. W. workers from Dubuque called a meeting in the High School Auditorium to organize Buchanan Co. About two dozen women were present. Miss Doris Campbell was chosen Sec-Treas. and I chairman. That afternoon Miss Campbell and I in her car began a tour of the newspaper offices of the county and that evening we had an organization meeting of prospective war leaders for Independence, the county seat. With the consent of the Red Cross officers we used their organization as a fulcrum throughout the county outside the Co. seat. Our method was to drive to every Red Cross group of workers; get permission to explain the need to them while they worked; arrange for some one of their number to take charge of a canvass in their town or township, or region; tell them of their share of the sum asked for from the county (basing this on population); and depart. The same method was used with any other groups we could get access to:—clubs, societies, etc. These groups received us with good will, and took our request as one of the war necessities that must be met, however weary and already over worked they felt. These visits were supplemented by letters, literature, posters, newspaper notices, announcements by townships of returns, etc., etc."

In the cities where there was a local branch of the Association the task was left to this organization. Accordingly, Dubuque was omitted from the plans made by the chairman of that district. The organization of Burlington became the center of the campaign in that city and its members were active workers in many Iowa cities. The scheme of the local campaigns was practically the same as that used by the men in their efforts—that is, competitive teams organized on military lines. Women served as captains, lieutenants, and privates; and at Fort Dodge they acted as "four minute men" presenting the merits of their cause in the theaters. In other places, however, women did not bear the entire responsibility. Sioux City had as its campaign manager, John O. Knutson, president of the Rotary Club; and on the executive and advisory committees appeared both men and women. Likewise, though the captains of the eighteen soliciting teams were women, many men served in the ranks. . . .

Just as the high school boys were an effective factor in the raising of the fund of the Young Men's Christian Association, so the high school girls contributed to the success of the women's endeavor. Indeed, at Fort Dodge the system was much the same. High school girls were organized on military lines, with a major and two captains. Each captain chose a lieutenant and a corporal from each class. A meeting was held at which time pledge cards, stating the willingness of the girls to give fifty cents a month for ten months, were passed out with instructions to take them home and have them countersigned by their parents. When the cards were returned it was found that $635 had been pledged. More than forty girls of the East High School in Waterloo pledged five dollars each toward the cause. In Washington the high school girls conducted the local campaign and received pledges of more than eight hundred dollars. . . .

Besides apathy and indifference there were in this campaign distinct objections to be overcome. Such was the "dancing girls story." A special article in a Chicago Sunday paper stated that the Young Women's Christian Association planned to bring several hundred girls to Camp Lewis, Washington, and pay them fifteen dollars weekly to dance with the soldiers of the cantonment who were to pay fifteen cents for each dance. In varying forms this story was widely copied and caused some people to hesitate in their giving, although it was immediately declared by campaign officials to be "absolutely false in every detail."

Even in remote rural districts rumors arose. The nature of the reports against which workers had to contend is illustrated by an incident occurring in one Iowa community. After considerable trouble a chairman was found for a township; but "later it was reported to us," states the narrative of the county chairman, "that she changed her mind and telephoned all around the neighborhood warning the women to have nothing to do with the movement as she had discovered (?) that it was all a scheme to collect money for building houses of ill fame for the soldiers of Camp Dodge!!! We bombarded her with publicity material, but got no returns from that township. In less virulent form we ran into this notion a number of times. The work for Red Cross nurses made instant appeal everywhere; but 'Hostess Houses' were either suspected or openly disapproved of. Work to keep safe young girls who flocked to Des Moines met with much criticism from country women who thought 'mothers should look after their own girls' 'that was what they were doing.'"

Questions

1. With which other voluntary organizations did the Young Women's Christian Association interact during wartime? What light does this shed on voluntary organizations? What were the effects of the war on these organizations?
2. What does the document reveal about concerns regarding morals under wartime conditions?

22-8   The Home Front: The Four Minute Men (1920)

George Creel

Washington fought the propaganda war through the Committee on Public Information, which was headed by journalist George Creel (1876–1953). As described in the textbook (pp. 722–725), the CPI used speakers, movies, posters, and pamphlets to spread its message. This excerpt on the "four minute men" comes from Creel's history of the CPI, *How We Advertised America.*

Source: George Creel, *How We Advertised America: The First Telling of the Amazing Story of the Committee on Public Information That Carried the Gospel of Americanism to Every Corner of the Globe* (New York: Harper and Bros., 1920), 84–88, 90–92.

There was nothing more time-wasting than the flood of people that poured into Washington during the war, each burdened with some wonderful suggestions that could be imparted only to an executive head. Even so, all of them had to be seen, for not only was it their right as citizens, but it was equally the case that the idea might have real value. Many of our best suggestions came from the most unlikely sources.

In the very first hours of the Committee, when we were still penned in the navy library, fighting for breath, a handsome, rosy-cheeked youth burst through the crowd and caught my lapel in a death-grip. His name was Donald Ryerson. He confessed to Chicago as his home, and the plan that he presented was the organization of volunteer speakers for the purpose of making patriotic talks in motion-picture theaters. He had tried out the scheme in

Chicago, and the success of the venture had catapulted him on the train to Washington and to me.

Being driven to the breaking-point has certain compensations, after all. It forces one to think quickly and confines thought largely to the positive values of a suggestion rather than future difficulties. Had I had the time to weigh the proposition from every angle, it may be that I would have decided against it, for it was delicate and dangerous business to turn loose on the country an army of speakers impossible of exact control and yet vested in large degree with the authority of the government. In ten minutes we had decided upon a national organization to be called the "Four Minute Men," and Mr. Ryerson rushed out with my appointment as its director.

When the armistice brought activities to a conclusion the Four Minute Men numbered 75,000 speakers, more than 7,555,190 speeches had been made, and a fair estimate of audiences makes it certain that a total of 134,454,514 people had been addressed. Notwithstanding the nature of the work, the infinite chances of blunder and bungle, this unique and effective agency functioned from first to last with only one voice ever raised to attack its faith and efficiency. As this voice was that of Senator Sherman of Illinois, this attack is justly to be set down as part of the general praise.

The form of presentation decided upon was a glass slide to be thrown on the theater-curtain, and worded as follows:

4 MINUTE MEN 4
(Copyright, 1917. Trade-mark.)

....

(Insert name of speaker)

will speak four minutes on a subject
of national importance. He speaks
under the authority of
THE COMMITTEE ON PUBLIC INFORMATION
GEORGE CREEL, CHAIRMAN
WASHINGTON, D. C.

A more difficult decision was as to the preparation of the matter to be sent out to speakers. We did not want stereotyped oratory, and yet it was imperative to guard against the dangers of unrestraint. It was finally agreed that regular bulletins should be issued, each containing a budget of material covering every phase of the question to be discussed, and also including two or three illustrative four-minute speeches. Mr. Waldo P. Warren of Chicago was chosen to write the first bulletin, and when he was called away his duties fell upon E. T. Gundlach, also of Chicago, the patriotic head of an advertising agency. These bulletins, however, prepared in close and continued consultation with the proper officials of each government depart-

ment responsible for them, were also gone over carefully by Professor Ford and his scholars.

The idea, from the very first, had the sweep of a prairie fire. Speakers volunteered by the thousand in every state, the owners of the motion-picture houses, after a first natural hesitancy, gave exclusive privileges to the organization, and the various government departments fairly clamored for the services of the Four Minute Men. The following list of bulletins will show the wide range of topics:

Topic	Period
Universal Service by Selective Draft	May 12–21, 1917
First Liberty Loan	May 22–June 15, 1917
Red Cross	June 18–25, 1917
Organization	
Food Conservation	July 1–14, 1917
Why We Are Fighting	July 23–Aug. 5, 1917
The Nation in Arms	Aug. 6–26, 1917
The Importance of Speed	Aug. 19–26, 1917
What Our Enemy Really Is	Aug. 27–Sept. 23, 1917
Unmasking German Propaganda	Aug. 27–Sept. 23, 1917 (supplementary topic)
Onward to Victory	Sept. 24–Oct. 27, 1917
Second Liberty Loan	Oct. 8–28, 1917
Food Pledge	Oct. 29–Nov. 4, 1917
Maintaining Morals and Morale	Nov. 12–25, 1917
Carrying the Message	Nov. 26–Dec. 22, 1917
War Savings Stamps	Jan. 2–19, 1918
The Shipbuilder	Jan. 28–Feb. 9, 1918
Eyes for the Navy	Feb. 11–16, 1918
The Danger to Democracy	Feb. 18–Mar. 10, 1918
Lincoln's Gettysburg Address	Feb. 12, 1918
The Income Tax	Mar. 11–16, 1918
Farm and Garden	Mar. 25–30, 1918
President Wilson's Letter to Theaters	Mar. 31–Apr. 5, 1918
Third Liberty Loan	Apr. 6–May 4, 1918
Organization	(Republished Apr. 23, 1918)
Second Red Cross Campaign	May 13–25, 1918
Danger to America	May 27–June 12, 1918
Second War Savings Campaign	June 24–28, 1918
The Meaning of America	June 29–July 27, 1918
Mobilizing America's Man Power	July 29–Aug. 17, 1918
Where Did You Get Your Facts?	Aug. 26–Sept. 7, 1918
Certificates to Theater Members	Sept. 9–14, 1918
Register	Sept. 5–12, 1918
Four Minute Singing	For general use
Fourth Liberty Loan	Sept. 28–Oct. 19, 1918
Food Program for 1919	Changed to Dec. 1–7; finally cancelled
Fire Prevention	Oct. 27–Nov. 2, 1918
United War Work Campaign	Nov. 3–18, 1918
Red Cross Home Service	Dec. 7, 1918
What Have We Won?	Dec. 8–14, 1918
Red Cross Christmas Roll Call	Dec. 15–23, 1918
A Tribute to the Allies	Dec. 24, 1918

Almost from the first the organization has the projectile force of a French "75," [a French artillery piece] and it was increasingly the case that government department heads turned to the Four Minute Men when they wished to arouse the nation swiftly and effectively. At a time when the Third Liberty Loan was lagging, President Wilson bought a fifty-dollar bond and challenged the men and women of the nation to "match" it. The Treasury Department asked the Committee to broadcast the message, and paid for the telegrams that went out to the state and county chairmen. Within a few days fifty thousand Four Minute Men were delivering the challenge to the people of every community in the United States, and the loan took a leap that carried it over the top. General Crowder followed the same plan in his registration campaign, putting up the money for the telegrams that went to the state and county chairmen, and like Secretary McAdoo, he obtained the same swift service and instant results. . . .

National arrangements were made to have Four Minute Men appear at the meetings of lodges, fraternal organizations, and labor unions, and this work progressed swiftly. In most cases these speakers were selected from the membership of the organizations to whom they spoke.

Under the authority of state lecturers of granges, four minute messages, based upon the official bulletins, were given also at all meetings of the granges in many states. The work was next extended to reach the lumber-camps of the country, some five hundred organizations being formed in such communities. Indian reservations were also taken in, and furnished some of the largest and most enthusiastic audiences.

The New York branch organized a church department to present four-minute speeches in churches, synagogues, and Sunday-schools. The idea spread from city to city, from state to state, and proved of particular value in rural communities. Some of the states, acting under authority from headquarters, organized women's divisions to bring the messages of the government to audiences at matinée performances in the motion-picture theaters, and to the members of women's clubs and other similar organizations.

College Four Minute Men were organized, under instructors acting as chairmen, to study the regular Four Minute Men bulletins, and practise speaking upon the sub-

jects thereof, each student being required to deliver at least one four-minute speech to the student body during the semester, in addition to securing satisfactory credits, in order to qualify as a Four Minute Man. This work was organized in 153 colleges. . . .

The Junior Four Minute Men was an expansion that proved to be almost as important as the original idea, for the youngsters of the country rallied with a whoop, and, what was more to the point, gave results as well as enthusiasm. Like so many other activities of the Committee, the Junior movement was more accidental than planned. At the request of the state of Minnesota the Washington office prepared a special War Savings Stamps bulletin. Results were so instant and remarkable that the idea had to be carried to other states, more than a million and a half copies of the bulletin being distributed to school-children during the campaign. Out of it all came the Junior Four Minute Men as a vital and integral part of the Committee on Public Information.

It was our cautious fear, at first, that regular school-work might be interrupted, but it soon developed that the idea had real educational value, helping teachers in their task instead of hindering. The general plan was for the teacher to explain the subject, using the bulletin as a text-book, and the children then wrote their speeches and submitted them to the teacher or principal. The best were selected and delivered as speeches or were read. In a few cases extemporaneous talks were given.

Details of the contests were left largely to the discretion of the teachers. In small schools there was generally one contest for the whole school. In schools of more than five or six classes it was usual to have separate contests for the higher and lower classes, and sometimes for each grade. There were many different ways of conducting these contests. Sometimes they were considered as a regular part of the school-work and were held in the class-room with no outsiders present, but more often they were made special events, the entire school, together with parents and other visitors, being present. Both boys and girls were eligible and the winners were given an official certificate from the government, commissioning them as four-minute speakers upon the specified topic of the contest. . . .

Questions

1. How did the "four minute men" program work?
2. Where is the potential for abuse in this program?
3. What significance do you see in the title of Creel's book?

22-9   Wartime Propaganda Poster

Posters propagandized the war for a number of purposes, both specific and general: to encourage the purchase of government bonds during Liberty loans, enlistment in the armed forces, and compliance with various wartime programs, such as food conservation, but above all to create support for the war (see text pp. 722–725).

Source: Historical Pictures/Stock Montage, Inc., in Henretta, vol. 2 (3rd ed.), 728.

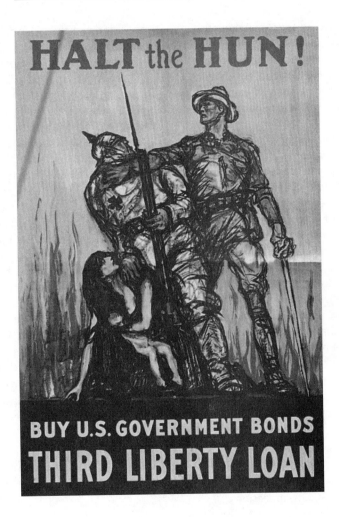

Questions

1. In what traditional ways does the poster portray gender roles?
2. What else strikes you about the poster?

22-10   Help Us to Help (1917)

The Crisis, a monthly magazine of the National Association for the Advancement of Colored People, edited by Dr. W. E. B. Du Bois, supported the war effort, as was revealed in Du Bois's editorials and in the publication of "Help Us to Help." Du Bois and the NAACP also sought support for the nondiscriminatory treatment of African American military personnel.

Source: "Help Us to Help," *The Crisis,* 16 (August 1918): 163–164.

From the petition of thirty-one Negro editors unanimously adopted at their meeting in Washington:
We American Negroes wish to affirm, first of all, our unalterable belief that the defeat of the German government and what it today represents is of paramount importance to the welfare of the world in general and to our people in particular.

We deem it hardly necessary, in view of the untarnished record of Negro Americans, to reaffirm our loyalty to Our Country and our readiness to make every sacrifice to win this war. We wish to use our every endeavor to keep all of these 12,000,000 people at the highest pitch, not simply of passive loyalty, but of active, enthusiastic and self-sacrificing participation in the war.

We are not unmindful of the recognition of our American citizenship in the draft, of the appointment of colored officers, of the designation of colored advisors to the Government departments and of other indications of a broadened public opinion; nevertheless, we believe today that justifiable grievances of the colored people are producing not disloyalty, but an amount of unrest and bitterness which even the best efforts of their leaders may not be always able to guide, unless they can have the active and sympathetic cooperation of the National and State governments. German propaganda among us is powerless, but the apparent indifference of our own Government may be dangerous.

The American Negro does not expect to have the whole Negro problem settled immediately; he is not seeking to hold-up a striving country and a distracted world by pushing irrelevant personal grievances as a price of loyalty; he is not disposed to catalogue, in this tremendous crisis, all his complaints and disabilities; he is more than willing to do his full share in helping to win the war for democracy and he expects his full share of the fruits thereof;—but he is today compelled to ask for that minimum of consideration which will enable him to be an efficient fighter for victory, namely:

(1) Better conditions of public travel.

(2) The acceptance of help where help is needed regardless of the color of the helper.

(3) The immediate suppression of lynching.

All these things are matters, not simply of justice, but of National and group efficiency; they are actions designed to still the natural unrest and apprehension among one-eighth of our citizens so as to enable them wholeheartedly and unselfishly to throw their every ounce of effort into this mighty and righteous war.

Questions

1. What is your assessment of this petition of thirty-one African American editors?
2. Drawing on the text (especially pp. 720–722) and this petition, compare and contrast the wartime strategy of the NAACP with that of the woman suffrage organizations.

Questions for Further Thought

1. Drawing on the text and documents from Chapters 20 and 22, make the case for or against this statement: the wartime period in America can be viewed as an extension of the Progressive Era.
2. Compare and contrast the depiction of women in the posters in Documents 22-5 and 22-9.

An Unsettled Peace, 1919–1920

One need only refer to the Reconstruction period after the Civil War (Chapter 15) to establish that America's major wars have sometimes been followed by intense conflict. The period of crisis after the First World War was brief, characterized by a range of conflicts that together made for two years of "unsettled peace" (see text pp. 727–733).

The terms of the peace proved politically divisive, as the U.S. Senate refused—on two votes late in 1919 and on a final roll call early the next year—to ratify the Treaty of Versailles, which would have involved the United States in the League of Nations. Meanwhile, nativism and racialism flourished, and wartime repression of dissent carried over into the postwar Red Scare, which provided the backdrop for bitter labor-management strife during the shift from a wartime economy to a peacetime economy.

Document 22-11 reproduces a portion of the Covenant of the League of Nations. Senator Henry Cabot Lodge states his position on the League of Nations in Document 22-12 and President Woodrow Wilson states his in Document 22-13. Document 22-14 reports on the postwar Chicago race riot, and Dr. W. E. B. Du Bois writes on "Returning Soldiers" in Document 22-15. Document 22-16 deals with Nebraska's 1919 school language law.

22-11   Covenant of the League of Nations, Articles 10 and 11 (1919)

The Allies were willing to base peace negotiations with Germany on President Woodrow Wilson's Fourteen Points, but British, French, and Italian leaders did not view the future of Europe and the world through Wilson's eyes. In part, then, the Treaty of Versailles bore the stamp of the American president and in part reflected the views of the European heads of state (see text pp. 727– 729).

The Covenant of the League of Nations was the handiwork of President Wilson, who drafted it in early 1919 before temporarily leaving Versailles for Washington, D.C., during mid-February. Wilson referred to Article 10 as the "Heart of the Covenant" and to Article 11 as his "favorite article in the treaty."

Source: Thomas G. Paterson and Dennis Merrill, eds., *Major Problems in American Foreign Relations: Since 1914,* vol. 2, 4th ed. (Lexington, Mass.: D. C. Heath, 1995), 39.

Article 10. The members of the League undertake to respect and preserve as against external aggression the territorial integrity and existing political independence of all Members of the League. In case of any such aggression or in case of any threat or danger of such aggression the Council shall advise upon the means by which this obligation shall be fulfilled.

Article 11. Any war or threat of war, whether immediately affecting any of the Members of the League or not, is hereby declared a matter of concern to the whole League, and the League shall take any action that may be deemed wise and effectual to safeguard the peace of nations. . . .

It is also declared to be the friendly right of each Member of the League to bring to the attention of the Assembly or of the Council any circumstance whatever affecting international relations which threatens to disturb international peace or the good understanding between nations upon which peace depends.

Questions

1. Review Wilson's Fourteen Points (Document 22-2) and the text coverage of "Negotiating the [Peace] Treaties" (pp. 727–729) to judge how the peace treaties' terms embody or do not embody Wilsonianism. Do Articles 10 and 11 of the League Covenant draw on Wilson's Fourteen Points?
2. Consider the commitments specified in Articles 10 and 11 of the League Covenant as you read Documents 22-12 and 22-13.

22-12   Speech before the Senate (1919)

Henry Cabot Lodge

Senator Henry Cabot Lodge (1850–1924) spoke after the drafting of the League Covenant ("constitution") and before President Wilson rejoined the Versailles Conference. He addressed an outgoing Senate still in Democratic hands.

When the Senate elected in 1918 convened later in 1919 to deal with the treaty, Republican control (49-47) of the body enabled Lodge to become majority leader and chair of the foreign relations committee.

Source: Henry Cabot Lodge, Speech to the U.S. Senate, February 28, 1919, in Henry Cabot Lodge, *The Senate and the League of Nations* (New York: Charles Scribner's Sons, 1925), 227–233.

Mr. President, all people, men and women alike, who are capable of connected thought abhor war and desire nothing so much as to make secure the future peace of the world. Everybody hates war. Everyone longs to make it impossible. We ought to lay aside once and for all the unfounded and really evil suggestion that because men differ as to the best method of securing the world's peace in the future, anyone is against permanent peace, if it can be obtained, among all the nations of mankind. . . . We all earnestly desire to advance toward the preservation of the world's peace, and difference in method makes no distinction in purpose. It is almost needless to say that the question now before us is so momentous that it transcends all party lines. . . . No question has ever confronted the United States Senate which equals in importance that which is involved in the league of nations intended to secure the future peace of the world. There should be no undue haste in considering it. My one desire is that not only the Senate, which is charged with responsibility, but that the press and the people of the country should investigate every proposal with the utmost thoroughness and weigh them all carefully before they make up their minds. If there is any proposition or any plan which will not bear, which will not court the most thorough and most public discussion, that fact makes it an object of suspicion at the very outset. . . .

In the first place, the terms of the league—the agreements which we make,—must be so plain and so explicit that no man can misunderstand them. . . . The Senate can take no action upon it, but it lies open before us for criticism and discussion. What is said in the Senate ought to be placed before the peace conference and published in Paris, so that the foreign Governments may be informed as to the various views expressed here.

In this draft prepared for a constitution of a league of nations, which is now before the world, there is hardly a clause about the interpretation of which men do not already differ. As it stands there is serious danger that the very nations which sign the constitution of the league will quarrel about the meaning of the various articles before a twelvemonth has passed. It seems to have been very hastily drafted, and the result is crudeness and looseness of expression, unintentional, I hope. There are certainly many doubtful passages and open questions obvious in the articles which can not be settled by individual inference, but which must be made so clear and so distinct that we may all understand the exact meaning of the instrument to which we are asked to set our hands. The language of these articles does not appear to me to have the precision and unmistakable character which a constitution, a treaty, or a law ought to present. The language only too frequently is not the language of laws or statutes. The article concerning mandatories, for example, contains an argument and a statement of existing conditions. Arguments and historical facts have no place in a statute or a treaty. Statutory and legal language must assert and command, not argue and describe. I press this point because there is nothing so vital to the peace of the world as the sanctity of treaties. The suggestion that we can safely sign because we can always violate or abrogate is fatal not only to any league but to peace itself. You can not found world peace upon the cynical "scrap of paper" doctrine so dear to Germany. To whatever instrument the United States sets its hand it must carry out the provisions of that instrument to the last jot and tittle, and observe it absolutely both in letter and in spirit. If this is not done the instrument will become a source of controversy instead of agreement, of dissension instead of harmony. This is all the more essential because it is evident, although not expressly stated, that this league is intended to be indissoluble, for there is no provision for its termination or for the withdrawal of any signatory. We are left to infer that any nation withdrawing from the league exposes itself to penalties and probably to war. Therefore, before we ratify, the terms and language in which the terms are stated must be exact and as precise, as free from any possibility of conflicting interpretations, as it is possible to make them.

The explanation or interpretation of any of these doubtful passages is not sufficient if made by one man, whether that man be the President of the United States, or a Senator, or anyone else. These questions and doubts must be answered and removed by the instrument itself.

It is to be remembered that if there is any dispute about the terms of this constitution there is no court provided that I can find to pass upon differences of opinion as to the terms of the constitution itself. There is no court to fulfill the function which our Supreme Court fulfills. There is provision for tribunals to decide questions submitted for arbitration, but there is no authority to decide differing interpretations as to the terms of the instrument itself.

What I have just said indicates the vast importance of the form and the manner in which the agreements which we are to sign shall be stated. I now come to questions of substance, which seem to me to demand the most careful thought of the entire American people, and particularly of those charged with the responsibility of ratification. We abandon entirely by the proposed constitution the policy laid down by Washington in his Farewell Address and the Monroe doctrine. It is worse than idle, it is not honest, to evade or deny this fact, and every fairminded supporter of this draft plan for a league admits it. I know that some of the ardent advocates of the plan submitted to us regard any suggestion of the importance of the Washington policy as foolish and irrelevant. Perhaps it is. Perhaps the time has come when the policies of Washington should be abandoned; but if we are to cast them aside I think that at least it should be done respectfully and with a sense of gratitude to the great man who formulated them. For nearly a century and a quarter the policies laid down in the Farewell Address have been followed and adhered to by the Government of the United States and by the American people. I

doubt if any purely political declaration has ever been observed by any people for so long a time. The principles of the Farewell Address in regard to our foreign relations have been sustained and acted upon by the American people down to the present moment. Washington declared against permanent alliances. He did not close the door on temporary alliances. He did not close the door on temporary alliances for particular purposes. Our entry in the great war just closed was entirely in accord with and violated in no respect the policy laid down by Washington. When we went to war with Germany we made no treaties with the nations engaged in the war against the German Government. The President was so careful in this direction that he did not permit himself ever to refer to the nations by whose side we fought as "allies," but always as "nations associated with us in the war." The attitude recommended by Washington was scrupulously maintained even under the pressure of the great conflict. Now, in the twinkling of an eye, while passion and emotion reign, the Washington policy is to be entirely laid aside and we are to enter upon a permanent and indissoluble alliance. That which we refuse to do in war we are to do in peace, deliberately, coolly, and with no war exigency. Let us not overlook the profound gravity of this step.

Washington was not only a very great man but he was also a very wise man. He looked far into the future and he never omitted human nature from his calculations. He knew well that human nature had not changed fundamentally since mankind had a history. Moreover, he was destitute of any personal ambitions to a degree never equaled by any other very great man known to us. In all the vital questions with which he dealt it was not merely that he thought of his country first and never thought of himself at all. He was so great a man that the fact that this country had produced him was enough of itself to justify the Revolution and our existence as a Nation. Do not think that I overstate this in the fondness of patriotism and with the partiality of one of his countrymen. The opinion I have expressed is the opinion of the world. . . .

That was the opinion of mankind then, and it is the opinion of mankind to-day, when his statue has been erected in Paris and is about to be erected in London. If we throw aside the political testament of such a man, which has been of living force down to the present instant, because altered circumstances demand it, it is a subject for deep regret and not for rejoicing. . . .

But if we put aside forever the Washington policy in regard to our foreign relations we must always remember that it carries with it the corollary known as the Monroe doctrine. Under the terms of this league draft reported by the committee to the peace conference the Monroe doctrine disappears. It has been our cherished guide and guard for nearly a century. The Monroe doctrine is based on the principle of self-preservation. To say that it is a question of protecting the boundaries, the political integrity, or the American States, is not to state the Monroe doctrine. . . .

The real essence of that doctrine is that American questions shall be settled by Americans alone; that the Americas shall be separated from Europe and from the interference of Europe in purely American questions. That is the vital principle of the doctrine.

I have seen it said that the Monroe doctrine is preserved under article 10 [calling for a collective security agreement among League members]; that we do not abandon the Monroe doctrine, we merely extend it to all the world. How anyone can say this passes my comprehension. The Monroe doctrine exists solely for the protection of the American Hemisphere, and to that hemisphere it was limited. If you extend it to all the world, it ceases to exist, because it rests on nothing but the differentiation of the American Hemisphere from the rest of the world. Under this draft of the constitution of the league of nations, American questions and European questions and Asian and African questions are all alike put within the control and jurisdiction of the league. Europe will have the right to take part in the settlement of all American questions, and we, of course, shall have the right to share in the settlement of all questions in Europe and Asia and Africa. Europe and Asia are to take part in policing the American continent and the Panama Canal, and in return we are to have, by way of compensation, the right to police the Balkans and Asia Minor when we are asked to do so. Perhaps the time has come when it is necessary to do this, but it is a very grave step, and I wish now merely to point out that the American people ought never to abandon the Washington policy and the Monroe doctrine without being perfectly certain that they earnestly wish to do so. Standing always firmly by these great policies, we have thriven and prospered and have done more to preserve the world's peace than any nation, league, or alliance which ever existed. For this reason I ask the press and the public and, of course, the Senate to consider well the gravity of this proposition before it takes the heavy responsibility of finally casting aside these policies which we have adhered to for a century and more and under which we have greatly served the cause of peace both at home and abroad. . . .

Questions

1. What aspect of the draft of the constitution for the League of Nations disturbs Lodge?
2. Why does he mention George Washington and other founders?
3. What was the supposed threat to the Monroe Doctrine?

22-13   Speech in Indianapolis, Indiana (1919)

Woodrow Wilson

President Wilson, at a disadvantage in the Senate battleground, sought to mobilize public support for the peace treaty by embarking on a major speaking tour during September 1919. He spoke in Indianapolis early in this effort, which ended when his health broke down late in the month.

Source: Thomas G. Paterson and Dennis Merrill, eds., *Major Problems in American Foreign Relations: Since 1914*, vol. 2, 4th ed. (Lexington, Mass.: D. C. Heath, 1995), 40–42.

You have heard a great deal about Article X of the Covenant of the League of Nations. Article X speaks the conscience of the world. Article X is the article which goes to the heart of this whole bad business, for that article says that the members of this League—and that is intended to be all the great nations of the world—engage to respect and to preserve against all external aggression the territorial integrity and political independence of the nations concerned. That promise is necessary in order to prevent this sort of war from recurring, and we are absolutely discredited if we fought this war and then neglect the essential safeguard against it.

You have heard it said, my fellow citizens, that we are robbed of some degree of our sovereign independence of choice by articles of that sort. Every man who makes a choice to respect the rights of his neighbors deprives himself of absolute sovereignty, but he does it by promising never to do wrong, and I cannot, for one, see anything that robs me of any inherent right that I ought to retain when I promise that I will do right.

We engage in the first sentence of Article X to respect and preserve from external aggression the territorial integrity and the existing political independence, not only of the other member states, but of all states. And if any member of the League of Nations disregards that promise, then what happens? The Council of the League advises what should be done to enforce the respect for that Covenant on the part of the nation attempting to violate it, and there is no compulsion upon us to take that advice except the compulsion of our good conscience and judgment. So that it is perfectly evident that if, in the judgment of the people of the United States, the Council adjudged wrong and that this was not an occasion for the use of force, there would be no necessity on the part of the Congress of the United States to vote the use of force. But there could be no advice of the Council on any such subject without a unanimous vote, and the unanimous vote would include our own, and if we accepted the advice we would be accepting our own advice. . . . There is in that Covenant not one note of surrender of the independent judgment of the government of the United States, but an expression of it, because that independent judgment would have to join with the judgment of the rest.

But when is that judgment going to be expressed, my fellow citizens? Only after it is evident that every other resource has failed, and I want to call your attention to the central machinery of the League of Nations. If any member of that League, or any nation not a member, refuses to submit the question at issue either to arbitration or to discussion by the Council, there ensues automatically by the engagements of this Covenant an absolute economic boycott. There will be no trade with that nation by any member of the League. There will be no interchange of communication by post or telegraph. There will be no travel to or from that nation. Its borders will be closed. No citizen or any other state will be allowed to enter it, and no one of its citizens will be allowed to leave it. It will be hermetically sealed by the united action of the most powerful nations in the world. And if this economic boycott bears with unequal weight, the members of the League agree to support

one another and to relieve one another in any exceptional disadvantages that may arise out of it.

And I want you to realize that this war was won not only by the armies of the world, but it was won by economic means as well. Without the economic means, the war would have been much longer continued. What happened was that Germany was shut off from the economic resources of the rest of the globe, and she could not stand it. A nation that is boycotted is a nation that is in sight of surrender. Apply this economic, peaceful, silent, deadly remedy, and there will be no need for force. It is a terrible remedy. It does not cost a life outside the nation boycotted, but it brings a pressure upon that nation which, in my judgment, no modern nation could resist. . . .

I therefore want to call your attention, if you will turn to it when you go home, to Article XI, following Article X, of the Covenant of the League of Nations. That Article XI, let me say, is the favorite article in the treaty, so far as I am concerned. It says that every matter which is likely to affect the peace of the world is everybody's business, and that it shall be the friendly right of any nation to call attention in the League to anything that is likely to affect the peace of the world or the good understanding between nations, upon which the peace of the world depends, whether that matter immediately concerns the nation drawing attention to it or not. . . .

There is not an oppressed people in the world which cannot henceforth get a hearing at that forum, and you know, my fellow citizens, what a hearing will mean if the cause of those people is just. The one thing which those who have reason to dread, have most reason to dread, is publicity and discussion, because if you are challenged to give a reason why you are doing a wrong that it has to be an exceedingly good reason, and if you give a bad reason you confess judgment, and the opinion of mankind goes against you.

Questions

1. What case does Wilson make for Article 10 of the League Covenant?
2. Why does Wilson view Article 11 so positively?
3. What role does Wilson foresee for "absolute economic boycott[s]"? How apt is his analogy between such a boycott and the blockade of 1914–1918?

22-14 Report on the Chicago Race Riot (1919)

Wartime and immediate postwar developments affecting African Americans (increased black migration and heightened black expectations due to their military service in the war) intensified racial fears and anger among whites (see text pp. 730–731). Lynchings increased, especially in the South; riots broke out in the North, the most serious of which occurred in East Saint Louis (1917) and Chicago (1919). The Chicago riot report excerpted here was published three years after the episode.

Source: Excerpted from *The Negro in Chicago: A Study of Race Relations and a Race Riot in 1919.* Copyright © 1922 by the University of Chicago Press. Reprinted by permission. (In reprint edition, New York: Arno Press and New York Times, 1968, 17–21).

. . . Racial outbreaks are often characterized by hangings, burnings, and mutilations, and frequently the cause given for them is a reported Negro attack upon a white woman. None of these features appeared in the Chicago riot. An attempted hanging was reported by a white detective but was unsubstantiated. A report that Joseph Lovings, one of the Negroes killed in the riot, was burned, was heralded abroad and even carried to the United States Senate, but it was false. The coroner's physicians found no burns on his body.

Reports of assaults upon women were at no time mentioned or even hinted at as a cause of the Chicago riot, but after the disorder started reports of such crimes were published in the white and Negro press, but they had no foundation in fact.

Of the ten women wounded in the Chicago riot, seven were white, two were Negroes, and the race of one is unknown. All but one of these ten injuries appears to have been accidental. The exception was the case of Roxy Pratt, a Negro woman who, with her brother, was chased down Wells Street from Forty-seventh by gangsters and was seriously wounded by a bullet. No cases of direct attacks upon white women by Negro men were reported.

The Commission has the record of numerous instances, principally during the first twenty-four hours, where individuals of opposing races met, knives or guns were drawn, and injury was inflicted without the element of mob stimulus.

On Monday mobs operated in sudden, excited assaults, and attacks on street cars provided outstanding cases, five persons being killed and many injured. Nicholas Kleinmark, a white assailant, was stabbed to death by a Negro named Scott, acting in self-defense. Negroes killed were Henry Goodman at Thirtieth and Union streets; John Mills, on Forty-seventy Street near Union; Louis Taylor at Root Street and Wentworth Avenue; and B. F. Hardy at Forty-sixth Street and Cottage Grove Avenue. All died from beatings.

Crowds armed themselves with stones, bricks, and baseball bats and scanned passing street cars for Negroes. Finding them, trolleys were pulled off wires and entrance to the cars forced. Negroes were dragged from under car seats and beaten. Once off the car the chase began. If possible, the vanguard of the mob caught the fleeing Negroes and beat them with clubs. If the Negro outran the pursuers, stones and bricks brought him down. Sometimes the chase led through back yards and over fences, but it was always short.

Another type of race warfare was the automobile raids carried on by young men crowded in cars, speeding across the dead line at Wentworth Avenue and the "Black Belt," and firing at random. Crowded colored districts, with people sitting on front steps and in open windows, were subjected to this menace. Strangely enough, only one person was killed in these raids, Henry Baker, Negro.

Automobile raids were reported wherever colored people had established themselves, in the "Black Belt," both on the main business streets and in the residence sections, and in the small community near Ada and Loomis streets in the vicinity of Ogden Park.

These raids began Monday night, continued spasmodically all day Tuesday, and were again prevalent that night. In spite of the long period, reports of motorcycle policeman show no white raiders arrested. One suspected raiding automobile was caught on State Street Tuesday night, after collision with a patrol wagon. One of the occupants, a white man, had on his person the badge and identification card of a policeman assigned to the Twenty-fourth Precinct. No case was worked up against him, and the other men in the machine were not heard of again in connection with the raid.

Most of the police motorcycle squad was assigned to the Stanton Avenue station, which was used as police headquarters in the "Black Belt." Several automobile loads of Negroes were arrested, and firearms were found either upon their persons or in the automobile.

In only two cases were Negroes aggressively rioting found outside of the "Black Belt." One of these was the case of the saloon-keeper already mentioned, and the other was that of a deputy sheriff, who, with a party of other men, said they were on the way to the Stock Yards to rescue some beleaguered members of their race. It is reported that they wounded five white people en route. Sheriff Peters said he understood that the deputy sheriff was attacked by white mobs and fired to clear the crowd. He was not convicted.

"Sniping" was a form of retaliation by Negroes which grew out of the automobile raids. These raiding automobiles were fired upon from yards, porches, and windows throughout the "Black Belt." One of the most serious cases reported was at Thirty-first and State Streets, where Negroes barricaded the streets with rubbish boxes. Motorcycle Policeman Cheney rammed through and was hit by a bullet. His companion officer following was knocked from his machine and the machine punctured with bullets.

After the wounding of Policeman Cheney and Sergeant Murray, of the Sixth Precinct, policemen made a thorough search of all Negro homes near the scene of the "sniping." Thirty-four Negroes were arrested. Of these, ten were discharged, ten were found not guilty, one was given one day in jail, one was given five days in jail, one was fined and put on probation, two were fined $10 and costs, one was fined $25; six were given thirty days each in the House of Correction, and one, who admitted firing twice but said he was firing at one of the automobiles, was sentenced to six months in the House of Correction. His case was taken to the appellate court.

Concerted retaliatory race action showed itself in the Italian district around Taylor and Loomis streets when rumor said that a little Italian girl had been killed or wounded by a shot fired by a Negro. Joseph Lovings, an innocent Negro, came upon the excited crowd of Italians. There was a short chase through back yards. Finally Lovings was dragged from his hiding-place in a basement and brutally murdered by the crowd. The coroner reported fourteen bullet wounds on his body, eight still having bullets in them; also various stab wounds, contusions of the head, and fractures of the skull. Rumor made the tale more hideous, saying that Lovings was burned after gasoline had been poured over the dead body. This was not true.

This same massing of race against race was shown in a similar clash between Italians and Negroes on the North Side. The results here, however, were not serious. It was reported in this last case that immediately after the fracas the Negroes and Italians were again on good terms. This was not true in the neighborhood of the Lovings outrage. Miss Jane Addams, of Hull-House, which is near the scene of Lovings' death, testified before the Commission that before the riot the Italians held no particular animosity toward Negroes, for those in the neighborhood were mostly from South Italy and accustomed to the dark-skinned races, but that they were developing antipathy. In the September following the riot, she said the neighborhood was still full of wild stories so stereotyped in character that they appeared to indicate propaganda spread for a purpose.

The gang which operated in the "Loop"[1] was composed partly of soldiers and sailors in uniform; they were boys of from seventeen to twenty-two, out for a "rough" time and using race prejudice as a shield for robbery. At times this crowd numbered 100. Its depredations began shortly after 2:00 A.M. Tuesday. The La Salle Street railroad station was entered twice, and Negro men were beaten and robbed. About 3:00 A.M. activities were transferred to Wabash Avenue. In the hunt for Negroes one restaurant was wrecked and the vandalism was continued in another restaurant where two Negroes were found. One was severely injured and the other was shot down. The gangsters rolled the body into the gutter and turned the pockets inside out; they stood on the corner of Wabash Avenue and Adams Street and divided the spoils, openly boasting later of having secured $52, a diamond ring, a watch, and a brooch.

Attacks in the "Loop" continued as late as ten o'clock Tuesday morning, Negroes being chased through the streets and beaten. Warned by the Pinkerton Detective Agency, business men with stores on Wabash Avenue came to protect their property. The rioting was reported to the police by the restaurant men. Policemen rescued two Negroes that morning, but so many policemen had been concentrated in and near the "Black Belt" that there were only a few patrolmen in the whole "Loop" district, and these did not actively endeavor to cope with the mob. In the meantime two Negroes were killed and others injured, while property was seriously damaged.

Tuesday's raids marked the peak of daring during the riot, and their subsidence was as gradual as their rise. For the next two days the gangs roamed the streets, intermittently attacking Negro homes. After Tuesday midnight their operations were not so open or so concerted. The riot gradually decreased in feeling and scope till the last event of a serious nature occurred, the incendiary fires back of the Stock Yards.

While there is general agreement that these fires were incendiary, no clue could be found to the perpetrators. Negroes were suspected, as all the houses burned belonged to whites. In spite of this fact, and the testimony of thirteen people who said they saw Negroes in the vicinity before or during the fires, a rumor persisted that the fires were set by white people with blackened faces. One of the men living in the burned district who testified to seeing a motor truck filled with Negroes said, when asked about the color of the men, "Sure, I know they were colored. Of course I don't know whether they were painted." An early milk-wagon driver said that he saw Negroes come out of a barn on Forty-third Street and Hermitage Avenue. Immediately afterward the barn burst into flames. He ran to a policeman and reported it. The policeman said he was "too busy" and "it is all right anyway." One of the colonels commanding a regiment of militia said he thought white people with blackened faces had set fire to the houses; he got this opinion from talking to the police in charge of that district.

Miss Mary McDowell, of the University of Chicago Settlement, which is located back of the Yards, said in testimony before the Commission:

> I don't think the Negroes did burn the houses. I think the white hoodlums burned them. The Negroes weren't back there, they stayed at home after that Monday. When we got hold of the firemen confidentially, they said no Negroes set fire to them at all, but the newspapers said so and the people were full of fear. All kinds of mythical stories were afloat for some time.

---

[1]*The Loop* is the business district in downtown Chicago (see Map 19-2, text p. 612).

The general superintendent of Armour & Company was asked, when testifying before the Commission, if he knew of any substantial reason why Negroes were accused of setting fires back of the Yards. He answered:

That statement was originated in the minds of a few individuals, radicals. It does not exist in the minds of the conservative and thinking people of the community, even those living in back of the Yards. They know better. I believe it goes without saying that there isn't a colored man, regardless of how little brains he'd have, who would attempt to go over into the Polish district and set fire to anybody's house over there. He wouldn't get that far.

The controlling superintendent of Swift & Company said he could not say it from his own experience, but he understood there was as much friction between the Poles and Lithuanians who worked together in the Yards as between the Negroes and the whites. The homes burned belonged to Lithuanians. The grand jury stated in its report: "The jury believes that these fires were started for the purpose of inciting race feeling by blaming same on the blacks."

The methods of attack used by Negroes and whites during the riot differed; the Negroes usually clung to individual attack and the whites to mob action. Negroes used chiefly firearms and knives, and the whites used their fists, bricks, stones, baseball bats, pieces of iron, hammers. Among the white men, 69 per cent were shot or stabbed and 31 per cent were beaten; among the Negroes almost the reverse was true, 35 per cent being shot and stabbed and 65 per cent beaten. A colonel in charge of a regiment of militia on riot duty says they found few whites but many Negroes armed. . . .

Questions

1. In general, how were people attacked during the riot?
2. What role did the automobile play in the rioting?
3. Consider the impact of the riot on the participants, the city government, and the middle class. How might the incident have affected the city a decade or more later?

22-15　Returning Soldiers (1919)

W. E. B. Du Bois

Less than twelve months after Dr. W. E. B. Du Bois published two editorials endorsing African American support for the war, he expressed the postwar disillusionment of African Americans who had hoped that the war would make America, as well as the world, "safe for democracy."

Source: "Returning Soldiers," *The Crisis,* 18 (May 1919): 13–14.

We are returning from war! THE CRISIS and tens of thousands of black men were drafted into a great struggle. For bleeding France and what she means and has meant and will mean to us and humanity and against the threat of German race arrogance, we fought gladly and to the last drop of blood; for America and her highest ideals, we fought in far-off hope; for the dominant southern oligarchy entrenched in Washington, we fought in bitter resignation. For the America that represents and gloats in lynching, disfranchisement, caste, brutality and devilish insult—for this, in the hateful upturning and mixing of things, we were forced by vindictive fate to fight, also.

But today we return! We return from the slavery of uniform which the world's madness demanded us to don to the freedom of civil garb. We stand again to look America squarely in the face and call a spade a spade. We sing: This country of ours, despite all its better souls have done and dreamed, is yet a shameful land.

It *lynches.*

And lynching is barbarism of a degree of contemptible nastiness unparalleled in human history. Yet for fifty years we have lynched two Negroes a week, and we have kept this up right through the war.

It *disfranchises* its own citizens.

Disfranchisement is the deliberate theft and robbery of the only protection of poor against rich and black against white. The land that disfranchises its citizens and calls itself a democracy lies and knows it lies.

It encourages *ignorance*.

It has never really tried to educate the Negro. A dominant minority does not want Negroes educated. It wants servants, dogs, whores and monkeys. And when this land allows a reactionary group by its stolen political power to force as many black folk into these categories as it possibly can, it cries in contemptible hypocrisy: "They threaten us with degeneracy; they cannot be educated."

It *steals* from us.

It organizes industry to cheat us. It cheats us out of our land: it cheats us out of our labor. It confiscates our savings. It reduces our wages. It raises our rent. It steals our profit. It taxes us without representation. It keeps us consistently and universally poor, and then feeds us on charity and derides our poverty.

It *insults* us.

It has organized a nation-wide and latterly a world-wide propaganda of deliberate and continuous insult and defamation of black blood wherever found. It decrees that it shall not be possible in travel nor residence, work nor play, education nor instruction for a black man to exist without tacit or open acknowledgment of his inferiority to the dirtiest white dog. And it looks upon any attempt to question or even discuss this dogma as arrogance, unwarranted assumption and treason.

This is the country to which we Soldiers of Democracy return. This is the fatherland for which we fought! But it is *our* fatherland. It was right for us to fight. The faults of *our* country are *our* faults. Under similar circumstances, we would fight again. But by the God of Heaven, we are cowards and jackasses if now that that war is over, we do not marshal every ounce of our brain and brawn to fight a sterner, longer, more unbending battle against the forces of hell in our own land.

We *return*.

We *return from fighting*.

We *return fighting*.

Make way for Democracy! We saved it in France, and by the Great Jehovah, we will save it in the United States of America, or know the reason why.

Questions

1. Compare and contrast the content and tone of "Help Us to Help" (Document 22-10) and this selection.
2. Drawing on the text (Chapters 18, 20, and 22, as appropriate), flesh out the charges in W. E. B. Du Bois's indictment.

22-16 Foreign Languages in the Schools: *Meyer v. Nebraska* (1923)

Nativism, fanned to a white heat by the war and the postwar Red Scare, found expression in many ways. The schools figured prominently in this crusade. More than twenty states made illegal the teaching of modern foreign languages in public, private, and religious schools through a specified grade, usually the eighth. This selection provides five arguments before the U.S. Supreme Court challenging and defending Nebraska's law, under which Meyer had been convicted; the majority opinion of Justice James McReynolds, striking down the law; and the dissenting opinion of Justice Oliver Wendell Holmes Jr. in a companion case, *Bartels v. State of Iowa*.

Source: Meyer v. State of Nebraska, 262 U.S. 390 (1923); *Bartels v. State of Iowa*, 262 U.S. 404 (1923).

ARGUMENT FOR PLAINTIFF IN ERROR.

Imparting knowledge in a foreign language is not inherently immoral or inimical to the public welfare, and not a legitimate subject for prohibitory legislation. In fact, an examination of the statute will show that the legislature did not regard the teaching of a pupil in some language other than English as vicious or inimical to the public welfare. It applies only to schools, leaving teachers and others at liberty to teach privately.

When the legislature by clear implication finds that the practice or pursuit against which the act is leveled does not of itself injuriously affect the public, a measure designed to prohibit it is unconstitutional. It being clear, therefore, both upon reason and legislative finding, that the prohibited acts are not harmful, this measure, insofar as it imposes upon teachers, both lay and clerical, penalties of fine and imprisonment for the giving of instruction in languages, is violative of their constitutional right to engage in the practice of their chosen profession or calling.

The statute in question is not a legitimate exercise of the police power. The exercise of the police power can be justified only when it adds, in a substantial way, to the security of the fundamental rights.

The relation to the common good of a law fixing a minimum of education is readily perceived, but how one fixing a maximum—limiting the field of human knowledge—can serve the public welfare or add substantially to the security of life, liberty or the pursuit of happiness is inconceivable.

One claim put forward is, that the statute forwards the work of Americanization. But in our desire for the Americanization of our foreign born population we should not overlook the fact that the spirit of America is liberty and toleration—the disposition to allow each person to live his own life in his own way, unhampered by unreasonable and arbitrary restrictions.

The law, as construed by the Supreme Court of Nebraska, operates to deny the plaintiff in error the equal protection of the law.

The law is directed against the teaching in or of a foreign language in public, private, denominational and parochial schools. It leaves those engaged in giving private lessons in such languages free to pursue their vocations.

ARGUMENT FOR DEFENDANT IN ERROR.

The federal constitutional question was injected into the case as an afterthought and too late to permit its review by this Court.

The statute was a legitimate exercise of the police power of the State.

The statute forbids the teaching of foreign languages to children of tender years before such children are grounded in the English tongue. It does not forbid the use of foreign languages by persons of maturity or prevent the study of foreign languages by persons who have passed the eighth grade. It does not in any way interfere with *bona fide* religious instruction or with any legitimate religion.

The object of the legislation . . . was to create an enlightened American citizenship in sympathy with the principles and ideals of this country, and to prevent children reared in America from being trained and educated in foreign languages and foreign ideals before they have had an opportunity to learn the English language and observe American ideals. It is a well known fact that the language first learned by a child remains his mother tongue and the language of his heart. The purpose of the statute is to insure that the English language shall be the mother tongue and the language of the heart of the children reared in this country who will eventually become the citizens of this country.

These foreign language statutes are no more difficult to sustain under the police power of the State than the Bank Guarantee Act, the Workmen's Compensation Acts, the Female Labor Laws, and Tenement Housing legislation.

Taking the test laid down as to the legitimate exercise of the police power by Freund (§ 143): A danger exists; of sufficient magnitude; concerning the public; the proposed measure tends to remove it; the restraint is a requirement in proportion to the danger; it is possible to secure the object sought without impairing essential rights and principles. If it is within the police power of the State to regulate wages, to legislate respecting housing conditions in crowded cities, to prohibit dark rooms in tenement houses, to compel landlords to place windows in their tenements which will enable their tenants to enjoy the sunshine, it is within the police power of the State to compel every resident of Nebraska so to educate his children that the sunshine of American ideals will permeate the life of the future citizens of this Republic. . . .

OPINION OF THE COURT.

. . . The problem for our determination is whether the statute as construed and applied unreasonably infringes the liberty guaranteed to the plaintiff in error by the Fourteenth Amendment. "No State shall . . . deprive any person of life, liberty, or property, without due process of law."

While this Court has not attempted to define with exactness the liberty thus guaranteed, the term has received much consideration and some of the included things have been definitely stated. Without doubt, it denotes not merely freedom from bodily restraint but also the right of the individual to contract, to engage in any of the common occupations of life, to acquire useful knowledge, to marry, establish a home and bring up children, to worship God according to the dictates of his own conscience, and generally to enjoy those privileges long recognized at common law as essential to the orderly pursuit of happiness by free men. The established doctrine is that this liberty may not be interfered with, under the guise of protecting the public interest, by legislative action which is arbitrary or without reasonable relation to some purpose within the competency of the State to effect. Determination by the legislature of what constitutes proper exercise of police power is not final or conclusive but is subject to supervision by the courts.

The American people have always regarded education and acquisition of knowledge as matters of supreme importance which should be diligently promoted. The Ordinance of 1787 declares, "Religion, morality, and knowledge being necessary to good government and the happiness of mankind, schools and the means of education shall forever be encouraged." Corresponding to the right of control, it is the natural duty of the parent to give his children education suitable to their station in life; and nearly all the States, including Nebraska, enforce this obligation by compulsory laws.

Practically, education of the young is only possible in schools conducted by especially qualified persons who devote themselves thereto. The calling always has been regarded as useful and honorable, essential, indeed, to the public welfare. Mere knowledge of the German language cannot reasonably be regarded as harmful. Heretofore it has been commonly looked upon as helpful and desirable. Plaintiff in error taught this language in school as part of his occupation. His right thus to teach and the right of parents to engage him so to instruct their children, we think, are within the liberty of the Amendment.

The challenged statute forbids the teaching in school of any subject except in English; also the teaching of any other language until the pupil has attained and successfully passed the eighth grade, which is not usually accomplished before the age of twelve. The Supreme Court of the State has held that "the so-called ancient or dead languages" are not "within the spirit or the purpose of the act." Latin, Greek, Hebrew are not proscribed; but German, French, Spanish, Italian and every other alien speech are within the ban. Evidently the legislature has attempted materially to interfere with the calling of modern language teachers, with the opportunities of pupils to acquire knowledge, and with the power of parents to control the education of their own.

It is said the purpose of the legislation was to promote civic development by inhibiting training and education of the immature in foreign tongues and ideals before they could learn English and acquire American ideals; and "that the English language should be and become the mother tongue of all children reared in this State." It is also affirmed that the foreign born population is very large, that certain communities commonly use foreign words, follow foreign leaders, move in a foreign atmosphere, and that the children are thereby hindered from becoming citizens of the most useful type and the public safety is imperiled.

That the State may do much, go very far, indeed, in order to improve the quality of its citizens, physically, mentally and morally, is clear; but the individual has certain fundamental rights which must be respected. The protection of the Constitution extends to all, to those who speak other languages as well as to those born with English on the tongue. Perhaps it would be highly advantageous if all

had ready understanding of our ordinary speech, but this cannot be coerced by methods which conflict with the Constitution—a desirable end cannot be promoted by prohibited means. . . .

The desire of the legislature to foster a homogeneous people with American ideals prepared readily to understand current discussions of civic matters is easy to appreciate. Unfortunate experiences during the late war and aversion toward every characteristic of truculent adversaries were certainly enough to quicken that aspiration. But the means adopted, we think, exceed the limitations upon the power of the State and conflict with rights assured to plaintiff in error. The interference is plain enough and no adequate reason therefor in time of peace and domestic tranquility has been shown. . . .

MR. JUSTICE HOLMES, DISSENTING.

We all agree, I take it, that it is desirable that all the citizens of the United States should speak a common tongue, and therefore that the end aimed at by the statute is a lawful and proper one. The only question is whether the means adopted deprive teachers of the liberty secured to them by the Fourteenth Amendment. It is with hesitation and unwillingness that I differ from my brethren with regard to a law like this but I cannot bring my mind to believe that in some circumstances, and circumstances existing it is said in Nebraska, the statute might not be regarded as a reasonable or even necessary method of reaching the desired result. The part of the act with which we are concerned deals with the teaching of young children. Youth is the time when familiarity with a language is established and if there are sections in the State where a child would hear only Polish or French or German spoken at home I am not prepared to say that it is unreasonable to provide that in his early years he shall hear and speak only English at school. But if it is reasonable it is not an undue restriction of the liberty either of teacher or scholar. No one would doubt that a teacher might be forbidden to teach many things, and the only criterion of his liberty under the Constitution that I can think of is "whether, considering the end in view, the statute passes the bounds of reason and assumes the character of a merely arbitrary fiat." I think I appreciate the objection to the law but it appears to me to present a question upon which men reasonably might differ and therefore I am unable to say that the Constitution of the United States prevents the experiment being tried.

Questions

1. What case is made for the Nebraska law by counsel for Defendant in Error? Against the Nebraska law by counsel for Plaintiff in Error?
2. Compare and contrast the opinions of Justice James McReynolds and Justice Oliver Wendell Holmes Jr. Does Holmes's dissent in *Lochner* (Document 20-3) contribute to your understanding of his dissent in *Bartels?*

Questions for Further Thought

1. What do the text and documents on the wartime and postwar periods suggest about the relationship between foreign and domestic developments between 1917 and 1920?

2. Consider why there have been recurring cultural-political conflicts over the schools (see Documents 18-3 to 18-6 and 22-16).

3. Compare and contrast the gains—or lack thereof—of women and African Americans during and after the First World War. How do you account for similarities and dissimilarities between the two groups?

CHAPTER 23

Modern Times: The 1920s

★   ★   ★

The Business-Government Partnership of the 1920s

The White House of the 1920s seemed different from the White House of the Progressive Era. Gone were Theodore Roosevelt and Woodrow Wilson, succeeded there by Warren Harding and Calvin Coolidge. Government policy seemed different, too, stressing cooperation with, rather than regulation of, business. Still, such cooperation had been one aspect of progressivism and was central to the conduct of the First World War. Moreover, the most important figure in the Harding and Coolidge administrations was Secretary of Commerce Herbert Hoover, a progressive and an important wartime administrator. A few social justice concerns were addressed during the 1920s—Congress enacted the Sheppard-Towner Federal Maternity and Infancy Act (see text pp. 740–742) and proposed a constitutional amendment to prohibit child labor, and the Harding administration prevailed on the steel industry to shorten workers' hours—but in the main, business received a sympathetic hearing from the Harding and Coolidge administrations, and agriculture and labor did not.

The United States prospered during the 1920s. It had emerged from World War I economically strengthened, not drained. Already the world's premier economic power, it was now the world's largest creditor, as well. However, not all Americans shared fully in prosperity. Workers' standard of living rose, but insecurity—due to unemployment, illness or injury, or old age—remained their lot. Employers, not government or labor unions, bore responsibility for such worker benefits as were provided. This was "welfare capitalism" before the birth of "the welfare state" and the revitalization of the labor movement during the 1930s (see text p. 743). Sectors of the agricultural economy—wheat, corn, and cotton farmers—also suffered economic declines during the 1920s (see text pp. 737–745).

In Document 23-1, Herbert Hoover reflects on and documents his policies toward business as secretary of commerce. Document 23-2 provides the advertising insight of Bruce Barton, who reveals "the Real Jesus" to have been "the founder of modern business."

23-1   Business-Government Relations (1921–1928)

Herbert Hoover

Secretary of Commerce Herbert Hoover (1874–1964) had been—and remained—a progressive, though of course not all progressives spoke or acted the same. Hoover's *Memoirs,* written many years after his presidency, provide his reflections on his life in government. They also incorporate Commerce Department documents dating to the 1920s so that we can learn about his policies to achieve the "associative state," as well as his later views of those policies (see text pp. 739–740).

Source: The Memoirs of Herbert Hoover: The Cabinet and the Presidency, 1920–1933 (New York: Macmillan, 1952), 66–68, 94–95, 167–170. Courtesy of the Herbert Hoover Presidential Library.

SIMPLIFICATION AND STANDARDIZATION

One of our early attacks upon the problem of elimination of industrial waste was to organize what we called "standardization" and "simplification." They were different in approach but complementary to each other. The activities of the Department were confined to staple products, style of articles being excluded as being matters of personal taste. In all this we had the constant co-operation of the Standards Committee appointed by the Engineering Societies.

My 1925 report to Congress described the simplification idea:

> By simplification we secure . . . elimination of the least necessary varieties, dimension, or grades of materials and products. The usefulness . . . is not limited in the application to materials and machines but extends . . . to business practices such as specifications, and . . . other documents. Uniformity in such specifications reinforces the demand for standardized and simplified products.

For instance, by simplification our automotive committee brought about the reduction of the number of sizes of automobile wheels from eight to three, and tires correspondingly. As an instance of standardization, the thread for bolts, nuts, pipes, and nipples had been agreed upon and adopted by all manufacturers. Previously, each manufacturer had his own standards, and any replacement must be made from him. The consequence of this cooperative action was of the utmost importance. Manufacturers were able to engage more fully in mass production, as they could produce for stocks instead of filling specific orders; the amount of inventories which must be carried by consumers was greatly reduced, and competition was enhanced in such articles.

Our method in this field, as in others, was a study of the particular subject, and a preliminary meeting of the trades concerned. If they were interested, committees were created which developed recommendations. A circular was sent out by the Department on behalf of the committees to all members of the trade, both producers and consumers, giving the recommendations and asking for acceptance. When acceptances were sufficient to warrant action, the recommendations were promulgated by the Department as the desirable simplification or standard for the trade. The interaction of consumers and producers upon each other secured rapid adoption. The committees were maintained to aid in adoption of any necessary revisions.

In addition to such articles as I have mentioned, we covered building materials (bricks, lumber, cement, doors, windows, and hardware); containers (wood, steel, and paper); bedsprings, mattresses; hospital linen and blankets; office furniture; tools and general hardware, plumbing fixtures, electric light sockets and electric bulbs; railway equipment and ship construction parts; ball bearings, brake linings, spark plugs, and scores of others. In all, probably three thousand articles were covered. . . .

Another phase of these activities was simplification and standardization of commercial documents, such as invoices, shippers' documents, and warehouse receipts. Still another phase was contractors' agreements. The 1925 report mentions that:

> Through the committee sponsored by the Secretary of Commerce, representing contractors' associations, architects, engineers, railways, public officials, and other large construction users, standard construction contract forms have been drawn up and are in wide and growing use, which afford better assurance to both contractor and owner, and which should eliminate much of the area of possible dispute and create a more uniform basis for competitive action.

ELIMINATION OF WASTE BY REDUCING SEASONAL OPERATION OF INDUSTRY

The 1926 report stated:

> In June, 1923, the Secretary appointed a committee of leading business and labor representatives upon "seasonal operation in the construction industries." This committee, after exhaustive investigation, made most important recommendations. The better understand-

ing of the problem brought about by the committee's report and the co-operative activities established in "follow-up" in the most important localities have had a marked effect. The annually enlarged building program of the country has been handled in large part by extension of the building season into the winter months; this has had a stabilizing effect upon prices and given increased annual earnings to workers, not only in construction but in the construction-material industries. The price of most building materials has, in fact, decreased despite the large increased demand. . . .

The building codes in our towns and cities had been largely dominated by contractors and labor organizations who greatly and unnecessarily increased costs. We called a national conference of public officials and technical experts to consider the question. In my Annual Report to Congress for 1922 I indicated the beginnings of this work:

Systematic measures of co-operation have been set in motion by the appointment of a committee to formulate a standard building code . . . as varying regulations in force in hundreds of different municipalities . . . imposed an unnecessary cost upon building of from 10 to 20 per cent. . . . A tentative draft was submitted to some 975 engineers, architects, municipal officials, and representatives of the building industry, whose useful criticisms were incorporated.

Finally, a standard code was formulated. We put on a campaign for its adoption and secured its acceptance in several hundred municipalities.

We inaugurated nation-wide zoning to protect home owners from business and factory encroachment into residential areas. We called a national conference of experts who drafted sample municipal codes for this purpose. When we started, there were only 48 municipalities with zoning laws; by 1928 there were 640.

The Department Report for 1928 said:

. . . Most gratifying results have come from the department's co-operation with business, civic, and labor groups, and local government officials toward solving various outstanding homebuilding problems. . . .

. . . At least 120 municipalities . . . have now made use of the recommendations prepared by the department's building code committee. . . . Savings up to 20 per cent of the cost are . . . made by the revision of obsolete requirements. . . .

. . . Campaigns to put construction more nearly on a year-round basis were inaugurated in a number of cities during the past year. . . . These voluntary efforts have helped to stabilize employment among more than 1,000,000 men engaged in construction, and several times as many engaged in the manufacture and transportation of building materials. . . .

Now more than 640 cities and towns [have adopted] zoning ordinances. . . . These communities

. . . now number ten times more than when the . . . committee . . .was created in the department seven years ago. . . .

We organized committees in the building trades, which included representatives of manufacturers, contractors, architects, and labor, to standardize and simplify building materials. . . .

Fixing the boundaries of governmental relations to business perplexed me daily and in innumerable ways during my twelve years as Secretary of Commerce and President. Fundamentally, this problem involved the destiny of the American scheme of life. Although business committed various abuses that were only marginal in an otherwise great productive system, the marginal wrongs had to be cured if the system was to survive—they were abuses of freedom, which grow like a cancer. . . .

The real cure of our marginal evils lay in the application, where necessary, of government regulation, which clearly and specifically prohibited an evil practice. But beyond and better than even that was cooperation in the business community to cure its own abuses. I considered it part of the duties of the Secretary of Commerce to help bring business to a realization of its responsibilities and to suggest methods of its own cures. . . .

The problem before the Department of Commerce could be divided into three parts: first, competition which could be abridged without violation of law; second, competition which could be destructive; and, third, recurrent abuses of the moral code by evil men.

In the first part—abridgment of competition which did not violate the laws—one effort of the Department lay in furnishing information and statistics which would put small business in as favorable a position as big business. . . .

The second part—destructive competition—was somewhat ameliorated by the elimination-of-waste programs. We tackled some of these practices, together with the third part—violations of the moral code—by securing action through cooperation of business and professional organizations.

Early in my term as Secretary of Commerce, I concluded that there was a form of organization in American business which could be made an instrumentality for all these three categories of action against some of the marginal faults.

Practically our entire American working world was now organized into some form of economic association. We had trade associations and trade institutes embracing practically every industry and occupation. We had chambers of commerce embracing representatives of different industries and commerce. We had the labor unions representing the different crafts. We had associations embracing all the different professions—law, engineering, medicine, banking, real estate, and what not. We had farmers' associations, and we had the enormous growth of farmers' cooperatives for actual dealing in commodities. Each of these associations had officers, paid staff, and annual conventions. . . .

We concluded that they [trade associations] could be made instrumental wholly for national benefit if they were given constructive things to do, and in doing it to be free from attack. It seemed to us that instead of keeping them under assault we should define their useful tasks and de-

velop within them definite ethical standards. Therefore, I submitted an informal memorandum on the question to the Department of Justice and the Federal Trade Commission. In this memorandum, I laid out the areas in which trade associations could take constructive action which not only would be of economic benefit, but also would lessen violations of the Anti-Trust laws. . . .

Questions

1. What is meant by the "associative state" (see text pp. 739–740)? How does Hoover seek to achieve it? How would it benefit participants and the public?
2. What is the significance of Hoover's characterization of "abuses," "wrongs," and "evils" in the system as "marginal"? To whom does he think the righting of wrongs should be entrusted?

23-2   The Man Nobody Knows (1925)

Bruce Barton

The advertising industry was not central to the "associative state" sought by Herbert Hoover, but it was obviously essential to the consumer goods–based economy and the "new national culture" of the 1920s.

Bruce Barton (1886–1967) was among advertising's leaders. The son of a Protestant clergyman, Barton, a Phi Beta Kappa graduate (voted "most likely to succeed") of Amherst College, worked as an editor and magazine sales manager. During the First World War, he did volunteer work for the Salvation Army and served as publicity director of the United War Work Agencies. It was then that he met Roy Durstine and Alex Osborne, with whom he founded an advertising agency in 1919. With a merger in 1928, the firm became even more famous as Batten, Barton, Durstine, and Osborne (BBD&O).

Barton's *The Man Nobody Knows,* excerpted here, led the nonfiction best-seller list in 1925 and 1926. ("Jeffries," to whom he refers, was James Jeffries, a heavyweight boxing champion.)

Source: Reprinted with the permission of Scribner, a division of Simon & Schuster from *The Man Nobody Knows: A Discovery of the Real Jesus* by Bruce Barton. Copyright © 1925 by The Bobbs-Merrill Company, Inc., renewed 1953 by Bruce Barton.

HOW IT CAME TO BE WRITTEN

The little boy's body sat bolt upright in the rough wooden chair, but his mind was very busy.

This was his weekly hour of revolt.

The kindly lady who could never seem to find her glasses would have been terribly shocked if she had known what was going on inside the little boy's mind.

"You must love Jesus," she said every Sunday, "and God."

The little boy did not say anything. He was afraid to say anything; he was almost afraid that something would happen to him because of the things he thought.

Love God! Who was always picking on people for having a good time, and sending little boys to hell because they couldn't do better in a world which he had made so hard! Why didn't God take some one his own size?

Love Jesus! The little boy looked up at the picture which hung on the Sunday-school wall. It showed a pale young man with flabby forearms and a sad expression. The young man had red whiskers.

Then the little boy looked across to the other wall. There was Daniel, good old Daniel, standing off the lions. The little boy liked Daniel. He liked David, too, with the trusty sling that landed a stone square on the forehead of Goliath. And Moses, with his rod and his big brass snake.

They were winners—those three. He wondered if David could whip Jeffries. Samson could! Say, that would have been a fight!

But Jesus! Jesus was the "lamb of God." The little boy did not know what that meant, but it sounded like Mary's little lamb. Something for girls—sissified. Jesus was also "meek and lowly," a "man of sorrows and acquainted with grief." He went around for three years telling people not to do things.

Sunday was Jesus' day; it was wrong to feel comfortable or laugh on Sunday.

The little boy was glad when the superintendent thumped the bell and announced: "We will now sing the closing hymn." One more bad hour was over. For one more week the little boy had got rid of Jesus.

Years went by and the boy grew up and became a business man.

He began to wonder about Jesus.

He said to himself: "Only strong magnetic men inspire great enthusiasm and build great organizations. Yet Jesus built the greatest organization of all. It is extraordinary."

The more sermons the man heard and the more books he read the more mystified he became.

One day he decided to wipe his mind clean of books and sermons.

He said, "I will read what the men who knew Jesus personally said about him. I will read about him as though he were a new historical character, about whom I had never heard anything at all."

The man was amazed.

A physical weakling! Where did they get that idea? Jesus pushed a plane and swung an adze; he was a successful carpenter. He slept outdoors and spent his days walking around his favorite lake. His muscles were so strong that when he drove the money-changers out, nobody dared to oppose him!

A kill-joy! He was the most popular dinner guest in Jerusalem! The criticism which proper people made was that he spent too much time with publicans and sinners (very good fellows, on the whole, the man thought) and enjoyed society too much. They called him a "wine bibber and a gluttonous man."

A failure! He picked up twelve men from the bottom ranks of business and forged them into an organization that conquered the world.

When the man had finished his reading he exclaimed, "This is a man nobody knows.

"Some day," said he, "some one will write a book about Jesus. Every business man will read it and send it to his partners and his salesmen. For it will tell the story of the founder of modern business."

So the man waited for some one to write the book, but no one did. Instead, more books were published about the "lamb of God" who was weak and unhappy and glad to die.

The man became impatient. One day he said, "I believe I will try to write that book, myself."

And he did.

Questions

1. Which view of Christ does Barton reject?
2. How does he portray Jesus instead?
3. How do you account for the popularity of Barton's best-selling book?

Questions for Further Thought

1. To what extent do the policies of Herbert Hoover (Document 23-1) appear to build on those of Bernard M. Baruch (Document 22-6)? To what extent does Hoover appear to differ from Baruch?
2. How might Bruce Barton's portrayal of Jesus (Document 23-2) have strengthened the self-esteem of businessmen (and of Barton himself)?

A New National Culture

During the 1920s, a national culture emerged, one that cut across (though it hardly obliterated) class, regional, racial, religious, and ethnic lines. To a considerable degree, this new mass culture was created by automobiles (and passable roads), radios, movies, mass-circulation magazines, and department and chain stores. Although large numbers of Americans did not share in the prosperity of the decade, living standards were rising in a society that stressed consumption and leisure. Advertising created wants, and various credit arrangements encouraged consumers to satisfy those wants. Sales of automobiles and electric household appliances boomed. Increasing numbers of Americans took to the road as tourists and attended movies and a range of athletic events, the stars of which became celebrities (see text pp. 745–755).

Documents 23-3 and 23-4 are advertisements from the period: the first is for Listerine, a consumer product; the second is for *The Wanderer,* a major film. Document 23-5 analyzes the impact of the automobile on the people of "Middletown" (Muncie, Indiana).

23-3   Advertisement for Listerine (1923)

During the 1920s, it has been noted, advertising copywriters increasingly emphasized the *consumers* to whom they hoped to sell products rather than the *products* themselves. Advertising for Listerine provided a classic and successful illustration of this strategy: the product's advertising budget rose by 5,000 percent, the producer's profits by 4,000 percent. Listerine was marketed as a treatment for colds, sore throats, and dandruff and as an astringent, aftershave, and deodorant, as well as a mouthwash.

Source: Listerine ad by Lambert Pharmacal Company, St. Louis, in *Literary Digest,* November 17, 1923. Courtesy of Warner-Lambert Company, the copyright and trademark owner.

Questions

1. What is the role of the dentist in this ad?
2. What are the various reasons given for buying the product?
3. What kind of gender stereotyping is involved in both the artwork and the ad copy?

In his discreet way he told her

It had never occurred to her before. But in his discreet, professional way he was able to tell her. And she was sensible enough to be grateful instead of resentful.

In fact, the suggestion he made came to mean a great deal to her.

It brought her greater poise—that feeling of self-assurance that adds to a woman's charm—and, moreover, a new sense of daintiness that she had never been quite so sure of in the past.

* * * * * *

Many people suffer in the same way. Halitosis (the scientific term for unpleasant breath) creeps upon you unawares. Usually you are not able to detect it yourself. And, naturally enough, even your best friends will not tell you.

Fortunately, however, halitosis is usually due to some local condition—often food fermentation in the mouth; something you have eaten; too much smoking. And it may be corrected by the systematic use of Listerine as a mouth wash and gargle.

Dentists know that this well-known antiseptic they have used for half a century, possesses these remarkable properties as a breath deodorant.

Your druggist will supply you. He sells lots of Listerine. It has dozens of other uses as a safe antiseptic. It is particularly valuable, too, at this time of year in combating sore throat. Read the circular that comes with each bottle.—*Lambert Pharmacal Company, Saint Louis, U. S. A.*

For HALITOSIS use LISTERINE

23-4   Advertisement for The Wanderer (1926)

For the price of a ticket, a moviegoer could be transported from New York City or Mason City, Iowa, to ancient Babylon. Meanwhile, as Thomas W. Lamb, who designed Columbus's elaborate Ohio Theatre, put it, palatial movie theaters helped customers "lift" themselves out of their "daily drudgery" by "cut[ting] them off from the rest of the city life." Movie theaters pioneered in providing air-conditioning, adding to customers' comfort and summer box-office receipts (see text pp. 750–753).

Source: This advertisement for *The Wanderer* appeared in the *Saturday Evening Post,* January 2, 1926. Copyright © 1926 by Universal City Studios, Inc. Courtesy of MCA Publishing Rights, a Division of MCA Inc. All rights reserved.

Questions

1. How does the advertisement draw the reader in?
2. What do the couple pictured at the top suggest?
3. How would a movie like *The Wanderer* homogenize disparate places like New York City and a small Iowa town?

Personalities of Paramount and their Paramount Pictures

ernest Torrence

—whose performance in The Covered Wagon as a Western Bad Man is excelled only by his Eastern Bad Man in The Wanderer, has a rare talent for rôles of sardonic villainy. Other Paramount Pictures showing his art are: Night Life of New York and The Pony Express.

Raoul Walsh

—is the director of The Wanderer. He also made The Thief of Bagdad. These two pictures are a story of marvellous art in themselves, spectacles literally unique of their kind. Mr. Walsh's next Paramount Picture will be: The Lucky Lady.

Greta Nissen

—is a new star of extraordinary charm. See her as Tisha the siren, in The Wanderer, and you will realize that this enchantress has an art all her own. Her other Paramount Pictures are: Lost—A Wife, The King on Main Street, and The Lucky Lady.

Wm. Collier Jr.

—is The Wanderer. He shows you the innocent and his money and their early parting. Many a mother's heart will beat quicker for her son because of the way this character is played. See William Collier, Jr., in: The Devil's Cargo, Eve's Secret and The Lucky Lady.

Esther Ralston

—is a rising favorite. She made a great impression as Wendy's mother in Peter Pan, and as the innocent cause of family dissension in The Trouble with Wives. Her other Paramount Pictures are: The Lucky Devil, Womanhandled, and The American Venus.

Bebe Daniels

—is admired by a host of fans for the sunny happiness she brings to the screen, seeming not to act but simply to live the stories. Paramount Pictures starring her are: Wild, Wild Susan, Lovers in Quarantine, and Miss Brewster's Millions.

Produced by
FAMOUS PLAYERS-LASKY CORP.
ADOLPH ZUKOR, President
New York City

The Wanderer

The Eternal Story of the Wandering Son

You see him leave home. You spend a fortune with him. Beautiful Greta Nissen, and Ernest Torrence as a shark of ancient days, take him, and you, to Babylon, and open the town with his fortune like an oyster.

Temptations no human being could resist, you see him fall for, and you hardly know whether to blame or envy, so nearly is the game worth the candle—until the dreadful bill of reckoning is presented, and then anyone can be wise—and you relax the dramatic spell thrown over you by the play, and tell yourself it is only a motion picture! But it is not, it is more, *and there are wanderers of 1926 who will see this* and have their eyes opened!

The scenes of life in ancient Babylon are as convincing as a certified check, and when the storm and the earthquake and the wrath of God flash upon the city you realize that none but an organization with resources as great as Paramount's could construct and destroy a city before your eyes for the simple betterment of one part of one plot of one Paramount Picture.

Great as this picture is in its spectacular sweep across your vision and imagination, and great as The Vanishing American, The Ten Commandments, A Kiss for Cinderella, and other Paramount Pictures are, not one of them, nor all of them together, are as great as the name that stands behind them, which is the sign of the organization steadily blazing the way to better and better pictures.

Paramount Pictures

"If it's a Paramount Picture it's the best show in town"

23-5   Remaking Leisure in Middletown (1929)

**Robert S. Lynd and
Helen Merrell Lynd**

Sociologists Robert S. Lynd (1892–1970) and Helen Merrell Lynd (1896–1982) wanted to study the effects of modernization on an urban community "in that common denominator of America, the Middle West." They chose Muncie, Indiana, which they referred to as Middletown (see text p. 737). The Lynds' work, first published in 1929, has become a classic in American sociology.

This selection considers the automobile (see text pp. 748–750), a new but already troubling phenomenon in Middletown.

Source: Excerpts from *Middletown: A Study in American Culture* by Robert S. Lynd and Helen Merrell Lynd, 253–260. Copyright 1929 by Harcourt, Inc., and renewed 1957 by Robert S. and Helen M. Lynd. Reprinted by permission of the publisher.

The first real automobile appeared in Middletown in 1900. About 1906 it was estimated that "there are probably 200 in the city and county." At the close of 1923 there were 6,221 passenger cars in the city, one for every 6.1 persons, or roughly two for every three families. Of these 6,221 cars, 41 per cent. were Fords; 54 per cent. of the total were cars of models of 1920 or later, and 17 per cent. models earlier than 1917. These cars average a bit over 5,000 miles a year. For some of the workers and some of the business class, use of the automobile is a seasonal matter, but the increase in surfaced roads and in closed cars is rapidly making the car a year-round tool for leisure-time as well as getting-a-living activities. As, at the turn of the century, business class people began to feel apologetic if they did not have a telephone, so ownership of an automobile has now reached the point of being an accepted essential of normal living.

Into the equilibrium of habits which constitutes for each individual some integration in living has come this new habit, upsetting old adjustments, and blasting its way through such accustomed and unquestioned dicta as "Rain or shine, I never miss a Sunday morning at church"; "A high school boy does not need much spending money"; "I don't need exercise, walking to the office keeps me fit"; "I wouldn't think of moving out of town and being so far from my friends"; "Parents ought always to know where their children are." The newcomer is most quickly and amicably incorporated into those regions of behavior in which men are engaged in doing impersonal, matter-of-fact things; much more contested is its advent where emotionally charged sanctions and taboos are concerned. No one questions the use of the auto for transporting groceries, getting to one's place of work or to the golf course, or in place of the porch for "cooling off after supper" on a hot summer evening; however much the activities concerned with getting a living may be altered by the fact that a factory can draw from workmen within a radius of forty-five miles, or however much old labor union men resent the intrusion of this new alternate way of spending an evening, these things are hardly major issues. But when auto riding tends to replace the traditional call in the family parlor as a way of approach between the unmarried, "the home is endangered," and all-day Sunday motor trips are a "threat against the church"; it is in the activities concerned with the home and religion that the automobile occasions the greatest emotional conflicts.

Group-sanctioned values are disturbed by the inroads of the automobile upon the family budget. A case in point is the not uncommon practice of mortgaging a home to buy an automobile. . . . That the automobile does represent a real choice in the minds of some at least is suggested by the acid retort of one citizen to the question about car ownership: "No, sir, we've *not* got a car. *That's* why we've got a home." According to an officer of a Middletown automobile financing company, 75 to 90 percent of the cars purchased locally are bought on time payment, and a working man earning $35.00 a week frequently plans to use one week's pay each month as payment for his car.

The automobile has apparently unsettled the habit of careful saving for some families. "Part of the money we spend on the car would go to the bank, I suppose," said more than one working class wife. A business man explained his recent inviting of social oblivion by selling his car by saying: "My car, counting depreciation and everything, was costing mighty nearly $100.00 a month, and my wife and I sat down together the other night and just figured that we're getting along, and if we're to have anything later on, we've just got to begin to save." The "moral" aspect of the competition between the automobile and certain accepted expenditures appears in the remark of another business man, "An automobile is a luxury, and no one has a right to one if he can't afford it. I haven't the slightest sympathy for any one who is out of work if he owns a car."

Men in the clothing industry are convinced that automobiles are bought at the expense of clothing, and the statements of a number of the working class wives bear this out:

"We'd rather do without clothes than give up the car," said one mother of nine children. "We used to go to his sister's to visit, but by the time we'd get the children shoed and dressed there wasn't any money left for carfare. Now no matter how they look, we just poke 'em in the car and take 'em along."

"We don't have no fancy clothes when we have the car to pay for," said another. "The car is the only pleasure we have."

Even food may suffer:

"I'll go without food before I'll see us give up the car," said one woman emphatically, and several who were out of work were apparently making precisely this adjustment. . . .

Many families feel that an automobile is justified as an agency holding the family group together. "I never feel as close to my family as when we are all together in the car," said one business class mother, and one or two spoke of giving up Country Club membership or other recreations to get a car for this reason. "We don't spend anything on recreation except for the car. We save every place we can and put the money into the car. It keeps the family together," was an opinion voiced more than once. Sixty-one per cent. of 337 boys and 60 per cent. of 423 girls in the three upper years of the high school say that they motor more often with their parents than without them.

But this centralizing tendency of the automobile may be only a passing phase; sets in the other direction are almost equally prominent. "Our daughters [eighteen and fifteen] don't use our car much because they are always with somebody else in their car when we go out motoring," lamented one business class mother. . . . "What on earth *do* you want me to do? Just sit around home all evening!" retorted a popular high school girl of today when her father discouraged her going out motoring for the evening with a young blade in a rakish car waiting at the curb. The fact that 348 boys and 382 girls in the three upper years of the high school placed "use of the automobile" fifth and fourth respectively in a list of twelve possible sources of disagreement between them and their parents suggests that this may be an increasing decentralizing agent.

An earnest teacher in a Sunday School class of working class boys and girls in their late teens was winding up the lesson on the temptations of Jesus: "These three temptations summarize all the temptations we encounter today: physical comfort, fame, and wealth. Can you think of any temptation we have today that Jesus didn't have?" "Speed!" rejoined one boy. . . . The boys who have cars "step on the gas," and those who haven't cars sometimes steal them: "The desire of youth to step on the gas when it has no machine of its own," said the local press, "is considered responsible for the theft of the greater part of the [154] automobiles stolen from [Middletown] during the past year."

The threat which the automobile presents to some anxious parents is suggested by the fact that of thirty girls brought before the juvenile court in the twelve months preceding September 1, 1924, charged with "sex crimes," for whom the place where the offense occurred was given in the records, nineteen were listed as having committed the offense in an automobile. Here again the automobile appears to some as an "enemy" of the home and society.

Sharp, also, is the resentment aroused by this elbowing new device when it interferes with old-established religious habits. The minister trying to change people's behavior in desired directions through the spoken word must compete against the strong pull of the open road strengthened by endless printed "copy" inciting to travel. Preaching to 200 people on a hot, sunny Sunday in midsummer on "The Supreme Need of Today," a leading Middletown minister denounced "automobilitis—the thing those people have who go off motoring on Sunday instead of going to church". . . .

"We had a fine day yesterday," exclaimed an elderly pillar of a prominent church, by way of Monday morning greeting. "We left home at five in the morning. By seven we swept into —. At eight we had breakfast at —, eighty miles from home. From there we went on to Lake —, the longest in the state. I had never seen it before, and I've lived here all my life, but I sure do want to go again. Then we went to — [the Y.M.C.A. camp] and had our chicken dinner. It's a fine thing for people to get out that way on Sundays. No question about it. They see different things and get a larger outlook."

"Did you miss church?" he was asked.

"Yes, I did, but you can't do both. I never missed church or Sunday school for thirteen years and I kind of feel as if I'd done my share. The ministers ought not to rail against people's driving on Sunday. They ought just to realize that they won't be there every Sunday during the summer, and make church interesting enough so they'll want to come."

But if the automobile touches the rest of Middletown's living at many points, it has revolutionized its leisure; more, perhaps, than the movies or any other intrusion new to Middletown since the nineties, it is making leisure-time enjoyment a regularly expected part of every day and week rather than an occasional event.

The readily available leisure-time options of even the working class have been multiplied many-fold. As one working class housewife remarked, "We just go to lots of things we couldn't go to if we didn't have a car." Beefsteak and watermelon picnics in a park or a near-by wood can be a matter of a moment's decision on a hot afternoon.

Not only has walking for pleasure become practically extinct, but the occasional event such as a parade on a holiday attracts far less attention now.

Questions

1. Why did the people of Middletown worry about the automobile's effect on religious worship?
2. What habits did the car seem to alter?
3. How did adolescents adapt to the automobile culture?

Questions for Further Thought

1. Are the ads reprinted as Documents 23-3 and 23-4 different in degree or content from current advertising? In what ways?
2. Cars, movies, and advertising—were the residents of Middletown (Document 23-5) right to feel uneasy about the changes they saw occurring in their community? Why or why not?
3. Chapter 23 begins by introducing America's "modern society" and "mass consumer culture." Reflect on these terms in light of your reading of the text and documents.

Dissenting Values and Cultural Conflict

We often think of the 1920s in terms of its writers and other creative individuals, some of them disillusioned by the Great War and the materialism of the postwar decade, who contributed greatly and enduringly to American culture. Among them we might name Ernest Hemingway, F. Scott Fitzgerald, Gertrude Stein, Langston Hughes, John Dos Passos, Edith Wharton, Eugene O'Neill, Robert Frost, Marianne Moore, and William Faulkner (see text pp. 762–765). However, the decade was also noteworthy for the intensity of its cultural conflicts. Some of these were long-standing; others had originated in the Progressive Era or during and immediately after the First World War. Nativism flourished. The immigration-restriction movement, which before World War I had sought enactment of a literacy test requirement for immigrants, now secured passage of laws that for the first time numerically restricted and imposed national quotas on immigration from Europe and prohibited immigration from Japan (1924). The second Ku Klux Klan, born in 1915, reached its short-lived peak during the mid-1920s. In Oregon, the Klan ("the most striking example of nativism in the 1920s") was instrumental in the 1922 passage of a popular initiative requiring children (ages eight to sixteen) to attend public schools, rather than permitting them to go to religious or private schools. Citing *Meyer v. Nebraska* (see Document 22-16), the U.S. Supreme Court struck down the law before it went into effect (in *Pierce, Governor of Oregon, et al. v. Society of Sisters*, 1925). Similar proposals failed in other states. Within private sectors of American life, religious and racial prejudice and discrimination were all too common (see text pp. 755–760).

Meanwhile, the nationwide enforcement of Prohibition, now part of the Constitution (the Eighteenth Amendment, ratified in 1919, had gone into effect one year later), publicly and deeply divided "dry" supporters and "wet" opponents. Moreover, growing differences between modernists and fundamentalists within Protestant denominations spilled over into politics as a few states, most famously Tennessee, legislated against the teaching of evolution in public schools (see text pp. 761–762).

A number of the cultural conflicts of the 1920s deeply affected national politics, especially as they divided the Democrats, already in a minority position, between southerners and westerners (largely old-stock, Protestant, "dry," and rural) and northeasterners (largely of immigrant stock, Catholic or Jewish, "wet," and urban). In 1924, the party's polarized and deadlocked national convention was ultimately reduced to nominating a sacrificial compromise presidential nominee, John W. Davis. Four years later, the Democrats nominated Alfred E. Smith for president. The four-term governor of New York was Catholic, of immigrant stock, "wet," and from New York City and Tammany Hall—in many ways the antithesis of Herbert Hoover, the Republican standard-bearer. After a bitter campaign, Smith went down to defeat—as any Democrat would have in 1928. The *pattern* of that defeat, however, revealed the potency of the cultural issues raised by Smith's candidacy (see text pp. 740, 765–767).

Document 23-6 reveals the nativism that fueled the debate over immigration restriction, Document 23-7 that which motivated the Ku Klux Klan. In Document 23-8, William Jennings Bryan expresses his concern over the threat posed by evolutionists. Document 23-9 is a political cartoon from the nasty presidential campaign of 1928. Document 23-10 provides an editorial by Marcus Garvey, who led the Universal Negro Improvement Association. Jane Addams reflects on Prohibition in Document 23-11.

23-6   Nativism in the Twenties (1930)

Madison Grant

John Higham, the foremost historian of American nativism, has termed Madison Grant (1865–1937) "intellectually the most important nativist in recent American history." In his writings, most famously *The Passing of the Great Race* (1916), Grant, an attorney and a naturalist, focused on the Nordic, Alpine, Mediterranean, and Jewish "races," with the last the most threatening of all. He influenced the immigration law passed by Congress in 1924 (see text pp. 756–760).

Source: Madison Grant, "Closing the Flood-Gates," in Madison Grant and Charles Steward Davison, eds., *The Alien in Our Midst or, Selling Our Birthright for a Mess of Pottage: The Written Views of a Number of Americans (Present and Former) on Immigration and Its Results* (New York: Galton, 1930), 13–21. Copyright 1930. Reprinted with permission.

Our Federal Republic has been more fortunate than other modern nations in the exceptional character of its founders. The end of the colonial period was marked by the appearance on the scene of action of an extraordinary group of statesmen. These men were deeply versed in the lessons taught by classical history as well as in the practical application of representative government, which had been slowly evolving in England. Thus equipped, they formulated a written constitution which has been sound enough and elastic enough to stand the strain of 150 years. During this period the nation, organized under its provisions, expanded across the continent and emerged from the scanty resources of the backwoods into one of the great powers of the world.

The group of men who formulated that constitution was drawn from a population scattered along the Eastern seaboard and numbering from three to four millions. It is doubtful whether our present one hundred millions could produce an equal number of statesmen—even if we admit that the best brains of the present are not devoted to the service of the state and have not been so devoted for the last fifty years.

The work of the founders was so well done that our chief concern today is to maintain the original spirit of the Constitution rather than to change or improve it. The last six or seven amendments have weakened rather than strengthened that instrument and certainly do not indicate any great degree of statesmanship.

The Revolution brought about by these Founders was political rather than social or religious. But ruling power was not taken from one class and given to another, though the governing classes of Colonial times were greatly weakened by the loss of many thousands of Loyalists who were driven from the country.

The Colonists were overwhelmingly Anglo-Saxon and were still more Nordic. Over ninety percent were British, including 82.1 per cent pure English and the balance Scotch and "Scotch-Irish." Over ninety-eight per cent were Nordic, including two and a half per cent Dutch and five and a half per cent German. This does not include the small Huguenot element, which was to a very great extent Nordic. Some, however, if not a majority, of the Pennsylvania Germans were Alpine. The only discordant elements were the Germans in Pennsylvania and small colonies of Portuguese at points on the New England coast, but the last were of little importance. The Founders, however, realized clearly that even these small minorities embodied a potential menace to the unity of the Republic. They realized also that the growth of the Colonial population was so rapid that there was no need of immigration.

Subsequent events have justified these opinions, and it is now known to the well-informed that the population of the United States would be as large as that of the present day, if there had been no immigration whatever. The originally large birth-rate of the native American falls wherever immigrants push in. Immigration means that for each new arrival from across the sea, one American is not born.

The introduction of serf labor to do rough work causes the withdrawal from such manual labor of the native Americans. One hears on every side, as an excuse for bringing in immigrants, that native Americans will not work in the field or in railroad gangs. It is true that they will not work alongside of Negroes or Slovaks or Mexicans, because a mean man makes the job a mean one. In the mountains of the South where there are no Negroes, and in those portions of the Northwest where there are few foreigners, native Americans can be seen today doing all the manual work, as was universally the case two generations ago.

A race that refuses to do manual work and seeks "white collar" jobs, is doomed through its falling birthrate to replacement by the lower races or classes. In other words, the introduction of immigrants as lowly laborers means a replacement of race. These immigrants drive out the native; they do not mix with him. The Myth of the Melting Pot was the great fallacy of the last generation—fortunately it is utterly discredited today.

If the considered and recorded views of the Founders

had prevailed and the nation after the Civil War had not made frantic efforts to "develop a continent" in a single generation and had not imported cheap serf labor for this purpose, the United States would have had today not only a population as large as its present one, but a population that was Nordic and Anglo-Saxon and homogeneous throughout.

Instead of a population homogeneous in race, religion, traditions and aspirations, as was the American nation down to 1840, we have—inserted into the body politic—an immense mass of foreigners, congregated for the most part in the large cities and in the industrial centers. The greater part of these foreigners, even if naturalized, are not in sympathy with American ideals, nor do they either understand or exercise the self-restraint necessary to govern a Republic. Many of these aliens, especially those from Eastern and Southern Europe were drawn from the lowest social strata of their homeland and mistake the liberty they find in America, and the easy-going tolerance of the native American, for an invitation to license and crime.

The closing years of the decade between 1840 and 1850 brought in the first of these foreigners. Germans, fleeing from their fatherland after the collapse of the revolutionary movements, for the most part took up unoccupied lands in the West, although some of them settled in the large cities, notably in St. Louis and Cincinnati. While it cannot be said that they improved the American population either physically or intellectually yet they accepted our form of government and made effort to maintain its traditions.

The Irish, on the other hand, who arrived a few years earlier, settled in the large cities and industrial centers of the North. These Irish were drawn from the submerged and primitive peasantry of South and West Ireland. In race they were partly Mediterranean and partly Nordic mixed with remnants of an aboriginal population. They were, for the most part, day laborers and domestic servants and Catholics. They came into conflict with the native Americans by trying to introduce their church institutions and parochial schools, which were and are regarded as hostile to the public school system of the United States.

When concentrated in large cities these Irish were responsive to the leadership of bosses and were organized in the solid blocs which demoralize our municipal politics. Our republican representative system, coupled with universal suffrage, does not work any too well even in rural districts, but it breaks down utterly in our cities. In recent decades the Irish have advanced somewhat in the social scale, because newcomers, the Poles, Slovaks, and Italians have in turn replaced them in the more menial tasks.

It must be noted that these later Irish differ racially, religiously and spiritually from the so-called "Scotch-Irish" immigrants of a century before. The name "Scotch-Irish" is a misnomer, for they were racially pure Scotch-English and had nothing in common with the native Irish of South Ireland. Being staunch Protestants, mostly Presbyterians, they were in antagonism to the Catholics from the South. The fathers or grandfathers of the so-called "Scotch-Irish" who migrated in the early part of the eighteenth century to America, were born in Scotland and England and had migrated to North Ireland. The descendants of these Scotch-English again migrated to these (then) colonies, mostly through Philadelphia, also to the Carolinas. From there they found their way into the backwoods beyond the old English settlements and southwest along the valleys of the Alleghenies. They formed a class of frontiersmen who settled Kentucky, Tennessee and the States beyond and were the chief Indian fighters of the later Colonial times. These facts were important at the time when the question of the quotas of Northern Ireland and Southern Ireland were being adjusted.

There were few Roman Catholics in the colonies. The Colonial laws were everywhere drastic against Catholics and even in Maryland, which is constantly referred to as a "Catholic colony," the Catholics were in such a great minority that in 1715, they were actually deprived of the franchise by the Protestant majority. John Fiske estimates the number of Roman Catholics at only one-twelfth of the population of Maryland in 1661–1689. The alleged tolerance said to have been exhibited by the Catholics of Maryland cannot be claimed as voluntary on their part for Lord Baltimore received his charter from a Protestant King on the express condition that no religious restrictions against Protestants were to be enacted.

Of their numbers in the United States the Official Catholic Year Book for the year 1928 says: "In 1775 there were only about 23,000 white Catholics in the country, administered to by thirty-four priests, the larger portion living in Maryland and Pennsylvania." In a book published in 1925, under the sanction of M. J. Curley, the Catholic Archbishop of Baltimore, in attempting to estimate the strength of the Catholic population in colonial times, it is stated that in 1790 the total Catholic population of the United States was 35,000 of which about 25,000 were Irish. From this it is obvious that a large proportion of the immigration even from Southern Ireland, and nearly all the immigration from Ulster in colonial times, was Protestant.

Undesirable as was substantially the whole of the immigration of the nineteenth century, it might have been partially Americanized, but, just when that transformation was beginning, two events of great portent happened. One was the exhaustion of free public land open to settlement, and the other was the extension of manufacturing with its call for cheap labor. America entered on a career of industrial development, which, while producing great wealth for a few, transformed whole countrysides and farming villages into factory towns.

The New England employer utilized the Irish who were at hand and imported French-Canadians. The mine owners in Pennsylvania imported Polish and Slovak miners. The industries of Ohio and of the adjoining states employed in large numbers members of nondescript races.

We may note, in passing, that the French-Canadians had nothing in common with the Colonial French Huguenots. The "habitant" from Quebec was and is a docile, sturdy undersized Breton peasant, speaking an archaic Norman dialect, while the early French Protestants, who escaped to America from persecution at home, were, to a very large extent, Nordic and were drawn from the skilled artisan and merchant classes and the lesser gentry.

In all the industrialized states, the replacement of the native American went on rapidly, but silently and unnoticed, except by a few patriotic men, until the drafts during the World War revealed that Vermont was full of French-Canadians; that farming lands along the Connecticut River Valley had been taken up by Poles; that Boston was overrun by the Irish; that New Haven had become almost an Italian city; that Rhode Island was swamped by aliens, and that Detroit and Chicago were to all intent foreign cities.

The native American element in New York City had been hopelessly submerged for half a century, but it came as a shock to the country to read the names in the draft lists, and to realize how complete was the transformation of some of the States. Massachusetts, Rhode Island, Connecticut and New Jersey are regarded by politicians as submerged areas and the effort, which was made in the 1928 election, was practically an effort to unite politically all these nonassimilated foreign and urban elements and to take over the control of the Federal government.

This new grouping has been for some time foreshadowed by the singular political alliance in Boston, and later in New York City, between the Jews and the Catholics but the alien elements in the North are still too weak to gain control of the Federal government without the support of the Southern states.

Americans were shocked to find what an utterly subordinate place was occupied by the American stock in the opinions of some aliens. An example of this was a poster issued by some thoughtless enthusiast in the Treasury Department in one of the appeals for Liberty Loans. It showed a Howard Chandler Christy girl of pure Nordic type, pointing with pride to a list of names and saying "AMERICANS ALL." Then followed the list:

DuBois	Villotto
Smith	Levy
O'Brien	Turovich
Cejka	Kowalski
Jaucke	Chriczanevicz
Pappandrikopolous	Knutson
Andrassi	Gonzales

The one "American" in that list, so far as he figures at all, is hidden under the sobriquet of "Smith," and there is, we must presume, an implied suggestion that the very beautiful lady is the product of this remarkable melting pot. . . .

Questions

1. How do Grant's ideas resemble or differ from those of Josiah Strong (Document 21-2) and the Social Darwinists?
2. What constitutes Grant's definition of *race?* How does he define *native Americans?*
3. What is Grant's hierarchy of European "races" and his characterization of each "race"?

23-7   The Ku Klux Klan (1924)

The Klan used print media to spread its message of white supremacy. State and local Klans reached followers through Klan publications; the piece excerpted here originally appeared in *The Good Citizen* (Zarephath, New Jersey). In 1926, Hiram W. Evans, Imperial Wizard of the Ku Klux Klan, explained "the Klan's fight for Americanism" to a cosmopolitan national audience through the prestigious *North American Review.*

Source: Reprinted with the permission of Macmillan Publishing Company from *The Challenge of the Clan* (pp. 133–136) by Stanley Frost. Copyright 1924 by The Bobbs Merrill Company, Inc., renewed 1952 by Marion Y. Frost; reprinted in Irwin Unger, ed., *American Issues: A Primary Source Reader in United States History,* vol. 2 (Englewood Cliffs, N.J.: Prentice Hall, 1994), 141–143.

THE RISING OF THE KU KLUX KLAN—THE NEW REFORMATION

On account of the abuses of religion by the Roman Catholic hierarchy, civilization had reached a universal crisis in the sixteenth century; and Martin Luther, the chosen instrument of God, was placed in the breach to prevent the wheels of progress from being reversed and the world from being plunged into greater darkness than that of the Dark Ages.

The thousand years preceding the Reformation, known by religious historians as Satan's Millennium, was brought on by the Romish Church with her paganistic worship and practices, during which time millions of men and women poured out their blood as martyrs of the Christian religion. . . .

THE WHITE-ROBED ARMY

Now come the Knights of the Ku Klux Klan in this crucial hour of our American history to contend for the faith of our fathers who suffered and died in behalf of freedom. At the psychological moment they have arrived to encourage the hearts of those who have been battling heroically for the rights and privileges granted them under the Constitution of the United States.

How our hearts have been thrilled at the sight of this army! Words fail to express the emotions of the soul at the appearance of this mighty throng upon the battle-field, where a few faithful followers of the lowly Nazarene have been contending for the faith once delivered to the Saints, against Papal mobs who have torn down gospel tabernacles, wrecked buildings and imprisoned Protestant worshipers.

OUR NATIONAL PERIL

The World War was the signal for greater alarm than the average American has been willing to admit. Notwithstanding the sacrifices that had to be made at home and the thousands of our young men who crossed the sea and laid down their lives on the battlefields of the Old World, it has taken the Ku Klux Klan to awaken even a portion of the population of the United States to our national peril. Our religious and political foes are not only within our gates, but are coming by the hundreds of thousands, bringing the chaos and ruin of old European and Asiatic countries to un-Americanize and destroy our nation, and to make it subserve the purposes of the Pope in his aspirations for world supremacy.

ROME WOULD OVERTHROW PUBLIC SCHOOLS

One of the great efforts of the Roman hierarchy toward this end is to get control of our public schools by placing

Roman Catholics on school boards and in the school-rooms and taking the Bible out of the schools. In the event of their success in their efforts to overthrow our present school system there would be a string of beads around every Protestant child's neck and a Roman Catholic cate-chism in his hand. 'Hail Mary, Mother of God,' would be on every child's lips, and the idolatrous worship of dead saints a part of the daily programme.

THE JEWISH AND CATHOLIC ALLIANCE

The money-grasping Jew, who has no use for the Christ of Calvary, does all in his power to bring discredit on Chris-tianity, and would be pleased to see the whole structure broken down, and in this way get rid of his responsibility for crucifying the Christ on Calvary and bringing the curse on his race, which they have had to suffer since the begin-ning of the Christian era. The sons of Abraham have there-fore become a strong ally to the Papacy, not because they have anything in common with it in religion, but in their political propaganda against American institutions and principles.

While no true Christian has anything against the Jew, it must be admitted that this alliance with the Papacy is a dangerous menace to our flag and country. The Jew is in-soluble and indigestible; and when he grows in numbers and power till he becomes a menace to Christianity and the whole moral fabric, drastic measures will have to be taken to counteract his destructive work, and more especially when he is in alliance with the old Papal religio-political machine.

Question

1. Why, according to the Klan, is "this [a] crucial hour of our American history"?
2. How do the public schools figure in the Protestant-Catholic conflict?
3. How does the Klan explain the alleged Catholic-Jewish alliance?

23-8   Back to God (1921)

William Jennings Bryan

Tennessee's trial of John T. Scopes in 1925 for teaching evolution focused public atten-tion on fundamentalism, modernism, secularism, and Darwinian evolution and on the courtroom duel between Clarence Darrow and William Jennings Bryan. However, the debate was long-standing and, as this document makes clear, Bryan had played the role of fundamentalism's advocate for some time before his appearance in Dayton, Ten-nessee (see text pp. 761–762).

Source: William Jennings Bryan, "Back to God," *The Commoner*, 10 (August 1921): 2; reprinted in Ray Ginger, ed., *William Jennings Bryan: Selections* (Indianapolis: Bobbs-Merrill, 1967), 229–231.

The supreme need of the day is to get back to God—to a love of God that fills the heart, the mind and the soul, and dominates every impulse and energy of the life.

Evolutionists are leading their followers away from the Creator, away from the Word of God, and away from the Son of God. They teach that man is the lineal descen-dant of the lower animals—that he has in him, not the breath of the Almighty but the blood of the brute. They tear out of the Old Testament the first chapter of Genesis, and then, having discarded the miracle, they tear out the first chapter of Matthew and deny the Virgin birth of the Saviour. They would, in effect, dethrone Jehovah, strip the Bible of its claim to inspiration and libel the Master, by branding him as the illegitimate son of an immoral woman. Their creed denudes life of its spiritual elements and make man a brother of the beast.

Materialism has so paralyzed the mental machinery of the evolutionists that they cannot comprehend spiritual things. They can understand how gravity, though an invisi-ble force, can draw all matter downward to the earth, but they cannot understand how an invisible God, all-power-ful, all-wise, and all-loving, can draw the souls of men up-ward toward his throne. Their minds arc open to the most absurd hypotheses advanced in the name of science, but their hearts are closed to the plainest spiritual truths.

These exponents of a brutish philosophy have entered our universities with boldness; they have crept into some of our Christian colleges by stealth; they have even wormed their way into a few of our theological seminaries. They make agnostics and atheists of a multitude of trusting students; they turn many young men away from the ministry; they palsy the zeal of some who stand behind the pulpit.

It is time the Christians of the country should understand the ravages that the groundless hypothesis of Darwin is making. It is depriving the church of the support of young men and young men who ought to be its leaders; it furnished Neitzsche [sic] with a basis for his Godless philosophy—a philosophy which led the world into its bloodiest war—and it is bringing chaos into the industrial world. What can be done to combat it and to save church and civilization from its benumbing influence?

First, those who preach and teach should be called upon to announce their views so that their positions may be clearly understood. Every citizen has a right to think as he pleases—to worship God according to the dictates of his conscience, or to refuse to worship him. That is an inalienable right that should not under any circumstances be interfered with, but those who employ a minister for themselves or an instructor for their children have a right to know what the preacher is to preach and what the teachers are to teach.

Second, only Christians should be permitted to teach in CHRISTIAN schools and colleges. If denominational schools cannot find Christian instructors to teach every branch of learning that needs to be taught they have no reason for existence.

Third, Christian taxpayers should insist upon a REAL neutrality in religion wherever neutrality is necessary. The Bible should not be attacked where it cannot be defended. Professors, paid by the public, should not be permitted to undermine the religious faith of students. No amount of education can compensate for the destruction of faith. Out of the hearts, not out of the head, are the issues of life; as a man thinketh in his heart, not as he thinketh in his head, so is he.

The sin of this generation is mind worship—a worship as destructive as any other form of idolatry. To your tents, O, Israel.

Questions

1. What threats to Christianity does Bryan identify?
2. How does he propose to meet those threats?

23-9   Cabinet Meeting—If Al Were President (1928)

Alfred E. Smith (1873–1944) unsuccessfully contended for the Democratic presidential nomination in 1924, then went on to his third and fourth gubernatorial election victories in New York State (1924, 1926). His presidential candidacy in 1928 touched off a national campaign unsurpassed in bitterness (see text pp. 765–767). This election-eve cartoon appeared in a publication of the Ku Klux Klan.

Source: The Fellowship Forum (Washington, D.C.), November 3, 1928, in New York State Library, Albany, New York; reprinted in Edmund A. Moore, *A Catholic Runs for President: The Campaign of 1928* (New York: Ronald Press, 1956), 109.

Questions

1. What are the central thrusts in this cartoon's attack on Al Smith?
2. How do the details fit into the broad pattern of this cartoon?

Cabinet Meeting—If Al Were President

23-10   Editorial in *Negro World* (1924)

Marcus Garvey

Just as writers and artists of the Harlem Renaissance, based in New York City's premier African American community, "championed racial pride and cultural identity" in a white society, so the Universal Negro Improvement Association, based in northern cities receiving large numbers of black migrants, "sought to challenge white political and cultural hegemony" by preaching black separatism, rather than a continued quest for racial integration (see text pp. 764–765).

Source: Marcus Garvey, editorial in *Negro World* (New York), September 2, 1924; reprinted in Robert A. Hill, ed., *The Marcus Garvey and Universal Negro Improvement Association Papers,* 6: 8–11. Copyright © 1989 by the Regents of the University of California. Reprinted by permission of the University of California Press and of the Marcus Garvey and UNIA Papers Project.

THE ENEMIES AT WORK

During the whole of the convention and a little prior thereto, the enemies of our cause tried to provoke and confuse our deliberation by the many unpleasant things they systematically published against the Universal Negro Improvement Association. Our enemies in America, especially the Negro Republican politicians of New York, used the general time fuse to explode on our tranquility and thereby destroy the purpose for which we were met, but as

is customary, the Universal Negro Improvement Association is always ready for the enemy. They had arranged among themselves to get certain individuals of the Liberian government along with Ernest Lyons, the Liberian Consul-General, in Baltimore, himself a reactionary Negro politician of the old school, to circulate through the Negro press and other agencies such unpleasant news purported to be from Liberia as to create consternation in our ranks and bring about the demoralization that they hoped and calculated for, but as usual, the idiots counted without their hosts. The Universal Negro Improvement Association cannot be destroyed that way, in that it is not only an organization, but is the expression of the spiritual desires of the four hundred million black peoples of the world.

OUR COLONIZATION PROGRAM

As everybody knows, we are preparing to carry out our Liberian colonization program during this and succeeding months. Every arrangement was practically made toward this end. . . . Unfortunately, after all arrangements had been made in this direction, our steamship secured to carry the colonists and all plans laid, these enemies of progress worked in every way to block the carrying out of the plan. For the purpose of deceiving the public and carrying out their obstruction, they tried to make out by the protest that was filed by Ernest Lyons of Baltimore, with the government of Washington, that our Association was of an incendiary character and that it was the intention of the organization to disturb the good relationship that existed between Liberia and other friendly powers. A greater nonsense could not have been advanced by any idiot. What could an organization like the Universal Negro Improvement Association do to destroy the peace of countries that are already established and recognized? It is supposed that England and France are the countries referred to when, in fact, the authors of that statement know that England and France are only waiting an opportunity to seize more land in Liberia and to keep Liberia in a state of stagnation, so as to justify their argument that the blacks are not competent of self-government in Africa as well as elsewhere. If Edwin Barclay had any sense, he would know that the Universal Negro Improvement Association is more friendly to Liberia, because it is made up of Negroes, than England and France could be in a thousand years. Lyons' protest was camouflage.

NEGROES DOUBLE-CROSSING

Everybody knows that the hitch in the colonization plan of the Universal Negro Improvement Association in Liberia came about because of double-crossing. The Firestone Rubber and Tire Company, of Ohio, has been spending large sums of money among certain people. The offer, no doubt, was so attractive as to cause certain persons to found the argument to destroy the Universal Negro Improvement Association, so as to favor the Firestone Rubber and Tire Company who, subsequently, got one million acres of Liberian land for actually nothing, to be exploited for rubber and minerals, and in the face of the fact that Liberia is one of the richest rubber countries in the world, an asset that should have been retained for the Liberian people and members of the black race, but now wantonly given over to a white company to be exploited in the interest of white capital, and to create another international complication, as evidenced in the subsequent subjugation of Haiti and the Haitians, after the New York City Bank

established itself in Haiti in a similar way as the Firestone Rubber and Tire Company will establish itself in Liberia. Why, every Negro who is doing a little thinking, knows that after the Firestone Rubber and Tire Company gets into Liberia to exploit the one million acres of land, it is only a question of time when the government will be taken out of the hands of the Negroes who rule it, and Liberia will become a white man's country in violation of the constitution of that government as guaranteeing its soil as a home for all Negroes of all climes and nationalities who desire to return to their native land. The thing is so disgraceful that we, ourselves, are ashamed to give full publicity to it, but we do hope that the people of Liberia, who control the government of Liberia, will be speedily informed so that they, through the Senate and House of Representatives, will repudiate the concessions granted to the Firestone Rubber and Tire Company, so as to save their country from eternal spoilation. If the Firestone Rubber and Tire Company should get the concessions in Liberia of one million acres of land, which should have been granted to the Universal Negro Improvement Association for development by Negroes for the good of Negroes, it simply means that in another short while thousands of white men will be sent away from America by the Firestone Rubber and Tire Company to exploit their concessions. These white men going out to colonize, as they generally regard tropical countries, will carry with them the spirit of all other white colonists, superiority over and subjugation of native peoples; hence it will only be a question of time when these gentlemen will change the black population of Liberia into a mongrel race, as they have done in America, [the] West Indies and other tropical countries, and there create another race problem such as is confusing us now in these United States of America. These white gentlemen are not going to allow black men to rule and govern them, so, like China and other places, there will be such complications as to ultimately lead to the abrogation of all native control and government and the setting up of new authority in a country that once belonged to the natives.

THE RAPE OF LIBERIA

It is the duty of every Negro in the world to protest against this rape of Liberia encouraged by those who are responsible for giving the concessions to the Firestone Rubber and Tire Company. Why, nearly one-half of the country has been given away and, when it is considered that out of the twelve million square miles of Africa, only Liberia is left as a free and independent black country, it becomes a shame and disgrace to see that men should be capable of giving away all this amount of land to the same people who have possession of over nine-tenths of the country's [continent's] area.

BRIGHT FUTURE FOR RACE

We beg to advise, however, the members and friends of the Universal Negro Improvement Association all over the world, that what has happened has not obstructed much the program of the Universal Negro Improvement Association as far as our colonization plans are concerned. All that we want is that everybody get behind the Black Cross Navigation and Trading Company and send us the necessary amount of money to pay for our first ship and secure other ships so as to carry out our trade contract with the Negroes of Africa, West Indies, South and Central America and these United States. The Association is devoting its time and energy now to building up an international commerce and trade so as to stabilize Negro industry. There is much for us to do. In taking the raw materials from our people in Africa to America, as well as materials [from] the West Indies, South and Central America to the United States[,] and taking back to them our finished and manufactured products in exchange, we have a whole world of industrial conquest to make and it can be done splendidly if each Negro will give us the support that is necessary. We want not only one, two or three ships, but we want dozens of ships, so that every week our ships can be going out of the ports of New York, Philadelphia, Boston, Baltimore, New Orleans, Savannah or Mobile for Liberia, Sierre [*sic*] Leone, Gold Coast, Lagos, Abyssinia, Brazil, Argentina, Costa Rica, Guatemala, Nicaragua, Honduras, Jamaica, Barbados, Trinidad, British Guiana and British Honduras. Let our ships be on the seven seas, taking our commerce to England, France, Germany, Italy, Japan, China and India. The chance of making good in commerce and trade is as much

ours as it is other races and so we call upon you everywhere to get behind the industrial program of the Universal Negro Improvement Association. If we can control the field of industry we can control the sentiment of the world and that is what the Universal Negro Improvement Association seeks for the four hundred millions of our race.

MOVE THE LITTLE BARRIERS

So, the little barriers that have been placed in the way by the envious and wicked of our own race can easily be removed if we will get together and work together. Now that the convention has risen, let us redouble our energy everywhere to put the program over. Let us work with our hearts, soul and minds to see that everything is accomplished for the good of the race. We must have our ship in action by next month. At least, we are calculating to have our ship sail out of New York by the 29th of October, laden with the first cargo for the tropics, and to bring back to us tropical fruits and produce, and from thence to sail for Africa, the land of our fathers. Help us make this possible. . . .

With very best wishes for your success, I have the honor to be, Your obedient servant,

MARCUS GARVEY
President-General
Universal Negro Improvement Association

Questions

1. What does Garvey propose?
2. Why does he consider black Republicans to be the enemy? What is his purpose in attacking the Firestone Company?
3. How do Garvey's views differ from those of Booker T. Washington (see Document 18-14) and W. E. B. Du Bois (see Document 18-15)? Does Garvey echo any of the points made by the others?

23-11   A Decade of Prohibition (1930)

Jane Addams

Support for Prohibition was strongest in rural areas but did not end once a person stepped inside city limits. Many urban social reformers welcomed the Eighteenth Amendment. Among them was Jane Addams (1860–1935; see Chapter 20), who discusses her views in the second installment of her autobiography, which was published in 1930.

Source: Reprinted with the permission of Scribner, a disivion of Simon & Schuster from *The Second Twenty Years at Hull-House* by Jane Addams, 223–229. Copyright 1930 by Macmillan Publishing Company. Copyright renewed © 1958 by John A. Brittain.

In the winter of 1911 the Juvenile Protective Association of Chicago made a very careful investigation of three hundred and twenty-eight public dance halls, and found that 86,000 people frequent them on a Saturday evening, of whom the majority were boys between the ages of sixteen and eighteen and girls between fourteen and sixteen—the very ages at which pleasure is most eagerly demanded as the prerogative of youth. One condition they found to be general; most of the dance halls existed for the sale of liquor and dancing was of secondary importance. One hundred and ninety halls had saloons opening into them, liquor was sold in two hundred and forty out of three hundred and twenty-eight, and in the others, except in rare instances, return checks were given to facilitate the use of the neighboring saloons. At the halls where liquor was sold, by twelve o'clock practically all the boys, who in many halls outnumbered the girls, showed signs of intoxication.

Peculiar dangers were to be found in connection with masquerade and fancy dress balls where the masks encouraged undue license, and where the prizes awarded for the best costumes were usually a barrel of beer to the best group of men, a dozen bottles of wine to the best group of girls, and a quart of whiskey for a single character. At one hall it was found that a cash prize of one hundred dollars had been offered to the girl who at the end of the month had the largest number of drinks placed to her credit. As the owner of the hall lived and thrived by the sale of liquor, the dances were short—four to five minutes; the intermissions were long—fifteen to thirty minutes; thus giving ample opportunity for drinking. There was but little ventilation; apparently on the theory that the hotter it was, the more thirst would be superinduced and the more liquor would be sold. In dance halls which did not have a connecting saloon the method of selling liquor was as follows: the dance-hall keeper procured a government license for which he paid twenty-five dollars a year; when an organization applied for permission to rent the hall the dance-hall keeper went with the officers of the association to the federal bureau or loaned them his government license, and with this they secured a special bar permit for which they paid six dollars each. This special bar permit allowed the sale of liquor from three o'clock in the afternoon until three o'clock the next morning, while under the city ordinances saloons were obliged to close at one o'clock. Because of this regulation, the patrons of the local saloons swarmed into the dance halls at midnight, paying of course an entrance fee and freely buying drinks. Many club dances came to depend upon the money thus brought in by late comers although they deprecated the "toughs" thus introduced. It was of course between these hours that the conduct became most obnoxious and that the dangers for young people were most apparent.

The carelessness of the city toward such social conditions was the more astounding in that we all know that public dance halls offered then as now the only opportunity open to thousands of young men for meeting the girls whom they will later marry. Nature, always anxious that human beings shall reveal themselves to each other, at no time makes the impulse so imperative as at that period when youth is dreaming of love and marriage. The imaginative powers, the sense that life possesses variety and color, are realized most easily in moments of pleasure and comradeship, and it is then that individual differences and variations are disclosed. All day long the young people work in factories where every effort is made that they shall conform to a common standard; as they walk upon the street they make painful exertions to appear in the prevailing mode of dress and to keep conventions. Only in moments of recreation does their sense of individuality expand; they are then able to reveal, as at no other time, that hidden self which is so important to each of us.

The owners of the dance halls were themselves sometimes touched by the helplessness of these young people who came to them in such numbers. They asked for help from the Juvenile Protective Association which at the request of individual dance halls, appointed social workers who with the aid of specially designated policemen endeavored to watch conditions in the halls. Not until after Prohibition was established in 1919, however, was it possible to do this for all the public dance halls within the city-wide Association of Dance Halls. The proprietors have come to pay the chaperon or investigator through the treasury of the J.P.A. The Association has also designated the person to be employed. Thus under Prohibition the large commercial dance halls in Chicago have come to be well chaperoned with a standard of conduct enforced by the dance-hall managers themselves. Every boy and man who pays an entrance fee is examined by an officer for a flask; if a flask is found, it is taken away from him and in his presence the contents are poured down the sewer. At one of the large dance halls a few months ago, in one evening, out of forty-five hundred persons examined, only three were found carrying flasks. Such a regulation of course would have been impossible unless the entire liquor business had been made illegal.

The entire dance-hall situation has been affected by it. Since there is no profit to be made from selling liquor, most of the public dances conducted by private organizations have been discontinued; therefore public dancing is more and more conducted in large halls by professional dance-hall promoters. This change has affected also the tactics of the politicians; some of them, since the abolition of the saloon, have hired vacant stores or other spaces, especially at election time, and established therein political clubs, paying the rent and in many ways putting the club members under obligations. They have even established such clubs for boys under voting age, in order to keep them in line. These organizations, however, since the abolition of the saloons, are not too successful, and political favors are gradually assuming other forms. One of the worst features of the pre-prohibition dance halls was drunkenness among the patrons, men and girls, who left the festivities late at night and whose condition was utilized by "runners" for houses of assignation. In many cases the men on the dance floor itself were procurers who had as far as possible placed their intended victims under the influence of liquor.

Drink was of course a leading lure and a necessary element in houses of prostitution, both from a financial and a social standpoint. Many students of the subject believed that professional houses of prostitution could not sustain themselves without the "vehicle of alcohol." Although the red light district of Chicago has been abolished, there are still of course many well-known houses, and it would be interesting to know how far their existence even now is dependent upon the liquor sold and consumed in them.

But if alcohol was associated intensively with these gross evils, it was also associated with homely and wholesome things. A certain type of treating had a social value which has disappeared, and doubtless large family parties have been less frequent, with the lure of drink and the consequent element of hilarity removed. Callers were then regaled with beer brought from the corner saloon, often illegally sold to a child who was hurriedly sent to get it for the visitor. Impecunious neighbors it was said sometimes called for the sake of the beer hospitality, and neighborliness has doubtless declined in those houses in which drink has disappeared. The Italians consider a wedding at which there is no wine for drinking the health of the bride to be an absolutely unnatural affair, and the substitute of "soft drinks" to be most unsatisfactory. Nevertheless, Bowen Hall, belonging to Hull-House, is used almost every weekend for a large Italian wedding party, although no alcoholic drinks are allowed there.

It is hard to exaggerate what excessive drinking did in the way of disturbing domestic relations and orderly family life. I knew for years a very charming Irish woman who with her three children led a dog's life because her recurrently deserting husband, when he returned from prolonged absences, always sold the accumulated household goods and clothing and reduced the family to absolute destitution and terror so long as he remained at home. Not until after his death, which occurred in a seizure of delirium tremens, was the capable mother able to establish a stable family life and to free her children from a fear which actually stunted their growth. But sometimes the mother of a family was not able to carry alone the burden of respectability and sobriety. I remember a wife and daughter who fell into drinking habits with the husband and father, and all three came to a disgraceful end. The father died in the so-called delirium tremens ward of the Cook County Hospital and the daughter in the venereal disease ward, the poor old mother surviving the loss of her family but a few months. This is a striking example of many similar family tragedies, not so often among the immigrants from southern Europe as among the families representing an older immigration.

Questions

1. What progress does Addams see with the coming of Prohibition? Does she acknowledge any losses?
2. What effect does she assume Prohibition will have on the drinking habits of immigrants?
3. Why do you think Prohibition failed in the end?

Questions for Further Thought

1. How do you account for the apparent explosion of cultural conflicts within a relatively brief period? Do any other periods of American history strike you as being marked by a number of such conflicts?
2. How might Madison Grant (Document 23-6) have reacted to immigration data (see Figure 23-1, text p. 760) from 1921 to 1930? How might someone who shares Grant's concerns view immigration data from 1953 to 1989?

CHAPTER 24

The Great Depression

★　　　　★　　　　★

The Coming of the Great Depression

The Great Depression of the 1930s was the worst economic crisis in American (and world) history. Jobs, savings, even homes were lost en masse; many who managed to retain their jobs suffered salary or wage cuts or were reduced to part-time work. Even those who came through the hard times personally unscathed felt the impact of the Great Depression on the American economy, society, and politics.

The initial and most dramatic economic shock came with the Great Crash of the stock market late in October 1929. Share prices, which had been rising from early in the 1920s, skyrocketed during 1928 and 1929, fueled by borrowing (itself facilitated initially by low interest rates), which permitted investors to acquire stock on credit (with these very shares serving as collateral). Not even signs that the economy was no longer robust halted the run-up in share prices. The stock market finally began to fall in September 1929, in part due to a large movement of funds to England. When the worsening stock market situation reached crisis proportions the following month, stocks that were serving as collateral had to be sold under panic conditions.

The Great Crash exposed basic weaknesses in the economy: the prolonged agricultural depression of the 1920s; hard times in the coal mining, textiles, and railroad industries; the shaky banking structure; and the fundamental problem that too many Americans lacked the money to purchase the output of the nation's productive industries. The crash had a serious impact on the economy. Diminished expectations discouraged would-be investors and consumers (see text pp. 771–774).

Before the crash, the celebrators of prosperity had far outnumbered the naysayers. At the beginning of his presidential campaign in 1928, Herbert Hoover prophesied that "with the help of God" and "if given a chance to go forward with the policies of the last eight years" America would shortly "be in sight of the day when poverty will be banished from this nation." John J. Raskob, whom Al Smith had chosen to head the Democratic National Committee during 1928, was also optimistic. Document 24-1 reproduces a magazine interview Raskob gave the following summer. In Document 24-2,

Stuart Chase's exercise in "balancing the books" leads him in a different direction. With the onset of hard times, harried spokesmen for business and business-government cooperation offered their assessments of the situation, as shown in Document 24-3.

24-1   Everybody Ought to Be Rich (1929)

John J. Raskob

John J. Raskob (1879–1950), associated with Du Pont and General Motors, served as chairman of the Democratic National Committee, the choice of Al Smith. Himself an investor in the stock market, here he provides some investment tips for one of the period's popular magazines, *Ladies' Home Journal* (see text p. 772).

Source: From Samuel Crowther, "Everybody Ought to Be Rich: An Interview with John J. Raskob," *Ladies' Home Journal* (August 1929). Copyright 1929, Meredith Corporation. All rights reserved. Used with permission of *Ladies' Home Journal*.

Being rich is, of course, a comparative status. A man with a million dollars used to be considered rich, but so many people have at least that much in these days, or are earning incomes in excess of a normal return from a million dollars, that a millionaire does not cause any comment.

Fixing a bulk line to define riches is a pointless performance. Let us rather say that a man is rich when he has an income from invested capital which is sufficient to support him and his family in a decent and comfortable manner—to give as much support, let us say, as has ever been given by his earnings. That amount of prosperity ought to be attainable by anyone. A greater share will come to those who have greater ability. . . .

It is quite true that wealth is not so evenly distributed as it ought to be and as it can be. And part of the reason for the unequal distribution is the lack of systematic investment and also the lack of even moderately sensible investment.

One class of investors saves money and puts it into savings banks or other mediums that pay only a fixed interest. Such funds are valuable, but they do not lead to wealth. A second class tries to get rich all at once, and buys any wildcat security that comes along with the promise of immense returns. A third class holds that the return from interest is not enough to justify savings, but at the same time has too much sense to buy fake stocks—and so saves nothing at all. Yet all the while wealth has been here for the asking.

The common stocks of this country have in the past ten years increased enormously in value because the business of the country has increased. Ten thousand dollars invested ten years ago in the common stock of General Motors would now be worth more than a million and a half dollars. And General Motors is only one of many first-class industrial corporations.

It may be said that this is a phenomenal increase and that conditions are going to be different in the next ten years. That prophecy may be true, but it is not founded on experience. In my opinion the wealth of the country is bound to increase at a very rapid rate. The rapidity of the rate will be determined by the increase in consumption, and under wise investment plans the consumption will steadily increase.

WE HAVE SCARCELY STARTED

Now anyone may regret that he or she did not have ten thousand dollars ten years ago and did not put it into General Motors or some other good company—and sigh over a lost opportunity. Anyone who firmly believes that the opportunities are all closed and that from now on the country will get worse instead of better is welcome to the opinion—and to whatever increment it will bring. I think that we have scarcely started, and I have thought so for many years.

In conjunction with others I have been interested in creating and directing at least a dozen trusts for investment in equity securities. This plan of equity investments is no mere theory with me. The first of these trusts was started in 1907 and the others in the years immediately following. Under all of these the plan provided for the saving of fifteen dollars per month for investment in equity securities only. There were no stocks bought on margin, no money borrowed, nor any stocks bought for a quick turn or re-sale. All stocks with few exceptions have been bought and held as permanent investments. The fifteen dollars was saved every month and the dividends from the stocks purchased were kept in the trust and reinvested. Three of these trusts are now twenty years old. Fifteen dollars per month equals one hundred and eighty dollars a year. In twenty years, therefore, the total savings amounted to thirty-six hundred dollars. Each of these three trusts is now worth well in excess of eighty thousand dollars. Invested at 6 per cent interest, this eighty thousand dollars would give the trust beneficiary an annual income of four hundred dollars per month, which ordinarily would represent more than the earning power of the beneficiary, because had he been able to earn as much as four hundred dollars per month he could have saved more than fifteen dollars.

Suppose a man marries at the age of twenty-three and begins a regular saving of fifteen dollars a month—and almost anyone who is employed can do that if he tries. If he invests in good common stocks and allows the dividends and rights to accumulate, he will at the end of twenty years have at least eighty thousand dollars and an income from investments of around four hundred dollars a month. He will be rich. And because anyone can do that I am firm in my belief that anyone not only can be rich but ought to be rich.

The obstacles to being rich are two: The trouble of saving, and the trouble of finding a medium for investment.

If Tom is known to have two hundred dollars in the savings bank then everyone is out to get it for some absolutely necessary purpose. More than likely his wife's sister will eventually find the emergency to draw it forth. But if he does withstand all attacks, what good will the money do him? The interest he receives is so small that he has no incentive to save, and since the whole is under his jurisdiction he can depend only upon his own will to save. To save in any such fashion requires a stronger will than the normal.

If he thinks of investing in some stock he has nowhere to turn for advice. He is not big enough to get much attention from his banker, and he has not enough money to go to a broker—or at least he thinks that he has not.

Suppose he has a thousand dollars; the bank can only advise him to buy a bond, for the officer will not take the risk of advising a stock and probably has not the experience anyway to give such advice. Tom can get really adequate attention only from some man who has a worthless security to sell, for then all of Tom's money will be profit.

The plan that I have had in mind for several years grows out of the success of the plans that we have followed for the executives in the General Motors and the Du Pont companies. In 1923, in order to give the executives of General Motors a greater interest in their work, we organized the Managers Securities Company, made up of eighty senior and junior executives. This company bought General Motors common stock to the then market value of thirty-three million dollars. The executives paid five million dollars in cash and borrowed twenty-eight million dollars. The stockholders of the Managers Securities Company are not stockholders of General Motors. They own stock in a company which owns stock in General Motors, so that, as far as General Motors is concerned, the stock is voted as a block according to the instructions of the directors of the

Managers Securities Company. This supplies an important interest which can exercise a large influence in shaping the policies of General Motors.

FROM $25,000 TO A MILLION

The holdings of the members in the securities company are adjusted in cases of men leaving the employ of the company. The plan of the Managers Securities Company contemplates no dissolution of that company, so that its holdings of General Motors stock will always be *en bloc*. The plan has been enormously successful, and much of the success of the General Motors Corporation has been due to the executives' having full responsibility and receiving financial rewards commensurate with that responsibility.

The participation in the Managers Securities Company was arranged in accordance with the position and salary of the executive. Minimum participation required a cash payment of twenty-five thousand dollars when the Managers Securities Company was organized. That minimum participation is now worth more than one million dollars.

Recently I have been advocating the formation of an equity securities corporation; that is, a corporation that will invest in common stocks only under proper and careful supervision. This company will buy the common stocks of first-class industrial corporations and issue its own stock certificates against them. This stock will be offered from time to time at a price to correspond exactly with the value of the assets of the corporation and all profit will go to the stockholders. The directors will be men of outstanding character, reputation and integrity. At regular intervals—say quarterly—the whole financial record of the corporation will be published together with all of its holdings and the cost thereof. The corporation will be owned by the public and with every transaction public. I am not at all interested in a private investment trust. The company would not be permitted to borrow money or go into any debt.

In addition to this company, there should be organized a discount company on the same lines as the finance companies of the motor concerns to be used to sell stock of the investing corporation on the installment plan. If Tom had two hundred dollars, this discount company would lend him three hundred dollars and thus enable him to buy five hundred dollars of the equity securities investment company stock, and Tom could arrange to pay off his loan just as he pays off his motor-car loan. When finished he would own outright five hundred dollars of equity stock. That would take his savings out of the free-will class and put them into the compulsory-payment class and his savings would no longer be fair game for relatives, for swindlers or for himself.

People pay for their motor car loans. They will also pay their loans contracted to secure their share in the nation's business. And in the kind of company suggested every increase in value and every right would go to the benefit of the stockholders and be reflected in the price and earning power of their stock. They would share absolutely in the nation's prosperity.

CONSTRUCTIVE SAVING

The effect of all this would, to my mind, be very far-reaching. If Tom bought five hundred dollars' worth of stock he would be helping some manufacturer to buy a new lathe or a new machine of some kind, which would add to the wealth of the country, and Tom, by participating in the profits of this machine, would be in a position to buy more goods and cause a demand for more machines. Prosperity is in the nature of an endless chain and we can break it only by our own refusal to see what it is.

Everyone ought to be rich, but it is out of the question to make people rich in spite of themselves.

The millennium is not at hand. One cannot have all play and no work. But it has been sufficiently demonstrated that many of the old and supposedly conservative maxims are as untrue as the radical notions. We can appraise things as they are.

Everyone by this time ought to know that nothing can be gained by stopping the progress of the world and dividing up everything—there would not be enough to divide, in the first place, and, in the second place, most of the world's wealth is not in such form it can be divided.

The socialistic theory of division is, however, no more irrational than some of the more hidebound theories of thrift or of getting rich by saving.

No one can become rich merely by saving. Putting aside a sum each week or month in a sock at no interest, or in a savings bank at ordinary interest, will not provide enough for old age unless life in the meantime be rigorously skimped down to the level of mere existence. And if everyone skimped in any such fashion then the country would be so poor that living at all would hardly be worth while.

Unless we have consumption we shall not have production. Production and consumption go together and a rigid national program of saving would, if carried beyond a point, make for general poverty, for there would be no consumption to call new wealth into being.

Therefore, savings must be looked at not as a present deprivation in order to enjoy more in the future, but as a constructive method of increasing not only one's future but also one's present income.

Saving may be a virtue if undertaken as a kind of mental and moral discipline, but such a course of saving is not to be regarded as a financial plan. Constructive saving in order to increase one's income is a financial operation and to be governed by financial rules; disciplinary saving is another matter entirely. The two have been confused.

Most of the old precepts contrasting the immorality of speculation with the morality of sound investment have no basis in fact. They have just been so often repeated as true that they are taken as true. If one buys a debt—that is,

takes a secured bond or mortgage at a fixed rate of interest—then that is supposed to be an investment. In the case of the debt, the principal sum as well as the interest is fixed and the investor cannot get more than he contracts for. The law guards against getting more and also it regulates the procedure by which the lender can take the property of the borrower in case of default. But the law cannot say that the property of the debtor will be worth the principal sum of the debt when it falls due; the creditor must take that chance.

The investor in a debt strictly limits his possible gain, but he does not limit his loss. He speculates in only one direction in so far as the actual return in dollars and cents is concerned. But in addition he speculates against the interest rate. If his security pays 4 per cent and money is worth 6 or 7 per cent then he is lending at less than the current rate; if money is worth 3 per cent, then he is lending at more than he could otherwise get.

The buyer of a common share in an enterprise limits neither his gains nor his losses. However, he excludes one element of speculation—the change in the value of money. For whatever earnings he gets will be in current money values. If he buys shares in a wholly new and untried enterprise, then his hazards are great, but if he buys into established enterprises, then he takes no more chance than does the investor who buys a debt.

It is difficult to see why a bond or mortgage should be considered as a more conservative investment than a good stock, for the only difference in practice is that the bond can never be worth more than its face value or return more than the interest, while a stock can be worth more than was paid for it and can return a limitless profit.

One may lose on either a bond or a stock. If a company fails it will usually be reorganized and in that case the bonds will have to give way to new money and possibly they will be scaled down. The common stockholders may lose all, or again they may get another kind of stock which may or may not eventually have a value. In a failure, neither the bondholders nor the stockholders will find any great cause for happiness—but there are very few failures among the larger corporations.

BENEFICIAL BORROWING

A first mortgage on improved real estate is supposedly a very safe investment, but the value of realty shifts quickly and even the most experienced investors in real-estate mortgages have to foreclose an appreciable percentage of their mortgages and buy in the properties to protect themselves. It may be years before the property can be sold again.

I would rather buy real estate than buy mortgages on it, for then I have the chance of gaining more than I paid. On a mortgage I cannot get back more than I lend, but I may get back less.

The line between investment and speculation is a very hazy one, and a definition is not to be found in the legal form of a security or in limiting the possible return on the money. The difference is rather in the approach.

Placing a bet is very different from placing one's money with a corporation which has thoroughly demonstrated that it can normally earn profits and has a reasonable expectation of earning greater profits. That may be called speculation, but it would be more accurate to think of the operation as going into business with men who have demonstrated that they know how to do business.

The old view of debt was quite as illogical as the old view of investment. It was beyond the conception of anyone that debt could be constructive. Every old saw about debt—and there must be a thousand of them—is bound up with borrowing instead of earning. We now know that borrowing may be a method of earning and beneficial to everyone concerned. Suppose a man needs a certain amount of money in order to buy a set of tools or anything else which will increase his income. He can take one of two courses. He can save the money and in the course of time buy his tools, or he can, if the proper facilities are provided, borrow the money at a reasonable rate of interest, buy the tools and immediately so increase his income that he can pay off his debt and own the tools within half the time that it would have taken him to save the money and pay cash. That loan enables him at once to create more wealth than before and consequently makes him a more valuable citizen. By increasing his power to produce he also increases his power to consume and therefore he increases the power of others to produce in order to fill his new needs and naturally increases their power to consume, and so on and on. By borrowing the money instead of saving it he increases his ability to save and steps up prosperity at once.

THE WAY TO WEALTH

That is exactly what the automobile has done to the prosperity of the country through the plan of installment pay-ments. The installment plan of paying for automobiles, when it was first launched, ran counter to the old notions of debt. It was opposed by bankers, who saw in it only an incentive for extravagance. It was opposed by manufacturers because they thought people would be led to buy automobiles instead of their products.

The results have been exactly opposite to the prediction. The ability to buy automobiles on credit gave an immediate step-up to their purchase. Manufacturing them, servicing them, building roads for them to run on, and caring for the people who used the roads have brought into existence about ten billion dollars of new wealth each year—which is roughly about the value of the farm crops. The creation of this new wealth gave a large increase to consumption and has brought on our present very solid prosperity.

But without the facility for going into debt or the facility for the consumer's getting credit—call it what you will—this great addition to wealth might never have taken place and certainly not for many years to come. Debt may be a burden, but it is more likely to be an incentive.

The great wealth of this country has been gained by the forces of production and consumption pushing each other for supremacy. The personal fortunes of this country have been made not by saving but by producing.

Mere saving is closely akin to the socialist policy of dividing and likewise runs up against the same objection that there is not enough around to save. The savings that count cannot be static. They must be going into the production of wealth. They may go in as debt and the managers of the wealth-making enterprises take all the profit over and above the interest paid. That has been the course recommended for saving and for the reasons that have been set out—the fallacy of conservative investment which is not conservative at all.

The way to wealth is to get into the profit end of wealth production in this country.

Questions

1. What essentially is Raskob's advice?
2. What challenges does he believe face those who want to be rich?
3. Which problems does Raskob ignore?

24-2   Balancing the Books (1929)

Stuart Chase   Stuart Chase (1888–1985), a social theorist and writer, appears to have had a better sense of timing than John J. Raskob. He submitted the manuscript of his book, *Prosperity: Fact or Myth,* shortly before the collapse of the stock market in October 1929; his work was rushed into print to capitalize on its timeliness.

Source: Stuart Chase, *Prosperity: Fact or Myth* (New York: C. Boni, 1929), 173–177, 186–188. Reprinted with permission.

BALANCING THE BOOKS

We have let us say an onion. The onion represents the total economic life of the United States at the present time. The heart of the onion is prosperity. How large does it bulk?

First, we must strip off all the states not included in the Middle Atlantic, East North Central, and Pacific states. The National Bureau of Economics finds that by and large these states have not prospered.

Second, in the prosperous belt, we strip off most of the farmers; they have not prospered.

Third, we strip off a large section of the middle class. The small business man, the independent storekeeper, the wholesaler, many professional men and women, have failed to keep income on a par with the new standard of living.

Fourth, we strip off the unemployed. Machinery appears to be displacing factory, railroad, and mining workers—and recently mergers are displacing executives, salesmen and clerks—faster than they can find employment in other fields. The net increase in "technological unemployment" since 1920 exceeds 650,000 men and women.

Fifth, we strip off the coal industry which has been in the doldrums throughout the period.

Sixth, we strip off the textile industry which has been seriously depressed.

Seventh, the boot and shoe industry. Ditto.

Eighth, the leather industry.

Ninth, the shipbuilding industry.

Tenth, the railroad equipment industry.

Eleventh, we strip off the excessive number of businesses which have gone bankrupt during the era.

Twelfth, we strip off those millions of unskilled workers who were teetering on the edge of a bare subsistence in 1922, and by no stretch of the imagination can be called prosperous to-day. The best that can be said is that their position is a little less precarious than it was.

In short only a part of the country has been prosperous, and even in that part are at least 11 soft spots—some of them very unpleasantly soft.

What then remains? . . .

The onion has shrunk, but it has not disappeared. We shall not list all the surviving leaves, but among the significant are:

1. A 20 per cent increase in the national income per capita from 1922 to 1928.
2. A 30 per cent increase in physical production.
3. A 100 per cent increase in the profits of the larger corporations.
4. A housing program expanding faster than population.
5. An increase in average health and longevity.
6. An increase in educational facilities greatly surpassing the growth of population.
7. A per capita increase in saving and insurance.
8. A booming stock market up to October 1929.
9. A 5-hour decline in the average working week.
10. A slowly rising wage scale against a fairly stationary price level.
11. An increasingly fecund, alert and intelligent science of management, resulting primarily in an ever growing productivity per worker. . . .

The trouble with nearly every item on this second list is that while it indicates that we are more prosperous than we were, nothing whatever is said about the *extent of prosperity* from which we started. The base line is missing. If we were barely comfortable in 1922, we ought to be reasonably comfortable to-day. But of course the fact is that some 80 per cent of all American families lived below the budget of health and decency in 1922, and the 20 per cent increase in per capita income since that date, while it has helped to be sure, still leaves probably two-thirds of all families below the line. Unfortunately, too, the 20 per cent cannot all go into intrinsically better food, housing and clothing, but must be applied to appease the clamoring salesmen of the new standard of living with their motor cars, radios, tootsie-rolls, silk stockings, moving pictures, near-fur coats and beauty shoppes. . . .

We have added a little real income and considerable fluff to the totally inadequate distribution of goods and services obtaining in 1922. Is this prosperity in the deeper sense? No. The most that can be said is that the last 7 or 8 years have registered a rate of advance in the direction of a prosperity which may some day be achieved. . . .

A beautiful technique this new science of management; the crowning achievement of prosperity. Given a free hand it might remake American industry humanly as well as technically. Given a free hand, it might abolish poverty, immeasurably diminish the stresses and strains which have dogged every step of the industrial revolution since the days of [James] Watt. It might flood the nation with essential and even beautiful goods at a fraction of their present cost, raise the curse of Adam, and lay the basis for, if not positively usher in, one of the noblest civilizations which the world has ever seen.

But the hands of management are not free. The technician is constantly undone by the sales department, which floundering in a pecuniary economy, sees no other way—and indeed there is no other way—to maintain capacity than by style changes, annual models, advertising misrepresentation, and high pressure merchandising. He is undone by the vested interests of the owners who demand their pound of flesh in rent, interest and dividends *now,* with no thought for the rounded perfection of engineering principles, and the time which they—and the physical laws which sanction them—demand. Foresters have worked out the technique for a perpetual lumber supply, with annual growth beautifully balanced against annual needs. But private enterprise cannot wait. Tear me down this grove tomorrow—and let the slash burn, and the soil run into the sea—I have a note maturing. So we cut our priceless heritage of forest four times as fast as it grows. In 30 years, at the present rate of exhaustion, it will be all but gone.

Above all, the technician is undone by failure to inaugurate a national system of super-management, whereby production might be articulated to consumptive needs, and the fabulous wastes of excess plants, excess machines, excess overhead costs, uneconomically located industries, cross hauling, jam, tangle and bottlenecks, brought under rational control. That such supermanagement is not beyond human capacity to operate, the experiences of the Supreme Economic Council during the War, and of the Russian Gosplan [the Soviet State Planning Committee] today, amply demonstrate. What a lordly science of engineering we might have, and to what great human benefit, if industrial anarchy gave way to industrial coördination and socialization in those fields where it logically belongs.

Prosperity in any deeper sense awaits the liberation of the engineer. If the owners will not get off his back—and why should they; they pay him little enough and he fills their safe deposit boxes?—I, for one, would not be sorry to see him combine with the wayfaring man to lift them off. A complicated technical structure should be run by engineers, not hucksters. But the technician is the modern Prometheus in chains.

Questions

1. Why does Chase compare the American economy in the 1920s to an onion?
2. What conclusion does Chase reach after "balancing the books" on the 1920s?
3. What is Chase's argument regarding prosperity's dependence on the "liberation of the engineer"? Does he echo in any way the points made by others who were prominent in the period?

24-3   Proposals for Recovery (1930–1931)

B. C. Forbes and Julius Klein

The impact of the depression was such that political and business leaders seemed at a loss to comprehend, let alone reverse, the economic decline. The following pieces by B. C. Forbes and Julius Klein appeared in *Forbes* during 1930 and 1931. B. C. Forbes (1880–1954) had founded the business magazine that bears his family name. Julius Klein (1886–1961) was educated at Harvard University in economics and history and then pursued a career in government, where he was closely identified with Herbert Hoover.

Sources: "Snap Out of It!" in B. C. Forbes, "Fact and Comment," *Forbes* (September 15, 1930): 11; excerpts from Julius Klein, "New Business Will Arise!" *Forbes* (September 15, 1930): 15–17; "National Sales Month Suggested," in B. C. Forbes, "Fact and Comment," *Forbes* (October 15, 1931): 10. Reprinted with permission.

(a) Snap Out of It! by B. C. Forbes

Snap out of it! Gloom has reigned long enough. It is time to drop cowardice and exercise courage. Deflation has run an ample course—to carry it much further would mean endless destruction, criminal destruction. The country is sound at the core, sound politically, sound financially, sound industrially, sound commercially. Agricultural prices, too, have been thoroughly deflated, even overdepressed. The nation has its health. It has lost little or none of its real wealth. It is living saner than when everyone was unrestrainedly optimistic. The time has come to cast off our doubts and fears, our hesitancy and timidity, our spasm of "nerves". Summer, the season for holiday-making, is over. The season for fresh planning, new enterprise, hard work, driving force, initiative, concentration on business, is here. Let's go.

Snap out of it!

(b) New Business Will Arise! by Julius Klein

A Storehouse of Facts for Men Who Seek to Utilize Nation's Latent and Enormous Buying Power— The Example of Miniature Golf

Vigilance and vigor (as one need hardly say) are among the prime essentials of any business victory. Seldom, indeed, is the American business man deficient in the vigor with which he attacks a commercial problem. His energy, his briskness, his whirlwind tactics are proverbial. But such robust vitality is unfortunately not accompanied, in all cases, by a maximum of vigilance—if one includes in that term the painstaking, pertinacious scrutiny of every single fact, every collection of relevant data, that might bear upon his efforts. The value of such study is being realized increasingly—but do we not all know the business man who can be considered only as a mere slap-dash empiricist, with a breezy confidence in hunches and a deep, ingrained dislike of statistical tables and bar-charts?

Yet statistics are quite capable of proving his salvation. His business, in many instances, is dependent absolutely on his knowing commercial trends, economic movements, broad and sweeping social forces. In few decades in all history have such startling changes taken place as those that we have witnessed in the past ten years. A thorough knowledge of those changes may well provide the firmest conceivable basis for encouragement right now. Especially conducive to such optimism are the facts about the steady growth in American income and buying power.

The National Bureau of Economic Research tells us that the total realized income of the people of continental United States in 1928 was more than $89,000,000,000. And that did not include the income that might be imputed to housewives and householders for services rendered to their families, nor employees' expense accounts, nor the money earned through odd-job employment. That means a

per capita income of $740. In the course of a year we are now earning nearly $25,000,000,000 more than we were ten years ago. And when we extend the comparison to 20 years ago, we find that the national income has more than trebled over that period. Even when we make all due allowance for price changes, the increase is very great.

Let us institute, for a moment, a comparison on the basis of "1913 dollars"—that is, dollars having a buying power equivalent to that which they had in 1913. We find that the purchasing power (in such 1913 dollars) of the total wages, salaries, pensions, etc., received by the employees of all American industries was $29,967,000,000 in 1928, as compared with $15,946,000,000 in 1909 and $18,822,000,000 in 1913. The purchasing power, in 1913 dollars, of the average annual earnings of the American wage-worker advanced from $556 in 1909, $594 in 1913, and $550 in 1921 to $705 in 1927 (the most recent year for which a dependable figure is available).

The National Bureau of Economic Research has well said that "the growth in per capita income since 1921 must be regarded as a remarkable phenomenon. The indications are that, in terms of immediate ability to buy goods for consumption purposes, the average American was approximately one-third better off in 1927 than he was in 1921." And the bureau goes on to draw the inevitable conclusions: "Under these circumstances it is not surprising that a tremendous market has developed for furs, automobiles, radios, and other luxuries which were previously beyond the reach of the masses of the population."

More recent, and undeniably significant, is the statement made just the other day by the United States Bureau of Labor Statistics, that the buying power of the dollar expanded more than a tenth in the year that ended June, 1930—and it is nearly a sixth greater than it was four years ago.

These are a few concrete facts (I shall speak later of certain "intangibles") that indicate the rise of new markets for manufacturers and merchants who possess the vision to discern and develop them. . . .

[The] Census of Distribution will throw light on numerous domains of business which have been shrouded hitherto in an almost impenetrable obscurity. When integrated and coordinated with other Census data and relevant facts collected by governmental and able private agencies, these data should make it possible for every business man to evaluate his own position and methods in relation to his competitors, his customers and his sources of supply. From such information, any wide-awake industrialist or merchant can draw concretely useful conclusions as to the dominant commercial currents of a tangible sort.

To be sure, he needs also to be *"en rapport"* with the intangible currents—and this is a bit more difficult. Of one thing, however, he may be very certain: Some of the most potent of those currents spring from the general rise in human standards, attendant upon the growth in income that I mentioned a moment ago.

Customers are constantly displaying more discrimination. They are demanding not alone that an article shall work (that primary pragmatic test)—they are requiring also that it shall possess those intangible but unmistakable factors of distinction and of style.

Good taste among the buying public has been incalculably heightened during this past decade. It has advanced in a rapidly ascending spiral. Any given achievement in the creation of artistic merchandise has enhanced the public receptivity to many others—possibly in unrelated lines. There has been a tremendous stimulation, a restless, eager stirring of what I may call, perhaps, the "mass aesthetic sense."

It is perfectly obvious, of course, that the basic cause of this has been the rise in living standards—the widespread elevation of the scale of creature comforts that prove satisfying to the average man. And we must not be led for a single moment to believe that such standards have suffered any grave, enduring damage through the temporary business recession that had its beginning last October. No—that upward surge is too insistent—the typical desires and aptitudes arising from it have become too ineradicably implanted—to permit of any lasting impairment in this land!

The American people have been traveling, at home and in foreign countries, to a previously inconceivable extent, and their observation has been keen. Travel has been revealing once-unimagined vistas—poignant beauty, arresting design, novel treatment and applications of the articles of common use.

The almost miraculous advance in communication has contributed to this greater sensitiveness to style. Radio descriptions have awakened curiosity—have excited lively interest. A new and fascinating factor has appeared in the radio transmission, even across the broad Atlantic, of pictures of designs of goods that are peculiarly susceptible to style.

Entertainment plays a vital role—no less influential because it is subtle and, in many cases, not immediately perceived. Motion pictures especially (both the purely amusement subjects and the frankly industrial films) have intensified the public consciousness of style.

The Census has disclosed, once more, the seemingly almost irresistible impulse toward urbanization. Our titanic cities are expanding. And in those enormous masses of humanity—with their quick interchanges of ideas, their swirling complexity and immediacy of movement—the influence of style is singularly acute. In the ferment of this urban life, new conceptions are being incessantly produced. Many of these are significant—potentially very valuable—to manufacturers and merchants, if they will keep their eyes open and grasp the opportunities.

We now need, in the city, many things that we once associated only with the seashore or the countryside. This statement may seem strange at first (and I admit quite frankly that its application is restricted), but it is supported by ample facts.

Take, merely as an example, the case of sporting goods of certain types. Let us consider bathing-suits. Not so long ago, these were used almost solely in the open—at the beaches and along our streams. But to-day that condition has been absolutely changed by the building of many splendid urban pools (both indoor and outdoor), adorned with impressive names such as "Plage Biarritz," provided with bronzed lifeguards, and necessitating the wearing of good, attractive bathing-suits. At the old swimming-hole to which we resorted in the days of our youth, we were happy and hilarious in a cheap dingy garment (or maybe none at all)—but that, of course, would never do at the glittering, resplendent "Pompeian Pool" that now allures our patronage. Here we see the creation of a new market, a new demand—and one in which that factor of style-consciousness plays assuredly a potent part.

So, too, with the amazing rise of those miniature golf courses that are springing up by the thousands. The players are the cynosure of many eyes, in near-by structures and on the street. I think there can be no doubt that this new game has stimulated a demand for handsome sports attire on the part of countless persons who would not otherwise have cared so much to garb themselves in gaudy raiment.

Our researchers at the Department of Commerce have estimated that there are now (in the middle of August) no fewer than 25,000 of these bantam-size golf courses in the country, with a value of perhaps $125,000,000 (not including the real estate involved), and by the time this article appears in print there will undoubtedly be thousands more. Think of the market thus created for some rather unusual construction materials—for paints and oils—for electricity—for golf balls and, more especially, for putters! And the end is not in sight. Our Textile Division at Washington is putting forward right now the thoroughly sound idea that, as a protection in inclement weather, these miniature courses need a covering of tent or awning material, which should prove a profitable investment at a cost of from $750 to $3,000 per course. This gives promise of developing a market for millions of dollars' worth of canvas, duck, and metal or wood supports. This entire situation illustrates forcefully the manner in which new businesses may arise unexpectedly and vigorously, in a way to hearten many trades. . . .

(c) National Sales Month Suggested by B. C. Forbes

H. E. Kranhold, vice-president of Brown & Bigelow, writes suggesting a National Sales Month. He says: "It is estimated that there are five million salesmen in the United States. Suppose it were possible to secure the interest and co-operation of every organization employing salesmen to put on a National Sales Month at the same time. Suppose that each one, through this extra effort, secured two additional orders during the month. Suppose these orders averaged $10. That would mean one hundred million dollars' worth of additional sales. It has been estimated that every dollar in a sale circulates approximately ten times in the course of producing what enters into the manufacture of the goods sold. That would represent, theoretically, a billion dollars. There isn't much question but what, if every organization in the United States did put on a National Sales and a National Buying Month, business immediately would turn for the better. Prosperity does not precede but follows sales."

He suggests December as the most appropriate month, as it is then that "thoughts are turning to Christmas, when retail stores are busy and the result of a big December business would make a happier Christmas for thousands and thousands of people. It would reflect itself in the new year by making business better in January."

Well, can it be organized?

Perhaps Mr. Gifford may see merit in this plan and, with his unique organizing ability, set in motion the machinery necessary for effective action, thus moving business off what Owen D. Young called its "dead center."

Doing nothing leads inevitably to everybody being undone.

Fear is failure—failure of faith.

Questions

1. Why would "snapping out of it" matter?
2. How would a National Sales Month work?
3. Explain how new businesses would have a ripple effect in generating prosperity.

Questions for Further Thought

1. Compare and contrast John J. Raskob's and Stuart Chase's readings of the American economy during the 1920s (Documents 24-1 and 24-2). Which would have been more likely to endorse the proposals offered in Document 24-3?
2. What is Julius Klein's basic line of argument in "New Business Will Arise"?
3. Compare and contrast the points made by Stuart Chase and Julius Klein relative to the growth of per capita income during the 1920s.

Hard Times

The Great Depression was recorded in statistics: unemployment, bank and business failures, mortgage foreclosures, stock market averages. Graphed from 1929 to 1933, these figures resemble the vital signs on the medical chart of a seriously ill patient, data that discloses periodic upticks but, ominously, an overall worsening condition. For patient, family, and friends, hard times were experienced and felt, as well as viewed on a chart.

As more and more businesses and farms failed, construction continued to fall off, and unemployment mounted, those who were affected and those who were not, increasingly fearful, reacted in such numbers that their responses became visible (see text pp. 774–782, including Figures 24-1 and 24-2). Marriage, birth, and divorce rates all fell. As the economy contracted, many whites were compelled to take jobs formerly held by blacks (such as office cleaning, laundry work, and domestic service); married women who worked were resented and discriminated against in government employment; high school attendance increased (especially among males) in the face of reduced job opportunities; and large numbers of young men and women, unable to contribute to meager family incomes, became tramps or hoboes.

Documents 24-4, 24-5, and 24-6 make painfully clear the impact of the Great Depression on individuals and families. (See, too, text pp. 775–782; "Voices from

Abroad: Breadlines and Beggars"; "American Voices: A Working-Class Family Encounters the Great Depression.") Document 24-7 addresses the birth-control movement during the depression in Connecticut, where state law was hostile to it (see text p. 781).

24-4   A Wise Economist Asks a Question (1932)

John T. McCutcheon

In a career that spanned forty-three years at the Chicago *Tribune,* John T. McCutcheon (1870–1949) demonstrated a sense of compassion that was rare in political cartoonists. There is nothing obvious or partisan in this drawing, which may explain why it won a Pulitzer Prize.

Source: Copyright 1932, reprinted by permission: Tribune Media Services.

Questions

1. How does McCutcheon make the man a sympathetic character?
2. Why does he have a squirrel ask the question?
3. What is McCutcheon saying about the American belief in personal responsibility?

24-5 Mr. Patterson (1940)

Mirra Komarovsky　　　　Barnard College sociologist Mirra Komarovsky measured the impact of hard times on men's self-esteem through case histories, such as that of "Mr. Patterson," in her 1940 book *The Unemployed Man and His Family*.

Source: Mirra Komarovsky, *The Unemployed Man and His Family* (New York: n.p., 1940; reprint, New York: Octagon, 1973), 26–28. Reprinted with permission.

Reaction to Unemployment and Relief. Prior to the depression Mr. Patterson was an inventory clerk earning from $35 to $40 a week. He lost his job in 1931. At the present time he does not earn anything, while his 18-year-old girl gets $12.50 a week working in Woolworth's, and his wife has part-time work cleaning a doctor's office. Unemployment and depression have hit Mr. Patterson much more than the rest of the family.

The hardest thing about unemployment, Mr. Patterson says, is the humiliation within the family. It makes him feel very useless to have his wife and daughter bring in money to the family while he does not contribute a nickel. It is awful to him, because now "the tables are turned," that is, he has to ask his daughter for a little money for tobacco, etc. He would rather walk miles than ask for carfare money. His daughter would want him to have it, but he cannot bring himself to ask for it. He had often thought that it would make it easier if he could have 25 cents a week that he could depend upon. He feels more irritable and morose than he ever did in his life. He doesn't enjoy eating. He hasn't slept well in months. He lies awake and tosses and tosses, wondering what he will do and what will happen to them if he doesn't ever get work any more. He feels that there is nothing to wake up for in the morning and nothing to live for. He often wonders what would happen if he put himself out of the picture, or just got out of the way of his wife. Perhaps she and the girl would get along better without him. He blames himself for being unemployed. While he tries all day long to find work and would take anything, he feels that he would be successful if he had taken advantage of his opportunities in youth and had secured an education.

Mr. Patterson believes that his wife and daughter have adjusted themselves to the depression better than he has. In fact, sometimes they seem so cheerful in the evening that he cannot stand it any more. He grabs his hat and says he is going out for a while, and walks hard for an hour before he comes home again. That is one thing he never did before unemployment, but he is so nervous and jumpy now he has to do something like that to prevent himself from exploding.

Mrs. Patterson says that they have not felt the depression so terribly themselves, or changed their way of living so very much.

Changes in Husband-Wife Relations Since Loss of Employment. The wife thinks it is her husband's fault that he is unemployed. Not that he doesn't run around and try his very best to get a job, but he neglected his opportunities when he was young. If he had had a proper education and had a better personality, he would not be in his present state. Besides, he has changed for the worse. He has become irritable and very hard to get along with. He talks of nothing else, and isn't interested in anything else but his troubles. She and her daughter try to forget troubles and have a good time once in a while, but he just sits and broods. Of course that makes her impatient with him. She cannot sit at home and keep him company, so that during the past couple of years she and her daughter just go out together without him. It isn't that they leave him out—he just isn't interested and stays at home.

Mr. Patterson insists that his child is as sweet as ever and always tries to cheer him up, but the tenor of his conversation about his wife is different. She does go out more with the daughter, leaving him alone. He cannot stand it, worrying so and having them so lighthearted. "When you are not bringing in any money, you don't get as much attention. She doesn't nag all the time, the way some women do," but he knows she blames him for being unemployed. He intimates that they have fewer sex relations—"It's nothing that I do or don't do—no change in me—but when I tell her that I want more love, she just gets mad." It came about gradually, he said. He cannot point definitely to any time when he noticed the difference in her. But he knows that his advances are rebuffed now when they would not have been before the hard times.

The wife gives the impression that there might have been some decrease in sex relations, but declines to discuss them. She tells the following episode:

The day before the interview she was kissing and hugging the daughter. "I like to keep the girl sweet and young, and in the habit of kissing her mother good-night." The father walked in and said, "Don't you get enough of that?" Mrs. Patterson went on at great length as to how terribly that statement hurt her.

The interviewer also witnessed another episode. Towards the end of the interview with the wife, the husband walked into the living room and asked his wife if she thought the interviewer would be interested in talking to their neighbors. The woman said, "Don't bother us, we are talking about something else just now." He got up quietly and went into the kitchen. In a moment she called after him, "Oh, you can sit in here if you *want* to." Nevertheless, he stayed in the kitchen. . . .

Questions

1. Judging from Mr. Patterson's experience, what was the impact of prolonged unemployment on American families?
2. Compare Mr. Patterson's reaction to the depression with that of his wife and daughter.
3. Some contemporary observers suggested that the solution to the depression would be for married women to stay in the home and not "take jobs away from men." Judging from the Patterson family's experience, was this a realistic solution?

24-6   Women on the Breadlines (1932)

Meridel Le Sueur

Meridel Le Sueur (1900–1996), born in Iowa, was a writer who remained active in radical circles throughout her life. "Women on the Breadlines" was published in *New Masses* but drew fire from communist editors for its defeatism and "nonrevolutionary spirit." After suffering through her "Dark Time" during the early Cold War, Le Sueur reemerged during the 1970s. Her writing continues to be of interest even today, some years after her death.

Source: Meridel Le Sueur, "Women on the Breadlines," *New Masses* (January 1932): 5–7, reprinted in Meridel Le Sueur, *Ripening: Selected Work*, ed. Elaine Hedges, with a new afterword by Meridel Le Sueur, 2nd ed. (New York: Feminist Press, 1990), 137–143.

I am sitting in the city free employment bureau. It's the women's section. We have been sitting here now for four hours. We sit here every day, waiting for a job. There are no jobs. Most of us have had no breakfast. Some have had scant rations for over a year. Hunger makes a human being lapse into a state of lethargy, especially city hunger. Is there any place else in the world where a human being is supposed to go hungry amidst plenty without an outcry, without protest, where only the boldest steal or kill for bread, and the timid crawl the streets, hunger like the beak of a terrible bird at the vitals?

We sit looking at the floor. No one dares think of the coming winter. There are only a few more days of summer. Everyone is anxious to get work to lay up something for that long siege of bitter cold. But there is no work. Sitting in the room we all know it. That is why we don't talk much. We look at the floor dreading to see that knowledge in each other's eyes. There is a kind of humiliation in it. We look away from each other. We look at the floor. It's too terrible to see this animal terror in each other's eyes.

So we sit hour after hour, day after day, waiting for a job to come in. There are many women for a single job. A thin sharp woman sits inside a wire cage looking at a book. For four hours we have watched her looking at that book. She has a hard little eye. In the small bare room there are half a dozen women sitting on the benches waiting. Many come and go. Our faces are all familiar to each other, for we wait here every day.

This is a domestic employment bureau. Most of the women who come here are middle-aged, some have families, some have raised their families and are now alone, some have men who are out of work. Hard times and the man leaves to hunt for work. He doesn't find it. He drifts on. The woman probably doesn't hear from him for a long time. She expects it. She isn't surprised. She struggles alone to feed the many mouths. Sometimes she gets help from the charities. If she's clever she can get herself a good living from the charities, if she's naturally a lick spittle, naturally a little docile and cunning. If she's proud then she starves silently, leaving her children to find work, coming home after a day's searching to wrestle with her house, her children.

Some such story is written on the faces of all these women. There are young girls too, fresh from the country. Some are made brazen too soon by the city. There is a great exodus of girls from the farms into the city now. Thousands of farms have been vacated completely in Minnesota. The girls are trying to get work. The prettier ones can get jobs in the stores when there are any, or waiting on table, but these jobs are only for the attractive and the adroit. The others, the real peasants, have a more difficult time.

Bernice sits next to me. She is a Polish woman of thirty-five. She has been working in people's kitchens for fifteen years or more. She is large, her great body in mounds, her face brightly scrubbed. She has a peasant mind and finds it hard even yet to understand the maze of the city where trickery is worth more than brawn. Her blue eyes are not clever but slow and trusting. She suffers from loneliness and lack of talk. When you speak to her, her face lifts and brightens as if you had spoken through a great darkness, and she talks magically of little things as if the weather were magic, or tells some crazy tale of her adventures on the city streets, embellishing them in bright colors until they hang heavy and thick like embroidery. She loves the city anyhow. It's exciting to her, like a bazaar. She loves to go shopping and get a bargain, hunting out the places where stale bread and cakes can be had for a few cents. She likes walking the streets looking for men to take her to a picture show. Sometimes she goes to five picture shows in one day, or she sits through one the entire day until she knows all the dialog by heart. . . .

She wants to get married but she sees what happens to her married friends, left with children to support, worn out before their time. So she stays single. She is virtuous. She is slightly deaf from hanging out clothes in winter. She had done people's washing and cooking for fifteen years and in that time saved thirty dollars. Now she hasn't worked steady for a year and she has spent the thirty dollars. She had dreamed of having a little house or a houseboat perhaps with a spot of ground for a few chickens. This dream she will never realize.

She has lost all her furniture now along with the dream. A married friend whose husband is gone gives her a bed for which she pays by doing a great deal of work for the woman. She comes here every day now sitting bewildered, her pudgy hands folded in her lap. She is hungry. Her great flesh has begun to hang in folds. She has been living on crackers. Sometimes a box of crackers lasts a week. She has a friend who's a baker and he sometimes steals the stale loaves and brings them to her.

A girl we have seen every day all summer went crazy yesterday at the YW. She went into hysterics, stamping her feet and screaming.

She hadn't had work for eight months. "You've got to give me something," she kept saying. The woman in charge flew into a rage that probably came from days and days of suffering on her part, because she is unable to give jobs, having none. She flew into a rage at the girl and there they were facing each other in a rage both helpless, help-

less. This woman told me once that she could hardly bear the suffering she saw, hardly hear it, that she couldn't eat sometimes and had nightmares at night.

So they stood there, the two women, in a rage, the girl weeping and the woman shouting at her. In the eight months of unemployment she had gotten ragged, and the woman was shouting that she would not send her out like that. "Why don't you shine your shoes?" she kept scolding the girl, and the girl kept sobbing and sobbing because she was starving.

"We can't recommend you like that," the harassed YWCA woman said, knowing she was starving, unable to do anything. And the girls and the women sat docilely, their eyes on the ground, ashamed to look at each other, ashamed of something.

Sitting here waiting for a job, the women have been talking in low voices about the girl Ellen. They talk in low voices with not too much pity for her, unable to see through the mist of their own torment. "What happened to Ellen?" one of them asks. She knows the answer already. We all know it.

A young girl who went around with Ellen tells about seeing her last evening back of a cafe downtown, outside the kitchen door, kicking, showing her legs so that the cook came out and gave her some food and some men gathered in the alley and threw small coin on the ground for a look at her legs. And the girl says enviously that Ellen had a swell breakfast and treated her to one too, that cost two dollars.

A scrub woman whose hips are bent forward from stooping with hands gnarled like watersoaked branches clicks her tongue in disgust. No one saves their money, she says, a little money and these foolish young things buy a hat, a dollar for breakfast, a bright scarf. And they do. If you've ever been without money, or food, something very strange happens when you get a bit of money, a kind of madness. You don't care. You can't remember that you had no money before, that the money will be gone. You can remember nothing but that there is the money for which you have been suffering. Now here it is. A lust takes hold of you. You see food in the windows. In imagination you eat hugely; you taste a thousand meals. You look in windows. Colors are brighter; you buy something to dress up in. An excitement takes hold of you. You know it is suicide but you can't help it. You must have food, dainty, splendid food, and a bright hat so once again you feel blithe, rid of that ratty gnawing shame.

"I guess she'll go on the street now," a thin woman says faintly, and no one takes the trouble to comment further. Like every commodity now the body is difficult to sell and the girls say you're lucky if you get fifty cents.

It's very difficult and humiliating to sell one's body.

Perhaps it would make it clear if one were to imagine having to go out on the street to sell, say, one's overcoat. Suppose you have to sell your coat so you can have breakfast and a place to sleep, say, for fifty cents. You decide to sell your only coat. You take it off and put it on your arm. The street, that has before been just a street, now becomes a mart, something entirely different. You must approach someone now and admit you are destitute and are now selling your clothes, your most intimate possessions. Everyone will watch you talking to the stranger showing him your overcoat, what a good coat it is. People will stop and watch curiously. You will be quite naked on the street. It is even harder to try to sell one's self, more humiliating. It is even humiliating to try to sell one's labor. When there is no buyer.

The thin woman opens the wire cage. There's a job for a nursemaid, she says. The old gnarled women, like old horses, know that no one will have them walk the streets with the young so they don't move. Ellen's friend gets up and goes to the window. She is unbelievably jaunty. I know she hasn't had work since last January. But she has a flare of life in her that glows like a tiny red flame and some tenacious thing, perhaps only youth, keeps it burning bright. Her legs are thin but the runs in her old stockings are neatly mended clear down her flat shank. Two bright spots of rouge conceal her pallor. A narrow belt is drawn tightly around her thin waist, her long shoulders stoop and the blades show. She runs wild as a colt hunting pleasure, hunting sustenance.

It's one of the great mysteries of the city where women go when they are out of work and hungry. There are not many women in the bread line. There are no flop houses for women as there are for men, where a bed can be had for a quarter or less. You don't see women lying on the floor at the mission in the free flops. They obviously don't sleep in the jungle or under newspapers in the park. There is no law I suppose against their being in these places but the fact is they rarely are.

Yet there must be as many women out of jobs in cities and suffering extreme poverty as there are men. What happens to them? Where do they go? Try to get into the YW without any money or looking down at heel. Charities take care of very few and only those that are called "deserving." The lone girl is under suspicion by the virgin women who dispense charity.

I've lived in cities for many months broke, without help, too timid to get in bread lines. I've known many women to live like this until they simply faint on the street from privations, without saying a word to anyone. A woman will shut herself up in a room until it is taken away from her, and eat a cracker a day and be as quiet as a mouse so there are no social statistics concerning her.

I don't know why it is, but a woman will do this unless she has dependents, will go for weeks verging on starvation, crawling in some hole, going through the streets ashamed, sitting in libraries, parks, going for days without speaking to a living soul like some exiled beast, keeping the runs mended in her stockings, shut up in terror in her own misery, until she becomes too super-sensitive and timid to even ask for a job.

Bernice says even strange men she has met in the park have sometimes, that is in better days, given her a loan to pay her room rent. She has always paid them back.

In the afternoon the young girls, to forget the hunger and the deathly torture and fear of being jobless, try to pick up a man to take them to a ten-cent show. They never go to more expensive ones, but they can always find a man willing to spend a dime to have the company of a girl for the afternoon.

Sometimes a girl facing the night without shelter will approach a man for lodging. A woman always asks a man for help. Rarely another woman. I have known girls to sleep in men's rooms for the night on a pallet without molestation and be given breakfast in the morning.

It's no wonder these young girls refuse to marry, refuse to rear children. They are like certain savage tribes, who, when they have been conquered, refuse to breed.

Not one of them but looks forward to starvation for the coming winter. We are in a jungle and know it. We are beaten, entrapped. There is no way out. Even if there were a job, even if that thin acrid woman came and gave everyone in the room a job for a few days, a few hours, at thirty cents an hour, this would all be repeated tomorrow, the next day and the next.

Not one of these women but knows that despite years of labor there is only starvation, humiliation in front of them.

Mrs. Gray, sitting across from me, is a living spokesman for the futility of labor. She is a warning. Her hands are scarred with labor. Her body is a great puckered scar. She has given birth to six children, buried three, supported them all alive and dead, bearing them, burying them, feeding them. Bred in hunger they have been spare, susceptible to disease. For seven years she tried to save her boy's arm from amputation, diseased from tuberculosis of the bone. It is almost too suffocating to think of that long close horror of years of child-bearing, child-feeding, rearing, with the bare suffering of providing a meal and shelter.

Now she is fifty. Her children, economically insecure, are drifters. She never hears of them. She doesn't know if they are alive. She doesn't know if she is alive. Such subtleties of suffering are not for her. For her the brutality of hunger and cold. Not until these are done away with can those subtle feelings that make a human being be indulged.

She is lucky to have five dollars ahead of her. That is her security. She has a tumor that she will die of. She is thin as a worn dime with her tumor sticking out of her side. She is brittle and bitter. Her face is not the face of a human being. She has borne more than it is possible for a human being to bear. She is reduced to the least possible denominator of human feelings.

It is terrible to see her little bloodshot eyes like a beaten hound's, fearful in terror.

We cannot meet her eyes. When she looks at any of us we look away. She is like a woman drowning and we turn away. We must ignore those eyes that are surely the eyes of a person drowning, doomed. She doesn't cry out. She goes down decently. And we all look away.

The young ones know though. I don't want to marry. I don't want any children. So they all say. No children. No marriage. They arm themselves alone, keep up alone. The man is helpless now. He cannot provide. If he propagates he cannot take care of his young. The means are not in his hands. So they live alone. Get what fun they can. The life risk is too horrible now. Defeat is too clearly written on it.

So we sit in this room like cattle, waiting for a nonexistent job, willing to work to the farthest atom of energy, unable to work, unable to get food and lodging, unable to bear children—here we must sit in this shame looking at the floor, worse than beasts at a slaughter.

It is appalling to think that these women sitting so listless in the room may work as hard as it is possible for a human being to work, may labor night and day, like Mrs. Gray wash streetcars from midnight to dawn and offices in the early evening, scrub for fourteen and fifteen hours a day, sleep only five hours or so, do this their whole lives, and never earn one day of security, having always before them the pit of the future. The endless labor, the bending back, the water-soaked hands, earning never more than a week's wages, never having in their hands more life than that.

It's not the suffering of birth, death, love that the young reject, but the suffering of endless labor without dream, eating the spare bread in bitterness, being a slave without the security of a slave.

Questions

1. What aspects of "Women on the Breadlines" likely led to the criticism by editors of *New Masses?*
2. What aspects of Le Sueur's work, revealed in this piece, do you think have led to renewed interest in the writer and to the recent publication of many of her works?
3. What most strikes you about the women Le Sueur describes and their experiences? What of the men who figure in the piece?

24-7   Birth Control in Connecticut during the Depression (1935–1939)

Hilda Crosby Standish

Connecticut's anticontraception law was highly restrictive, prohibiting the use of contraceptives. The state legislature repeatedly rejected liberalization of the law, and the state judiciary balked at liberalizing its reading of the law. Not until 1965 did the U.S. Supreme Court, in *Griswold v. Connecticut,* overturn the Connecticut law. (See text pp. 633–635, 650; also Document 20-6.)

The birth-control clinic discussed in this selection by Dr. Hilda Crosby Standish functioned from 1935 to 1939. The "Mrs. Hepburn" to whom she refers is Katharine Martha Houghton Hepburn, an activist in a range of women's causes, the wife of Dr. James N. Hepburn, and the mother of Katharine Houghton Hepburn, the celebrated actress.

Source: Interview of Dr. Hilda Crosby Standish by Carol Nichols, July 28, 1980, in Oral History Project, "The Political Activities of the First Generation of Fully Enfranchised Connecticut Women, 1920–1945," 28–38, Center for Oral History and the Women's Studies Program, University of Connecticut, excerpted in Ruth Barnes Moynihan, Cynthia Russett, and Laurie Crumpacker, eds., *Second to None: A Documentary History of American Women,* vol. 2: *From 1865 to the Present* (Lincoln and London: University of Nebraska Press, 1993), 197–199. Reprinted with permission.

Standish: After I came back from China, I was very fortunate. It was at a time when the [birth control] movement in Connecticut had gotten to the point of not being able to get anywhere in the legislature. Therefore, the leaders decided that this law on the books probably would not hold

anyway, so why not open a clinic and see. Mrs. Hepburn, who was the leader in the movement in Hartford, and a friend of Margaret Sanger's, decided to get a board of directors and actually open a clinic here. This was all taking place just as I came back from China. I don't remember through whom I heard about it, but at any rate I was asked if I would be interested in being the medical director of this new clinic that was forming. Well, I was. This was before I was married; the clinic was to be open only two or three days a week. We organized, found the place and all the things we needed and so forth, and opened on July ninth of 1935, which was little over a year after I came back. It was called the Maternal Health Center and was at 100 Retreat Avenue where the Medical Arts Building now stands. . . .

The office was on the first floor of a brownstone on Retreat Avenue, right across from the Hartford Hospital entrance to the clinic. This proved interesting, because while the Hartford Hospital could not sponsor us, nor could the Board of Health or anything else, openly, many of the nurses in the outpatient department, the postpartum department particularly, would say, "Well, you've just had a baby, and it would be wise to wait a while before you have another. If you just follow that white line across the street, and look up you'll see a sign there, and you might be interested in going in and talking with them." So, we really had quite a few referrals from the Hartford Hospital. [Laughs.]

Nichols: The sign said, "Birth Control League" or "Maternal Health Center"?

Standish: The sign said, "Maternal Health Center." The nurses said, "They will help you, perhaps, in understanding how to wait a while before you have another child."

And actually we trained some interns from the Hartford Hospital who were in the obstetrical division—because this was at a time when it was a rotating service there—these interns would come across, most of them for one or two sessions with us, to see how to fit diaphragms, which was the chief method that we had—oh, 95 percent in those days.

Nichols: All this was illegal, of course.

Standish: We didn't think it was, honestly. It was such a strange old law, because it was a law that would not permit you to *use* methods of birth control. Now, how do you know whether anybody's using them or not! But a doctor or a nurse by aiding and abetting a person to break a law is himself or herself responsible and liable to fine or imprisonment. So, it got back to us. But we thought that if the lawyers ever really judged this or the court did, that they would say, "This is simply ridiculous, and this law does not hold." We really thought that. . . .

Nichols: Did you ever feel that your own professional status was in any way threatened by what you were doing?

Standish: No, not in the least. Practically all of the doctors on the staff that I knew were very much for it. Many of them didn't dare say so, but this was true of our doctors in the public health group, too. They just dared not in their positions. Even the Catholic doctors were, many of them, in favor of it. They sent us patients. Of course, in those days we were very careful as to the patients we took. They had to be married. They had to have had one child. Now, as I think of it, it was just ghastly to have been so strict.

Nichols: They had to have had a child already?

Standish: Yes, and they had to be referred by a minister or a social worker or a doctor. These references, well, we had to have them. It was sad, for many of the women wanted to come and just didn't dare because they couldn't seem to feel it was right or find a sponsor. The priest, of course, couldn't send them or wouldn't send them, and yet they'd come sometimes on their own. We'd say, "There must be a sponsor somewhere." We didn't dare take people on their own. We had plenty of patients. The clinic ran 50 percent Catholic women. This has been true in most places, that you have the same percentage as you have in the population, and in those days Hartford was just about 50 percent Catholic. They'd say, "The priest doesn't know what we're up against. We just can't have more children. We love the ones we have, but we can't have any more. We can't support them." Or, "I'm just worn out." . . .

Nichols: Did you see many patients?

Standish: Yes, in the four years that we were there, we had over three thousand patients. . . .

Nichols: If you had to say what were the most common reasons why women came to you—because of finances? Or because of health? What were the reasons why they came to you?

Standish: Both.

Nichols: Even increased sexual pleasure? I would assume that these are all interrelated.

Standish: We didn't hear much of that. It was primarily, "I just can't have another child." "I'm tired." "I don't have enough money to support another child." "I can't take care of the ones I have in the way I want to." "We don't have a good enough home," etc. I would say for 99 percent these were the reasons.

Questions

1. Why would a facility like the Maternal Health Center be of greater importance to poor women than to well-to-do women?

2. Compare and contrast the positions of Standish and Margaret Sanger (Document 20-6) on birth control.

Questions for Further Thought

1. Drawing on documents and text, reflect on the position of men during hard times.
2. Doing likewise, reflect on the position of women during hard times.

Harder Times

For farmers, African Americans, and Mexican Americans, the Great Depression meant that hard times became harder still. Large numbers of farmers and others from the Dust Bowl of the Great Plains migrated to California. Their plight there was most famously treated by novelist John Steinbeck. An excerpt from his *Grapes of Wrath* appears in Document 24-8. During the 1930s, three-quarters of all African Americans still resided in the South, but the ongoing northward migration since 1910 had carried many into cities. In New York City, the major African American neighborhood, Harlem, exploded into riot early in 1935, as described in Document 24-9. (On Mexican Americans' lives during the period, see text pp. 789–793, including "American Lives: Bert Corona and the Mexican American Generation.")

24-8   The Grapes of Wrath (1939)

John Steinbeck

In his popular and Pulitzer Prize–winning novel, *The Grapes of Wrath,* John Steinbeck (1902–1968) sympathetically portrayed the Joad family, "Okies" who sought to build new lives for themselves as agricultural laborers in California. (For balanced coverage of Dust Bowl migrations, see text pp. 787–789.)

Source: Chapter 25 from *The Grapes of Wrath* (pp. 473–477) by John Steinbeck. Copyright 1939, renewed © 1967 by John Steinbeck. Used by permission of Viking Penguin, a division of Penguin Putnam, Inc.

CHAPTER TWENTY-FIVE

The spring is beautiful in California. Valleys in which the fruit blossoms are fragrant pink and white waters in a shallow sea. Then the first tendrils of the grapes, swelling from the old gnarled vines, cascade down to cover the trunks. The full green hills are round and soft as breasts. And on the level vegetable lands are the mile-long rows of pale green lettuce and the spindly little cauliflowers, the gray-green unearthly artichoke plants.

And then the leaves break out on the trees, and the petals drop from the fruit trees and carpet the earth with pink and white. The centers of the blossoms swell and grow and color: cherries and apples, peaches and pears, figs which close the flower in the fruit. All California quickens with produce, and the fruit grows heavy, and the limbs bend gradually under the fruit so that little crutches must be placed under them to support the weight.

Behind the fruitfulness are men of understanding and knowledge and skill, men who experiment with seed, endlessly developing the techniques for greater crops of plants whose roots will resist the million enemies of the earth: the molds, the insects, the rusts, the blights. These men work carefully and endlessly to perfect the seed, the roots. And there are the men of chemistry who spray the trees against pests, who sulphur the grapes, who cut out disease and rots, mildews and sicknesses. Doctors of preventive medicine, men at the borders who look for fruit flies, for Japanese beetle, men who quarantine the sick trees and root them out and burn them, men of knowledge. The men who graft the young trees, the little vines, are the cleverest of all, for theirs is a surgeon's job, as tender and delicate; and these men must have surgeons' hands and surgeons' hearts to slit the bark, to place the grafts, to bind the wounds and cover them from the air. These are great men.

Along the rows, the cultivators move, tearing the spring grass and turning it under to make a fertile earth, breaking the ground to hold the water up near the surface, ridging the ground in little pools for the irrigation, destroying the weed roots that may drink the water away from the trees.

And all the time the fruit swells and the flowers break out in long clusters on the vines. And in the growing year the warmth grows and the leaves turn dark green. The prunes lengthen like little green bird's eggs, and the limbs sag down against the crutches under the weight. And the hard little pears take shape, and the beginning of the fuzz comes out on the peaches. Grape blossoms shed their tiny petals and the hard little beads become green buttons, and the buttons grow heavy. The men who work in the fields, the owners of the little orchards, watch and calculate. The year is heavy with produce. And men are proud, for of their knowledge they can make the year heavy. They have transformed the world with their knowledge. The short, lean wheat has been made big and productive. Little sour apples have grown large and sweet, and that old grape that grew among the trees and fed the birds its tiny fruit has mothered a thousand varieties, red and black, green and pale pink, purple and yellow; and each variety with its own flavor. The men who work in the experimental farms have made new fruits: nectarines and forty kinds of plums, walnuts with paper shells. And always they work, selecting, grafting, changing, driving themselves, driving the earth to produce.

And first the cherries ripen. Cent and a half a pound. Hell, we can't pick 'em for that. Black cherries and red cherries, full and sweet, and the birds eat half of each cherry and the yellowjackets buzz into the holes the birds made. And on the ground the seeds drop and dry with black shreds hanging from them.

The purple prunes soften and sweeten. My God, we can't pick them and dry and sulphur them. We can't pay wages, no matter what wages. And the purple prunes carpet the ground. And first the skins wrinkle a little and swarms of flies come to feast, and the valley is filled with the odor of sweet decay. The meat turns dark and the crop shrivels on the ground.

And the pears grow yellow and soft. Five dollars a ton. Five dollars for forty fifty-pound boxes; trees pruned and sprayed, orchards cultivated—pick the fruit, put it in boxes, load the trucks, deliver the fruit to the cannery—forty boxes for five dollars. We can't do it. And the yellow fruit falls heavily to the ground and splashes on the ground. The yellowjackets dig in the soft meat, and there is a smell of ferment and rot.

Then the grapes—we can't make good wine. People can't buy good wine. Rip the grapes from the vines, good grapes, rotten grapes, wasp-stung grapes. Press stems, press dirt and rot.

But there's mildew and formic acid in the vats.

Add sulphur and tannic acid.

The smell from the ferment is not the rich odor of wine, but the smell of decay and chemicals.

Oh, well. It has alcohol in it, anyway. They can get drunk.

The little farmers watched debt creep up on them like the tide. They sprayed the trees and sold no crop, they pruned and grafted and could not pick the crop. And the men of knowledge have worked, have considered, and the fruit is rotting on the ground, and the decaying mash in the wine vats is poisoning the air. And taste the wine—no grape flavor at all, just sulphur and tannic acid and alcohol.

This little orchard will be a part of a great holding next year, for the debt will have choked the owner.

This vineyard will belong to the bank. Only the great owners can survive, for they own the canneries too. And four pears peeled and cut in half, cooked and canned, still cost fifteen cents. And the canned pears do not spoil. They will last for years.

The decay spreads over the State, and the sweet smell is a great sorrow on the land. Men who can graft the trees and make the seed fertile and big can find no way to let the hungry people eat their produce. Men who have created new fruits in the world cannot create a system whereby their fruits may be eaten. And the failure hangs over the State like a great sorrow.

The works of the roots of the vines, of the trees, must be destroyed to keep up the price, and this is the saddest, bitterest thing of all. Carloads of oranges dumped on the ground. The people came for miles to take the fruit, but this could not be. How would they buy oranges at twenty cents a dozen if they could drive out and pick them up? And men with hoses squirt kerosene on the oranges, and they are angry at the crime, angry at the people who have come to take the fruit. A million people hungry, needing the fruit— and kerosene sprayed over the golden mountains.

And the smell of rot fills the country.

Burn coffee for fuel in the ships. Burn corn to keep warm, it makes a hot fire. Dump potatoes in the rivers and place guards along the banks to keep the hungry people from fishing them out. Slaughter the pigs and bury them, and let the putrescence drip down into the earth.

There is a crime here that goes beyond denunciation. There is a sorrow here that weeping cannot symbolize. There is a failure here that topples all our success. The fertile earth, the straight tree rows, the sturdy trunks, and the ripe fruit. And children dying of pellagra[1] must die because a profit cannot be taken from an orange. And coroners must fill in the certificates—died of malnutrition—because the food must rot, must be forced to rot.

The people come with nets to fish for potatoes in the river, and the guards hold them back; they come in rattling

---

[1] *Pellagra* is a disease caused by a deficiency of niacin in the diet. It produces lesions as well as gastrointestinal and mental problems.

cars to get the dumped oranges, but the kerosene is sprayed. And they stand still and watch the potatoes float by, listen to the screaming pigs being killed in a ditch and covered with quicklime, watch the mountains of oranges slop down to a putrefying ooze; and in the eyes of the peo- ple there is the failure; and in the eyes of the hungry there is a growing wrath. In the souls of the people the grapes of wrath are filling and growing heavy, growing heavy for the vintage.

Questions

1. How does this chapter illustrate the paradox of hunger and want amid plenty?
2. Why did it seem more economical to the growers to destroy their crops than to bring them to market?
3. What does Steinbeck mean in his concluding warning that "the grapes of wrath are filling and growing heavy, growing heavy for the vintage"? Are you familiar with an earlier American reference to the biblical "grapes of wrath" and "vintage"?

24-9   The Harlem Riot of 1935

Introducing a report on the Harlem riot, the editors of a documentary history, Richard Hofstadter and Michael Wallace, categorize the episode as the first in a series of "ghetto riots," which differed from "race riots" like the one that occurred in Chicago in 1919 (see text pp. 785–787; compare with pp. 730–732 and Document 22-14). Mayor Fiorello La Guardia of New York created a commission to investigate the riot, but he balked at making public its report. The *Amsterdam News,* the city's major African American newspaper, published it.

Source: The Mayor's Commission on Conditions in Harlem, "The Negro in Harlem: A Report on the Social and Economic Conditions Responsible for the Outbreak," printed as "The Complete Harlem Riot Report," *New York Amsterdam News* (July 18, 1936); excerpted in Richard Hofstadter and Michael Wallace, eds., *American Violence: A Documentary History* (New York: Vintage, 1971), 258–262. Later published as *The Complete Report of Mayor La Guardia's Commission on the Harlem Riot of March 19, 1935* (New York: Arno Press, 1969).

At about 2:30 on the afternoon of March 19, 1935, Lino Rivera, a 16-year-old colored boy, stole a knife from a counter in the rear of E. H. Kress and Company on 125th Street. He was seen by the manager of the store, Jackson Smith, and an assistant, Charles Hurley, who were on the balcony at the time. Mr. Hurley and another employee overtook the boy before he was able to make his escape through the front door. When the two men took the knife from Rivera's pocket and threatened him with punish- ment, the boy in his fright tried to cling to a pillar and bit the hands of his captors. Rivera was finally taken to the front entrance, where Mounted Patrolman Donahue was called. The boy was then taken back into the store by the officer, who asked the manager if an arrest was desired. While Mr. Smith, the manager, instructed the officer to let the culprit go free—as he had done in many cases before—

an officer from the Crime Prevention Bureau was sent to the store.

This relatively unimportant case of juvenile pilfering would never have acquired the significance which it later took on had not a fortuitous combination of subsequent events made it the spark that set aflame the smouldering resentments of the people of Harlem against racial discrim- ination and poverty in the midst of plenty. Patrolman Don- ahue, in order to avoid the curious and excited spectators, took the boy through the basement to the rear entrance on 124th Street. But his act only confirmed the outcry of a hysterical Negro woman that they had taken "the boy to the basement to beat him up." Likewise, the appearance of the ambulance which had been summoned to dress the wounded hands of the boy's captors not only seemed to substantiate her charge, but, when it left empty, gave color to another rumor that the boy was dead. By an odd trick of fate, still another incident furnished the final confirmation of the rumor of the boy's death to the excited throng of shoppers. A hearse which was usually kept in a garage opposite the store on 124th Street was parked in front of the store entrance while the driver entered the store to see his brother-in-law. The rumor of the death of the boy, which became now to the aroused Negro shoppers an established fact, awakened the deep-seated sense of wrongs and denials and even memories of injustices in the South. One woman was heard to cry out that the treatment was "just like down South where they lynch us." The deep sense of wrong expressed in this remark was echoed in the rising resentment which turned the hundred or more shoppers into an indignant crowd.

The sporadic attempts on the part of the police to assure the crowd within the store that no harm had been done the boy fell upon unbelieving ears, partly because no systematic attempt was made to let representatives of the crowd determine the truth for themselves, and partly because of the attitude of the policemen. According to the testimony of one policeman, a committee of women from among the shoppers was permitted to search the basement, but these women have never been located. On the other hand, when the crowd became too insistent about learning the fate of the boy, the police told them that it was none of their business and attempted to shove them towards the door. This only tended to infuriate the crowd and was interpreted by them as further evidence of the suppression of a wronged race. At 5:30 it became necessary to close the store.

The closing of the store did not stay the rumors that were current inside. With incredible swiftness the feelings and attitude of the outraged crowd of shoppers was communicated to those on 125th Street and soon all of Harlem was repeating the rumor that a Negro boy had been murdered in the basement of Kress' store. The first sign of the reaction of the community appeared when a group of men attempted to start a public meeting at a nearby corner. When the police ordered the group to move from the corner, they set up a stand in front of Kress' store. A Negro who acted as chairman introduced a white speaker. Scarcely had the speaker uttered the first words of his address to the crowd when someone threw a missile through the window of Kress' store. This was the signal for the police to drag the speaker from the stand and disperse the crowd. Immediately, the crowd reassembled across the street and another speaker attempted to address the crowd from a perch on a lamp-post. He was pulled down from his post and arrested along with the other speaker on a charge of "unlawful assemblage." . . . the extreme barbarity which was shown towards at least one of these speakers was seemingly motivated by the fact that these policemen who made derogatory and threatening remarks concerning Negroes were outraged because white men dared to take the part of Ne-

groes. . . . These actions on the part of the police only tended to arouse resentment in the crowd which was increasing all the time along 125th Street. From 125th Street the crowds spread to Seventh Avenue and Lenox Avenue and the smashing of windows and looting of shops gathered momentum as the evening and the night came on. . . .

From its inception, as we have pointed out, the outbreak was a spontaneous and unpremeditated action on the part, first, of women shoppers in Kress's store and, later, of the crowds on 125th Street that had been formed as the result of the rumor of a boy's death in the store. As the fever of excitement based upon this rumor spread to other sections of the community, other crowds, formed by many unemployed standing about the streets and other onlookers, sprang up spontaneously. At no time does it seem that these crowds were under the direction of any single individual or that they acted as a part of a conspiracy against law and order. The very susceptibility which the people in the community showed towards this rumor—which was more or less vague, depending upon the circumstances under which it was communicated—was due to the feeling of insecurity produced by years of unemployment and deep-seated resentment against the many forms of discrimination which they had suffered as a racial minority.

While it is difficult to estimate the actual number of persons who participated in the outburst, it does not seem, from available sources of information, that more than a few thousand were involved. These were not concentrated at any time in one place. Crowds formed here and there as the rumors spread. When a crowd was dispersed by the police, it often re-formed again. These crowds constantly changed their make-up. When bricks thrown through store windows brought the police, the crowds would often dissolve, only to gather again and continue their assaults upon property. Looting often followed the smashing of store windows. The screaming of sirens, the sound of pistol shots and the cracking of glass created in many a need for destruction and excitement. Rubbish, flower pots, or any object at hand were tossed from windows into the street. People seized property when there was no possible use which it would serve. They acted as if there were a chance to seize what rightfully belonged to them, but had long been withheld. The crowds showed various needs and changed their mood from time to time. Some of the destruction was carried on in a playful spirit. Even the looting, which has furnished many an amusing tale, was sometimes done in the spirit of children taking preserves from a closet to which they have accidentally found the key. The mood of these crowds was determined in many cases by the attitude of the police towards their unruly conduct. But, in the end, neither the threats nor the reassurances of the police could restrain these spontaneous outbursts until the crowds had spent themselves in giving release to their pent-up emotions. . . .

Questions

1. What are the most important points that this report makes? What is the perspective of the commission that researched and reported on the riot?
2. What role did rumors play during the riot? How do you account for the importance of rumors in such a situation?

Questions for Further Thought

1. Compare and contrast the circumstances of farmers, African Americans, and Mexican Americans during the depression, and explain the factors that accounted for these circumstances.
2. Drawing on the text and documents, consider what led Richard Hofstadter and Michael Wallace to distinguish between a "ghetto riot" (Harlem, 1935) and a "race riot" (Chicago, 1919).

Herbert Hoover and the Great Depression

The stock market crashed little more than seven months into Herbert Hoover's presidency. During the final two years of his term, Hoover confronted a series of dilemmas posed by an economic crisis unprecedented in severity and ever worsening. That crisis, moreover, had major political and diplomatic implications (see text pp. 791–796). Only during 1860 and 1861 had the nation and its chief executive faced a comparable crisis. Document 24-10 provides a statement by President Hoover during 1932.

Popular discontent that focused on President Hoover and the Republican Party could—and would—express itself at the polls in 1932, but farmers, workers, and the unemployed sometimes took direct action against conditions that they regarded as intolerable (see text pp. 795–796; also "American Voices: The Despair of the Unemployed"). Document 24-11 provides the views of one direct action leader, Milo Reno, of the Farm Holiday Association. Neither communism nor fascism generated truly mass support in the United States during the Great Depression, but each (especially communism) had its following. Document 24-12 offers the testimony of a temporary recruit of communism, Richard Wright, who was to become a prominent African American novelist (see text p. 823).

24-10   Countering the Depression (1932)

Herbert Hoover

In this statement, read at a press conference on May 13, 1932, President Herbert Hoover (1874–1964) compared the actions his administration was taking to counter the effects of the depression with those the government would use in wartime. In the same statement, however, Hoover identified balancing the budget (never a wartime priority) as the most important single step government could take to advance economic recovery.

Source: State Papers of Herbert Hoover (Garden City, N.Y.: Doubleday, Doran, 1934), 188–189.

Our job in the Government is unity of action to do our part in an unceasing campaign to reëstablish public confidence. That is fundamental to recovery. The imperative and immediate step is to balance the Budget and I am sure the Government will stay at this job until it is accomplished.

When our people recover from frozen confidence then our credit machinery will begin to function once more on a normal basis and there will be no need to exercise the emergency powers already vested in any of our governmental agencies or the further extensions we are proposing for the Reconstruction Corporation [The Reconstruction Corporation was the Reconstruction Finance Corporation, created in 1932. See text p. 794.]. If by unity of action these extensions of powers are kept within the limits I have proposed they do not affect the Budget. They do not constitute a drain on the taxpayer. They constitute temporary mobilization of timid capital for the positive and definite purpose of speeding the recovery of business, agriculture and employment.

I have, however, no taste for any such emergency powers in the Government. But we are fighting the economic consequences of over liquidation and unjustified fear as to the future of the United States. The battle to set our economic machine in motion in this emergency takes new forms and requires new tactics from time to time. We used such emergency powers to win the war; we can use them to fight the depression, the misery and suffering from which are equally great.

Questions

1. Why does President Hoover believe that the restoration of public "confidence" is the solution to the country's economic problems?
2. Why does Hoover compare the country's economic crisis to the crisis of wartime?
3. Is there any contradiction between Hoover's call for balancing the budget and his request for "emergency" measures to combat the depression?

24-11   Why the Farmers' Holiday? (1932)

Milo Reno

Milo Reno (1866–1936), a veteran of the Farmers' Union and the unsuccessful 1920s campaign to secure federal legislation to increase farm prices, led the Farmers' Holiday movement, which gained prominence during 1932 and 1933 (see text p. 796).

Source: Milo Reno, radio broadcast "Why the Farmers' Holiday?" (July 20, 1932).
In [R. White], *Milo Reno, Farmers Union Pioneer: The Story of a Man and a Movement,* a memorial volume (Iowa City: Iowa Farmers Union, 1941), 148–153. Reprinted with permission.

In presenting to the listeners of KFNF the Farmers' National Holiday program, it is necessary to, as briefly as possible, review the causes which have led up to the most amazing and confounding situation in the history of the world—people starving in a land with an abundance of food; naked, because of a surplus of clothing; people bankrupt in the richest nation in the world.

This situation did not just happen. It is not because of an act of Providence! But is the result of a conspiracy as destructive and damnable as has ever occurred in this history of mankind.

Its correction can only be accomplished through heroic measures; a patriotic determination to faithfully carry out the objective for which this government was formed—a guarantee of life, liberty and the pursuit of happiness for the citizens of this Republic.

In 1920 as a result of the world's war, the debts of all nations engaged therein were multiplied many times, vast fortunes were made, with the power that attends the accumulation of great wealth. The conspirators against the peace and tranquility of this Republic, determined upon an unwarranted and drastic deflation that began with agriculture and that in eighteen months had destroyed thirty billion dollars of farm values.

Farm organizations pled with congress for the correction of the situation that was strangling American agriculture, was destroying America's farm homes and which could only mean the final destruction of the foundation principles upon which this Government rests.

Many measures were proposed, alibis carefully prepared to excuse the pernicious program of the money lords of the nation, but the requests and prayers of the American farmer for economic equality were ignored.

In 1924, a pernicious program of propaganda, designed to excuse the do-nothing policy of those responsible for legislation was begun, leading the public to believe that the farmer himself was to blame that he had not received the consideration that he was so evidently entitled to; that he was so contrary that he would not co-operate with his fellow farmer; that the farm leadership was selfish, envious, and jealous of each other to the extent that they could not agree upon a definite, positive legislative program and that, if the farm leaders would get together, lay aside their differences of opinion, their organization jealousies, and agree upon an agricultural program, how happy they would be to concede it.

The farm leadership of the United States met the challenge, and, in response to a call sent out by the national Farmers Union, a meeting was held in Des Moines, Iowa, on the 12th day of May 1925, in which 24 farm groups were represented. In this memorable conference, the Corn Belt committee was formed and a legislative program adopted, which embodied the McNary-Haugen bill. Splendid men were selected from all farm organizations, to present this legislative program to congress. So earnestly and valiantly the representatives of this group battled for the farmer's right to a square deal, that the bill twice passed the House and Senate and was twice vetoed by a unfriendly president. The second time the McNary-Haugen bill was vetoed, it had passed the house and senate by an overwhelming majority, in fact, it only lacked one vote of the necessary two-thirds to pass the measure over the president' veto.

The Corn Belt committee was called into session on July 6th, 1927, and after serious consideration of the situation and after fully realizing the money lords of the country, controlling the eastern vote, would never willingly grant the farmer an equal opportunity to exist with industry, the following resolution was passed:

"If we cannot obtain justice by legislation, the time will have arrived when no other course remains than organized refusal to deliver the products of the farm at less than production costs."

We had hoped in the nomination and election of a president in 1928 the country would concede the right of production costs, to those who produced the food and raw material for the rest of society, and the splendid representatives of 36 organized farm groups unanimously declared to the world in this resolution that unless we were conceded economic equality we would organize and refuse to deliver the products of our farms for less than production costs.

The absolute failure of the present congress, whether because of intellectual ability or a lack of patriotic courage, has miserably failed to correct a situation in this republic, unparalleled in history, consequently, we feel the time has arrived for the men and women, who live upon the farms, to resort to drastic measures to protect their homes from confiscation.

A meeting was called for May 3rd, 1932, in the city of Des Moines, Iowa, to which all groups were invited, both agriculture, business, professional and labor, to discuss the action necessary to save the farmers of this nation from complete destruction. It was a monster meeting of earnest men and women, and in this meeting the Farmers' Holiday association was born, and I wish to assure you that it is the last stand of American agriculture in defense of their rights and their homes. . . .

Congress has just ended a long and arduous session, but, seemingly, the objective aimed at by both the major political parties, was to prepare for the campaign of 1932, instead of relieving the situation of despair and desolation of the present time. Not a single measure of relief was passed that did not carry with it an increased burden of debt and usury. The one thing that would restore prosperity again to this nation was defeated each time it was proposed, that is, an inflation of the currency to that point that would reduce the value of the dollar as measured in other things practically to the same point that it was in 1920.

If we are ever able to obtain the legislation necessary to place agriculture on an economic equality with industry, it will be, when we use our economic power, which is the only power left the farmer today.

The Farmers' Holiday association proposes to fix a fair valuation on farm products, based on production costs, and to refuse to deliver until those prices are conceded. Some may call this a strike. Very well. If it is a strike for the farmers to refuse to deliver his products for less than production costs, it is also a strike when the merchant declines to deliver his goods for less than cost and carriage.

We propose that society, as a whole, shall recognize the farmer's right to be considered the same as other serving groups of society. Railroad corporations, because of the fact that they were performing a public service, were conceded by the federal government the cost of operation, plus a five and one-fourth per cent profit on their investment, and I wish to ask my listeners—Is it more of a public service to transport the food products of this nation than it is to produce them?

The utility corporations have, by the federal courts, been conceded the right to fix the price for their services, that, after all operating expenses are paid, they shall have from six to eight per cent return on their capital investment, and this is true of every other business.

Why should other groups of society expect the American farmer, to produce the food and raw material that makes existence possible for them, and deliver his product at a price below production costs, which inevitably means bankruptcy and destruction?

In calling a farmers' holiday, we are simply putting into operation a program that has been adopted by many cities in the middle west, to protect the assets of their banks.

No one should criticize either the banks or the officials of those cities, that adopted drastic methods to protect the property of those institutions from depreciation, in fact, destruction, neither should any group criticize the farmers for refusing to see the value of their holdings depreciated to the extent that the labor of a lifetime is destroyed and in their old age, they are left homeless and in poverty.

The governor of our state joined in with a group of Iowa farmers last September in an effort to stabilize the corn prices. This effort was commendable, but its failure was inevitable, because of its lack of militancy and universal support. For a movement of this kind to succeed, it should have the support and encouragement of the commercial and professional groups, as well as agriculture. It should be entirely divorced from any particular organization, because in order to succeed, it must have the same individual and organization support that prevailed in the old Corn Belt committee. This program means the restoration of the farmer's purchasing power, the power to pay his debts, the ability to purchase the things he so sadly needs, in the operation of his home and his farm. This will mean prosperity to the business institutions and to the professional world. For example, concede to the farmer production costs and he will pay his grocer, the grocer will pay the wholesaler, the wholesaler will pay the manufacturer and the manufacturer will be able to meet his obligations at the bank. Restore the farmer's purchasing power and you have re-established an endless chain of prosperity and happiness in this country. Continue the present policy and you will not only wreck the farmer's home, but in such wrecking, you will wreck every institution that is dependent upon the prosperity of the farmer.

We are at the parting of the ways. The time is too short to temporize longer. The people of the United States must be saved from the destructive desolation that is due us in the coming winter. Therefore, the national Farmers' Holiday association is appealing to the individual farmers, to the co-operative groups, and to all farm organizations to forget all their differences and join in a united effort to correct the situation before it is everlastingly too late to save the farm home, that has been built by the sweat, the toil, the sacrifice, of those who occupy them.

To achieve these ends, some legislation will be necessary. There were a few bills introduced in the last session of congress that if enacted into law would have very materially corrected the present situation. It is not difficult to determine as to the effect of a bill that would provide an increase in the volume of money. . . .

The direct cause of the present distress was deflation of the currency or monopolization of the economic life blood of this nation. Any measure that would inflate the currency and assure us an honest dollar is the remedy. The legislators serving the money lords of the country very frequently use the term "honest dollar" in their opposition to the government exercising its sovereign prerogative to provide the nations' currency.

In 1920, it required $3.00 to measure a bushel of wheat. Through the process of deflation or making money scarce, $1.00 would measure the same quantity of wheat. We did not hear this group of money servers, talking about a dishonest dollar, but, when we proposed to reverse the situation and bring the value of a dollar back to where it was when the great majority of our debts were created, immediately they sent up the cry for an "honest dollar".

Senator Borah, as reported in yesterday's paper (July 19th) says: "We can never pay out under the present program and under present conditions. There is nothing ahead but chaos and disaster, unless we boldly undertake to bring prices back to what they were when a substantial portion of our current debts were obligated, and that only an expansion of the currency would enable us to avoid chaos and disaster." In fact, every thinking man realizes that prices must be brought back by an expansion of the currency.

The farmer has a perfect right to insist that he be permitted to pay his obligation with a dollar of the same purchasing power as the one he borrowed.

How will we go about to accomplish this desired end?

Economists everywhere realize and frankly admit that the present economic system is entirely broken down—that not only the farmer is facing desolation and disaster, but our business and financial institutions are on the verge of universal collapse.

The farmer, by withholding his product, can not only restore a price that will cover production costs, but will have a powerful influence in shaping desired legislation.

In the perfecting of this Farmers' Holiday plan, we will have a marketing committee starting from the townships to the county, from the county to the state, and from the state to the national, without intervention, and it will be a farmer's marketing program built by himself, owned, controlled and operated by himself, without the obstruction of cumbersome federal machinery, that invariably degenerates into a political machine.

Farmers of the middle west, you are standing with your backs to the wall, you have pinned your faith in the past to parties and institutions provided for you by the men higher up. They have failed you in your hour of need—the time has arrived when, if your problems are solved and your right to prosperity and happiness restored, it will be through your own efforts.

Let's take the Farmers' Holiday program into every state, county and township that produces human food. I thank you.

Questions

1. What did the Farmers' Holiday Association hope to accomplish?
2. Why does Reno compare farmers to banks?
3. Which parts of this document make Reno appear to be radical?

24-12   Communism in the 1930s

Richard Wright

With the publication of *Native Son* in 1940, Richard Wright (1908–1960) became the best-known African American novelist of his generation. In the mid-1930s, Wright was attracted to the Communist Party. In this excerpt from his memoir, *American Hunger*, he suggests why communism appealed to him for a time and why its appeal proved limited.

Source: Pages 60–65 from *American Hunger* by Richard Wright. Copyright © 1944 by Richard Wright. Copyright renewed 1977 by Ellen Wright. Reprinted by permission of HarperCollins, Publishers, Inc.

One Thursday night I received an invitation from a group of white boys I had known in the post office to meet in a South Side hotel and argue the state of the world. About ten of us gathered and ate salami sandwiches, drank beer, and talked. I was amazed to discover that many of them had joined the Communist party. I challenged them by reciting the antics of the Negro Communists I had seen in the parks, and I was told that those antics were "tactics" and were all right. I was dubious.

Then one Thursday night Sol, a Jewish chap, startled us by announcing that he had had a short story accepted by a little magazine called the *Anvil*, edited by Jack Conroy, and that he had joined a revolutionary artists' organization, the John Reed Club. Sol repeatedly begged me to attend the meetings of the club, but I always found an easy excuse for refusing.

"You'd like them," Sol said.

"I don't want to be organized," I said.

"They can help you to write," he said.

"Nobody can tell me how or what to write," I said.

"Come and see," he urged. "What have you to lose?"

I felt that Communists could not possibly have a sincere interest in Negroes. I was cynical and I would rather have heard a white man say that he hated Negroes, which I could have readily believed, then to have heard him say that he respected Negroes, which would have made me doubt him. I did not think that there existed many whites who, through intellectual effort, could lift themselves out of the traditions of their times and see the Negro objectively.

One Saturday night, sitting home idle, not caring to visit the girls I had met on my former insurance route,

bored with reading, I decided to appear at the John Reed Club in the capacity of an amused spectator. I rode to the Loop and found the number. A dark stairway led upwards; it did not look welcoming. What on earth of importance could transpire in so dingy a place? Through the windows above me I saw vague murals along the walls. I mounted the stairs to a door that was lettered:

THE CHICAGO JOHN REED CLUB

I opened it and stepped into the strangest room I had ever seen. Paper and cigarette butts lay on the floor. A few benches ran along the walls, above which were vivid colors depicting colossal figures of workers carrying streaming banners. The mouths of the workers gaped in wild cries; their legs were sprawled over cities.

"Hello."

I turned and saw a white man smiling at me.

"A friend of mine, who's a member of this club, asked me to visit here. His name is Sol———," I told him.

"You're welcome here," the white man said. "We're not having an affair tonight. We're holding an editorial meeting. Do you paint?" He was slightly gray and he had a mustache.

"No," I said. "I try to write."

"Then sit in on the editorial meeting of our magazine, *Left Front*," he suggested.

"I know nothing of editing," I said.

"You can learn," he said.

I stared at him, doubting.

"I don't want to be in the way here," I said.

"My name's Grimm," he said

I told him my name and we shook hands. He went to a closet and returned with an armful of magazines.

"Here are some back issues of the *Masses*," he said "Have you ever read it?"

"No," I said.

"Some of the best writers in America publish in it," he explained. He also gave me copies of a magazine called *International Literature*. "There's stuff here from Gide, Gorky . . ."

I assured him that I would read them. He took me to an office and introduced me to a Jewish boy who was to become one of the nation's leading painters, to a chap who was to become one of the eminent composers of his day, to a writer who was to create some of the best novels of his generation, to a young Jewish boy who was destined to film the Nazi invasion of Czechoslovakia. I was meeting men and women whom I would know for decades to come, who were to form the first sustained relationships in my life.

I sat in a corner and listened while they discussed their magazine, *Left Front*. Were they treating me courteously because I was a Negro? I must let cold reason guide me with these people, I told myself. I was asked to contribute something to the magazine, and I said vaguely that I would consider it. After the meeting I met an Irish girl who worked for an advertising agency, a girl who did social work, a schoolteacher, and the wife of a prominent university professor. I had once worked as a servant for people like these and I was skeptical. I tried to fathom their motives, but I could detect no condescension in them.

I went home full of reflection, probing the sincerity of the strange white people I had met, wondering how they *really* regarded Negroes. I lay on my bed and read the magazines and was amazed to find that there did exist in the world an organized search for the truth of the lives of the oppressed and the isolated. When I had begged bread from the officials, I had wondered dimly if the outcasts could become united in action, thought, and feeling. Now I knew. It was being done in one-sixth of the earth already. The revolutionary words leaped from the printed page and struck me with tremendous force.

It was not the economics of Communism, nor the great power of trade unions, nor the excitement of underground politics that claimed me; my attention was caught by the similarity of the experiences of workers in other lands, by the possibility of uniting scattered but kindred peoples into a whole. My cynicism—which had been my protection against an America that had cast me out—slid from me and, timidly, I began to wonder if a solution of unity was possible. My life as a Negro in America had led me to feel—though my helplessness had made me try to hide it from myself—that the problem of human unity was more important than bread, more important than physical living itself; for I felt that without a common bond uniting men, without a continuous current of shared thought and feeling circulating through the social system, like blood coursing through the body, there could be no living worthy of being called human.

I hungered to share the dominant assumptions of my time and act upon them. I did not want to feel, like an animal in a jungle, that the whole world was alien and hostile. I did not want to make individual war or individual peace. So far I had managed to keep humanly alive through transfusions from books. In my concrete relations with others I had encountered nothing to encourage me to believe in my feelings. It had been by denying what I saw with my eyes, disputing what I felt with my body, that I had managed to keep my identity intact. But it seemed to me that here at least in the realm of revolutionary expression was where Negro experience could find a home, a functioning value and role. Out of the magazines I read came a passionate call for the experiences of the disinherited, and there were none of the same lispings of the missionary in it. It did not say: "Be like us and we will like you, maybe." It said: "If you possess enough courage to speak out what you are, you will find that you are not alone." It urged life to believe in life.

I read on into the night; then, toward dawn, I swung from bed and inserted paper into the typewriter. Feeling for the first time that I could speak to listening ears, I wrote a wild, crude poem in free verse, coining images of black hands playing, working, holding bayonets, stiffening finally in death . . . I read it and felt that in a clumsy way it linked white life with black, merged two streams of common experience.

I heard someone poking about the kitchen.

"Richard, are you ill?" my mother called.

"No. I'm reading."

My mother opened the door and stared curiously at the pile of magazines that lay upon my pillow.

"You're not throwing away money buying these magazines, are you?" she asked.

"No. They were given to me."

She hobbled to the bed on her crippled legs and picked up a copy of the *Masses* that carried a lurid May Day cartoon. She adjusted her glasses and peered at it for a long time.

"My God in heaven," she breathed in horror.

"What's the matter, mama?"

"What is this?" she asked, extending the magazine to me, pointing to the cover. "What's wrong with that man?"

With my mother standing at my side, lending me her eyes, I stared at a cartoon drawn by a Communist artist; it was the figure of a worker clad in ragged overalls and holding aloft a red banner. The man's eyes bulged; his mouth gaped as wide as his face; his teeth showed; the muscles of his neck were like ropes. Following the man was a horde of nondescript men, women, and children, waving clubs, stones, and pitchforks.

"What are those people going to do?" my mother asked.

"I don't know," I hedged.

"Are these Communist magazines?"

"Yes."

"And do they want people to act like this?"

"Well . . ." I hesitated.

My mother's face showed disgust and moral loathing. She was a gentle woman. Her ideal was Christ upon the cross. How could I tell her that the Communist party wanted her to march in the streets, chanting, singing?

"What do Communists think people are?" she asked.

"They don't quite mean what you see there," I said, fumbling with my words.

"Then what do they mean?"

"This is symbolic," I said.

"Then why don't they speak out what they mean?"

"Maybe they don't know how."

"Then why do they print this stuff?"

"They don't quite know how to appeal to people yet," I admitted, wondering whom I could convince of this if I could not convince my mother.

"That picture's enough to drive a body crazy," she said, dropping the magazine, turning to leave, then pausing at the door.

"You're not getting mixed up with those people?"

"I'm just reading, mama," I dodged.

Questions

1. Many Americans became dissatisfied with the status quo during the Great Depression. Which grievances shaped the response of African Americans to the social and economic hardships of that era?
2. Why did communism appeal to Wright as a possible solution to the problems he faced?
3. Judging from Wright's account, what factors prevented communism from becoming a more popular movement?

Questions for Further Thought

1. Compare and contrast the ideas expressed by President Hoover (Document 24-10), Milo Reno (Document 24-11), and Richard Wright (Document 24-12).
2. Review Documents 16-6, 18-10, and 24-11. In what ways did the Farmers' Holiday resemble the Grangers and the Populists? In what ways did it differ?

The New Deal, 1933–1939

★   ★   ★

The New Deal Takes Over, 1933–1935

From the beginning of his presidency, Franklin Delano Roosevelt demonstrated that his personality and voice would figure prominently in his presidency. Indeed, even before his election, he had dramatically broken with precedent by flying to the Democratic National Convention and personally accepting his nomination. In his speech there, he had referred to a "new deal," a term that quickly gained currency. In his inaugural address (Document 25-1) the following March, President Roosevelt sought to rally a shaken nation at the very depths of the Great Depression. The New Deal was not to rest on any single ideology. Its major players differed widely regarding means and even ends: like other public figures before and since, they sought to advance themselves as well as their agendas. To do so, they almost always had to gain the president's support or acquiescence (see text pp. 801–806).

Broad public and congressional support did not mean that the New Deal lacked significant opposition (see text pp. 807–808). To its right, for example, the Supreme Court began to invalidate federal and state laws enacted by the Democrats. The Court's decision striking down the national Industrial Recovery Act drew fire from the frustrated president (Document 25-2). To the left of the New Deal, the likes of Senator Huey P. Long, a Democrat from Louisiana, advanced populistic schemes (Document 25-3).

25-1   First Inaugural Address (1933)

Franklin D. Roosevelt   With so many Americans suffering in poverty through the winter of 1932–1933, President Roosevelt (1882–1945) knew that he had to find a way to rekindle their spirits. Assisted by advisor Raymond Moley, Roosevelt crafted an inaugural address toward that end. The speech, given on March 4, 1933, was a resounding success.

Source: In Samuel I. Rosenman, ed., *The Public Papers and Addresses of Franklin D. Roosevelt,* 2 (New York: Random House, 1938).

President Hoover, Mr. Chief Justice, my friends:

This is a day of national consecration, and I am certain that my fellow Americans expect that on my induction into the Presidency I will address them with a candor and a decision which the present situation of our nation impels.

This is pre-eminently the time to speak the truth, the whole truth, frankly and boldly. Nor need we shrink from honestly facing conditions in our country today. This great nation will endure as it has endured, will revive and will prosper.

So first of all let me assert my firm belief that the only thing we have to fear is fear itself—nameless, unreasoning, unjustified terror which paralyzes needed efforts to convert retreat into advance.

In every dark hour of our national life a leadership of frankness and vigor has met with that understanding and support of the people themselves which is essential to victory. I am convinced that you will again give that support to leadership in these critical days.

In such a spirit on my part and on yours we face our common difficulties. They concern, thank God, only material things. Values have shrunken to fantastic levels; taxes have risen; our ability to pay has fallen, government of all kinds is faced by serious curtailment of income; the means of exchange are frozen in the currents of trade; the withered leaves of industrial enterprise lie on every side; farmers find no markets for their produce; the savings of many years in thousands of families are gone.

More important, a host of unemployed citizens face the grim problem of existence, and an equally great number toil with little return. Only a foolish optimist can deny the dark realities of the moment.

Yet our distress comes from no failure of substance. We are stricken by no plague of locusts. Compared with the perils which our forefathers conquered because they believed and were not afraid, we have still much to be thankful for. Nature still offers her bounty and human efforts have multiplied it. Plenty is at our doorstop, but a generous use of it languishes in the very sight of the supply.

Primarily, this is because the rulers of the exchange of mankind's goods have failed through their own stubbornness and their own incompetence, have admitted their fail-ure and abdicated. Practices of the unscrupulous money changers stand indicted in the court of public opinion, rejected by the hearts and minds of men.

True, they have tried, but their efforts have been cast in the pattern of an outworn tradition. Faced by failure of credit, they have proposed only the lending of more money.

Stripped of the lure of profit by which to induce our people to follow their false leadership, they have resorted to exhortations, pleading tearfully for restored confidence. They know only the rules of a generation of self-seekers.

They have no vision, and when there is no vision the people perish.

The money changers have fled from their high seats in the temple of our civilization. We may now restore that temple to the ancient truths.

The measure of the restoration lies in the extent to which we apply social values more noble than mere monetary profit.

Happiness lies not in the mere possession of money; it lies in the joy of achievement, in the thrill of creative effort.

The joy and moral stimulation of work no longer must be forgotten in the mad chase of evanescent profits. These dark days will be worth all they cost us if they teach us that our true destiny is not to be ministered unto but to minister to ourselves and to our fellow men.

Recognition of the falsity of material wealth as the standard of success goes hand in hand with the abandonment of the false belief that public office and high political position are to be valued only by the standards of pride of place and personal profit; and there must be an end to a conduct in banking and in business which too often has given to a sacred trust the likeness of callous and selfish wrongdoing.

Small wonder that confidence languishes, for it thrives only on honesty, on honor, on the sacredness of obligations, on faithful protection, on unselfish performance. Without them it cannot live.

Restoration calls, however, not for changes in ethics alone. This nation asks for action, and action now.

Our greatest primary task is to put people to work. This is no unsolvable problem if we face it wisely and courageously.

It can be accomplished in part by direct recruiting by the government itself, treating the task as we would treat the emergency of a war, but at the same time, through this employment, accomplishing greatly needed projects to stimulate and reorganize the use of our natural resources.

Hand in hand with this, we must frankly recognize the overbalance of population in our industrial centers and, by engaging on a national scale in the redistribution, endeavor to provide a better use of the land for those best fitted for the land.

The task can be helped by definite efforts to raise the values of agricultural products and with this the power to purchase the output of our cities.

It can be helped by preventing realistically the tragedy of the growing loss, through foreclosure, of our small homes and our farms.

It can be helped by insistence that the Federal, State and local governments act forthwith on the demand that their cost be drastically reduced.

It can be helped by the unifying of relief activities which today are often scattered, uneconomical and unequal. It can be helped by national planning for and supervision of all forms of transportation and of communications and other utilities which have a definitely public character.

There are many ways in which it can be helped, but it can never be helped merely by talking about it. We must act, and act quickly.

Finally, in our progress toward a resumption of work we require two safeguards against a return of the evils of the old order; there must be a strict supervision of all banking and credits and investments; there must be an end to speculation with other people's money, and there must be provision for an adequate but sound currency.

There are the lines of attack. I shall presently urge upon a new Congress in special session detailed measures for their fulfillment, and I shall seek the immediate assistance of the several States.

Through this program of action we address ourselves to putting our own national house in order and making income balance outgo.

Our international trade relations, though vastly important, are, in point of time and necessity, secondary to the establishment of a sound national economy.

I favor as a practical policy the putting of first things first. I shall spare no effort to restore world trade by international economic readjustment, but the emergency at home cannot wait on that accomplishment.

The basic thought that guides these specific means of national recovery is not narrowly nationalistic.

It is the insistence, as a first consideration, upon the interdependence of the various elements in, and parts of, the United States——a recognition of the old and permanently important manifestation of the American spirit of the pioneer.

It is the way to recovery. It is the immediate way. It is the strongest assurance that the recovery will endure.

In the field of world policy I would dedicate this nation to the policy of the good neighbor—the neighbor who resolutely respects himself and, because he does so, respects the rights of others—the neighbor who respects his obligations and respects the sanctity of his agreements in and with a world of neighbors.

If I read the temper of our people correctly, we now realize as we have never before, our interdependence on each other; that we cannot merely take, but we must give as well; that if we are to go forward we must move as a trained and loyal army willing to sacrifice for the good of a common discipline, because, without such discipline, no progress is made, no leadership becomes effective.

We are, I know, ready and willing to submit our lives and property to such discipline because it makes possible a leadership which aims at a larger good.

This I propose to offer, pledging that the larger purposes will bind upon us all as a sacred obligation with a unity of duty hitherto evoked only in time of armed strife.

With this pledge taken, I assume unhesitatingly the leadership of this great army of our people, dedicated to a disciplined attack upon our common problems.

Action in this image and to this end is feasible under the form of government which we have inherited from our ancestors.

Our Constitution is so simple and practical that it is possible always to meet extraordinary needs by changes in emphasis and arrangement without loss of essential form.

That is why our constitutional system has proved itself the most superbly enduring political mechanism the modern world has produced. It has met every stress of vast expansion of territory, of foreign wars, of bitter internal strife, of world relations.

It is to be hoped that the normal balance of executive and legislative authority may be wholly adequate to meet the unprecedented task before us. But it may be that an unprecedented demand and need for undelayed action may call for temporary departure from that normal balance of public procedure.

I am prepared under my constitutional duty to recommend the measures that a stricken nation in the midst of a stricken world may require.

These measures, or such other measures as the Congress may build out of its experience and wisdom, I shall seek, within my constitutional authority, to bring to speedy adoption.

But in the event that the Congress shall fail to take one of these two courses, and in the event the national emergency is still critical, I shall not evade the clear course of duty that will then confront me.

I shall ask the Congress for the one remaining instrument to meet the crisis—broad executive power to wage a war against the emergency as great as the power that would be given me if we were in fact invaded by a foreign foe.

For the trust reposed in me I will return the courage and the devotion that befit the time, I can do no less.

We face the arduous days that lie before us in the warm courage of national unity; with the clear consciousness of seeking old and precious moral values; with the clean satisfaction that comes from the stern performance of duty by old and young alike.

We aim at the assurance of a rounded and permanent national life.

We do not distrust the future of essential democracy.

The people of the United States have not failed. In their need they have registered a mandate that they want direct, vigorous action.

They have asked for discipline and direction under leadership. They have made me the present instrument of their wishes. In the spirit of the gift I take it.

In this dedication of a nation we humbly ask the blessing of God. May He protect each and every one of us! May He guide me in the days to come!

Questions

1. What does Roosevelt seek to achieve in this address?
2. What do you make of his analogy between wartime and depression circumstances?
3. How do you interpret Roosevelt's religious references?

25-2   Criticism of a Supreme Court Decision (1935)

Franklin D. Roosevelt

In a press conference on May 31, 1935, the president commented at length on a May 27 Supreme Court decision, *Schechter v. United States,* which completed the dismantling of the National Industrial Recovery Act (NIRA) begun in *Panama Refining Co. v. Ryan.* Key issues included the "delegation of legislative power to the executive," the distinction between interstate and intrastate commerce, and the extent of emergency government power. Chief Charles Evans Hughs wrote the unanimous opinion.

This press conference was Roosevelt's 209th. Like his less frequent radio addresses and "fireside chats," these conferences were weapons in FDR's political arsenal. "Mr. Stephenson" is Francis Stephenson, a journalist, and "Mr. Early" is Stephen Early, Roosevelt's press secretary. The "old Knight case" to which FDR refers is *U.S. v. E. C. Knight,* decided in 1895, not 1885. (On the NIRA and *Schechter,* see text pp. 805, 807, 810–811.)

Source: "The Two Hundred and Ninth Press Conference, May 31, 1935," in Samuel I. Rosenman, ed., *The Public Papers and Addresses of Franklin D. Roosevelt,* 4, *The Court Disapproves, 1935* (New York: Random House, 1938), 200–222.

. . . Now, coming down to the decision itself. What are the implications? For the benefit of those of you who haven't read it through I think I can put it this way: the implications of this decision are much more important than almost certainly any decision of my lifetime or yours, more important than any decision probably since the Dred Scott case, because they bring the country as a whole up against a very practical question. That is in spite of what one gentleman said in the paper this morning, that I resented the decision. Nobody resents a Supreme Court decision. You can deplore a Supreme Court decision, and you can point out the effect of it. You can call the attention of the coun-

try to what the implications are as to the future, what the results of that decision are if future decisions follow this decision. . . .

Now, they [the justices] have pointed out in regard to this particular Act that it was unconstitutional because it delegated certain powers which should have been written into the Act itself. And then there is this interesting language that bears that out. It is on page eight.

"We are told that the provisions of the statute authorizing the adoption of the codes must be viewed in the light of the grave national crisis with which Congress was confronted. Undoubtedly, the conditions to which power is addressed are always to be considered when the exercise of power is challenged. Extraordinary conditions may call for extraordinary remedies. But the argument necessarily stops short of an attempt to justify action which lies outside the sphere of constitutional authority. Extraordinary conditions do not create or enlarge constitutional power."

Of course, that is a very interesting implication. Some of us are old enough to remember the war days—the legislation that was passed in April, May and June of 1917. Being a war, that legislation was never brought before the Supreme Court. Of course, as a matter of fact, a great deal of that legislation was far more violative of the strict interpretation of the Constitution than any legislation that was passed in 1933. All one has to do is to go back and read those war acts which conferred upon the Executive far greater power over human beings and over property than anything that was done in 1933. But the Supreme Court has finally ruled that extraordinary conditions do not create or enlarge constitutional power! It is a very interesting statement on the part of the Court.

However, the question of the delegation of legislative power is not so very important in this particular case because the Supreme Court has at least intimated that in so far as the delegation of power was concerned, the language of the Act could have been so improved as to give definite directions to administrative or quasi-judicial bodies and in that respect it refers to the methods already used in the case of the Federal Trade Commission and cites that with approval.

In other words, for the future the delegation of power is not an unsurmountable object, and undoubtedly an Act could be written which would in general conform to this opinion of the Supreme Court as to delegated powers—get that! So that is not the most serious implication yet.

However, you come down to something else which is the most important implication, and that relates to interstate commerce. . . .

Let's put the decision in plain lay language in regard to at least the dictum of the Court and never mind this particular sick chicken or whatever they call it. That was a question of fact, but of course the Court in ruling on the question of fact about these particular chickens said they were killed in New York and sold and probably eaten in New York, and therefore it was probably intrastate commerce. But of course the Court does not stop there. In fact the Court in this decision, at least by dictum—and remember that dictum is not always followed in the future—has gone back to the old Knight case in 1885, which in fact limited any application of interstate commerce to goods in transit—nothing else!

Since 1885 the Court in various decisions has enlarged on the definition of interstate commerce—railroad cases, coal cases and so forth and so on. It was clearly the opinion of the Congress before this decision and the opinion of various attorneys-general, regardless of party, that the words "interstate commerce" applied not only to an actual shipment of goods but also to a great many other things that affected interstate commerce. . . .

The whole tendency over these years has been to view the interstate commerce clause in the light of present-day civilization. The country was in the horse-and-buggy age when that clause was written and if you go back to the debates on the Federal Constitution you will find in 1787 that one of the impelling motives for putting in that clause was this: There wasn't much interstate commerce at all—probably 80 or 90 percent of the human beings in the thirteen original States were completely self-supporting within their own communities. . . .

In other words, the whole picture was a different one when the interstate commerce clause was put into the Constitution from what it is now. Since that time, because of the improvement in transportation, because of the fact that, as we know, what happens in one State has a good deal of influence on the people in another State, we have developed an entirely different philosophy.

The prosperity of the farmer does have an effect today on the manufacturer in Pittsburgh. The prosperity of the clothing worker in the city of New York has an effect on the prosperity of the farmer in Wisconsin, and so it goes. We are interdependent—we are tied in together. And the hope has been that we could, through a period of years, interpret the interstate commerce clause of the Constitution in the light of these new things that have come to the country. It has been our hope that under the interstate commerce clause we could recognize by legislation and by judicial decision that a harmful practice in one section of the country could be prevented on the theory that it was doing harm to another section of the country. That was why the Congress for a good many years, and most lawyers, have had the thought that in drafting legislation we could depend on an interpretation that would enlarge the Constitutional meaning of interstate commerce to include not only those matters of direct interstate commerce, but also those matters which indirectly affect interstate commerce. . . .

You see the implications of the decision. That is why I say it is one of the most important decisions ever rendered in this country. And the issue is not going to be a partisan issue for a minute. The issue is going to be whether we go one way or the other. Don't call it right or left; that is just first-year high-school language, just about. It is not right or left—it is a question for national decision on a very important problem of Government. We are the only Nation in the world that has not solved that problem. We thought we were solving it, and now it has been thrown right straight in our faces. We have been relegated to the horse-and-buggy definition of interstate commerce. . . .

Q. (Mr. Stephenson) Can we use the direct quotation on that horse-and-buggy stage?

THE PRESIDENT: I think so.

MR. EARLY: Just the phrase.

Q. You referred to the Dred Scott decision. That was followed by the Civil War and by at least two amendments to the Constitution.

THE PRESIDENT: Well, the reason for that, of course, was the fact that the generation of 1856 did not take action during the next four years.

Questions

1. How does Roosevelt criticize key arguments of the Supreme Court?
2. Why does he refer to the Dred Scott decision? To the "horse-and-buggy age" and the "horse-and-buggy definition of interstate commerce"? To laws passed during 1917?

25-3   The Long Plan (1933)

Huey P. Long

To his supporters, Senator Huey P. Long (1893–1935) of Louisiana (see text pp. 807–808) was a saint; to his enemies, he was Satan. Long simply referred to himself as "the Kingfish." Until an assassin murdered him, Long and his brand of Populism seemed strong enough to pose a threat to FDR's winning a second term. Long titled his autobiography *Every Man a King*. Following is his plan to make that vision a reality.

Source: Huey P. Long, *Every Man a King: The Autobiography of Huey P. Long* (New Orleans: National Book, 1933; reprint, Chicago: Quadrangle Books, 1964), 338–340. Reprinted with permission.

THE MADDENED FORTUNE HOLDERS AND THEIR INFURIATED PUBLIC PRESS!

The increasing fury with which I have been, and am to be, assailed by reason of the fight and growth of support for limiting the size of fortunes can only be explained by the madness which human nature attaches to the holders of accumulated wealth.

What I have proposed is:—

THE LONG PLAN

1. A capital levy tax on the property owned by any one person of 1% of all over $1,000,000; 2% of all over $2,000,000 etc., until, when it reaches fortunes of over $100,000,000, the government takes all above that figure; which means a limit on the size of any one man's fortune to something like $50,000,000—the balance to go to the government to spread out in its work among all the people.

2. An inheritance tax which does not allow any one person to receive more than $5,000,000 in a lifetime without working for it, all over that amount to go to the government to be spread among the people for its work.

3. An income tax which does not allow any one man to make more than $1,000,000 in one year, exclusive of taxes, the balance to go to the United States for general work among the people.

The foregoing program means all taxes paid by the fortune holders at the top and none by the people at the bottom; the spreading of wealth among all the people and the breaking up of a system of Lords and Slaves in our economic life. It allows the millionaires to have, however, more than they can use for any luxury they can enjoy on earth. But, with such limits, all else can survive.

That the public press should regard my plan and effort as a calamity and me as a menace is no more than should be expected, gauged in the light of past events. . . .

In 1932, the vote for my resolution showed possibly a half dozen other Senators back of it. It grew in the last Congress to nearly twenty Senators. Such growth through one other year will mean the success of a venture, the completion of everything I have undertaken,—the time when I can and will retire from the stress and fury of my public life, maybe as my forties begin,—a contemplation so serene as to appear impossible.

That day will reflect credit on the States whose Senators took the early lead to spread the wealth of the land among all the people.

Then no tear dimmed eyes of a small child will be lifted into the saddened face of a father or mother unable to give it the necessities required by its soul and body for life; then the powerful will be rebuked in the sight of man for holding that which they cannot consume, but which is craved to sustain humanity; the food of the land will feed, the raiment clothe, and the houses shelter all the people; the powerful will be elated by the well being of all, rather than through their greed.

Then, those of us who have pursued that phantom of Jefferson, Jackson, Webster, Theodore Roosevelt and Bryan may hear wafted from their lips in Valhalla:
EVERY MAN A KING

Questions

1. What is Long proposing?
2. Who was most likely to support him? Why?
3. Is Long arguing for reform or revolution? In your answer consider the status of the rich under the Long Plan.

Questions for Further Thought

1. Compare FDR's inaugural address (Document 25-1) with the *Forbes* magazine editorial "Snap Out Of It!" (Document 24-3). To what extent do they make the same argument? Why did one succeed where the other failed?
2. How does the Long Plan compare with the ideas of William Jennings Bryan (Document 18-11) and the Progressive Party platform of 1912 (Document 20-10)? What makes an idea "radical"?

The Second New Deal, 1935–1938

The Second New Deal initially involved a leftward shift in Congress (the Democrats had gained additional House seats in 1934) and by the administration, which was under attack from the right for what it had done and under pressure from the left for what it had not done. In 1935, Congress took the lead in enacting the National Labor Relations Act to assist the labor movement, and the administration took the lead in passing the Social Security Act to provide old-age pensions, unemployment compensation, and assistance to the "deserving poor." These laws were to become part of the New Deal's legacy. In a landslide victory one year later, Roosevelt won reelection, while his party added to its congressional majority.

Roosevelt's second term proved to be less successful than his first. His early 1937 proposal to enlarge the Supreme Court aroused widespread opposition. A sharp economic downturn during 1937 and 1938, the so-called Roosevelt recession, damaged the president, his administration, and his party. The Democratic Party itself was increasingly divided between liberals (mostly northern and urban) and conservatives (mostly southern and rural). As a consequence, in 1937 and 1938, only a few New Deal measures passed Congress. During 1938, FDR failed to unseat conservative Democratic congressional opponents in party primary elections and the Republicans registered gains in midterm elections. Clearly, the New Deal tide that had flowed in 1935 and 1936 ebbed in 1937 and 1938, resulting in a lasting political stalemate (see text pp. 808–812).

Document 25-4 offers the dissenting opinion of Justice Harlan F. Stone in the 1936 decision of the Supreme Court that struck down the Agricultural Adjustment Act of 1933. Stone defended the constitutionality of this key piece of New Deal legislation. Document 25-5 provides portions of the 1936 Republican and Democratic national platforms. Document 25-6 reveals the concern of southern Democrats over a proposed federal antilynching law early in 1938.

25-4 Dissenting Opinion, *U.S. v. Butler* (1936)

Harlan F. Stone

Unlike *Schechter,* a number of controversial cases before the Supreme Court during the mid-1930s were decided, one way or the other, by divided votes. (Before FDR's first appointment to the high court in 1937, it comprised four justices predictably opposed to the New Deal, two generally but not always opposed, and three sometimes though by no means always supportive of New Deal measures.) In *Butler,* a six-justice majority declared unconstitutional a tax on agricultural processors that was central to the Agricultural Adjustment Act of 1933 (see text pp. 805, 810–811). Justice Harlan F. Stone (1872–1946) sharply dissented from that opinion.

Source: U.S. v. Butler, 297 U.S. 1 (1936), excerpted in Donald O. Dewey, ed., *Union and Liberty: A Documentary History of American Constitutionalism* (New York: McGraw-Hill, 1969), 236.

1. The power of courts to declare a statute unconstitutional is subject to two guiding principles of decision which ought never to be absent from judicial consciousness. One is that courts are concerned only with the power to enact statutes, not with their wisdom. The other is that while unconstitutional exercise of power by the executive and legislative branches of the government is subject to judicial restraint, the only check upon our own exercise of power is our own sense of self-restraint. For the removal of unwise laws from the statute books appeal lies not to the courts but to the ballot and to the processes of democratic government.

2. The constitutional power of Congress to levy an excise tax upon the processing of agricultural products is not questioned. The present levy is held invalid, not for any want of power in Congress to lay such a tax to defray public expenditures, including those for the general welfare, but because the use to which its proceeds are put is disapproved.

. . . "Let the end be legitimate," said the great Chief Justice, "let it be within the scope of the Constitution, and all means which are appropriate, which are plainly adapted to that end, which are not prohibited, but consistent with the letter and spirit of the Constitution, are constitutional." *McCulloch v. Maryland.* This cardinal guide to constitutional exposition must now be rephrased so far as the spending power of the federal government is concerned. Let the expenditure be to promote the general welfare, still, if it is needful in order to insure its use for the intended purpose to influence any action which Congress cannot command because within the sphere of state government, the expenditure is unconstitutional. And taxes otherwise lawfully levied are likewise unconstitutional if they are appropriated to the expenditure whose incident is condemned. . . .

. . . Courts are not the only agency of government that must be assumed to have capacity to govern. Congress and the courts both unhappily may falter or be mistaken in the performance of their constitutional duty. But interpretation of our great charter of government which proceeds on any assumption that the responsibility for the preservation of our institutions is the exclusive concern of any one of the three branches of government, or that it alone can save them from destruction is far more likely, in the long run, "to obliterate the constituent members" of "an indestructible union of indestructible states" than the frank recognition that language, even of a constitution, may mean what it says: that the power to tax and spend includes the power to relieve a nationwide economic maladjustment by conditional gifts of money.

Questions

1. What is the thrust of Stone's argument regarding judicial "self-restraint"?
2. In what ways, if any, does Stone's opinion resemble President Roosevelt's press conference remarks (Document 25-2)?

25-5 Republican and Democratic National Platforms (1936)

In 1936, the Republicans nominated Alfred M. Landon and Colonel Frank Knox for president and vice-president, each on the first ballot. The Democrats renominated Franklin D. Roosevelt and John Nance Garner by acclamation. Before his nomination, Landon telegraphed the Republican convention expressing agreement with the platform but advocating a constitutional amendment to safeguard women and children in the workplace and to establish wage and hour standards in case the courts struck down pending legislation. The Democratic platform chided the Republican document for proposing state action to cope with national problems and recommended a "clarifying amendment" if necessary to ensure that federal and state governments could constitutionally enact necessary legislation. The portions of the national platforms excerpted here reveal the depths of partisan differences over the New Deal.

Source: Donald Bruce Johnson, comp., *National Party Platforms,* rev. ed., 2 vols. (Urbana: University of Illinois Press, 1978), 1: *1840–1956,* 360, 365–366.

REPUBLICAN

America is in peril. The welfare of American men and women and the future of our youth are at stake. We dedicate ourselves to the preservation of their political liberty, their individual opportunity and their character as free citizens, which today for the first time are threatened by Government itself.

For three long years the New Deal Administration has dishonored American traditions and flagrantly betrayed the pledges upon which the Democratic Party sought and received public support.

The powers of Congress have been usurped by the President.

The integrity and authority of the Supreme Court have been flouted.

The rights and liberties of American citizens have been violated.

Regulated monopoly has displaced free enterprise.

The New Deal Administration constantly seeks to usurp the rights reserved to the States and to the people.

It has insisted on the passage of laws contrary to the Constitution.

It has intimidated witnesses and interfered with the right of petition.

It has dishonored our country by repudiating its most sacred obligations.

It has been guilty of frightful waste and extravagance, using public funds for partisan political purposes.

It has promoted investigations to harass and intimidate American citizens, at the same time denying investigations into its own improper expenditures.

It has created a vast multitude of new offices, filled them with its favorites, set up a centralized bureaucracy, and sent out swarms of inspectors to harass our people.

It has bred fear and hesitation in commerce and industry, thus discouraging new enterprises, preventing employment and prolonging the depression.

It secretly has made tariff agreements with our foreign competitors, flooding our markets with foreign commodities.

It has coerced and intimidated voters by withholding relief to those opposing its tyrannical policies.

It has destroyed the morale of our people and made them dependent upon government.

Appeals to passion and class prejudice have replaced reason and tolerance.

To a free people, these actions are insufferable. This campaign cannot be waged on the traditional differences between the Republican and Democratic parties. The responsibility of this election transcends all previous political divisions. We invite all Americans, irrespective of party, to join us in defense of American institutions.

DEMOCRATIC

We hold this truth to be self-evident—that the test of a representative government is its ability to promote the safety and happiness of the people.

We hold this truth to be self-evident—that 12 years of Republican leadership left our Nation sorely stricken in body, mind, and spirit: and that three years of Democratic leadership have put it back on the road to restored health and prosperity.

We hold this truth to be self-evident—that 12 years of Republican surrender to the dictatorship of a privileged few have been supplanted by a Democratic leadership which has returned the people themselves to the places of authority, and has revived in them new faith and restored the hope which they had almost lost.

We hold this truth to be self-evident—that this three-year recovery in all the basic values of life and the reestablishment of the American way of living has been brought about by humanizing the policies of the Federal Government as they affect the personal, financial, industrial, and agricultural well-being of the American people.

We hold this truth to be self-evident—that government in a modern civilization has certain inescapable obligations to its citizens, among which are:

(1) Protection of the family and the home.

(2) Establishment of a democracy of opportunity for all the people.

(3) Aid to those overtaken by disaster.

These obligations, neglected through 12 years of the old leadership, have once more been recognized by American Government. Under the new leadership they will never be neglected.

Questions

1. What appeals to emotion do the platforms make?
2. Identify New Deal measures indicted by the Republicans.
3. Identify New Deal measures that fit into one or more of the three "inescapable obligations" of government enumerated by the Democrats.

25-6   The Federal Antilynching Bills (1938)

Changes in the national Democratic Party and the federal government during the New Deal cost the Democrats' southern wing a measure of influence. However, that wing remained potent, especially when, beginning in 1937, it could work with other conservative Democrats and the Republicans to thwart New Deal initiatives and even reverse programs. When Republicans and northern Democrats (*not* the administration) pushed a federal antilynching measure through the House of Representatives during 1937, southern Democrats blocked its enactment in the Senate the next year. In doing so, they revealed the importance of race to their wing of the party (see text pp. 808, 816).

This selection comprises *Time*'s coverage of the Wagner-Van Nuys bill in the Senate and the *New York Times*'s report of the January 10, 1938, speech of Senator Pat Harrison, a Mississippi Democrat.

Source: Time (January 24, 1938): 7–8; *New York Times* (January 11, 1938), 18. Reprinted by permission of the *New York Times*.

(a) The Wagner-Van Nuys Bill

. . . Last spring under the spur of the two blow-torch lynchings at Duck Hill, Miss. (TIME, April 26), the Gavagan Bill, a similar anti-lynching measure, passed the House. Passage by the Senate therefore meant that the bill would become law barring the unlikely event of a Presidential veto. So as predicted, Texas' Tom Connally promptly organized a filibuster. Not as predicted, that filibuster last week rounded out ten days and had gathered so much momentum that Tom Connally jubilantly announced he would keep it going if necessary until Christmas.

Filibuster. The actual contents of the Wagner-Van Nuys Bill, as simple as they were familiar, would scarcely keep the U.S. Senate busy for that period. Like its predecessors, it provided for Federal prosecution, and a $5,000 fine or up to five years' imprisonment, or both, for sheriffs & peace officers who did not afford criminals and suspected criminals reasonable protection from mobs (any gatherings of more than three persons). Its other principal provision, the payment of an indemnity up to $10,000 to the family of a victim of mob violence by the county whose officials are responsible, is already in the statute books of twelve States. . . .

(b) The 1938 Speech of Senator Pat Harrison

ANTI-LYNCH BILL SPLITS LEADERS
Harrison, Using Bitter Irony, Says Some Back Measure
for Political Gain

GIVES WARNING TO PARTY
Asks It Keep Faith With South—Assails Plan as Wedge
for New Curbs on States

Special to THE NEW YORK TIMES.
WASHINGTON, Jan. 10.—The racial issue over which the
North and South have long differed drove today a deep
cleavage in the Senate leadership when Senator Harrison
assailed colleagues with whom he long had worked closely
for sponsoring the Wagner Anti-lynching Bill. He spoke
with blunt irony of members to whom he ascribed Presidential or Supreme Court ambitions and asked them if for
the sake of votes they would "betray" the South.

"Is the faith of the South to be broken?" he asked. "Is
its love for the Democratic party to be shattered and its devotion to those who have made that party great to be dissipated?"

But while he pleaded in this manner, the greater part
of his speech, which consumed an hour, was scathing in its
comment and as blunt as any he ever delivered in his attacks on former Republican Administrations.

"Let me say to all aspiring gentlemen in this body who
may retain some hope of becoming the nominee of the Democratic party," he declared, "that they had best stop,
look and listen. It is always better to put advocacy of a
question upon better and higher grounds than that."

WARNS AMBITIOUS

"And those sweet, amiable gentlemen who every time a
newspaper correspondent calls them go out with a flutter-
ing of the heart because they think news has come from

the White House that their nomination is going to be sent
to the Senate to fill the vacancy on the Supreme Court
caused by the resignation of Mr. Justice Sutherland, had
better beware. They do not add to their standing as
lawyers or their qualifications for places on the highest tri-
bunal in this land by voting for such a legislative monstros-
ity as that now pending before the Senate, which destroys
the dual form of government and robs the States of their
sovereignty."

Senator Harrison maintained that "this bill will not
appease anybody," and that, despite that, "we see the people of the South confronted with the terrible situation of a
Democratic majority betraying the trust of the Southern
people, destroying the things that they have idolized and in
which they believe.

"The groups that form the Society for the Advancement of the Colored Race and others may be satisfied with
it for a little while; those who are advocating the bill here
may win favor with them for a little while, but paid lobbyists and representatives of these organized groups are never
quiet; they must be active. They must be busy and when
they have had this work performed, they must get to work
upon another thing.

PICTURES POSIBILITIES [sic.]

"I read the other day that the Negro Representative from
Illinois had introduced a bill to abolish Jim Crow car laws
in the States, to abolish those laws which provide for the
segregation of the races. The next thing in all probability
will be a bill to provide that miscegenation of the races
cannot be prohibited, and when that has been accomplished they will come back here and seek the help of the
majority party in power to take away from the States the
right to say who shall vote in their elections, to say that
every colored man in every Southern State should take part
in the primaries in the State."

Questions

1. On what fears does Harrison play to gain support for opposition to the federal
   antilynching bill?
2. Harrison refers to "primaries" as well as "elections" in his speech. What was the
   importance of Democratic Party primary elections in the South during the 1930s?

Questions for Further Thought

1. Compare the dissenting opinion of Justice Harlan P. Stone in *Butler* (Document
   25-4) with that of Justice Oliver Wendell Holmes Jr. in *Lochner* (Document 20-3).
2. To what extent did Senator Pat Harrison, speaking in 1938, sound notes similar
   to or different from southern Democrats during the 1890s (see text pp. 594–603;
   Document 18-12).

The New Deal's Impact on American Society

New Deal governmental policies would affect the nation for decades, even to the present. The federal government assumed a larger role in the economy, which continued to be based on the private sector, and with it a larger presence in the lives and minds of Americans. Agriculture and labor organizations received lasting recognition; for a time, the creative and performing arts were encouraged by government. A rudimentary welfare state came into existence, and the Democratic Party, which had come to national power during the Great Depression, remained the nation's majority party for more than two decades following the death of FDR (see text pp. 812–827).

A range of groups that contributed to and benefited from the New Deal merit attention in their own right. Women, ethnic and religious minorities, and African Americans came to play larger public roles, some in government, others in private organizations. With Eleanor Roosevelt (Document 25-7) in the White House; Francis Perkins in the cabinet; Mary McLeod Bethune, an African American, in the National Youth Administration; and Genora Johnson Dollinger in the labor movement, women figured in the events of the period (see text pp. 815–816; "American Lives: Mary McLeod Bethune," text pp. 818–819; "American Voices: Genora Johnson Dollinger," text p. 814). Similarly, the government employed Jews and Catholics at a time when the private labor market was tight because of the depression and jobs were frequently closed to them because of prejudice. (See "American Voices: Joe Marcus," text p. 804. On blacks, Mexican Americans, and Native Americans, see text pp. 816–817; "American Lives: Bert Corona," text pp. 792–793.)

Document 25-8 deals with working men and women (Genora Johnson Dollinger among them) during the General Motors sit-down strike in Flint, Michigan, in 1936 and 1937. Document 25-9 offers the reflections of Alfred Kazin, an intellectual who came of age during the 1930s.

25-7   The State's Responsibility for Fair Working Conditions (1933)

Eleanor Roosevelt

Eleanor Roosevelt (1884–1962) brought to the White House her public and organizational experience in reform causes during the 1920s. As wife of the president, she advised him and advocated causes important to her (though not necessarily to him), including youth, women, and African Americans.

Source: "The State's Responsibility for Fair Working Conditions" by Eleanor Roosevelt is reprinted with the permission of Scribner, a Division of Simon & Schuster, from *Scribner's Magazine,* March 1933, 140. Copyright 1933 by Charles Scribner's Sons; copyright renewed © 1961 by Charles Scribner's Sons. In Allida M. Black, ed., *What I Hope to Leave Behind: The Essential Essays of Eleanor Roosevelt* (Brooklyn, N.Y.: Carlson, 1995), 57–58.

No matter how fair employers wish to be, there are always some who will take advantage of times such as these to lower unnecessarily the standards of labor, thereby subjecting him to unfair competition. It is necessary to stress the regulation by law of these unhealthy conditions in industry. It is quite obvious that one cannot depend upon the worker in such times as these to take care of things in the usual way. Many women, particularly, are not unionized and even unions have temporarily lowered their standards in order to keep their people at work. If you face starvation, it is better to accept almost anything than to feel that you and your children are going to be evicted from the last and the cheapest rooms which you have been able to find and that there will be no food.

Cut after cut has been accepted by workers in their wages, they have shared their work by accepting fewer days a week in order that others might be kept on a few days also, until many of them have fallen far below what I would consider the normal and proper standard for healthful living. If the future of our country is to be safe and the next generation is to grow up to healthy and good citizens, it is absolutely necessary to protect the health of our workers now and at all times.

It has been found, for instance, in Germany, in spite of the depression and the difficulty in making wages cover good food, that sickness and mortality rates have been surprisingly low amongst the workers, probably because of the fact that they have not been obliged to work an unhealthy number of hours.

Limiting the number of working hours by law has a twofold result. It spreads the employment, thereby giving more people work, and it protects the health of the work- ers. Instead of keeping a few people working a great many hours and even asking them to share their work with others by working fewer days, it limits all work to a reasonable number of hours and makes it necessary to employ the number of people required to cover the work.

Refusing to allow people to be paid less than a living wage preserves to us our own market. There is absolutely no use in producing anything if you gradually reduce the number of people able to buy even the cheapest products. The only way to preserve our markets is to pay an adequate wage.

It seems to me that all fair-minded people will realize that it is self-preservation to treat the industrial worker with consideration and fairness at the present time and to uphold the fair employer in his efforts to treat his employees well by preventing unfair competition.

Questions

1. What group is Roosevelt attacking?
2. Who is she aligning herself with?
3. What kind of political fallout could such views have for her husband? Should that have been a consideration for her? Why or why not?

25-8   The Sit-Down Strike at General Motors (1937)

Mary Heaton Vorse

The Flint, Michigan, sit-down strike against General Motors was among the most dramatic and significant episodes in American labor history (see text pp. 812–815). Defying court injunctions and police attacks, workers occupied the General Motors plant from December 31, 1936 to February 11, 1937. The strike led to the recognition of the United Automobile Workers by GM and Chrysler, though Ford continued to resist unionization for some time. Journalist Mary Heaton Vorse (1874–1966) here reports on the GM sit-down strike, the men and women involved in it, and labor's day of triumph.

Source: Mary Heaton Vorse, *Labor's New Millions* (New York: Modern Age, 1938; reprint, New York: Ayer, 1969), 76–77, 88–90. Reprinted with permission.

I went down to the Chevrolet plant with two members of the Emergency Brigade. The workers had now captured plant No. 4. The street was full of people—there were about twenty policemen between the bridge and the high gate of the plant. They were quiet and unprovocative, so the crowd of pickets was good-natured. The sound car was directing operations.

The use of the sound truck is new in strike procedure and it is hard to know how a strike was ever conducted without it. As we came down past the policemen a great voice, calm and benign, proclaimed that everything was in hand—the plant was under control.

Next the great disembodied voice, really the voice of auburn-haired young Roy Reuther [a young organizer of the United Automobile Workers], urged the men in the plant to barricade themselves from tear gas. Every now and then the voice boomed:

"Protection squad. Attention! Guard your sound car. Protection squad. Attention!"

Then the voice addressed the workers who crowded

the windows of the lower levels. At the top of the steep flight of steps were the workers of the plant, lunch buckets under their arms, waving at the pickets in the street. A crowd of workers fringed the roof. The sound car inquired if they were union men. They shouted, "Yes." The crowd cheered.

The measured soothing voice of the sound car boomed:

"Word has come to us that there are men in the crowd anxious to join the union. Go to the last car, you will find the cards ready to sign. If you have no money for dues with you you can come to Pengally Hall later." The sound car struck up *Solidarity* and the men at the top of the steps, on top of the plant, in the street, all sang.

A woman's voice next—Genora Johnson [organizer of the Women's Emergency Brigade]. She told the crowd that the women had gone to the Hall to wipe their eyes clear of tear gas and would soon be back. "We don't want any violence; we don't want any trouble. We are going to do everything we can to keep from trouble, but we are going to protect our husbands."

Down the hill presently came a procession, preceded by an American flag. The women's bright red caps showed dramatically in the dark crowd. They were singing, *Hold the Fort*.

To all the crowd there was something moving about seeing the women return to the picket line after having been gassed in front of plant No. 9. A cheer went up; the crowd took up the song. The line of bright-capped women spread itself out in front of the high gate. Clasping hands, they struck up the song, *We Shall Not Be Moved*. Some of the men who had jumped over the gate went back, amid the cheers of the crowd.

I went to the top of the little hill and a file of men were coming out of the back of the building.

"Are you going home?"

"Home—Hell no! We're going back to picket the plant. Half of us are sitting down inside, and half of us are coming out to picket from the street."

"How many of you are for the sit-down?"

"Ninety per cent," a group of them chorused.

What happened that day [the day the workers left in victory—February 11, 1937] in Flint was something that no one who ever saw it could possibly forget. Never since Armistice Day has anything been seen comparable to its intensity. A mighty emotion shook the working people of that town. Joy and freedom dominated Flint's commonplace streets.

It was as if Flint had been under a spell for a long time, perhaps always. Fear and suspicion had walked through Flint's streets. People didn't dare to join unions. They'd get fired, they'd lose their jobs. Your next door neighbor might be a spy. No one knew who the stool pigeons were. The people who had got used to living that way didn't know how maimed they were.

General Motors had come into Flint and made a city out of a crossroads. General Motors had dominated the town. It had ruled its political life and it had set its face against unions. Men had organized on their peril. Unions were kept out by fear. And now that fear was over. No wonder that the people marching in the line stretched out their hands to their friends on the sidewalk and said:

"You can join now, you can join now, we are free!"

Freedom to join your own union seems a little thing. But one has to live in a town dominated by a great industry to see how far off a union can seem and how powerful the industry.

Now General Motors had bargained with the union officials. The long days of suspended violence were over. Here was the antithesis of a mob: the gathering together of people to express a great emotion. Such gathering together is at the very basis of civilization. It is the intensification of the individual, the raising of his power for good to a thousandth degree.

No one in that crowd remained isolated. People's small personalities were lost in this great Halleluiah.

When the men from Fisher No. 1 had accepted the agreement they marched in a parade to the plants at the other end of the town which were still guarded by the militia. The barrier of soldiers drew aside.

The crowd with flags marched cheering into the guarded zone.

The strikers were coming out of Chevrolet No. 4, flags preceding them. There were flags on the steps and flags on the street. Flares lighted up the scene. Cheers for Governor Murphy[1] filled the air. Strikers' wives were waving to husbands they had not seen for days. A woman held up a baby. The procession marched down the street. Another roar filled all space.

The Fisher No. 2 boys marched out. They marched out in military formation from the quiet of the empty, waiting plant, carrying neat bundles of their things. They became part of the crowd that was now bright with confetti. People carried toy balloons. The whole scene was lit up by the burst of glory of the photographers' flares. The big flags punctuated the crowd with color.

They shouted to the rhythm of "Freedom, Freedom, Freedom!"

Chevrolet Avenue was packed from bridge to bridge. People swarmed over the murky little Flint River with its new barbed wire fences. They came past Chevrolet No. 4 and they came up the street past Fisher No. 2. They came, flags at their head, singing. They marched from the plants back to union headquarters. The streets were lined all the way with cheering people. Men and women from the cars and marchers shouted to the groups of other working people who lined the streets, "Join the union! We are free!"

---

[1]*Governor Frank Murphy*, a Democrat, risked his political career by refusing to employ the National Guard to force the sit-down strikers to evacuate the plants.

The marchers arrived in front of Pengally Hall. They gathered in increasing thousands. The hall itself was jammed. They no longer let people into the building. Inside and outside, the loud speakers were going. Homer Martin, Wyndham Mortimer, Bob Travis and the other strike leaders addressed the roaring crowds.

The joy of victory tore through Flint. It was more than the joy of war ceasing, it was the joy of creation. The workers were creating a new life. The wind of Freedom had roared down Flint's streets. The strike had ended! The working people of Flint had begun to forge a new life out of their historic victory.

Questions

1. According to Vorse, why had Flint's workers remained nonunionized for so many years?
2. Which tactics brought victory to the union? What strikes you about the male and female participants?
3. Why does Vorse compare the emotions of the workers after winning the strike to those on Armistice Day (the day on which the Great War ended)?

25-9 Starting Out in the Thirties (1936–1939)

Alfred Kazin

Alfred Kazin (1915–1998) grew up in New York City during the depression. He supported himself through a variety of literary odd jobs, including working for *The New Republic*. The excerpt that follows, from Kazin's memoir, *Starting Out in the Thirties* (1965), suggests how radical political idealism gave way to disillusionment among many intellectuals when Soviet Russia negotiated a nonaggression pact with Nazi Germany (see text pp. 822–824, 829).

Source: Alfred Kazin, *Starting Out in the Thirties* (Boston: Little, Brown, 1965), 82–87, 138–139. Reprinted with permission.

[1936]

History was going our way, and in our need was the very lifeblood of history. Everything in the outside world seemed to be moving toward some final decision, for by now the Spanish Civil War had begun, and every day felt choked with struggle. It was as if the planet had locked in combat. In the same way the unrest and unemployment, the political struggles inside the New Deal, suddenly became part of the single pattern of struggle in Europe against Franco and his allies Hitler and Mussolini, so I sensed that I could become a writer without giving up my people. The unmistakable and surging march of history might yet pass through me. There seemed to be no division between my effort at personal liberation and the apparent effort of humanity to deliver itself. Reading [Italian Communist novelist Ignazio] Silone and [French novelist André] Malraux, discovering the Beethoven string quartets and having love affairs were part of the great pattern in Spain, in Nazi concentration camps, in Fontamars and in the Valley of the Ebro, in the Salinas Valley of California that Steinbeck was describing with love for the oppressed,

in the boilers of Chinese locomotives where Chiang Kai-shek was burning the brave and sacrificial militants of the Chinese Communists. Wherever I went now, I felt the moral contagion of a single idea. . . .

More than twenty years later, I was to hear young intellectuals in Moscow laugh at the show trials of the Thirties, and in their proud American English dismiss them as "phonies." The Moscow airfield was lined with gleaming white jets, and the young intellectuals born in 1936 now know all about Stalin. But in 1936 the issue was not quite so simple even for those who knew that the trials were *wrong*. The danger was Hitler, Mussolini, Franco. And because the Fascist assault on Spain and the ever-growing strength of Hitler had made the United Front necessary, I found myself more sympathetic to the Communists. They had, they had just had, they still seemed to have, Silone, Malraux, Hemingway, Gide, [Romain] Rolland, Gorky, [Louis] Aragon, Picasso, [Paul] Eluard, Auden, Spender, Barbusse, Dreiser, [James T.] Farrell, while the Socialists seemed to have only their own virtue. I was tired of virtue, and now wanted to see some action. In the midst of the violent labor unrest in France, the great sitdown strikes in American factories, the beginnings of the CIO, everything at home and abroad seemed to call for the same revolutionary energy. On Inaugural Day 1937, I went down to Washington to do an article on the great day, and though that morning of rain the flags flapped wetly against the posts and the streets seemed strangely empty, there, in the back of the car as it came out of the White House drive, was the fixedly smiling face that presided over our generation, and standing in the rain we cheered our President and all our own hopes. Like all my friends, I distrusted Roosevelt as a wily politician and a professional charmer. Who was he behind that ever-smiling public face, and what reason did *he* have to care? But I could almost believe in him now, there was so much need of him to do the right thing. FDR's historical function was destined; everybody's was. Not even the hack jobs I did for a living now seemed unworthy, for the issue raised in a book review, a street scene studied for an article, always fitted into my sense of the destiny and inclusiveness of history. So my parents' poverty had a mystique for me, and our loneliness a definite heroism—we were usually unhappy and always on each other's necks, but I saw us all moving forward on the sweep of great events. I believed that everyone was engulfed in politics, absorbed in issues that were the noble part of themselves. Despite the daily anxiety of trying to get a push up the inhumanly smooth wall of other people's jobs, I felt, with the outbreak of the Spanish Civil War, that the outrage of Franco, Mussolini and Hitler working together was a challenge, not a defeat; I trusted to the righteousness of history. Just as I was trying to break through, so history was seeking its appointed consummation. My interest and the genius of history simply had to coincide. It did not matter how deceitful and murderous Stalin was showing himself to be in the purges; the Soviet Union, a "workers' state" stained only with the unaccountable sins of its leadership, still represented the irreversible movement of human progress. Even Hitler, by his total infamy, obviously represented a *deliberate* attempt to put the clock back; believing that the Jews, and especially Jewish intellectuals, had a mission to humanity, I never wondered why Jewish intellectuals particularly were hated by the Nazis. We were a moral ferment; easy to kill off, but an unsettling influence. Hitler destroyed German democracy, Dollfuss the Austrian Socialists, Franco was destroying the Spanish Republic and Mussolini thousands of Ethiopians: the daily onrush of events fitted so easily into a general pattern of meaning, seemingly supplied by the age itself, that every day was like a smoothly rushing movie of the time—and I loved newsreels, the documentary novels of Dos Passos with their own newsreels, documentary movies, especially now that in tribute to the emergency of the times there were movie houses in Times Square that showed nothing but newsreels. I was as excited by history as if it were a newsreel, and I saw history in every newsreel, my love and hatred of the historical actors rising to the music on the sound track like a swimmer to the surf. . . .

[1938, 1939]

I could not believe that Fascism was anything but a temporary aberration; given a fair chance, the people under Nazi rule and Fascist rule would get rid of their oppressors and give themselves to the historical destiny so clearly forseen by liberals and socialists in the nineteenth century. When a classmate of mine just back from the front told me of the massacre by the GPU in Barcelona of Anarchists and anti-Stalinist Communists, I was reluctant to believe him. Although, after years of writing for Cowley at the *New Republic,* I liked him as little as ever and resented his protective benevolence toward "proletarian" literature, which I despised, I shared his feeling that Fascism was the main enemy and I feared any division on the left that might limit maximum resistance to Franco and Hitler. As an influence in literature, the Communists seemed to me idiotic; even Party members now made a point of laughing at the obtuseness of the professional Communist critics. My teaching in the evening session at City College became wearisome as the faithful in my classes resisted every example of free thought, of literary originality. In giving a course on modern fiction, I found to my disgust that half the class refused to read anything by H. G. Wells—he was a "bourgeois liberal." The arrogant stupidity of Communist instructors at this time passed beyond anything I had ever known before. The college *Führer* of the Party was an English instructor with a bad stammer, large spectacles, and a little beard; his middle name was Ulysses, and as he horribly choked out each word in a pronunciamento on the relation of *The Canterbury Tales* to the wool trade in fourteenth-century England, his bearded chin would quiver with agony and his weak frightened eyes would stare up at you while obstinately he ground out the literary law. And one day, when I was offered an editor's job in Washington with the WPA Writers' Project, I went down for my interview in the New York office, somewhere along the waterfront, to enter a room crowded with men and women lying face down on the floor, screaming that they were on strike. In order to get to the supervisor's office at the other end of the hall, I had to make my way over bodies stacked as if after a battle; and as I sat in the supervisor's office, he calmly discussed the job while shouts and screams came from the long hall outside. I made my way out again between and over the bodies.

It was the summer of 1939 now. After Hitler's seizure of Czechoslovakia in March, it still seemed to me inconceivable that Russia would not come out against Hitler, and in August, when English and French military missions arrived in Moscow, I took it for granted that some agreement would be made, since of course the Soviet Union wanted peace. On the morning of August 22, I was working happily away at my book and had interrupted myself at noon for a cup of coffee and the news broadcast when it was announced that Ribbentrop [the German minister] was flying to Moscow to sign a non-aggression pact with Stalin the next day, and that the Swastika was already flying over Moscow airport. "No!" I shouted at the radio. "It's not true!" The announcer calmly went on giving the details. . . .

Questions

1. What does Kazin mean when he writes about the "moral contagion of a single idea"?
2. Why does Kazin "love" the newsreels of the 1930s?
3. Why was the Nazi-Soviet pact of August 1939 so shocking to Kazin?

Questions for Further Thought

1. Drawing on the text and the documents for Chapter 25, compare and contrast the roles of women, African Americans, Mexican Americans, and Native Americans in government and the private sector during the New Deal and the effects of government policies on these groups.
2. The supporters of the New Deal were a political coalition that included industrial workers, professionals, and intellectuals. Why did the New Deal appeal to so varied a coalition? What problems were likely to strain the coalition?

America and an Insecure World Peace

Although the United States sought to increase foreign trade during the Great Depression, isolationism—an aversion to international involvements that ran the risk of war—ran deep in the nation and found expression in Congress (see text pp. 827–829). But even as the Roosevelt administration confronted stormy domestic economic and political situations during 1937 and 1938, it had to take into account darkening international skies—civil war (with foreign involvement) in Spain, an openly rearming Nazi Germany, and, particularly, Japanese aggression in China.

Document 25-10 is a powerful isolationist cartoon from 1936. Document 25-11 excerpts President Roosevelt's "Quarantine" speech of the following year.

25-10   Editorial Cartoon in the *New York Daily News* (1936)

C. D. Batchelor

C. D. Batchelor's editorial cartoon earned him a Pulitzer Prize in 1937. The *New York Daily News,* for which Batchelor drew, was a highly successful tabloid newspaper during the period. The billboard on the wall reads "Follies of 1936" and lists European heads of state in the cast.

"COME ON IN. I'LL TREAT YOU RIGHT.
I USED TO KNOW YOUR DADDY."

BATCHELOR, NEW YORK *DAILY NEWS*

Source: New York Daily News, 1936, reprinted with permission in Walter LaFeber, *The American Age: United States Foreign Policy at Home and Abroad,* 2nd ed. (New York and London: W. W. Norton, 1994), 384.

Questions

1. What significance do you attach to the depiction of war as a female and a prostitute?
2. To whom does the woman refer when she speaks of the youth's "daddy"?

25-11   Quarantine Speech (1937)

Franklin D. Roosevelt

President Roosevelt spoke on October 5, 1937, in Chicago, located in the heart of the isolationist Midwest and home of the influential *Chicago Tribune,* a newspaper hostile to both the New Deal and internationalism (see text pp. 827–829). At the time, Japan alone the among major powers was at war—with China. The submarine attacks to which FDR refers were mounted by unidentified (German and Italian) U–boats off Spain during that nation's civil war.

Source: Samuel I. Rosenman, ed., *The Public Papers and Addresses of Franklin D. Roosevelt, 1937* (New York: Macmillan, 1941), 406–411.

SPEECH AT CHICAGO

October 5, 1937

. . . On my trip across the continent and back. . . . I have seen with my own eyes the prosperous farms, the thriving factories, and the busy railroads, as I have seen the happiness and security and peace which covers our wide land, [and] almost inevitably I have been compelled to contrast our peace with very different scenes being enacted in other parts of the world.

It is because the people of the United States under modern conditions must, for the sake of their own future, give thought to the rest of the world, that I, as the responsible executive head of the nation, have chosen this great inland city . . . to speak to you on a subject of definite national importance.

The political situation in the world, which of late has been growing progressively worse, is such as to cause grave concern and anxiety to all the peoples and nations who wish to live in peace and amity with their neighbors.

Some fifteen years ago the hopes of mankind for a continuing era of international peace were raised to great heights when more than sixty nations solemnly pledged themselves not to resort to arms in furtherance of their national aims and policies. The high aspirations expressed in the Briand-Kellogg Peace Pact, and the hopes for peace thus raised, have of late given way to a haunting fear of calamity. The present reign of terror and international lawlessness began a few years ago.

It began through unjustified interference in the internal affairs of other nations or the invasion of alien territory in violation of treaties; and has now reached a stage where the very foundations of civilization are seriously threatened. The landmarks and traditions which have marked the progress of civilization toward a condition of law, order, and justice are being wiped away.

Without a declaration of war, and without warning or justification of any kind, civilians, including vast numbers of women and children, are being ruthlessly murdered with bombs from the air. In times of so-called peace, ships are being attacked and sunk by submarines without cause or notice. Nations are fomenting and taking sides in civil warfare in nations that have never done them any harm. Nations claiming freedom for themselves deny it to others.

Innocent peoples, innocent nations, are being cruelly sacrificed to a greed for power and supremacy which is devoid of all sense of justice and humane considerations. . . .

If those things come to pass in other parts of the world, let no one imagine that America will escape, that America may expect mercy, that this Western Hemisphere will not be attacked, and that it will continue tranquilly and peacefully to carry on the ethics and the arts of civilization. . . . if we are to have a world in which we can breathe freely and live in amity without fear—the peace-loving nations must make a concerted effort to uphold laws and principles on which alone peace can rest secure.

The peace-loving nations must make a concerted effort in opposition to those violations of treaties and those ignorings of humane instincts which today are creating a state of international anarchy and instability from which there is no escape through mere isolation or neutrality.

Those who cherish their freedom and recognize and respect the equal right of their neighbors to be free and live in peace must work together for the triumph of law and moral principles in order that peace, justice, and confidence may prevail in the world. There must be a return to a belief in the pledged word, in the value of a signed treaty. There must be recognition of the fact that national morality is as vital as private morality. . . .

There is a solidarity and interdependence about the modern world, both technically and morally, which makes it impossible for any nation completely to isolate itself from economic and political upheavals in the rest of the world, especially when such upheavals appear to be spreading and not declining. There can be no stability or peace either within nations or between nations except under laws and moral standards adhered to by all. International anarchy destroys every foundation for peace. It jeopardizes either the immediate or the future security of every nation, large or small. It is, therefore, a matter of vital interest and concern to the people of the United States that the sanctity of international treaties and the maintenance of international morality be restored.

The overwhelming majority of the peoples and nations of the world today want to live in peace. They seek the removal of barriers against trade. They want to exert themselves in industry, in agriculture, and in business that they may increase their wealth through the production of wealth-producing goods rather than striving to produce military planes and bombs and machine guns and cannon for the destruction of human lives and useful property.

In those nations of the world which seem to be piling armament on armament for purposes of aggression, and those other nations which fear acts of aggression against them and their security, a very high proportion of their national income is being spent directly for armaments. It runs from thirty to as high as fifty per cent. We are fortunate. The proportion that we in the United States spend is far less—eleven or twelve per cent. . . .

I am compelled and you are compelled . . . to look ahead. The peace, the freedom, and the security of ninety per cent of the population of the world is being jeopardized by the remaining ten per cent who are threatening a breakdown of all international order and law. Surely the ninety per cent who want to live in peace under law and in accordance with moral standards that have received almost universal acceptance through the centuries can and must find some way to make their will prevail.

The situation is definitely of universal concern. The questions involved relate not merely to violations of specific provisions of particular treaties; they are questions of war and of peace, of international law and especially of principles of humanity. It is true that they involve definite violations of agreements, and especially of the Covenant of the League of Nations, the Briand-Kellogg Pact, and the Nine Power Treaty. But they also involve problems of world economy, world security, and world humanity.

It is true that the moral consciousness of the world must recognize the importance of removing injustices and well-founded grievances; but at the same time it must be aroused to the cardinal necessity of honoring sanctity of treaties, of respecting the rights and liberties of others, and of putting an end to acts of international aggression.

It seems to be unfortunately true that the epidemic of world lawlessness is spreading.

When an epidemic of physical disease starts to spread, the community approves and joins in a quarantine of the patients in order to protect the health of the community against the spread of the disease.

It is my determination to pursue a policy of peace. It is my determination to adopt every practicable measure to avoid involvement in war. It ought to be inconceivable that in this modern era, and in the face of experience, any nation could be so foolish and ruthless as to run the risk of plunging the whole world into war by invading and violating, in contravention of solemn treaties, the territory of other nations that have done them no real harm and are too weak to protect themselves adequately. Yet the peace of the world and the welfare and security of every nation, including our own, is today being threatened by that very thing.

No nation which refuses to exercise forbearance and to respect the freedom and rights of others can long remain strong and retain the confidence and respect of other nations. No nation ever loses its dignity or its good standing by conciliating its differences, and by exercising great patience with, and consideration for, the rights of other nations.

War is a contagion, whether it be declared or undeclared. It can engulf states and peoples remote from the original scene of hostilities. We are determined to keep out of war, yet we cannot insure ourselves against the disastrous effects of war and the dangers of involvement. We are adopting such measures as will minimize our risk of involvement, but we cannot have complete protection in a world of disorder in which confidence and security have broken down.

If civilization is to survive, the principles of the Prince of Peace must be restored. Trust between nations must be revived.

Most important of all, the will for peace on the part of peace-loving nations must express itself to the end that nations that may be tempted to violate their agreements and the rights of others will desist from such a course. There must be positive endeavors to preserve peace.

America hates war. America hopes for peace. Therefore, America actively engages in the search for peace.

Questions

1. Which world events convinced Roosevelt that peace was in jeopardy and that the United States should feel threatened?
2. What specific benefits could the United States and other nations expect to enjoy in a world where peace reigned?
3. What specific steps (if any) does Roosevelt propose to take to preserve peace?

Questions for Further Thought

1. Franklin Roosevelt had served in the administration of President Woodrow Wilson. Does his "Quarantine" speech echo Wilsonianism in any respects? In addressing this question, review Chapter 22 and Documents 22-2 and 22-13.
2. The *London Times* said of Roosevelt and the "Quarantine" speech that he "was defining an *attitude* and not a *program*" (emphasis added). What did the *Times* mean by so characterizing this speech?

CHAPTER 26

The World at War, 1939–1945

★   ★   ★

American Neutrality, 1939–1941

World War II began on September 3, 1939, when Germany invaded Poland; Great Britain and France declared war on Germany two days later. Japan of course, had been at war with China since 1937. For the time being Italy, the Soviet Union, and the United States remained out of the European war. The Roosevelt administration and the American public favored both the Allies and America's nonparticipation in the conflict.

Germany's smashing victory over France and accompanying developments during June 1940 dramatically changed the international situation. Germany was paramount in Europe; Italy had joined the war on Germany's side; and the Soviet Union continued to assist Germany, as it had since the August 1939 German-Soviet pact. Great Britain stood alone and on the defensive, and the Asian colonies of France, the Netherlands (also overrun by the Germans), and Great Britain were more vulnerable than ever to the Japanese, who continued their war against the Chinese.

Alarmed by the implications of the altered international equation following France's defeat, in 1940 and 1941 the Roosevelt administration moved to assist Great Britain by various means short of war—exchanging American destroyers for leases on British military bases in the Western Hemisphere (1940) and securing congressional passage of the Lend-Lease Act, which authorized shipment of war matériel to nations deemed vital to American security (1941). Administration policy touched off heated public debate in the United States. Meanwhile, during 1940, the president added two supportive Republicans to his Cabinet: Henry Stimson, former secretary of war (under Taft) and secretary of state (under Hoover), as secretary of war, and Frank Knox, the GOP vice-presidential candidate in 1936, as secretary of the Navy. In the same year, Congress authorized sharply increased spending to enlarge and modernize the American military and provided the first peacetime draft in the nation's history.

America's new stance, and their own ambitions, led Japan, Germany, and Italy to draw closer together. In June 1941, Germany and its European allies suddenly invaded the Soviet Union. They had three motivations: to secure *lebensraum* (territory deemed essential to the future well-being of Nazi Germany), to destroy a Communist state, and to deprive embattled Great Britain of its only possible future European ally. That August, Prime Minister Winston Churchill of Great Britain and President Franklin D. Roosevelt issued the Atlantic Charter. By autumn, the United States and Germany were waging an undeclared Atlantic war, which neither side moved to escalate. Meanwhile, Japan decided to seize the European colonial empires in the Far East, which were rich in vital natural resources, above all petroleum in the Dutch East Indies (now Indonesia). To do so without American interference, Japan attacked the U.S. Pacific fleet at Pearl Harbor early in the morning of December 7. The United States declared war on Japan, and when Germany and Italy declared war on the U.S. in response, the United States reciprocated. What had begun as wars in East Asia and Europe was now truly a world war (see text pp. 833–837).

Two documents present the pro-involvement arguments of President Roosevelt: his Fireside Chat on the "Great Arsenal of Democracy" (Document 26-1) and his "Four Freedoms" speech (Document 26-2). Documents 26-3 and 26-4 offer the opinions of two opponents of Roosevelt's foreign policy, Charles A. Lindbergh and Senator Burton K. Wheeler. Document 26-5 is the Atlantic Charter of President Roosevelt and Prime Minister Churchill.

26-1   Fireside Chat on the Great Arsenal of Democracy (1940)

Franklin D. Roosevelt

During late 1939, President Roosevelt (1882–1945) persuaded Congress to repeal the arms embargo of earlier neutrality legislation. Belligerents could now purchase weapons from American manufacturers on a strict cash-and-carry basis—as the Neutrality Act of 1937 had allowed for other goods. This step, which favored Britain and France, touched off debate in the United States (see text pp. 827, 834–835).

By December 29, 1940, when the president delivered this Fireside Chat, France had long since fallen, Great Britain had survived the aerial Battle of Britain, and Greece was (as FDR notes) resisting an Italian invasion. Twelve days earlier, during a press conference, Roosevelt had strongly advocated the policy that would be embodied in the Lend-Lease Act (see text pp. 835–836).

Source: Samuel I. Rosenman, ed., *The Public Papers and Addresses of Franklin D. Roosevelt, 1940* (New York: Macmillan, 1941), 633–644.

Never before since Jamestown and Plymouth Rock has our American civilization been in such danger as now.

For, on September 27, 1940, by an agreement signed in Berlin, three powerful nations, two in Europe and one in Asia, joined themselves together in the threat that if the United States of America interfered with or blocked the expansion program of these three nations—a program aimed at world control—they would unite in ultimate action against the United States.

The Nazi masters of Germany have made it clear that they intend not only to dominate all life and thought in their own country, but also to enslave the whole of Europe,

and then to use the resources of Europe to dominate the rest of the world. . . .

Some of our people like to believe that wars in Asia and in Europe are of no concern to us. But it is a matter of most vital concern to us that European and Asiatic warmakers should not gain control of the oceans which lead to this hemisphere. . . .

Does anyone seriously believe that we need to fear attack anywhere in the Americas while a free Britain remains our most powerful naval neighbor in the Atlantic? Does anyone seriously believe, on the other hand, that we could rest easy if the Axis powers were our neighbors there?

If Great Britain goes down, the Axis powers will control the continents of Europe, Asia, Africa, Australia, and the high seas—and they will be in a position to bring enormous military and naval resources against this hemisphere. It is no exaggeration to say that all of us, in all the Americas, would be living at the point of a gun—a gun loaded with explosive bullets, economic as well as military.

We should enter upon a new and terrible era in which the whole world, our hemisphere included, would be run by threats of brute force. To survive in such a world, we would have to convert ourselves permanently into a militaristic power on the basis of war economy.

Some of us like to believe that even if Great Britain falls, we are still safe, because of the broad expanse of the Atlantic and of the Pacific.

But the width of those oceans is not what it was in the days of clipper ships. At one point between Africa and Brazil the distance is less than from Washington to Denver, Colorado—five hours for the latest type of bomber. And at the North end of the Pacific Ocean America and Asia almost touch each other. . . .

There are those who say that the Axis powers would never have any desire to attack the Western Hemisphere. That is the same dangerous form of wishful thinking which has destroyed the powers of resistance of so many conquered peoples. The plain facts are that the Nazis have proclaimed, time and again, that all other races are their inferiors and therefore subject to their orders. And most important of all, the vast resources and wealth of this American Hemisphere constitute the most tempting loot in all the round world. . . .

The experience of the past two years has proven beyond doubt that no nation can appease the Nazis. . . . There can be no appeasement with ruthlessness. There can be no reasoning with an incendiary bomb. We know now that a nation can have peace with the Nazis only at the price of total surrender. . . .

The history of recent years proves that shootings and chains and concentration camps are not simply the transient tools but the very altars of modern dictatorships. They may talk of a "new order" in the world, but what they have in mind is only a revival of the oldest and the worst tyranny. In that there is no liberty, no religion, no hope.

The proposed "new order" is the very opposite of a United States of Europe or a United States of Asia. It is not a Government based upon the consent of the governed. It is not a union of ordinary, self-respecting men and women to protect themselves and their freedom and their dignity from oppression. It is an unholy alliance of power and pelf to dominate and enslave the human race.

The British people and their allies today are conducting an active war against this unholy alliance. Our own future security is greatly dependent on the outcome of that fight. Our ability to "keep out of war" is going to be affected by that outcome.

Thinking in terms of today and tomorrow, I make the direct statement to the American people that there is far less chance of the United States getting into war, if we do all we can now to support the nations defending themselves against attack by the Axis than if we acquiesce in their defeat, submit tamely to an Axis victory, and wait our turn to be the object of attack in another war later on.

If we are to be completely honest with ourselves, we must admit that there is risk in any course we may take. But I deeply believe that the great majority of our people agree that the course that I advocate involves the least risk now and the greatest hope for world peace in the future.

The people of Europe who are defending themselves do not ask us to do their fighting. They ask us for the implements of war . . . which will enable them to fight for their liberty and for our security. Emphatically we must get these weapons to them in sufficient volume and quickly enough, so that we and our children will be saved the agony and suffering of war which others have had to endure. . . .

We must be the great arsenal of democracy. For us this is an emergency as serious as war itself. We must apply ourselves to our task with the same resolution, the same sense of urgency, the same spirit of patriotism and sacrifice as we would show were we at war.

We have furnished the British great material support and we will furnish far more in the future.

There will be no "bottlenecks" in our determination to aid Great Britain. No dictator, no combination of dictators, will weaken that determination by threats of how they will construe that determination.

The British have received invaluable military support from the heroic Greek army, and from the forces of all the governments in exile. Their strength is growing. It is the strength of men and women who value their freedom more highly than they value their lives.

Questions

1. According to Roosevelt, how have events in Europe and Asia threatened American interests?
2. How does Roosevelt describe Great Britain's role in the international conflict?
3. What actions does Roosevelt propose?

26-2   Four Freedoms Speech (1941)

Franklin D. Roosevelt   President Roosevelt stated his opposition to isolationism more strongly than ever in his State of the Union message to Congress. In this speech, he tied Lend-Lease and other international initiatives to his agenda for domestic politics. His concluding paragraphs on the "four freedoms" soon became the most famous rationale for American participation in the war (see text pp. 835–836).

Source: Samuel I. Rosenman, ed., *The Public Papers and Addresses of Franklin D. Roosevelt, 1940* (New York: Macmillan, 1941), 663–672.

I address you, the Members of the Seventy-Seventh Congress, at a moment unprecedented in the history of the Union. I use the word "unprecedented," because at no previous time has American security been as seriously threatened from without as it is today. . . .

It is true that prior to 1914 the United States often had been disturbed by events in other Continents. We had even engaged in two wars with European nations and in a number of undeclared wars in the West Indies, in the Mediterranean and in the Pacific for the maintenance of American rights and for the principles of peaceful commerce. In no case, however, had a serious threat been raised against our national safety or our independence.

What I seek to convey is the historic truth that the United States as a nation has at all times maintained opposition to any attempt to lock us in behind an ancient Chinese wall while the procession of civilization went past. Today, thinking of our children and their children, we oppose enforced isolation for ourselves or for any part of the Americas.

Even when the World War broke out in 1914, it seemed to contain only small threat of danger to our own American future. But, as time went on, the American people began to visualize what the downfall of democratic nations might mean to our own democracy.

We need not over-emphasize imperfections in the Peace of Versailles. We need not harp on failure of the democracies to deal with problems of world deconstruction. We should remember that the Peace of 1919 was far less unjust than the kind of "pacification" which began even before Munich, and which is being carried on under the new order of tyranny that seeks to spread over every continent today. The American people have unalterably set their faces against that tyranny.

Every realist knows that the democratic way of life is at this moment being directly assailed in every part of the world—assailed either by arms, or by secret spreading of poisonous propaganda by those who seek to destroy unity and promote discord in nations still at peace. During sixteen months this assault has blotted out the whole pattern of democratic life in an appalling number of independent nations, great and small. The assailants are still on the march, threatening other nations, great and small.

Therefore, as your President, performing my constitutional duty to "give to the Congress information of the state of the Union," I find it necessary to report that the future and the safety of our country and of our democracy are overwhelmingly involved in events far beyond our borders.

Armed defense of democratic existence is now being gallantly waged in four continents. If that defense fails, all the population and all the resources of Europe, Asia, Africa and Australasia will be dominated by the conquerors. The total of those populations and their resources greatly exceeds the sum total of the population and resources of the whole of the Western Hemisphere—many times over.

In times like these it is immature—and incidentally untrue—for anybody to brag that an unprepared America, single-handed, and with one hand tied behind its back, can hold off the whole world. . . .

A free nation has the right to expect full cooperation from all groups. A free nation has the right to look to the leaders of business, of labor, and of agriculture to take the lead in stimulating effort, not among other groups but within their own groups. The best way of dealing with the few slackers or trouble makers in our midst is, first, to shame them by patriotic example, and, if that fails, to use the sovereignty of government to save government.

As men do not live by bread alone, they do not fight by armaments alone. Those who man our defenses, and those behind them who build our defenses, must have the stamina and courage which come from an unshakable belief in the manner of life which they are defending. The mighty action which we are calling for cannot be based on a disregard of all things worth fighting for.

The Nation takes great satisfaction and much strength from the things which have been done to make its people conscious of their individual stake in the preservation of democratic life in America. Those things have toughened the fibre of our people, have renewed their faith and strengthened their devotion to the institutions we make ready to protect. Certainly this is no time to stop thinking about the social and economic problems which are the root cause of the social revolution which is today a supreme factor in the world.

There is nothing mysterious about the foundations of a healthy and strong democracy. The basic things expected by our people of their political and economic systems are simple. They are: equality of opportunity for youth and for others; jobs for those who can work; security for those who need it; the ending of special privilege for the few; the preservation of civil liberties for all; the enjoyment of the fruits of scientific progress in a wider and constantly rising standard of living.

These are the simple and basic things that must never be lost sight of in the turmoil and unbelievable complexity of our modern world. The inner and abiding strength of our economic and political systems is dependent upon the degree to which they fulfill these expectations.

Many subjects connected with our social economy call for immediate improvement. As examples: We should bring more citizens under the coverage of old age pensions and unemployment insurance. We should widen the opportunities for adequate medical care. We should plan a better system by which persons deserving or needing gainful employment may obtain it.

I have called for personal sacrifice. I am assured of the willingness of almost all Americans to respond to that call. . . .

In the future days, which we seek to make secure, we look forward to a world founded upon four essential human freedoms.

The first is freedom of speech and expression—everywhere in the world.

The second is freedom of every person to worship God in his own way—everywhere in the world.

The third is freedom from want—which, translated into world terms, means economic understandings which will secure to every nation a healthy peace time life for its inhabitants—everywhere in the world.

The fourth is freedom from fear—which, translated into world terms, means a world-wide reduction of armaments to such a point and in such a thorough fashion that no nation will be in a position to commit an act of physical aggression against any neighbor—anywhere in the world.

That is no vision of a distant millennium. It is a definite basis for a kind of world attainable in our own time and generation. That kind of world is the very antithesis of the so-called new order of tyranny which the dictators seek to create with the crash of a bomb.

To that new order we oppose the greater conception—the moral order. A good society is able to face schemes of world domination and foreign revolutions alike without fear.

Since the beginning of our American history we have been engaged in change—in a perpetual peaceful revolution—a revolution which goes on steadily, quietly adjusting itself to changing conditions—without the concentration camp or the quick-lime in the ditch. The world order which we seek is the cooperation of free countries, working together in a friendly, civilized society.

This nation has placed its destiny in the hands and heads and hearts of its millions of free men and women; and its faith in freedom under the guidance of God. Freedom means the supremacy of human rights everywhere. Our support goes to those who struggle to gain those rights or keep them. Our strength is in our unity of purpose.

To that high concept there can be no end save victory.

Questions

1. What "four freedoms" does Roosevelt identify?
2. How does Roosevelt link domestic and foreign concerns in this speech? Why does he link them?
3. How does Roosevelt extend his argument against the principles of the Neutrality Acts and in favor of an internationalist foreign policy?

26-3   Aviation, Geography, and Race (1939)

Charles A. Lindbergh   Charles A. Lindbergh (1902–1974), a major American hero since his epochal 1927 solo aircraft flight from Long Island to Paris, joined the national America First Committee during April 1941 after enactment of Lend-Lease. He had already written, spoken, and testified before Congress for the anti-interventionist cause; his America First speeches generated controversy and prompted an administration campaign to discredit him. (It should also be noted that Lindbergh's father, a Minnesota congressman, had voted against war in 1917.) This selection shows Lindbergh's thinking during the first months of the European war—thinking that influenced his stand from 1939 to 1941.

Source: Charles A. Lindbergh, "Aviation, Geography, and Race," *Reader's Digest,* 35 (November 1939): 64–67.

Aviation has struck a delicately balanced world, a world where stability was already giving way to the pressure of new dynamic forces, a world dominated by a mechanical, materialistic, Western European civilization. Aviation is a product of that civilization, borne on the crest of its conquest, developed by its spirit of adventure, typical of its science, its industry, its outlook. Typical also of its strength and its weakness, its vanity and its self-destruction—man flung upward in the face of God, another Icarus to dominate the sky, and, in turn, to be dominated by it; for eventually the laws of nature determine the success of human effort and measure the value of human inventions in that divinely complicated, mathematically unpredictable, development of life at which Science has shied the name of Evolution.

Aviation seems almost a gift from heaven to those Western nations who were already the leaders of their era, strengthening their leadership, their confidence, their dominance over other peoples. It is a tool specially shaped for Western hands, a scientific art which others only copy in a mediocre fashion, another barrier between the teeming millions of Asia and the Grecian inheritance of Europe—one of those priceless possessions which permit the White race to live at all in a pressing sea of Yellow, Black, and Brown.

But aviation, using it symbolically as well as in its own right, brings two great dangers, one peculiar to our modern civilization, the other older than history. Since aviation is dependent on the intricate organization of life and industry, it carries with it the environmental danger of a people too far separated from the soil and from the sea—the danger of that physical decline which so often goes with a high intellectual development, of that spiritual decline which seems invariably to accompany an industrial life, of that racial decline which follows physical and spiritual mediocrity. . . .

But the other great danger is more easily recognized, because it has occurred again and again through history. It is the ember of war, fanned by every new military weapon, flaming today as it has never flamed before. It is the old internal struggle among a dominant people for power, blind, insatiable, suicidal. Western nations are again at war, a war likely to be more prostrating than any in the past, a war in which the White race is bound to lose, and the others bound to gain, a war which may easily lead our civilization through more Dark Ages if it survives at all. . . .

Military strength has become more dynamic and less tangible. A new alignment of power has taken place, and there is no adequate peacetime measure for its effect on the influence of nations. There seems no way to agree on the rights it brings to some and takes from others. The rights of men within a nation are readjusted in each generation by laws of inheritance—land changes hands as decades pass, fortunes are taxed from one generation to the next, ownership is no more permanent than life. But among nations themselves there is no similar provision to reward virility and penalize decay, no way to reapportion the world's wealth as tides of human character ebb and flow—except by the strength of armies. In the last analysis, military strength is measurable only by its own expenditure, by the prostration of one contender while the other can still stagger on the field—and all about the wolves of lesser stature abide their time to spring on both the warriors.

We, the heirs of European culture, are on the verge of a disastrous war, a war within our own family of nations, a war which will reduce the strength and destroy the treasures of the White race, a war which may even lead to the end of our civilization. And while we stand poised for battle, Oriental guns are turning westward, Asia presses towards us on the Russian border, all foreign races stir restlessly. It is time to turn from our quarrels and to build our White ramparts again. This alliance with foreign races means nothing but death to us. It is our turn to guard our heritage from Mongol and Persian and Moor, before we become engulfed in a limitless foreign sea. Our civilization depends on a united strength among ourselves; on a strength too great for foreign armies to challenge; on a Western Wall of race and arms which can hold back either a Genghis Khan or the infiltration of inferior blood; on an English fleet, a German air force, a French army, an American nation, standing together as guardians of our common heritage, sharing strength, dividing influence.

Our civilization depends on peace among Western nations, and therefore on united strength, for Peace is a virgin who dare not show her face without Strength, her father, for protection. We can have peace and security only so long as we band together to preserve that most priceless possession, our inheritance of European blood, only so long as we guard ourselves against attack by foreign armies and dilution by foreign races.

We need peace to let our best men live to work out those more subtle, but equally dangerous, problems brought by this new environment in which we dwell, to give us time to turn this materialistic trend, to stop prostrating ourselves before this modern Idol of mechanical efficiency, to find means of combining freedom, spirit, and beauty with industrial life—a peace which will bring character, strength, and security back to Western peoples.

With all the world around our borders, let us not commit racial suicide by internal conflict. We must learn from Athens and Sparta before all of Greece is lost.

Questions

1. What dangers to "Western European civilization" concern Lindbergh?
2. What is his thinking regarding race?
3. What policies would Lindbergh likely wish to see the European powers and the United States follow?

26-4   Speech Opposing Lend-Lease (1941)

Senator Burton K. Wheeler

The Lend-Lease bill, designated H.R. 1776, touched off a major national debate, during which Senator Burton K. Wheeler (1882–1975), a Montana Democrat, delivered one of the bitterest speeches against the measure. Wendell Willkie, to whom Wheeler disparagingly refers, had been the head of Commonwealth & Southern, an important electric utilities holding company, and the Republican presidential candidate the previous year. In the end, Lend-Lease passed 60-31 in the Senate, 317-71 in the House.

Source: Congressional Record, 77th Congress, 1st Session, *Appendix,* 87: part 10 (January 12, 1941), A178–A179.

. . . The lend-lease policy, translated into legislative form, stunned a Congress and a nation wholly sympathetic to the cause of Great Britain. The Kaiser's blank check to Austria-Hungary in the first World War was a piker compared to the Roosevelt blank check of World War II. It warranted my worst fears for the future of America, and it definitely stamps the President as war-minded.

The lend-lease-give program is the New Deal's triple A foreign policy; it will plow under every fourth American boy.

Never before have the American people been asked or compelled to give so bounteously and so completely of their tax dollars to any foreign nation. Never before has the Congress of the United States been asked by any President to violate international law. Never before has this Nation resorted to duplicity in the conduct of its foreign affairs. Never before has the United States given to one man the power to strip this Nation of its defenses. Never before has a Congress coldly and flatly been asked to abdicate.

If the American people want a dictatorship—if they want a totalitarian form of government and if they want war—this bill should be steam-rollered through Congress, as is the wont of President Roosevelt.

Approval of this legislation means war, open and complete warfare. I, therefore, ask the American people before they supinely accept it. Was the last World War worth while?

If it were, then we should lend and lease war materials. If it were, then we should lend and lease American boys. President Roosevelt has said we would be repaid by England. We will be. We will be repaid, just as England repaid her war debts of the first World War—repaid those dollars wrung from the sweat of labor and the toil of farmers with cries of "Uncle Shylock." Our boys will be returned—returned in caskets, maybe; returned with bodies maimed; returned with minds warped and twisted by sights of horrors and the scream and shriek of high-powered shells.

Considered on its merits and stripped of its emotional appeal to our sympathies, the lend-lease-give bill is both ruinous and ridiculous. Why should we Americans pay for war materials for Great Britain who still has $7,000,000,000 in credit or collateral in the United States? Thus far England has fully maintained rather than depleted her credits in the United States. The cost of the lend-lease-give program is high in terms of American tax dollars, but it is even higher in terms of our national defense. Now it gives to the President the unlimited power to completely strip our air forces of its every bomber, of its every fighting plane.

It gives to one man—responsible to no one—the power to denude our shores of every warship. It gives to one individual the dictatorial power to strip the American

Army of our every tank, cannon, rifle, or antiaircraft gun. No one would deny that the lend-lease-give bill contains provisions that would enable one man to render the United States defenseless, but they will tell you, "The President would never do it." To this I say, "Why does he ask the power if he does not intend to use it?" Why not, I say, place some check on American donations to a foreign nation?

Is it possible that the farmers of America are willing to sell their birthright for a mess of pottage?

Is it possible that American labor is to be sold down the river in return for a place upon the Defense Commission, or because your labor leaders are entertained at pink teas?

Is it possible that the American people are so gullible that they will permit their representatives in Congress to sit supinely by while an American President demands totalitarian powers—in the name of saving democracy?

I say in the kind of language used by the President— shame on those who ask the powers—and shame on those who would grant them.

You people who oppose war and dictatorship, do not be dismayed because the war-mongers and interventionists control most of the avenues of propaganda, including the motion-picture industry.

Do not be dismayed because Mr. Willkie, of the Commonwealth & Southern, agrees with Mr. Roosevelt. This merely puts all the economic and foreign "royalists" on the side of war.

Remember, the interventionists control the money bags, but you control the votes. . . .

Questions

1. What criticisms of President Roosevelt and Lend-Lease does Wheeler voice?
2. For whom does Wheeler claim to speak?
3. How does Wheeler characterize supporters of FDR's policy? What do you make of his characterizations of friends and foes?

26-5   The Atlantic Charter (1941)

Following their initial conference, off Newfoundland, President Roosevelt and Prime Minister Churchill issued the Atlantic Charter (August 14, 1941), a joint statement of war aims—even though the United States had not yet joined the war (see text p. 836). In the final version, Roosevelt shied away from specific reference to an "effective international organization," and Churchill sought to preserve British imperial trading preferences by adding "with due respect for their existing obligations" to the fourth point.

Source: Samuel I. Rosenman, ed., *The Public Papers and Addresses of Franklin D. Roosevelt, 1941* (New York: Harper and Brothers, 1950), 314.

The President of the United States of America and the Prime Minister, Mr. Churchill, representing His Majesty's Government in the United Kingdom, being met together, deem it right to make known certain common principles in the national policies of their respective countries on which they base their hopes for a better future for the world.

First, their countries seek no aggrandizement, territorial or other;

Second, they desire to see no territorial changes that do not accord with the freely expressed wishes of the peoples concerned;

Third, they respect the right of all peoples to choose the form of government under which they will live; and they wish to see sovereign rights and self government restored to those who have been forcibly deprived of them;

Fourth, they will endeavor, with due respect for their existing obligations to further the enjoyment by all States, great or small, victor or vanquished, of access, on equal terms, to the trade and to the raw materials of the world which are needed for their economic prosperity;

Fifth, they desire to bring about the fullest collaboration between all nations in the economic field with the object of securing, for all, improved labor standards, economic advancement and social security;

Sixth, after the final destruction of the Nazi tyranny, they hope to see established a peace which will afford to all nations the means of dwelling in safety within their own boundaries, and which will afford assurance that all the men in all the lands may live out their lives in freedom from fear and want;

Seventh, such a peace should enable all men to traverse the high seas and oceans without hindrance;

Eighth, they believe that all of the nations of the world, for realistic as well as spiritual reasons must come to the abandonment of the use of force. Since no future peace can be maintained if land, sea or air armaments continue to be employed by nations which threaten, or may threaten, aggression outside of their frontiers, they believe, pending the establishment of a wider and permanent system of general security, that the disarmament of such nations is essential. They will likewise aid and encourage all other practicable measures which will lighten for peace-loving peoples the crushing burden of armaments.

FRANKLIN D. ROOSEVELT
WINSTON S. CHURCHILL

Questions

1. How does the Atlantic Charter balance economic and political concerns?
2. How do Roosevelt and Churchill envision the world order that will follow the war?

Questions for Further Thought

1. Compare and contrast President Roosevelt's "Four Freedoms" speech with President Wilson's "Fourteen Points" speech (Document 22-2). How, in particular, do you account for some differences in emphasis in FDR's message?
2. Did Senator Burton K. Wheeler echo sentiments and arguments expressed during debate over U.S. entry into the First World War?

Organizing for Victory

Mobilizing the nation's human and material resources to win the Second World War required organization that involved the interaction of governmental agencies, some old, others newly created, and private organizations (business, labor, and agricultural). Under changing circumstances, adversarial relations between government and business largely gave way to cooperation. Obviously, the government's role expanded, as well as changed, as it recruited, trained, and fielded large military forces; spent lavishly to equip and maintain our armed forces and assist our allies; and taxed and borrowed to finance the war. Wartime economics achieved the prosperity that had eluded the Hoover and Roosevelt administrations during peacetime and established precedents for the postwar era (see text pp. 837–843, including "American Lives: Henry J. Kaiser").

The war created opportunities for women, African Americans, and Mexican Americans, though all confronted obstacles even as they and the war cleared some away. Women served in all four military services; others filled positions vacated by men entering the armed forces or jobs newly created by wartime demands. Yet the government and employers did not provide women with equal job opportunities or necessary support (child care, flexible work schedules), and organizations to articulate their needs and press for policies to address them. African Americans and Mexican Americans served in large numbers in the armed forces. The former were largely segregated; the latter were not. Both groups experienced gains, but also prejudice and discrimination, in the wartime labor market. During the war, African Americans and Mexican Americans protested segregation and discrimination. Blacks led in this regard: the National Association for the Advancement of Colored People (NAACP) gained markedly in membership, and the Congress of Racial Equality (CORE) was founded. Both organizations would, of course, figure prominently in the later civil rights movement.

Wartime federal action in behalf of minorities was limited: Congress was unsupportive; the president's 1941 executive order prohibiting discrimination in war industries and government, issued under blacks' threat to mount a "march on Washington," did break new ground, but little more. The Supreme Court, increasingly liberal, took the most decisive action, striking down Texas's white Democratic primary election (*Smith v. Allwright*, 1944) (see text pp. 837-846).

Document 26-6 reports the wartime experiences, on the job and at home, of one female worker. Document 26-7 is the significant Supreme Court decision in *Smith v. Allwright*. Propaganda was deemed essential to motivating the armed forces and the civilian population, as Document 26-8 illustrates.

26-6   Women Working at the Home Front (1944)

Norma Yerger Queen

Responding to a request form the U. S. Office of War Information for the observations of wartime female workers, Norma Yerger Queen—a Utahan married to a professional and employed in a military hospital—wrote about her work, community, and home life.

Source: Norma Yerger Queen to the Office of War Information, 1944.

The people of this community all respect women who work regardless of the type of work. Women from the best families & many officers' wives work at our hospital. It is not at all uncommon to meet at evening parties in town women who work in the kitchens or offices of our hospital (Army-Bushnell-large general). The city mayor's wife too works there.

The church disapproves of women working who have small children. The church has a strong influence in our county.

For the canning season in our county men's & women's clubs & the church all recruited vigorously for women for the canneries. . . .

I personally have encouraged officers' wives who have no children to get out and work. Those of us who have done so have been highly respected by the others and we have not lost social standing. In fact many of the social affairs are arranged at our convenience.

Some husbands do not approve of wives working & this has kept home some who do not have small children. Some of the women just do not wish to put forth the effort.

The financial incentive has been the strongest influence among most economic groups but especially among those families who were on relief for many years. Patriotic motivation is sometimes present but sometimes it really is a front for the financial one. A few women work to keep

their minds from worrying about sons or husbands in the service.

In this county, the hospital is the chief employer of women. A few go to Ogden (20 miles away) to work in an arsenal, the depot, or the air field. When these Ogden plants first opened quite a few women started to work there, but the long commuting plus the labor at the plants plus their housework proved too much.

Many women thoroughly enjoy working & getting away from the home. They seem to get much more satisfaction out of it than out of housework or bringing up children. Those who quit have done so because of lack of good care for their children, or of inability to do the housework & the job. . . .

I am convinced that if women could work 4 days a week instead of 5½ or 6 that more could take jobs. I found it impossible to work 5½ days & do my housework but when I arranged for 4 days I could manage both. These days one has to do everything—one cannot buy services as formerly. For instance—laundry. I'm lucky. I can send out much of our laundry to the hospital but even so there is a goodly amount that must be done at home—all the ironing of summer dresses is very tiring. I even have to press my husband's trousers—a thing I never did in all my married life. The weekly housecleaning—shoe shining—all things we formerly had done by others. Now we also do home canning. I never in the 14 yrs. of my married life canned 1 jar. Last summer I put up dozens of quarts per instructions of Uncle Sam. I'm only one among many who is now doing a lot of manual labor foreign to our usual custom. I just could not take on all that & an outside job too. It is no fun to eat out—you wait so long for service & the restaurants cannot be immaculately kept—therefore it is more pleasant & quicker to cook & eat at home even after a long day's work. I've talked with the personnel manager at the hospital & he agrees that fewer days a week would be better. The canneries finally took women for as little as 3 hrs. a day.

This is a farming area & many farm wives could not under any arrangements take a war job. They have too much to do at their farm jobs & many now have to go into the fields, run tractors & do other jobs formerly done by men. I marvel at all these women are able to do & feel very inadequate next to them. . . .

Here is the difference between a man working & a woman as seen in our home—while I prepare the evening meal, my husband reads the evening paper. We then do the dishes together after which he reads his medical journal or cogitates over some lecture he is to give or some problem at his lab. I have to make up grocery lists, mend, straighten up a drawer, clean out the ice box, press clothes, put away anything strewn about the house, wash bric a brac, or do several of hundreds of small "woman's work is never done stuff." This consumes from 1 to 2 hrs. each evening after which I'm too weary to read any professional social work literature & think I'm lucky if I can keep up with the daily paper, Time Life or Reader's Digest. All this while my husband is relaxing & resting. When I worked full time, we tried doing the housecleaning together but it just didn't click. He is responsible for introducing penicillin into Bushnell & thus into the army & there were so many visiting brass hats & night conferences he couldn't give even one night a week to the house. Then came a mess of lectures of all kinds of medical meetings—he had to prepare those at home. I got so worn out it was either quit work or do it part time.

This has been a lot of personal experience but I'm sure we are no exception. I thought I was thro[ugh] working in 1938. My husband urged me to help out for the war effort—he's all out for getting the war work done & he agreed to do his share of the housework. He is not lazy but he found we could not do it. I hope this personal experience will help to give you an idea of some of the problems.

Questions

1. According to Queen, why did women take jobs during the war? Which reasons were especially important?
2. What practical factors limited women's participation in the labor force? How did practical factors affect women who came from different circumstances—farms, towns, the military base?
3. How did their outside jobs affect women's work at home? What problems and options does Queen mention?

26-7   The Supreme Court on White Primaries in the South (1944)

Stanley Reed

For several decades across much of the South, Democratic primary elections were more important than general elections, in which Republican opposition was token or nonexistent. In 1927, in *Nixon v. Herndon,* the Supreme Court struck down a Texas law that excluded African Americans from Democratic primaries. Texas ultimately moved to circumvent further court action by allowing political parties to act on their own as private groups. The high court initially accepted this (*Grovey v. Townsend,* 1935), but in 1941 it held, in a case involving flagrant election fraud in a Louisiana congressional district (*United States v. Classic*), that party primaries for federal office, integral parts of the election process, were subject to federal law. Here, in *Smith v. Allwright,* the Supreme Court, through the opinion of Justice Stanley Reed (1884–1980), overturns *Grovey* (see text p. 844).

Source: Smith v. Allwright, 321 U.S. 649 (1944).

The State of Texas by its Constitution and statutes provides that every person, if certain other requirements are met which are not here in issue, qualified by residence in the district or county "shall be deemed a qualified elector." Primary elections for United States Senators, Congressmen and state officers are provided for by Chapters Twelve and Thirteen of the statutes. Under these chapters, the Democratic Party was required to hold the primary which was the occasion of the alleged wrong to petitioned. . . . These nominations are to be made by the qualified voters of the party.

The Democratic Party of Texas is held by the Supreme Court of that state to be a "voluntary association," protected by Section 27 of the Bill of Rights, Art. 1, Constitution of Texas, from interference by the state except that:

"In the interest of fair methods and a fair expression by their members of their preferences in the selection of their nominees, the State may regulate such elections by proper laws."

The Democratic party on May 24, 1932 in a State Convention adopted the following resolution, which has not since been "amended, abrogated, annulled or avoided":

"Be it resolved that all white citizens of the State of Texas who are qualified to vote under the Constitution and laws of the State shall be eligible to membership in the Democratic party and, as such, entitled to participate in its deliberations."

It was by virtue of this resolution that the respondents refused to permit the petitioner to vote.

Texas is free to conduct her elections and limit her electorate as she may deem wise, save only as her action may be affected by the prohibitions of the United States Constitution or in conflict with powers delegated to and exercised by the National Government. The Fourteenth Amendment forbids a state from making or enforcing any law which abridges the privileges or immunities of citizens of the United States and the Fifteenth Amendment specifi-

cally interdicts any denial or abridgement by a state of the right of citizens to vote on account of color. . . .

When *Grovey v. Townsend* was written, the Court looked upon the denial of a vote in a primary as a mere refusal by a party of party membership. As the Louisiana statutes for holding primaries are similar to those of Texas, our ruling in *Classic* as to the unitary character of the electoral process calls for a reëxamination as to whether or not the exclusion of Negroes from a Texas party primary was state action.

It may now be taken as a postulate that the right to vote in such a primary for the nomination of candidates without discrimination by the State, like the right to vote in a general election, is a right secured by the Constitution.

We are thus brought to an examination of the qualifications for Democratic primary electors in Texas, to determine whether state action or private action has excluded Negroes from participation.

We think that this statutory system for the selection of party nominees for inclusion on the general election ballot makes the party which is required to follow these legislative directions an agency of the state in so far as it determines the participants in a primary election. The party takes its character as a state agency from the duties imposed upon it by state statutes; the duties do not become matters of private law because they are performed by a political party. . . .

The United States is a constitutional democracy. Its organic law grants to all citizens a right to participate in the choice of elected officials without restriction by any state because of race. This grant to the people of the opportunity for choice is not to be nullified by a state through casting its electoral process in a form which permits a private organization to practice racial discrimination in the election. Constitutional rights would be of little value if they could be thus indirectly denied. . . .

Questions

1. According to this Supreme Court decision, what limits was Texas bound to observe in arranging its primary elections?
2. Texas had argued that the all-white Democratic primary was a *private,* not a public, activity. How did it make this argument? Why did the Court rule against it?
3. What influence, if any, might U.S. war aims, as stated by President Roosevelt, have had on the Supreme Court's decision to hear this case or on the language used in the decision?

26-8 Wartime Posters: The Japanese and Venereal Disease as Enemies

Second World War propaganda took many forms: radio broadcasts, films, and print media. As during World War I, posters played a role, whether directed against the United States' wartime enemies, especially the Japanese, or against the threat of venereal disease (see text pp. 839, 847–848).

Sources: "This Is the Enemy," shown at the Museum of Modern Art (New York City), reprinted in *Life*, from John W. Dower, *War without Mercy: Race and Power in the Pacific War* (New York: Pantheon, 1986), p. 189; "V. D.: Worst of the Three," National Archives, Washington, D.C., from Allan M. Brandt, *No Magic Bullet: A Social History of Venereal Disease in the United States,* exp. ed. (New York: Oxford University Press, 1987), following p. 164.

Questions

1. Compare and contrast the depiction of a Japanese soldier of World War II (Document 26-8) with depictions of German soldiers during World War I (Document 22-9) and World War II (see text p. 839).
2. Compare and contrast the depiction of women in World War I posters (Document 22-5), a 1936 political cartoon (Document 25-10), and a World War II poster (Document 26-8).

Questions for Further Thought

1. What light does Norma Yerger Queen (Document 26-6) shed on issues of gender, class, and status in her community?
2. Why, during the prewar and World War II years, was it more likely that court decisions, rather than legislative enactments, would advance the cause of African Americans?

Life on the Home Front

In describing life in the United States during World War II, the text makes clear that Japanese Americans, most of them American-born citizens, suffered as no other group did during the war—or during World War I, for that matter, for all its intolerance and repression (see text pp. 850–853). Document 26-9 is President Roosevelt's executive order authorizing the prescribing of military areas. Document 26-10 offers opposing opinions in a Supreme Court case arising out of wartime restrictions on Japanese Americans. (Also see "American Voices: Monica Sone," text p. 852).

As noted earlier, African Americans and Mexican Americans shared, though not fully, in wartime prosperity. Members of both groups confronted prejudice and discrimination as they took new jobs and moved into new locales. Tensions spilled over into violence in a number of instances, including attacks on Mexican Americans in Los Angeles and a bloody race riot in Detroit (Document 26-11), both during 1943 (see text pp. 843–845).

Americans' life on the home front involved neither heavy civilian casualties nor widespread property destruction, as it did in other warring nations. For Americans with loved ones in the armed forces, of course, there was fear; for those losing loved ones in the war, grief. But rationing and wartime shortages of consumer products were inconveniences, rarely hardships in a nation experiencing war-based prosperity. Publicized drives to secure blood, collect scrap metal, and sell government bonds, and the widespread planting of "victory gardens," contributed to the war effort and reminded the home front that indeed, there was a war on (see text pp. 846–850). Document 26-12 offers the reminiscences of a woman on the home front during the Second World War.

26-9   Executive Order 9066 to Prescribe Military Areas (1942)

After the surprise attack on Pearl Harbor, amid rumors of espionage and subversion in Hawaii, the American people grew fearful of enemy aliens. On February 19, 1942, President Roosevelt issued an executive order authorizing the secretary of war to identify areas of the country where movements of people could be controlled or restricted. Prescription was followed by executive and military orders that resulted in the internment of Japanese and Japanese Americans in relocation camps (see text pp. 850–853).

Source: Executive Order No. 9066, "Authorizing the Secretary of War to Prescribe Military Areas," *Federal Register* 7, no. 38 (February 25, 1942): 1407.

AUTHORIZING THE SECRETARY OF WAR TO
PRESCRIBE MILITARY AREAS

WHEREAS the successful prosecution of the war requires every possible protection against espionage and against sabotage to national-defense material, national-defense premises, and national-defense utilities. . . .

NOW, THEREFORE, by virtue of the authority vested in me as President of the United States, and Commander in Chief of the Army and Navy, I hereby authorize and direct the Secretary of War, and the Military Commanders whom he may from time to time designate, whenever he or any designated Commander deems such actions necessary or desirable, to prescribe military areas in such places and of such extent as he or the appropriate Military Commanders may determine, from which any or all persons may be excluded, and with such respect to which, the right of any person to enter, remain in, or leave shall be subject to whatever restrictions the Secretary of War or the appropriate Military Commander may impose in his discretion. The Secretary of War is hereby authorized to provide for residents of any such area who are excluded therefrom, such transportation, food, shelter, and other accommodations as may be necessary, in the judgement of the Secretary of War or the said Military Commander, and until other arrangements are made, to accomplish the purpose of this order. The designation of military areas in any region or locality shall supersede designations of prohibited and restricted areas by the Attorney General under the Proclamations of December 7 and 8, 1941, and shall supersede the responsibility and authority of the Attorney General under the said Proclamations in respect of such prohibited and restricted areas.

I hereby further authorize and direct the Secretary of War and the said Military Commanders to take such other steps as he or the appropriate Military Commander may deem advisable to enforce compliance with the restrictions applicable to each Military area hereinabove authorized to be designated, including the use of Federal troops and other Federal Agencies, with authority to accept assistance of state and local agencies.

I hereby further authorize and direct all Executive Departments, independent establishments and other Federal Agencies, to assist the Secretary of War or the said Military Commanders in carrying out this Executive Order, including the furnishing of medical aid, hospitalization, food, clothing, transportation, use of land, shelter, and other supplies, equipment, utilities, facilities and services.

This order shall not be construed as modifying or limiting in any way the authority heretofore granted under Executive Order No. 8972, dated December 12, 1941, nor shall it be construed as limiting or modifying the duty and responsibility of the Federal Bureau of Investigation, with respect to the investigation of alleged acts of sabotage or the duty and responsibility of the Attorney General and the Department of Justice under the Proclamations of December 7 and 8, 1941, prescribing regulations for the conduct and control of alien enemies, except as such duty and responsibility is superseded by the designation of military areas hereunder.

FRANKLIN D. ROOSEVELT
The White House
February 19, 1942.

Questions

1. What specific concerns about national security led to the issuance of Executive Order 9066?
2. Is the order restricting the actions of residents of prescribed military areas specific in identifying individuals or groups? In your opinion, why was it written this way?
3. What limitations does the order place on the secretary of war and others authorized to enforce its provisions?

26-10   Japanese American Exclusion: *Korematsu v. United States* (1944)

**Hugo Black and
Frank Murphy**

Following promulgation of Executive Order 9066, military authorities issued orders that restricted and ultimately took away the freedom of Japanese Americans within the prescribed area of the Far West. The Supreme Court upheld such policy, but its decision in *Korematsu v. United States* was divided, 6-3. Justice Hugo Black (1886–1971) delivered the majority opinion; Justice Frank Murphy (1890–1949), one of the dissents. In referring to "the very brink of constitutional power" (now overstepped), Murphy quoted his own *concurring* opinion, originally drafted as a *dissent,* in *Hirabayashi v. United States* (1943). In that opinion, Murphy had warned that U.S. policy regarding Japanese Americans had "a melancholy resemblance" to Nazi policy regarding Jews.

Source: Korematsu v. United States, 323 U.S. 214, excerpted in Donald O. Dewey, ed., *Union and Liberty: A Documentary History of American Constitutionalism* (New York: McGraw-Hill, 1969), 264–266.

(a) Majority Opinion: Justice Hugo Black

The petitioner, an American citizen of Japanese descent, was convicted in a federal district court for remaining in San Leandro, California, a "Military Area," contrary to Civilian Exclusion Order No. 34 of the Commanding General of the Western Command, U.S. Army, which directed that after May 9, 1942, all persons of Japanese ancestry should be excluded from that area. No question was raised as to the petitioner's loyalty to the United States. The Circuit Court of Appeals affirmed, and the importance of the constitutional question involved caused us to grand certiorari.

It should be noted, to begin with, that all legal restrictions which curtail the civil rights of a single racial group are immediately suspect. That is not to say that all such restrictions are unconstitutional. It is to say that courts must subject them to the most rigid scrutiny. Pressing public necessity may sometimes justify the existence of such restrictions; racial antagonism never can. . . .

In the light of the principles we announced in the *Hirabayashi* case, we are unable to conclude that it was beyond the war power of Congress and the Executive to exclude those of Japanese ancestry from the West Coast war area at the time they did. . . . But exclusion from a threatened area, no less than curfew, has a definite and close relationship to the prevention of espionage and sabotage. The military authorities, charged with the primary responsibility of defending our shores, concluded that curfew provided inadequate protection and ordered exclusion. They did so, as pointed out in our *Hirabayashi* opinion, in accordance with Congressional authority to the military to say who should, and who should not, remain in the threatened areas. . . .

Like curfew, exclusion of those of Japanese origin was deemed necessary because of the presence of an unascertained number of disloyal members of the group, most of whom we have no doubt were loyal to this country. It was because we could not reject the finding of the military authorities that it was impossible to bring about an immediate segregation of the disloyal from the loyal that we sustained the validity of the curfew order as applying to the whole group. In the instant case, temporary exclusion of the entire group was rested by the military on the same ground. The judgment that exclusion of the whole group was for the same reason a military imperative answers the contention that the exclusion was in the nature of group punishment based on antagonism to those of Japanese origin. . . . [We] are not unmindful of the hardships imposed by it upon a large group of American citizens. But hardships are part of war, and war is an aggregation of hardships. All citizens alike, both in and out of uniform, feel the impact of war in greater or lesser measure. Citizenship has its responsibilities as well as its privileges, and in time of war the burden is always heavier. Compulsory exclusion of large groups of citizens from their homes, except under circumstances of direst emergency and peril, is inconsistent with our basic governmental institutions. But when under conditions of modern warfare our shores are threatened by hostile forces, the power to protect must be commensurate with the threatened danger. . . .

It is said that we are dealing here with the case of imprisonment of a citizen in a concentration camp solely because of his ancestry, without evidence or inquiry concerning his loyalty and good disposition towards the United States. Our task would be simple, our duty clear, were this a case involving the imprisonment of a loyal citizen in a concentration camp because of racial prejudice. Regardless of the true nature of the assembly and relocation centers—and we deem it unjustifiable to call them concentration camps with all the ugly connotations that term implies—we are dealing specifically with nothing but an exclusion order. To cast this case into outlines of racial prejudice, without reference to the real military dangers which were presented, merely confuses the issue. Korematsu was not excluded from the military area because of hostility to him or his race. He was excluded because we are at war with the Japanese Empire, because the properly constituted military authorities feared an invasion of our West Coast and felt constrained to take proper security measures, because they decided that the military urgency of the situation demanded that all citizens of Japanese ancestry be segregated from the West Coast temporarily, and finally, because Congress, reposing its confidence in this time of war in our military leaders—as inevitably it must—determined that they should have the power to do just this. There was evidence of disloyalty on the part of some, the military authorities considered that the need for action was great, and time was short. We cannot—by availing ourselves of the calm perspective of hindsight—now say that at that time these actions were unjustified.

(b) Dissent: Justice Frank Murphy

This exclusion of "all persons of Japanese ancestry, both alien and non-alien," from the Pacific Coast area on a plea of military necessity in the absence of martial law ought not to be approved. Such exclusion goes over "the very brink of constitutional power" and falls into the ugly abyss of racism.

. . . it is essential that there be definite limits to military discretion, especially where martial law has not been declared. Individuals must not be left impoverished of their constitutional rights on a plea of military necessity that has neither substance nor support. Thus, like other claims conflicting with the asserted constitutional rights of the individual, the military claim must subject itself to the judicial process of having its reasonableness determined and its conflicts with other interests reconciled. "What are the allowable limits of military discretion, and whether or not they have been overstepped in a particular case, are judicial questions."

The judicial test of whether the Government, on a plea of military necessity, can validly deprive an individual of any of his constitutional rights is whether the deprivation is reasonably related to a public danger that is so "immediate, imminent, and impending" as not to admit of delay and not to permit the intervention of ordinary constitutional processes to alleviate the danger. Civilian Exclusion Order No. 34, banishing from a prescribed area of the Pacific Coast "all persons of Japanese ancestry, both alien and non-alien," clearly does not meet that test. Being an obvious racial discrimination, the order deprives all those within its scope of the equal protection of the laws as guaranteed by the Fifth Amendment. It further deprives these individuals of their constitutional rights to live and work where they will, to establish a home where they choose and to move about freely. In excommunicating them without benefit of hearings, this order also deprives them of all their constitutional rights to procedural due process. Yet no reasonable relation to an "immediate, imminent, and impending" public danger is evident to support this racial restriction which is one of the most sweeping and complete deprivations of constitutional rights in the history of this nation in the absence of martial law.

. . . the exclusion order necessarily must rely for its reasonableness upon the assumption that all persons of Japanese ancestry may have a dangerous tendency to commit sabotage and espionage and to aid our Japanese enemy in other ways. It is difficult to believe that reason, logic or experience could be marshaled in support of such an assumption.

That this forced exclusion was the result in good measure of this erroneous assumption of racial guilt rather than bona fide military necessity is evidence by the Commanding General's Final Report on the evacuation from the Pacific Coast area. In it he refers to all individuals of Japanese descent as "subversive," as belonging to "an enemy race" whose "racial strains are undiluted," and as constituting "over 112,000 potential enemies . . . at large today" along the Pacific Coast. . . .

. . . But to infer that examples of individual disloyalty prove group disloyalty and justify discriminatory action against the entire group is to deny that under our system of law individual guilt is the sole basis for deprivation of rights. Moreover, this inference, which is at the very heart of the evacuation orders, has been used in support of the abhorrent and despicable treatment of minority groups by the dictatorial tyrannies which this nation is now pledged to destroy. To give constitutional sanction to that inference in this case, however well-intentioned may have been the military command on the Pacific Coast, is to adopt one of the cruelest of the rationales used by our enemies to destroy the dignity of the individual and to encourage and open the door to discriminatory actions against other minority groups in the passions of tomorrow.

No adequate reason is given for the failure to treat these Japanese Americans on an individual basis by holding investigations and hearings to separate the loyal from the disloyal, as was done in the case of persons of German and Italian ancestry. It is asserted merely that the loyalties of this group "were unknown and time was of the essence." Yet nearly four months elapsed after Pearl Harbor before the first exclusion order was issued; nearly eight months went by until the last order was issued; and the last of these "subversive" persons was not actually removed until almost eleven months had elapsed. Leisure and deliberation seem to have been more of the essence than speed. And the fact that conditions were not such as to warrant a declaration of martial law adds strength to the belief that the factors of time and military necessity were not as urgent as they have been represented to be. . . .

I dissent, therefore, from this legalization of racism. Racial discrimination in any form and in any degree has no justifiable part whatever in our democratic way of life. It is unattractive in any setting but it is utterly revolting among a free people who have embraced the principles set forth in the Constitution of the United States. All residents of this nation are kin in some way by blood or culture to a foreign land. Yet they are primarily and necessarily a part of the new and distinct civilization of the United States. They must accordingly be treated at all times as the heirs of the American experiment and as entitled to all the rights and freedoms guaranteed by the Constitution.

Questions

1. How does Black make the case that *Korematsu* involves "military necessity," not "racism"?
2. How does Murphy make the case that *Korematsu* involves "racism," not "military necessity"?
3. Which case do you find more persuasive? Why?

26-11   The Gestapo in Detroit (1943)

Thurgood Marshall

Underlying racial tensions and exacerbating factors—the migration of large numbers of whites and African Americans into centers of war production and the increasing presence of African Americans in the work force—led to group conflict, which sometimes spilled over into violence (see text p. 850). The worst outbreak occurred in Detroit, Michigan, June 20–22, 1943. Thurgood Marshall (1908–1993), then chief counsel of the National Association for the Advancement of Colored People, reported on the Detroit riot in *The Crisis,* the NAACP's monthly magazine. Marshall later became the first African American justice of the U. S. Supreme Court.

Source: Thurgood Marshall, "The Gestapo in Detroit," *The Crisis* 50 (August 1943); 232–233, 246–247.

Riots are usually the result of many underlying causes, yet no single factor is more important than the attitude and efficiency of the police. When disorder starts, it is either stopped quickly or permitted to spread into serious proportions, depending upon the actions of the local police.

Much of the blood spilled in the Detroit riot is on the hands of the Detroit police department. In the past the Detroit police have been guilty of both inefficiency and an attitude of prejudice against Negroes. Of course, there are several individual exceptions.

The citizens of Detroit, white and Negro, are familiar with the attitude of the police as demonstrated during the trouble in 1942 surrounding the Sojourner Truth housing project. At that time a mob of white persons armed with rocks, sticks and other weapons attacked Negro tenants who were attempting to move into the project. Police were called to the scene. Instead of dispersing the mob which was unlawfully on property belonging to the federal government and leased to Negroes, they directed their efforts toward dispersing the Negroes who were attempting to get into their own homes. All Negroes approaching the project were searched and their automobiles likewise searched. White people were neither searched nor disarmed by the police. This incident is typical of the one-sided law enforcement practiced by Detroit police. White hoodlums were justified in their belief that

the police would act the same way in any further disturbances.

In the June riot of this year, the police ran true to form. The trouble reached riot proportions because the police once again enforced the law with an unequal hand. They used "persuasion" rather than firm action with white rioters, while against Negroes they used the ultimate in force: night sticks, revolvers, riot guns, sub-machine guns, and deer guns. As a result, 25 of the 34 persons killed were Negroes. Of the latter, 17 were killed by police.

The excuse of the police department for the disproportionate number of Negroes killed is that the majority of them were shot while committing felonies: namely, the looting of stores on Hastings Street. On the other hand, the crimes of arson and felonious assaults are also felonies. It is true that some Negroes were looting stores and were shot while committing these crimes. It is equally true that white persons were turning over and burning automobiles on Woodward Avenue. This is arson. Others were beating Negroes with iron pipes, clubs, and rocks. This is felonious assault. Several Negroes were stabbed. This is assault with intent to murder.

All these crimes are matters of record: Many were committed in the presence of police officers, several on the pavement around the City Hall. Yet the record remains: Negroes kill[ed] by police--17; white persons killed by police—none. The entire record, both of the riot killings and of previous disturbances, reads like the story of the Nazi Gestapo.

Evidence of tension in Detroit has been apparent for months. The *Detroit Free Press* sent a reporter to the police department. When Commissioner Witherspoon was asked how he was handling the situation he told the reporter: "We have given orders to handle it with kid gloves. The policemen have taken insults to keep trouble from breaking out. I doubt if you or I could have put up with it." This weak-kneed policy of the police commissioner coupled with the anti-Negro attitude of many members of the force helped to make a riot inevitable.

SUNDAY NIGHT ON BELLE ISLE

Belle Isle is a municipal recreation park where thousands of white and Negro war workers and their families go on Sundays for their outings. There had been isolated instances of racial friction in the past. On Sunday night, June 20, there was trouble between a group of white and Negro people. The disturbance was under control by midnight. During the time of the disturbance and after it was under control, the police searched the automobiles of all Negroes and searched the Negroes as well. They did not search the white people. One Negro who was to be inducted into the army the following week was arrested because another person in the car had a small pen knife. This youth was later sentenced to 90 days in jail before his family could locate him. Many Negroes were arrested during this period and rushed to local police stations. At the very beginning the police demonstrated that they would continue to handle racial disorders by searching, beating and arresting Negroes while using mere persuasion on white people.

THE RIOT SPREADS

A short time after midnight disorder broke out in a white neighborhood near the Roxy theatre on Woodward Avenue. The Roxy is an all night theatre attended by white and Negro patrons. Several Negroes were beaten and others were forced to remain in the theatre for lack of police protection. The rumor spread among the white people that a Negro had raped a white woman on Belle Island and that the Negroes were rioting.

At about the same time a rumor spread around Hastings and Adams Streets in the Negro area that white sailors had thrown a Negro woman and her baby into the lake at Belle Isle and that the police were beating Negroes. This rumor was also repeated by an unidentified Negro at one of the night spots. Some Negroes began to attack white persons in the area. The police immediately began to use their sticks and revolvers against them. The Negroes began to break out the windows of stores of white merchants on Hastings Street.

The interesting thing is that when the windows in the stores on Hastings Street were first broken, there was no

looting. An officer of the Merchants' Association walked the length of Hastings Street, starting 7 o'clock Monday morning and noticed that none of the stores with broken windows had been looted. It is thus clear that the original breaking of windows was not for the purpose of looting.

Throughout Monday the police, instead of placing men in front of the stores to protect them from looting, contented themselves with driving up and down Hastings Street from time to time, stopping in front of the stores. The usual procedure was to jump out of the squad cars with drawn revolvers and riot guns to shoot whoever might be in the store. The policemen would then tell the Negro bystanders to "run and not look back." On several occasions, persons running were shot in the back. In other instances, bystanders were clubbed by police. To the police, all Negroes on Hastings Street were "looters." This included war workers returning from work. There is no question that many Negroes were guilty of looting, just as there is always looting during earthquakes or as there was when English towns were bombed by the Germans.

CARS DETOURED INTO MOBS

Woodward Avenue is one of the main thoroughfares of the city of Detroit. Small groups of white people began to rove up and down Woodward beating Negroes, stoning cars containing Negroes, stopping street cars and yanking Negroes from them, and stabbing and shooting Negroes. In no case did the police do more than try to "reason" with these mobs, many of which were, at this stage, quite small. The police did not draw their revolvers or riot guns, and never used any force to disperse these mobs. As a result of this, the mobs got larger and bolder and even attacked Negroes on the pavement of the City Hall in demonstration not only of their contempt for Negroes, but of their contempt for law and order as represented by the municipal government.

During this time, Mayor Jeffries was in his office in the City Hall with the door locked and the window shade drawn. The use of night sticks or the drawing of revolvers would have dispersed these white groups and saved the lives of many Negroes. It would not have been necessary to shoot, but it would have been sufficient to threaten to shoot into the white mobs. The use of a fire hose would have dispersed many of the groups. None of these things was done and the disorder took on the proportions of a major riot. The responsibility rests with the Detroit police.

At the height of the disorder on Woodward Avenue, Negroes driving north on Brush Street (a Negro street) were stopped at Vernor Highway by a policeman who forced them to detour to Woodward Avenue. Many of these cars are automobiles which appeared in the pictures released by several newspapers showing them overturned and burned on Woodward Avenue.

While investigating the riot, we obtained many affidavits from Negroes concerning police brutality during the riot. It is impossible to include the facts of all of these affidavits. However, typical instances may be cited. A Negro soldier in uniform who had recently been released from the army with a medical discharge, was on his way down Brush Street Monday morning, toward a theatre on Woodward Avenue. This soldier was not aware of the fact that the riot was still going on. While in the Negro neighborhood on Brush Street, he reached a corner where a squad car drove up and discharged several policemen with drawn revolvers who announced to a small group on the corner to run and not look back. Several of the Negroes who did not move quite fast enough for the police were struck with night sticks and revolvers. The soldier was yanked from behind by one policeman and struck in the head with a blunt instrument and knocked to the ground, where he remained in a stupor. The police then returned to their squad car and drove off. A Negro woman in the block noticed the entire incident from her window, and she rushed out with a cold, damp towel to bind the soldier's head. She then hailed two Negro postal employees who carried the soldier to a hospital where his life was saved.

There are many additional affidavits of similar occurrences involving obviously innocent civilians throughout many Negro sections in Detroit where there had been no rioting at all. It was characteristic of these cases that the policemen would drive up to a corner, jump out with drawn revolvers, striking at Negroes indiscriminately, ofttimes shooting at them, and in all cases forcing them to run. At the same time on Woodward Avenue, white civilians were seizing Negroes and telling them to "run, nigger, run." At least two Negroes, "shot while looting," were innocent persons who happened to be in the area at that time.

One Negro who had been an employee of a bank in Detroit for the past eighteen years was on his way to work on a Woodward Avenue street car when he was seized by one of the white mobs. In the presence of at least four policemen, he was beaten and stabbed in the side. He also heard several shots fired from the back of the mob. He managed to run to two of the policemen who proceeded to "protect" him from the mob. The two policemen, followed by two mounted policemen, proceeded down Woodward Avenue. While he was being escorted by these policemen, the man was struck in the face by at least eight of the mob, and at no time was any effort made to prevent him from being struck. After a short distance this man noticed a squad car parked on the other side of the street. In sheer desperation, he broke away from the two policemen who claimed to be protecting him and ran to the squad car, begging for protection. The officer in the squad car put him in the back seat and drove off, thereby saving his life.

During all this time, the fact that the man was either shot or stabbed was evident because of the fact that blood was spurting from his side. Despite this obvious felony, committed in the presence of at least four policemen, no effort was made at that time either to protect the victim or to arrest the persons guilty of the felony.

In addition to the many cases of one-sided enforcement of the law by the police, there are two glaring examples of criminal aggression against innocent Negro citizens and workers by members of the Michigan state police and Detroit police.

SHOOTING IN YMCA

On the night of June 22 at about 10 o'clock, some of the residents of the St. Antoine Branch of the Y.M.C.A. were returning to the dormitory. Several were on their way home from the Y.W.C.A. across the street. State police were searching some other Negroes on the pavement of the Y.M.C.A. when two of the Y.M.C.A. residents were stopped and searched for weapons. After none was found they were allowed to proceed to the building. Just as the last of the Y.M.C.A. men was about to enter the building, he heard someone behind him yell what sounded to him like, "Hi, Ridley." (Ridley is also a resident of the Y.) Another resident said he heard someone yell what sounded to him like "Heil, Hitler."

A state policeman, Ted Anders, jumped from his car with his revolver drawn, ran to the steps of the Y.M.C.A., put one foot on the bottom step and fired through the outside door. Immediately after firing the shot he entered the building. Other officers followed. Julian Witherspoon, who had just entered the building, was lying on the floor, shot in the side by the bullet that was fired through the outside door. There had been no show of violence or weapons of any kind by anyone in or around the Y.M.C.A.

The officers with drawn revolvers ordered all those residents of the Y.M.C.A. who were in the lobby of their building, to raise their hands in the air and line up against the wall like criminals. During all this time these men were called "black b——— and monkeys," and other vile names by the officers. At least one man was struck, another was forced to throw his lunch on the floor. All the men in the lobby were searched.

The desk clerk was also forced to line up. The officers then went behind the desk and into the private offices and searched everything. The officers also made the clerk open all locked drawers, threatening to shoot him if he did not do so.

Witherspoon was later removed to the hospital and has subsequently been released. . . .

Justification for our belief that the Detroit police could have prevented the trouble from reaching riot proportions is evidenced in at least two recent instances. During the last month in the town of Atlanta, Georgia, several white youths organized a gang to beat up Negroes. They first encountered a young Negro boy on a bicycle and threw him to the ground. However, before they could beat this lone Negro, a squad car drove up. The police promptly arrested several of the white boys, and dispersed the group immediately, thus effectively forestalling and preventing what might have resulted in a riot. On the Sunday preceding the Detroit riots, Sheriff Baird, of Wayne County, Michigan, with jurisdiction over the area just outside Detroit, suppressed a potential riot in a nearby town. A large group of Negroes and a large group of white people were opposing each other and mob violence was threatened. The sheriff and his deputies got between the two groups and told them that in case of any violence, the guilty parties would be handled and that the law enforcement officers would do everything possible to prevent the riot. Because of this firm stand, the members of both groups dispersed.

If similar affirmative action had been taken by the Detroit police when the small groups were running up and down Woodward Avenue beating, cutting and shooting Negroes, the trouble never would have reached the bloody and destructive magnitude which has shocked the nation.

This record by the Detroit police demonstrates once more what all Negroes know only too well: that nearly all police departments limit their conception of checking racial disorders to surrounding, arresting, maltreating, and shooting Negroes. Little attempt is made to check the activities of whites.

The certainty of Negroes that they will not be protected by police, but instead attacked by them is a contributing factor to racial tensions leading to overt acts. The first item on the agenda of any group seeking to prevent rioting would seem to be a critical study of the police department of the community, its record in handling Negroes, something of the background of its personnel, and the plans of its chief officers for meeting possible racial disorders.

Questions

1. What does Marshall say about the actions of whites during the Detroit riot?
2. What does he say about the actions of African Americans during the riot?
3. How does Marshall describe the conduct of the police? Why does he liken the police to the Gestapo?

26-12   Remembering the War Years on the Home Front (1984)

Decades after World War II, a retired music teacher in Los Angeles reminisced about her life during the war years for Studs Terkel's oral history of the war. After the war, she divorced her husband, with whom she had had two children.

Source: Studs Terkel, *"The Good War": An Oral History of World War Two* (New York: Pantheon, 1984), 117–122. Reprinted with permission.

While my conscience told me the war was a terrible thing, bloodshed and misery, there was excitement in the air. I had just left college and was working as a substitute teacher. Life was fairly dull. Suddenly, single women were of tremendous importance. It was hammered at us through the newspapers and magazines and on the radio. We were needed at USO, to dance with the soldiers.

A young woman had a chance to meet hundreds of men in the course of one or two weeks, more than she would in her entire lifetime, because of the war. Life became a series of weekend dates.

I became a nurse's aide, working in the hospital. Six or eight weeks of Red Cross training. The uniform made us special people.

I had a brother three years younger than I. He was a cadet at the Santa Ana Air Base. Your cadet got to wear these great hats, with the grommets taken out. Marvelous uniform.

I met my future husband. I really didn't care that much for him, but the pressure was so great. My brother said, "What do you mean you don't like Glenn? You're going to marry him, aren't you?" The first time it would occur to me that I would marry anybody. The pressure to marry a soldier was so great that after a while I didn't question it. I have to marry sometime and I might as well marry him.

That women married soldiers and sent them overseas happy was hammered at us. We had plays on the radio, short stories in magazines, and the movies, which were a tremendous influence in our lives. The central theme was the girl meets the soldier, and after a weekend of acquaintanceship they get married and overcome all difficulties. Then off to war he went. Remember Judy Garland and Robert Walker in *The Clock?*

I knew Glenn six weekends, not weeks. They began on Saturday afternoon. We'd go out in herds and stay up all night. There was very little sleeping around. We were still at the tail-end of a moral generation. Openly living together was not condoned. An illegitimate child was a horrendous handicap. It was almost the ruination of your life. I'm amazed and delighted the way it's accepted now, that a girl isn't a social outcast any more.

The OWI, Office of War Information, did a thorough job of convincing us our cause was unquestionably right. We were stopping Hitler, and you look back at it and you had to stop him. We were saving the world. We were allied with Russia, which was great at that time. Germany had started World War One and now it had started World War Two, and Germany would be wiped off the face of the map. A few years later, when we started to arm Germany, I was so shocked. I'd been sold a bill of goods—I couldn't believe it. I remember sitting on the back porch here, I picked up the paper, and I read that our sworn enemy was now our ally. The disillusionment was so great, that was the beginning of distrusting my own government.

Russia was the enemy from the time I was born right up to '40. Then Russia became our ally. It's funny nobody stopped to think that this was a complete turnabout. As soon as the war was over, we dropped Russia. During the war, I never heard any anti-Russian talk. . . .

I had one of those movie weddings, because he couldn't get off the base. My parents approved. My mother had a talk with the head of the army base. She wanted to know why the guy I was to marry was restricted to quarters. He said they were having nothing but trouble with this guy. The major advised her to think twice before permitting her daughter to marry a man like this: he was totally irresponsible. My mother told me this, and we both laughed about it. He was a soldier. He could not be anything but a marvelous, magnificent human being. I couldn't believe for one minute what this major had said. He was given a weekend pass and we were married.

Shortly after that he was thrown out of the air force. This was my first doubt that he was magnificent. So he became a sergeant, dusting off airplanes. He was sent to various parts of the country: Panama City, Florida; Ypsilanti, Michigan; Amarillo, Texas. I followed him.

That's how I got to see the misery of the war, not the excitement. Pregnant women who could barely balance in a rocking train, going to see their husbands for the last time before the guys were sent overseas. Women coming back from seeing their husbands, traveling with small children. Trying to feed their kids, diaper their kids. I felt sorriest for them. It suddenly occurred to me that this wasn't half as much fun as I'd been told it was going to be. I just thanked God I had no kids. . . .

I ran across a lot of women with husbands overseas. They were living on allotment. Fifty bucks a month wouldn't support you. Things were relatively cheap, but then we had very little money, too. It wasn't so much the cost of food as points. I suspected the ration system was a patriotic ploy to keep our enthusiasm at a fever pitch. If you wanted something you didn't have points for, it was the easiest thing in the world . . . Almost everybody had a cynical feeling about what we were told was a food shortage.

When it started out, this was the greatest thing since the Crusades. The patriotic fervor was such at the beginning that if "The Star-Spangled Banner" came on the radio, everybody in the room would stand up at attention. As the war dragged on and on and on, we read of the selfish actions of guys in power. We read stories of the generals, like MacArthur taking food right out of the guys' mouths when he was in the Philippines, to feed his own family. Our enthusiasm waned and we became cynical and very tired and sick of the bloodshed and killing. It was a completely different thing than the way it started. At least, this is the way I felt. . . .

There were some movies we knew were sheer bullshit. There was a George Murphy movie where he gets his draft induction notice. He opens the telegram, and he's in his pajamas and bare feet, and he runs around the house and jumps over the couch and jumps over the chair, screaming and yelling. His landlady says, "What's going on?" "I've been drafted! I've been drafted." Well, the whole audience howled. 'Cause they know you can feed 'em only so much bullshit.

If a guy in a movie was a civilian, he always had to say—what was it? Gene Kelly in *Cover Girl?* I remember this line: "Well, Danny, why aren't you in the army?" "Hell, I was wounded in North Africa, and now all I can do is keep people happy by putting on these shows." They had to explain why the guy wasn't in uniform. Always. There was always a line in the movie: "Well, I was turned down." "Oh, tough luck." There were always soldiers in the audience, and they would scream. So we recognized a lot of the crap. . . .

The good war? That infuriates me. Yeah, the idea of World War Two being called a good war is a horrible thing. I think of all the atrocities. I think of a madman who had all this power. I think of the destruction of the Jews, the misery, the horrendous suffering in the concentration camps. In 1971, I visited Dachau. I could not believe what I saw. There's one barracks left, a model barracks. You can reconstruct the rest and see what the hell was going on. It doesn't take a visit to make you realize the extent of human misery.

I know it had to be stopped and we stopped it. But I don't feel proud, because the way we did it was so devious. How many years has it been? Forty years later? I feel I'm standing here with egg on my face. I was lied to. I was cheated. I was made a fool of If they had said to me, Look, this has to be done and we'll go out and do the job . . . we'll all get our arms and legs blown off but it has to be done, I'd understand. If they didn't hand me all this shit with the uniforms and the girls in their pompadours dancing at the USO and all those songs—"There'll Be Bluebirds over the White Cliffs of Dover"—bullshit! . . .

My brother was killed. Not even overseas. He was killed in North Carolina on a fight exercise. It ruined my mother, because she just worshipped my brother. He was the only boy. I don't think she ever recovered from it.

There was *one* good thing came out of it. I had friends whose mothers went to work in factories. For the first time in their lives, they worked outside the home. They realized that they were capable of doing something more than cook a meal. I remember going to Sunday dinner one of the older women invited me to. She and her sister at the dinner table were talking about the best way to keep their drill sharp in the factory. I had never heard anything like this in my life. It was just marvelous. I was tickled.

But even here we were sold a bill of goods. They were hammering away that the woman who went to work did it temporarily to help her man, and when he came back, he took her job and she cheerfully leaped back to the home. . . .

I think a lot of women said, Screw that noise. 'Cause they had a taste of freedom, they had a taste of making their own money, making their own decisions. I think the beginning of the women's movement had its seeds right there in World War Two.

Question

1. What strikes you about this woman's memories of World War II, the home front, and herself during the war?

Questions for Further Thought

1. How do you account for differences between the treatment of Japanese Americans and of German Americans and Italian Americans during the Second World War?
2. In *American Violence,* editors Richard Hofstadter and Michael Wallace characterize the Detroit episode as a race riot (like Chicago's in 1919), rather than as a ghetto riot (like Harlem's in 1935). Why? (See text pp. 730–731, 787, and Documents 22-14 and 24-9.)
3. Review Documents 26-6 and 26-12, and compare and contrast the two women's accounts of their lives on the home front during World War II.

Fighting and Winning the War

Even before the United States entered the Second World War, President Roosevelt had conferred with Prime Minister Winston Churchill off Newfoundland. During the war he met Churchill, Joseph Stalin of the Soviet Union, Chiang Kai-shek of China, and lesser heads of state in meetings of varying sizes. These dealt with strategizing to win the war, with maintaining unity in the coalition, which was essential to winning the war, and (as victory drew closer) with shaping the peace and postwar world (see text pp. 836, 853–854, 858–860). Document 26-13 offers President Roosevelt's address on the Yalta Conference of early 1945. As Allied armies advanced during the final stages of the European war, they overran Nazi German extermination and concentration camps. Document 26-14 provides American eyewitness accounts of concentration camps—and dead and surviving prisoners. The dropping of two atomic bombs and the entry of the Soviet Union into the Pacific-Asian war brought about Japan's surrender during August 1945. In Document 26-15, Henry L. Stimson, then secretary of war, makes the case for employing the A-bomb against Japan.

26-13   The Yalta Conference (1945)

Franklin D. Roosevelt

Addressing Congress and the nation on March 1, 1945, President Roosevelt admitted that he was doing so sitting down, rather than standing, to save himself from having to wear his leg braces, "about ten pounds of steel." The speech offered Roosevelt's public reading of the February British-Soviet-American conference at Yalta, in the Crimea, which had dealt more with the peace to come than with the war still raging (see text pp. 857–860). The President died in April; the European war ended the following month.

Source: Samuel I. Rosenman, ed., *The Public Papers and Addresses of Franklin D. Roosevelt, 1944–1945* (New York: Harper and Brothers, 1950), 571–586.

I come from the Crimea Conference with a firm belief that we have made a good start on the road to a world of peace.

There were two main purposes in this Crimea Conference. The first was to bring defeat to Germany with the greatest possible speed, and the smallest possible loss of Allied men. That purpose is now being carried out in great force. The German Army, and the German people, are feeling the ever-increasing might of our fighting men and of the Allied armies. Every hour gives us added pride in the heroic advance of our troops in Germany—on German soil—toward a meeting with the gallant Red Army.

The second purpose was to continue to build the foundation for an international accord that would bring order and security after the chaos of the war, that would give some assurance of lasting peace among the Nations of the world.

Toward that goal also, a tremendous stride was made. . . .

When we met at Yalta, in addition to laying our strategic and tactical plans for the complete and final military victory over Germany, there were other problems of vital political consequence.

For instance, first, there were the problems of the occupation and control of Germany—after victory—the complete destruction of her military power, and the assurance that neither the Nazis nor Prussian militarism could again be revived to threaten the peace and the civilization of the world.

Second—again for example—there was the settlement of the few differences that remained among us with respect to the International Security Organization after the Dumbarton Oaks Conference. As you remember, at that time, I said that we had agreed ninety percent. Well, that's a pretty good percentage. I think the other ten percent was ironed out at Yalta.

Third, there were the general political and economic problems common to all of the areas which had been or would be liberated from the Nazi yoke. This is a very special problem. We over here find it difficult to understand the ramifications of many of these problems in foreign lands, but we are trying to.

Fourth, there were the special problems created by a few instances such as Poland and Yugoslavia.

Days were spent in discussing these momentous matters and we argued freely and frankly across the table. But at the end, on every point, unanimous agreement was reached. And more important even than the agreement of words, I may say we achieved a unity of thought and a way of getting along together.

Of course, we know that it was Hitler's hope—and the German war lords'—that we would not agree—that some slight crack might appear in the solid wall of Allied unity, a crack that would give him and his fellow gangsters one last hope of escaping their just doom. That is the objective for which his propaganda machine has been working for many months.

But Hitler has failed.

Never before have the major allies been more closely united—not only in their war aims but also in their peace aims. And they are determined to continue to be united with each other—and with all peace-loving Nations—so that the ideal of lasting peace will become a reality.

The Soviet, British, and United States Chiefs of Staff held daily meetings with each other. They conferred frequently with Marshal Stalin, and with Prime Minister Churchill and with me, on the problem of coordinating the strategic and tactical efforts of the Allied powers. They completed their plans for the final knock-out blows to Germany. . . .

Of equal importance with the military arrangements at the Crimea Conference were the agreements reached with respect to a general international organization for lasting world peace. The foundations were laid at Dumbarton Oaks. There was one point, however, on which agreement was not reached at Dumbarton Oaks. It involved the procedure of voting in the Security Council. . . .

At the Crimea Conference, the Americans made a proposal on this subject which, after full discussion was, I am glad to say, unanimously adopted by the other two Nations.

It is not yet possible to announce the terms of that agreement publicly, but it will be in a very short time.

When the conclusions reached with respect to voting in the Security Council are made known, I think and I hope you will find them a fair solution of this complicated and difficult problem. They are founded in justice, and will go far to assure international cooperation in the maintenance of peace.

A conference of all the United Nations of the world will meet in San Francisco on April 25, 1945. There, we all hope, and confidently expect, to execute a definite charter of organization under which the peace of the world will be preserved and the forces of aggression permanently outlawed.

This time we are not making the mistake of waiting until the end of the war to set up the machinery of peace. This time, as we fight together to win the war finally, we work together to keep it from happening again. . . .

One outstanding example of joint action by the three major Allied powers in the liberated areas was the solution reached on Poland. The whole Polish question was a potential source of trouble in postwar Europe—as it has been sometimes before—and we came to the Conference determined to find a common ground for its solution. And we did—even though everybody does not agree with us, obviously.

Our objective was to help create a strong, independent, and prosperous Nation. That is the thing we must always remember, those words, agreed to by Russia, by Britain, and by the United States: the objective of making Poland a strong, independent, and prosperous Nation, with a government ultimately to be selected by the Polish people themselves.

To achieve that objective, it was necessary to provide for the formation of a new government much more representative than had been possible while Poland was enslaved. There were, as you know, two governments—one in London, one in Lublin—practically in Russia. Accordingly, steps were taken at Yalta to reorganize the existing Provisional Government in Poland on a broader democratic basis, so as to include democratic leaders now in Poland and those abroad. This new, reorganized government will be recognized by all of us as the temporary government of Poland. Poland needs a temporary government in the worst way—an ad interim government, I think is another way of putting it.

However, the new Polish Provisional Government of National Unity will be pledged to holding a free election as soon as possible on the basis of universal suffrage and a secret ballot.

Throughout history, Poland has been the corridor through which attacks on Russia have been made. Twice in this generation, Germany has struck at Russia through this corridor. To insure European security and world peace, a strong and independent Poland is necessary to prevent that from happening again.

The decision with respect to the boundaries of Poland was, frankly, a compromise. I did not agree with all of it, by any means, but we did not go as far as Britain wanted, in certain areas; we did not go as far as Russia wanted, in certain areas; and we did not go as far as I wanted, in certain areas. It *was* a compromise. The decision is one, however, under which the Poles will receive compensation in territory in the North and West in exchange for what they lose by the Curzon Line in the East. The limits of the western border will be permanently fixed in the final Peace Conference. We know, roughly, that it will include—in the new, strong Poland—quite a large slice of what now is called Germany. And it was agreed, also, that the new Poland will have a large and long coast line, and many new harbors. Also, that most of East Prussia will go to Poland. A corner of it will go to Russia. Also, that the anomaly of the Free State of Danzig [now Gdansk] will come to an end; I think Danzig would be a lot better if it were Polish.

It is well known that the people east of the Curzon Line—just for example, here is why I compromised—are predominantly white Russian and Ukranian—they are not Polish; and a very great majority of the people west of the line are predominantly Polish, except in that part of East Prussia and eastern Germany, which will go to the new Poland. As far back as 1919, representatives of the Allies agreed that the Curzon Line represented a fair boundary between the two peoples. And you must remember, also, that there had not been any Polish government before 1919 for a great many generations.

I am convinced that the agreement on Poland, under the circumstances, is the most hopeful agreement possible for a free, independent, and prosperous Polish state. . . .

The Conference in the Crimea was a turning point—I hope in our history and therefore in the history of the world. There will soon be presented to the Senate of the United States and to the American people a great decision that will determine the fate of the United States—and of the world—for generations to come.

Questions

1. What does Roosevelt believe he accomplished at Yalta?
2. What problems does he acknowledge were still unresolved?
3. Why does Poland figure so prominently in discussions at Yalta and in Roosevelt's speech?

26-14   Remembering the Holocaust (1945)

**William McConahey and
Dorothy Wahlstrom**

During the winter of 1944–1945, the advancing Red Army seized German extermination or death camps, which had been built in eastern Europe to slaughter Jews and others, from all areas of German-occupied Europe. The following spring, the advancing armies of the western Allies liberated German concentration camps within the Reich itself (see text pp. 856–857). Originally built to terrorize "enemies" of the Nazi regime, these had increasingly become forced and slave labor camps during the war. Large numbers of those imprisoned within them died—from overwork, malnutrition, disease, and brutal treatment—or were murdered. Here, two Americans recall the concentration camps that they helped free during the final weeks of the war in Europe.

Source: Recollections of Dr. William McConahey and Dorothy Wahlstrom, excerpted from *Witnesses to the Holocaust: An Oral History,* edited by Rhoda G. Lewin, 202–203, 214–215. Copyright © 1990 by Jewish Community Relations Council/Anti-Defamation League of Minnesota and the Dakotas. Used by permission.

(a) Dr. William McConahey, Medical Officer at Flossenburg with the 337th Infantry

. . . As we moved into Germany we started hearing about the concentration camps at army briefings. April 23 our division liberated Flossenburg, and I went in there next day.

Flossenburg held 15,000 prisoners but there were only about 1,500 left. The German guards had marched out about 13,000 toward Dachau, to get away from our advancing army. It was a very poignant, sad-looking road because they were marched out carrying blankets or maybe a jacket, but they were too weak to carry things, and they'd dropped them along the way.

A few very emaciated prisoners were wandering around in blue and white striped prison garb. My jeep driver spoke German, so he had conversations with many of the prisoners. They were from all over Europe—Poles, Russians, Czechs, French, Belgian, Spanish. They had a lot of Jewish people there, of course, but many were political prisoners, from the underground, or just people picked up by the Gestapo because they thought they were anti-Hitler. They all bore the scars of beatings and being knocked around.

The camp was laid out in very neat barracks style, with two big barbed wire fences around it. Running through it was a little railroad with a little pushcart like you see in coal mines, pushed by hand, to haul bodies to the crematory.

Three inmates, pretty much zombies, were still burning bodies in the crematory because prisoners were still dying left and right, and for sanitation you had to do something! About sixteen corpses were lined up to be burned. They were just skin and bone, each one weighing about forty pounds, I'd guess, because you could pick them up with one hand. One fellow opened the furnace door, and there were a couple of bodies in there, sizzling away.

We saw the beautiful houses where the S.S. guards lived with their women. Then I walked into the barracks, very drab and cold, with three tiers of bunks on each side. It was nothing but boards—no mattresses, no straw, nothing. Each bunk was big enough for one, but they said three slept there every night.

I visited the "hospital" where they brought prisoners to die. They'd put them on the bare wooden floor with straw on it, and they'd lie there in their own excrement and vomitus, until they died.

Some prisoners, their spirits were broken, they were just shells and they'd lost the will to live. Some were so close to death you couldn't feed them because they hadn't eaten for so long their stomachs were atrophied, and if they got food in, they vomited and bloated and obstructed. We tried to get them back on small feedings very slowly, over a period of weeks, but we couldn't save them. We felt terrible. They were dying under our eyes, and there was nothing we could do.

After the war ended, we drove to Dachau one day. Dachau was much bigger than Flossenburg. Again, we toured the barracks and saw the crematories, six big ovens. Outside were thousands of jars stacked up, the charred bones and ashes of people who had been burned there. I was told they used these for fertilizing the gardens, and that sometimes they would send a political prisoner's family a box of bones, anybody's bones. We saw the whipping posts, the torture chambers. It was obviously degradation and terror and horror and suffering, just like Flossenburg, only on a bigger scale.

It was those concentration camps that made us realize what we were fighting for. We really felt this was a holy crusade to wipe out this diabolical regime. We have sadistic bums and misfits and psychopaths in this country who could do what the S.S. did in Germany, but Hitler gave them a rank, a uniform, a purpose and a mission, and encouraged them.

The infantry medical corps was not like "M.A.S.H." or the movies. Unless you're there, unless you're in combat, and fight the battle, and crawl on your belly under machine gun bullets, and dig a foxhole in the rain, and get shelled, you can't understand what it's like. We were with the infantry, having the same life as they were having, and the same death they were having, too.

The war marked me for life. I realized that making a lot of money or being a big shot, that wasn't as important as doing something worthwhile. To really be a person was what counted.

(b) Dorothy Wahlstrom, a Captain with the 127th Evac Hospital, Whose Unit Entered Dachau on May 3, 1945

The dead and dying were all around us. Piles of naked dead were stacked beside the crematorium and inside.

Dachau was certainly a calculated attempt by the Nazis to desecrate not only the body, but also the mind and spirit.

We set up ward units in the S.S. barracks. Dead dogs lay in the kennels nearby, killed by our military after survivors told us they were used to tear away parts of prisoners' bodies on command. Survivors told us infants were torn limb from limb as their mothers watched. They told us that prisoners who could no longer work were used as live targets for machine gun practice. They mentioned other unspeakable atrocities—medical experiments, torture chambers—horrors too terrible to think up without having experienced them.

Each of the two hospital units at Dachau, the 127th and the 116th, was equipped to care for 450 patients at one time, but each unit cared for 1,500 or more at peak times.

We felt we were dancing with death. We couldn't get away from it, and wondered if it would ever stop. We couldn't care for everyone, and often we could not admit a patient until another one died or was discharged from the hospital. It was truly heartbreaking for our medical officers to have to choose the people they thought might live and leave the sickest ones to die. Of those we thought would live, seven or eight stretchers were lined up in front of each ward in the morning—people who had died during the night.

The severely malnourished did not tolerate increased rations too well, and dysentery was out of control. We had double bunk beds for our patients, and the diarrhea was so severe it leaked from bed to bed. Many were so emaciated that even with the care we gave them, it was too late.

The diseases were those that go with filth and lack of sanitation. One and one-half tons of DDT powder were used in dusting the camp to get control of the infected lice that spread typhus. Perhaps 20 percent of the camp population had active tuberculosis.

I wish I could describe the smells and the silence of death. Even now, certain sights and sound can remind me of that pain, that suffering, that sorrow and loss and anguish and degradation.

I find comfort in the sacred Scriptures that record that the Lord will vindicate His Israel, and that there will always be a House of David. I am truly grateful to the Lord for having allowed me to serve His people.

Questions

1. Which sights and smells affected McConahey and Wahlstrom the most as they toured the death camps?
2. Why did medical personnel feel so frustrated in their efforts to save the victims they found in the camps?
3. How did their experiences with the victims of the Holocaust change the lives of McConahey and Wahlstrom?

26-15   The Decision to Use the Atomic Bomb (1945)

Henry L. Stimson

Given the increasing bloodiness and brutality of the Second World War and the massive scientific and engineering investment in developing the atomic bomb, it was well-nigh inevitable that, once built, the atomic bomb would be used. Given that Germany had surrendered (in May 1945) before the successful testing of the atomic bomb, the first—and to date, only—atomic bombs employed in war were dropped on Japan that August (see text pp. 860–862). Secretary of War Henry L. Stimson (1867–1950) served Presidents Roosevelt and Truman throughout World War II. His postwar account of the decision to employ the bomb includes an assessment of the war written shortly before the testing of the atomic bomb.

Sources: Henry L. Stimson, "The Decision to Use the Atomic Bomb," *Harper's Magazine* 194 (February 1947): 102–107. Copyright 1947 by *Harper's Magazine*. All rights rerserved. Reprinted by special permission.

It was already clear in July that even before the invasion we should be able to inflict enormously severe damage on the Japanese homeland by the combined application of "conventional" sea and air power. The critical question was whether this kind of action would induce surrender. It therefore became necessary to consider very carefully the probable state of mind of the enemy, and to assess with accuracy the line of conduct which might end his will to resist.

With these considerations in mind, I wrote a memorandum for the President, on July 2, which I believe fairly represents the thinking of the American government as it finally took shape in action. This memorandum was prepared after discussion and general agreement with Joseph C. Grew, Acting Secretary of State, and Secretary of the Navy Forrestal, and when I discussed it with the President, he expressed his general approval.

July 2, 1945.

Memorandum for the President.

PROPOSED PROGRAM FOR JAPAN

1. The plans of operation up to and including the first landing have been authorized and the preparation for the operation are now actually going on. This situation was accepted by all members of your conference on Monday, June 18.

2. There is reason to believe that the operation for the occupation of Japan following the landing may be a very long, costly, and arduous struggle on our part. The terrain, much of which I have visited several times, has left the impression on my memory of being one which would be susceptible to a last ditch defense such as has been made on Iwo Jima and Okinawa and which of course is very much larger than either of those two areas. According to my recollection it will be much more unfavorable with regard to tank maneuvering than either the Philippines or Germany.

3. If we once land on one of the main islands and begin a forceful occupation of Japan, we shall probably have cast the die of last ditch resistance. The Japanese are highly patriotic and certainly susceptible to calls for fanatical resistance to repel an invasion. Once started in actual invasion, we shall in my opinion have to go through with an even more bitter finish fight than in Germany. We shall incur the losses incident to such a war and we shall have to leave the Japanese islands even more thoroughly destroyed than was the case with Germany. This would be due both to the difference in the Japanese and German personal character and the differences in the size and character of the terrain through which the operations will take place.

4. A question then comes: Is there any alternative to such a forceful occupation of Japan which will secure for us the equivalent of an unconditional surrender of her forces and a permanent destruction of her power again to strike an aggressive blow at the "peace of the Pacific"? I am inclined to think that there is enough such chance to make it well worthwhile our giving them a warning of what is to come and a definite opportunity to capitulate. As above suggested, it should be tried before the actual forceful occupation of the homeland islands is begun and furthermore the warning should be given in ample time to permit a national reaction to set in.

We have the following enormously favorable factors on our side—factors much weightier than those we had against Germany:

- Japan has no allies.
- Her navy is nearly destroyed and she is vulnerable to a surface and underwater blockade which can deprive her of sufficient food and supplies for her population.

- She is terribly vulnerable to our concentrated air attack upon her crowded cities, industrial and food resources.
- She has against her not only the Anglo-American forces but the rising forces of China and the ominous threat of Russia.
- We have inexhaustible and untouched industrial resources to bring to bear against her diminishing potential.
- We have great moral superiority through being the victim of her first sneak attack.

The problem is to translate these advantages into prompt and economical achievement of our objectives. I believe Japan is susceptible to reason in such a crisis to a much greater extent than is indicated by our current press and other current comment. Japan is not a nation composed wholly of mad fanatics of an entirely different mentality from ours. On the contrary, she has within the past century shown herself to possess extremely intelligent people, capable in an unprecedentedly short time of adopting not only the complicated technique of Occidental civilization but to a substantial extent their culture and their political and social ideas. Her advance in all these respects during the short period of sixty or seventy years has been one of the most astounding feats of national progress in history—a leap from the isolated feudalism of centuries into the position of one of the six or seven great powers of the world. She has not only built up powerful armies and navies. She has maintained an honest and effective national finance and respected position in many of the sciences in which we pride ourselves. Prior to the forcible seizure of power over her government by the fanatical military group in 1931, she had for ten years lived a reasonably responsible and respectable international life.

My own opinion is in her favor on the two points involved in this question:

a. I think the Japanese nation has the mental intelligence and versatile capacity in such a crisis to recognize the follow of a fight to the finish and to accept the proffer of what will amount to an unconditional surrender; and

b. I think she has within her population enough liberal leaders (although now submerged by the terrorists) to be depended upon for her reconstruction as a responsible member of the family of nations. I think she is better in this last respect than Germany was. Her liberals yielded only at the point of pistol and, so far as I am aware, their liberal attitude has not been personally subverted in the way which was so general in Germany.

On the other hand, I think that the attempt to exterminate her armies and her population by gunfire or other means will tend to produce a fusion of race so-

lidity and antipathy which has no analogy in the case of Germany. We have a national interest in creating, if possible, a condition wherein the Japanese nation may live as a peaceful and useful member of the future Pacific community.

5. It is therefore my conclusion that a carefully timed warning be given to Japan by the chief representatives of the United States, Great Britain, China, and, if then a belligerent, Russia by calling upon Japan to surrender and permit the occupation of her country in order to insure its complete demilitarization for the sake of the future peace.

This warning should contain the following elements:

The varied and overwhelming character of the force we are about to bring to bear on the islands.

The inevitability and completeness of the destruction which the full application of this force will entail.

The determination of the Allies to destroy permanently all authority and influence of those who have deceived and misled the country into embarking on world conquest.

The determination of the Allies to limit Japanese sovereignty to her main islands and to render them powerless to mount and support another war.

The disavowal of any attempt to extirpate the Japanese as a race or to destroy them as a nation.

A statement of our readiness, once her economy is purged of its militaristic influence, to permit the Japanese to maintain such industries, particularly of a light consumer character, as offer no threat of aggression against their neighbors, but which can produce a sustaining economy, and provide a reasonable standard of living. The statement should indicate our willingness, for this purpose, to give Japan trade access to external raw materials, but no longer any control over the sources of supply outside her main islands. It should also indicate our willingness, in accordance with our now established foreign trade policy, in due course to enter into mutually advantageous trade relations with her.

The withdrawal from their country as soon as the above objectives of the Allies are accomplished, and as soon as there has been established a peacefully inclined government, of a character representative of the masses of the Japanese people. I personally think that if in saying this we should add that we do not exclude a constitutional monarchy under her present dynasty, it would substantially add to the chances of acceptance.

6. Success of course will depend on the potency of the warning which we give her. She has an extremely sensitive national pride and, as we are now seeing every day, when actually locked with the enemy will fight to the very death. For that reason the warning must be tendered before the actual invasion has occurred and while the impending destruction, though

clear beyond peradventure, has not yet reduced her to fanatical despair. If Russia is a part of the threat, the Russian attack, if actual, must not have progressed too far. Our own bombing should be confined to military objectives as far as possible.

It is important to emphasize the double character of the suggested warning. It was designed to promise destruction if Japan resisted, and hope, if she surrendered.

It will be noted that the atomic bomb is not mentioned in this memorandum. On grounds of secrecy the bomb was never mentioned except when absolutely necessary, and furthermore, it had not yet been tested. It was of course well forward in our minds, as the memorandum was written and discussed, that the bomb would be the best possible sanction if our warning were rejected.

THE USE OF THE BOMB

The adoption of the policy outlined in the memorandum of July 2 was a decision of high politics; once it was accepted by the President, the position of the atomic bomb in our planning became quite clear. I find that I stated in my diary, as early as June 19, that "the last chance warning . . . must be given before an actual landing of the ground forces in Japan, and fortunately the plans provide for enough time to bring in the sanctions to our warning in the shape of heavy ordinary bombing attack and an attack of S-1." S-1 was a code name for the atomic bomb.

There was much discussion in Washington about the timing of the warning to Japan. The controlling factor in the end was the date already set for the Potsdam meeting of the Big Three. It was President Truman's decision that such a warning should be solemnly issued by the U.S. and the U.K. from this meeting, with the concurrence of the head of the Chinese government, so that it would be plain that *all* of Japan's principal enemies were in entire unity. This was done, in the Potsdam ultimatum of July 26, which very closely followed the above memorandum of July 2, with the exception that it made no mention of the Japanese Emperor.

On July 28 the Premier of Japan, Suzuki, rejected the Potsdam ultimatum by announcing that it was "unworthy of public notice." In the face of this rejection we could only proceed to demonstrate that the ultimatum had meant exactly what it said when it stated that if the Japanese continued the war, "the full application of our military power, backed by our resolve, will mean the inevitable and complete destruction of the Japanese armed forces and just as inevitably the utter devastation of the Japanese homeland."

For such a purpose the atomic bomb was an eminently suitable weapon. The New Mexico test occurred while we were at Potsdam, on July 16. It was immediately clear that the power of the bomb measured up to our highest estimates. We had developed a weapon of such a revolutionary character that its use against the enemy might well be

expected to produce exactly the kind of shock on the Japanese ruling oligarchy which we desired, strengthening the position of those who wished peace, and weakening that of the military party.

Because of the importance of the atomic mission against Japan, the detailed plans were brought to me by the military staff for approval. With President Truman's warm support I struck off the list of suggested targets the city of Kyoto. Although it was a target of considerable military importance, it had been the ancient capital of Japan and was a shrine of Japanese art and culture. We determined that it should be spared. I approved four other targets including the cities of Hiroshima and Nagasaki.

Hiroshima was bombed on August 6, and Nagasaki on August 9. These two cities were active working parts of the Japanese war effort. One was an army center; the other was naval and industrial. Hiroshima was the headquarters of the Japanese Army defending southern Japan and was a major military storage and assembly point. Nagasaki was a major seaport and it contained several large industrial plants of great wartime importance. We believed that our attacks had struck cities which must certainly be important to the Japanese military leaders, both Army and Navy, and we waited for a result. We waited one day.

Many accounts have been written about the Japanese surrender. After a prolonged Japanese cabinet session in which the deadlock was broken by the Emperor himself, the offer to surrender as made on August 10. It was based on the Potsdam terms, with a reservation concerning the sovereignty of the Emperor. While the Allied reply made no promises other than those already given, it implicitly recognized the Emperor's position by prescribing that his power must be subject to the orders of the Allied Supreme Commander. These terms were accepted on August 14 by the Japanese, and the instrument of surrender was formally signed on September 2, in Tokyo Bay. Our great objective was thus achieved, and all the evidence I have seen indicates that the controlling factor in the final Japanese decision to accept our terms of surrender was the atomic bomb.[*]

The two atomic bombs which we had dropped were the only ones we had ready, and our rate of production at the time was very small. Had the war continued until the projected invasion on November 1, additional fire raids of B-29's would have been more destructive of life and property than the very limited number of atomic raids which we could have executed in the same period. But the atomic bomb was more than a weapon of terrible destruction; it was a psychological weapon. In March 1945 our Air Force

[*] Report of United States Strategic Bombing Survey; "Japan's Struggle to End the War"; "If the Atomic Bomb Had Not Been Used," by K. T. Compton, *Atlantic Monthly,* December 1946; unpublished material of historical division, War Department Special Staff, June 1946.

had launched its first great incendiary raid on the Tokyo area. In this raid more damage was done and more casualties were inflicted than was the case at Hiroshima. Hundreds of bombers took part and hundreds of tons of incendiaries were dropped. Similar successive raids burned out a great part of the urban area of Japan, but the Japanese fought on. On August 6 one B-29 dropped a single atomic bomb on Hiroshima. Three days later a second bomb was dropped on Nagasaki and the war was over. So far as the Japanese could know, our ability to execute atomic attacks, if necessary by many planes at a time, was unlimited. As Dr. Karl Compton has said, it was not one atomic bomb, or two, which brought surrender; it was the experience of what an atomic bomb will actually do to a community, *plus the dread of many more*, that was effective."

The bomb thus served exactly the purpose we intended. The peace party was able to take the path of surrender, and the whole weight of the Emperor's prestige was exerted in favor of peace. When the Emperor ordered surrender, and the small but dangerous group of fanatics who opposed him were brought under control, the Japanese became so subdued that the great undertaking of occupation and disarmament was completed with unprecedented ease.

A PERSONAL SUMMARY

In the foregoing pages I have tried to give an accurate account of my own personal observations of the circumstances which led up to the use of the atomic bomb and the reasons which underlay our use of it. To me they have always seemed compelling and clear, and I cannot see how any person vested with such responsibilities as mine could have taken any other course or given any other advice to his chiefs.

Two great nations were approaching contact in a fight to a finish which would begin on November 1, 1945. Our enemy, Japan, commanded forces of somewhat over 5,000,000 armed men. Men of these armies had already inflicted upon us, in our breakthrough of the outer perimeter of their defenses, over 300,000 battle casualties. Enemy armies still unbeaten had the strength to cost us a million more. *As long as the Japanese government refused to surrender,* we should be forced to take and hold the ground, and smash the Japanese ground armies, by close-in fighting of the same desperate and costly kind that we had faced in the Pacific islands for nearly four years.

In the light of the formidable problem which thus confronted us, I felt that every possible step should be taken to compel a surrender of the homelands, and a withdrawal of all Japanese troops from the Asiatic mainland and from other positions, before we had commenced an invasion. We held two cards to assist us in such an effort. One was the traditional veneration in which the Japanese Emperor was held by his subjects and the power which was thus vested in him over his loyal troops. It was for this reason that I suggested in my memorandum of July 2 that his dynasty should be continued. The second card was the use of the atomic bomb in the manner best calculated to persuade that Emperor and the counselors about him to submit to our demand for what was essentially unconditional surrender, placing his immense power over his people and his troops subject to our orders.

In order to end the war in the shortest possible time and to avoid the enormous losses of human life which otherwise confronted us, I felt that we must use the Emperor as our instrument to command and compel his people to cease fighting and subject themselves to our authority through him, and that to accomplish this we must give him and his controlling advisers a compelling reason to accede to our demands. This reason furthermore must be of such a nature that his people could understand his decision. The bomb seemed to me to furnish a unique instrument for that purpose.

My chief purpose was to end the war in victory with the least possible cost in the lives of the men in the armies which I had helped to raise. In the light of the alternatives which, on a fair estimate, were open to us I believe that no man, in our position and subject to our responsibilities, holding in his hands a weapon of such possibilities for accomplishing this purpose and saving those lives, could have failed to use it and afterwards looked his countrymen in the face.

As I read over what I have written, I am aware that much of it, in this year of peace, may have a harsh and unfeeling sound. It would perhaps be possible to say the same things and say them more gently. But I do not think it would be wise. As I look back over the five years of my service as Secretary of War, I see too many stern and heartrending decisions to be willing to pretend that war is anything else than what it is. The face of war is the face of death; death is an inevitable part of every order that a wartime leader gives. The decision to use the atomic bomb was a decision that brought death to over a hundred thousand Japanese. No explanation can change that fact and I do not wish to gloss it over. But this deliberate, premeditated destruction was our lease abhorrent choice. The destruction of Hiroshima and Nagasaki put an end to the Japanese war. It stopped the fire raids, and the strangling blockade; it ended the ghastly specter of a clash of great land armies.

In this last great action of the Second World War we were given final proof that war is death. War in the twentieth century has grown steadily more barbarous, more destructive, more debased in all its aspects. Now, with the release of atomic energy, man's ability to destroy himself is very nearly complete. The bombs dropped on Hiroshima and Nagasaki ended a war. They also made it wholly clear that we must never have another war. This is the lesson men and leaders everywhere must learn, and I believe that when they learn it they will find a way to lasting peace. There is no other choice.

Questions

1. What is the case Stimson makes for using the atomic bomb?
2. Are his postwar reflections consistent with his wartime assessment of the war against Japan, as revealed in the memorandum of July 2, 1945?
3. What were Stimson's views of the Japanese in 1945 and 1947?

Questions for Further Thought

1. Compare and contrast President Roosevelt's report on the Yalta Conference (Document 26-13) with his "Four Freedoms" speech (Document 26-2) and Roosevelt and Churchill's Atlantic Charter (Document 26-5). How do you account for similarities (if any) and differences (if any) between the 1941 speech and charter and the 1945 speech?
2. Compare and contrast the international situation as viewed by President Woodrow Wilson in his "Fourteen Points" speech (Document 22-2) early in 1918 with that as seen by President Roosevelt in his speech on the Yalta Conference (Document 26-13) early in 1945.
3. Drawing on the text, reflect on Documents 26-14 and 26-15. How do they contribute to your understanding of the Second World War?

CHAPTER **27**

Cold War America, 1945–1960

★   ★   ★

The Early Cold War

As the Second World War drew to a close, the United States, by now the world's most powerful nation, appeared ready to lead in the creation of a postwar international order that, leaders hoped, would prevent a recurrence of the disastrous economic, political, and diplomatic breakdowns of the 1930s (see text pp. 857–860, 904–905). But the United States emerged victorious from World War II only to enter a Cold War against a ravaged, but powerful, wartime ally (the Soviet Union), other Communist nations (most significantly Red China after the Chinese Communists' victory), and the Communist movement in many countries, some considered vital to American strategic, economic, and ideological interests.

Over the span of five years, 1945 to 1950, developments in the very complex postwar world prompted American policy makers to shape plans to meet various threats to the interests of the United States and other nations with shared interests. Containment of the Soviet Union became central to American foreign policy, a doctrine articulated by George Kennan in 1946 and 1947 (Document 27-1). Communists' prominent role in a civil war in Greece, Soviet pressure on Turkey, and a continued Soviet presence in Iran (dating to World War II) led to increased pressure on the Soviets to withdraw from Iran and to the enunciation of the Truman Doctrine (Document 27-2), which provided economic and military assistance to Greece and Turkey. The Marshall Plan was formulated to stimulate Europe's depressed postwar economy, thereby undercutting the appeal of Communist parties and making possible an economic recovery that would benefit the United States as well as the European participants (see text pp. 871–875, including "Voices from Abroad: Jean Monnet"). To shield America's European allies from Soviet-bloc military threats or action, the United States and eleven other nations created the North Atlantic Treaty Organization (NATO), though not without debate in the U.S. Senate (Documents 27-3 and 27-4). Finally, ominous developments during 1949—the Communists' triumph over the Nationalists in China's civil war and the

Soviets' detonation of an atomic bomb—led the National Security Council (NSC) to prepare a strategic plan for waging the Cold War (see text pp. 867–877). Two months after President Truman received the report, NSC-68 (Document 27-5), the Cold War became a hot war, not in Europe, but in Asia, where Communist North Korea invaded South Korea (see text pp. 877–878). For President Truman's response, see Document 27-6.

27-1   Containment Policy (1947)

George F. Kennan

George F. Kennan (b. 1904), a career diplomat attached to the American embassy in Moscow, assessed the Soviet Union and its foreign policy in a "long telegram" to the U.S. government in 1946 and in an anonymous article the next year. In doing so, he helped to define America's policy of containment, which was to remain important throughout the Cold War. (On containment and Kennan, see text p. 870; and "American Lives: George F. Kennan," text pp. 872–873.)

Source: X [George Kennan], "The Sources of Soviet Conduct." Reprinted by permission of *Foreign Affairs,* July 1947, 566–582. Copyright © 1947 by the Council on Foreign Relations, Inc.

The political personality of Soviet power as we know it today is the product of ideology and circumstances: ideology inherited by the present Soviet leaders from the movement in which they had their political origin, and circumstances of the power which they now have exercised for nearly three decades in Russia. . . .

It is difficult to summarize the set of ideological concepts with which the Soviet leaders came into power. Marxian ideology, in its Russian-Communist projection, has always been in process of subtle evolution. The materials on which it bases itself are extensive and complex. But the outstanding features of Communist thought as it existed in 1916 may perhaps be summarized as follows: (a) that the central factor in the life of man, the factor which determines the character of public life and the "physiognomy of society," is the system by which material goods are produced and exchanged; (b) that the capitalist system of production is a nefarious one which inevitably leads to the exploitation of the working class by the capital-owning class and is incapable of developing adequately the economic resources of society or of distributing fairly the material goods produced by human labor; (c) that capitalism contains the seeds of its own destruction and must, in view of the inability of the capital-owning class to adjust itself to economic change, result eventually and inescapably in a revolutionary transfer of power to the working class; and (d) that imperialism, the final phase of capitalism, leads directly to war and revolution.

The rest may be outlined in Lenin's own words: "Unevenness of economic and political development is the in-flexible law of capitalism. It follows from this that the victory of Socialism may come originally in a few capitalist countries or even in a single capitalist country. The victorious proletariat of that country, having expropriated the capitalists and having organized Socialist production at home, would rise against the remaining capitalist world, drawing to itself in the process the oppressed classes of other countries." It must be noted that there was no assumption that capitalism would perish without proletarian revolution. A final push was needed from a revolutionary proletariat movement in order to tip over the tottering structure. But it was regarded as inevitable that sooner or later that push be given. . . .

The circumstances of the immediate post-revolution period—the existence in Russia of civil war and foreign intervention, together with the obvious fact that the Communists represented only a tiny minority of the Russian people—made the establishment of dictatorial power a necessity. The experiment with "war Communism" and the abrupt attempt to eliminate private production and trade had unfortunate economic consequences and caused further bitterness against the new revolutionary régime. While the temporary relaxation of the effort to communize Russia, represented by the New Economic Policy, alleviated some of this economic distress and thereby served its purpose, it also made evident that the "capitalist sector of society" was still prepared to profit at once from any relaxation of governmental pressure, and would, if permitted to continue to exist, always constitute a powerful opposing element to the Soviet régime and a serious rival for influence in the country. Somewhat the same situation prevailed with respect to the individual peasant who, in his own small way, was also a private producer. . . .

Now the outstanding circumstance concerning the Soviet régime is that down to the present day this process of political consolidation has never been completed and the men in the Kremlin have continued to be predominantly absorbed with the struggle to secure and make absolute the power which they seized in November 1917. They have endeavored to secure it primarily against forces at home, within Soviet society itself. But they have also endeavored to secure it against the outside world. For ideology, as we have seen, taught them that the outside world was hostile and that it was their duty eventually to overthrow the political forces beyond their borders. The powerful hands of Russian history and tradition reached up to sustain them in this feeling. Finally, their own aggressive intransigence with respect to the outside world began to find its own reaction; and they were soon forced, to use another Gibbonesque phrase, "to chastise the contumacy" which they themselves had provoked. It is an undeniable privilege of every man to prove himself right in the thesis that the world is his enemy; for if he reiterates it frequently enough and makes it the background of his conduct he is bound eventually to be right. . . .

Now the maintenance of this pattern of Soviet power, namely, the pursuit of unlimited authority domestically, accompanied by the cultivation of the semi-myth of implacable foreign hostility, has gone far to shape the actual machinery of Soviet power as we know it today. Internal organs of administration which did not serve this purpose withered on the vine. Organs which did serve this purpose became vastly swollen. The security of Soviet power came to rest on the iron discipline of the Party, on the severity and ubiquity of the secret police, and on the uncompromising economic monopolism of the state. The "organs of suppression," in which the Soviet leaders had sought security from rival forces, became in large measure the masters of those whom they were designed to serve. Today the major part of the structure of Soviet power is committed to the perfection of the dictatorship and to the maintenance of the concept of Russia as in a state of siege, with the enemy lowering beyond the walls. And the millions of human beings who form that part of the structure of power must defend at all costs this concept of Russia's position, for without it they are themselves superfluous.

As things stand today, the rulers can no longer dream of parting with these organs of suppression. The quest for absolute power, pursued now for nearly three decades with a ruthlessness unparalleled (in scope at least) in modern times, has again produced internally, as it did externally, its own reaction. The excesses of the police apparatus have fanned the potential opposition to the régime into something far greater and more dangerous than it could have been before those excesses began.

But least of all can the rulers dispense with the fiction by which the maintenance of dictatorial power has been defended. For this fiction has been canonized in Soviet philosophy by the excesses already committed in its name; and it is now anchored in the Soviet structure of thought by bonds far greater than those of mere ideology.

II

. . . Once a given party line has been laid down on a given issue of current policy, the whole Soviet governmental machine, including the mechanism of diplomacy, moves inexorably along the prescribed path, like a persistent toy automobile wound up and headed in a given direction, stopping only when it meets with some unanswerable force. The individuals who are the components of this machine are unamenable to argument or reason which comes to them from outside sources. Their whole training has taught them to mistrust and discount the glib persuasiveness of the outside world. Like the white dog before the phonograph, they hear only the "master's voice." And if they are to be called off from the purposes last dictated to them, it is the master who must call them off. Thus the foreign representative cannot hope that his words will make any impression on them. The most that he can hope is that they will be transmitted to those at the top, who are capable of changing the party line. But even those are not likely to be swayed by any normal logic in the words of the bourgeois representative. Since there can be no appeal to common purposes, there can be no appeal to common mental approaches. For this reason, facts speak louder than words to the ears of the Kremlin; and words carry the greatest weight when they have the ring of reflecting, or being backed up by, facts of unchallengeable validity.

But we have seen that the Kremlin is under no ideological compulsion to accomplish its purposes in a hurry. Like the Church, it is dealing in ideological concepts which are of long-term validity, and it can afford to be patient. It has no right to risk the existing achievements of the revolution for the sake of vain baubles of the future. The very teachings of Lenin himself require great caution and flexibility in the pursuit of Communist purposes. Again, these precepts are fortified by the lessons of Russian history: of centuries of obscure battles between nomadic forces over the stretches of a vast unfortified plain. Here caution, circumspection, flexibility and deception are the valuable qualities; and their value finds natural appreciation in the Russian or the oriental mind. Thus the Kremlin has no compunction about retreating in the face of superior force. And being under the compulsion of no timetable, it does not get panicky under the necessity for such retreat. Its political action is a fluid stream which moves constantly, wherever it is permitted to move, toward a given goal. Its main concern is to make sure that it has filled every nook and cranny available to it in the basin of world power. But if it finds unassailable barriers in its path, it accepts these philosophically and accommodates itself to them. The main thing is that there should always be pressure, unceasing constant pressure, toward the desired goal. . . .

In these circumstances it is clear that the main element of any United States policy toward the Soviet Union must be that of a long-term, patient but firm and vigilant containment of Russian expansive tendencies. It is important to note, however, that such a policy has nothing to do with outward histrionics: with threats or blustering or superfluous gestures of outward "toughness." . . .

III

In the light of the above, it will be clearly seen that the Soviet pressure against the free institutions of the western world is something that can be contained by the adroit and vigilant application of counter-force at a series of constantly shifting geographical and political points, corresponding to the shifts and manœuvres of Soviet policy, but which cannot be charmed or talked out of existence. . . .

Thus the future of Soviet power may not be by any means as secure as Russian capacity for self-delusion would make it appear to the men in the Kremlin. That they can keep power themselves, they have demonstrated. That they can quietly and easily turn it over to others remains to be proved. Meanwhile, the hardships of their rule and the vicissitudes of international life have taken a heavy toll of the strength and hopes of the great people on whom their power rests. . . . This cannot be proved. And it cannot be disproved: But the possibility remains (and in the opinion of this writer it is a strong one) that Soviet power, like the capitalist world of its conception, bears within it the seeds of its own decay, and that the sprouting of these seeds is well advanced.

IV

It is clear that the United States cannot expect in the foreseeable future to enjoy political intimacy with the Soviet régime. It must continue to regard the Soviet Union as a rival, not a partner, in the political arena. It must continue to expect that Soviet policies will reflect no abstract love of peace and stability, no real faith in the possibility of a permanent happy coexistence of the Socialist and capitalist worlds, but rather a cautious, persistent pressure toward the disruption and weakening of all rival influence and rival power.

Balanced against this are the facts that Russia, as opposed to the western world in general, is still by far the weaker party, that Soviet policy is highly flexible, and that Soviet society may well contain deficiencies which will eventually weaken its own total potential. This would of itself warrant the United States entering with reasonable confidence upon a policy of firm containment, designed to confront the Russians with unalterable counter-force at every point where they show signs of encroaching upon the interests of a peaceful and stable world.

But in actuality the possibilities for American policy are by no means limited to holding the line and hoping for the best. It is entirely possible for the United States to influence by its actions the internal developments, both within Russia and throughout the international Communist movement, by which Russian policy is largely determined. This is not only a question of the modest measure of informational activity which this government can conduct in the Soviet Union and elsewhere, although that, too, is important. It is rather a question of the degree to which the United States can create among the peoples of the world generally the impression of a country which knows what it wants, which is coping successfully with the problems of its internal life and with the responsibilities of a World Power, and which has a spiritual vitality capable of holding its own among the major ideological currents of the time. To the extent that such an impression can be created and maintained, the aims of Russian Communism must appear sterile and quixotic, the hopes and enthusiasm of Moscow's supporters must wane, and added strain must be imposed on the Kremlin's foreign policies. For the palsied decrepitude of the capitalist world is the keystone of Communist philosophy. Even the failure of the United States to experience the early economic depression which the ravens of the Red Square have been predicting with such complacent confidence since hostilities ceased would have deep and important repercussions throughout the Communist world. . . .

It would be an exaggeration to say that American behavior unassisted and alone could exercise a power of life and death over the Communist movement and bring about the early fall of Soviet power in Russia. But the United States has it in its power to increase enormously the strains under which Soviet policy must operate, to force upon the Kremlin a far greater degree of moderation and circumspection than it has had to observe in recent years, and in this way to promote tendencies which must eventually find their outlet in either the break-up or the gradual mellowing of Soviet power. For no mystical, Messianic movement— and particularly not that of the Kremlin—can face frustration indefinitely without eventually adjusting itself in one way or another to the logic of that state of affairs.

Thus the decision will really fall in large measure in this country itself. The issue of Soviet-American relations is in essence a test of the over-all worth of the United States as a nation among nations. To avoid destruction the United States need only measure up to its own best traditions and prove itself worthy of preservation as a great nation.

Surely, there was never a fairer test of national quality than this. In the light of these circumstances, the thoughtful observer of Russian-American relations will find no cause for complaint in the Kremlin's challenge to American society. He will rather experience a certain gratitude to a Providence which, by providing the American people with this implacable challenge, has made their entire security as a nation dependent on their pulling themselves together and accepting the responsibilities of moral and political leadership that history plainly intended them to bear.

Questions

1. How does Kennan explain "the sources of Soviet conduct"?
2. What strategies does he propose for implementing the policy of containment?
3. What does Kennan see as the outcome of containment?

27-2   Remembering the Truman Doctrine (1947)

Harry S. Truman

Crises involving Iran, Turkey, and Greece provided early tests of the containment policy. In his memoirs, former President Harry S. Truman (1884–1972) recalls these crises and his responses, especially the response that became known as the Truman Doctrine (see text pp. 870–871).

Source: Harry S. Truman, *Memoirs by Harry S. Truman,* vol. 2, *Years of Trial and Hope* (Garden City, N.Y.: Doubleday, 1956), 93, 95–106. Reprinted with permission.

In early 1946 Russian activities in Iran threatened the peace of the world. . . .

As I saw it, three things were involved. One was the security of Turkey. Russia had been pressing Turkey for special privileges and for territorial concessions for several months. The Turks had resisted all these demands, but their position would be infinitely more difficult if Russia, or a Russian puppet state, were able to outflank her in the east.

The second problem was the control of Iran's oil reserves. That Russia had an eye on these vast deposits seemed beyond question. If the Russians were to control Iran's oil, either directly or indirectly, the raw-material balance of the world would undergo a serious change, and it would be a serious loss for the economy of the Western world.

What perturbed me most, however, was Russia's callous disregard of the rights of a small nation and of her own solemn promises. International co-operation was impossible if national obligations could be ignored and the U.N. bypassed as if it did not exist.

I talked over all these points with Secretary Byrnes and Admiral Leahy. Then I told Byrnes to send a blunt message to Premier Stalin. On March 24 Moscow announced that all Russian troops would be withdrawn from Iran at once. The threat to Turkey had been removed, although it had not vanished and continued to demand our attention. Iran could negotiate with Russia without feeling threatened; indeed, its parliament rejected later the accord entered into by its government, a clear sign that fear had been removed from the land.

The world was now able to look more hopefully toward the United Nations. But Russia's ambitions would not be halted by friendly reminders of promises made. The Russians would press wherever weakness showed—and we would have to meet that pressure wherever it occurred, in a manner that Russia and the world would understand. When Communist pressure began to endanger Greece and Turkey, I moved to make this policy clear and firm.

It was not long before the same issue was presented to us again in the same part of the world. Turkey and Greece had become subjected to heavy pressures from the Russian bloc. Each of them had valiantly sought to repel these pressures, but now their strength was waning and they were in need of aid.

Turkey was, of course, an age-old objective of Russian ambitions. The Communists were only continuing what the Czars had practiced when they tried to gain control of the area that blocked Russian exit into the Mediterranean Sea. . . .

[T]he Russians, in addition to their efforts to outflank Turkey through Iran, were beginning to exert pressure on Turkey for territorial concessions. In July 1946, Moscow sent a note to Ankara proposing a new regime for the Dardanelles that would have excluded all nations except the Black Sea powers. In other words, both we and the British would have been eliminated from any future agreement, and Turkey would have been faced by a combination of three Communist states: Russia, Rumania, and Bulgaria. The second and far more ominous part of the Soviet proposal was that the straits should be put under joint Turkish-Russian defense.

This was indeed an open bid to obtain control of Turkey. If Russian troops entered Turkey with the ostensible purpose of enforcing joint control of the straits, it would only be a short time before these troops would be used for the control of all of Turkey. We had learned from the experience of the past two years that Soviet intervention inevitably meant Soviet occupation and control. To allow Russia to set up bases in the Dardanelles or to bring troops into Turkey, ostensibly for the defense of the straits, would, in the natural course of events, result in Greece and the whole Near and Middle East falling under Soviet control.

The Turkish government sought our advice, and Acting Secretary of State Acheson placed the matter before me. I directed the State, War, and Navy Departments to make a careful study of the situation. The Secretaries of the three departments, with the Chiefs of Staff, moved with speed and brought me a unanimous recommendation that we take a strong position. I met with the Secretaries and the Chiefs of Staff and discussed the development thoroughly around a map on my desk to evaluate the situation in the Middle East. I approved the recommendations submitted. We co-ordinated our views with those of our allies, taking a strong position, which was at once communicated to the Turkish government. At the same time, the Turkish government received similar views and support from the British and French. . . .

While Turkey's plight was entirely due to Russia's postwar intransigence, the condition of Greece had its beginning in the World War II occupation of that nation.

Greece had suffered tragically in World War II. Her people had offered heroic resistance to Mussolini's army, but at last the combined might of Germany and Italy had broken the Greek armies.

Resistance continued, however, throughout the country, and soon it had come to crystallize around two principal groups. One of these, the so-called EAM, was under Communist domination; the other remained loyal to the King and his government in exile. Between the vicious practices of the German forces of occupation and the constant fighting between the resistance groups, normal life in Greece virtually ceased. Fields and factories were idle. People starved, and disease took untold numbers. . . .

The Communists, of course, thrived on the continuing conditions of misery, starvation, and economic ruin. Moscow and the Balkan satellite countries were now rendering open support to the EAM. Intelligence reports which I received stated that many of the insurgents had been trained, indoctrinated, armed, and equipped at various camps beyond the Greek borders. Under Soviet direction, the reports said, Greece's northern neighbors—Yugoslavia, Bulgaria, and Albania—were conducting a drive to establish a Communist Greece.

What little stability and order could be found in Greece was due primarily to the presence there of forty thousand British troops and to the counsel and support given to the Greek government by the British. But as early as the fall of 1945 the British had suggested to us that they would like our assistance in Greece, especially financial help to the Greek government.

I had authorized the State Department to enter into discussions with the British on terms of economic aid to Greece. . . .

Greece needed aid, and needed it quickly and in substantial amounts. The alternative was the loss of Greece and the extension of the iron curtain across the eastern Mediterranean. If Greece was lost, Turkey would become an untenable outpost in a sea of Communism. Similarly, if Turkey yielded to Soviet demands, the position of Greece would be extremely endangered.

But the situation had even wider implications. Poland, Rumania, and the other satellite nations of eastern Europe had been turned into Communist camps because, in the course of the war, they had been occupied by the Russian Army. We had tried, vainly, to persuade the Soviets to permit political freedom in these countries, but we had no means to compel them to relinquish their control, unless we were prepared to wage war.

Greece and Turkey were still free countries being challenged by Communist threats both from within and without. These free peoples were now engaged in a valiant struggle to preserve their liberties and their independence.

America could not, and should not, let these free countries stand unaided. To do so would carry the clearest implications in the Middle East and in Italy, Germany, and France. The ideals and the traditions of our nation demanded that we come to the aid of Greece and Turkey and that we put the world on notice that it would be our policy to support the cause of freedom wherever it was threatened.

The risks which such a course might entail were risks which a great nation had to take if it cherished freedom at all. The studies which Marshall and Acheson brought to me and which we examined together made it plain that serious risks would be involved. But the alternative would be disastrous to our security and to the security of free nations everywhere.

What course the free world should take in the face of the threat of Russian totalitarianism was a subject I had discussed with my foreign policy advisers on many occasions in the year just passed. To foster our thinking in long-range terms I had approved the establishment in the State Department of a Policy Planning Staff. George F. Kennan, one of our foremost experts on Russia, was to head this group.

A President has little enough time to meditate, but whenever such moments occurred I was more than likely to turn my thoughts toward this key problem that confronted our nation.

We had fought a long and costly war to crush the totalitarianism of Hitler, the insolence of Mussolini, and the arrogance of the warlords of Japan. Yet the new menace facing us seemed every bit as grave as Nazi Germany and her allies had been.

I could never quite forget the strong hold which isolationism had gained over our country after World War I. Throughout my years in the Senate I listened each year as one of the senators would read Washington's Farewell

Address. It served little purpose to point out to the isolationists that Washington had advised a method suitable under the conditions of *his* day to achieve the great end of preserving the nation, and that although conditions and our international position had changed, the objectives of our policy—peace and security—were still the same. For the isolationists this address was like a biblical text. The America First organization of 1940–41, the Ku Klux Klan, Pelley and his Silver Shirts—they all quoted the first President in support of their assorted aims.

I had a very good picture of what a revival of American isolationism would mean for the world. After World War II it was clear that without American participation there was no power capable of meeting Russia as an equal. If we were to turn our back on the world, areas such as Greece, weakened and divided as a result of the war, would fall into the Soviet orbit without much effort on the part of the Russians. The success of Russia in such areas and our avowed lack of interest would lead to the growth of domestic Communist parties in such European countries as France and Italy, where they were already significant threats. Inaction, withdrawal, "Fortress America" notions could only result in handing to the Russians vast areas of the globe now denied to them.

This was the time to align the United States of America clearly on the side, and the head, of the free world. I knew that George Washington's spirit would be invoked against me, and Henry Clay's, and all the other patron saints of the isolationists. But I was convinced that the policy I was about to proclaim was indeed as much required by the conditions of my day as was Washington's by the situation in his era and Monroe's doctrine by the circumstances which he then faced. . . .

The drafting of the actual message which I would deliver to the Congress had meanwhile been started by the State Department. . . . I wanted no hedging in this speech. This was America's answer to the surge of expansion of Communist tyranny. It had to be clear and free of hesitation or double talk.

On Wednesday, March 12, 1947, at one o'clock in the afternoon, I stepped to the rostrum in the hall of the House of Representatives and addressed a joint session of the Congress. I had asked the senators and representatives to meet together so that I might place before them what I believed was an extremely critical situation.

To cope with this situation, I recommended immediate action by the Congress. But I also wished to state, for all the world to know, what the position of the United States was in the face of the new totalitarian challenge. This declaration of policy soon began to be referred to as the "Truman Doctrine." This was, I believe, the turning point in America's foreign policy, which now declared that wherever aggression, direct or indirect, threatened the peace, the security of the United States was involved.

Questions

1. What specific concerns did Truman have in mind when he began to consider the need to provide financial aid to Greece and Turkey? Were these new problems, or did they reflect long-term issues?
2. What in Truman's view, is the strategic importance of Iran, Turkey, and Greece?
3. In Truman's mind, why is traditional isolationism no longer a viable policy for the United States?
4. Why does Truman view this moment as a "turning point" for the United States?

27-3   On NATO (1949)

Arthur Vandenberg   Senator Arthur Vandenberg (1884-1951), a Michigan Republican and a prewar noninterventionist, shifted position during the postwar period to support containment. His championing of American involvement in the North Atlantic Treaty Organization helped make Senate ratification of the NATO treaty bipartisan. During the debate, he explained his position in correspondence with constituents and others.

Source: Excerpts from *The Private Papers of Senator Vandenberg,* edited by Arthur H. Vandenberg Jr. with the collaboration of Joe Alex Morris, 475, 477–480, 499–500. Copyright 1952 by Arthur Vandenberg Jr., © renewed 1980. Reprinted by permission of Houghton Mifflin Company. All rights reserved.

January 27, 1949

There is no doubt about the fact that it is a "calculated risk" for us to even partially arm the countries of Western Europe. It is also very much of a "calculated risk" if we do *not*. One risk will have to be weighed against the other. You suggest that it will be a safe thing to do "when the economic stability of these countries shall have improved." The basic question we have to settle is whether "economic stability" can precede the creation of a greater sense of physical security. I am inclined to think that "physical security" is a prerequisite to the kind of long-range economic planning which Western Europe requires. The fact remains that the problem is fraught with many hazardous imponderables. I am withholding my own final judgment until I see the precise terms of the treaty under which this new co-operation will be proposed. I think we ought to have wit enough to write it on a basis which is relatively safe. . . .

February 21, 1949

. . . In my opinion, when Mr. Hitler was contemplating World War Two, I believe he would have never launched it if he had had any serious reasons to believe that it might bring him into armed collision with the United States. I think he was sure it would not do so because of our then existing neutrality laws. If an appropriate North Atlantic Pact is written, I think it will exactly reverse this psychology so far as Mr. Stalin is concerned if, as and when he contemplates World War Three. Under such circumstances, I very much doubt whether World War Three happens. . . .

February 22, 1949

I am one of its [the Pact's] authors. I heartily believe in it. I want to give it a maximum chance to help prevent World War Three before it starts. But this requires absolute candor as to what it does and does not promise. I can think of no greater tragedy than to permit our friends in Western Europe to interpret the Pact beyond its actual realities. One reality is that we cannot commit ourselves to automatic war in the future. . . . We are recognizing facts of life as established in the Constitution of the United States. I will go as far as I can within the Constitution. I will not go

farther because it would be an imposition upon our own good faith and a false reliance for our friends abroad. I hasten to add that I think we can achieve every essential result for the North Atlantic Pact by staying strictly within the Constitution of the United States and within the Charter of the United Nations. . . .

March 18, 1949

. . . I am glad to know your preliminary reaction to the North Atlantic Pact. I agree with you one thousand percent that "this world cannot stand another war." Every effort of my remaining days will be dedicated to this truth. My greatest fear in this connection is that we will somehow drift into another war. . . . If Soviet Russia does start to march it would seem to be completely inevitable that the United States will be the ultimate target and that we shall inevitably be in that war—Pact or no Pact. So it seems to me that our best insurance is to make our position plan in advance. This includes above all else a clear demonstration that our objectives are totally defensive; that we have no goal except peace with honor and justice in a live-and-let-live world.

If you are right and this proposed North Atlantic Pact is "another provocation to another World War" then the Pact ought to be rejected. If I am right in believing that the Pact is our best protection against another World War then the Pact ought to be ratified. Therefore, our current problem is to fully and publicly explore every phase and every angle of the Pact. You may be very sure that I shall insist upon extensive public hearings which will clarify the issue. I want everything ventilated in this connection so that we may reach the wisest possible decision in a situation where we must take a "calculated risk" whichever way the decision goes. . . .

[July 21, 1949]

Well—as you know we won the big battle [over the North Atlantic Treaty] today by a vote of 82 to 13 . . . It's a great relief to have the battle over—yet I seem to feel a greater responsibility than ever tonight—how will it all work out? At best, it's a calculated risk. But I have a feeling that this day will go down in history as one of the big dates. . . .

Questions

1. According to Vandenberg, what kinds of dangers does the United States face in the Cold War?
2. What risks does the United States run by aligning itself so closely with the states of Western Europe? What kinds of gains does NATO make possible?
3. What lessons did Vandenberg learn from the events preceding World War II? How does he put them to use in his support for NATO?

27-4   Against NATO (1949)

Robert A. Taft

Robert A. Taft (1889–1953), son of President William Howard Taft, was elected to the Senate from Ohio in the Republican comeback of 1938. Between 1940 and 1952, he was a contender for the Republican presidential nomination. A noninterventionist between 1939 and 1941, he was also critical of aspects of postwar American foreign policy and their domestic implications.

Source: Congressional Record, 81st Congress, 1st Session, vol. 95, part 7 (July 11, 1949), 9205–9210.

Mr. President, I listened with great interest to the speech made today by the distinguished Senator from Iowa [Mr. GILLETTE]. I wish to assure the Senate that I have not consulted with the Senator from Iowa; but the arguments I shall make against the Atlantic Pact are very similar to the ones he made, and I agree thoroughly with the very effective argument and very effective speech he made on that subject. However, the same arguments have led me to the conclusion that I must vote against the pact, rather than for it, as he has announced he intends to do.

It is with great regret that I have come to my conclusion, but I have come to it because I think the pact carries with it an obligation to assist in arming, at our expense, the nations of western Europe, because with that obligation I believe it will promote war in the world rather than peace, and because I think that with the arms plan it is wholly contrary to the spirit of the obligations we assumed in the United Nations Charter. I would vote for the pact if a reservation were adopted denying any legal or moral obligation to provide arms.

The purpose of American foreign policy, as I see it, is to maintain the freedom of the people of this country and, insofar as consistent with that purpose, to keep this country at peace. We are, of course, interested in the welfare of the rest of the world because we are a humane nation. Our huge economic aid, however, is based on the belief that a world which is prosperous and well off is less likely to engage in war than one in which there are great inequities in the economic condition of different people.

In the past, we have considered that the best method of preserving the peace and security of this country is the maintenance of American armed forces sufficient to defend us against attack, and a wise diplomatic policy which does not antagonize other nations. Those still are the main essentials to the maintenance of peace in the world of today.

But as the world shrinks in size, as new weapons are developed, as we inevitably become more involved in the affairs of other countries, it has become apparent that these weapons alone will not assure peace. And so we have committed ourselves to the principle of an association of sovereign nations banded together to preserve peace by preventing and punishing aggression. In the United Nations Charter we accepted the principle that we would go to war in association with other nations against a nation found by the Security Council to be an aggressor. That was a tremendous departure from our previous policy, but one which I have always urged and approved from the days of the League of Nations. I believe that all nations must ultimately agree, if we are to have peace, to an international law defining the duties and obligations of such nations, particularly with reference to restraint from aggression and war. I believe that there should be international courts to determine whether nations are abiding by that law, and I believe that there should be a joint armed force to enforce that law and the decisions of that court. I believe that in the end, the public opinion of the world will come to support the principle that nations like individuals are bound by law, and will insist that any nation which violates the law be promptly subjected to the joint action of nations guided by a determination to enforce the laws of peace.

It is quite true that the United Nations Charter as drafted does not as yet reach the ideals of international' peace and justice which I have described, but it goes a long way in that direction. It is defective principally because any one of the large nations can veto the action of the Security Council, and because there is not sufficient emphasis on law and justice as a guide to the action of the Security Council. But we have advised the President that prompt action should be taken to improve the Charter. . . .

The North Atlantic Treaty might have been so drafted as to create a small United Nations within the larger group, improving upon the United Nations Charter, eliminating its defects, and furnishing an example of an improved international organization which could be followed by the United Nations itself. . . .

But, the State Department did not adopt any of these suggestions and has shown no intention of doing so. We have to consider here the North Atlantic Treaty as it has been drafted. without the improvements Senators would like to see made, but which 12 nations probably would not agree to once this treaty is ratified. We abandoned the chance of getting those when we signed the treaty in its present form. The Atlantic Treaty as drawn is certainly no improvement over the United Nations, nor can it by any stretch of the imagination be regarded as a perfection of or supplement to that Charter. From the point of view of an international organization, it is a step backward. Apart from the obligation to provide arms, the treaty is permitted by the Charter, which says:

> Nothing in the present Charter shall impair the inherent right of individual or collective self-defense if an armed attack occurs against a member of the United Nations until the Security Council has taken the measures necessary to maintain international peace and security.

The Charter merely recognizes this inherent right as necessary because the veto provision of the Charter may result in complete inaction on the part of the Security Council. But certainly in all other respects the treaty far more resembles a military alliance than it does any international association of nations. As the Senator from Iowa so forcefully said, it is a step backward in the progress toward international peace and justice.

What is the nature of that treaty?

It is obviously, and I do not think it can be questioned, a defensive military alliance between certain nations, the essence of which is an obligation under article 5 to go to war if necessary with any nation which attacks any one of the signers of the treaty. Such an attack may come from outsiders or it may come from one of the signers of the treaty itself. The obligation is completely binding for a period of 20 years. It imposes an obligation upon the United States to each member nation whether or not there is consultation or joint action by the Council, or a finding by any court that an unjustified armed attack has occurred. Our obligation is self-executing upon the occurrence of an armed attack.

Some doubt will always remain as to whether the Congress must declare war before our armed forces actually take part. I am inclined to think such action is not necessary if the President chooses to use our armed forces when an ally is attacked. But whether it is or not, the obligation to go to war seems to me binding upon the United States as a nation, so that Congress would be obligated to declare war if that were necessary to comply with the provisions of the treaty. It is pointed out that the President could fail to act and Congress could refuse to declare war, but certainly we are not making a treaty on the theory that we expect to violate it in accordance with our own sweet will.

It is correctly pointed out that the exact measures which we are obligated to take will be determined by us, and that it may not be necessary to go to the extent of a declaration of war. We do reserve a certain discretion, but as I see it, we do not reserve any discretion on the question,

for instance, whether the armed attack is justified, as a reason for supporting it. If one of the members of the pact provides an attack, even by conduct which we disapprove, we would still apparently be bound to go to its defense. By executing a treaty of this kind, we put ourselves at the mercy of the foreign policies of 11 other nations, and do so for a period of 20 years. The Charter is obviously aimed at possible Russian aggression against western Europe, but the obligation assumed is far broader than that. I emphasize again that the obligation is much more unconditional, much less dependent on legal processes and much less dependent on joint action than the obligation of the United Nations Charter.

And yet in spite of these dangers, I have wanted to vote in favor of the Atlantic Pact for one reason and would still do so if the question of arms were not involved. I fully agree with the effective argument in favor of the pact made by the distinguished Senator from Michigan because of its warning to the U. S. S. R. I think we should make it clear to the U. S. S. R. that if it attacks western Europe, it will be at war with us. I fully agree with the statement of the distinguished Senator from Michigan:

> It is not the military forces in being which measure the impact of this knock-out admonition. Its invincible power for peace is the awesome fact that any aggressor upon the North Atlantic community knows in advance from the very moment he launches his conquest, he will forthwith face whatever cumulative opposition these united allies in their own wisdom deem necessary to beat him to his knees and to restore peace and security. It is this total concept which, in my view, would give even a reincarnated Hitler cause.

I agree that if the Kaiser had known that England and the United States would be in the war, the First World War might never have begun. I agree that if Hitler had known the United States would be in the war, the Second World War might not have begun. I favor the extension of the Monroe Doctrine under present circumstances to western Europe.

It is said that the Atlantic Treaty is simply another Monroe Doctrine. I wish it were. That would be much more acceptable to me than the Atlantic pact, arms or no arms. Let me point out the vital differences. The Monroe Doctrine was a unilateral declaration. We were free to modify it or withdraw from it at any moment. This treaty, adopted to deal with a particular emergency today, is binding upon us for 20 years to cover all kinds of circumstances which cannot possibly be foreseen. The Monroe Doctrine left us free to determine the merits of each dispute which might arise and to judge the justice and the wisdom of war in the light of the circumstances at the time. The present treaty obligates us to go to war if certain facts occur. The Monroe Doctrine imposed no obligation whatever to assist any American Nation by giving it arms or even economic aid. We were free to fight the war in such a manner as we might determine, or not at all. This treaty imposes on us a continuous obligation for 20 years to give aid to all the other members of the pact, and, I believe, to give military aid to all the other members of the pact. . . .

The present treaty is a military alliance. The present treaty does contemplate a peacetime renewal of the old, open-ended lend-lease formula. The present treaty assumes unilateral responsibility for the fate of western Europe. We are obligated to go to the defense of any nation whether the other members of the pact do so or not, or whatever their consultation may advise. . . . And yet, in spite of my belief that the treaty goes much too far and should have been confined to a mere declaration on our part that we would go to war if Russia attacked western Europe, I would still vote for the treaty except for my belief that the pact commits us to the arming of all the other signers of the pact. There is no question that the arms program and the treaty were negotiated together. There is no question in my mind that foreign nations which signed the treaty regarded the providing of arms as an essential part of it. Several of their leaders have expressed that view in public in Europe. . . . The pact standing by itself would clearly be a deterrent to war. If Russia knows that if it starts a war it will immediately find itself at war with the United States, it is much less likely to start a war. I see and believe in the full force of that argument. That is why I would favor the extension of the Monroe Doctrine to Europe. But if Russia sees itself ringed about gradually by so-called defensive arms, from Norway and Denmark to Turkey and Greece, it may form a different opinion. It may decide that the arming of western Europe, regardless of its present purpose, looks to an attack upon Russia. Its view may be unreasonable, and I think it is. But from the Russian standpoint it may not seem unreasonable. They may well decide that if war is the certain result, that war might better occur now rather than after the arming of Europe is completed. In 1941, Secretary Hull sent a message to Japan in the nature of an ultimatum which said, in effect, that if Japan did not withdraw from China, sooner or later they would face a war with the United States. The Japanese appear to have concluded that if ultimately there was to be such a war, it was to their interest to have it occur at once.

The arming of western Europe cannot be achieved overnight--in fact, it will be years before the European nations could resist an all-out Russian attack. During that period, I feel that the arms policy is more likely to incite war than to deter it. . . .

. . . I do not mind saying now that once we enter into the pact, or do not enter into the pact, I am quite willing to consider providing arms for a particular nation to meet a particular emergency. I voted for the Greek and Turkish loans to provide arms. There may be other cases. I think today the providing of arms in support of Nationalist China, where war is actually going on is something that I would approve, but that is a very different thing from building up a tremendous armament for 11 different nations, implying so far as I can see, the obligation to do the same thing in the rest of the world.

In any war the result will not come from the battle put up by the western European countries. The outcome will finally depend on the armed forces of America. Let us keep our forces strong. Let us use the money we have for armament in building up the American Army, the American Air Forces, and the American Navy. Let us keep our forces strong, and spend the money that is available for arms for those forces, because in the last analysis, we will win a war only if the United States wins the war, no matter how we assist other nations. They may be of assistance here and there. We cannot be certain that they will fight. We cannot be sure what their position may be at the time. We cannot be sure that Communists will not take control in those nations. I believe very strongly, as Winston Churchill said, that the world depends on the strength of the American Army, and the weapons which the American Army has.

We have chosen to give economic assistance. That assistance is given on the theory that the Russians do not contemplate aggressive war, but intend to fight their battle by propaganda and a production of chaotic economic conditions. I believe the undertaking of both types of assistance is beyond the economic capacity of the United States. I believe we will have to choose whether we give economic assistance or arms. The first, I believe, has contributed and will contribute to peace. The second, I think will make war more likely. . . .

Mr. President, since I feel that this pact is inextricably linked with the arms program, and since I believe that, so linked, the program is a threat to the welfare of the people of the United States, I shall vote against the treaty.

I am quite willing to consider the providing of assistance to particular countries, at particular times, if such aid seems at that time a real deterrent to war, and on that principle I voted for aid to Greece and Turkey. But that is a very different thing from an obligation to build up the armed forces of 11 countries, and a commitment on the American taxpayer for 20 years to give continued aid under circumstances of which we have not the slightest conception today. It is a very different thing from arming half the world against the other half.

My conclusion has been reached with the greatest discomfort. When so many disagree with that conclusion, I must admit that I may be completely wrong. I do not claim to be an expert in questions of foreign policy. I would like to be able to vote for a policy that will commit us to war if Russia attacks western Europe. I would be glad to join in an agreement to occupy Germany indefinitely to guard against a third attack from that quarter. I would waive my other objections to the Atlantic Pact if I did not feel that it was inextricably involved with the arms program. But I cannot escape the logic of the situation as I see it, and therefore I cannot vote for a treaty which, in my opinion, will do far more to bring about a third world war than it will ever maintain the peace of the world.

Questions

1. Which American Cold War policies does Taft support? Which proposed policies would he support?
2. What aspect of the treaty creating NATO leads Taft to oppose it?
3. In what ways can Taft be said to echo noninterventionists of 1939 to 1941? In what ways can he be said to differ from them? (See Documents 26-3 and 26-4.)

27-5 NSC-68 (1950)

The National Security Council had come into existence in 1947 as a result of the Cold War. In the wake of the victory of the Communists in China's civil war and the Soviet Union's detonation of an atomic device, the council prepared NSC-68, a paper that marked Communism as the enemy and suggested possible military strategies. Meanwhile, George Kennan, increasingly concerned over the implementation of containment and opposed to the development of the hydrogen bomb, had resigned as head of the Department of State's Policy Planning Staff. He was to criticize NSC-68's militarization of the containment policy (see text pp. 871–873, 875–877; also Figure 27-1, text p. 895).

Source: Foreign Relations of the United States, no. 1 (1950), 237–292.

Analysis
  I. Background of the Present World Crisis
 II. The Fundamental Purpose of the United States
III. The Fundamental Design of the Kremlin
 IV. The Underlying Conflict in the Realm of Ideas and Values between the U.S. Purpose and the Kremlin Design
    A. Nature of Conflict
    B. Objectives
    C. Means
  V. Soviet Intentions and Capabilities—Actual and Potential
    A. Political and Psychological
    B. Economic
    C. Military
 VI. U.S. Intentions and Capabilities—Actual and Potential
    A. Political and Psychological
    B. Economic
    C. Military
VII. Present Risks
    A. General
    B. Specific
VIII. Atomic Armaments
    A. Military Evaluation of U.S. and U.S.S.R. Atomic Capabilities

    B. Stockpiling and Use of Atomic Weapons
    C. International Control of Atomic Energy
 IX. Possible Course of Action
    Introduction
    The Role of Negotiation
    A. The First Course—Continuation of Current Policies, with Current and Currently Projected Programs for Carrying Out These Policies
    B. The Second Course—Isolation
    C. The Third Course—War
    D. The Remaining Course of Action—A Rapid Build-up of Political, Economic, and Military Strength in the Free World
Conclusions
Recommendations

ANALYSIS

I. Background of the Present Crisis

. . . During the span of one generation, the international distribution of power has been fundamentally altered. . . .

Two complex sets of factors have now basically altered this historical distribution of power. First, the defeat of Germany and Japan and the decline of the British and French Empires have interacted with the development of the United States and the Soviet Union in such a way that power has increasingly gravitated to these two centers. Second, the Soviet Union, unlike previous aspirants to hegemony, is animated by a new fanatic faith, antithetical to our own, and seeks to impose its absolute authority over the rest of the world. Conflict has, therefore, become endemic and is waged, on the part of the Soviet Union, by violent or non-violent methods in accordance with the dictates of expediency. With the development of increasingly terrifying weapons of mass destruction, every individual faces the ever-present possibility of annihilation should the conflict enter the phase of total war.

On the one hand, the people of the world yearn for relief from the anxiety arising from the risk of atomic war. On the other hand, any substantial further extension of the area under the domination of the Kremlin would raise the possibility that no coalition adequate to confront the Kremlin with greater strength could be assembled. It is in this context that this Republic and its citizens in the ascendancy of their strength stand in their deepest peril. . . .

II. Fundamental Purpose of the United States

The fundamental purpose of the United States is laid down in the Preamble to the Constitution. . . . In essence, the fundamental purpose is to assure the integrity and vitality of our free society, which is founded upon the dignity and worth of the individual.

Three realities emerge as a consequence of this purpose: Our determination to maintain the essential elements of individual freedom, as set forth in the Constitution and Bill of Rights; our determination to create conditions under which our free and democratic system can live and prosper; and our determination to fight if necessary to defend our way of life. . . .

III. Fundamental Design of the Kremlin

The fundamental design of those who control the Soviet Union and the international communist movement is to retain and solidify their absolute power, first in the Soviet Union and second in the areas now under their control. In the minds of the Soviet leaders, however, achievement of this design requires the dynamic extension of their authority and the ultimate elimination of any effective opposition to their authority.

The design, therefore, calls for the complete subversion or forcible destruction of the machinery of government and structure of society in the countries of the non-Soviet world and their replacement by an apparatus and structure subservient to and controlled from the Kremlin. To that end Soviet efforts are now directed toward the domination of the Eurasian land mass. The United States, as the principal center of power in the non-Soviet world and the bulwark of opposition to Soviet expansion, is the principal enemy whose integrity and vitality must be subverted or destroyed by one means or another if the Kremlin is to achieve its fundamental design.

IV. The Underlying Conflict in the Realm of Ideas and Values between the U.S. Purpose and the Kremlin Design

A. NATURE OF CONFLICT

The Kremlin regards the United States as the only major threat to the achievement of its fundamental design. There is a basic conflict between the idea of freedom under a government of laws, and the idea of slavery under the grim oligarchy of the Kremlin, which has come to a crisis with the polarization of power described in Section I, and the exclusive possession of atomic weapons by the two protagonists. The idea of freedom, moreover, is peculiarly and intolerably subversive of the idea of slavery. But the converse is not true. The implacable purpose of the slave state to eliminate the challenge of freedom has placed the two great powers at opposite poles. It is this fact which gives the present polarization of power the quality of crisis. . . .

B. OBJECTIVES

In a shrinking world, which now faces the threat of atomic warfare, it is not an adequate objective merely to seek to check the Kremlin design, for the absence of order among nations is becoming less and less tolerable. This fact imposes on us, in our own interests, the responsibility of world leadership. It demands that we make the attempt, and accept the risks inherent in it, to bring about order and justice by means consistent with the principles of freedom and democracy. We should limit our requirement of the Soviet Union to its participation with other nations on the basis of equality and respect for the rights of others. Subject to this requirement, we must with our allies and the former subject peoples, seek to create a world society based on the principle of consent. Its framework cannot be inflexible. It will consist of many national communities of great and varying abilities and resources, and hence of war potential. The seeds of conflicts will inevitably exist or will come into being. To acknowledge this is only to acknowledge the impossibility of a final solution. Not to acknowledge it can be fatally dangerous in a world in which there are no final solutions. . . .

V. Soviet Intentions and Capabilities— Actual and Potential

A. POLITICAL AND PSYCHOLOGICAL

. . . Soviet ideas and practices run counter to the best and potentially the strongest instincts of men, and deny their most fundamental aspirations. Against an adversary which effectively affirmed the constructive and hopeful instincts of men and was capable of fulfilling their fundamental aspirations, the Soviet system might prove to be fatally weak. . . .

C. MILITARY

The Soviet Union is developing the military capacity to support its design for world domination. The Soviet Union actually possesses armed forces far in excess of those necessary to defend its national territory. These armed forces are probably not yet considered by the Soviet Union to be sufficient to initiate a war which would involve the United States. This excessive strength, coupled now with an atomic capability, provides the Soviet Union with great coercive power for use in time of peace in furtherance of its objectives and serves as a deterrent to the victims of its aggression from taking any action in opposition to its tactics which would risk war.

Should a major war occur in 1950 the Soviet Union and its satellites are considered by the Joint Chiefs of Staff to be in a sufficiently advanced state of preparation immediately to undertake and carry out the following campaigns.

a. To overrun Western Europe, with the possible exception of the Iberian and Scandinavian Peninsulas; to drive toward the oil-bearing areas of the Near and Middle East; and to consolidate Communist gains in the Far East;

b. To launch air attacks against the British Isles and air and sea attacks against the lines of communications of the Western Powers in the Atlantic and the Pacific;

c. To attack selected targets with atomic weapons, now including the likelihood of such attacks against targets in Alaska, Canada, and the United States. Alternatively, this capability, coupled with other actions open to the Soviet Union, might deny the United Kingdom as an effective base of operations for allied forces. It also should be possible for the Soviet Union to prevent any allied "Normandy" type amphibious operations intended to force a reentry into the continent of Europe.

After the Soviet Union completed its initial campaigns and consolidated its positions in the Western European area, it could simultaneously conduct:

a. Full-scale air and limited sea operations against the British Isles;

b. Invasions of the Iberian and Scandinavian Peninsulas;

c. Further operations in the Near and Middle East, continued air operations against the North American continent, and air and sea operations against Atlantic and Pacific lines of communication; and

d. Diversionary attacks in other areas. . . .

For planning purposes, therefore, the date the Soviets possess an atomic stockpile of 200 bombs would be a critical date for the United States, for the delivery of 100 atomic bombs on targets in the United States would seriously damage this country.

At the time the Soviet Union has a substantial atomic stockpile and if it is assumed that it will strike a strong surprise blow and if it is assumed further that its atomic attacks will be met with no more effective defense opposition than the United States and its allies have programmed, results of those attacks could include:

a. Laying waste to the British Isles and thus depriving the Western Powers of their use as a base;

b. Destruction of the vital centers and of the communications of Western Europe, thus precluding effective defense by the Western Powers; and

c. Delivering devastating attacks on certain vital centers of the United States and Canada.

The possession by the Soviet Union of a thermonuclear capability in addition to this substantial atomic stockpile would result in tremendously increased damage.

During this decade, the defensive capabilities of the Soviet Union will probably be strengthened, particularly by the development and use of modern aircraft, aircraft warning and communications devices, and defensive guided missiles. . . .

VI. U.S. Intentions and Capabilities—Actual and Potential

A. POLITICAL AND PSYCHOLOGICAL

In a world of polarized power, policies designed to develop a healthy international community are more than ever necessary to our own strength.

As for the policy of "containment," it is one which seeks by all means short of war to (1) block further expansion of Soviet power, (2) expose the falsities of Soviet pretensions, (3) induce a retraction of the Kremlin's control and influence, and (4) in general, so foster the seeds of destruction within the Soviet system that the Kremlin is brought at least to the point of modifying its behavior to conform to generally accepted international standards.

It was and continues to be cardinal in this policy that we possess superior overall power in ourselves or in dependable combination with other like-minded nations. One of the most important ingredients of power is military strength. In the concept of "containment," the maintenance of a strong military posture is deemed to be essential for two reasons: (1) as an ultimate guarantee of our national security and (2) as an indispensable backdrop to the conduct of the policy of "containment." Without superior aggregate military strength, in being and readily mobilizable, a policy of "containment"—which is in effect a policy of calculated and gradual coercion—is no more than a policy of bluff. . . .

VII. Present Risks

B. SPECIFIC

It is quite clear from Soviet theory and practice that the Kremlin seeks to bring the free world under its dominion by the methods of the cold war. The preferred technique is to subvert by infiltration and intimidation. Every institution of our society is an instrument which it is sought to stultify and turn against our purposes. Those that touch most closely our material and moral strength are obviously the prime targets, labor unions, civic enterprises, schools, churches, and all media for influencing opinion. The effort is not so much to make them serve obvious Soviet ends as to prevent them from serving our ends, and thus to make them sources of confusion in our economy, our culture, and our body politic. The doubts and diversities that in terms of our values are part of the merit of a free system, the weaknesses and the problems that are peculiar to it, the rights and privileges that free men enjoy, and the disorganization and destruction left in the wake of the last attack on our freedoms, all are but opportunities for the Kremlin to do its evil work. Every advantage is taken of the fact that our means of prevention and retaliation are limited by those principles and scruples which are precisely the ones that give our freedom and democracy its meaning for us. None of our scruples deter those whose only code is "morality is that which serves the revolution."

Since everything that gives us or others respect for our institutions is a suitable object for attack, it also fits the Kremlin's design that where, with impunity, we can be insulted and made to suffer indignity the opportunity shall not be missed, particularly in any context which can be used to cast dishonor on our country, our system, our motives, or our methods. Thus the means by which we sought to restore our own economic health in the '30's, and now seek to restore that of the free world, come equally under attack. The military aid by which we sought to help the free world was frantically denounced by the Communists in the early days of the last war, and of course our present efforts to develop adequate military strength for ourselves and our allies are equally denounced.

At the same time the Soviet Union is seeking to create overwhelming military force, in order to back up infiltration with intimidation. In the only terms in which it understands strength, it is seeking to demonstrate to the free world that force and the will to use it are on the side of the Kremlin, that those who lack it are decadent and doomed. In local incidents it threatens and encroaches both for the sake of local gains and to increase anxiety and defeatism in all the free world. . . .

VIII. Atomic Armaments

A. MILITARY EVALUATION OF U.S. AND USSR ATOMIC CAPABILITIES

. . . As the atomic capability of the USSR increases, it will have an increased ability to hit at our atomic bases and installations and thus seriously hamper the ability of the United States to carry out an attack such as that outlined above. It is quite possible that in the near future the USSR will have a sufficient number of atomic bombs and a sufficient deliverability to raise a question whether Britain with its present inadequate air defense could be relied upon as an advance base from which a major portion of the U.S. attack could be launched.

It is estimated that, within the next four years, the USSR will attain the capability of seriously damaging vital centers of the United States, provided it strikes a surprise blow and provided further that the blow is opposed by no more effective opposition than we now have programmed. Such a blow could so seriously damage the United States as to greatly reduce its superiority in economic potential.

Effective opposition to this Soviet capability will require among other measures greatly increased air warning systems, air defenses, and vigorous development and implementation of a civilian defense program which has been thoroughly integrated with the military defense systems.

In time the atomic capability of the USSR can be expected to grow to a point where, given surprise and no more effective opposition than we now have programmed, the possibility of a decisive initial attack [by the USSR] cannot be excluded. . . .

B. STOCKPILING AND USE OF ATOMIC WEAPONS

In the event the USSR develops by 1954 the atomic capability which we now anticipate, it is hardly conceivable that, if war comes, the Soviet leaders would refrain from the use of atomic weapons unless they felt fully confident of attaining their objectives by other means.

In the event we use atomic weapons either in retaliation for their prior use by the USSR or because there is no alternative method by which we can attain our objectives, it is imperative that the strategic and tactical targets against which they are used be appropriate and the manner in which they are used be consistent with those objectives.

It appears to follow from the above that we should produce and stockpile thermonuclear weapons in the event they prove feasible and would add significantly to our net capability. Not enough is yet known of their potentialities to warrant a judgment at this time regarding their use in war to attain our objectives. . . .

C. INTERNATIONAL CONTROL OF ATOMIC ENERGY

The principal immediate benefit of international control would be to make a surprise atomic attack impossible, assuming the elimination of large reactors and the effective disposal of stockpiles of fissionable materials. But it is almost certain that the Soviet Union would not agree to the elimination of large reactors, unless the impracticability of producing atomic power for peaceful purposes had been demonstrated beyond a doubt. By the same token, it would not now agree to elimination of its stockpile of fissionable materials. . . .

[T]he absence of good faith on the part of the USSR must be assumed until there is concrete evidence that there has been a decisive change in Soviet policies. It is to be doubted whether such a change can take place without a change in the nature of the Soviet system itself. . . .

IX. Possible Courses of Action

Introduction. Four possible courses of action by the United States in the present situation can be distinguished. They are:

a. Continuation of current policies, with current and currently projected programs for carrying out these policies;

b. Isolation;

c. War; and

d. A more rapid building up of the political, economic, and military strength of the free world than provided under a, with the purpose of reaching, if possible, a tolerable state of order among nations without war and of preparing to defend ourselves in the event that the free world is attacked. . . .

The Kremlin will have three major objectives in negotiations with the United States. The first is to eliminate the atomic capabilities of the United States; the second is to prevent the effective mobilization of the superior potential of the free world in human and material resources; and the third is to secure a withdrawal of United States forces from, and commitments to, Europe and Japan. Depending on its evaluation of its own strengths and weaknesses as against the West's (particularly the ability and will of the West to sustain its efforts), it will or will not be prepared to make important concessions to achieve these major objectives. It is unlikely that the Kremlin's evaluation is such that it would now be prepared to make significant concessions.

It must be presumed that for some time the Kremlin will accept agreements only if it is convinced that by acting in bad faith whenever and wherever there is an opportunity to do so with impunity, it can derive greater advantage from the agreements than the free world. For this reason, we must take care that any agreements are enforceable or that they are not susceptible of violation without detection and the possibility of effective countermeasures. . . .

A. THE FIRST COURSE—CONTINUATION OF CURRENT POLICIES, WITH CURRENT AND CURRENTLY PROJECTED PROGRAMS FOR CARRYING OUT THESE POLICIES

1. Military aspects. . . . A review of Soviet policy shows that the military capabilities, actual and potential, of the United States and the rest of the free world, together with the apparent determination of the free world to resist further Soviet expansion, have not induced the Kremlin to relax its pressures generally or to give up the initiative in the cold war. On the contrary, the Soviet Union has consistently pursued a bold foreign policy, modified only when its probing revealed a determination and an ability of the free world to resist encroachment upon it. The relative military capabilities of the free world are declining, with the result that its determination to resist may also decline and that the security of the United States and the free world as a whole will be jeopardized.

From the military point of view, the actual and potential capabilities of the United States, given a continuation of current and projected programs, will become less and less effective as a war deterrent. Improvement of the state of readiness will become more and more important not only to inhibit the launching of war by the Soviet Union but also to support a national policy designed to reverse the present ominous trends in international relations. A building up of the military capabilities of the United States and the free world is a pre-condition to the achievement of the objectives outlined in this report and to the protection of the United States against disaster.

Fortunately, the United States military establishment has been developed into a unified and effective force as a result of the policies laid down by the Congress and the vigorous carrying out of these policies by the Administration in the fields of both organization and economy. It is, therefore, a base upon which increased strength can be rapidly built with maximum efficiency and economy.

2. Political aspects. . . . Politically, recognition of the military implications of a continuation of present trends will mean that the United States and especially other free countries will tend to shift to the defensive, or to follow a dangerous policy of bluff, because the maintenance of a firm initiative in the cold war is closely related to aggregate strength in being and readily available. . . .

3. Economic and social aspects. As was pointed out in Chapter VI, the present foreign economic policies and programs of the United States will not produce a solution to the problem of international economic equilibrium, notably the problem of the dollar gap, and will not create an economic base conducive to political stability in many important free countries. . . .

The Executive Branch is now undertaking a study of the problem of the United States balance of payments and of the measures which might be taken by the United States to assist in establishing international economic equilibrium. This is a very important project and work on it should have a high priority. However, unless such an economic program is matched and supplemented by an equally far-sighted and vigorous political and military program, we will not be successful in checking and rolling back the Kremlin's drive.

4. Negotiation. In short, by continuing along its present course the free world will not succeed in making effective use of its vastly superior political, economic, and military potential to build a tolerable state of order among nations. On the contrary, the political, economic, and military situation of the free world is already unsatisfactory and will become less favorable unless we act to reverse present trends. . . .

The idea that Germany or Japan or other important areas can exist as islands of neutrality in a divided world is unreal, given the Kremlin design for world domination.

B. THE SECOND COURSE—ISOLATION

[A policy of isolation] overlooks the relativity of capabilities. With the United States in an isolated position, we would have to face the probability that the Soviet Union would quickly dominate most of Eurasia, probably without meeting armed resistance. It would thus acquire a potential far superior to our own, and would promptly proceed to develop this potential with the purpose of eliminating our power, which would, even in isolation, remain as a challenge to it and as an obstacle to the imposition of its kind of order in the world. There is no way to make ourselves inoffensive to the Kremlin except by complete submission to its will. Therefore isolation would in the end condemn us to capitulate or to fight alone and on the defensive, with drastically limited offensive and retaliatory capabilities in comparison with the Soviet Union. (These are the only possibilities, unless we are prepared to risk the future on the hazard that the Soviet Empire, because of overextension or other reasons, will spontaneously destroy itself from within. . . .

C. THE THIRD COURSE—WAR

. . . [A] surprise attack upon the Soviet Union, despite the provocativeness of recent Soviet behavior, would be repugnant to many Americans. Although the American people would probably rally in support of the war effort, the shock of responsibility for a surprise attack would be morally corrosive. . . .

. . . If the argument of Chapter IV is accepted, it follows that there is no "easy" solution and that the only sure victory lies in the frustration of the Kremlin design by the steady development of the moral and material strength of the free world and its projection into the Soviet world in such a way as to bring about an internal change in the Soviet system.

D. THE REMAINING COURSE OF ACTION—A RAPID BUILD-UP OF POLITICAL, ECONOMIC, AND MILITARY STRENGTH IN THE FREE WORLD

A more rapid build-up of political, economic, and military strength and thereby of confidence in the free world than is now contemplated is the only course which is consistent with progress toward achieving our fundamental purpose. . . .

The threat to the free world involved in the development of the Soviet Union's atomic and other capabilities will rise steadily and rather rapidly. For the time being, the United States possesses a marked atomic superiority over the Soviet Union which, together with the potential capabilities of the United States and other free countries in other forces and weapons, inhibits aggressive Soviet action. This provides an opportunity for the United States, in cooperation with other free countries, to launch a build-up of strength which will support a firm policy directed to the frustration of the Kremlin design. The immediate goal of our efforts to build a successfully functioning political and economic system in the free world backed by adequate military strength is to postpone and avert the disastrous situation which, in light of the Soviet Union's probable fission bomb capability and possible thermonuclear bomb capability, might arise in 1954 on a continuation of our present programs. By acting promptly and vigorously in such a way that this date is, so to speak, pushed into the future, we would permit time for the process of accommodation, withdrawal and frustration to produce the necessary changes in the Soviet system. Time is short, however, and the risks of war attendant upon a decision to build up strength will steadily increase the longer we defer it.

CONCLUSIONS

The foregoing analysis indicates that the probable fission bomb capability and possible thermonuclear bomb capability of the Soviet Union have greatly intensified the Soviet threat to the security of the United States. This threat is of the same character as that described in NSC 20/4 (approved by the President on November 24, 1948) but is more immediate than had previously been estimated. In particular, the United States now faces the contingency that within the next four or five years the Soviet Union will possess the military capability of delivering a surprise atomic attack of such weight that the United States must have substantially increased general air, ground, and sea strength, atomic capabilities, and air and civilian defenses to deter war and to provide reasonable assurance, in the event of war, that it could survive the initial blow and go on to the eventual attainment of its objectives. In return, this contingency requires the intensification of our efforts in the fields of intelligence and research and development. . . .

Allowing for the immediacy of the danger, the following statement of Soviet threats contained in NSC 20/4, remains valid:

14. The gravest threat to the security of the United States within the foreseeable future stems from the hostile designs and formidable power of the USSR, and from the nature of the Soviet system.

15. The political, economic, and psychological warfare which the USSR is now waging has dangerous potentialities for weakening the relative world position of the United States and disrupting its traditional institutions by means short of war, unless sufficient resistance is encountered in the policies of this and other non-communist countries.

16. The risk of war with the USSR is sufficient to warrant, in common prudence, timely and adequate preparation by the United States.

    a. Even though present estimates indicate that the Soviet leaders do not intend deliberate armed action involving the United States at this time, the possibility of such deliberate resort to war cannot be ruled out.

    b. Now and for the foreseeable future there is a continuing danger that war will arise either through Soviet miscalculation of the determination of the United States to use all the means at its command to safeguard its security, through Soviet misinterpretation of our intentions, or through U.S. miscalculation of Soviet reactions to measures which we might take.

17. Soviet domination of the potential power of Eurasia, whether achieved by armed aggression or by political and subversive means, would be strategically and politically unacceptable to the United States.

18. The capability of the United States either in peace or in the event of war to cope with threats to its security or to gain its objectives would be severely weakened by internal development, important among which are:

    a. Serious espionage, subversion and sabotage, particularly by concerted and well-directed communist activity.

    b. Prolonged or exaggerated economic instability.

    c. Internal political and social disunity.

    d. Inadequate or excessive armament or foreign aid expenditures.

    e. An excessive or wasteful usage of our resources in time of peace.

    f. Lessening of U.S. prestige and influence through vacillation or appeasement or lack of skill and imagination in the conduct of its foreign policy or by shirking world responsibilities.

    g. Development of a false sense of security through a deceptive change in Soviet tactics. . . .

19.

    a. To reduce the power and influence of the USSR to limits which no longer constitute a threat to the peace, national independence, and stability of the world family of nations.

    b. To bring about a basic change in the conduct of international relations by the government in power in Russia, to conform with the purposes and principles set forth in the UN Charter.

In pursuing these objectives, due care must be taken to avoid permanently impairing our economy and the fundamental values and institutions inherent in our way of life.

20. We should endeavor to achieve our general objectives by methods short of war through the pursuit of the following aims:

    a. To encourage and promote the gradual retraction of undue Russian power and influence from the present perimeter areas around traditional Russian boundaries and the emergence of the satellite countries as entities independent of the USSR.

    b. To encourage the development among the Russian peoples of attitudes which may help to modify current Soviet behavior and permit a revival of the national life of groups evidencing the ability and determination to achieve and maintain national independence.

    c. To eradicate the myth by which people remote from Soviet military influence are held in a position of subservience to Moscow and to cause the world at large to see and understand the true nature of the USSR and the Soviet-directed world communist party, and to adopt a logical and realistic attitude toward them.

    d. To create situations which will compel the Soviet Government to recognize the practical undesirability of acting on the basis of its present concepts and the necessity of behaving in accordance with precepts of international conduct, as set forth in the purposes and principles of the UN Charter.

21. Attainment of these aims requires that the United States:

    a. Develop a level of military readiness which can be maintained as long as necessary as a deterrent to Soviet aggression, as indispensable support to our political attitude toward the USSR, as a source of encouragement to nations resisting Soviet political aggression, and as an adequate basis for immediate military commitments and for rapid mobilization should war prove unavoidable.

    b. Assure the internal security of the United States against dangers of sabotage, subversion, and espionage.

    c. Maximize our economic potential, including the strengthening of our peacetime economy and the establishment of essential reserves readily available in the event of war.

    d. Strengthen the orientation toward the United States of the non-Soviet nations; and help such of those nations as are able and willing to make an important contribution to U.S. security, to increase their economic and political stability and their military capability.

e. Place the maximum strain on the Soviet structure of power and particularly on the relationship between Moscow and the satellite countries.

f. Keep the U.S. public fully informed and cognizant of the threats to our national security so that it will be prepared to support the measures which we must accordingly adopt.

In the light of present and prospective Soviet atomic capabilities, the action which can be taken under present programs and plans, however, becomes dangerously inadequate, in both timing and scope, to accomplish the rapid progress toward the attainment of the United States political, economic, and military objectives which is now imperative.

A continuation of present trends would result in a serious decline in the strength of the free world relative to the Soviet Union and its satellites. This unfavorable trend arises from the inadequacy of current programs and plans rather than from any error in our objectives and aims. These trends lead in the direction of isolation, not by deliberate decision but by lack of the necessary basis for a vigorous initiative in the conflict with the Soviet Union.

Our position as the center of power in the free world places a heavy responsibility upon the United States for leadership. We must organize and enlist the energies and resources of the free world in a positive program for peace which will frustrate the Kremlin design for world domination by creating a situation in the free world to which the Kremlin will be compelled to adjust. Without such a cooperative effort, led by the United States, we will have to make gradual withdrawals under pressure until we discover one day that we have sacrificed positions of vital interest.

It is imperative that this trend be reversed by a much more rapid and concerted build-up of the actual strength of both the United States and the other nations of the free world. The analysis shows that this will be costly and will involve significant domestic financial and economic adjustments.

The execution of such a build-up, however, requires that the United States have an affirmative program beyond the solely defensive one of countering the threat posed by the Soviet Union. This program must light the path of peace and order among nations in a system based on freedom and justice, as contemplated in the Charter of the United Nations. Further, it must envisage the political and economic measures with which and the military shield behind which the free world can work to frustrate the Kremlin design by the strategy of the cold war; for every consideration of devotion to our fundamental values and to our national security demands that we achieve our objectives by the strategy of the cold war, building up our military strength in order that it may not have to be used. The only sure victory lies in the frustration of the Kremlin design by the steady development of the moral and material strength of the free world and its projection into the Soviet world in such a way as to bring about an internal change in the Soviet system. Such a positive program—harmonious with our fundamental national purpose and our objectives—is necessary if we are to regain and retain the initiative and to win and hold the necessary popular support and cooperation in the United States and the rest of the free world.

This program should include a plan for negotiation with the Soviet Union, developed and agreed with our allies and which is consonant with our objectives. The United States and its allies, particularly the United Kingdom and France, should always be ready to negotiate with the Soviet Union on terms consistent with our objectives. The present world situation, however, is one which militates against successful negotiations with the Kremlin—for the terms of agreements on important pending issues would reflect present realities and would therefore be unacceptable, if not disastrous, to the United States and the rest of the free world. After a decision and a start on building up the strength of the free world has been made, it might then be desirable for the United States to take an initiative in seeking negotiations in the hope that it might facilitate the process of accommodation by the Kremlin to the new situation. Failing that, the unwillingness of the Kremlin to accept equitable terms or its bad faith in observing them would assist in consolidating popular opinion in the free world in support of the measures necessary to sustain the build-up.

In summary, we must, by means of a rapid and sustained build-up of the political, economic, and military strength of the free world, and by means of an affirmative program intended to wrest the initiative from the Soviet Union, confront it with convincing evidence of the determination and ability of the free world to frustrate the Kremlin design of a world dominated by its will. Such evidence is the only means short of war which eventually may force the Kremlin to abandon its present course of action and to negotiate acceptable agreements on issues of major importance.

The whole success of the proposed program hangs ultimately on recognition by this Government, the American people, and all free peoples, that the cold war is in fact a real war in which the survival of the free world is at stake. Essential prerequisites to success are consultations with Congressional leaders designed to make the program the object of non-partisan legislative support, and a presentation to the public of a full explanation of the facts and implications of the present international situation. The prosecution of the program will require of us all the ingenuity, sacrifice, and unity demanded by the vital importance of the issue and the tenacity to persevere until our national objectives have been attained. . . .

Questions

1. According to the authors of NCS-68, what are the fundamental sources of conflict between the Soviet Union and the United States?
2. Why does NSC-68 rule out, for the present, negotiations between the United States and its allies and the Soviet Union?
3. Given these circumstances, what policies do the authors of NSC-68 believe should be undertaken? What alternative policies do they reject?

27-6   Statement on the North Korean Invasion of South Korea (1950)

Harry S. Truman

In moving to reunify Korea by force late in June 1950, Kim Il Sung of North Korea reckoned that the North's military superiority over South Korea, led by Syngman Rhee, would enable the North to win quickly enough that even American intervention could not save the South. Judging that much was at stake in the war, President Truman promptly ordered American military forces to intervene. Later in 1950, of course, the threat of a South Korean–American reunification of Korea would prompt Chinese Communist intervention in the war (see text pp. 877–879).

Source: Department of State Bulletin, vol. 23 (July 3, 1950), 5.

In Korea, the Government forces, which were armed to prevent border raids and to preserve internal security, were attacked by invading forces from North Korea. The Security Council of the United Nations called upon the invading troops to cease hostilities and to withdraw to the 38th Parallel. This they have not done but, on the contrary, have pressed the attack. The Security Council called upon all members of the United Nations to render every assistance to the United Nations in the execution of this resolution. In these circumstances, I have ordered United States air and sea forces to give the Korean Government troops cover and support.

The attack upon Korea makes it plain beyond all doubt that communism has passed beyond the use of subversion to conquer independent nations and will now use armed invasion and war. It has defied the orders of the Security Council of the United Nations issued to preserve international peace and security. In these circumstances, the occupation of Formosa by Communist forces would be a direct threat to the security of the Pacific area and to United States forces performing their lawful and necessary functions in that area.

Accordingly, I have ordered the Seventh Fleet to prevent any attack on Formosa. As a corollary of this action, I am calling upon the Chinese Government on Formosa to cease all air and sea operations against the mainland. The Seventh Fleet will see that this is done. The determination of the future status of Formosa must await the restoration of security in the Pacific, a peace settlement with Japan, or consideration by the United Nations.

I have also directed that United States forces in the Philippines be strengthened and that military assistance to the Philippine Government be accelerated.

I have similarly directed acceleration in the furnishing of military assistance to the forces of France and the Associated States in Indochina and the dispatch of a military mission to provide close working relations with those forces.

I know that all members of the United Nations will consider carefully the consequences of this latest aggression in Korea in defiance of the Charter of the United Nations. A return to the rule of force in international affairs would have far-reaching effects. The United States will continue to uphold the rule of law.

I have instructed Ambassador Austin, as the representative of the United States to the Security Council, to report these steps to the Council.

Questions

1. What, to Truman, is the broader significance of the outbreak of war in Korea?
2. What is the significance of Truman's statements and instructions relative to other areas of Asia?
3. Why does Truman refer to South Korean forces being "armed to prevent border raids and to preserve internal security"?

Question for Further Thought

1. After reviewing Documents 27-1 through 27-6 and the relevant text (especially "American Lives: George F. Kennan," pp. 872–873), critically assess American foreign policy during the early Cold War (1945–1950). How do you judge Kennan's formulation of containment policy (Document 27-1) and NSC-68 (Document 27-5)? How do they resemble one another? How do they differ?

Harry Truman and the Cold War at Home

With the death of Franklin Roosevelt, Harry Truman became president after less than three months as vice-president; he had been seen, but not heard or even informed. He occupied the White House not only during the early Cold War, but also during the period of reconversion to a peacetime economy and society. The postwar period was marked by inflation (which had been partially contained during wartime by price and wage controls) and by a wave of strikes (called by labor unions, which had gained in membership during the immediate prewar and wartime years). President Truman took a hard line toward labor during critical strikes; Congress, captured by the Republicans in 1946, moved the next year to clip the wings of organized labor in the Taft-Hartley Act, passed over a presidential veto (thanks to conservative Democrats, who voted with the Republicans).

Throughout the prosperous wartime period, political and private leaders had expressed their concern that the postwar nation might return to the economic stagnation of the 1930s. Indeed, the Servicemen's Readjustment Act of 1944 (the GI Bill of Rights) was in part an antidepression measure. (Unlike the First World War veteran's bonus, to be paid at a future date, the GI Bill promptly provided an impressive array of veterans' benefits.) In 1946, Congress passed the Employment Act (Document 27-7), path breaking, though limited, to influence peacetime federal economic policy (see text pp. 845–846, 879–881).

President Truman confronted difficulties in his efforts to achieve his Fair Deal, an expansion of the New Deal that would lead to the attainment of civil rights for African Americans—this in a postwar period very different from the 1930s. Not only did the Republicans control Congress during the second half of his "accidental" term, but both the left and right wings of his own party staged revolts in 1948, running national tickets of their own. The issue of civil rights was central to the growing anger of Deep South Democrats with the national Democratic Party. Still, Truman won reelection, and his party recaptured Congress. Document 27-8 offers the 1948 national party platform planks on the civil rights issue (see text pp. 881–883).

Even when President Truman faced a Democratic Congress during his full term (1949–1953), the conservative congressional coalition that had emerged during the late 1930s thwarted initiatives like national health insurance and the repeal of the Taft-Hartley Act. Truman was more successful in expanding programs that were already in place: increasing the minimum wage and Social Security benefits and extending Social Security to hitherto uncovered workers. His full term was also marked by the Korean War and other Cold War developments and by "the Great Fear," one aspect of which was McCarthyism (Document 27-9). (See text pp. 877–879, 882–887.)

27-7   The Employment Act (1946)

The Employment Act of 1946 was passed not during a crisis, whether of depression or of war, but with both of those part of recent memory. It went beyond pre-1929 thinking regarding government's economic policy-making role, but not as far as advocates of government planning wished (see text p. 880).

Source: United States, *Statutes at Large*, 60: 23–26.

DECLARATION OF POLICY

SEC. 2. The Congress hereby declares that it is the continuing policy and responsibility of the Federal Government to use all practicable means consistent with its needs and obligations and other essential considerations of national policy, with the assistance and cooperation of industry, agriculture, labor, and State and local governments, to coordinate and utilize all its plans, functions, and resources for the purpose of creating and maintaining, in a manner calculated to foster and promote free competitive enterprise and the general welfare, conditions under which there will be afforded useful employment opportunities, including self-employment, for those able, willing, and seeking to work, and to promote maximum employment, production, and purchasing power.

ECONOMIC REPORT OF THE PRESIDENT

SEC. 3. (a) The President shall transmit to the Congress within sixty days after the beginning of each regular session (commencing with the year 1947) an economic report (hereinafter called the "Economic Report") setting forth (1) the levels of employment, production, and purchasing power obtaining in the United States and such levels needed to carry out the policy declared in section 2; (2) current and foreseeable trends in the levels of employment, production, and purchasing power; (3) a review of the economic program of the Federal Government and a review of economic conditions affecting employment in the United States or any considerable portion thereof during the preceding year and of their effect upon employment, production, and purchasing power; and (4) a program for carrying out the policy

declared in section 2, together with such recommendations for legislation as he may deem necessary or desirable.

(b) The President may transmit from time to time to the Congress reports supplementary to the Economic Report, each of which shall include such supplementary or revised recommendations as he may deem necessary or desirable to achieve the policy declared in section 2.

(c) The Economic Report, and all supplementary reports transmitted under subsection (b), shall, when transmitted to Congress, be referred to the joint committee created by section 5.

COUNCIL OF ECONOMIC ADVISERS TO THE PRESIDENT

SEC. 4. (a) There is hereby created in the Executive Office of the President, a Council of Economic Advisers (hereinafter called the "Council"). The Council shall be composed of three members who shall be appointed by the President, by and with the advice and consent of the Senate, and each of whom shall be a person who, as a result of his training, experience, and attainments, is exceptionally qualified to analyze and interpret economic developments, to appraise programs and activities of the Government in the light of the policy declared in section 2, and to formulate and recommend national economy policy to promote employment, production, and purchasing power under free competitive enterprise. Each member of the Council shall receive compensation at the rate of $15,000 per annum. The President shall designate one of the members of the Council as chairman and one as vice chairman, who shall act as chairman in the absence of the chairman.

(b) The Council is authorized to employ, and fix the compensation of, such specialists and other experts as may be necessary for the carrying out of its functions under this Act, without regard to the civil-service laws and the Classification Act of 1923, as amended, and is authorized, subject to the civil-service laws, to employ such other officers and employees as may be necessary for carrying out its functions under this Act, and fix their compensation in accordance with the Classification Act of 1923, as amended.

(c) It shall be the duty and function of the Council—

(1) to assist and advise the President in the preparation of the Economic Report;

(2) to gather timely and authoritative information concerning economic developments and economic trends, both current and prospective, to analyze and interpret such information in the light of the policy declared in section 2 for the purpose of determining whether such developments and trends are interfering, or are likely to interfere, with the achievement of such policy, and to compile and submit to the President studies relating to such developments and trends;

(3) to appraise the various programs and activities of the Federal Government in the light of the policy declared in section 2 for the purpose of determining the extent to which such programs and activities are contributing, and the extent to which they are not contributing, to the achievement of such policy, and to make recommendations to the President with respect thereto;

(4) to develop and recommend to the President national economic policies to foster and promote free competitive enterprise, to avoid economic fluctuations or to diminish the effects thereof, and to maintain employment, production, and purchasing power;

(5) to make and furnish such studies, report thereon, and recommendations with respect to matters of Federal economic policy and legislation as the President may request.

(d) The Council shall make an annual report to the President in December of each year.

(e) In exercising its powers, functions and duties under this Act—

(1) the Council may constitute such advisory committees and may consult with such representatives of industry, agriculture, labor, consumers, State and local governments, and other groups, as it deems advisable;

(2) the Council shall, to the fullest extent possible, utilize the services, facilities, and information (including statistical information) of other Government agencies as well as of private research agencies, in order that duplication of effort and expense may be avoided.

(f) To enable the Council to exercise its powers, functions, and duties under this Act, there are authorized to be appropriate (except for the salaries of the members and the salaries of officers and employees of the Council) such sums as may be necessary. For the salaries of the members and the salaries of officers and employees of the Council, there is authorized to be appropriated not exceeding $345,000 in the aggregate for each fiscal year.

JOINT COMMITTEE ON THE ECONOMIC REPORT

Sec. 5. (a) There is hereby established a Joint Committee on the Economic Report, to be composed of seven Members of the Senate, to be appointed by the President of the Senate, and seven Members of the House of Representatives, to be appointed by the Speaker of the House of Representatives. The party representation on the joint committee shall as nearly as may be feasible reflect the relative membership of the majority and minority parties in the Senate and House of Representatives.

(b) It shall be the function of the joint committee—

(1) to make a continuing study of matters relating to the Economic Report;

(2) to study means of coordinating programs in order to further the policy of this Act; and

(3) as a guide to the several committees of the Congress dealing with legislation relating to the Economic Report, not later than May 1 of each year (beginning with the year 1947) to file a report with the Senate and the House of Representatives containing its findings and recommendations with respect to each of the main recommendations made by the President in the Economic Report, and from time to time to make such other reports and recommendations to the Senate and House of Representatives as it deems advisable.

(c) Vacancies in the membership of the joint committee shall not affect the power of the remaining members to execute the functions of the joint committee, and shall be filled in the same manner as in the case of the original selection. The joint committee shall select a chairman and a vice chairman from among its members.

(d) The joint committee, or any duly authorized subcommittee thereof, is authorized to hold such hearings as it deems advisable, and, within the limitations of its appropriations, the joint committee is empowered to appoint and fix the compensation of such experts, consultants, technicians, and clerical and stenographic assistants, to procure such printing and binding, and to make such expenditures, as it deems necessary and advisable. The cost of stenographic services to report hearings of the joint committee, or any subcommittee thereof, shall not exceed 25 cents per hundred words. The joint committee is authorized to utilize the services, information, and facilities of the departments and establishments of the Government, and also of private research agencies.

(e) There is hereby authorized to be appropriated for each fiscal year, the sum of $50,000, or so much thereof as may be necessary, to carry out the provisions of this section, to be disbursed by the Secretary of the Senate on vouchers signed by the chairman or vice chairman.

Approved February 20, 1946.

Questions

1. In what respects is the Employment Act of 1946 an important milestone?
2. In what respects is the legislation weak?
3. What responsibilities does the act assign to the president? To the Council of Economic Advisers? To the Joint Committee on the Economic Report? To the Congress?

27-8   Civil Rights and the National Party Platforms (1948)

A growing, but still far from nationally dominant, concern over civil rights figured in the 1948 presidential campaign (see text pp. 881–883). The Democratic Party was particularly affected. Its national convention rejected southerners' efforts to weaken a general civil rights plank (largely based on the 1944 platform), then strengthened that plank (in its two final paragraphs) by a vote of 651½–582½. This precipitated the creation of the States' Rights Democratic (Dixiecrat) party. At that time, the Republican Party had no significant base in the South, and the Progressive party of 1948 barely existed there. For a 1948 statement—and a 1980s recollection—of Strom Thurmond of South Carolina, the Dixiecrats' presidential candidate, see *Instructor's Resource Manual, America's History*, vol. 2, *Since 1865*, 4th ed., 391–392.

Source: Kirk H. Porter and Donald Bruce Johnson, comps., *National Party Platforms, 1840–1968* (Urbana: University of Illinois Press, 1970), 435, 437, 441, 442, 447, 450, 452, 453, 468.

DEMOCRATS

. . . The Democratic Party is responsible for the great civil rights gains made in recent years in eliminating unfair and illegal discrimination based on race, creed or color.

The Democratic Party commits itself to continuing its efforts to eradicate all racial, religious and economic discrimination.

We again state our belief that racial and religious minorities must have the right to live, the right to work, the right to vote, the full and equal protection of the laws, on the basis of equality with all citizens as guaranteed by the Constitution.

We highly commend President Harry S. Truman for his courageous stand on the issue of civil rights.

We call upon the Congress to support our President in guaranteeing these basic and fundamental American Principles: (1) the right of full and equal political participation; (2) the right to equal opportunity of employment; (3) the right of security of person; (4) and the right of equal treatment in the service and defense of our nation.[1] . . .

[1] When this platform was presented to the Convention, this section stated: "We again call upon the Congress to exert its full authority to the limit of its constitutional powers to assure and protect these rights." The last two paragraphs in the text above were inserted as an amendment to the platform by a vote of 651½ to 582½.

PROGRESSIVES

. . . The American people cherish freedom.

But the old parties, acting for the forces of special privilege, conspire to destroy traditional American freedoms.

They deny the Negro people the rights of citizenship. They impose a universal policy of Jim Crow and enforce it with every weapon of terror. They refuse to outlaw its most bestial expression—the crime of lynching.

They refuse to abolish the poll tax, and year after year they deny the right to vote to Negroes and millions of white people in the South. . . .

The Progressive Party condemns segregation and discrimination in all its forms and in all places.

We demand full equality for the Negro people, the Jewish people, Spanish-speaking Americans, Italian Americans, Japanese Americans, and all other nationality groups.

We call for a Presidential proclamation ending segregation and all forms of discrimination in the armed services and Federal employment.

We demand Federal anti-lynch, anti-discrimination, and fair-employment-practices legislation, and legislation abolishing segregation in interstate travel.

We call for immediate passage of anti-poll tax legislation, enactment of a universal suffrage law to permit all citizens to vote in Federal elections, and the full use of Federal enforcement powers to assure free exercise of the right to franchise.

We call for a Civil Rights Act for the District of Columbia to eliminate racial segregation and discrimination in the nation's capital.

We demand the ending of segregation and discrimination in the Panama Canal Zone and all territories, possessions and trusteeships. . . .

We will develop special programs to raise the low standards of health, housing, and educational facilities for Negroes, Indians and nationality groups, and will deny Federal funds to any state or local authority which withholds opportunities or benefits for reasons of race, creed, color, sex or national origin.

We will initiate a Federal program of education, in cooperation with state, local, and private agencies to combat racial and religious prejudice.

We support the enactment of legislation making it a Federal crime to disseminate anti-Semitic, anti-Negro, and all racist propaganda by mail, radio, motion picture or other means of communication. . . .

. . . The Progressive Party demands abolition of Jim Crow in the armed forces. . . .

The Progressive Party proposes to guarantee, free from segregation and discrimination, the inalienable right to a good education to every man, woman, and child in America. Essential to good education are the recognized principles of academic freedom—in particular, the principle of free inquiry into and discussion of controversial issues by teachers and students.

We call for the establishment of an integrated Federal grant-in-aid program to build new schools, libraries, raise teachers' and librarians' salaries, improve primary and secondary schools, and assist municipalities and states to establish free colleges.

We call for a system of Federal scholarships, fellowships, and cost-of-living grants, free from limitations or quotas based on race, creed, color, sex or national origin, in order to enable all those with necessary qualifications but without adequate means of support to obtain higher education in institutions of their own choice.

We call for a national program of adult education in cooperation with state and local authorities.

We oppose segregation in education and support legal action on behalf of Negro students and other minorities aimed at securing their admission to state-supported graduate and professional schools which now exclude them by law.

REPUBLICANS

. . . Constant and effective insistence on the personal dignity of the individual, and his right to complete justice without regard to race, creed or color, is a fundamental American principle.

We aim always to unite and to strengthen; never to weaken or divide. In such a brotherhood will we Americans get results. Thus we will overcome all obstacles. . . .

. . . Lynching or any other form of mob violence anywhere is a disgrace to any civilized state, and we favor the prompt enactment of legislation to end this infamy.

One of the basic principles of this Republic is the equality of all individuals in their right to life, liberty, and the pursuit of happiness. This principle is enunciated in the Declaration of Independence and embodied in the Constitution of the United States; it was vindicated on the field of battle and became the cornerstone of this Republic. This right of equal opportunity to work and to advance in life should never be limited in any individual because of race, religion, color, or country of origin. We favor the enactment and just enforcement of such Federal legislation as may be necessary to maintain this right at all times in every part of this Republic.

We favor the abolition of the poll tax as a requisite to voting.

We are opposed to the idea of racial segregation in the armed services of the United States. . . .

STATES' RIGHTS DEMOCRATS

. . . 1. We believe that the Constitution of the United States is the greatest charter of human liberty ever conceived by the mind of man.

2. We oppose all efforts to invade or destroy the rights vouchsafed by it to every citizen of this republic.

3. We stand for social and economic justice, which we believe can be vouchsafed to all citizens only by a strict adherence to our Constitution and the avoidance of any invasion or destruction of the constitutional rights of the states and individuals. We oppose the totalitarian, centralized, bureaucratic government and the police state called for by the platforms adopted by the Democratic and Republican conventions.

4. We stand for the segregation of the races and the racial integrity of each race; the constitutional right to choose one's associates; to accept private employment without governmental interference, and to earn one's living in any lawful way. We oppose the elimination of segregation employment by Federal bureaucrats called for by the misnamed civil rights program. We favor home rule, local self-government and a minimum interference with individual rights.

5. We oppose and condemn the action of the Democratic convention in sponsoring a civil rights program calling for the elimination of segregation, social equality by Federal fiat, regulation of private employment practices, voting and local law enforcement.

6. We affirm that the effective enforcement of such a program would be utterly destructive of the social, economic and political life of the Southern people, and of

other localities in which there may be differences in race, creed or national origin in appreciable numbers.

7. We stand for the checks and balances provided by the three departments of our Government. We oppose the usurpation of legislative functions by the executive and judicial departments. We unreservedly condemn the effort to establish nation-wide a police state in this republic that would destroy the last vestige of liberty enjoyed by a citizen.

8. We demand that there be returned to the people, to whom of right they belong, those powers needed for the preservation of human rights and the discharge of our responsibility as Democrats for human welfare. We oppose a denial of those rights by political parties, a barter or sale of those rights by a political convention, as well as any invasion or violation of those rights by the Federal Government.

We call upon all Democrats and upon all other loyal Americans who are opposed to totalitarianism at home and abroad to unite with us in ignominiously defeating Harry S. Truman and Thomas E. Dewey, and every other candidate for public office who would establish a police state in the United States of America.

Questions

1. What do the Democrats call for in the civil rights plank of their national platform? What demands of the civil rights movement of the 1950s and 1960s are not part of the 1948 Democratic platform?
2. In what respects does the Progressive party platform go beyond the Democratic and Republican platforms in dealing with civil rights?
3. What did the States' Rights Democratic party platform mean by "social equality"? Why did it term the Democratic and Republican platforms as favoring "totalitarian, centralized, bureaucratic government and the police state"?

27-9   Communists in the U.S. Government (1950)

Joseph R. McCarthy

Joseph R. McCarthy (1908–1957), a freshman Republican senator from Wisconsin, joined the anti-communist crusade during February 1950, in a speech delivered in Wheeling, West Virginia. He read the version of that speech excerpted here into the *Congressional Record* on February 20, 1950. The secretary of state whom he excoriated and caricatured was Dean Acheson; the individual whom Acheson had refused to disown was Alger Hiss. Hiss, accused as early as 1948 of having been a Communist spy while in government, had been convicted of perjury the previous month. (On "the Great Fear" of the 1940s and 1950s, see text pp. 883–887, including "American Voices: Mark Goodson.")

Source: Congressional Record, 81st Congress, 2nd Session, vol. 96, part 2, 1954–1957.

Five years after a world war has been won, men's hearts should anticipate a long peace, and men's minds should be free from the heavy weight that comes with war. But this is not such a period—for this is not a period of peace. This is a time of the "cold war." This is a time when all the world is split into two vast, increasingly hostile armed camps—a time of a great armaments race.

Today we can almost physically hear the mutterings and rumblings of an invigorated god of war. You can see it, feel it, and hear it all the way from the hills of Indochina, from the shores of Formosa, right over into the very heart of Europe itself. . . .

[W]e are now engaged in a show-down fight—not the usual war between nations for land areas or other material gains, but a war between two diametrically opposed ideologies.

The great difference between our western Christian world and the atheistic Communist world is not political, ladies and gentlemen, it is moral. . . .

The real, basic difference, however, lies in the religion of immoralism—invented by Marx, preached feverishly by Lenin, and carried to unimaginable extremes by Stalin. This religion of immoralism, if the Red half of the world wins—and well it may—this religion of immoralism will more deeply wound and damage mankind than any conceivable economic or political system.

Karl Marx dismissed God as a hoax, and Lenin and Stalin have added in clear-cut, unmistakable language their resolve that no nation, no people who believe in a God, can exist side by side with their communistic state.

Karl Marx, for example, expelled people from his Communist Party for mentioning such things as justice, humanity, or morality. He called this soulful ravings and sloppy sentimentality.

While Lincoln was a relatively young man in his late thirties, Karl Marx boasted that the Communist specter was haunting Europe. Since that time, hundreds of millions of people and vast areas of the world have fallen under Communist domination. Today, less than 100 years after Lincoln's death, Stalin brags that this Communist specter is not only haunting the world, but is about to completely subjugate it.

Today we are engaged in a final, all-out battle between communistic atheism and Christianity. The modern champions of communism have selected this as the time. And, ladies and gentlemen, the chips are down—they are truly down. . . .

Ladies and gentlemen, can there be anyone here tonight who is so blind as to say that the war is not on? Can there be anyone who fails to realize that the Communist world has said, "The time is now"—and that this is the time for the show-down between the democratic Christian world and the Communist atheistic world?

Unless we face this fact, we shall pay the price that must be paid by those who wait too long.

Six years ago, at the time of the first conference to map out the peace—Dumbarton Oaks—there was within the Soviet orbit 180,000,000 people. Lined up on the anti-totalitarian side there were in the world at that time roughly 1,625,000,000 people. Today only 6 years later, there are 800,000,000 people under the absolute domination of Soviet Russia—an increase of over 400 percent. On our side, the figure has shrunk to around 500,000,000. In other words, in less than 6 years the odds have changed from 9 to 1 in our favor to 8 to 5 against us. This indicates the swiftness of the tempo of Communist victories and American defeats in the cold war. As one of our outstanding historical figures once said, "When a great democracy is destroyed, it will not be because of enemies from without, but rather because of enemies from within."

The truth of this statement is becoming terrifyingly clear as we see this country each day losing on every front.

At war's end we were physically the strongest nation on earth and, at least potentially, the most powerful intellectually and morally. Ours could have been the honor of being a beacon in the desert of destruction, a shining living proof that civilization was not yet ready to destroy itself. Unfortunately, we have failed miserably and tragically to arise to the opportunity.

The reason why we find ourselves in a position of impotency is not because our only powerful potential enemy has sent men to invade our shores, but rather because of the traitorous actions of those who have been treated so well by this Nation. It has not been the less fortunate or members of minority groups who have been selling this Nation out, but rather those who have had all the benefits that the wealthiest nation on earth has had to offer—the finest homes, the finest college education, and the finest jobs in Government we can give.

This is glaringly true in the State Department. There the bright young men who are born with silver spoons in their mouths are the ones who have been worst. . . .

When Chiang Kai-shek [Jiang Jieshi] was fighting our war, the State Department had in China a young man named John S. Service. His task, obviously, was not to work for the communization of China. Strangely, however, he sent official reports back to the State Department urging that we torpedo our ally Chiang Kai-shek and stating, in effect, that communism was the best hope of China.

Later, this man—John Service—was picked up by the Federal Bureau of Investigation for turning over to the Communists secret State Department information. Strangely, however, he was never prosecuted. However, Joseph Grew, the Under Secretary of State, who insisted on his prosecution, was forced to resign. Two days after Grew's successor, Dean Acheson, took over as Under Secretary of State, this man—John Service—who had been picked up by the FBI and who had previously urged that communism was the best hope of China, was not only reinstated in the State Department but promoted. And finally, under Acheson, placed in charge of all placements and promotions.

Today, ladies and gentlemen, this man Service is on his way to represent the State Department and Acheson in Calcutta—by far and away the most important listening post in the Far East. . . .

This, ladies and gentlemen, gives you somewhat of a picture of the type of individuals who have been helping to shape our foreign policy. In my opinion the State Department, which is one of the most important government departments, is thoroughly infested with Communists.

I have in my hand 57 cases of individuals who would appear to be either card carrying members or certainly loyal to the Communist Party, but who nevertheless are still helping to shape our foreign policy.

One thing to remember in discussing the Communists in our Government is that we are not dealing with spies who get 30 pieces of silver to steal the blueprints of a new weapon. We are dealing with a far more sinister type of activity because it permits the enemy to guide and shape our policy. . . .

It is the result of an emotional hang-over and a temporary moral lapse which follows every war. It is the apathy to evil which people who have been subjected to the tremendous evils of war feel. As the people of the world see mass murder, the destruction of defenseless and innocent people, and all of the crime and lack of morals which go with war, they become numb and apathetic. It has always been thus after war.

However, the morals of our people have not been destroyed. They still exist. This cloak of numbness and apathy has only needed a spark to rekindle them. Happily, this spark has finally been supplied.

As you know, very recently the Secretary of State proclaimed his loyalty to a man guilty of what has always been considered as the most abominable of all crimes—of being a traitor to the people who gave him a position of great trust. The Secretary of State in attempting to justify his continued devotion to the man who sold out the Christian world to the atheistic world, referred to Christ's Sermon on the Mount as a justification and reason therefor, and the reaction of the American people to this would have made the heart of Abraham Lincoln happy.

When this pompous diplomat in striped pants, with a phony British accent, proclaimed to the American people that Christ on the Mount endorsed communism, high treason, and betrayal of a sacred trust, the blasphemy was so great that it awakened the dormant indignation of the American people.

He has lighted the spark which is resulting in a moral uprising and will end only when the whole sorry mess of twisted, warped thinkers are swept from the national scene so that we may have a new birth of national honesty and decency in Government.

Questions

1. How does McCarthy characterize the opposing sides in the Cold War?
2. How does he explain the successes of the Communists in the Cold War?
3. Who are the villains in his account?

Questions for Further Thought

1. How would you explain President Truman's winning the election in 1948 yet failing to win passage of important components of his program ("Fair Deal" liberalism)?
2. How would you compare and contrast the Red Scare following World War I with the Great Fear of the 1940s and 1950s?
3. What events and developments, at home and abroad, likely contributed to the meteoric rise of Senator McCarthy?

"Modern Republicanism"

Dwight Eisenhower became the first Republican president to serve two full terms since Ulysses S. Grant. His "Modern Republicanism" largely accepted, but did not enthusiastically embrace, the government that Presidents Roosevelt and Truman had led. The Democrats were the majority party in Congress during all but the first two years of Eisenhower's presidency. Reducing inflation and budget deficits took precedence over stimulating economic growth during the Eisenhower years, but Social Security coverage was broadened, and the minimum wage was raised (neither necessitating increased federal spending). Economic interest groups were encouraged to act in the public interest, with government serving as public referee (see text pp. 887–889). (On a major initiative of the Eisenhower administration, the National Interstate and Defense Highway Act of 1956, see text pp. 889, 909–910, and Document 28–4.)

Civil rights emerged as a national issue during the 1950s, one on which President Eisenhower did not provide leadership. The unanimous decision of the Supreme Court in *Brown v. Board of Education of Topeka* (1954) declared racial segregation in public schools to be unconstitutional, but it was not until the following year that the Supreme Court provided guidelines for implementing the decision, and it was not for several years that local school boards, closely overseen by federal district court judges, significantly desegregated public schools. Meanwhile, the Montgomery, Alabama, bus boycott of 1955–1956 demonstrated the potential of local, nonviolent civil rights protest. Triggered by Rosa Parks, a black woman who was arrested after refusing to give up her bus seat to a white, the boycott brought the Reverend Martin Luther King Jr. to national attention. In 1957, King and others founded the Southern Christian Leadership Conference (SCLC), which played a major role in the civil rights movement. In Document 27-10, Parks describes her arrest (see text pp. 889–891). (Also see *Brown v. Board of Education* [1954] and "The Southern Manifesto" [1956], both in *Instructor's Resource Manual: America's History*, vol. 2, *Since 1865*, 4th ed., 444–445, 393–394.)

The Korean War was brought to a conclusion, in an uneasy armistice, under President Eisenhower, but the Cold War, in which it had been but one campaign, remained central to administration thinking. Committed to both containment and the limiting of military spending (which had risen sharply during the Korean War and had remained high afterward), Eisenhower's administration stressed a "New Look" foreign policy that emphasized the threat of massive retaliation with nuclear weapons; selective intervention, covert and overt, from Latin America to Asia; and additional bilateral and multilateral regional security pacts (see text pp. 892–895). In Document 27-11, Secretary of State John Foster Dulles discusses Cold War policy before a meeting of Baghdad Pact nations.

27-10   Describing My Arrest (1955)

Rosa Parks

By refusing to give up her seat on a segregated local bus in Montgomery, Alabama, Rosa Parks (b. 1913), a seamstress and a member of the National Association for the Advancement of Colored People, played a pioneering role in community-based, nonviolent resistance to Jim Crow. Nonviolent resistance became highly important to the emerging civil rights movement. E. D. Nixon, an African American, was active in the NAACP; Clifford and Virginia Durr were local whites who supported the civil rights cause. (See text pp. 891–892, 918–921; also "American Voices: Anne Moody," text p. 928.)

Source: Rosa L. Parks interview by Howell Raines. Reprinted by permission of Putnam Berkley, a division of Penguin Putnam, Inc., from *My Soul Is Rested: The Story of the Civil Rights Movement in the Deep South* by Howell Raines, 40–41. Copyright © 1977 by Howell Raines.

I had left my work at the men's alteration shop . . . in the Montgomery Fair department store . . . . I came across the street and looked for a Cleveland Avenue bus that apparently had some seats on it. At that time it was a little hard to get a seat on the bus. . . .

As I got up on the bus and walked to the seat I saw there was only one vacancy that was just back of where it was considered the white section. So this was the seat that I took, next to the aisle, and a man was sitting next to me. Across the aisle there were two women, and there were a few seats at this point in the very front of the bus that was called the white section. . . . And on the third stop there were some people getting on, and at this point all of the front seats were taken. Now in the beginning, at the very first stop I had got on the bus, the back of the bus was filled up with people standing in the aisle and I don't know why this one vacancy that I took was left, because there were quite a few people already standing toward the back of the bus. The third stop is when all the front seats were taken, and this one man was standing and when the driver looked around and saw he was standing, he asked the four of us, the man in the seat with me and the two women across the aisle, to let him have those front seats.

At his first request, didn't any of us move. Then he spoke again and said, "You'd better make it light on yourselves and let me have those seats." At this point, of course, the passenger who would have taken the seat hadn't said anything. In fact, he never did speak to my knowledge. When the three people, the man who was in the seat with me and the two women, stood up and moved into the aisle, I remained where I was. When the driver saw that I was still sitting there, he asked if I was going to stand up. I told him, no, I wasn't. He said, "Well, if you don't stand up, I'm going to have you arrested." I told him to go on and have me arrested.

He got off the bus and came back shortly. A few minutes later, two policemen got on the bus, and they approached me and asked if the driver had asked me to stand

up, and I said yes, and they wanted to know why I didn't. I told them I didn't think I should have to stand up. . . . They placed me under arrest then and had me get in the police car, and I was taken to jail and booked on suspicion. . . . They had to determine whether or not the driver wanted to press charges or swear out a warrant, which he did. Then they took me to jail and I was placed in a cell. In a little while I was taken from the cell, and my picture was made and fingerprints taken. I went back to the cell then, and a few minutes later I was called back again, and when this happened I found out that Mr. E. D. Nixon and Attorney and Mrs. Clifford Durr had come to make bond for me.

Questions

1. What elements of nonviolent protest are evident in Parks's recollection?
2. Do you think that the fact that Parks was a woman was an important element in this event? Why or why not?
3. What does Parks's story indicate about whites in Montgomery?

27-11   Cold War Foreign Policy (1958)

John Foster Dulles

In opening remarks before the fourth session of the Council of Ministers of the Baghdad Pact, a defensive alliance between Turkey, Iraq, Iran, Pakistan, and Great Britain, Secretary of State John Foster Dulles (1888–1959) stressed the importance of "defensive security" and "economic health" in "meeting the Communist threat." He spoke in Ankara, Turkey, on January 27, 1958. The United States had encouraged Turkey and Iraq to enter into a defensive alliance, which the other three nations later joined. Iraqi nationalists soon overthrew the regime that had supported the pact.

Source: Department of State Bulletin, vol. 38 (February 17, 1958), 251–254.

Gentlemen, the close of World War II raised mankind's hopes that a new era of peace and security for all might now prevail. Unfortunately, these hopes were soon dashed. Instead, free men and free nations found themselves faced with a struggle to preserve their independence from the predatory ambitions of Communist imperialism. Moscow and Peiping [Beijing] directly or through local Communist parties, have relentlessly sought to extend their control in every direction. Where they have succeeded, freedom of choice has become a sham, the dignity of the individual a hollow mockery. The list of once free and proud nations that must today wear the Communist yoke is painful to recall. They are nearly a score in number. Coercion alone keeps them in this state of bondage, as was demonstrated by the recent revolt of the Hungarian people against their alien masters. Yet the parties of international communism continue openly to proclaim their

goal of world domination. They did so again, only last November, at Moscow.

Currently the use and threat of military power are supplemented by intensified and enlarged efforts at subversion and seduction. These efforts are insidious and deceptive. They seize upon mankind's yearning for economic and social betterment to undermine his vigilance to resist enslavement. . . .

Fortunately, there is, in general, a clear perception of the threat to independence posed by Communist imperialism. Around the world, the free nations have drawn together in collective regional associations as authorized and encouraged by the charter of the United Nations. These associations would, I believe, profit from exchange of information and of experience as between themselves. . . .

We are well aware of the fact that in this general area political independence, always an aspiration, has sometimes been lost and oftentimes been threatened, as indeed it is threatened today.

Also we recognize that it is not enough merely to want, or now have, independence. Reliable independence rests on two pillars: the pillar of defensive security and the pillar of economic health. The United States is prepared to cooperate, where desired, in assisting in these two ways any nation or group of nations in the general area of the Middle East to maintain national independence.

DEFENSIVE SECURITY

Let me speak first of security.

Security cannot be taken for granted. It must be won by positive efforts. It is not won by pacifism, by weakness, or by appeasement. That has been demonstrated time after time. Security is won by conditions which make it apparent that aggression does not pay. If a potential aggressor realizes that he will, by aggression, lose more than he could gain, it can be reliably assumed that he will not attempt aggression. That is where collective security plays its indispensable role. Few nations, by themselves, possess the resources needed to deter aggression. Collectively they can do so. Therefore, sometimes by treaty, sometimes by congressional resolution, the United States has associated itself with over 40 nations in defense of national independence and of peace. . . .

The Baghdad Pact group of countries can be confident that mobile power of great force would, as needed, be brought to bear against any Communist aggressor. And by the same token any such potential aggressor knows in advance that his losses from aggression would far exceed any possible gains. That is an effective deterrent to aggression and a guaranty of peace.

Also, it is vital that there be forces of national defense. These constitute indispensable, visible evidence of the will of people to fight and die, if need be, for their homes, their nation, and their faith. There is no "pushbutton" substitute for this. Furthermore, such forces, with the reinforcement where needed of mobile power, can save the people from the scourge of invasion if, perchance, deterrence fails. The United States has contributed, and will contribute, to this aspect of defense. . . .

I assure you that the United States strives earnestly both to end the nuclear menace and to limit conventional armaments. I recall that a decade ago the United States, possessing a monopoly of atomic weapons, offered to forgo that monopoly and to join in establishing a system to assure that atomic power would be used only for peaceful purposes. The Soviet Union alone blocked that peaceful and humanitarian measure.

And we act in the same spirit today. Outer space is becoming, for the first time, usable, and both the United States and the Soviet Union are experimentally using outer space for weapons purposes. So the United States has proposed to the Soviet Union that the nations forgo the use of outer space for war and dedicate it for all time to the peaceful purposes of mankind, to man's fuller life, not to his greater peril. So far that proposal remains without positive response.

The Soviet Union has, however, by a statement made last week, advanced the grotesque theory that only atheistic governments, as are the Communists, can properly possess modern weapons. The argument is that it would be a sacrilege for religious peoples, for defenders of the faith, to have such weapons; thus only the atheists, the Communists, can have them.

The United States ardently seeks limitation of armament on the basis of equality. But never will the United States accept the Soviet Communist thesis that men, because they are religious, must deny themselves the means to defend their religious freedom.

ECONOMIC HEALTH

Let me speak now of economic health. This is an equally indispensable pillar of independence. Without it no nation can maintain adequate and dependable security forces or be able surely to resist subversion.

Large military establishments are not easily reconciled with economic welfare. One of the merits of collective self-defense is that it reduces the requirements for individual self-defense. For under a collective system the mobile power that protects one can equally protect many. In this way, and only in this way, is it made possible for nations confronted by superior hostile power to avoid making the people fear an excessive nonproductive military burden and enable them to combine military security with economic health.

Military authorities can advise us about military security. But there is need also for a broad political judgment that comprehends both military and economic factors. Some economic sacrifices are needed for military security. We dare not give so absolute a priority to military requirements that economic health collapses. Indeed a sound and developing economy is the indispensable foundation for sustained military effort. Furthermore, given the deterrent military power that exists in the world today, there may be greater risk to independence in economic weakness than in local military weakness. It is not easy to strike the proper balance between military and economic effort. To achieve that is, however, the paramount duty of statesmanship. . . .

Social and economic progress is a universal desire. It is understandably most acute among those peoples who, for various historical reasons, do not yet fully share in the benefits of modern technology and science. These improve man's health, ease his labor, and afford him greater opportunities to develop his own talents and spiritual resources. . . .

MEETING THE COMMUNIST THREAT

Gentlemen, we live in difficult days. By great efforts over the centuries—efforts marked by successes and failures—

men have reached a great appreciation of the dignity of the human individual and the need for an organization of the society of nations in accordance with the tested principles of collective security and friendly cooperation. Yet at the moment, when so much seems possible, all is endangered. A small group believes fanatically in a materialistic, atheistic society. It believes in mechanistic conformity, both in terms of human beings and of national groups. It would turn men into cogs in a materialistic machine, thinking and acting under central dictatorship. It boasts that it is "internationalist" in the sense of bringing all governments everywhere under the domination of a single power, that of international communism, acting under the guiding direction of the Communist Party of the Soviet Union.

This fanatical group, using every device without moral restraint—for they deny the existence of a moral law—by use of revolution, military conquest, and subversion have come to rule a great part of the world, and they exploit the human and material resources they now control to extend their domination over the rest of us.

That is a threat of immense proportions. We need not, however, be dismayed. The greatest danger is always the danger which comes from blindness to danger. Today we see the danger, and we are allied with forces that have repeatedly demonstrated their ability to prevail as against materialistic despotisms. There are, we know, God-given aspirations for freedom of mind and spirit and for opportunity. These are beyond the power of man to destroy. So long as we ally ourselves loyally and sacrificially with what is good, what is true, our cause surely will prevail.

Gentlemen, the United States observer delegation, animated by these sentiments, will endeavor to make a constructive contribution to your deliberations.

Thank you.

Questions

1. Dulles sees a significant difference between what had been anticipated at the end of World War II and what had actually occurred. How does he account for that difference?

2. How does Dulles explain that military strength and economic well-being are in opposition to each other? What economic benefits of collective security does he mention?

Question for Further Thought

1. Does Dulles echo any earlier American Cold War declarations (Documents 27-1, 27-2, 27-5)? Does he strike any new notes?

The Impact of the Cold War

Wars, cold as well as hot, affect the societies that wage them. So it was that the lengthening and still indecisive Cold War had important effects on American society during the 1940s and 1950s. The salience of foreign relations and military policy increased the power of the executive branch of the federal government even more than the Great Depression and the New Deal had done. A struggle that involved the clash of ideologies, subversion, and espionage also placed a premium on conformity (see text pp. 883–887).

The continuing confrontation with Communist powers meant long-term and large-scale military commitments. The military draft, reinstituted during the early Cold War, affected successive cohorts of young men over a quarter century, not just during the wars in Korea and Vietnam. With the American and Soviet buildup of nuclear arsenals went the testing of weapons, with radioactive fallout a threatening consequence. Defense spending, on research and development, as well as production, was an economic stimulus, but it also overspent on some sectors of the economy while shortchanging others (see text pp. 895–900, including Figure 27-1, Map 27-4, and "American Voices"). In Document 27-12, President Eisenhower, about to leave office, expresses his concern about "the impact of the Cold War" on the United States.

27-12   Farewell Address (1961)

Dwight D. Eisenhower   Speaking on national television on January 17, 1961, just three days before the inauguration of his youthful successor, John F. Kennedy, President Dwight D. Eisenhower (1890–1969) reflected on the Cold War and its impact on the United States.

Source: Public Papers of the Presidents of the United States: Dwight D. Eisenhower, 1960–1961 (Washington, D.C.: U.S. Government Printing Office, 1961), 1035–1040.

We now stand ten years past the midpoint of a century that has witnessed four major wars among great nations. Three of these involved our own country. Despite these holocausts America is today the strongest, the most influential and most productive nation in the world. Understandably proud of this pre-eminence, we yet realize that America's leadership and prestige depend, not merely upon our unmatched material progress, riches and military strength, but on how we use our power in the interests of world peace and human betterment.

Throughout America's adventure in free government, our basic purposes have been to keep the peace; to foster progress in human achievement; and to enhance liberty, dignity and integrity among people and among nations. To strive for less would be unworthy of a free and religious people. Any failure traceable to arrogance, or our lack of comprehension or readiness to sacrifice would inflict upon us grievous hurt both at home and abroad.

Progress toward these noble goals is persistently threatened by the conflict now engulfing the world. It commands our whole attention, absorbs our very beings. We face a hostile ideology—global in scope, atheistic in character, ruthless in purpose, and insidious in method. Unhappily the danger it poses promises to be of indefinite duration. To meet it successfully, there is called for, not so much the emotional and transitory sacrifices of crisis, but rather those which enable us to carry forward steadily, surely, and without complaint the burdens of a prolonged and complex struggle—with liberty the stake. Only thus shall we remain, despite every provocation, on our charted course toward permanent peace and human betterment. . . .

A vital element in keeping the peace is our military establishment. Our arms must be mighty, ready for instant action, so that no potential aggressor may be tempted to risk his own destruction.

Our military organization today bears little relation to that known by any of my predecessors in peacetime, or indeed by the fighting men of World War II or Korea.

Until the latest of our world conflicts, the United States had no armaments industry. American makers of plowshares could, with time and as required, make swords as well. But now we can no longer risk emergency improvisation of national defense; we have been compelled to create a permanent armaments industry of vast proportions. Added to this, three and a half million men and women are directly engaged in the defense establishment. We annually spend on military security more than the net income of all United States corporations.

This conjunction of an immense military establishment and a large arms industry is new in the American experience. The total influence—economic, political, even spiritual—is felt in every city, every State house, every office of the Federal government. We recognize the imperative need for this development. Yet we must not fail to comprehend its grave implications. Our toil, resources and livelihood are all involved; so is the very structure of our society.

In the councils of government, we must guard against the acquisition of unwarranted influence, whether sought or unsought, by the military-industrial complex. The potential for the disastrous rise of misplaced power exists and will persist.

We must never let the weight of this combination endanger our liberties or democratic processes. We should take nothing for granted. Only an alert and knowledgeable citizenry can compel the proper meshing of the huge industrial and military machinery of defense with our peaceful methods and goals, so that security and liberty may prosper together.

Akin to, and largely responsible for the sweeping changes in our industrial-military posture, has been the technological revolution during recent decades.

In this revolution, research has become central; it also becomes more formalized, complex, and costly. A steadily increasing share is conducted for, by, or at the direction of, the Federal government.

Today, the solitary inventor, tinkering in his shop, has been overshadowed by task forces of scientists in laboratories and testing fields. In the same fashion, the free university, historically the fountainhead of free ideas and scientific discovery, has experienced a revolution in the conduct of research. Partly because of the huge costs involved, a government contract becomes virtually a substitute for intellectual curiosity. For every old blackboard there are now hundreds of new electronic computers.

The prospect of domination of the nation's scholars by Federal employment, project allocations, and the power of money is ever present—and is gravely to be regarded.

Yet, in holding scientific research and discovery in respect, as we should, we must also be alert to the equal and opposite danger that public policy could itself become the captive of a scientific-technological elite.

It is the task of statesmanship to mold, to balance, and to integrate these and other forces, new and old, within the principles of our democratic system—ever aiming toward the supreme goals of our free society.

Another factor in maintaining balance involves the element of time. As we peer into society's future, we—you and I, and our government—must avoid the impulse to live only for today, plundering, for our own ease and convenience, the precious resources of tomorrow. We cannot mortgage the material assets of our grandchildren without risking the loss also of their political and spiritual heritage. We want democracy to survive for all generations to come, not to become the insolvent phantom of tomorrow.

Down the long lane of the history yet to be written America knows that this world of ours, ever growing smaller, must avoid becoming a community of dreadful fear and hate, and be, instead, a proud confederation of mutual trust and respect.

Such a confederation must be one of equals. The weakest must come to the conference table with the same confidence as do we, protected as we are by our moral, economic, and military strength. That table, though scarred by many past frustrations, cannot be abandoned for the certain agony of the battlefield.

Disarmament, with mutual honor and confidence, is a continuing imperative. Together we must learn how to compose differences, not with arms, but with intellect and decent purpose. Because this need is so sharp and apparent I confess that I lay down my official responsibilities in this field with a definite sense of disappointment. As one who has witnessed the horror and the lingering sadness of war—as one who knows that another war could utterly destroy this civilization which has been so slowly and painfully built over thousands of years—I wish I could say tonight that a lasting peace is in sight.

Happily, I can say that war has been avoided. Steady progress toward our ultimate goal has been made. But, so much remains to be done. As a private citizen, I shall never cease to do what little I can to help the world advance along that road. . . .

You and I—my fellow citizens—need to be strong in our faith that all nations, under God, will reach the goal of peace with justice. May we be ever unswerving in devotion to principle, confident but humble with power, diligent in pursuit of the Nation's great goals.

To all the peoples of the world, I once more give expression to America's prayerful and continuing aspiration:

We pray that peoples of all faiths, all races, all nations, may have their great human needs satisfied; that those now denied opportunity shall come to enjoy it to the full; that all who yearn for freedom may experience its spiritual blessings; that those who have freedom will understand, also, its heavy responsibilities; that all who are insensitive to the needs of others will learn charity; that the scourges of poverty, disease and ignorance will be made to disappear from the earth, and that, in the goodness of time, all peoples will come to live together in a peace guaranteed by the binding force of mutual respect and love.

Questions

1. Eisenhower seems to see a threat to the independence of universities and the sciences as a result of governmental invasion of university laboratories. How does he describe changes in laboratories that would make them subject to such an invasion?

2. Eisenhower's use of the term *military-industrial complex* suggests the potential for a conspiracy against the public interest. How does he relate the military to public and governmental concerns? What role does government play in the development of industrial power?

3. Liberty, Eisenhower states, is at stake. From his speech, which institutions seem to be involved? Who is threatening liberty, and what can be done to protect it?

Questions for Further Thought

1. John Foster Dulles (Document 27-11) and President Eisenhower (Document 27-12) discern both foreign and domestic threats to which they want to call attention. What are those threats, and what responses do they want their audiences to have?

2. Both Dulles and Eisenhower are concerned with the expansion of American military power and its effect on the national and international roles of the United States. This is a new, post–World War II issue for Americans. How does each man define it? Are they saying essentially the same things?

3. How do you judge the diplomatic and military policies of the Eisenhower administration in the light of the concerns expressed by President Eisenhower in his Farewell Address?

CHAPTER **28**

The Affluent Society and the Liberal Consensus, 1945–1965

★ ★ ★

The Affluent Society

The decades after the Second World War were marked not only by the Cold War, but also by increasing prosperity for most, though not all, Americans. The war had strengthened, not damaged, the nation's economy. After experiencing want during the depression and then rationing and shortages during the prosperous war years, Americans were now ready and able to go on postwar buying sprees—to purchase homes and automobiles, household appliances (including newly available television sets), and the like. Government lent a helping hand: the GI Bill of Rights assisted veterans (most of whom were male) to purchase homes, start businesses, and acquire higher educations or technical training; spending on highway construction helped open suburban areas, where lower land costs encouraged home ownership. The powerful American economy both dominated and sustained the war-ravaged world, further contributing to domestic prosperity. Again, government played a role, with the Marshall Plan assisting European nations' recovery from the war and their purchase of American exports (see text pp. 903–917).

Prosperity (like depression) involves the society as well as the economy. Long before World War II ended, businesses began to extol their products for the postwar civilian market as well as their wartime production for the military. One such advertisement (Document 28-1) portrays a postwar society that would be very different from that of wartime, with many implications for women. Still, more women worked after the Second World War than before, though they were concentrated in some occupations and largely absent from others. Document 28-2 presents job ads for women in Chicago, twelve years into the postwar period (see text pp. 913–915).

As noted earlier, a number of interacting factors contributed to the postwar expansion of suburbia. Innovative developers played their role in this "suburban explosion," as Document 28-3, advertising the Green Acres housing development, makes clear. The federal government's interest in fostering automobile-based transportation is stated in

Document 28-4, Secretary of the Treasury George M. Humphrey's testimony regarding highway construction (see text pp. 906-910, including "Voices from Abroad").

The postwar "consumer culture" was broader than that of the 1920s, including working-class, as well as middle-class, families. It rested on rising real incomes, increased leisure time, new consumer appliances, consumer credit (including credit cards, introduced during the 1950s), and skillful (and costly) advertising. Television not only was a consumer appliance in demand, but also shaped consumer culture, as much in the programs it presented as in the commercials it carried (see text pp. 910–912). Document 28-5 offers Vance Packard's criticism of the marketing of goods and services during the 1950s. However dominant the conformism of the 1950s, it was not without its dissenters. In Document 28-6, John Clellon Holmes speaks for the Beat generation.

28-1   Mother, When Will You Stay Home Again? (1944)

Wartime advertising encouraged married women with children to work in war industries, but increasingly such messages included references to the postwar lives of such women. This advertisement appeared a year before Germany's surrender, fifteen months before Japan's. (Far more American military casualties were suffered during this period than during the first twenty-nine months of America's involvement.)

Source: Advertisement, Adel Manufacturing Company, *Saturday Evening Post,* May 6, 1944. Courtesy Gaslight Advertising Archives, Inc.

Questions

1. What role does the child play in the advertisement?
2. What purposes are served by placing the husband-father in military service?
3. How will the wartime experience of the wife-mother contribute to her postwar life, according to the ad?

Mother, when will you stay home again?

Some jubilant day mother *will* stay home again, doing the job she likes best—making a home for you and daddy, when he gets back. She knows that all the hydraulic valves, line support clips and blocks and electric anti-icing equipment that ADEL turns out for airplanes are helping bring that day closer.

Meanwhile she's learning the vital importance of precision in equipment made by ADEL. In her postwar home she'll want appliances with the same high degree of precision and she will get them when ADEL converts its famous *Design Simplicity* to products of equal dependability for home and industry.

ADEL

ADEL PRECISION PRODUCTS CORP.
BURBANK, CALIFORNIA, HUNTINGTON, WEST VIRGINIA
SERVICE OFFICES: DETROIT, HAGERSTOWN, SEATTLE

FOR WAR (AND PEACE) BUY BONDS

ADEL 'ISOdraulic REMOTE CONTROLS
Built for large aircraft, ADEL's 'ISOdraulic Controls answer remote control problems encountered in rail, marine and industrial applications. Precise positive control thru immediate response of "slave" unit irrespective of vibration, system pressure fluctuations, temperature (−67°F. to +200°F.). Send for booklet.

ADEL FLUID METERING EQUIPMENT
Fluid metering pumps with output ranges from .5 to 30 gph per outlet. Suitable for alcohol-glycerine and many other fluids. Maximum efficiency, minimum maintenance assured thru Design Simplicity plus service-testing during 7 years involving millions of miles of operation in all parts of the globe.

ADEL HYDRAULIC VALVES
Over 150 types and sizes predicated on six basic Design Simplicity models with standardized, interchangeable parts. Illustrated "Mighty Midget" 4-way selector valve. Weight 11 oz. Measures 1⅜" x 2⅜" x 2½". Handle loads as low as 20 in. pounds for 800 psi operations. Available in multiple units.

ADEL EQUIPMENT SERVES UNITED NATIONS' AIR FORCES ON EVERY BATTLE FRONT

28-2   Help Wanted—Women (1957)

After the war, married women, especially mothers, confronted difficult questions over whether to work. All women considering work faced dilemmas relating to the job market. Consider these want ads in the light of Documents 28-6 and 28-1 and text pp. 913–915, including the *Saturday Evening Post* cover and "American Voices."

Source: Classified ads, *Chicago Sunday Tribune,* May 12, 1957, part 5, 36, 40.

Executive Secretary $100 Week

$100 paid weekly to the PRESIDENT'S private secretary. Your own carpeted private office. Average skills nec. as you'll be handling most of your own correspondence. Ability to deal with people important, heavy public contact work involved. FREE at CHICAGO Personnel. 6 E. Randolph [Above Walgreens.] RAndolph 6-2355.

Arrange Social Functions

Famous college fraternity needs you to take over in their beautiful new national headquarters office. Make arrangements for social functions, send invitations to members, handle enrollments and all convention plans. $70 to start with raise in 30 days for this unusually different position. FREE at LAKE Personnel. 29 E. Madison.
RAndolph 6-4650   11th Fl.

RECEPTION LITE TYPING

No exp. nec. for this front office reception position. Answer pushbutton phones, greet visitors in beautiful modern office from 9-5. Lt. typing. Sal. high. FREE at LAKE Personnel. 29 E. Madison.
RAndolph 6-4650   11th Fl.

Reservation Secretary

Lite steno desired for unique position as secretary in charge of reservations for beautiful hotel. Handle accommodations for important people in the public eye. Poise and ability to deal with people important. Extremely high starting salary. FREE at LAKE Personnel. 29 E. Madison.
RAndolph 6-4650   11th Fl.

AIRLINE TICKET SALES GIRL

$305 mo. even during 10 day training period as ticket sales girl with high paying airline. All public contact—no office skills. Single girls receive travel passes for themselves and their families. Absolutely no exp. nec. For details see
BOULEVARD   22 W. Madison st.
5th Floor   FInancial 6-3780

RECEPTION WILL TEACH SWBD.

No experience or typing needed to be front office girl in well known commercial art studio. Your nice appearance, friendly manner, interest in public contact qualify. Salary open and high! Vacation this summer! Beginner qualifies. No fee at
BOULEVARD   22 W. Madison st.
5th Floor   FInancial 6-3780

SECRETARY

Permanent position available for girl to perform secretarial work of a varied nature. Requires person with pleasing personality, experience and ability. Modern air conditioned office located for convenient transportation.

GOSS
PRINTING PRESS CO.
5601 W. 31ST-ST.
BIshop 2-3300   Ext. 311

SECRETARY
PUBLIC RELATIONS DIR.

Must have good stenographic skills and like to do a variety of work. Age 22-30. Paid vacations, holidays, company cafeteria, and other employee benefits.
ILLINOIS TOOL WORKS
2501 N. Keeler [4200 W.]

SECRETARY

VACATION WITH PAY THIS SUMMER!

If you're not happy where you are, but don't want to lose your vacation this summer, here's your chance. We need a secretary for a vice president of this advertising agency, one who's neat, accurate taking and transcribing heavy copy dictation on electric typewriter, who can handle details herself, keep her boss on the beam, help out elsewhere in this six-girl office. We're in a spanking new office just a few steps from Van Buren I. C. station. A happy place to work in an expanding organization. Salary starts at $70 per week, but you must work 1 month before vacation starts. We'll test you before hiring—to start at once.

CALL MR. DEAN
WAbash 2-8056

Questions

1. What is the significance of separate want-ad sections for women and men?
2. What kinds of jobs predominate in these ads for women? What kinds are absent?
3. What strikes you about the language of the want ads (regarding prospective jobs, applicants, work environments, etc.)?

28-3   Green Acres (1950)

Suburbanization, the movement of people, institutions, and activities out of the city, was one of the central developments of the postwar period. The newspaper ad on page 357 carries the message of Long Island developers to potential home-buyers in New York City (see text pp. 906–911; also pp. 748–750, 754–755).

Source: Advertisement, Green Acres, *New York Times,* June 25, 1950, sec. 8, p. 6.

Questions

1. What strikes you about the home described in the ad?
2. How does the ad try to sell the house?
3. What appears to be the relationship between the Green Acres development in Valley Stream, Long Island, and New York City, at least as of 1950?

A New Home by CHANIN

Six rooms, all on one floor, attached garage, full basement, 34x25, exclusive of laundry space, make this a *complete* home for all the family—comfortable to live in, easy to keep, interesting and inviting to your friends.

Chanin skill of design has given it graciousness and luxury. Rooms are well-proportioned. Friendly entrance vestibule with guest closet, picture windows, front and rear, venetian blinds, china closet with service bar between dining room and kitchen, combination linen closet and laundry hamper, color-harmonized bath with vanitory, medicine cabinet with 14 feet of shelf-room, ceramic tile wainscoting and floor add finish and charm.

The basement easily becomes a recreation or hobby room, a play place for the children.

Chanin precision construction—poured concrete foundation and basement walls, full insulation, weather stripping, copper piping—mean low-cost maintenance. Oil-fired hot water circulating heat provides winter comfort; keeps down fuel bills.

The Hotpoint all-electric kitchen lightens housework. Steel cabinets have 23 square feet of textolite work surfaces. Refrigerator, range, dishwasher, ventilating fan and washing machine (in the basement) all are included in the purchase price.

But more important than details are the experience and integrity of the designer and builder. The Chanin Organization has created more than 6,000 dwelling units. Chanin "know-how" means lasting charm, sturdy lifetime quality.

The purchase price is less than you may think— $14,790 for everything mentioned, plus your choice of several exteriors, 6,000-square foot landscaped plot, sewers, curb, paved street, sidewalk. Veterans pay nothing down. Their 30-year mortgages bear 4 percent interest. Terms to nonveterans are equally attractive.

Compare this house with anything you have seen anywhere near its price range. Compare its location, in a planned, established community, 5 minutes walk from the Valley Stream station, 29 minutes from Penn Station, 17 miles from midtown New York or Brooklyn, near main highways, parkways, schools, churches, stores.

Then walk around Green Acres a bit. Hundreds of other homes, now 8 to 14 years old themselves will tell you that "Chanin-built is well-built" and much more than a phrase. It is a hallmark, a guarantee of building perfection.

Hotpoint appliances used exclusively

BY TRAIN: *Long Island train from Penn Station or Brooklyn to Valley Stream; walk back through park to property.* BY CAR: *Sunrise Highway to Central Avenue; from Merrick Road or Southern State Parkway, turn on Central Avenue to Sunrise Highway.* BY SUBWAY AND BUS: *6th Avenue or 8th Avenue IND train to Parsons Boulevard, Queens. Change to Bee Line's Grant Park bus which passes entrance gates.*

• GREEN ACRES •

"The Planned Residential Community"

SUNRISE HIGHWAY AT CENTRAL AVE., VALLEY STREAM, L. I.

28-4   The Interstate Highway System (1955)

George M. Humphrey   Federal construction of the interstate highway system made clear the interrelationships between interested businesses, the public, and the government (see text pp. 908–910). On May 16, 1955, testifying before the Subcommittee on Roads of the House Committee on Public Works, Secretary of the Treasury George M. Humphrey (1890–1970) made the case for the proposal that became the National Interstate and Defense Highway Act of 1956.

Source: Treasury Secretary George M. Humphrey, testimony before a House Subcommittee, 1955. In Nathaniel Howard, ed., *The Basic Papers of George M. Humphrey* (Cleveland: Western Reserve Historical Society, 1965), 513–515.

In my view, the new highways will be earning assets, making possible a continuation of expansion in the case of motor transportation which would otherwise be seriously handicapped by the growing inadequacy of our highway network. You already know of the savings possible from improved safety, reduced time delays, greater vehicle efficiency, and lower repair and maintenance costs. . . .

There is probably . . . no thinking person in America who does not know that the nation needs better highways. We need them for the daily business and safety of everyone. And we need them to help our defense should this nation ever be attacked by a foreign power. This being the

case, I believe that men of good will and good intentions must be able to get together on a plan for starting these better highways—not on a small scale, and not just a little amount a year—but on a major scale, and right now. Every year, every month lost in having these extra miles of better highways means loss to our economy and so less better living for our citizens. It means loss of lives through loss of the safety these better highways would bring. It means loss of the best possible transportation of our defense equipment and evacuation of our people in the event of an enemy attack.

Questions

1. According to Humphrey, why will the proposed highways become "earning assets"?
2. What role does Humphrey believe the highways will play in national defense? (How did the highways in the South Atlantic states fare in this role during 1999's Hurricane Floyd?)
3. What interests would be positively affected by the highways? What interests would be negatively affected?

28-5   The Hidden Persuaders (1957)

Vance Packard   During the 1950s, as during the 1920s, the advertising industry sought to stimulate demand for the consumer products and services of businesses (see text pp. 910–912, and, on the 1920s, pp. 745–750). The marketing campaign was not without its critics, among them Vance Packard. The following excerpt is from his book *The Hidden Persuaders*.

Source: Vance Packard, *The Hidden Persuaders* (New York: Van Rees Press, 1957), 72–82. Estate of Vance Packard.

MARKETING EIGHT HIDDEN NEEDS

. . . Selling emotional security. The Weiss and Geller advertising agency became suspicious of the conventional reasons people gave for buying home freezers. In many cases it found that economically, the freezers didn't make sense when you added up the initial cost, the monthly cost added on the electric bill, and the amount of frozen leftovers in the box that eventually would be thrown out. When all factors were added, the food that was consumed from the freezer often became very costly indeed.

Its curiosity aroused, the agency made a psychiatric pilot study. The probers found significance in the fact that the home freezer first came into widespread popularity after World War II when many families were filled with inner anxieties because of uncertainties involving not only food but just about everything else in their lives. These people began thinking fondly of former periods of safety and security, which subconsciously took them back to childhood where there was the mother who never disappointed and love was closely related with the giving of food. The probers concluded: "The freezer represents to many the assurance that there is always food in the house, and food in the home represents security, warmth, and safety." People who feel insecure, they found, need more food around than they can eat. The agency decided that the merchandising of freezers should take this squirrel factor into account in shaping campaigns. . . .

Selling reassurance of worth. In the mid-fifties *The Chicago Tribune* made a depth study of the detergent and soap market to try to find out why these products had failed to build brand loyalty, as many other products have done. Housewives tend to switch from one brand to another. This, the *Tribune* felt, was lamentable and concluded that the soap and detergent makers were themselves clearly to blame. They had been old-fashioned in their approach. "Most advertising," it found, "now shows practically no awareness that women have any other motive for using their products than to be clean, to protect the hands, and to keep objects clean." The depth-wise soap maker, the report advised, will realize that many housewives feel they are engaged in unrewarded and unappreciated drudgery when they clean. The advertiser should thus foster the wife's feeling of "worth and esteem." His "advertising should exalt the role of housekeeping—not in self-conscious, stodgy ways or with embarrassingly direct praise—but by various implications making it known what an important and proud thing it is or should be to be a housewife performing a role often regarded . . . as drudgery." . . .

Selling ego-gratification. This in a sense is akin to selling reassurance or worth. A maker of steam shovels found that sales were lagging. It had been showing in its ads magnificent photos of its mammoth machines lifting great loads of rock and dirt. A motivation study of prospective customers was made to find what was wrong. The first fact uncovered was that purchasing agents, in buying such ma-

chines, were strongly influenced by the comments and recommendations of their steam-shovel operators, and the operators showed considerable hostility to this company's brand. Probing the operators, the investigators quickly found the reason. The operators resented pictures in the ad that put all the glory on the huge machine and showed the operator as a barely visible figure inside the distant cab. The shovel maker, armed with this insight, changed its ad approach and began taking its photographs from over the operator's shoulder. He was shown as the complete master of the mammoth machine. This new approach, *Tide* magazine reported, is "easing the operators' hostility." . . .

Selling creative outlets. The director of psychological research at a Chicago ad agency mentioned casually in a conversation that gardening is a "pregnancy activity." When questioned about this she responded, as if explaining the most obvious thing in the world, that gardening gives older women a chance to keep on growing things after they have passed the child-bearing stage. This explains, she said, why gardening has particular appeal to older women and to men, who of course can't have babies. She cited the case of a woman with eleven children who, when she passed through menopause, nearly had a nervous collapse until she discovered gardening, which she took to for the first time in her life and with obvious and intense delight.

Housewives consistently report that one of the most pleasurable tasks of the home is making a cake. Psychologists were put to work exploring this phenomenon for merchandising clues. James Vicary made a study of cake symbolism and came up with the conclusion that "baking a cake traditionally is acting out the birth of a child" so that when a woman bakes a cake for her family she is symbolically presenting the family with a new baby, an idea she likes very much. Mr. Vicary cited the many jokes and old wives tales about cake making as evidence: the quip that brides whose cakes fall obviously can't produce a baby yet; the married jest about "leaving a cake in the oven"; the myth that a cake is likely to fall if the woman baking it is menstruating. A psychological consulting firm in Chicago also made a study of cake symbolism and found that "women experience making a cake as making a gift of themselves to their family," which suggests much the same thing.

The food mixes—particularly the cake mixes—soon found themselves deeply involved in this problem of feminine creativity and encountered much more resistance than the makers, being logical people, ever dreamed possible. The makers found themselves trying to cope with negative and guilt feelings on the part of women who felt that use of ready mixes was a sign of poor housekeeping and threatened to deprive them of a traditional source of praise.

In the early days the cake-mix packages instructed, "Do not add milk, just add water." Still many wives insisted on adding milk as their creative touch, overloaded the cakes or muffins with calcium, and often the cakes or muffins fell, and the wives would blame the cake mix. Or the package would say, "Do not add eggs." Typically the milk and eggs had already been added by the manufacturer in dried form. But wives who were interviewed in depth studies would exclaim: "What kind of cake is it if you just need to add tap water!" Several different psychological firms wrestled with this problem and came up with essentially the same answer. The mix makers should always leave the housewife something to do. Thus Dr. Dichter counseled General Mills that it should start telling the housewife that she and Bisquick *together* could do the job and not Bisquick alone. Swansdown White Cake Mix began telling wives in large type: "You Add Fresh Eggs . . ." Some mixes have the wife add both fresh eggs and fresh milk. . . .

Selling love objects. This might seem a weird kind of merchandising but the promoters of Liberace, the TV pianist, have manipulated—with apparent premeditation—the trappings of Oedipus symbolism in selling him to women past the child-bearing age (where much of his following is concentrated). The TV columnist John Crosby alluded to this when he described the reception Liberace was receiving in England, where, according to Mr. Crosby, he was "visible in all his redundant dimples" on British commercial TV. Mr. Crosby quoted the *New Statesman and Nation* as follows: "Every American mom is longing to stroke the greasy, roguish curls. The wide, trustful child-like smile persists, even when the voice is in full song." TV viewers who have had an opportunity to sit in Mr. Liberace's TV presence may recall that in his TV presentations a picture of his real-life mom is frequently flashed on the screen, beaming in her rocking chair or divan while her son performs.

Selling sense of power. The fascination Americans show for any product that seems to offer them a personal extension of power has offered a rich field for exploitation by merchandisers. Automobile makers have strained to produce cars with ever-higher horsepower. After psychiatric probing a Midwestern ad agency concluded that a major appeal of buying a shiny new and more powerful car every couple of years is that "it gives him [the buyer] a renewed sense of power and reassures him of his own masculinity, an emotional need which his old car fails to deliver."

One complication of the power appeal of a powerful new car, the Institute for Motivational Research found, was that the man buying it often feels guilty about indulging himself with power that might be regarded as needless. The buyer needs some rational reassurance for indulging his deep-seated desires. A good solution, the institute decided, was to give the power appeals but stress that all that wonderful surging power would provide "the extra margin of safety in an emergency." This, an institute official explains, provides "the illusion of rationality" that the buyer needs.

The McCann-Erickson advertising agency made a study for Esso gasoline to discover what motivates consumers, in order more effectively to win new friends for Esso. The agency found there is considerable magic in the word power. After many depth interviews with gasoline buyers the agency perfected an ad strategy that hammered at two words, with all letters capitalized: TOTAL POWER. . . .

Selling a sense of roots. When the Mogen David wine people were seeking some way to add magic to their wine's sales appeal (while it was still an obscure brand), they turned to motivation research via its ad agency. Psychiatrists and other probers listening to people talk at random about wine found that many related it to old family-centered or festive occasions. Some talked in an almost homesick way about wine and the good old days that went with it. A hard-hitting copy platform was erected based on these homey associations. The campaign tied home and mother into the selling themes. One line was: "The good old days—the home sweet home wine—the wine that grandma used to make." As a result of these carefully "motivated" slogans, the sales of Mogen David doubled within a year and soon the company was budgeting $2,000,000 just for advertising—the biggest ad campaign in the history of the wine industry.

Selling immortality. Perhaps the most astounding of all the efforts to merchandise hidden needs was that proposed to a conference of Midwestern life-insurance men. The conference invited Edward Weiss, head of Weiss and Geller, to tell members of the assembled North Central Life Advertisers Association (meeting in Omaha in April, 1955) how to put more impact into their messages advertising insurance. In his speech, called "Hidden Attitudes Toward Life Insurance" he reported on a study in depth made by several psychologists. . . .

The heart of his presentation was the findings on selling life insurance to the male, who is the breadwinner in most families and the one whose life is to be insured. Weiss criticized many of the current selling messages as being blind to the realities of this man who usually makes the buying decision. Typically, he demonstrated, current ads either glorified the persistence and helpfulness of the insurance agent or else portrayed the comfortable pattern of life the family had managed to achieve after the breadwinner's death, thanks to the insurance. Both approaches, said Mr. Weiss, are dead wrong. In a few cases, he conceded, the breadwinner may be praised for his foresight, but still he is always depicted as someone now dead and gone.

One of the real appeals of life insurance to a man, his probers found, is that it assures the buyer of "the prospect of immortality through the perpetuation of his influence for it is not the fact of his own *physical* death that is inconceivable; it is the prospect of his *obliteration*." The man can't stand the thought of obliteration. Weiss reported that when men talked at the conscious and more formal level about insurance they talked of their great desire to protect their loved ones in case of any "eventuality." In this their desire for immortality was plain enough. But Weiss said there was strong evidence that this socially commendable acceptance of responsibility was not always the real and main desire of the prospective customer. Weiss said it appeared to be true for many men but not all. "In many instances," he went on, "our projective tests revealed the respondent's fierce desire to achieve immortality in order to *control* his family after death. These men obtain insurance against obliteration through the knowledge that they will continue to *dominate* their families; to *control* the family standard of living, and to guide the education of their children long after they are gone."

Questions

1. What is the significance of Packard's choice for the title of his book? What concerns Packard about the marketing on which he reports?
2. How did the marketing studies reported by Packard lead businesses to reorient advertising and even to modify products?
3. Do you see evidence of marketing strategies being employed on behalf of political candidates and positions in political debates?

28-6   Nothing More to Declare (1958)

John Clellon Holmes

Although John Clellon Holmes (1926–1988) did not enjoy as much public recognition as Allen Ginsberg *(Howl)* and Jack Kerouac *(On the Road)*, he was a highly regarded writer of the Beat Generation. The essay excerpted here first appeared in 1958. Although the Beats were cultural, rather than political, rebels, they influenced a number of rebels in the next decade, including Bob Dylan and Tom Hayden (see text pp. 914–915).

Source: John Clellon Holmes, *Nothing More to Declare* (New York: Dutton, 1967), 116–120, 122–126. Reprinted by permission of Sterling Lord Literistic, Inc. Copyright 1967 by the Estate of John Clellon Holmes. Reprinted from David E. Shi and Holly A. Mayer, eds., *For the Record: A Documentary History of America*, vol. 2, *From Reconstruction through Contemporary Times* (New York and London: W. W. Norton, 1999), 312–315.

Last September a novel was published which *The New York Times* called "the most beautifully executed, the clearest and most important utterance" yet made by a young writer; a book likely to represent the present generation. . . . It was called *On the Road,* by Jack Kerouac, and it described the experiences and attitudes of a restless group of young Americans, "mad to live, mad to talk, mad to be saved," whose primary interests seemed to be fast cars, wild parties, modem jazz, sex, marijuana, and other miscellaneous "kicks." Kerouac said they were members of a Beat Generation.

No one seemed to know exactly what Kerouac meant, and, indeed, some critics insisted that these wild young hedonists were not really representative of anything, but were only "freaks," "mental and moral imbeciles," "bourgeois rebels." Nevertheless, something about the book, and something about the term, would not be so easily dismissed. The book became the object of heated discussion, selling well as a consequence; and the term stuck—at least in the craw of those who denied there was any such thing.

Providing a word that crystallizes the characteristics of an entire generation has always been a thankless task. . . . But to find a word that will describe the group that is now roughly between the ages of eighteen and twenty-eight (give or take a year in either direction) is even more difficult, because this group includes veterans of three distinct kinds of modern war: a hot war, a cold war, and a war that was stubbornly not called a war at all, but a police action.

Everyone who has lived through a war, any sort of war, knows that Beat means not so much weariness, as rawness of the nerves; not so much being "filled up to *here,*" as being emptied out. It describes a state of mind from which all unessentials have been stripped, leaving it receptive to everything around it, but impatient with trivial obstructions. To be Beat is to be at the bottom of your personality, looking up; to be existential in the Kierkegaard,[1] rather than the Jean-Paul Sartre, sense.

What differentiated the characters in *On the Road* from the slum-bred petty criminals and icon-smashing Bohemians which have been something of a staple in much modern American fiction—what made them Beat—was something which seemed to irritate critics most of all. It was Kerouac's insistence that actually they were on a quest, and that the specific object of their quest was spiritual. Though they rushed back and forth across the country on the slightest pretext, gathering kicks along the way, their real journey was inward; and if they seemed to trespass most boundaries, legal and moral, it was only in the hope of finding a belief on the other side. "The Beat Generation," he said, "is basically a religious generation."

On the face of it, this may seem absurd when you consider that parents, civic leaders, law-enforcement officers and even literary critics most often have been amused, irritated or downright shocked by the behavior of this generation. They have noted more delinquency, more excess, more social irresponsibility in it than in any generation in recent years, and they have seen less interest in politics, community activity, and the orthodox religious creeds. They have been outraged by the adulation of the late James Dean, seeing in it signs of a dangerous morbidity, and they have been equally outraged by the adulation of Elvis Presley, seeing in it signs of a dangerous sensuality. They have read statistics on narcotics addiction, sexual promiscuity and the consumption of alcohol among the young and blanched. They have lamented the fact that "the most original work[2] being done in this country has come to depend on the bizarre and the offbeat for its creative stimulus"; and they have expressed horror at the disquieting kind of juvenile crime—violent and without an object—which has erupted in most large cities.

They see no signs of a search for spiritual values in a generation whose diverse tragic heroes have included jazzman Charlie Parker, actor Dean and poet Dylan Thomas; and whose interests have ranged all the way from bebop to rock and roll; from hipsterism to Zen Buddhism; from vision-inducing drugs to Method Acting. To be told that this is a generation whose almost exclusive concern is the discovery of something in which to believe seems to them to fly directly in the face of all the evidence.

Perhaps all generations feel that they have inherited "the worst of all possible worlds," but the Beat Generation probably has more claim to the feeling than any that have come before it. The historical climate which formed its attitudes was violent, and it did as much violence to ideas as it did to the men who believed in them. One does not have to be consciously aware of such destruction to feel it. Conventional notions of private and public morality have been steadily atrophied in the last ten or fifteen years by the exposure of treason in government, corruption in labor and business, and scandal among the mighty of Broadway and Hollywood. The political faiths which sometimes seem to justify slaughter have become steadily less appealing as slaughter has reached proportions that stagger even the mathematical mind. Orthodox religious conceptions of good and evil seem increasingly inadequate to explain a world of science-fiction turned fact, past enemies turned bosom friends, and honorable diplomacy turned brink-of-war. Older generations may be distressed or cynical or apathetic about this world, or they may have somehow adjusted their conceptions to it. But the Beat Generation is specifically the product of this world, and it is the only world its members have ever known.

It is the first generation in American history that has grown up with peacetime military training as a fully accepted fact of life. It is the first generation for whom the catch phrases of psychiatry have become such intellectual pabulum that it can dare to think they may not be the final yardstick of the human soul. It is the first generation for whom genocide, brainwashing, cybernetics, motivational research—and the resultant limitation of the concept of human volition which is inherent in them have been as familiar as its own face. It is also the first generation that has grown up since the possibility of the nuclear destruction of the world has become the final answer to all questions.

But instead of the cynicism and apathy which accompanies the end of ideals, and which gave the Lost Generation a certain poetic, autumnal quality, the Beat Generation is altogether too vigorous, too intent, too indefatigable, too curious to suit its elders. Nothing seems to satisfy or interest it but extremes, which, if they have included the criminality of narcotics, have also included the sanctity of monasteries. Everywhere the Beat Generation seems occupied with the feverish production of answers—some of them frightening, some of them foolish—to a single question: how are we to live? And if this is not immediately recognizable in leather-jacketed motorcyclists and hipsters "digging the street," it is because we assume that only answers which recognize man as a collective animal have any validity; and do not realize that this generation cannot conceive of the question in any but personal terms, and knows that the only answer it can accept will come out of the dark night of the individual soul.

Before looking at some of those answers, it would be well to remember what Norman Mailer, in a recent article on the hipster, said about the hip language: "What makes [it] a special language is that it cannot really be taught—if one shares none of the experiences of elation and exhaustion which it is equipped to describe, then it seems merely arch or vulgar or irritating." This is also true to a large extent of the whole reality in which the members of the Beat Generation have grown. If you can't see it the way they do, you can't understand the way they act. One way to see it,

---

[1] *Søren Kierkegaard* was a nineteenth-century Danish theologian and philosopher.

[2] I.e., Literary work.

perhaps the easiest, is to investigate the image they have of themselves.

A large proportion of this generation lived vicariously in the short, tumultuous career of actor James Dean. He was their idol in much the same way that Valentino was the screen idol of the twenties and Clark Gable was the screen idol of the thirties. But there was a difference, and it was all the difference. In Dean, they saw not a daydream Lothario who was more attractive, mysterious and wealthy than they were, or a virile man of action with whom they could fancifully identify to make up for their own feelings of powerlessness, but a wistful, reticent youth, looking over the abyss separating him from older people with a level, saddened eye; living intensely in alternate explosions of tenderness and violence; eager for love and a sense of purpose, but able to accept them only on terms which acknowledged the facts of life as he knew them: in short, themselves.

To many people, Dean's mumbling speech, attenuated silences, and rash gestures seemed the ultimate in empty mannerisms, but the young generation knew that it was not so much that he was inarticulate or affected as it was that he was unable to believe in some of the things his scripts required him to say. He spoke to them right through all the expensive make-believe of million-dollar productions, saying with his sighs, and the prolonged shifting of his weight from foot to foot: "Well, I suppose there's no way out of this, but we know how it *really* is. . . ." They knew he was lonely, they knew he was flawed, they knew he was confused. But they also knew that he "dug," and so they delighted in his sloppy clothes and untrimmed hair and indifference to the proprieties of fame. He was not what they wanted to be; he was what they were. He lived hard and without complaint; and he died as he lived, going fast. Or as Kerouac's characters express it: "We gotta go and never stop going till we get there." "Where we going, man?" "I don't know, but we gotta go."

Only the most myopic, it seems to me, can view this need for mobility (and it is one of the distinguishing characteristics of the Beat Generation) as a flight rather than a search.

The reaction to this on the part of young people, even those in a teen-age gang, is not a calculated immorality, however, but a return to an older, more personal, but no less rigorous code of ethics, which includes the inviolability of comradeship, the respect for confidences, and an almost mystical regard for courage—all of which are the ethics of the tribe, rather than community; the code of a small compact group living in an indifferent or a hostile environment, which it seeks not to conquer or change, but only to elude.

On a slightly older level, this almost primitive will to survive gives rise to the hipster, who moves through our cities like a member of some mysterious, nonviolent Underground, not plotting anything, but merely keeping alive an unpopular philosophy, much like the Christian of the first century. He finds in bop, the milder narcotics, his secretive language and the night itself, affirmation of an individuality (more and more besieged by the conformity of our national life), which can sometimes only be expressed by outright eccentricity. But his aim is to be asocial, not antisocial; his trancelike "digging" of jazz or sex or marijuana is an effort to free himself, not exert power over others. In his most enlightened state, the hipster feels that argument, violence and concern for attachments are ultimately Square, and he says, "Yes, man, yes!" to the Buddhist principle that most human miseries arise from these emotions. I once heard a young hipster exclaim wearily to the antagonist in a barroom brawl: "Oh, man, you don't want to interfere with him, with his kick. I mean, man, what a *drag!*"

. . . But it is perhaps in poetry where the attitude of the Beat Generation, and its exaggerated will to find beliefs at any cost, is most clearly articulated. In San Francisco, a whole school of young poets has made a complete break with their elegant, university-imprisoned forebears. Some of them subscribe to Zen Buddhism, which is a highly sophisticated, nonrational psychology of revelation, and wait for satori (wisdom, understanding, reconciliation). . . . All of them believe that only that which cries to be said, no matter how "unpoetic" it may seem; only that which is unalterably true to the sayer, and bursts out of him in a flood, finding its own form as it comes, is worth the saying in the first place. Literary attitudes, concern about meter or grammar, everything self-conscious and artificial that separates literature from life (they say) has got to go. . . .

The suggestion, at least in Kerouac's book, is that beyond the violence, the drugs, the jazz, and all the other "kicks" in which it frantically seeks its identity, this generation will find a faith and become consciously—he believes that it is unconsciously already—a religious generation. Be that as it may, there are indications that the Beat Generation is not just an American phenomenon. England has its Teddy Boys, Japan its Sun Tribers, and even in Russia there are hipsters of a sort. Everywhere young people are reacting to the growing collectivity of modern life, and the constant threat of collective death, with the same disturbing extremity of individualism. Everywhere they seem to be saying to their elders: "We are different from you, and we can't believe in the things you believe in—if only because this is the world you have wrought." Everywhere, they are searching for their own answers.

For many of them, the answer may well be jail or madness or death. They may never find the faith that Kerouac believes is at the end of their road. But on one thing they would all agree: the valueless abyss of modern life is unbearable. And if other generations have lamented the fact that theirs was "the worst of all possible worlds," young people today seem to know that it is the only one that they will ever have, and that [it] is how a man lives, not why, that makes all the difference. Their assumption—that the foundation of all systems, moral or social, is the indestructible unit of the single individual—may be nothing but a rebellion against a century in which this idea has fallen into disrepute. But their recognition that what sustains the individual is belief—and their growing conviction that only spiritual beliefs have any lasting validity in a world such as ours—should put their often frenzied behavior in a new light, and will certainly figure large in whatever future they may have.

Questions

1. According to Holmes, against what in America was the Beat Generation reacting during the 1950s?
2. What, according to Holmes, did members of the Beat Generation embrace?

Questions for Further Thought

1. Applying the ideas in Vance Packard's *The Hidden Persuaders* (Document 28-5), evaluate advertising from the 1920s (see Documents 23-3 and 23-4, and text pp. 744–748).
2. Drawing on the text (pp. 904–917, including "American Voices: Joy Wilner" and "American Lives: Elvis Presley"), and the documents, recreate the lives of a 1950s family and its members, including a person of your age group.
3. Drawing on the text (pp. 914–917) and Document 28-6, consider youth culture and cultural dissenters during the 1950s. What did they share? How did they differ?

The Other America

John Kenneth Galbraith did not celebrate the affluent society about which he wrote in 1958. Rather, he contrasted private affluence with public squalor and questioned the society that tolerated the discrepancy. Not everyone shared the widespread affluence of the 1950s and 1960s. Furthermore, both countless private decisions (such as those that led businesses and individuals to locate in suburbia) and important governmental policies (especially highway construction and urban renewal) worked to the disadvantage of urban groups that were part of "the other America" (see text pp. 918–921). In Document 28-7 Herbert Gans writes sympathetically of "the urban villagers" who lived in Boston's West End before urban renewal began there. Document 28-8 offers Chicago city government's case for urban renewal. Early in the 1960s, Michael Harrington wrote powerfully about an America that contained within it "an affluent society" *and* "an underdeveloped nation, a culture of poverty" (Document 28-9).

28-7   Boston's West Enders (1962)

Herbert Gans

Herbert Gans (b. 1927) wrote of the people whose neighborhood was Boston's West End. These "urban villagers" and "true urbanites," as he termed them, were predominantly working-class Italian Americans. Urban renewal razed the tenements of the West End, displacing those who had dwelled in them, in favor of high-rent apartment houses and those who could afford them (see text pp. 918–921, esp. p. 920).

Source: Abridged with the permission of The Free Press, a division of Simon & Schuster, from *The Urban Villagers,* Revised and Expanded Edition, by Herbert J. Gans, 20–24. Copyright © 1982 by Herbert J. Gans.

West Enders did not think of their area as a slum and resented the city's description of the area because it cast aspersions on them as slum dwellers. They were not pleased that the apartment buildings were not well kept up outside, but, as long as the landlord kept the building clean, maintained the mechanical system, and did not bother his tenants, they were not seriously disturbed about it. People kept their apartments up-to-date as they could afford to, and most of the ones I saw differed little from lower-middle-class ones in urban and suburban neighborhoods.

Housing is not the same kind of status symbol for the West Enders that it is for middle-class people. They are as concerned about making a good impression on others as anyone else, but the people to be impressed and the ways of impressing them do differ. The people who are entertained in the apartment are intimates. Moreover, they all live in similar circumstances. As a result they evaluate the host not on the basis of his housing, but on his friendliness, his moral qualities, and his ability as a host. Not only are acquaintances and strangers invited less freely to the home than in the middle class, but they are also less important to the West Enders' way of life, and therefore less significant judges of their status. Thus, West Enders, unlike the middle class, do not have to put on as impressive a front for such people. . . .

Whereas most West Enders have no objection to the older suburban towns that surround the Boston city limits, they have little use for the newer suburbs. They described these as too quiet for their tastes, lonely—that is, without street life—and occupied by people concerned only with trying to appear better than they are. West Enders avoid "the country." . . . They do not like its isolation. . . . I was told by one social worker of an experiment some years back to expose West End children to nature by taking them on a trip to Cape Cod. The experiment failed, for the young West Enders found no pleasure in the loneliness of natural surroundings and wanted to get back to the West End as quickly as possible. They were incredulous that anyone could live without people around them. . . .

Many West Enders impressed me as being true urbanites, with empathy for the pace, crowding, and excitement of city life. . . . They are not [cosmopolitan], however; the parts of the city that they use and enjoy are socially, culturally, and physically far different from those frequented by the upper-middle class. . . .

Questions

1. What does Gans mean by "urban villagers"? Why, to him, were the West Enders "true urbanites"?
2. Why did West Enders feel uncomfortable in suburban and rural surroundings, according to Gans?
3. What institutions were likely to have played important roles in the West End? What might have happened to them following urban renewal?

28-8   What Does Chicago's Renewal Program Mean? (1963)

By the early 1960s, American cities were using urban renewal as a weapon of desperation in an attempt to hold on to their middle-class population (see text p. 920). The city of Chicago printed this pamphlet in the hope that the upbeat tone would allay fears of urban decline.

Source: Pamphlet *What Does Chicago's Renewal Program Mean . . . to You . . . to Your Family . . . Your Neighbors . . . and Your Chicago?* (Chicago: City of Chicago, 1963). Courtesy of the Municipal Reference Collection, Chicago Public Library.

What Does Chicago's Renewal Program Mean . . .

To You . . . To Your Family . . . Your Neighbors . . . And Your Chicago?

IT MEANS MANY THINGS

Chicago is a great city. It is a city of fine neighborhoods, providing its citizens with homes and apartments of all sizes and at all prices. It is a city of magnificent parks. It offers unequalled cultural activities. Your children are provided with good schools. Good public transportation, super highways and well-lighted, clean streets provide easy access to and from your job.

But as great as Chicago is, it needs constant improvement and renewal to serve its people well.

Chicago—like all cities—must keep pace in the modern world BY SOLVING PROBLEMS of congestion and blight, BY PROTECTING THE GOOD THINGS we have, and by TAKING ADVANTAGE OF THE BIG OPPORTUNITIES that Chicago enjoys. This can mean better homes, more and better jobs, a better life for everyone. And the job of making Chicago a better place in which to live is a team effort requiring the help of all its citizens. It is the responsibility of each neighborhood and community.

In this great effort there is a role for all citizens.

They can do their part through their local neighborhood organization, civic groups, perhaps as a member of the conservation community councils, and various other citizen boards and commissions. Through these groups people work with those agencies directly concerned with the overall planning and execution of renewal and conservation.

Only when people—tenants, homeowners, businessmen, industrialists—all of them taxpayers—participate, is renewal and community improvement truly representative of their desires and needs for a better life.

Every taxpayer should be aware of the fact that slums and blight cost Chicago money.

More than 75 per cent of Chicago's corporate budget goes for police, fire, health, sanitation and Building Department operations.

To render these services in slums costs much more than it does in good neighborhoods.

RENEWAL CLEARS AND PREVENTS SLUMS.

DO YOU KNOW—the Chicago Renewal Program has already added $18,700,000 in new assessed valuation and current projects are expected to add $13,000,000 in the next two years.

Renewal ENCOURAGES PRIVATE INVESTMENT IN EXISTING NEIGHBORHOODS AND PROVIDES LAND FOR NEW INDUSTRIAL, COMMERCIAL, AND RESIDENTIAL DEVELOPMENT.

The Chicago Renewal Program costs money. BUT— MONEY SPENT FOR RENEWAL IS QUICKLY RECAPTURED THROUGH TAX RETURNS FROM THE ADDED VALUE OF THE NEW BUILDINGS WHICH ARE BUILT.

AFTER REDEVELOPMENT

$4,794,368

BEFORE REDEVELOPMENT

$2,321,442

Tax yields in clearance projects before and after redevelopment.

IF YOU ARE A HOMEOWNER . . .

Chances are your home represents the biggest single purchase you will ever make. Renewal protects not only your home but that of your neighbor as well. Enforcement of the building, housing and zoning codes prevents blight. Conservation projects and slum clearance in any neighborhood improves all of Chicago by providing space for schools, parks, streets, street lighting, and churches.

IF YOU ARE A TENANT . . .

Renewal, whether slum clearance or conservation, helps YOU by eliminating dilapidated buildings and replacing them with apartments and homes thus giving everyone a bigger choice of housing accommodations, or by rehabilitation of existing buildings. Renewal brings about street improvements, helps with parking problems, and provides you with all types of public improvements you need for good city living.

IF YOU ARE A BUSINESSMAN . . .

Either as an industrialist or a merchant, Chicago's Renewal Program benefits you directly. To-date, Chicago's Renewal Program means that $150,000,000 worth of investment has gone into industrial plants, commercial properties and homes.

Renewal can provide major new industrial sites.

Renewal can aid in the conservation of industrial districts.

Renewal provides the new homes and conserves existing neighborhoods from which business and factories draw for their labor force.

To the merchant, renewal adds in modernizing your business district.

Renewal improves traffic and parking conditions.

Renewal helps you and your customers.

Renewal helps provide jobs and assists Chicago's economy so that people in your community can continue to patronize your store, your bank and your place of entertainment.

IF YOU ARE A WAGE EARNER . . .

Renewal means more jobs and better jobs.

Renewal not only adds jobs, but saves jobs through industrial redevelopment that otherwise might be lost.

IF YOU ARE A CONSTRUCTION WORKER . . .

The renewal program is a major factor in rebuilding—homes and other construction projects requiring large amounts of land—which has already generated over $150,000,000 worth of building activity.

IF YOU ARE A PARENT . . .

Physical—Renewal eliminates conditions that breed juvenile delinquency and disease.

Social—Renewal provides land for improved parks, schools, churches and provides safer streets. It plays a vital role in reducing juvenile delinquency and contributes directly in making a better, cleaner, healthier neighborhood environment.

Your youngsters will benefit from renewal by attending the University of Illinois, the University of Chicago, Illinois Institute of Technology, DePaul University, Chicago Teachers College, and other fine colleges which are directly benefiting from Chicago's Renewal program.

Questions

1. How is urban renewal defined here?
2. What does it promise?
3. Which consequences of urban renewal are ignored?

28-9   The Other America (1962)

Michael Harrington

Like Walter Rauschenbusch (Document 20-2), Michael Harrington (1928–1989) believed that religious conviction should lead to social action. As a member of the Catholic Worker Movement, he had come to see Christ even in "the pathetic, shambling, shivering creature who would wander in off the streets." Here, he focuses on the "millions who are poor in the United States [and who] tend to become increasingly invisible"—in urban slums, Appalachian backwaters, migrant labor camps, and native American reservations (see text pp. 918–921, 934–935).

Source: Reprinted with the permission of Scribner, a division of Simon & Schuster from *The Other America: Poverty in the United States* by Michael Harrington, 158–162. Copyright © 1962, 1969, 1981 by Michael Harrington.

The United States in the sixties contains an affluent society within its borders. Millions and tens of millions enjoy the highest standard of life the world has ever known. This blessing is mixed. It is built upon a peculiarly distorted economy, one that often proliferates pseudo-needs rather than satisfying human needs. For some, it has resulted in a sense of spiritual emptiness, of alienation. Yet a man would be a fool to prefer hunger to satiety, and the material gains at least open up the possibility of a rich and full existence.

At the same time, the United States contains an underdeveloped nation, a culture of poverty. Its inhabitants do not suffer the extreme privation of the peasants of Asia or the tribesmen of Africa, yet the mechanism of the misery is similar. They are beyond history, beyond progress, sunk in a paralyzing, maiming routine.

The new nations, however, have one advantage: poverty is so general and so extreme that it is the passion of the entire society to obliterate it. Every resource, every policy, is measured by its effect on the lowest and most impoverished. There is a gigantic mobilization of the spirit of the society: aspiration becomes a national purpose that penetrates to every village and motivates a historical transformation.

But this country seems to be caught in a paradox. Because its poverty is not so deadly, because so many are enjoying a decent standard of life, there are indifference and blindness to the plight of the poor. There are even those who deny that the culture of poverty exists. It is as if Disraeli's famous remark about the two nations of the rich and the poor had come true in a fantastic fashion. At precisely the moment in history where for the first time a people have the material ability to end poverty, they lack the will to do so. They cannot see; they cannot act. The consciences of the well-off are the victims of affluence; the lives of the poor are the victims of a physical and spiritual misery.

The problem, then, is to a great extent one of vision. The nation of the well-off must be able to see through the wall of affluence and recognize the alien citizens on the other side. And there must be vision in the sense of purpose, of aspiration: if the word does not grate upon the ears of a gentile America, there must be a passion to end poverty, for nothing less than that will do.

In this summary chapter, I hope I can supply at least some of the material for such a vision. Let us try to understand the other America as a whole, to see its perspective for the future if it is left alone, to realize the responsibility and the potential for ending this nation in our midst.

But, when all is said and done, the decisive moment occurs after all the sociology and the description is in. There is really no such thing as "the material for a vision." After one reads the facts, either there are anger and shame, or there are not. And, as usual, the fate of the poor hangs upon the decision of the better-off. If this anger and shame are not forthcoming, someone can write a book about the other America a generation from now and it will be the same, or worse.

I

Perhaps the most important analytic point to have emerged in this description of the other America is the fact that poverty in America forms a culture, a way of life and feeling, that it makes a whole. It is crucial to generalize this idea, for it profoundly affects how one moves to destroy poverty.

The most obvious aspect of this interrelatedness is in the way in which the various subcultures of the other America feed into one another. This is clearest with the aged. There the poverty of the declining years is, for some millions of human beings, a function of the poverty of the earlier years. If there were adequate medical care for everyone in the United States, there would be less misery for old people. It is as simple as that. Or there is the relation between the poor farmers and the unskilled workers. When a man is driven off the land because of the impoverishment worked by technological progress, he leaves one part of the culture of poverty and joins another. If something were done about the low-income farmer, that would immediately tell in the statistics of urban unemployment and the economic underworld. The same is true of the Negroes. Any gain for America's minorities will immediately be translated into an advance for all the unskilled workers. One cannot raise the bottom of a society without benefiting everyone above.

Indeed, there is a curious advantage in the wholeness of poverty. Since the other America forms a distinct system within the United States, effective action at any one decisive point will have a "multiplier" effect; it will ramify through the entire culture of misery and ultimately through the entire society.

Then, poverty is a culture in the sense that the mechanism of impoverishment is fundamentally the same in every part of the system. The vicious circle is a basic pattern. It takes different forms for the unskilled workers, for the aged, for the Negroes, for the agricultural workers, but in each case the principle is the same. There are people in the affluent society who are poor because they are poor; and who stay poor because they are poor.

To realize this is to see that there are some tens of millions of Americans who are beyond the welfare state. Some of them are simply not covered by social legislation: they are omitted from Social Security and from minimum wage. Others are covered, but since they are so poor they do not know how to take advantage of the opportunities, or else their coverage is so inadequate as not to make a difference.

The welfare state was designed during that great burst of social creativity that took place in the 1930's. As previously noted its structure corresponds to the needs of those who played the most important role in building it: the middle third, the organized workers, the forces of urban liberalism, and so on. At the worst, there is "socialism for the rich and free enterprise for the poor," as when the huge corporation farms are the main beneficiaries of the farm program while the poor farmers get practically nothing; or when public funds are directed to aid in the construction of luxury housing while the slums are left to themselves (or become more dense as space is created for the well-off).

So there is the fundamental paradox of the welfare state: that it is not built for the desperate, but for those who are already capable of helping themselves. As long as the illusion persists that the poor are merrily freeloading on the public dole, so long will the other America continue unthreatened. The truth, it must be understood, is the exact opposite. The poor get less out of the welfare state than any group in America.

This is, of course, related to the most distinguishing mark of the other America: its common sense of hopelessness. For even when there are programs designed to help the other Americans, the poor are held back by their own pessimism.

On one level this fact has been described in this book as a matter of "aspiration." Like the Asian peasant, the impoverished American tends to see life as a fate, an endless cycle from which there is no deliverance. Lacking hope (and he is realistic to feel this way in many cases), that famous solution to all problems—let us educate the poor—becomes less and less meaningful. A person has to feel that education will do something for him if he is to gain from it. Placing a magnificent school with a fine faculty in the middle of a slum is, I suppose, better than having a run-down building staffed by incompetents. But it will not really make a difference so long as the environment of the tenement, the family, and the street counsels the children to leave as soon as they can and to disregard schooling.

On another level, the emotions of the other America are even more profoundly disturbed. Here it is not lack of aspiration and of hope; it is a matter of personal chaos. The drunkenness, the unstable marriages, the violence of the other America are not simply facts about individuals. They are the description of an entire group in the society who react this way because of the conditions under which they live.

In short, being poor is not one aspect of a person's life in this country; it is his life. Taken as a whole, poverty is a culture. Taken on the family level, it has the same quality. These are people who lack education and skill, who have bad health, poor housing, low levels of aspiration and high levels of mental distress. They are, in the language of sociology, "multiproblem" families. Each disability is the more intense because it exists within a web of disabilities. And if one problem is solved, and the others are left constant, there is little gain.

One might translate these facts into the moralistic language so dear to those who would condemn the poor for their faults. The other Americans are those who live at a level of life beneath moral choice, who are so submerged in their poverty that one cannot begin to talk about free choice. The point is not to make them wards of the state. Rather, society must help them before they can help themselves.

Questions

1. Why is Harrington critical of the welfare state?
2. What does he mean by saying that "poverty is a culture"?
3. What is the difference between helping the poor and making them wards of the state?

Questions for Further Thought

1. To what extent would Michael Harrington's treatment of poverty in his own time (Document 28-9) be relevant to understanding poverty during the 1930s? During the 1990s?
2. According to Harrington's analysis, why might the poor "tend to become increasingly invisible"?
3. Do "the urban villagers" of Boston's West End (Document 28-7) fit Harrington's definition of those in "The Other America"?

John F. Kennedy and the Politics of Expectation

The transfer of power from President Eisenhower to President Kennedy struck many Americans as it appeared to strike Kennedy himself in his Inaugural Address: "The torch has been passed to a new generation of Americans." (Not only was Kennedy twenty-seven years younger than his predecessor, he had been born later than four of the next five presidents to follow him.)

Television, which had grown remarkable in importance during the 1950s (see text pp. 911–912), was Kennedy's medium of choice. The next three documents deal with important episodes in the public career of John Kennedy, all of which reached large television audiences. Senator Kennedy's four debates with Vice-President Richard Nixon, his opponent for the presidency in 1960, were, of course, staged for television (Document 28-10). Kennedy's inaugural address the following January (Document 28-11) conveyed his hopes for the nation and his administration; and his address to Americans during the Cuban missile crisis of 1962 (Document 28-12) deals with the most dangerous Soviet-American confrontation of the Cold War. Document 28-13 excerpts a Kennedy speech dealing with domestic policy, undramatic but no less important for that.

28-10 The Television Debates (1960)

Theodore H. White

Journalist Theodore H. White (1915–1986) believed that "the central fact of politics has always been the quality of leadership under the pressure of great forces." White tested his hypothesis during the presidential campaign of 1960, when the television cameras created their own great pressure during a series of debates between John F. Kennedy and Richard M. Nixon (see text pp. 922–923).

Source: Excerpted from Theodore H. White, *The Making of the President, 1960* (New York: Atheneum, 1961), 279–287. Reprinted with permission.

At 8:30 P.M., Chicago time, on the evening of September 26th, 1960, the voice and shadow of the previous show faded from the screen; in a few seconds it was followed by another voice and by a visual clip extolling the virtues of Liggett and Myers cigarettes; fifteen seconds were then devoted to Maybelline, the mascara "devoted exclusively to eye beauty, velvety soft and smooth." Then a deep voice regretfully announced that the viewers who turned to this channel would tonight be denied the privilege of viewing the Andy Griffith Show—and the screen dissolved to three men who were about to confirm a revolution in American Presidential politics.

This revolution had been made by no one of the three men on screen—John F. Kennedy, Richard M. Nixon or Howard K. Smith, the moderator. It was a revolution born of the ceaseless American genius in technology; its sole agent and organizer had been the common American television set. Tonight it was to permit the simultaneous gathering of all the tribes of America to ponder their choice between two chieftains in the largest political convocation in the history of man.

Again, it is the census that best describes this revolution. Ten years earlier (in 1950) of America's then 40,000,000 families only 11 percent (or 4,400,000) enjoyed the pleasures of a television set. By 1960 the number of American families had grown to 44,000,000, and of these *no less than 88 per cent, or 40,000,000, possessed a television set.* The installation of this equipment had in some years of the previous decade partaken of the quality of stampede—and in the peak stampede years of 1954–1955–1956 no fewer than 10,000 American homes had each been installing a new television set for the first time *every single day of the year.* The change that came about with this stampede is almost immeasurable. By the summer of 1960 the average use of the television set in the American home was four or five hours out of the twenty-four in each day. The best judgment on what television had done to America comes from the research departments of the large television networks. According to them, it is now possible for the first time to answer an inquiring foreign visitor as to what Americans do in the evening. The answer is clear: *they watch television.* Within a single decade the medium has exploded to a dimension in shaping the American mind that rivals that of America's schools and churches. . . .

In 1960 this yearning of the television networks to show their best was particularly acute. For the men who direct television are sensitive to public criticism; they wince and weep in public like adolescents at the slightest touch of hostility in print—and in 1959 they had suffered the worst round of public criticism and contempt since their industry was founded. The shock of the "payola" scandals of 1959; the Congressional hearings on these scandals; the editorial indignation in the "Gutenberg" media not only at these scandals but at the drenching of the air by violence, vulgarity and horse opera—all these had not only given the masters of television an inferiority complex but also frightened them with the prospect that the franchise on the air given to them so freely in return for their legal obligation of "public service" might be withdrawn, curtailed or abolished. It was a time for the "upgrading" of television; and the Presidential campaign of 1960 seemed to offer a fine opportunity for public service—if only Congress would relax those regulations and laws that had manacled and *prevented* television from doing its best. . . .

It is important to understand why the debates of 1960 were to be different from previous political use of the medium.

Television had already demonstrated its primitive power in politics from, at least, the fall of 1952, when, in one broadcast, it had transformed Richard M. Nixon from a negative Vice-Presidential candidate, under attack, into a martyr and an asset to Dwight D. Eisenhower's Presidential campaign. But from 1952 until 1960 television could be used only as an expensive partisan instrument; its time had to be bought and paid for by political parties for their own candidates. The audiences such partisan broadcasts assembled, like the audiences at political rallies, were audiences of the convinced—of convinced Republicans for Republican candidates, of convinced Democrats for Democratic candidates. Generally, the most effective political broadcast could assemble hardly more than half the audience of the commercial show that it replaced. This was why so many candidates and their television advisers sought two-minute or five-minute spots tacked on to the major programs that engaged the nation's fancy; the general audience would not tune out a hostile candidate if he appeared for only two or three minutes, and thus a candidate, using TV "spots" had a much better chance of reaching the members of the opposition party and the "independents," whom he must lure to listen to and then vote for him. The 1960 idea of a "debate," in which both major candidates would appear simultaneously, thus promised to bring both Democrats and Republicans together in the same viewing audience for the first time. Some optimists thought the debates would at least double the exposure of both candidates. How much more they would do than "double" the exposure no one, in the summer of 1960, dreamed.

The future was thus still obscure when the representatives of the two candidates and the spokesmen for the broadcasting networks first met at the Waldorf-Astoria Hotel in New York in September to discuss the conditions and circumstances of the meetings. By this time each of the two major networks had offered eight hours of free time to the campaign, and the third had offered three hours, for a total of nineteen hours of nationwide broadcasting, worth about $2,000,000; they had also made it clear to the candidates that this was not "gift" time but time over which they, the networks, meant to exercise an editorial control to insure maximum viewing interest. Slowly, in discussion, the shape and form of the debates emerged—a controlled panel of four press interlocutors; no notes; dignity to be safeguarded; opening statements of eight minutes by each candidate in the first and last debates; two-and-one-half minute responses to questions. The Nixon negotiators fought to restrict the number of debates—their man, they felt, was the master of the form and one "sudden-death" debate could eliminate Kennedy with a roundhouse swing. They viewed the insistence of the Kennedy negotiators on the maximum possible number of debates as weakness. ("If they weren't scared," said one Nixon staffman, "why shouldn't they be willing to pin everything on one show?") The Kennedy negotiators insisted on at least five debates, then let themselves be whittled to four. ("Every time we get those two fellows on the screen side by side," said J. Leonard Reinsch, Kennedy's TV maestro, "we're going to gain and he's going to lose.")

By mid-September all had been arranged. There would be four debates—on September 26th, October 7th, October 13th and October 21st. The first would be produced by CBS out of Chicago, the second by NBC out of Washington, the third by ABC out of New York and Los Angeles and the fourth, again by ABC, out of New York.

In the event, when all was over, the audience exceeded the wildest fancies and claims of the television networks. Each individual broadcast averaged an audience set at a low of 65,000,000 and a high of 70,000,000. The greatest previous audience in television history had been for the climactic game of the 1959 World Series, when an estimated 90,000,000 Americans had tuned in to watch the White Sox play the Dodgers. When, finally, figures were assembled for all four debates, the total audience for the television debates on the Presidency exceeded even this figure.

All this, of course, was far in the future when, on Sunday, September 25th, 1960, John F. Kennedy arrived in Chicago from Cleveland, Ohio, to stay at the Ambassador East Hotel, and Richard M. Nixon came from Washington, D.C., to stop at the Pick-Congress Hotel, to prepare, each in his own way, for the confrontation.

Kennedy's preparation was marked by his typical attention to organization and his air of casual self-possession; the man behaves, in any crisis, as if it consisted only of a sequence of necessary things to be done that will become complicated if emotions intrude. His personal Brain Trust of three had arrived and assembled at the Knickerbocker Hotel in Chicago on Sunday, the day before. The chief of these three was, of course, Ted Sorensen; with Sorensen was Richard Goodwin, a twenty-eight-year-old lawyer, an elongated elfin man with a capacity for fact and reasoning that had made him Number One man only two years before at the Harvard Law School; and Mike Feldman, a burly and impressive man, a one-time instructor of law at the University of Pennsylvania, later a highly successful businessman, who had abandoned business to follow Kennedy's star as Chief of the Senator's Legislative Research. With them, they had brought the portable Kennedy campaign research library—a Sears Roebuck foot locker of documents—and now, for a twenty-four-hour session at the Knickerbocker Hotel, stretching around the clock, they operated like young men at college cramming for an exam. When they had finished, they had prepared fifteen pages of copy boiling down into twelve or thirteen subject areas the relevant facts and probable questions they thought the correspondents on the panel, or Mr. Nixon, might raise. All three had worked with Kennedy closely for years. They knew that as a member of the House and the Senate Com-

mittees on Labor he was fully familiar with all the issues that might arise on domestic policy (the subject of the first debate) and that it was necessary to fix in his mind, not the issues or understanding, but only the latest data.

Early on Monday they met the candidate in his suite for a morning session of questions and answers. The candidate read their suggestions for his opening eight-minute statement, disagreed, tossed their suggestions out, called his secretary, dictated another of his own; and then for four hours Kennedy and the Brain Trust considered together the Nixon position and the Kennedy position, with the accent constantly on fact: What was the latest rate of unemployment? What was steel production rate? What was the Nixon stand on this or that particular? The conversation, according to those present, was not only easy but rather comic and rambling, covering a vast number of issues entirely irrelevant to the debate. Shortly before one o'clock Goodwin and Feldman disappeared to a basement office in the Ambassador East to answer new questions the candidate had raised, and the candidate then had a gay lunch with Ted Sorensen, his brother Robert and public-opinion analyst Louis Harris. The candidate left shortly thereafter for a quick address to the United Brotherhood of Carpenters and Joiners of America (which Nixon had addressed in the morning) and came back to his hotel room for a nap. About five o'clock he rose from his nap, quite refreshed, and assembled brother Robert, Sorensen, Harris, Goodwin and Feldman for another Harvard tutorial skull session.

Several who were present remember the performance as vividly as those who were present at the Hyannisport meeting in October, 1959. The candidate lay on his bed in a white, open-necked T shirt and army suntan pants, and fired questions at his intimates. He held in his hand the fact cards that Goodwin and Feldman had prepared for him during the afternoon, and as he finished each, he sent it spinning off the bed to the floor. Finally, at about 6:30, he rose from his bed and decided to have dinner. He ate what is called "a splendid dinner" all by himself in his room, then emerged in a white shirt and dark-gray suit, called for a stop watch and proceeded to the old converted sports arena that is now CBS Station WBBM at McClurg Court in Chicago, to face his rival for the Presidency of the United States.

Richard M. Nixon had preceded him to the studio. Nixon had spent the day in solitude without companions in the loneliness of his room at the Pick-Congress. The Vice-President was tired; the drive of campaigning in the previous two weeks had caused him to lose another five pounds since he had left the hospital; his TV advisers had urged that he arrive in Chicago on Saturday and have a full day of rest before he went on the air on Monday, but they had been unable to get through to him, and had not even been able to reach his press secretary, Herbert Klein. Mr. Nixon thus arrived in Chicago late on Sunday evening, unbriefed on the magnitude of the trial he was approaching;

on Monday he spoke during the morning to the United Brotherhood of Carpenters and Joiners, an appearance his TV advisers considered a misfortune—the Brotherhood was a hostile union audience, whose negative reaction, they knew, would psychologically disturb their contender.

When Nixon returned to his hotel from the Brotherhood appearance at 12:30, he became incommunicado while his frantic TV technicians tried to reach him or brief him on the setting of the debate, the staging, the problems he might encounter. The Vice-President received one visitor for five minutes that afternoon in his suite, and he received one long telephone call—from Henry Cabot Lodge, who, reportedly, urged him to be careful to erase the "assassin image" when he went on the air. For the rest, the Vice-President was alone, in consultation with no one. Finally, as he emerged from the hotel to drive through Chicago traffic to the studio, one TV adviser was permitted to ride with him and hastily brief him in the ten-minute drive. The adviser urged that the Vice-President come out swinging—that this was a contest, a fight, and that Kennedy must be jolted at the first exchange. The Vice-President was of another mind, however—and wondered whether the suggestion had originated with his adviser or with someone else, like Frank Stanton, President of CBS, who, said the Vice-President, only wanted a good show. Thus they arrived at the studio; as Nixon got out, he struck his knee again—a nasty crack—on the edge of the automobile door, just as he had on his first accident to the knee at Greensboro, North Carolina. An observer reports that his face went all "white and pasty" but that he quickly recovered and entered the studio. . . .

Mr. Nixon's advisers and representatives, understandably nervous since they could not communicate with their principal, had made the best preparation they could. They had earlier requested that both candidates talk from a lectern, standing—and Kennedy had agreed. They had asked several days earlier that the two candidates be seated farther apart from each other than originally planned—and that had been agreed on too. Now, on the day of the debate, they paid meticulous attention to each detail. They

were worried about the deep eye shadows in Nixon's face and they requested and adjusted two tiny spotlights ("inkies" in television parlance) to shine directly into his eye wells and illuminate the darkness there; they asked that a table be placed in front of the moderator, and this was agreed to also; they requested that no shots be taken of Nixon's left profile during the debate; and this was also agreed to.

The Kennedy advisers had no requests; they seemed as cocky and confident as their chief.

Nixon entered the studio about an hour before air time and inspected the setting, let himself be televised on an interior camera briefly for the inspection of his advisers, then paced moodily about in the back of the studio. He beckoned the producer to him at one point as he paced and asked as a personal favor that he not be on camera if he happened to be mopping sweat from his face. (That night, contrary to most reports, Nixon was wearing no theatrical make-up. In order to tone down his dark beard stubble on the screen, an adviser had applied only a light coating of "Lazy Shave," a pancake make-up with which a man who has heavy afternoon beard growth may powder his face to conceal the growth.)

Senator Kennedy arrived about fifteen minutes after the Vice-President; he inspected the set; sat for the camera; and his advisers inspected him, then declared they were satisfied. The producer made a remark about the glare of the Senator's white shirt, and Kennedy sent an aide back to his hotel to bring back a blue one, into which he changed just before air time. The men took their seats, the tally lights on the cameras blinked red to show they were live now.

"Good evening," said Howard K. Smith, the gray and handsome moderator. "The television and radio stations of the United States . . . are proud to provide for a discussion of issues in the current political campaign by the two major candidates for the Presidency. The candidates need no introduction. . . ."

And they were on air, before seventy million Americans.

Questions

1. By 1960, how important had television become in national politics?
2. What problems did Nixon experience going into the debate that might have affected viewers' perception of his performance?
3. Are televised debates a fair and accurate measure of a candidate's abilities? Why or why not?

28-11   Inaugural Address (1961)

John F. Kennedy

Standing coatless in the subfreezing cold of Inauguration Day, January 20, 1961, the youthful president delivered an inaugural address that historian Allen J. Matusow terms "the best campaign speech Kennedy ever gave" (see text p. 921). Kennedy subsequently became the first president to have his press conferences televised live.

Source: Public Papers of the Presidents of the United States: John F. Kennedy, 1961 (Washington, D.C.: U.S. Government Printing Office, 1962), 1–3.

We observe today not a victory of party but a celebration of freedom—symbolizing an end as well as a beginning—signifying renewal as well as change. For I have sworn before you and Almighty God the same solemn oath our forebears prescribed nearly a century and three quarters ago.

The world is very different now. For man holds in his mortal hands the power to abolish all forms of human poverty and all forms of human life. And yet the same revolutionary beliefs for which our forebears fought are still at issue around the globe—the belief that the rights of man come not from the generosity of the state but from the hand of God.

We dare not forget today that we are the heirs of that first revolution. Let the word go forth from this time and place, to friend and foe alike, that the torch has been passed to a new generation of Americans—born in this century, tempered by war, disciplined by a hard and bitter peace, proud of our ancient heritage—and unwilling to witness or permit the slow undoing of those human rights to which this nation has always been committed, and to which we are committed today at home and around the world.

Let every nation know, whether it wishes us well or ill, that we shall bear any burden, meet any hardship, support any friend, oppose any foe, to assure the survival and the success of liberty.

This we pledge and more.

To those allies whose cultural and spiritual origins we share, we pledge the loyalty of faithful friends. United,

there is little we cannot do in a host of cooperative ventures. Divided, there is little we can do—for we do not meet a powerful challenge at odds and split asunder.

To those new states whom we welcome to the ranks of the free, we pledge our word that one form of colonial control shall not have passed away merely to be replaced by a far more iron tyranny. We shall not always expect to find them supporting our view. But we shall always hope to find them strongly supporting their own freedom—and to remember that in the past, those who foolishly sought power by riding the back of the tiger ended up inside.

To those peoples in the huts and villages of half the globe struggling to break the bonds of mass misery, we pledge our best efforts to help them help themselves . . . not because the Communists may be doing it, not because we seek their votes, but because it is right. If a free society cannot help the many who are poor, it cannot save the few who are rich. . . .

Finally, to those nations who would make themselves our adversary, we offer not a pledge but a request: that both sides begin anew the quest for peace, before the dark powers of destruction unleashed by science engulf all humanity in planned or accidental self-destruction.

We dare not tempt them with weakness. For only when our arms are sufficient beyond doubt can we be certain beyond doubt that they will never be employed. . . .

In the long history of the world, only a few generations have been granted the role of defending freedom in its hour of maximum danger. I do not shrink from this responsibility—I welcome it.

Questions

1. Kennedy begins his speech with appeals to the "revolutionary beliefs for which our forebears fought." How could those beliefs be used to fight the Cold War in the Third World?
2. What parts of the address are aimed at the communist superpowers, and what is Kennedy's posture toward them?

28-12   Address on the Cuban Missile Crisis (1962)

John F. Kennedy   During 1961 and 1962, the fledgling Kennedy administration confronted serious Cold War crises in various locales, the most immediately threatening of which reached its climax in the Cuban missile crisis of October 1962 (see text pp. 923–926, 943–944).

On October 22, President Kennedy provided the nation with the government's reading of the situation and laid out its *"initial"* response: "a strict quarantine on all offensive military equipment under shipment to Cuba"; "continued and increased surveillance of Cuba," with instructions to the Armed Forces "to prepare for any eventualities"; and the warning that "any nuclear missile launched from Cuba," whatever its hemispheric target, would be regarded "as an attack by the Soviet Union on the United States, requiring a full retaliatory response upon the Soviet Union."

Source: Public Papers of the Presidents of the United States: John F. Kennedy, 1962 (Washington, D.C.: U.S. Government Printing Office, 1963), 806–809.

This government, as promised, has maintained the closest surveillance of the Soviet military build-up on the island of Cuba. Within the past week, unmistakable evidence has established the fact that a series of offensive missile sites is now in preparation on that imprisoned island. The purpose of these bases can be none other than to provide a nuclear strike capability against the Western Hemisphere. . . .

For many years, both the Soviet Union and the United States . . . have deployed strategic nuclear weapons with great care, never upsetting the precarious status quo which insured that these weapons would not be used in the absence of some vital challenge. Our own strategic missiles have never been transferred to the territory of any other nation under a cloak of secrecy and deception; and our history—unlike that of the Soviets since the end of World War II—demonstrates that we have no desire to dominate or conquer any other nation or impose our system upon its people. Nevertheless, American citizens have become adjusted to living daily on the bull's-eye of Soviet missiles located inside the U.S.S.R. or in submarines.

In that sense, missiles in Cuba add to an already clear and present danger. . . .

But this secret, swift, and extraordinary buildup of Communist missiles—in an area well known to have a special and historical relationship to the United States and the nations of the Western Hemisphere, in violation of Soviet assurances, and in defiance of American and hemispheric policy—this sudden, clandestine decision to station strategic weapons for the first time outside of Soviet soil—is a deliberately provocative and unjustified change in the status quo which cannot be accepted by this country, if our courage and our commitments are ever to be trusted again by either friend or foe. . . .

Our policy has been one of patience and restraint, as befits a peaceful and powerful nation, which leads a worldwide alliance. . . . We will not prematurely or unnecessarily risk the costs of worldwide nuclear war in which even the fruits of victory would be ashes in our mouth—but neither will we shrink from that risk at any time it must be faced. . . .

The path we have chosen for the present is full of hazards, as all paths are—but it is the one most consistent with our character and our courage as a nation and our commitments around the world. The cost of freedom is always high—but Americans have always paid it. And one path we shall never choose, and that is the path of surrender or submission.

Questions

1. What purpose, according to Kennedy, would be served by Soviet missiles in Cuba?
2. What, in Kennedy's view, made the Soviets' placing of nuclear missiles in Cuba unacceptable to the American government?

28-13   Address at Yale University (1962)

John F. Kennedy   The early on-the-job education of President Kennedy involved his coping with domestic, as well as foreign policy, issues. Through 1962, at least, he spoke out more forcefully regarding economics than civil rights (see text pp. 926–930, also pp. 984, 1009, Figures 30-2 and 31-1). On June 11, 1962, Kennedy delivered the commencement address at Yale University, which awarded him an honorary Doctor of Laws degree. The address revealed both his wit and his growing sophistication regarding government, business, and the economy of the early 1960s. Among those to whom he referred were Roger Blough, president of the United States Steel Corporation, with whom he had recently clashed over steel price increases, and publishers John Hay Whitney *(New York Herald-Tribune)* and Henry Luce *(Life, Time, Fortune).* William F. Buckley is a widely known conservative intellectual.

Source: Public Papers of the Presidents of the United States: John F. Kennedy, 1962 (Washington, D.C.: U.S. Government Printing Office, 1963), 470–475.

Let me begin by expressing my appreciation for the very deep honor that you have conferred upon me. As General de Gaulle occasionally acknowledges America to be the daughter of Europe, so I am pleased to come to Yale, the daughter of Harvard. It might be said now that I have the best of both worlds, a Harvard education and a Yale degree.

I am particularly glad to become a Yale man because as I think about my troubles, I find that a lot of them have come from other Yale men. Among businessmen, I have had a minor disagreement with Roger Blough, of the law school class of 1931, and I have had some complaints, too, from my friend Henry Ford, of the class of 1940. In journalism I seem to have a difference with John Hay Whitney, of the class of 1926—and sometimes I also displease Henry Luce of the class of 1920, not to mention also William F. Buckley, Jr., of the class of 1950. I even have some trouble with my Yale advisers. I get along with them, but I am not always sure how they get along with each other. . . .

. . . As every past generation has had to disenthrall itself from an inheritance of truisms and stereotypes, so in our own time we must move on from the reassuring repetition of stale phrases to a new, difficult, but essential confrontation with reality. . . .

Mythology distracts us everywhere—in government as in business, in politics as in economics, in foreign affairs as in domestic affairs. But today I want to particularly consider the myth and reality in our national economy. In recent months many have come to feel, as I do, that the dialog between the parties—between business and government, between the government and the public—is clogged by illusion and platitude and fails to reflect the true realities of contemporary American society. . . .

There are three great areas of our domestic affairs in which, today, there is a danger that illusion may prevent effective action. They are, first, the question of the size and the shape of government's responsibilities; second, the question of public fiscal policy; and third, the matter of confidence, business confidence or public confidence, or simply confidence in America. I want to talk about all three, and I want to talk about them carefully and dispassionately—and I emphasize that I am concerned here not with political debate but with finding ways to separate false problems from real ones. . . .

Let us take first the question of the size and shape of government. The myth here is that government is big, and bad—and steadily getting bigger and worse. Obviously this myth has some excuse for existence. It is true that in recent history each new administration has spent much more money than its predecessor. Thus President Roosevelt outspent President Hoover, and with allowances for the special case of the Second World War, President Truman outspent President Roosevelt. Just to prove that this was not a partisan matter, President Eisenhower then outspent President Truman by the handsome figure of $182 billion. It is even possible, some think, that this trend may continue.

But does it follow from this that big government is growing relatively bigger? It does not—for the fact is for the last 15 years, the Federal Government—and also the Federal debt—and also the Federal bureaucracy—have grown less rapidly than the economy as a whole. If we leave defense and space expenditures aside, the Federal Government since the Second World War has expanded less than any other major sector of our national life—less than industry, less than commerce, less than agriculture, less than higher education, and very much less than the noise about big government.

The truth about big government is the truth about any other great activity—it is complex. Certainly it is true that size brings dangers—but it is also true that size can bring benefits. Here at Yale which has contributed so much to our national progress in science and medicine, it may be proper for me to mention one great and little noticed expansion of government which has brought strength to our whole society—the new role of our Federal Government as the major patron of research in science and in medicine. Few people realize that in 1961, in support of all university research in science and medicine, three dollars out of every four came from the Federal Government. I need hardly point out that this has taken place without undue enlargement of Government control—that American scientists remain second to none in their independence and in their individualism.

I am not suggesting that Federal expenditures cannot bring some measure of control. The whole thrust of Federal expenditures in agriculture have been related by purpose and design to control, as a means of dealing with the problems created by our farmers and our growing productivity. Each sector, my point is, of activity must be approached on its own merits and in terms of specific national needs. Generalities in regard to Federal expenditures, therefore, can be misleading—each case, science, urban renewal, education, agriculture, natural resources, each case must be determined on its merits if we are to profit from our unrivaled ability to combine the strength of public and private purpose.

Next, let us turn to the problem of our fiscal policy. Here the myths are legion and the truth hard to find. But let me take as a prime example the problem of the Federal budget. We persist in measuring our Federal fiscal integrity today by the conventional or administrative budget—with results which would be regarded as absurd in any business firm—in any country of Europe—or in any careful assessment of the reality of our national finances. The administrative budget has sound administrative uses. But for wider purposes it is less helpful. It omits our special trust funds and the effect that they have on our economy; it neglects changes in assets or inventories. It cannot tell a loan from a straight expenditure—and worst of all it cannot distinguish between operating expenditures and long term investments.

This budget, in relation to the great problems of Federal fiscal policy which are basic to our economy in 1962, is not simply irrelevant; it can be actively misleading. And yet there is a mythology that measures all of our national soundness or unsoundness on the single simple basis of this same annual administrative budget. If our Federal budget is to serve not the debate but the country, we must and will find ways of clarifying this area of discourse.

Still in the area of fiscal policy, let me say a word about deficits. The myth persists that Federal deficits create inflation and budget surpluses prevent it. Yet sizeable budget surpluses after the war did not prevent inflation, and persistent deficits for the last several years have not upset our basic price stability. Obviously deficits are sometimes dangerous—and so are surpluses. But honest assessment plainly requires a more sophisticated view than the old and automatic cliché that deficits automatically bring inflation.

There are myths also about our public debt. It is widely supposed that this debt is growing at a dangerously rapid rate. In fact, both the debt per person and the debt as a proportion of our gross national product have declined sharply since the Second World War. In absolute terms the national debt since the end of World War II has increased only 8 percent, while private debt was increasing 305 percent, and the debts of State and local governments—on whom people frequently suggest we should place additional burdens—the debts of State and local governments have increased 378 percent. Moreover, debts, public and private, are neither good nor bad, in and of themselves. Borrowing can lead to over-extension and collapse—but it can also lead to expansion and strength. There is no single, simple slogan in this field that we can trust.

Finally, I come to the problem of confidence. Confidence is a matter of myth and also a matter of truth—and this time let me take the truth of the matter first. . . .

Corporate plans are not based on a political confidence in party leaders but on an economic confidence in the Nation's ability to invest and produce and consume. Business had full confidence in the administrations in power in 1929, 1954, 1958, and 1960—but this was not enough to prevent recession when business lacked full confidence in the economy. What matters is the capacity of the Nation as a whole to deal with its economic problems and its opportunities. . . .

What is at stake in our economic decisions today is not some grand warfare of rival ideologies which will sweep the country with passion but the practical management of a modern economy. What we need is not labels and clichés but more basic discussion of the sophisticated and technical questions involved in keeping a great economic machinery moving ahead.

The national interest lies in high employment and steady expansion of output, in stable prices, and a strong dollar. The declaration of such an objective is easy; their attainment in an intricate and interdependent economy and world is a little more difficult. To attain them, we require not some automatic response but hard thought. Let me end by suggesting a few of the real questions on our national agenda.

First, how can our budget and tax policies supply adequate revenues and preserve our balance of payments position without slowing up our economic growth?

Two, how are we to set our interest rates and regulate the flow of money in ways which will stimulate the economy at home, without weakening the dollar abroad? Given the spectrum of our domestic and international responsibilities, what should be the mix between fiscal and monetary policy? . . .

I am suggesting that the problems of fiscal and monetary policies in the sixties as opposed to the kinds of problems we faced in the thirties demand subtle challenges for which technical answers, not political answers, must be provided. These are matters upon which government and business may and in many cases will disagree. They are certainly matters that government and business should be discussing in the most sober, dispassionate, and careful way if we are to maintain the kind of vigorous economy upon which our country depends.

How can we develop and sustain strong and stable world markets for basic commodities without unfairness to the consumer and without undue stimulus to the producer? How can we generate the buying power which can consume what we produce on our farms and in our factories? How can we take advantage of the miracles of automation with the great demand that it will put upon highly skilled labor and yet offer employment to the half million of unskilled school dropouts each year who enter the labor market, eight million of them in the 1960's?

How do we eradicate the barriers which separate substantial minorities of our citizens from access to education and employment on equal terms with the rest?

How, in sum, can we make our free economy work at full capacity—that is, provide adequate profits for enterprise, adequate wages for labor, adequate utilization of plant, and opportunity for all?

These are the problems that we should be talking about—that the political parties and the various groups in our country should be discussing. They cannot be solved by incantations from the forgotten past. But the example of Western Europe shows that they are capable of solution—that governments, and many of them are conservative governments, prepared to face technical problems without ideological preconceptions, can coordinate the elements of a national economy and bring about growth and prosperity—a decade of it.

Some conversations I have heard in our own country sound like old records, long-playing, left over from the middle thirties. The debate of the thirties had its great significance and produced great results, but it took place in a different world with different needs and different tasks. It is our responsibility today to live in our own world, and to identify the needs and discharge the tasks of the 1960's. . . .

Questions

1. What were the three "illusion[s]" or "myths" that Kennedy discusses? (See text pp. 926, 984, 1009.)
2. How does Kennedy distinguish between the discussion of public issues during the 1930s and the 1960s? Why do you think he stresses the distinction?
3. What do you think of Kennedy's argument that questions relating to 1960s economic policy require "technical answers, not political answers."

Questions for Further Thought

1. Compare and contrast the inaugural addresses of Presidents Franklin Roosevelt (Document 25-1) and John F. Kennedy (Document 28-11). Does either speech offer insight into the presidency that followed?
2. Why does historian Allen Matusow term Kennedy's inaugural address a "campaign speech"? Might one say the same of Roosevelt's?
3. Compare and contrast the farewell address of President Dwight D. Eisenhower (Document 27-12) and the inaugural address of President Kennedy—speeches delivered only days apart.

Lyndon B. Johnson and the Great Society

Lyndon Johnson succeeded to the presidency upon the assassination of John Kennedy in November 1963. Before becoming vice-president, he had served nearly a quarter of a century in the U.S. House of Representatives and the Senate. Even before scoring a landslide victory in the election of 1964, President Johnson had won passage of civil rights, social welfare, and other legislation (see text p. 932, Table 28-1). After that victory, Johnson, now leading enlarged Democratic congressional majorities, achieved other legislative successes to create the Great Society (see text pp. 926–935).

Still, the showings of segregationist governor George Wallace of Alabama in the 1964 Democratic presidential primaries in Wisconsin, Indiana, and Maryland and those of the conservative Republican senator Barry Goldwater of Arizona in five Deep South states in that year's presidential election demonstrated the explosiveness of the race issue as the civil rights movement reached high tide (see text pp. 927–936).

Document 28-14 excerpts Dr. Martin Luther King Jr.'s "Letter from Birmingham City Jail." Document 28-15 is the acceptance speech of Barry Goldwater at the Republican National Convention in 1964. Document 28-16 includes portions of a 1965 address by President Johnson.

28-14   Letter from Birmingham Jail (1963)

Martin Luther King Jr.

The struggle for civil rights intensified across the South during the early 1960s, marked by grassroots nonviolent efforts by civil rights supporters and increasingly harsh and violent responses by white segregationists (see text pp. 927–930, including "American Voices: Anne Moody;" also "An Appeal for Human Rights" in *Instructor's Resource Manual,* vol. 2, *Since 1865,* 4th ed., Document 14, pp. 259–261). Dr. Martin Luther King Jr. (1929–1968), arrested and jailed in Birmingham, Alabama, on Good Friday, April 12, 1963, for heading a protest in violation of a judge's injunction, explained his actions and his thoughts about nonviolent resistance in a letter addressed to other clergymen.

Source: Excerpted from Martin Luther King Jr., "Letter from Birmingham City Jail," April 16, 1963. In *A Testament of Hope: The Essential Writings of Martin Luther King, Jr.,* ed. James Melvin Washington (New York: HarperCollins, 1991), 289–302. Reprinted by arrangement with The Heirs to the Estate of Martin Luther King Jr., c/o Joan Daves Agency, as agent for the proprietor. Copyright 1963 by Martin Luther King Jr.; copyright renewed 1991 by Coretta Scott King.

My dear Fellow Clergymen,

While confined here in the Birmingham city jail, I came across your recent statement calling our present activities "unwise and untimely." Seldom, if ever, do I pause to answer criticism of my work and ideas. If I sought to answer all of the criticisms that cross my desk, my secretaries would be engaged in little else in the course of the day, and I would have no time for constructive work. But since I feel that you are men of genuine good will and your criticisms are sincerely set forth, I would like to answer your statement in what I hope will be patient and reasonable terms.

I think I should give the reason for my being in Birmingham, since you have been influenced by the argument of "outsiders coming in." I have the honor of serving as president of the Southern Christian Leadership Conference, an organization operating in every southern state, with headquarters in Atlanta, Georgia. We have some eighty-five affiliate organizations all across the South—one being the Alabama Christian Movement for Human Rights. Whenever

necessary and possible we share staff, educational and financial resources with our affiliates. Several months ago our local affiliate here in Birmingham invited us to be on call to engage in a nonviolent direct-action program if such were deemed necessary. We readily consented and when the hour came we lived up to our promises. So I am here, along with several members of my staff, because we were invited here. I am here because I have basic organizational ties here. . . .

In any nonviolent campaign there are four basic steps: (1) collection of the facts to determine whether injustices are alive, (2) negotiation, (3) self-purification, and (4) direct action. We have gone through all of these steps in Birmingham. There can be no gainsaying of the fact that racial injustice engulfs this community.

Birmingham is probably the most thoroughly segregated city in the United States. Its ugly record of police brutality is known in every section of this country. Its injust treatment of Negroes in the courts is a notorious reality. There have been more unsolved bombings of Negro homes and churches in Birmingham than any city in this nation. These are the hard, brutal and unbelievable facts. On the basis of these conditions Negro leaders sought to negotiate with the city fathers. But the political leaders consistently refused to engage in good faith negotiation.

Then came the opportunity last September to talk with some of the leaders of the economic community. In these negotiating sessions certain promises were made by the merchants—such as the promise to remove the humiliating racial signs from the stores. On the basis of these promises Rev. Shuttlesworth and the leaders of the Alabama Christian Movement for Human Rights agreed to call a moratorium on any type of demonstrations. As the weeks and months unfolded we realized that we were the victims of a broken promise. The signs remained. Like so many experiences of the past we were confronted with blasted hopes, and the dark shadow of a deep disappointment settled upon us. So we had no alternative except that of preparing for direct action, whereby we would present our very bodies as a means of laying our case before the conscience of the local and national community. We were not unmindful of the difficulties involved. So we decided to go through a process of self-purification. We started having workshops on nonviolence and repeatedly asked ourselves the questions, "Are you able to accept blows without retaliating?" "Are you able to endure the ordeals of jail?" We decided to set our direct-action program around the Easter season, realizing that with the exception of Christmas, this was the largest shopping period of the year. . . .

You may well ask, "Why direct action? Why sit-ins, marches, etc.? Isn't negotiation a better path?" You are exactly right in your call for negotiation. Indeed, this is the purpose of direct action. Nonviolent direct action seeks to create such a crisis and establish such creative tension that a community that has constantly refused to negotiate is forced to confront the issue. It seeks so to dramatize the issue that it can no longer be ignored. . . . So the purpose of the direct action is to create a situation so crisis-packed that it will inevitably open the door to negotiation. We, therefore, concur with you in your call for negotiation. Too long has our beloved Southland been bogged down in the tragic attempt to live in monologue rather than dialogue.

My friends, I must say to you that we have not made a single gain in civil rights without determined legal and nonviolent pressure. History is the long and tragic story of the fact that privileged groups seldom give up their privileges voluntarily. Individuals may see the moral light and voluntarily give up their unjust posture; but as Reinhold Niebuhr[1] has reminded us, groups are more immoral than individuals.

We know through painful experience that freedom is never voluntarily given by the oppressor; it must be demanded by the oppressed. Frankly, I have never yet engaged in a direct action movement that was "well-timed," according to the timetable of those who have not suffered unduly from the disease of segregation. For years now I have heard the words "Wait!" It rings in the ear of every Negro with a piercing familiarity. This "Wait" has almost always meant "Never." . . . We must come to see with the distinguished jurist of yesterday that "justice too long delayed is justice denied." We have waited for more than 340 years for our constitutional and God-given rights. The nations of Asia and Africa are moving with jetlike speed toward the goal of political independence, and we still creep at horse and buggy pace toward the gaining of a cup of coffee at a lunch counter. I guess it is easy for those who have never felt the stinging darts of segregation to say, "Wait." But when you have seen vicious mobs lynch your mothers and fathers at will and drown your sisters and brothers at whim; when you have seen hate-filled policemen curse, kick, brutalize and even kill your black brothers and sisters with impunity; when you see the vast majority of your twenty million Negro brothers smothering in an airtight cage of poverty in the midst of an affluent society; when you suddenly find your tongue twisted and your speech stammering as you seek to explain to your six-year-old daughter why she can't go to the public amusement park that has just been advertised on television, and see tears welling up in her little eyes when she is told that Funtown is closed to colored children, and see the depressing clouds of inferiority begin to form in her little mental sky, and see her begin to distort her little personality by unconsciously developing a bitterness toward white people; when you have to concoct an answer for a five-year-old son asking in agonizing pathos: "Daddy, why do white people treat colored people so mean?"; when you take a cross-country drive and find it necessary to sleep night after night in the uncomfortable corners of your automobile because no motel will accept you; when you are humiliated day in and day out by nagging signs reading "white" and "colored"; when your first name becomes "nigger" and your middle name becomes "boy" (however old you are) and your last name becomes "John," and when your wife and mother are never given the respected title "Mrs."; when you are harried by day and haunted by night by the fact that you are a Negro, living constantly at tiptoe stance never quite knowing what to expect next, and plagued with inner fears and outer resentments; when you are forever fighting a degenerating sense of "nobodiness"; then you will understand why we find it difficult to wait. There comes a time when the cup of endurance runs over, and men are no longer willing to be plunged into an abyss of injustice where they experience the blackness of corroding despair. I hope, sirs, you can understand our legitimate and unavoidable impatience. . . .

We must come to see that human progress never rolls in on wheels of inevitability. It comes through the tireless efforts and persistent work of men willing to be co-workers with God, and without this hard work time itself becomes an ally of the forces of social stagnation. We must

---

[1]*Reinhold Niebuhr* (1892–1971) was a prominent American theologian who, for many years, was a professor at Union Theological Seminary in New Your City.

use time creatively, and forever realize that the time is always ripe to do right. Now is the time to make real the promise of democracy, and transform our pending national elegy into a creative psalm of brotherhood. Now is the time to lift our national policy from the quicksand of racial injustice to the solid rock of human dignity.

You spoke of our activity in Birmingham as extreme. At first I was rather disappointed that fellow clergymen would see my nonviolent efforts as those of the extremist. I started thinking about the fact that I stand in the middle of two opposing forces in the Negro community. One is a force of complacency made up of Negroes who, as a result of long years of oppression, have been so completely drained of self-respect and a sense of "somebodiness" that they have adjusted to segregation, and, of a few Negroes in the middle class who, because of a degree of academic and economic security, and because at points they profit by segregation, have unconsciously become insensitive to the problems of the masses. The other force is one of bitterness and hatred, and comes perilously close to advocating violence. It is expressed in the various black nationalist groups that are springing up over the nation, the largest and best known being Elijah Muhammad's Muslim movement. This movement is nourished by the contemporary frustration over the continued existence of racial discrimination. It is made up of people who have lost faith in America, who have absolutely repudiated Christianity, and who have concluded that the white man is an incurable "devil." I have tried to stand between these two forces, saying that we need not follow the "do-nothingism" of the complacent or the hatred and despair of the black nationalist. There is the more excellent way of love and nonviolent protest. I'm grateful to God that, through the Negro church, the dimension of nonviolence entered our struggle. If this philosophy had not emerged, I am convinced that by now many streets of the South would be flowing with floods of blood. And I am further convinced that if our white brothers dismiss us as "rabble-rousers" and "outside agitators" those of us who are working through the channels of nonviolent direct action and refuse to support our nonviolent efforts, millions of Negroes, out of frustration and despair, will seek solace and security in black nationalist ideologies, a development that will lead inevitably to a frightening racial nightmare.

Oppressed people cannot remain oppressed forever. The urge for freedom will eventually come. This is what happened to the American Negro. Something within has reminded him of his birthright of freedom; something without has reminded him that he can gain it. . . .

In spite of my shattered dreams of the past, I came to Birmingham with the hope that the white religious leadership of this community would see the justice of our cause, and with deep moral concern, serve as the channel through which our just grievances would get to the power structure. I had hoped that each of you would understand. But again I have been disappointed. I have heard numerous religious leaders of the South call upon their worshippers to comply with a desegregation decision because it is the *law,* but I have longed to hear white ministers say, "Follow this decree because integration is morally *right* and the Negro is your brother." In the midst of blatant injustice inflicted upon the Negro, I have watched white churches stand on the sideline and merely mouth pious irrelevancies and sanctimonious trivialities. In the midst of a mighty struggle to rid our nation of racial and economic injustice, I have heard so many ministers say, "Those are social issues with which the gospel has no real concern," and I have watched so many churches commit themselves to a completely otherworldly religion which made a strange distinction between body and soul, the sacred and the secular. . . .

I'm sorry that I can't join you in your praise for the police department.

It is true that they have been rather disciplined in their public handling of the demonstrators. In this sense they have been rather publicly "nonviolent." But for what purpose? To preserve the evil system of segregation. Over the last few years I have consistently preached that nonviolence demands that the means we use must be as pure as the ends we seek. So I have tried to make it clear that it is wrong to use immoral means to attain moral ends. But now I must affirm that it is just as wrong, or even more so, to use moral means to preserve immoral ends. Maybe Mr. Connor and his policemen have been rather publicly nonviolent, as Chief Pritchett was in Albany, Georgia, but they have used the moral means of nonviolence to maintain the immoral end of flagrant racial injustice. T.S. Eliot has said that there is no greater treason than to do the right deed for the wrong reason.

I wish you had commended the Negro sit-inners and demonstrators of Birmingham for their sublime courage, their willingness to suffer and their amazing discipline in the midst of the most inhuman provocation. . . .

One day the South will know that when these disinherited children of God sat down at lunch counters they were in reality standing up for the best in the American dream and the most sacred values in our Judeo-Christian heritage, and thusly, carrying our whole nation back to those great wells of democracy which were dug deep by the Founding Fathers in the formulation of the Constitution and the Declaration of Independence. . . .

I hope this letter finds you strong in the faith. I also hope that circumstances will soon make it possible for me to meet each of you, not as an integrationist or a civil rights leader, but as a fellow clergyman and a Christian brother. Let us all hope that the dark clouds of racial prejudice will soon pass away and the deep fog of misunderstanding will be lifted from our fear-drenched communities and in some not too distant tomorrow the radiant stars of love and brotherhood will shine over our great nation with all of their scintillating beauty.

Yours for the cause of Peace and Brotherhood,
Martin Luther King, Jr.

Questions

1. What does this letter indicate about the major tenets of King's philosophy of non-violence?
2. What is King's attitude toward moderate members of the white clergy? How does he hope to alter the position of his white colleagues?
3. Do you find the overall tone of the letter to be optimistic or pessimistic? What evidence can you cite to support your conclusion? What does this tell you about the civil rights movement in 1963?

28-15   Acceptance Speech at the Republican National Convention (1964)

Barry Goldwater

A variety of circumstances contributed to the easy victory of Senator Barry Goldwater (1909–1998) of Arizona at the divisive Republican National Convention of 1964. The party's platform promised "full implementation and faithful execution" of the 1964 civil rights law. In an effort to further strengthen the civil rights plank, northeastern convention delegates proposed the inclusion of an expression of pride in Republican support for the recent enactment of the law. The delegates failed, 409-897. Goldwater had been among only five (of thirty-three) Republican senators to oppose the original 1964 civil rights law. He delivered his acceptance speech as the Republican nominee on July 16.

Source: Excerpted with the express permission of the Republican National Committee from "Acceptance Speech by Senator Barry Goldwater, Republican National Convention, San Francisco, California," in Barry Goldwater, *Where I Stand* (New York: McGraw-Hill, 1964), 9–16.

From this moment, united and determined, we will go forward together—dedicated to the ultimate and undeniable greatness of the whole man.

I accept your nomination with a deep sense of humility. I accept the responsibility that goes with it. I seek your continued help and guidance.

Our cause is too great for any man to feel worthy of it.

Our task would be too great for any man, did he not have with him the hearts and hands of this great Republican Party.

I promise you that every fibre of my being is consecrated to our cause, that nothing shall be lacking from the struggle that can be brought to it by enthusiasm and devotion—and hard work!

In this world, no person—no party—can guarantee anything. What we *can* do, and what we *shall* do, is to *deserve* victory.

The good Lord raised up this mighty Republic to be a home for the brave and to flourish as the land of the free—*not* to stagnate in the swampland of collectivism—*not* to cringe before the bullying of Communism.

The tide has been running against freedom. Our people have followed false prophets. We must and we *shall* return to proven ways—*not* because they are old, but because they are *true*. We must and we shall set the tides running again in the cause of freedom.

This Party, with its every action, every word, every breath, and every heartbeat, has but a single resolve:

Freedom!

Freedom—made orderly for this nation by our Constitutional government.

Freedom—under a government limited by the laws of nature and of nature's God.

Freedom—balanced so that order, lacking liberty, will not become the slavery of the prison cell; balanced so that liberty, lacking order, will not become the license of the mob and the jungle.

We Americans understand freedom. We have earned it, lived for it, and died for it.

This nation and its people *are* freedom's model in a searching world. We *can be* freedom's missionaries in a doubting world. But first we *must renew* freedom's vision in our own hearts and in our own homes.

During four futile years, the Administration which we shall replace has distorted and lost that vision.

It has talked and talked and talked the *words* of freedom. But it has failed and failed and failed in the *works* of freedom.

Failures cement the wall of shame in Berlin. Failures blot the sands of shame at the Bay of Pigs. Failures mark the slow death of freedom in Laos. Failures infest the jungles of Vietnam. Failures haunt the houses of our once great alliances, and undermine the greatest bulwark ever erected by free nations—the NATO community.

Failures proclaim lost leadership, obscure purpose, weakening will, and the risk of inciting our sworn enemies to new aggressions and new excesses.

Because of this Administration, we are a world divided—we are a nation becalmed.

We have lost the brisk pace of diversity and the genius of individual creativity. We are plodding at a pace set by centralized planning, red tape, rules without responsibility, and regimentation without recourse.

Rather than useful jobs, our people have been offered bureaucratic make-work. Rather than moral leadership, they have been given bread and circuses, spectacle and even scandal.

There is violence in our streets, corruption in our highest offices, aimlessness among our youth, anxiety among our elders. There is virtual despair among the many who look beyond material success for the inner meaning of their lives.

Where examples of morality should be set, the opposite is seen. Small men, seeking great wealth or power, have too often and too long turned even the highest levels of public service into mere personal opportunity.

Certainly, simple honesty is not too much to demand of men in government. We find it in most. Republicans demand it from everyone—no matter how exalted or protected his position.

The growing menace to personal safety, to life, limb, and property, in homes, churches, playgrounds, and places of business, particularly in our great cities, is the mounting concern of every thoughtful citizen. Security from domestic violence, no less than from foreign aggression, is the most elementary and fundamental purpose of any government. A government that cannot fulfill this purpose is one that cannot long command the loyalty of its citizens. History demonstrates that nothing prepares the way for tyranny more than the failure of public officials to keep the streets safe from bullies and marauders.

We Republicans see all this as more, *much* more than the result of mere political differences, or mere political mistakes. We see this as the result of a fundamentally and absolutely wrong view of man, his nature, and his destiny.

Those who seek to live your lives for you, to take your liberties in return for relieving you of your responsibilities—those who elevate the state and downgrade the citizen—must see ultimately a world in which earthly power can be substituted for divine will. This nation was founded upon the rejection of that notion and upon the acceptance of God as the author of freedom.

Those who seek absolute power, even though they seek it to do what they regard as good, are simply demanding the right to enforce *their* version of heaven on earth. They are the very ones who always create the most hellish tyrannies.

Absolute power *does* corrupt. And those who seek it must be suspect and must be opposed.

Their mistaken course stems from false notions of equality.

Equality, rightly understood, as our Founding Fathers understood it, leads to liberty and to the emancipation of creative differences.

Wrongly understood, as it has been so tragically in our time, it leads first to conformity and then to despotism.

It is the cause of Republicanism to resist concentrations of power, *private* or *public,* which enforce such conformity and inflict such despotism.

It is the cause of Republicanism to ensure that power remains in the hands of the people. And, so help us God, that is exactly what a Republican President will do—with the help of a Republican Congress.

It is the cause of Republicanism to restore a clear understanding of the tyranny of man over man in the world at large. It is our cause to dispel the foggy thinking which avoids hard decisions in the delusion that a world of conflict will mysteriously resolve itself into a world of harmony—if we just don't rock the boat or irritate the forces of aggression.

It is the cause of Republicanism to remind ourselves and the world that only the strong *can* remain free—that only the strong *can* keep the peace!

Republicans have shouldered this hard responsibility and marched in this cause before. It was Republican leadership under Dwight David Eisenhower that kept the peace and passed along to this Administration the mightiest arsenal for defense the world has ever known.

It was the strength and believable will of the Eisenhower years that kept the peace by using our strength—by using it in the Formosa Straits and in Lebanon, and by showing it *courageously* at all times.

It was during those Republican years that the thrust of Communist imperialism was blunted. It was during those years of Republican leadership that this world moved closer to *peace* than at any other time in the last three decades.

It has been during *Democratic* years that our strength to deter war has stood still and even gone into a planned decline.

It has been during *Democratic* years that we have weakly stumbled into conflict—*timidly* refusing to draw our own lines against aggression—*deceitfully* refusing to tell even our own people of our full participation—and *tragically* letting our finest men die on battlefields unmarked by purpose, pride, or the prospect of victory.

Yesterday it was Korea. Today it is Vietnam.

We are at war in Vietnam—yet the President who is the Commander in Chief of our forces refuses to say whether or not the objective is victory. His Secretary of Defense continues to mislead and misinform the American people.

It has been during *Democratic* years that a billion persons were cast into Communist captivity and their fate cynically sealed. Today, we have an Administration which seems eager to deal with Communism in every coin known—from gold to wheat, from consulates to confidences, and even human freedom itself.

The Republican cause demands that we brand Communism as the principal disturber of peace in the world today—indeed, the only significant disturber of the peace. We must make clear that until its goals of conquest are absolutely renounced, and its relations with all nations tempered, Communism and the governments it now controls are enemies of every man on earth who is or wants to be free. . . .

I can see, and I suggest that all thoughtful men must contemplate, the flowering of an Atlantic civilization: the *whole* of Europe reunified and freed, trading openly across its borders, communicating openly across the world.

This is a goal more meaningful than a moon shot—a truly inspiring goal for all free men to set for themselves during the latter half of the twentieth century.

I can see, and all free men must thrill to, the advance of this Atlantic civilization joined by its great ocean highway to the United States. What a destiny can be ours—to stand as a great central pillar linking Europe, the Americas, and the venerable and vital peoples and cultures of the Pacific.

I can see a day when all the Americas, North and South, will be linked in a mighty system, a system in which the errors and misunderstandings of the past will be submerged, one by one, in a rising tide of prosperity and interdependence. We know that the misunderstandings of centuries are not to be wiped away in a day or an hour. But we pledge that human sympathy—what our neighbors to the South call an attitude that is *simpatico*—no less than enlightened self-interest, will be our guide.

I can see this Atlantic civilization galvanizing and *guiding* emergent nations everywhere. . . .

During Republican years this again will be a nation of men and women, of families proud of their roles, jealous of their responsibilities, unlimited in their aspirations—a nation where all who *can, will* be self-reliant. . . .

We see, in private property and an economy based upon and fostering private property, the one way to make government a durable ally of the whole man, rather than his determined enemy. We see, in the sanctity of private property, the only durable foundation for Constitutional government in a free society.

And beyond that, we see and cherish diversity of ways, diversity of thoughts, of motives and accomplishments. We do not seek to live anyone's life for him—we seek only to secure his rights, guarantee him opportunity to strive, with government performing only those needed and Constitutionally-sanctioned tasks which cannot otherwise be performed.

We seek a government that attends to its inherent responsibilities of maintaining a stable monetary and fiscal climate—encouraging a free and competitive economy, and enforcing law and order.

Thus do we seek inventiveness, diversity, and creative difference within a stable order. For we Republicans define government's role, where needed, at *many* levels, preferably the one *closest* to the people involved.

Our towns and our cities, then our counties and states, then our regional compacts—and *only then* the national government! *That* is the ladder of liberty built by decentralized power. On it, also, we must have balance *between* branches of government at *every* level.

Balance, diversity, creative difference—*these* are the elements of the Republican equation. Republicans agree on these elements and they heartily agree to disagree on many, many of their applications.

This is a party for free men—*not* for blind followers and *not* for conformists. . . .

Any who join us in all sincerity, we welcome. Those who do not care for our cause we do not expect to enter our ranks in any case.

And let our Republicanism, so focused and so dedicated, not be made fuzzy and futile by unthinking labels.

Extremism in the defense of liberty is no vice. Moderation in the pursuit of justice is no virtue. . . .

Questions

1. What is Goldwater's definition of freedom?
2. Is his speech partisan or accurate in its treatment of the Democrats? Explain.
3. What are the enemies of freedom at home and abroad, according to Goldwater? Can they be fought with the same weapons?

28-16   Address at Howard University (1965)

Lyndon Johnson

Within three months during 1965, President Lyndon Johnson delivered three highly important speeches. The first, a nationally televised special message to Congress, "The American Promise" (March 15), dealt movingly with the voting rights proposal that Johnson was sending to Congress, this against the backdrop of crisis in Selma, Alabama (see text pp. 933–934).

Although his March address focused on "the right to vote," on "the privileges of citizenship regardless of race," the president also declared that "to exercise these privileges takes much more than just legal right. It requires a trained mind and a healthy body. It requires a decent home, and the chance to find a job, and the opportunity to escape the clutches of poverty."

The second speech, dealing with the war in Vietnam, is excerpted as Document 29-2.

In his commencement address at Howard University, "To Fulfill These Rights," delivered June 4 and excerpted here, Johnson explored issues central to the long-term dilemma of race in America. His case bore the imprint of Assistant Secretary of Labor Daniel Patrick Moynihan, who had prepared a report on "The Negro Family: The Case for National Action." Johnson spoke at a time when African American protest had been rising for a while in the urban North; the summer would bring rioting in Watts (Los Angeles) and ground war in Vietnam (see text pp. 920, 934–936, 944–947, 954–957). Making public the Moynihan Report that summer generated a storm. Such was the changing racial-political climate that the autumn conference, "To Fulfill These Rights," to which Johnson had referred in his speech, was not held until the following June. (Moynihan would later serve in the presidential administration of Richard Nixon and as a Democratic senator from New York.)

Source: Public Papers of the Presidents of the United States: Lyndon B. Johnson, 1965, Book 2 (Washington, D.C.: U.S. Government Printing Office, 1966), 635–639.

. . . Our earth is the home of revolution. In every corner of every continent men charged with hope contend with ancient ways in the pursuit of justice. They reach for the newest of weapons to realize the oldest of dreams, that each may walk in freedom and pride, stretching his talents, enjoying the fruits of the earth.

Our enemies may occasionally seize the day of change, but it is the banner of our revolution they take. And our own future is linked to this process of swift and turbulent change in many lands in the world. But nothing in any country touches us more profoundly, and nothing is more freighted with meaning for our own destiny than the revolution of the Negro American.

In far too many ways American Negroes have been another nation: deprived of freedom, crippled by hatred, the doors of opportunity closed to hope.

In our time change has come to this Nation, too. The American Negro, acting with impressive restraint, has peacefully protested and marched, entered the courtrooms and the seats of government, demanding a justice that has long been denied. The voice of the Negro was the call to action. But it is a tribute to America that, once aroused, the courts and the Congress, the President and most of the people, have been the allies of progress. . . .

The voting rights bill will be the latest, and among the most important, in a long series of victories. But this victory—as Winston Churchill said of another triumph for freedom—"is not the end. It is not even the beginning of the end. But it is, perhaps, the end of the beginning."

That beginning is freedom; and the barriers to that freedom are tumbling down. Freedom is the right to share, share fully and equally, in American society—to vote, to hold a job, to enter a public place, to go to school. It is the right to be treated in every part of our national life as a person equal in dignity and promise to all others. . . .

But freedom is not enough. You do not wipe away the scars of centuries by saying: Now you are free to go where you want, and do as you desire, and choose the leaders you please.

You do not take a person who, for years, has been hobbled by chains and liberate him, bring him up to the starting line of a race and then say, "you are free to compete with all the others," and still justly believe that you have been completely fair.

Thus it is not enough just to open the gates of opportunity. All our citizens must have the ability to walk through those gates.

This is the next and the more profound stage of the battle for civil rights. We seek not just freedom but opportunity. We seek not just legal equity but human ability, not just equality as a right and a theory but equality as a fact and equality as a result.

For the task is to give 20 million Negroes the same chance as every other American to learn and grow, to work and share in society, to develop their abilities—physical, mental and spiritual, and to pursue their individual happiness.

To this end equal opportunity is essential, but not enough, not enough. Men and women of all races are born with the same range of abilities. But ability is not just the product of birth. Ability is stretched or stunted by the family that you live with, and the neighborhood you live in—by the school you go to and the poverty or the richness of your surroundings. It is the product of a hundred unseen forces playing upon the little infant, the child, and finally the man. . . .

This graduating class at Howard University is witness to the indomitable determination of the Negro American to win his way in American life.

The number of Negroes in schools of higher learning has almost doubled in 15 years. The number of nonwhite professional workers has more than doubled in 10 years. The median income of Negro college women tonight exceeds that of white college women. And there are also the enormous accomplishments of distinguished individual Negroes—many of them graduates of this institution, and one of them the first lady ambassador in the history of the United States.

These are proud and impressive achievements. But they tell only the story of a growing middle class minority, steadily narrowing the gap between them and their white counterparts. . . .

But for the great majority of Negro Americans—the poor, the unemployed, the uprooted, and the dispossessed—there is a much grimmer story. They still, as we meet here tonight, are another nation. Despite the court orders and the laws, despite the legislative victories and the speeches, for them the walls are rising and the gulf is widening.

Here are some of the facts of this American failure.

Thirty-five years ago the rate of unemployment for Negroes and whites was about the same. Tonight the Negro rate is twice as high. . . .

Between 1949 and 1959, the income of Negro men relative to white men declined in every section of this country. . . .

In the years 1955 through 1957, 23 percent of experienced Negro workers were out of work at some time dur-

ing the year. In 1961 through 1963 that proportion had soared to 29 percent.

Since 1947 the number of white families living in poverty has decreased 27 percent while the number of poorer nonwhite families decreased only 3 percent.

The infant mortality of nonwhites in 1940 was 70 percent greater than whites. Twenty-two years later it was 90 percent greater.

Moreover, the isolation of Negro from white communities is increasing, rather than decreasing as Negroes crowd into the central cities and become a city within a city.

Of course Negro Americans as well as white Americans have shared in our rising national abundance. But the harsh fact of the matter is that in the battle for true equality too many—far too many—are losing ground every day. . . .

We are not completely sure why this is. We know the causes are complex and subtle. But we do know the two broad basic reasons. And we do know that we have to act.

First, Negroes are trapped—as many whites are trapped—in inherited, gateless poverty. They lack training and skills. They are shut in, in slums, without decent medical care. Private and public poverty combine to cripple their capacities.

We are trying to attack these evils through our poverty program, through our education program, through our medical care and our other health programs, and a dozen more of the Great Society programs that are aimed at the root causes of this poverty.

We will increase, and we will accelerate, and we will broaden this attack in years to come until this most enduring of foes finally yields to our unyielding will.

But there is a second cause—much more difficult to explain, more deeply grounded, more desperate in its force. It is the devastating heritage of long years of slavery; and a century of oppression, hatred, and injustice. . . .

For Negro poverty is not white poverty. Many of its causes and many of its cures are the same. But there are differences—deep, corrosive, obstinate differences—radiating painful roots into the community, and into the family, and the nature of the individual.

These differences are not racial differences. They are solely and simply the consequence of ancient brutality, past injustice, and present prejudice. . . .

Nor can we find a complete answer in the experience of other American minorities. They made a valiant and a largely successful effort to emerge from poverty and prejudice.

The Negro, like these others, will have to rely mostly upon his own efforts. But he just can not do it alone. For they did not have the heritage of centuries to overcome, and they did not have a cultural tradition which had been twisted and battered by endless years of hatred and hopelessness, nor were they excluded—these others—because of race or color—a feeling whose dark intensity is matched by no other prejudice in our society.

Nor can these differences be understood as isolated infirmities. They are a seamless web. They cause each other. They result from each other. They reinforce each other. . . .

One of the differences is the increased concentration of Negroes in our cities. More than 73 percent of all Negroes live in urban areas compared with less than 70 percent of the whites. Most of these Negroes live in slums. Most of these Negroes live together—a separated people.

Men are shaped by their world. When it is a world of decay, ringed by an invisible wall, when escape is arduous and uncertain, and the saving pressures of a more hopeful society are unknown, it can cripple the youth and it can desolate the men.

There is also the burden that a dark skin can add to the search for a productive place in our society. Unemployment strikes most swiftly and broadly at the Negro, and this burden erodes hope. Blighted hope breeds despair. Despair brings indifferences to the learning which offers a way out. And despair, coupled with indifferences, is often the source of destructive rebellion against the fabric of society.

There is also the lacerating hurt of early collision with white hatred or prejudice, distaste or condescension. Other groups have felt similar intolerance. But success and achievement could wipe it away. They do not change the color of a man's skin. . . .

Perhaps most important—its influence radiating to every part of life—is the breakdown of the Negro family structure. For this, most of all, white America must accept responsibility. It flows from centuries of oppression and persecution of the Negro man. It flows from the long years of degradation and discrimination, which have attacked his dignity and assaulted his ability to produce for his family.

This, too, is not pleasant to look upon. But it must be faced by those whose serious intent is to improve the life of all Americans.

Only a minority—less than half—of all Negro children reach the age of 18 having lived all their lives with both of their parents. At this moment, tonight, little less than two-thirds are at home with both of their parents. Probably a majority of all Negro children receive federally-aided public assistance sometime during their childhood.

The family is the cornerstone of our society. More than any other force it shapes the attitude, the hopes, the ambitions, and the values of the child. And when the family collapses it is the children that are usually damaged. When it happens on a massive scale the community itself is crippled.

So, unless we work to strengthen the family, to create conditions under which most parents will stay together—all the rest: schools, and playgrounds, and public assistance, and private concern, will never be enough to cut completely the circle of despair and deprivation. . . .

There is no single easy answer to all of these problems.

Jobs are part of the answer. They bring the income which permits a man to provide for his family.

Decent homes in decent surroundings and a chance to learn—an equal chance to learn—are part of the answer.

Welfare and social programs better designed to hold families together are part of the answer.

Care for the sick is part of the answer.

An understanding heart by all Americans is another big part of the answer.

And to all of these fronts—and a dozen more—I will dedicate the expanding efforts of the Johnson administration.

But there are other answers that are still to be found. Nor do we fully understand even all of the problems. Therefore, I want to announce tonight that this fall I intend to call a White House conference of scholars, and experts, and outstanding Negro leaders—men of both races—and officials of Government at every level.

This White House conference's theme and title will be "To Fulfill These Rights."

Its object will be to help the American Negro fulfill the rights which, after the long time of injustice, he is finally about to secure.

To move beyond opportunity to achievement.

Questions

1. Why did President Johnson choose to deliver this address at Howard University?
2. What was the significance of Johnson's calling his speech and the planned conference "To Fulfill These Rights"?
3. What was most controversial about the speech and the Moynihan Report on which it drew?

Questions for Further Thought

1. How do the letter of Dr. Martin Luther King Jr. (Document 28-14) and the addresses of Senator Barry Goldwater (Document 28-15) and President Lyndon Johnson (Document 28-16) contribute to your understanding of public debate over issues that confronted the United States between 1960 and 1965 and beyond?

2. To what did Senator Goldwater refer when he discussed "domestic violence"? To what did he not refer?

CHAPTER 29

War Abroad and at Home: The Vietnam Era, 1961–1975

★　　　　★　　　　★

Into the Quagmire, 1945–1968

America's costly, divisive, and inconclusive war in Vietnam—along with racial conflict and disorder and violence in black neighborhoods, on campuses, and outside the 1968 Democratic National Convention in Chicago (to all of which the war contributed)—was central to the coming apart of the nation and the dissolving of "the liberal consensus" during the mid and late 1960s. The United States had long been involved in Vietnam when Lyndon Johnson became president. As early as the Truman administration, the United States began helping to underwrite France's war against a Communist-nationalist war for independence. This aid increased during the Korean War. Following the failure of France's war in 1954, in the climactic battle of which the Eisenhower administration had decided against aerial intervention, Vietnam was divided into Communist North Vietnam and non-Communist South Vietnam, supposedly to be reunited after free elections. South Vietnam's leader, Ngo Dinh Diem, called off reunification elections; the United States, supplanting France, sent aid and military advisers to Diem. The Kennedy administration increased America's commitment to South Vietnam (with advisors suffering casualties in the field), but Diem's regime was unsuccessful in its war against the National Liberation Front (NLF, or Vietcong) and its Communist North Vietnamese backers. So it was that the United States gave a green light to the South Vietnamese army coup that deposed and killed Diem just weeks before the assassination of President Kennedy (see text pp. 941–944; also *Instructor's Resource Manual*, vol. 2, *Since 1865*, 4th ed., Document 13, pp. 478–479).

Still, the fateful escalation of American military involvement in Southeast Asia occurred during the presidency of Lyndon Johnson. In August 1964, President Johnson secured congressional approval of the Gulf of Tonkin Resolution, at once enabling him to appear strong, though prudent, as he ran for reelection and securing for him congressional authorization for future military action. Document 29-1 excerpts this resolution. The following March, the United States launched a sustained aerial bombardment (Operation Rolling Thunder) of North Vietnam and the Ho Chi Minh Trail. (The trail, named for North Vietnam's leader, ran from North Vietnam through Laos and Cambodia into South Vietnam.) A week after the bombing began, U.S. ground combat forces arrived in South Vietnam, originally to protect an American air base, but increasingly to mount search-and-destroy operations against the Vietcong (see text pp. 942–947, including Map 29-1 and Figure 29-1). Document 29-2 provides President Johnson's public justification of his escalation of the war. As the war intensified and American casualties mounted, with draftees fighting and dying in larger numbers and with television bringing nightly images of the war home to Americans, the anti-war movement grew. Document 29-3 offers passages from a 1967 interview with Dr. Martin Luther King Jr., who criticized the war in part because of its effects on the Great Society and African Americans (see text pp. 944–950, including "American Voices"; also pp. 970–971, "American Lives," pp. 970–971).

29-1   The Gulf of Tonkin Resolution (1964)

After two ambiguous naval skirmishes in the Gulf of Tonkin, President Johnson ordered retaliatory air strikes and sought congressional support for future actions if necessary. In doing so, Johnson sent a warning to North Vietnam and a message to Americans on the eve of the 1964 presidential campaign. On August 7, overwhelming bipartisan congressional majorities granted the president extraordinary authority in the Gulf of Tonkin Resolution (see text pp. 944–945).

Source: Department of State Bulletin (August 29, 1964), 268.

Whereas naval units of the Communist regime in Vietnam, in violation of the principles of the Charter of the United Nations and of international law, have deliberately and repeatedly attacked the United States naval vessels present in international waters, and have thereby created a serious threat to international peace;

Whereas these attacks are part of a deliberate and systematic campaign of aggression that the Communist regime in North Vietnam has been waging against its neighbors and the nations joined with them in the collective defense of their freedom;

Whereas the United States is assisting the peoples *of southeast Asia to protect their political freedom and has not territorial, military or political ambitions in that area, but desires only that these peoples should be left in peace to work out their own destinies in their own way: Now, therefore, be it*

Resolved by the Senate and House of Representatives of the United States of America in Congress assembled, That the Congress approves and supports the determination of the President, as Commander in Chief, to take all necessary measures to repel any armed attack against the forces of the United States and to prevent further aggression.

SEC. 2. The United States regards as vital to its national interests and to world peace the maintenance of international peace and security in southeast Asia. . . . The United States is, therefore, prepared, as the President determines, to take all necessary steps, including the use of armed force, to assist any member or protocol state of the Southeast Asia Collective Defense Treaty requesting assistance in defense of its freedom.

SEC. 3. This resolution shall expire when the President shall determine that the peace and security of the area is reasonably assured. . . .

Questions

1. What are the North Vietnamese accused of in this resolution?
2. What are the American interests in the region, according to the resolution?
3. In what ways does the resolution grant a free hand to the president?

29-2   Peace without Conquest (1965)

Lyndon Johnson

President Lyndon Johnson (1908–1973) spoke at Johns Hopkins University on April 7, 1965, shortly after American air and ground forces escalated the military effort in Viet-nam. Support for administration policies was still widespread; the anti-war movement had not yet hit its stride (see text pp. 945–947, 949–950).

Source: Public Papers of the Presidents of the United States: Lyndon Johnson, 1965 (Washington, D.C.: U.S. Government Printing Office, 1966), 394–397.

. . . Tonight Americans and Asians are dying for a world where each people may choose its own path to change.

This is the principle for which our ancestors fought in the valleys of Pennsylvania. It is the principle for which our sons fight tonight in the jungles of Viet-Nam.

Viet-Nam is far away from this quiet campus. We have no territory there, nor do we seek any. The war is dirty and brutal and difficult. And some 400 young men, born into an America that is bursting with opportunity and promise, have ended their lives on Viet-Nam's steaming soil.

Why must we take this painful road? . . .

The first reality is that North Viet-Nam has attacked the independent nation of South Viet-Nam. Its object is total conquest.

Of course, some of the people of South Viet-Nam are participating in attack on their own government. But trained men and supplies, orders and arms, flow in a constant stream from north to south.

This support is the heartbeat of the war. . . .

Over this war—and all Asia—is another reality: the deepening shadow of Communist China. The rulers in Hanoi are urged on by Peking. This is a regime which has destroyed freedom in Tibet, which has attacked India, and has been condemned by the United Nations for aggression in Korea. It is a nation which is helping the forces of violence in almost every continent. The contest in Viet-Nam is part of a wider pattern of aggressive purposes. . . .

Why are these realities our concern? Why are we in South Viet-Nam?

We are there because we have a promise to keep. Since 1954 every American President has offered support to the people of South Viet-Nam. We have helped to build, and we have helped to defend. Thus, over many years, we have made a national pledge to help South Viet-Nam defend its independence.

And I intend to keep that promise.

To dishonor that pledge, to abandon this small and brave nation to its enemies, and to the terror that must follow, would be an unforgivable wrong.

We are also there to strengthen world order. Around the globe, from Berlin to Thailand, are people whose well-being rests, in part, on the belief that they can count on us if they are attacked. To leave Viet-Nam to its fate would shake the confidence of all these people in the value of an American commitment and in the value of America's word. The result would be increased unrest and instability, and even wider war.

We are also there because there are great stakes in the balance. Let no one think for a moment that retreat from Viet-Nam would bring an end to conflict. The battle would be renewed in one country and then another. The central lesson of our time is that the appetite of aggression is never satisfied. To withdraw from one battlefield means only to prepare for the next. We must say in southeast Asia—as we did in Europe—in the words of the Bible: "Hitherto shalt thou come, but no further." . . .

Our objective is the independence of South Viet-Nam, and its freedom from attack. We want nothing for ourselves—only that the people of South Viet-Nam be allowed to guide their own country in their own way.

We will do everything necessary to reach that objective. And we will do only what is absolutely necessary.

In recent months attacks on South Viet-Nam were stepped up. Thus, it became necessary for us to increase our response and to make attacks by air. This is not a change of purpose. It is a change in what we believe that purpose requires.

We do this in order to slow down aggression.

We do this to increase the confidence of the brave people of South Viet-Nam who have bravely borne this brutal battle for so many years with so many casualties.

And we do this to convince the leaders of North Viet-Nam—and all who seek to share their conquest—of a very simple fact:

We will not be defeated.

We will not grow tired.

We will not withdraw, either openly or under the cloak of a meaningless agreement. . . .

Once this is clear, then it should also be clear that the only path for reasonable men is the path of peaceful settlement.

Such peace demands an independent South Viet-Nam—securely guaranteed and able to shape its own relationships to all others—free from outside interference—tied to no alliance—a military base for no other country.

These are the essentials of any final settlement.

We will never be second in the search for such a peaceful settlement in Viet-Nam.

There may be many ways to this kind of peace: in discussion or negotiation with the governments concerned; in large groups or in small ones; in the reaffirmation of old agreements or their strengthening with new ones. . . .

These countries of southeast Asia are homes for millions of impoverished people. . . .

Stability and peace do not come easily in such a land. Neither independence nor human dignity will ever be won, though, by arms alone. It also requires the work of peace. The American people have helped generously in times past in these works. Now there must be a much more massive effort to improve the life of man in that conflict-torn corner of our world.

The first step is for the countries of southeast Asia to associate themselves in a greatly expanded cooperative effort for development. We would hope that North Viet-Nam would take its place in the common effort just as soon as peaceful cooperation is possible.

The United Nations is already actively engaged in development in this area. . . .

For our part I will ask the Congress to join in a billion dollar American investment in this effort as soon as it is underway.

And I would hope that all other industrialized countries, including the Soviet Union, will join in this effort to replace despair with hope, and terror with progress.

The task is nothing less than to enrich the hopes and the existence of more than a hundred million people. And there is much to be done.

The vast Mekong River can provide food and water and power on a scale to dwarf even our own TVA.

The wonders of modern medicine can be spread through villages where thousands die every year from lack of care.

Schools can be established to train people in the skills that are needed to manage the process of development.

And these objectives, and more, are within the reach of a cooperative and determined effort.

I also intend to expand and speed up a program to make available our farm surpluses to assist in feeding and clothing the needy in Asia. We should not allow people to go hungry and wear rags while our own warehouses overflow with an abundance of wheat and corn, rice and cotton. . . .

In areas that are still ripped by conflict, of course development will not be easy. Peace will be necessary for final success. But we cannot and must not wait for peace to begin this job. . . .

This will be a disorderly planet for a long time. In Asia, as elsewhere, the forces of the modern world are shaking old ways and uprooting ancient civilizations. There will be turbulence and struggle and even violence. Great social change—as we see in our own country now—does not always come without conflict. . . .

Questions

1. What, according to Johnson, underlies the war in Vietnam?
2. What are America's objectives in Vietnam? Why must the United States persevere in seeking to attain them? Do any of Johnson's arguments draw on earlier American experience and policies?
3. Why do you think Johnson discusses "the work of peace" in his speech?

29-3   Joining the Anti-War Movement (1967)

Martin Luther King Jr.

As early as the summer of 1965, Dr. Martin Luther King Jr. (1929–1968) had questioned American escalation of the war in Vietnam, but it was not until early 1967 that he broke with the Johnson administration regarding American involvement in that conflict. On March 30, between anti-war speeches in Los Angeles and Chicago (where he participated in his first anti-war march) and two addresses in New York City (one at an anti-war demonstration), Dr. King was interviewed by John Herbers of the *New York Times*. In the interview, Dr. King made clear the connections between the war abroad and the plight of African Americans at home. Incidentally, both the Student Nonviolent Coordinating Committee (SNCC) and the Congress of Racial Equality (CORE) had long since officially declared against the war. (On the context in which

King joined the anti-war movement, see text pp. 920, 935–938, 947–957, including "Voices from Abroad: Che Guevara").

Source: Interview by John Herbers in *New York Times,* April 2, 1967.

Following are questions and answers from the interview:

Q. Dr. King, in recent days you have become increasingly outspoken against the war in Vietnam. Why the increased opposition at this particular time?

A. Well, I would say there are at least three reasons why I felt compelled to take a stronger stand against the war in Vietnam. First, I feel this war is playing havoc with our domestic destinies. As long as the war in Vietnam goes on, the more difficult it will be to implement the programs that will deal with the economic and social problems that Negro people confront in our country and poor people generally.

So in a real sense, the Great Society has been shot down on the battlefields of Vietnam. I feel it is necessary to take a stand against it or at least arouse the conscience of the nation against it so that at least we can move more and more toward a negotiated settlement of that terrible conflict.

There is another reason why I feel compelled at this time to take a stand against the war and that is that the constant escalation of the war in Vietnam can lead to a grand war with China and to a kind of full world war that could mean the annihilation of the human race.

And I think those of us who are concerned about the survival of mankind, those of us who feel and know that mankind should survive must take a stand against this war because it is more than just a local conflict on Asian soil. . . .

The other reason is I have preached nonviolence in the movement in our country, and I think it is very consistent for me to follow a nonviolent approach in international affairs. . . .

Q. In 1965, there was an influx of civil rights workers, mostly those identified with the more radical groups such as the Student Nonviolent Coordinating Committee, into the peace movement. At that time I believe you condemned the war but kept your organization and energies pretty well channeled in the civil rights movement.

Recently, one of your assistants, the Rev. James Bevel, moved full time into the peace movement and is now organizing a protest in New York April 15 in which he will participate. Do you foresee a mass migration from civil rights to the peace movement?

A. No, I don't think there will be a mass migration from the civil rights movement if by that you mean leaving civil rights. I think more and more of them will become involved in both kinds of programmatic action.

There are many Negroes who now feel the two problems, the two issues, are inextricably bound together and that you can't really have freedom without justice, you can't have peace without justice, and you can't have justice without peace, so it is more of a realization of the interrelatedness of racism and militarism and the need to attack both problems rather than leaving one.

Certainly we will continue to work in both areas, but I feel, and many others that I have talked to agree, that we are merely marking time in the civil rights movement if we do not take a stand against the war. The fact is that while it may be true technically and from a monetary point of view that you can have guns and butter, it is a fact of life that where your heart is there your money will go, and the heart of the Administration is in that war in Vietnam.

The heart of the Congress is in that war. As long as that is true, that is where the money will go, and I feel that we are in need of a radical reorientation of our national priorities. This war is keeping us to the point where we aren't really reordering things.

Q. If the war continues and worsens despite peaceful demonstrations against it in this country, do you think the peace movement should engage in civil disobedience of the kind the civil rights movement has used with some success in the past?

A. I have not yet gone that far. But I wouldn't say it won't be necessary. It depends on developments over the next few months. I feel like the United States must take the first steps. I mean the initiative, to create an atmosphere for negotiations. We are so much more powerful than Vietnam. . . .

Now if our nation insists on escalating the war and if we don't see any changes it may be necessary to engage in civil disobedience to further arouse the conscience of the nation and make it clear we feel this is hurting our country.

And I might say this is another basic reason why I am involved and concerned. It is because I love America. I am not engaged in a hate America campaign. . . .

Q. Dr. King, I understand you have been away for some time writing a new book and contemplating where to go from here. Did you reach any conclusions on where the civil rights movement is headed?

A. Well, I reached several conclusions which will be stated in the book. One of the things I tried to state in the first chapter is that for more than a decade we worked mainly to remove the stigma and humiliation of legal segregation. We have made some significant victories in this area. Many people in the nation, whites, joined in taking a stand against this kind of humiliation of the Negro.

But what we are faced with now is the fact that the struggle must be and actually is at this point a struggle for genuine equality. The struggle over the last 10 or 12 years has been a struggle for decency, a struggle to get rid of extremist behavior towards Negroes, and I think we are moving into a period which is much more difficult, because it is dealing with hard economic problems which will cost the nation something to solve.

It did not cost the nation anything to integrate lunch counters or public accommodations. It did not cost the nation anything to guarantee the right to vote. The problem is now—in order to end the long night of poverty and economic insecurity—it would mean billions of dollars. In order to end slums it would mean billions of dollars. In order to get rid of bad education, education devoid of poverty, it means lifting the educational level of the whole public school system, which would mean billions of dollars.

This, I feel, is much more difficult than the period we have gone through. There will be more resistance because it means the privileged groups will have to give up some of their billions. And I think the so-called white backlash is expressed right here.

It is a reaction to the demands that are presently being made by Negroes now demanding genuine equality, and not just integration of the lunch counters but an adequate wage; not just integration of the classrooms, but a decent sanitary house in which to live. It is much easier to integrate a restaurant than it is to demand an annual income. I think the growing debate is recognition of this difficulty.

The next conclusion I reached is that the great need in the Negro community and the civil rights movement is to organize the Negro community for the amassing of real political and economic power. The question now is not merely developing programs because we have put many programs on paper.

What is needed now is the undergirding power to bring about enough pressure so that these programs can become a reality, that they can become concretized in our everyday lives; not only under the legislative process but under all the processes necessary to make them real. This just means the hard job of organizing tenants, organizing welfare recipients, organizing the unemployed and the underemployed.

It is for this reason that I am recommending to the Southern Christian Leadership Conference that we begin to train more field organizers so that we can really go out and organize these people and thereby move into the area of political action. I think the Negro can improve his economic resources much more if these resources are pooled, and I intend to do much more in this area so that we can make an economic thrust. . . .

Q. What about the President's civil rights bills now before Congress? Are they relevant to today's problems?

A. They are all relevant to today's problems, but they are not adequate. One aspect of the inadequacy is the failure to call for immediacy.

The housing problem, I believe, is one of the greatest problems facing our nation. There is a no more dangerous trend than the constant growth of predominantly Negro central cities ringed by white suburbs. I think this is only inviting social disaster.

I don't see any answer to it but an open housing law that is vigorously enforced. The Administration's bill does not call this year for a housing bill that is immediately enforcible. It would take three years to become nationally and universally applicable.

Q. What in your opinion is the current state of race relations in this country? Have there been gains? Do you still have hope?

A. We have certainly made some gains. The greatest gain is that we have brought the issue out into the open so that nobody can escape it, nobody can say there isn't a race problem.

For years, many people deluded themselves and argued that the Negro was satisfied, that conditions were well. But now everybody knows that things aren't right and the Negro is not satisfied. We have exposed the injustices and brought the evils out in the open. This is probably the greatest achievement.

The other is a psychological achievement and many people overlook this, and that is the new sense of dignity, the new sense of manhood within the Negro himself. And I think this is probably the greatest victory, that the Negro has a new sense of dignity, a new sense of destiny, a new sense of self-respect as the result of the struggle over the last few years.

Also, we have made very significant legislative strides. The Civil Rights Bill of 1964 represented progress; the Voting Rights Bill of 1965 represented real progress. The problem is that these particular gains are legislative victories that did very little to rectify conditions facing millions of Negroes in the teeming ghettos of the North.

They rectified wrongs and evils in the South, but did very little to penetrate the lower depths of Negro deprivation in the North. Consequently, we do see worse slums today in many parts. The schools in the North are more segregated today than they were in 1954. And, as I said earlier, the Negroes' economic problem is at many points worse today because of Negro unemployment and growing gulfs between white and Negro income.

Now this tells us that we still have a long way to go. But I'm not one to lose faith in the future or lose hope because I think the minute you do that you defeat the force that makes a revolution powerful. A revolution cannot survive on despair. It always must move on a wave of rising expectations and the feeling that you can win.

The minute you begin to feel that you can't win, you begin to adopt a no-win policy and to develop a nihilistic approach. I refuse to engage in that kind of hopelessness.

I still believe that we have in this country forces of goodwill that can be mobilized and that can direct the condition of conscience that will finally bring about the day when racism is no longer at the center of our society.

Questions

1. What most strikes you about King's criticism of America's war in Vietnam?
2. What connections does King draw between that war and America itself?
3. What are King's readings of "where the civil rights movement is headed" and "the current state of race relations"?

Questions for Further Thought

1. Compare and contrast the Vietnam policy of President John F. Kennedy with that of President Lyndon Johnson.
2. Compare and contrast the arguments of President Johnson (Document 29-2) and Dr. Martin Luther King Jr. (Document 29-3) regarding military involvement in the war in Vietnam.
3. What risks were involved for Dr. King, the Southern Christian Leadership Conference, and the civil rights movement in Dr. King's assuming a prominent role in the anti-war movement?

The Challenge of Youth, 1962–1970

The post–World War II baby boom meant that there were growing numbers of college- and military-age youths during the 1960s. Prosperity and changing economic and social expectations fairly ensured that the nation's universities, colleges, and junior colleges would experience an enrollment boom. Escalation of the war in Vietnam carried with it increased draft calls (see text pp. 912–917, 946–949; also Appendix pp. A–6, A–7, A–11). A mass youth culture antedated the 1960s, of course, but now the civil rights movement, the liberal appeal of the Kennedy and Johnson administrations, the anti-war movement, and other causes engaged sufficient young people—a minority, to be sure, but influential beyond their numbers—that one can refer to "the challenge of youth" (see text pp. 950–961).

Youths figured prominently in liberal and radical movements and organizations during the 1960s. Document 29-4 provides the Port Huron statement of the founders of Students for a Democratic Society, a "New Left" organization that challenged both liberalism, then dominant, and the "Old Left" of communism and socialism. As the civil rights movement shifted its campaign to northern cities, where discrimination and de facto segregation were widespread and intractable, separatism and black nationalism gained ground among both young veterans of the civil rights movement and young urban blacks. Document 29-5 offers the remarks of Malcolm X to Mississippi students visiting New York City and a poem by Yusef Iman. The period was also marked by increasing group awareness among Chicanos and native Americans. Although the two groups' histories differed and native Americans were diverse, both had long-standing grievances and had fought for their rights before the 1960s. Now, younger Chicanos and native Americans were prominent in protests. See Document 29-6 for Inés Hernández's "Para Teresa." Document 29-7 presents testimony of Menominee native American activists from Wisconsin regarding the adverse effects of a government policy on their tribe.

The years 1964 to 1968 were marked by violent protests by African Americans in cities across the nation—ghetto riots that involved arson, looting, and clashes with police troops, but with few attacks on whites (see Map 29-2, text p. 956). Document 29-8 is a newspaper interview of a youthful Detroit rioter.

Feminism revived in the 1960s, led by politically active older women but also influenced by younger women, many of them radicalized by their subordination in civil rights, student, and anti-war protest groups. Document 29-9 provides the National Organization for Women's statement of purpose. (For criticism by two white female activists of the subordination of women in the SNCC, see Mary King and Casey Hayden, "Sex and Caste" (1965) in the *Instructor's Resource Manual*, vol. 2, *Since 1865*, Document 12, pp. 297–298. The *Manual* also offers additional remarks by Malcolm X, Document 15, pp. 262–263.)

29-4   The Port Huron Statement (1962)

Students for a Democratic Society

The Students for a Democratic Society (SDS) played a leading role in the youth movement. In 1962, two University of Michigan activists, Al Haber and Tom Hayden, organized the founding meeting of SDS, held at a United Auto Workers center in Port Huron, Michigan (see text pp. 950–952). The students approved the following manifesto.

Source: Students for a Democratic Society, *Port Huron Statement*, 1962. Reprinted by permission of Senator Tom Hayden. A copy of the third printing is available in the Labadie Collection, Hatcher Graduate Library, University of Michigan.

INTRODUCTION: AGENDA FOR A GENERATION

We are people of this generation, bred in at least modest comfort, housed now in universities, looking uncomfortably to the world we inherit.

When we were kids the United States was the wealthiest and strongest country in the world; the only one with the atom bomb, the least scarred by modern war, an initiator of the United Nations that we thought would distribute Western influence throughout the world. Freedom and equality for each individual, government of, by, and for the people—these American values we found good, principles by which we could live as men. Many of us began maturing in complacency.

As we grew, however, our comfort was penetrated by events too troubling to dismiss. First, the permeating and victimizing fact of human degradation, symbolized by the Southern struggle against racial bigotry, compelled most of us from silence to activism. Second, the enclosing fact of the Cold War, symbolized by the presence of the Bomb, brought awareness that we ourselves, and our friends, and millions of abstract "others" we knew more directly because of our common peril, might die at any time. We might deliberately ignore, or avoid, or fail to feel all other human problems, but not these two, for these were too immediate and crushing in their impact, too challenging in the demand that we as individuals take the responsibility for encounter and resolution.

While these and other problems either directly oppressed us or rankled our consciences and became our own subjective concerns, we began to see complicated and disturbing paradoxes in our surrounding America. The declaration "all men are created equal . . ." rang hollow before the facts of Negro life in the South and the big cities of the North. The proclaimed peaceful intentions of the United States contradicted its economic and military investments in the Cold War status quo. . . .

Not only did tarnish appear on our image of American virtue, not only did disillusion occur when the hypocrisy of American ideals was discovered, but we began to sense that what we had originally seen as the American Golden Age was actually the decline of an era. The worldwide outbreak of revolution against colonialism and imperialism, the entrenchment of totalitarian states, the menace of war, overpopulation, international disorder, supertechnology—these trends were testing the tenacity of our own commitment to democracy and freedom and our abilities to visualize their application to a world in upheaval.

Our work is guided by the sense that we may be the last generation in the experiment with living. But we are a minority—the vast majority of our people regard the temporary equilibriums of our society and world as eternally-functional parts. In this is perhaps the outstanding paradox: we ourselves are imbued with urgency, yet the message of our society is that there is no viable alternative to the present. Beneath the reassuring tones of the politicians, beneath the common opinion that America will "muddle through," beneath the stagnation of those who have closed their minds to the future, is the pervading feeling that there simply are no alternatives, that our times have witnessed the exhaustion not only of Utopias, but of any new departures as well. Feeling the press of complexity upon the emptiness of life, people are fearful of the thought that at any moment things might be thrust out of control. They fear change itself, since change might smash whatever invisible framework seems to hold back chaos for them now. For most Americans, all crusades are suspect, threatening. The fact that each individual sees apathy in his fellows perpetuates the common reluctance to organize for change. The dominant institutions are complex enough to blunt the minds of their potential critics, and entrenched enough to swiftly dissipate or entirely repel the energies of protest and reform, thus limiting human expectancies. Then, too, we are a materially improved society, and by our own improvements we seem to have weakened the case for further change. . . .

The search for truly democratic alternatives to the present, and a commitment to social experimentation with them, is a worthy and fulfilling human enterprise, one which moves us and, we hope, others today. On such a basis do we offer this document of our convictions and analysis: as an effort in understanding and changing the conditions of humanity in the late twentieth century, an effort rooted in the ancient, still unfulfilled conception of man attaining determining influence over his circumstances of life.

VALUES

Making values explicit—an initial task in establishing alternatives—is an activity that has been devalued and corrupted. The conventional moral terms of the age, the politician moralities—"free world," "people's democracies"—reflect realities poorly, if at all, and seem to function more as ruling myths than as descriptive principles. But neither has our experience in the universities brought us moral enlightenment. Our professors and administrators sacrifice controversy to public relations; their curriculums change more slowly than the living events of the world; their skills and silence are purchased by investors in the arms race; passion is called unscholastic. The questions we might want raised—what is really important? can we live in a different and better way? if we wanted to change society, how would we do it?—are not thought to be questions of a "fruitful, empirical nature," and thus are brushed aside. . . .

Men have unrealized potential for self-cultivation, self-direction, self-understanding, and creativity. It is this potential that we regard as crucial and to which we appeal, not to the human potentiality for violence, unreason, and submission to authority. The goal of man and society should be human independence: a concern not with image of popularity but with finding a meaning in life that is personally authentic; a quality of mind not compulsively driven by a sense of powerlessness, nor one which unthinkingly adopts status values, nor one which represses all threats to its habits, but one which has full, spontaneous access to present and past experiences, one which easily unites the fragmented parts of personal history, one which openly faces problems which are troubling and unresolved; one with an intuitive awareness of possibilities, an active sense of curiosity, an ability and willingness to learn.

This kind of independence does not mean egotistic individualism—the object is not to have one's way so much as it is to have a way that is one's own. Nor do we deify man—we merely have faith in his potential.

Human relationships should involve fraternity and honesty. Human interdependence is contemporary fact; human brotherhood must be willed, however, as a condition of future survival and as the most appropriate form of social relations. Personal links between man and man are needed, especially to go beyond the partial and fragmentary bonds of function that bind men only as worker to worker, employer to employee, teacher to student, American to Russian. . . .

We would replace power rooted in possession, privilege, or circumstance by power and uniqueness rooted in love, reflectiveness, reason, and creativity. As a *social system* we seek the establishment of a democracy of individual participation, governed by two central aims: that the individual share in those social decisions determining the quality and direction of his life; that society be organized to encourage independence in men and provide the media for their common participation. . . .

Questions

1. What indictments does the Port Huron statement bring against mainstream American society?
2. How does the statement address generational differences?
3. What does the statement say about civil rights? What does it say about academia?

29-5   Black Nationalism (1964)

Malcolm X
Yusef Iman

Black Muslim leader Malcolm X (1925–1965) became a major spokesperson for black nationalism, a viewpoint that appealed especially to young urban African Americans (see text pp. 954–955). Some elements of Malcolm X's views are expressed in a speech he gave to Mississippi students visiting New York in 1964. Malcolm X had a tremendous impact on Stokely Carmichael and others associated with black power. The ideas expressed in Yusef Iman's poem "Love Your Enemy" are clearly influenced by Malcolm X's philosophy.

Sources: Malcolm X, excerpts from speech "To Mississippi Youth," given at the Hotel Theresa, Harlem, January 1, 1965. In *Malcolm X Speaks: Selected Speeches and Statements,* ed. George Breitman, 137–146. Reprinted by permission of Pathfinder Press. Copyright © 1965, 1989 by Betty Shabazz and Pathfinder Press. Yusef Iman, "Love Your Enemy," in Amiri Baraka's *Black Fire: An Anthology of Afro-American Writing,* ed. LeRoi Jones and Larry Neal (New York: Morrow, 1968), 387–388. Reprinted by permission of Sterling Lord Literistic, Inc. Copyright 1968 by Amiri Baraka.

(a) To Mississippi Youth, by Malcolm X

One of the first things I think young people, especially nowadays, should learn is how to see for yourself and listen for yourself and think for yourself. Then you can come to an intelligent decision for yourself. If you form the habit of going by what you hear others say about someone, or going by what others think about someone, instead of searching that thing out for yourself and seeing for yourself, you will be walking west when you think you're going east, and you will be walking east when you think you're going west. This generation, especially of our people, has a burden, more so than any other time in history. The most important thing that we can learn to do today is think for ourselves. . . .

I myself would go for nonviolence if it was consistent, if everybody was going to be nonviolent all the time. I'd say, okay, let's get with it, we'll all be nonviolent. But I don't go along with any kind of nonviolence unless everybody's going to be nonviolent. If they make the Ku Klux Klan nonviolent, I'll be nonviolent. If they make the White Citizens Council nonviolent, I'll be nonviolent. But as long as you've got somebody else not being nonviolent, I don't want anybody coming to me talking any nonviolent talk. I don't think it is fair to tell our people to be nonviolent unless someone is out there making the Klan and the Citizens Council and these other groups also be nonviolent. . . .

If the leaders of the nonviolent movement can go into the white community and teach nonviolence, good. I'd go along with that. But as long as I see them teaching nonviolence only in the black community, we can't go along with that. We believe in equality, and equality means that you have to put the same thing over here that you put over there. And if black people alone are going to be the ones who are nonviolent, then it's not fair. We throw ourselves

off guard. In fact, we disarm ourselves and make ourselves defenseless. . . .

[W]e of the Organization of Afro-American Unity realized that the only time the black man in this country is given any kind of recognition, or even listened to, is when America is afraid of outside pressure, or when she's afraid of her image abroad. So we saw that it was necessary to expand the problem and the struggle of the black man in this country until it went above and beyond the jurisdiction of the United States. . . .

And today you'll find in the United Nations, and it's not an accident, that every time the Congo question or anything on the African continent is being debated, they couple it with what is going on, or what is happening to you and me, in Mississippi and Alabama and these other places. In my opinion, the greatest accomplishment that was made in the struggle of the black man in America in 1964 toward some kind of real progress was the successful linking together of our problem with the African problem, or making our problem a world problem. Because now, whenever anything happens to you in Mississippi, it's not just a case of somebody in Alabama getting indignant, or somebody in New York getting indignant. The same repercussions that you see all over the world when an imperialist or foreign power interferes in some section of Africa— you see repercussions, you see the embassies being bombed and burned and overturned—nowadays, when something happens to black people in Mississippi, you'll see the same repercussions all over the world.

I wanted to point this out to you because it is important for you to know that when you're in Mississippi, you're not alone. As long as you think you're alone, then you take a stand as if you're a minority or as if you're outnumbered, and that kind of stand will never enable you to win a battle. You've got to know that you've got as much power on your side as that Ku Klux Klan has on its side. And when you know that you've got as much power on your side as the Klan has on its side, you'll talk the same kind of language with that Klan as the Klan is talking with you. . . .

I think in 1965, whether you like it, or I like it, or they like it, or not, you will see that there is a generation of black people becoming mature to the point where they feel that they have no more business being asked to take a peaceful approach than anybody else takes, unless everybody's going to take a peaceful approach.

So we here in the Organization of Afro-American Unity are with the struggle in Mississippi one thousand percent. We're with the efforts to register our people in Mississippi to vote one thousand per cent. But we do not go along with anybody telling us to help nonviolently. We think that if the government says that Negroes have a right to vote, and then some Negroes come out to vote, and some kind of Ku Klux Klan is going to put them in the river, and the government doesn't do anything about it, it's time for us to organize and band together and equip ourselves and qualify ourselves to protect ourselves. And once you can protect yourself, you don't have to worry about being hurt. . . .

You get freedom by letting your enemy know that you'll do anything to get your freedom; then you'll get it. It's the only way you'll get it. When you get that kind of attitude, they'll label you as a "crazy Negro," or they'll call you a "crazy nigger"—they don't say Negro. Or they'll call you an extremist or a subversive, or seditious, or a red or a radical. But when you stay radical long enough, and get enough people to be like you, you'll get your freedom. . . .

(b) Love Your Enemy, by Yusef Iman

Brought here in slave ships and pitched over board.
Love your enemy.
Language taken away, culture taken away.
Love your enemy.
Work from sun up to sun down.

Love your enemy.
Work for no pay.
Love your enemy.
Last hired, first fired.
Love your enemy.
Rape your mother.
Love your enemy.
Lynch your father.
Love your enemy.
Bomb your churches.
Love your enemy.
Kill your children.
Love your enemy.
Forced to fight his wars.
Love your enemy.
Pay the highest rent.

Love your enemy.
Sell you rotten foods.
Love your enemy.
Sell dope to your children.
Love your enemy.
Forced to live in the slums.
Love your enemy.
Dilapidated schools.
Love your enemy.
Puts you in jail.
Love your enemy.
Bitten by dogs.
Love your enemy.
Water hose you down.
Love your enemy.
    Love.
    Love.
    Love.
    Love.
    Love.
    Love, for everybody else.
But when will we love ourselves?

Questions

1. What is Malcolm X's opinion of the philosophy of nonviolence?
2. What strategy does Iman use to convey his message, and what is that message? How is Malcolm X's advice reflected in the poem "Love Your Enemy"?
3. What emotions do you believe Malcolm X and Iman hope to stir in their readers?

29-6   Para Teresa[1]

Inés Hernández

Like African Americans, Chicanos experienced feelings of being treated like outsiders and interlopers in American society. As was true for all minority groups, there were differences in the Hispanic community as to what strategy would best overcome this prejudice and discrimination. Inés Hernández's poem about a confrontation with a schoolmate illustrates some of those differences (see text p. 958).

Source: Inés Hernández, "Para Teresa," in *Con Razon, Corazon: Poetry,* rev. ed. (San Antonio: Texas: M & A Editions, n.d.). Inés Hernández-Avila is Chicana and Nez Perce; she is an Associate Professor of Native American Studies at the University of California, Davis. Used by permission.

A tí-Teresa
Te dedico las palabras estás
que explotan de mi corazón[2]

That day during lunch hour
at Alamo which-had-to-be-its-name
Elementary
my dear raza
That day in the bathroom
Door guarded
Myself cornered
I was accused by you, Teresa
Tú y las demás de tus amigas
Pachucas todos
Eran Uds. cinco.[3]

Me gritaban que porque me creía tan grande[4]
What was I trying to do, you growled
Show you up?
Make the teachers like me, pet me,
Tell me what a credit to my people I was?
I was playing right into their hands, you challenged
And you would have none of it.
I was to stop.
I was to be like you
I was to play your game of deadly defiance
Arrogance, refusal to submit.
The game in which the winner takes nothing
Asks for nothing
Never lets his weakness show.

But I didn't understand.
My fear salted with confusion
Charged me to explain to you
I did nothing for the teachers.
I studied for my parents and for my grandparents
Who cut out honor roll lists
Whenever their nietos'[5] names appeared
For my shy mother who mastered her terror
to demand her place in mother's clubs
For my carpenter-father who helped me patiently with my math.
For my abuelos que me regalaron lápices en la Navidad[6]
And for myself.

Porque reconocí en aquel entonces
una verdad tremenda
que me hizo mi un rebelde
Aunque tú no te habías dado cuenta[7]
We were not inferior
You and I, y las demás de tus amigas
Y los demás de nuestra gente[8]
I knew it the way I knew I was alive
We were good, honorable, brave
Genuine, loyal, strong

And smart.
Mine was a deadly game of defiance, also.
My contest was to prove
beyond any doubt
that we were not only equal but superior to them.
That was why I studied.
If I could do it, we all could.

---

[1]For Teresa. [Author's note]

[2]To you, Teresa, I dedicate these words that explode from my heart. [Author's note]

[3]You and the rest of your friends, all Pachucas (female natives of Pachuca, capital of the Mexican state of Hidalgo), there were five of you. [Author's note]

[4]You were screaming at me, asking me why I thought I was so hot. [Author's note]

[5]Grandchildren's [Author's note]

[6]Grandparents who gave me gifts of pencils at Christmas [Author's note]

[7]Because I recognized a great truth then that made me a rebel, even though you didn't realize it [Author's note]

[8]And the rest of your friends / And the rest of our people [Author's note]

You let me go then.
Your friends unblocked the way
I who-did-not-know-how-to-fight
was not made to engage with you-who-grew-up-fighting
Tu y yo, Teresa[9]
We went in different directions
Pero fuimos juntas.[10]

In sixth grade we did not understand
Uds. with the teased, dyed-black-but-reddening hair,
Full petticoats, red lipsticks
and sweaters with the sleeves
pushed up
Y yo conformándome con lo que deseaba mi mama[11]

Certainly never allowed to dye, to tease, to paint myself
I did not accept your way of anger,
Your judgements
You did not accept mine.

But now in 1975, when I am twenty-eight
Teresa
I remember you.
Y sabes—
Te comprendo,
Es más, te respeto.
Y, si me permites,
Te nombro—"hermana."[12]

[9]You and I [Author's note]

[10]But we were together [Author's note]

[11]And I conforming to my mother's wishes [Author's note]

[12]And do you know what, I understand you. Even more, I respect you. And, if you permit me, I name you my sister. [Author's note]

Questions

1. What did the poem's speaker do to combat racism, and what did Teresa advocate?
2. How did the speaker's attitude toward Teresa change, and how do you account for this change?
3. Which position do you think was most effective—that of Teresa or the poem's speaker?

29-7   The Consequences of Termination for the Menominee of Wisconsin (1971)

DRUMS Committee of the Menominee

In the 1950s, Congress endorsed a new policy for native Americans. It was called termination and was intended to end "the legal standing of native tribes and move their members off reservations" (see text pp. 919–920, 958, 960). But what looked good in Washington did not necessarily work for people such as the Menominee of Wisconsin.

Source: DRUMS Committee, Menominee, chronology from DRUMS testimony, Hearings on Senate Concurrent Resolution Number 26, Senate Committee on Interior and Insular Affairs, July 21, 1971; in Peter Nabokov, ed., *Native American Testimony: A Chronicle of Indian-White Relations from Prophecy to the Present, 1492–1992* (New York: Viking Penguin, 1991), 344–347.

Early in 1953, we Menominee wanted a portion of our 1951 settlement—about $5,000,000—distributed among ourselves on a $1,500 per capita basis. Since Congressional approval was required for such disbursement of our assets, [then] Representative Melvin Laird and Senator Joseph McCarthy introduced in Congress on behalf of our Tribe a bill to authorize the payment of *our* money to us.

This bill passed the House, but in hearings before the Senate Committee on Interior and Insular Affairs, it ran up against an amendment sponsored by the late Senator Arthur V. Watkins (R. Utah) calling for "termination" of federal supervision and assistance to the Menominee. Watkins and the Committee refused to report the bill favorably, calling upon us Menominee to submit a termination plan *before* we would be given *our* money! "Termination!" What did *that* mean? Certainly at that time, none of us Menominee realized what it meant! . . . In June, 1953, we Menominee invited Senator Watkins to visit the Reservation and explain "termination" to us.

Senator Watkins badly wanted our termination. He was firmly convinced that factors such as our status as Reservation Indians, our tribal ownership of land, and our tax exemption were blocking our initiative, our freedom, and our development of private enterprise. He wished to see us rapidly assimilated into the mainstream of American society—as tax paying, hard working, "emancipated" citizens. . . .

On June 20, 1953, Senator Watkins spoke for 45 minutes to our General Council. He told us that Congress had already decided on terminating us, and that at most we could have three years before our "affairs would be turned over to us"—and that we would not receive our per capitas until *after* termination.

After he left, our Council had the opportunity to vote on the "principle of termination!" Some opportunity! What little understanding we had of what termination would mean! The vote was 169 to 5 in favor of the "principle of termination." A mere 5 percent of the 3,200 Menominee people participated in this vote. Most of our people chose to be absent from the meeting in order to express their negative reaction to termination. Many who did vote affirmatively that day believed that termination was coming from Congress whether the Menominee liked it or not. Others thought that they were voting *only* in favor of receiving their per capitas. . . .

We then set about preparing a termination plan, which the BIA [Bureau of Indian Affairs] subsequently emasculated, and we received word that Senator Watkins was pressing ahead with his *own* termination bill. *Another* general council meeting was called, one which is seldom mentioned, but at which the Menominee voted 197 to 0 to *oppose and reject* termination. But our feelings did not matter—and although the Watkins bill met a temporary defeat on technical grounds in the House in late 1953, Senator Watkins re-introduced it in 1954.

We became convinced that there was *no* alternative to accepting termination. Therefore, all we pleaded for was adequate time to plan this sudden and revolutionary change in our lives! On June 17, 1954, the Menominee Termination Act was signed into law by President Eisenhower. . . .

Termination represented a gigantic and revolutionary *forced* change in the traditional Menominee way of life. Congress expected us to replace our Indian way of life with a complicated corporate style of living. Congress expected immediate Menominee assimilation of non-Indian culture, values, and life styles. . . .

The immediate effect of termination on our tribe was the loss of most of our hundred-year-old treaty rights, protections, and services. No amount of explanation or imagination prior to termination could have prepared us for the shock of what these losses meant.

Congress withdrew its trusteeship of our lands, transferring to MEI [Menominee Enterprises, Inc., the corporation which was to supervise Menominee holdings after termination] the responsibility for protecting these lands, our greatest assets. As we shall explain, far from being able to preserve our land, MEI has been forced to sell it. And because our land is now being sold to non-Menominee, termination is doing to us what allotment has done to other Indian tribes.

Congress also extinguished our ancient system of tribal "ownership" of land (under which no individual had separate title to his home) and transferred title to MEI. Consequently, we individual Menominee suddenly discovered that we would be forced to buy from MEI the land which had always been considered our own, and to pay title to our homesites. Thus began the tragic process of our corporation "feeding off" our people.

We Menominee lost our right to tax exemption. Both MEI and individual Menominee found themselves saddled with tax burdens particularly crushing to a small tribe struggling to develop economically.

BIA health, education and utility services ceased. We lost all medical and dental care within the Reservation. Both our reservation and hospital were closed because they failed to meet state standards. Individual Menominee were forced to pay for electricity and water that they previously received at no cost. Our county found it had to renovate at high cost its substandard sewerage system.

Finally, with termination and the closing of our tribal rolls, our children born since 1954 have been legally deprived of their birthright as Menominee Indians. Like all other Menominee, they have lost their entitlement to United States Government benefits and services to Indians. . . . The only major Menominee treaty right which the government has allowed us to retain has been our hunting and fishing right. Wisconsin had tried to deprive us of this right, but in 1968, after costly litigation, the United States Supreme Court ruled that this treaty right had "survived" termination. . . .

We hope you can appreciate the magnitude of these treaty losses to us. Visualize a situation similar to ours happening in one of your home states. Imagine the outrage of the people in one of your own communities if Congress should attempt to terminate their basic property, inheritance, and civil rights. . . .

Today Menominee County is the poorest county in Wisconsin. It has the highest birthrate in the state and ranks at or near the bottom of Wisconsin counties in income, housing, property value, education, employment, sanitation and health. The most recent figures available (1967) show that the annual income of nearly 80 percent of our families falls below the federal poverty level of $3,000. The per capita annual income of our wage earners in 1965 was estimated at $881, the lowest in the state. . . .

This lack of employment opportunities, combined with our high birthrate, forced nearly 50 percent of our county residents to go on welfare in 1968. Welfare costs in the county for 1968 were over $766,000 and our per capita welfare payment was the highest in the state. The majority of Menominee who have left our county to seek work in the cities have become trapped in poverty there also.

With the closing of the BIA hospital, we lost most of our health services, and most Menominee continue to suffer from lack of medical care. There have been no full-time doctors or dentists in Menominee County since termination. Shortly before termination, our people were stricken by a TB epidemic which caused great suffering and hardship because of the lack of local medical facilities. . . .

The loss of the BIA school required that our youth be sent to Shawano County for their high school training. The Shawano school system had assumed that Menominee children possess the same cultural and historical background as [children from the] middle-class white community. . . . Since 1961, our high school drop-out rates have increased substantially, absenteeism has soared, and our children apparently are suffering a downward trend in achievement. . . .

We have told a story which is very tragic, yet it is a true story of the Menominee people since termination. We have told how termination has meant the loss of treaty benefits, has pushed our already poor community further into the depths of poverty, forced our sale of assets; and denied us a democratic community.

DRUMS COMMITTEE, *Menominee*

Questions

1. Who decided on termination?
2. What were the consequences of this policy?

29-8   The Detroit Race Riot (1967)

Ray Rogers

The 1960s were marked by violence in many forms and settings: the war in Vietnam, of course, and the assassinations that punctuated the decade; the acts of diehard segregationists and those of extremist radicals, white and African American; campus disorder, which reached its bloody climax in 1970; and a spate of riots in African American inner-city neighborhoods (see text pp. 956–957, including Map 29-2, and 964–967). The Detroit ghetto riot was touched off by early morning police raids on drinking and gambling clubs, which dated to Prohibition. Police cars were stoned; window-smashing, looting, and arson followed. Police, national guardsmen, and federal troops suppressed the riot, which left forty-three dead. Ray Rogers of the *New York Post* interviewed an African American youth who said that he had been among those who sniped at the police and the National Guard.

(On radicals and violence during the period, see Angela Davis, "Letter from Prison" [1970], in *Instructor's Resource Manual*, vol. 2, *Since 1865*, 4th ed., Document 16, pp. 264–265; also see Document 31-9 for debate over comparisons and contrasts between the anger and violence of the Left during the 1960s and the anger and violence of the Right during the 1990s.)

Source: "A Sniper's Story: I'm Just Getting Even," *New York Post*, July 7, 1967, reprinted in Richard Hofstadter and Michael Wallace, eds., *American Violence: A Documentary History* (New York: Vintage, 1971), 267–269.

A teenage Negro who identified himself as one of the elusive Detroit snipers says "the war" will not be over until "they kill all of us."

But, he insisted yesterday, his activities were not organized.

"When the thing broke out me and my main man [best friend] were out there helping. We threw some cocktails. But after a while we got tired of that so we decided to go home and get our pieces [guns]," he explained.

"We knew they were going to try and step on this thing before it got out of hand so we figured we would give them something to think about," he giggled.

"GOT ONE OR TWO"

"We had them — cops so scared that first night they were shooting at one another. I know I got one or two of them, but I don't think I killed them. I wish I had, the dirty —."

The young man explained that he went and got his "piece" after he and his buddy had looted a liquor store.

"We drank a little. And after a while—boom, just like that we decided to do some shootin'."

Did he realize he could be killed?

"I'm not crazy—I'm not crazy to be killed. I'm just gettin' even for what they did to us. Really. That's where it's at.

"Man, they killed Malcolm X just like that. So I'm gonna take a few of them with me. They may get me later on, but somebody else will take my place—just like that."

He explained that he avoided the area patrolled by the airborne troops because of the intensity with which they returned fire.

"They got a lot of soul brothers in their outfit too and I'm not trying to waste my own kind. I am after them honkies . . ." he said.

MOTHER DIED

His mother had died years ago leaving him and his sister in a dilapidated apartment, he said.

"Man, that place was so bad that I hated to come home at night. My sister became a hustler for a guy I grew up with." He said he had heard that she had been shot Wednesday night while looting a store.

"That makes me mad. Why they have to shoot somebody for takin' something out of a store during a riot? These white mothers are something else," he said angrily as he rubbed his long, powerful fingers together.

He said he wished he had a better weapon than the U.S. M-I-automatic carbine because it lacked range and fire power. Thus he could not fire more than one or two rounds at most before National Guardsmen laid down a heavy barrage.

"But I know I got two of them. I saw them mothers fall.

"One was a honky-tonk cop with a big belly and he couldn't run too fast. And when I hit him he hollered and hit the pavement.

"And them stupid mothers fired all over the place except the place where I was—I was laying among some bricks in a burnt-out store. It was beautiful, baby, so beautiful I almost cried with joy."

He said he never carried the carbine with him and he hid it in a different place after each time he used it.

He laughed and said:

"Twice they had their hands on me and searched me but they let me go. That's why I say that the war ain't over until they put all of us in jail or kill us. . . . I mean all of us soul brothers. But they can't do that because there's too many of us."

Suddenly he began talking about his early life.

"I went to school just like you did. I believed in all that oakie-doak and then I woke up one day and said later for that stuff because that stuff would just mess up my mind, just mess up my mind. I hustled and did a little bit of everything to stay alive.

"I got a couple of kids by some sister on the other side of town but I never see them. What can I say to them?"

He said that he and his buddy paid his 10-year-old cousin to watch for National Guard patrols while they were staked out on roofs. They communicated with him by a toy walkie-talkie.

"It was funny for a while because all they could do was lay there and holler at one another. Man, it was beautiful. We controlled the scene.

"We were just like guerrillas—real ones."

Questions

1. What strikes you about the life of the self-described sniper?
2. What do you think about the teenager's comments on his thoughts and actions during the riot?

29-9   Statement of Purpose (1966)

National Organization for Women

The National Organization for Women (NOW) was founded in 1966 by a small group of women. One of the founders, Betty Friedan, had gained widespread recognition with the publication of her book *The Feminine Mystique* three years earlier. The organizers of NOW hoped the group would serve women as the NAACP had long served African Americans.

Source: Betty Friedan, *It Changed My Life* (New York: W. W. Norton, 1976), pp. 87–91. Copyright, © 1963, 1964, 1966, 1970, 1971, 1972, 1973, 1974, 1975, 1976, 1985, 1991, 1998 by Betty Friedan. Originally published by Random House, Inc. Reprinted by permission of Curtis Brown, Ltd.

We, men and women who hereby constitute ourselves as the National Organization for Women, believe that the time has come for a new movement toward true equality for all women in America, and toward a fully equal partnership of the sexes, as part of the world-wide revolution of human rights now taking place within and beyond our national borders.

The purpose of NOW is to take action to bring women into full participation in the mainstream of American society now, exercising all the privileges and responsibilities thereof in truly equal partnership with men. . . .

There is no civil rights movement to speak for women, as there has been for Negroes and other victims of discrimination. The National Organization for Women must therefore begin to speak.

WE BELIEVE that the power of American law, and the protection guaranteed by the U.S. Constitution to the civil rights of all individuals, must be effectively applied and enforced to isolate and remove patterns of sex discrimination, to ensure equality of opportunity in employment and education, and equality of civil and political rights and responsibilities on behalf of women, as well as for Negroes and other deprived groups. . . .

WE DO NOT ACCEPT the token appointment of a few women to high-level positions in government and industry as a substitute for a serious continuing effort to recruit and advance women according to their individual abilities. To this end, we urge American government and industry to mobilize the same resources of ingenuity and command with which they have solved problems of far greater difficulty than those now impeding the progress of women.

WE BELIEVE that this nation has a capacity at least as great as other nations, to innovate new social institutions which will enable women to enjoy true equality of opportunity and responsibility in society, without conflict with their responsibilities as mothers and homemakers. In such innovations, America does not lead the Western world, but lags by decades behind many European countries. We do not accept the traditional assumption that a woman has to choose between marriage and motherhood, on the one

hand, and serious participation in industry or the professions on the other. We question the present expectation that all normal women will retire from job or profession for ten or fifteen years, to devote their full time to raising children, only to reenter the job market at a relatively minor level. This in itself is a deterrent to the aspirations of women, to their acceptance into management or professional training courses, and to the very possibility of equality of opportunity or real choice, for all but a few women. Above all, we reject the assumption that these problems are the unique responsibility of each individual woman, rather than a basic social dilemma which society must solve. True equality of opportunity and freedom of choice for women requires such practical and possible innovations as a nationwide network of child-care centers, which will make it unnecessary for women to retire completely from society until their children are grown, and national programs to provide retraining for women who have chosen to care for their own children full time.

WE BELIEVE that it is as essential for every girl to be educated to her full potential of human ability as it is for every boy—with the knowledge that such education is the key to effective participation in today's economy and that, for a girl as for boy [*sic*], education can only be serious where there is expectation that it will be used in society. We believe that American educators are capable of devising means of imparting such expectations to girl students. Moreover, we consider the decline in the proportion of women receiving higher and professional education to be evidence of discrimination. This discrimination may take the form of quotas against the admission of women to colleges and professional schools; lack of encouragement by parents, counselors and educators; denial of loans or fellowships; or the traditional or arbitrary procedures in graduate and professional training geared in terms of men, which inadvertently discriminate against women. We believe that the same serious attention must be given to high school dropouts who are girls as to boys.

WE REJECT the current assumptions that a man must carry the sole burden of supporting himself, his wife, and family, and that a woman is automatically entitled to life-long support by a man upon her marriage, or that marriage, home and family are primarily woman's world and responsibility—hers, to dominate, his to support. We believe that a true partnership between the sexes demands a different concept of marriage, an equitable sharing of the responsibilities of home and children and of the economic burdens of their support. We believe that proper recognition should be given to the economic and social value of homemaking and child care. To these ends, we will seek to open a reexamination of laws and mores governing marriage and divorce, for we believe that the current state of "half-equality" between the sexes discriminates against both men and women, and is the cause of much unnecessary hostility between the sexes.

WE BELIEVE that women must now exercise their political rights and responsibilities as American citizens. They must refuse to be segregated on the basis of sex into separate-and-not-equal ladies' auxiliaries in the political parties, and they must demand representation according to their numbers in the regularly constituted party committees—at local, state, and national levels—and in the informal power structure, participating fully in the selection of candidates and political decision-making, and running for office themselves.

IN THE INTERESTS OF THE HUMAN DIGNITY OF WOMEN, we will protest and endeavor to change the false image of women now prevalent in the mass media, and in the texts, ceremonies, laws, and practices of our major social institutions. Such images perpetuate contempt for women by society and by women for themselves. We are similarly opposed to all policies and practices—in church, state, college, factory, or office—which, in the guise of protectiveness, not only deny opportunities but also foster in women self-denigration, dependence, and evasion of responsibility, undermine their confidence in their own abilities and foster contempt for women. . . .

WE BELIEVE THAT women will do most to create a new image of women by *acting* now, and by speaking out in behalf of their own equality, freedom, and human dignity—not in pleas for special privilege, nor in enmity toward men, who are also victims of the current half-equality between the sexes—but in an active, self-respecting partnership with men. By so doing, women will develop confidence in their own ability to determine actively, in partnership with men, the conditions of their life, their choices, their future and their society.

Questions

1. What major issues does NOW identify in its statement of purpose?
2. How, according to NOW, should these issues be addressed?
3. Compare and contrast NOW's statement of purpose with Mary King and Casey Hayden's "Sex and Caste" (*Instructor's Resource Manual,* vol. 2: 297–298).

Questions for Further Thought

1. Based on your reading of the text (pp. 950–961) and Documents 29-4 through 29-9, what similarities and dissimilarities do you see among these activists?
2. What factors would you cite in seeking to explain the "wave of [racial] riots" that swept across black ghettos between 1964 and 1968?
3. Compare and contrast the feminist movement and the earlier woman's suffrage movement.

The Long Road Home, 1968–1975

Before the United States set out on its "long road home," it endured a "year of shocks" in 1968, arguably as painful and difficult a year as any in the history of the republic. That year witnessed the Vietcong's Tet Offensive, the withdrawal of President Johnson from the presidential race, the anti-war Democratic presidential candidacies of Eugene McCarthy and Robert Kennedy, the assassinations of Dr. Martin Luther King Jr. and Robert Kennedy, African American ghetto riots after the murder of Dr. King, campus disorder, the Democrats' nomination of Vice-President Hubert Humphrey for president in riot-torn Chicago, and the independent presidential candidacy of Governor George C. Wallace of Alabama. In the end, Richard Nixon, the Republicans' presidential nominee, defeated Humphrey and Wallace. Although the Democrats retained control of Congress, their coalition had been shattered in the national race (see text pp. 961–964). The presidency was now Richard Nixon's, but so was the American war in Vietnam.

The long road home was just that, long and, like 1968, difficult and painful, too. President Nixon's policy of Vietnamization increased South Vietnamese involvement and reduced American involvement in the ground war, but Americans continued to fight and die in Southeast Asia, over 20,000 falling between 1969 and 1973. Vietnamization also involved an intensification of America's aerial bombing campaign in the war and, together with South Vietnamese troops, an invasion of Cambodia (1970) to root out enemy bases. This "incursion" touched off campus anti-war demonstrations, which escalated beyond earlier protests when Ohio national guardsmen killed students at Kent State University and Mississippi state policemen did likewise at Jackson State University, a black school. Strikes, arson, and bombings forced the closing of numerous campuses (see Figure 29-1, text p. 946, 964–968). Still, America's long war in Vietnam did end, in 1973, and two years later, Vietnam's even longer civil war also ended, in victory for North Vietnam's Communists. The costs of the war, human and material, ran high for Vietnam, Cambodia, and Laos and for the United States. The war's wounds would be long in healing (see text pp. 968–972).

Documents 29-10 and 29-11 provide war policy statements by President Nixon, the first on Vietnamization and the Nixon Doctrine, the second justifying the invasion of Cambodia. Document 29-12 recounts the return to the United States from Vietnam of an army nurse. Document 29-13 conveys the words of a mother to her son, fifteen years after his death in Vietnam.

29-10   Vietnamization and the Nixon Doctrine (1969)

Richard Nixon

Addressing Americans on November 3, 1969, President Richard Nixon (1913–1994) made the case for his administration's policy in Vietnam (Vietnamization) and, more broadly, Asia (the Nixon Doctrine). (See text pp. 964–967; also Figure 29-1, p. 946.)

Source: Department of State Bulletin, November 24, 1969.

Let me briefly explain what has been described as the Nixon doctrine—a policy which not only will help end the war in Viet-Nam but which is an essential element of our program to prevent future Viet-Nams.

We Americans are a do-it-yourself people. We are an impatient people. Instead of teaching someone else to do a job, we like to do it ourselves. And this trait has been carried over into our foreign policy.

In Korea and again in Viet-Nam, the United States furnished most of the money, most of the arms, and most of the men to help the people of those countries defend their freedom against Communist aggression.

Before any American troops were committed to Viet-Nam, a leader of another Asian country expressed this opinion to me when I was traveling in Asia as a private citizen. He said: "When you are trying to assist another nation defend its freedom, U.S. policy should be to help them fight the war, but not to fight the war for them."

Well, in accordance with this wise counsel, I laid down in Guam three principles as guidelines for future American policy toward Asia:

—First, the United States will keep all of its treaty commitments.

—Second, we shall provide a shield if a nuclear power threatens the freedom of a nation allied with us or of a nation whose survival we consider vital to our security.

—Third, in cases involving other types of aggression, we shall furnish military and economic assistance when requested in accordance with our treaty commitments. But we shall look to the nation directly threatened to assume the primary responsibility of providing the manpower for its defense. . . .

The defense of freedom is everybody's business—not just America's business. And it is particularly the responsibility of the people whose freedom is threatened. In the previous administration we Americanized the war in Viet-Nam. In this administration we are Vietnamizing the search for peace.

The policy of the previous administration not only resulted in our assuming the primary responsibility for fighting the war but, even more significantly did not adequately stress the goal of strengthening the South Vietnamese so that they could defend themselves when we left.

The Vietnamization plan was launched following Secretary [of Defense Melvin R.] Laird's visit to Viet-Nam in March. Under the plan, I ordered first a substantial increase in the training and equipment of South Vietnamese forces.

In July, on my visit to Viet-Nam, I changed General Abrams' orders so that they were consistent with the objectives of our new policies. Under the new orders, the primary mission of our troops is to enable the South Vietnamese forces to assume the full responsibility for the security of South Viet-Nam. . . .

We have adopted a plan which we have worked out in cooperation with the South Vietnamese for the complete withdrawal of all U.S. combat ground forces and their replacement by South Vietnamese forces on an orderly scheduled timetable. This withdrawal will be made from strength and not from weakness. As South Vietnamese forces become stronger, the rate of American withdrawal can become greater. . . .

If the level of infiltration or our casualties increase while we are trying to scale down the fighting, it will be the result of a conscious decision by the enemy.

Hanoi could make no greater mistake than to assume that an increase in violence will be to its advantage. If I conclude that increased enemy action jeopardizes our remaining forces in Viet-Nam, I shall not hesitate to take strong and effective measures to deal with that situation.

This is not a threat. This is a statement of policy which as Commander in Chief of our Armed Forces I am making in meeting my responsibility for the protection of American fighting men wherever they may be.

My fellow Americans, I am sure you can recognize from what I have said that we really only have two choices open to us if we want to end this war:

—I can order an immediate, precipitate withdrawal of all Americans from Viet-Nam without regard to the effects of that action.

—Or we can persist in our search for a just peace, through a negotiated settlement if possible or through continued implementation of our plan for Vietnamization if necessary—a plan in which we will withdraw all of our forces from Viet-Nam on a schedule in accordance with our program, as the South Vietnamese become strong enough to defend their own freedom.

I have chosen this second course. It is not the easy way. It is the right way. It is a plan which will end the war and serve the cause of peace, not just in Viet-Nam but in the Pacific and in the world.

In speaking of the consequences of a precipitate withdrawal, I mentioned that our allies would lose confidence in America.

Far more dangerous, we would lose confidence in ourselves. Oh, the immediate reaction would be a sense of relief that our men were coming home. But as we saw the consequences of what we had done, inevitable remorse and divisive recrimination would scar our spirit as a people. . . .

If [the plan for peace] does succeed, what the critics say now won't matter. If it does not succeed, anything I say then won't matter.

I know it may not be fashionable to speak of patriotism or national destiny these days. But I feel it is appropriate to do so on this occasion.

Two hundred years ago this nation was weak and poor. But even then, America was the hope of millions in the world. Today we have become the strongest and richest nation in the world. The wheel of destiny has turned so that any hope the world has for the survival of peace and freedom will be determined by whether the American people have the moral stamina and the courage to meet the challenge of free-world leadership.

Let historians not record that when America was the most powerful nation in the world we passed on the other side of the road and allowed the last hopes for peace and freedom of millions of people to be suffocated by the forces of totalitarianism.

And so tonight—to you, the great silent majority of my fellow Americans—I ask for your support.

I pledged in my campaign for the Presidency to end the war in a way that we could win the peace. I have initiated a plan of action which will enable me to keep that pledge.

The more support I can have from the American people, the sooner that pledge can be redeemed; for the more divided we are at home, the less likely the enemy is to negotiate at Paris.

Let us be united for peace. Let us also be united against defeat. Because let us understand: North Viet-Nam cannot defeat or humiliate the United States. Only Americans can do that.

Questions

1. How does Nixon generalize his Vietnamization policy into the "Nixon Doctrine"?
2. According to Nixon, how does his Vietnamization policy differ from the policy followed by President Johnson?
3. What arguments does Nixon use to persuade Americans to support Vietnamization?

29-11   The Invasion of Cambodia (1970)

Richard Nixon

On April 30, 1970, American and South Vietnamese forces invaded Cambodia. That very day, President Nixon justified the "incursion" to a nation divided over the war and anti-war dissent (see text pp. 965–972).

Source: Department of State Bulletin, May 18, 1970.

Ten days ago, in my report to the Nation on Viet-Nam, I announced a decision to withdraw an additional 150,000 Americans from Viet-Nam over the next year. I said then that I was making that decision despite our concern over increased enemy activity in Laos, in Cambodia, and in South Viet-Nam.

At that time, I warned that if I concluded that increased enemy activity in any of these areas endangered the lives of Americans remaining in Viet-Nam, I would not hesitate to take strong and effective measures to deal with that situation.

Despite that warning, North Viet-Nam has increased its military aggression in all these areas, and particularly in Cambodia.

After full consultation with the National Security Council . . . and my other advisers, I have concluded that the actions of the enemy in the last 10 days clearly endanger the lives of Americans who are in Viet-Nam now and would constitute an unacceptable risk to those who will be there after withdrawal of another 150,000.

To protect our men who are in Viet-Nam and to guarantee the continued success of our withdrawal and Vietnamization programs, I have concluded that the time has come for action. . . .

For the past 5 years . . . North Viet-Nam has occupied military sanctuaries all along the Cambodian frontier with South Viet-Nam. Some of these extend up to 20 miles into Cambodia. The sanctuaries . . . are on both sides of the border. They are used for hit-and-run attacks on American and South Vietnamese forces in South Viet-Nam.

These Communist-occupied territories contain major base camps, training sites, logistics facilities, weapons and ammunition factories, airstrips, and prisoner of war compounds. . . .

Tonight American and South Vietnamese units will attack the headquarters for the entire Communist military operation in South Viet-Nam. This key control center has been occupied by the North Vietnamese and Viet Cong for 5 years in blatant violation of Cambodia's neutrality.

This is not an invasion of Cambodia. The areas in which these attacks will be launched are completely occupied and controlled by North Vietnamese forces. Our purpose is not to occupy the areas. Once enemy forces are driven out of these sanctuaries and once their military supplies are destroyed, we will withdraw.

These actions are in no way directed at the security interests of any nation. Any government that chooses to use these actions as a pretext for harming relations with the United States will be doing so on its own responsibility and on its own initiative, and we will draw the appropriate conclusions.

Now, let me give you the reasons for my decision.

A majority of the American people, a majority of you listening to me, are for the withdrawal of our forces from Viet-Nam. The action I have taken tonight is indispensible for the continuing success of that withdrawal program.

A majority of the American people want to end this war rather than to have it drag on interminably. The action I have taken tonight will serve that purpose.

A majority of the American people want to keep the

casualties of our brave men in Viet-Nam at an absolute minimum. The action I take tonight is essential if we are to accomplish that goal.

We take this action not for the purpose of expanding the war into Cambodia, but for the purpose of ending the war in Viet-Nam and winning the just peace we all desire. We have made and we will continue to make every possible effort to end this war through negotiation at the conference table rather than through more fighting on the battlefield. . . .

My fellow Americans, we live in an age of anarchy, both abroad and at home. We see mindless attacks on all the great institutions which have been created by free civilizations in the last 500 years. Even here in the United States, great universities are being systematically destroyed. Small nations all over the world find themselves under attack from within and from without.

If, when the chips are down, the world's most powerful nation, the United States of America, acts like a pitiful, helpless giant, the forces of totalitarianism and anarchy will threaten free nations and free institutions throughout the world.

It is not our power but our will and character that is being tested tonight. The question all Americans must ask and answer tonight is this: Does the richest and strongest nation in the history of the world have the character to meet a direct challenge by a group which rejects every effort to win a just peace, ignores our warning, tramples on solemn agreements, violates the neutrality of an unarmed people, and uses our prisoners as hostages?

If we fail to meet this challenge, all other nations will be on notice that despite its overwhelming power the United States, when a real crisis comes, will be found wanting.

During my campaign for the Presidency, I pledged to bring Americans home from Viet-Nam. They are coming home.

I promised to end this war. I shall keep that promise.

I promised to win a just peace. I shall keep that promise.

We shall avoid a wider war. But we are also determined to put an end to this war. . . .

Questions

1. How does Nixon seek to persuade Americans that the attack was not "an invasion of Cambodia"?
2. How does he try to persuade his listeners that he is avoiding a "wider war"?
3. What does Nixon mean by his reference to "the forces of totalitarianism and anarchy"?

29-12   Coming Home (1983)

Lynda Van Devanter

After graduating from nursing school, Lynda Van Devanter served a year as an army nurse in Vietnam, where she came to resent American policymakers and despise both "Saigon warriors" (Americans whose administrative duties largely kept them out of harm's way) and "lily-livered" South Vietnamese troops. Medical personnel like Van Devanter felt the pain and stress of treating and caring for the wounded—soldiers who were astonishingly young, some of whom died despite every effort, others of whom survived but were grievously maimed. Van Devanter's homecoming was difficult (see text pp. 968–969).

Source: Excerpted from Lynda Van Devanter, with Christopher Morgan, *Home before Morning: The Story of an Army Nurse in Vietnam* (New York: Beaufort Books, 1983), 209–212. Reprinted with permission.

When the soldiers of World War II came home, they were met by brass bands, ticker-tape parades, and people so thankful for their service that even those who had never heard a shot fired in anger were treated with respect. It was a time when words like honor, glory, and duty held some value, a time when a returning GI was viewed with esteem so high it bordered on awe. To be a veteran was to be seen as a person of courage, a champion of democracy, an ideal against which all citizens could measure themselves. If you had answered your country's call, you were a hero. And in those days, heroes were plentiful.

But somewhere between 1945 and 1970, words like bravery, sacrifice, and valor had gone out of vogue. . . . When I returned to my country in June of 1970, I began to learn a very bitter lesson. The values with which I had been raised had changed; in the eyes of most Americans, the military services had no more heroes, merely babykillers, misfits, and fools. I was certain that I was neither a babykiller nor a misfit. Maybe I was a fool. . . .

Perhaps if I hadn't expected anything at all when I returned to the States, I would not have been disappointed. Maybe I would have been contented simply to be on American soil. Maybe all of us who arrived at Travis Air Force Base on June 16 had unrealistic expectations.

But we didn't ask for a b[r]ass band. We didn't ask for a parade. We didn't even ask for much of a thank you. All we wanted was some transportation to San Francisco International Airport so we could hop connecting flights to get home to our families. We gave the Army a year of our lives, a year with more difficulties than most Americans face in fifty years. The least the Army could have done was to give us a ride.

At Travis we were herded onto buses and driven to the Oakland Army Terminal where they dumped us around 5 A.M. with a "so long, suckers" from the driver and a feeling that we were no more than warm bodies who had outlived their usefulness. Unfortunately, San Francisco International was at least twenty miles away. Since most of us had to get flights from there, wouldn't it have been logical to drop us at the airport? Or was I expecting too much out of the Army when I asked it to be logical?

I checked into commercial buses and taxis, but none were running. There was a transit strike on, and it was nearly impossible to get public transportation of any kind. So I hung one of my suitcases from my left shoulder, hefted my duffel bag onto my right shoulder, grabbed my overnight case with my left hand and my purse with my right, and struggling under the weight, walked out to the highway, where I stuck out my thumb and waited. I was no stranger to hitchhiking. It was the only way to get around in Vietnam. Back in 'Nam, I would usually stand on the flight line in my fatigues, combat boots, jungle hat, pigtails, and a smile. Getting a ride there was a cinch. In fact, planes would sometimes reach the end of the runway, then return to offer me a lift.

But hitchhiking in the real world, I was quickly find-ing out, was nowhere near as easy—especially if you were wearing a uniform. The cars whizzed past me during rush hour, while I patiently waited for a good Samaritan to stop. A few drivers gave me the finger. I tried to ignore them. Some slowed long enough to yell obscenities. One threw a carton of trash and another nearly hit me with a half-empty can of soda. Finally, two guys stopped in a red and yellow Volkswagen bus. The one on the passenger side opened his door. I ran to the car, dragging the duffel bag and other luggage behind me. I was hot, tired, and dirty.

"Going anywhere near the airport?" I asked.

"Sure am," the guy said. He had long brown hair, blue eyes framed by wire-rimmed glasses, and a full curly beard. There [were] patches on his jeans and a peace sign on his T-shirt. His relaxed, easy smile was deceptive.

I smiled back and lifted my duffel bag to put it inside the van. But the guy slammed the door shut. "We're going past the airport, sucker, but we don't take Army pigs." He spit on me. I was stunned. . . .

[The driver] floored the accelerator and they both laughed uncontrollably as the VW spun its wheels for a few seconds, throwing dirt and stones back at me before it roared away. The drivers of other passing cars also laughed.

I looked down at my chest. On top of my nametag sat a big glob of brownish-colored saliva. I couldn't touch it. I didn't have the energy to wipe it away. Instead, I watched as it ran down my name tag and over a button before it was absorbed into the green material of my uniform.

I wasn't angry, just confused. I wanted to know why. Why would he spit on me? What had I done to him? To either of them? It might have been simple to say I had gone to war and they blamed me for killing innocent people, but didn't they understand that I didn't want this war any more than the most vocal of peace marchers? Didn't they realize that those of us who had seen the war firsthand were probably more antiwar than they were? That we had seen friends suffer and die? That we had seen children destroyed? That we had seen futures crushed?

Were they that naive?

Or were they merely insensitive creeps who used the excuse of my uniform to vent their hostility toward all people?

I waited a few more hours, holding my thumb out until I thought my arm would fall off. After awhile, I stopped watching people as they hurled their insults. I had begun noticing the people who didn't scream as they drove by. I soon realized they all had something in common. It was what I eventually came to refer to as "the look." It was a combination of surprise at seeing a woman in uniform, and hatred for what they assumed I represented. Most of them never bothered to try to conceal it. "The look" would start around the eyes, as if they were peering right through me. Their faces would harden into stone. I was a pariah, a nonperson so low that they believed they could squash me underfoot. . . .

While I stood there alone, I almost wished I was back in 'Nam. At least there you expected some people to hate you. That was a war. But here, in the United States, I guess I wanted everything to be wonderful. I thought that life would be different, that there would be no more pain. No more death. No more sorrow. It was all going to be good again. It had to be good again. I had had enough of fighting, and hatred, and bitterness.

Around 10:30 A.M., when I had given up hope and was sitting on my duffel bag. . . . an old black man in a beat up '58 Chevy stopped and got out of his car. He walked with a limp and leaned forward as if he couldn't stand straight. His clothes were frayed and his face deeply lined. He ran his bony fingers through his gray-black hair, then shook his head and smiled. "I don't know where you're going, little girl," he said. "But I been by here four times since early morning and you ain't got a ride yet. I can't let you spend your whole life on this road." He was only headed for the other side of Oakland, but he said he'd rather go out of his way than see me stranded. He even carried my duffel bag to the trunk. As we drove south on 101, I didn't say much other than thank you, but my disillusionment was obvious.

"People ain't all bad, little girl," he said. "It's just some folks are crazy mixed up these days. You keep in mind that it's gotta get better, cause it can't get any worse."

Questions

1. Compare the different homecomings of veterans returning from World War II and Vietnam veterans coming home to "the world." How do you explain these differences?

2. Why is Van Devanter so surprised at the "welcome" she received? Why does she wish she was back in Vietnam rather than home?

3. The "old black man" who picks up Van Devanter assures her that things "can't get any worse." In fact, for many Vietnam veterans life got much worse after their return home. What kinds of problems did Vietnam veterans suffer after coming home?

29-13   A Mother Remembers Her Son at "The Wall" (1984)

Eleanor Wimbish

For some families who lost sons and daughters in Vietnam, the pain and suffering of the war continue to be part of daily life (see text pp. 968–969). They anguish over the loss of their loved ones and wonder why their nation did not mourn with them during the war. A few find comfort in the healing powers of the Vietnam Veterans Memorial, which commemorates all the men and women who served in Vietnam as well as the 58,000 who died during the war. In this letter from Eleanor Wimbish to her son Bill at "the Wall," a mother expresses both grief and love for her child who did not come home from the war. Bill's mother has sent him more than two dozen letters addressed to the Wall.

Source: Reprinted from *Dear America: Letters Home from Vietnam*, 299–300, edited by Bernard Edelman for the New York Vietnam Veterans Memorial Commission; published originally by W. W. Norton, 1985.

Dear Bill,

Today is February 13, 1984. I came to this black wall again to see and touch your name, and as I do I wonder if anyone ever stops to realize that next to your name, on this black wall, is your mother's heart. A heart broken 15 years ago today, when you lost your life in Vietnam.

And as I look at your name, William R. Stocks, I think of how many, many times I used to wonder how scared and homesick you must have been in that strange country called Vietnam. And if and how it might have changed you, for you were the most happy-go-lucky kid in the world, hardly ever sad or unhappy. And until the day I die,

I will see you as you laughed at me, even when I was very mad at you, and the next thing I knew, we were laughing together.

But on the past New Year's Day, I had my answer. I talked by phone to a friend of yours from Michigan, who spent your last Christmas and the last four months of your life with you. Jim told me how you died, for he was there and saw the helicopter crash. He told me how you had flown your quota and had not been scheduled to fly that day. How the regular pilot was unable to fly, and had been replaced by someone with less experience. How they did not know the exact cause of the crash. How it was either hit by enemy fire, or they hit a pole or something unknown. How the blades went through the chopper and hit you. How you lived about a half hour, but were unconscious and therefore did not suffer.

He said how your jobs were like sitting ducks. They would send you men out to draw the enemy into the open and *then* they would send in the big guns and planes to take over. Meantime, death came to so many of you.

He told me how, after a while over there, instead of a yellow streak, the men got a mean streak down their backs. Each day the streak got bigger and the men became meaner. Everyone but *you*, Bill. He said how you stayed the same, happy-go-lucky guy that you were when you arrived in Vietnam. How your warmth and friendliness drew the guys to you. How your [lieutenant] gave you the nickname of "Spanky," and soon your group, Jim included, were all known as "Spanky's gang." How when you died it made it so much harder on them for you were their moral support. And he said how you of all people should never have been the one to die.

Oh, God, how it hurts to write this. But I must face it and then put it to rest. I know that after Jim talked to me, he must have relived it all over again and suffered so. Before I hung up the phone I told Jim I loved him. Loved him for just being your close friend, and for sharing the last days of your life with you, and for being there with you when you died. How lucky you were to have him for a friend, and how lucky he was to have had you.

Later that same day I received a phone call from a mother in Billings, Montana. She had lost her daughter, her only child, a year ago. She needed someone to talk to for no one would let her talk about the tragedy. She said she had seen me on [television] on New Year's Eve, after the Christmas letter I wrote to you and left at this memorial had drawn newspaper and television attention. She said she had been thinking about me all day, and just had to talk to me. She talked to me of her pain, and seemingly needed me to help her with it. I cried with this heartbroken mother, and after I hung up the phone, I laid my head down and cried as hard for her. Here was a mother calling me for help with her pain over the loss of her child, a grown daughter. And as I sobbed I thought, how can I help her with her pain when I have never completely been able to cope with my own?

They tell me the letters I write to you and leave here at this memorial are waking others up to the fact that there is still much pain left, after all these years, from the Vietnam War.

But this I know, I would rather to have had you for 21 years, and all the pain that goes with losing you, than never to have had you at all.

Mom

Questions

1. In Vietnam there was great camaraderie between soldiers. How does this come home to Bill's mother?
2. How has Wimbish been able to help other parents who have lost children? What does she think of this new role?

Questions for Further Thought

1. Compare and contrast Richard Nixon's rationale for continuing American involvement in Vietnam (Documents 29-10 and 29-11) with Lyndon Johnson's rationale (Document 29-2).
2. Compare the experience and feelings of Lynda Van Devanter (Document 29-12) and Eleanor Wimbish (Document 29-13). How do you account for differences between them?
3. What are your thoughts regarding the Vietnam Veterans Memorial? (If you have visited the memorial, how did the experience affect you?)

CHAPTER 30

The Lean Years, 1969–1980

★   ★   ★

The Nixon Years

The years of Richard Nixon's presidency, 1969–1974, were eventful abroad and at home and painful, too, climaxed as they were by the first presidential resignation in the nation's history. Nixon involved himself deeply in foreign policy, which had been central to presidencies since Franklin Roosevelt's. Assisted by adviser Henry Kissinger, he sought Vietnamization of the war in Southeast Asia, which reduced American casualties there and anti-war protests at home, and the easing of tensions (détente) with Soviet Russia and Communist China, including seeking their assistance in ending the war in Southeast Asia on acceptable terms. He also thought in terms of allies, such as Iran, playing larger regional policing roles (the Nixon Doctrine). All the while, he was willing to intensify the aerial war in Southeast Asia and to invade Cambodia to achieve the peace he sought.

Domestic policy did not engage President Nixon in quite the same way as foreign policy, but this is not to say that he was disengaged. Nixon sought to scale down Great Society antipoverty programs and compiled a mixed record regarding race. However, he also offered a welfare program of his own, the Family Assistance Plan, and supported, or at least accepted, entitlement and regulatory policies that enlarged, rather than reduced, the role of the federal government (see text pp. 964–968, 976–977).

Richard Nixon and Spiro Agnew, who had won a narrow popular vote victory in 1968, were reelected in a landslide four years later. During 1973, however, Agnew was compelled to resign over kickbacks he had received while governor of Maryland and vice-president. The next year Nixon resigned to avoid impeachment and conviction for offenses so serious that a substantial minority of Republicans on the Judiciary Committee of the House of Representatives had joined Democrats in support of three articles of impeachment after the release, ordered by the Supreme Court, of incriminating audiotapes. Neither Gerald Ford, who succeeded first Agnew and then Nixon, nor Nelson Rockefeller, whom President Ford selected as his vice-president, had been popularly elected to national office (see text pp. 978–981).

Document 30-1 provides a position paper on African Americans sent to President Nixon by Daniel Patrick Moynihan, a domestic policy adviser. Document 30-2 offers portions of transcripts of secretly taped presidential conversations during the Watergate affair.

30-1   Memorandum on Benign Neglect (1970)

Daniel Patrick Moynihan

As a member of the Johnson administration, Daniel Patrick Moynihan (b. 1927) had prepared a memorandum that informed President Johnson's address at Howard University (Document 28-16). As a domestic policy adviser in the Nixon administration, he once again returned to the subject of African Americans in this memorandum to President Nixon (see text pp. 976–977).

Source: Daniel Patrick Moynihan, "Memorandum for the President" (1970). In "Text of the Moynihan Memorandum on the Status of Negroes," *New York Times,* March 1, 1970.

As the new year begins, it occurs to me that you might find useful a general assessment of the position of Negroes at the end of the first year of your Administration, and of the decade in which their position has been the central domestic political issue.

In quantitative terms, which are reliable, the American Negro is making extraordinary progress. In political terms, somewhat less reliable, this would also appear to be true. In each case, however, there would seem to be countercurrents that pose a serious threat to the welfare of the blacks and the stability of the society, white and black.

1. Employment and Income

The nineteen-sixties saw the great breakthrough for blacks. A third (32 per cent) of all families of Negro and other races earned $8,000 or more in 1968 compared, in constant dollars, with 15 per cent in 1960.

The South is still a problem. Slightly more than half (52 per cent) of the Negro population lived in the South in 1969. There, only 19 per cent of families of Negro and other races earned over $8,000.

Young Negro families are achieving income parity with young white families. Outside the South, young husband-wife Negro families have 99 per cent of the income of whites! For families headed by a male age 25 to 34 the proportion was 87 per cent. Thus, it may be this ancient gap is finally closing.

Income reflects employment, and this changed dramatically in the nineteen-sixties. Blacks continued to have twice the unemployment rates of whites, but these were down for both groups. In 1969, the rate for married men of Negro and other races was only 2.5 per cent. Teen-

agers, on the other hand, continued their appalling rates: 24.4 per cent in 1969.

Black occupations improved dramatically. The number of professional and technical employees doubled in the period 1960-68. This was two and a half times the increase for whites. In 1969, Negro and other races provided 10 per cent of the other-than-college teachers. This is roughly their proportion of the population (11 per cent).

2. Education

In 1968, 19 per cent of Negro children 3 and 4 years old were enrolled in school, compared to 15 per cent of white children. Forty-five per cent of Negroes 18 and 19 years old were in school, almost the equal of the white proportion of 51 per cent. Negro college enrollment rose 85 per cent between 1964 and 1968, by which time there were 434,000 Negro college students. (The total full-time university population of Great Britain is 200,000.)

Educational achievement should not be exaggerated. Only 16 per cent of Negro high school seniors have verbal test scores at or above grade level. But blacks are staying in school.

3. Female-Headed Families

This problem does not get better, it gets worse. In 1969, the proportion of husband-wife families of Negro and other races declined once again, this time to 68.7 per cent. The illegitimacy ratio rose once again, this time to 29.4 per cent of all live births. (The white ratio rose more sharply, but was still only 4.9 per cent.)

Increasingly, the problem of Negro poverty is the problem of the female-headed family. In 1968, 56 per cent of Negro families with income under $3,000 were female-headed. In 1968, for the first time, the number of poor Negro children in female-headed families (2,241,000) was greater than the number in male-headed families (1,947,000).

4. Social Pathology

The incidence of antisocial behavior among young black males continues to be extraordinarily high. Apart from white racial attitudes, this is the biggest problem black Americans face, and in part it helps shape white racial attitudes. Black Americans injure one another. Because blacks live in de facto segregated neighborhoods and go to de facto segregated schools, the socially stable elements of the black population cannot escape the socially pathological ones. Routinely, their children get caught up in the antisocial patterns of the others.

You are familiar with the problem of crime. Let me draw your attention to another phenomenon, exactly parallel, and originating in exactly the same social circumstances: Fire. Unless I mistake the trends, we are heading for a genuinely serious fire problem in American cities. . . .

Many of these fires are the result of population density. But a great many are more or less deliberately set. (Thus, on Monday, welfare protestors set two fires in the New York State Capitol.) Fires are in fact a "leading indicator" of social pathology for a neighborhood. They come first. Crime, and the rest, follows. The psychiatric interpretation of fire-setting is complex, but it relates to the types of personalities which slums produce. (A point of possible interest: Fires in the black slums peak in July and August. The urban riots of 1964–1968 could be thought of as epidemic conditions of an endemic situation.)

5. Social Alienation

With no real evidence, I would nonetheless suggest that a great deal of the crime, the fire-setting, the rampant school violence and other such phenomenon in the black community have become quasi-politicized. Hatred—revenge—against whites is now an acceptable excuse for doing what might have been done anyway. This is bad news for any society, especially when it takes forms which the Black Panthers seem to have adopted.

This social alienation among the black lower classes is matched and probably enhanced, by a virulent form of anti-white feeling among portions of the large and prosperous black middle class. It would be difficult to overestimate the degree to which young, well-educated blacks detest white America.

6. The Nixon Administration

As you have candidly acknowledged, the relation of the Administration to the black population is a problem. I think it ought also to be acknowledged that we are a long way from solving it. During the past year, intense efforts have been made by the Administration to develop programs that will be of help to the blacks. I dare say, as much or more time and attention goes into this effort in this Administration than any in history. But little has come of it. There has been a great deal of political ineptness in some departments, and you have been the loser.

I don't know what you can do about this. Perhaps nothing. But I do have four suggestions.

First. Sometime early in the year, I would gather together the Administration officials who are most involved with these matters and talk out the subject a bit. There really is a need for a more coherent Administration approach to a number of issues. (Which I can list for you, if you like.)

Second. The time may have come when the issue of race could benefit from a period of "benign neglect." The subject has been too much talked about. The forum has been too much taken over to hysterics, paranoids and boodlers on all sides. We may need a period in which Negro progress continues and racial rhetoric fades. The Administration can help bring this about by paying close attention to such progress—as we are doing—while seeking to avoid situations in which extremists of either race are given opportunities for martyrdom, heroics, histrionics or whatever. Greater attention to Indians, Mexican-Americans and Puerto Ricans would be useful. A tendency to ignore provocations from groups such as the Black Panthers might also be useful. (The Panthers were apparently almost defunct until the Chicago police raided one of their headquarters and transformed them into culture heroes for the white—and black—middle class. You perhaps did not note on the society page of yesterday's Times that Mrs. Leonard Bernstein gave a cocktail party on Wednesday to raise money for the Panthers. Mrs. W. Vincent Astor was among the guests. Mrs. Peter Duchin, "the rich blonde wife of the orchestra leader," was thrilled. "I've never met a Panther," she said. "This is a first for me.")

Third. We really ought to be getting on with research on crime. We just don't know enough. It is a year now since the Administration came to office committed to doing something about crime in the streets. But frankly, in that year I don't see that we have advanced either our understanding of the problem, or that of the public at large. (This of course may only reveal my ignorance of what is going on.)

At the risk of indiscretion, may I put it that lawyers are not professionally well-equipped to do much to prevent crime. Lawyers are not managers, and they are not researchers. The logistics, the ecology, the strategy and tactics of reducing the incidence of certain types of behavior in large urban populations simply are not things lawyers think about often.

We are never going to "learn" about crime in a laboratory sense. But we almost certainly could profit from limited, carefully done studies. I don't think these will be done unless you express a personal interest.

Fourth. There is a silent black majority as well as a white one. It is mostly working class, as against lower middle class. It is politically moderate (on issues other than racial equality) and shares most of the concerns of its white counterpart. This group has been generally ignored by the Government and the media. The more recognition we can give to it, the better off we shall all be. (I would take it, for example, that Ambassador [Jerome H.] Holland is a natural leader of this segment of the black community. There are others like him.)

Questions

1. What advances for African Americans does Moynihan cite? What problems continue, in his view?
2. What is Moynihan's view of race relations?
3. Moynihan's memorandum generated controversy. Why? What does he mean by "benign neglect"? How might critics read the phrase?

30-2   Watergate: Taped White House Conversations (1972)

Watergate, a "third-rate burglary attempt" that became a national crisis, ultimately forced Richard Nixon to resign the presidency to avoid certain impeachment and conviction (and possible criminal charges). It also resulted in criminal convictions of several of the president's advisers and in the enactment of a number of reforms (see text pp. 978–981).

Secretly taped White House conversations between President Nixon and various associates proved to be central to the exposure of Watergate. Two important conversations are excerpted here, the first involving H. R. Haldeman, the president's chief of staff, the second John Dean, White House counsel. Among those referred to but not fully identified in the following passages were John Mitchell, a former attorney general who headed the Committee to Re-elect the President; Maurice Stans, finance chair of the committee; John Ehrlichman, domestic affairs assistant to the president; and E. Howard Hunt and G. Gordon Liddy, former operatives of the Central Intelligence Agency, who were security consultants to the Nixon White House.

Source: White House transcripts of conversations between H. R. Haldeman and Richard Nixon in the Oval Office of the President, June 23, 1972; and between John Dean and Richard Nixon, September 15, 1972. U.S. Congress, House, *Hearings before the Committee on the Judiciary,* 93rd Congress, 2nd session, 1974.

JUNE 23, 1972

HALDEMAN: Now, on the investigation, you know the Democratic break-in thing, we're back in the problem area because the FBI is not under control, because [Director Patrick] Gray doesn't exactly know how to control it and they have—their investigation is now leading into some productive areas. . . . They've been able to trace the money—not through the money itself—but through the bank sources—the banker. And it goes in some directions we don't want it to go. Ah, also there have been some [other] things—like an informant came in off the street to the FBI in Miami who was a photographer or has a friend who is a photographer who developed some films through this guy [Bernard] Barker and the films had pictures of Democratic National Committee letterhead documents and things. So it's things like that are filtering in. . . . [John] Mitchell came up with yesterday, and John Dean analyzed very carefully last night and concludes, concurs now with Mitchell's recommendation that the only way to solve this . . . is for us to have [CIA Assistant Director Vernon] Walters call Pat Gray and just say, "Stay to hell out of this—this is ah, [our] business here. We don't want you to go any further on it." That's not an unusual development, and ah, that would take care of it.

PRESIDENT: What about Pat Gray—you mean Pat Gray doesn't want to?

HALDEMAN: Pat does want to. He doesn't know how to, and he doesn't have any basis for doing it. Given this, he will then have the basis. He'll call [FBI Assistant Director] Mark Felt in, and the two of them—and Mark Felt wants to cooperate because he's ambitious—

PRESIDENT: Yeah.

HALDEMAN: He'll call him in and say, "We've got the signal from across the river to put the hold on this." And that will fit rather well because the FBI agents who are working the case, at this point, feel that's what it is.

PRESIDENT: This is CIA? They've traced the money? Who'd they trace it to? . . .

HALDEMAN: Ken Dahlberg.

PRESIDENT: Who the hell is Ken Dahlberg?

HALDEMAN: He gave $25,000 in Minnesota and, ah, the check went directly to this guy Barker.

PRESIDENT: It isn't from the Committee though, from [Maurice] Stans?

HALDEMAN: Yeah. It is. It's directly traceable and there's some more through some Texas people that went to the Mexican bank which can also be traced to the Mexican bank—they'll get their names today.

PRESIDENT: Well, I mean, there's no way—I'm just thinking if they don't cooperate, what do they say? That they were approached by the Cubans? That's what Dahlberg has to say, the Texans too.

HALDEMAN: Well, if they will. But then we're relying on more and more people all the time. That's the problem and they'll [the FBI] . . . stop if we could take this other route.

PRESIDENT: All right.

HALDEMAN: [Mitchell and Dean] say the only way to do that is from White House instructions. And it's got to be to [CIA Director Richard] Helms and to—ah, what's his name? . . . Walters. . . . And the proposal would be that . . . [John] Ehrlichman and I call them in, and say, ah—

PRESIDENT: All right, fine. How do you call him in—I mean you just—well, we protected Helms from one hell of a lot of things.

HALDEMAN: That's what Ehrlichman says.

PRESIDENT: Of course; this [Howard] Hunt [business.] That will uncover a lot of things. You open that scab there's a hell of a lot of things and we just feel that it would be very detrimental to have this thing go any further. This involves these Cubans, Hunt, and a lot of hanky-panky that we have nothing to do with ourselves. Well, what the hell, did Mitchell know about this?

HALDEMAN: I think so. I don't think he knew the details, but I think he knew.

PRESIDENT: He didn't know how it was going to be handled though—with Dahlberg and the Texans and so

forth? Well who was the asshole that did? Is it [G. Gordon] Liddy? Is that the fellow? He must be a little nuts!

HALDEMAN: He is.

PRESIDENT: I mean he just isn't well screwed on, is he? Is that the problem?

HALDEMAN: No, but he was under pressure, apparently, to get more information, and as he got more pressure, he pushed the people harder.

PRESIDENT: Pressure from Mitchell?

HALDEMAN: Apparently. . . .

PRESIDENT: All right, fine, I understand it all. We won't second-guess Mitchell and the rest. Thank God it wasn't [special White House counsel Charles] Colson.

HALDEMAN: The FBI interviewed Colson yesterday. They determined that would be a good thing to do. To have him take an interrogation, which he did, and the FBI guys working the case concluded that there were one or two possibilities—one, that this was a White House (they don't think that there is anything at the Election Committee) they think it was either a White House operation and they had some obscure reasons for it—non-political, or it was a—Cuban [operation] and [involved] the CIA. And after the interrogation of Colson yesterday, they concluded it was not the White House, but are now convinced it is a CIA thing, so the CIA turnoff would—

PRESIDENT: Well, not sure of their analysis, I'm not going to get that involved. I'm (unintelligible).

HALDEMAN: No, sir, we don't want you to.

PRESIDENT: You call them in.

HALDEMAN: Good deal.

PRESIDENT: Play it tough. That's the way they play it and that's the way we are going to play it. . . .

PRESIDENT: O.K. . . . Just say (unintelligible) very bad to have this fellow Hunt, ah, he knows too damned much. . . . If it gets out that this is all involved, the Cuba thing, it would be a fiasco. It would make the CIA look bad, it's going to make Hunt look bad, and it is likely to blow the whole Bay of Pigs thing which we think would be very unfortunate—both for CIA, and for the country, at this time, and for American foreign policy. Just tell him to lay off. Don't you [think] so?

HALDEMAN: Yep. That's the basis to do it on. Just leave it at that. . . .

SEPTEMBER 15, 1972

PRESIDENT: We are all in it together. This is a war. We take a few shots and it will be over. We will give them a few shots and it will be over. Don't worry. I wouldn't want to be on the other side right now. Would you?

DEAN: Along that line, one of the things I've tried to do, I have begun to keep notes on a lot of people who are emerging as less than our friends because this will be over some day and we shouldn't forget the way some of them have treated us.

PRESIDENT: I want the most comprehensive notes on

all those who tried to do us in. They didn't have to do it. If we had had a very close election and they were playing the other side I would understand this. No—they were doing this quite deliberately and they are asking for it and they are going to get it. We have not used the power in this first four years, as you know. . . . We have not used the Bureau, and we have not used the Justice Department, but things are going to change now. And they are either going to do it right or go.

DEAN: What an exciting prospect.

PRESIDENT: Thanks. It has to be done. We have been (adjective deleted) fools for us to come into this election campaign, and not do anything with regard to the Democratic Senators who are running, et cetera. And who the hell are they after? They are after us. It is absolutely ridiculous. It is not going to be that way any more.

Questions

1. According to these transcripts, how much did President Nixon know about the financial and security operations of his reelection campaign?
2. According to the transcripts, what did Nixon know on June 23, 1972, about the Watergate break-in and related matters? What evidence do the transcripts provide that Nixon ordered the CIA and the FBI to participate in the cover-up?
3. Do the transcripts reveal other matters that Nixon might not have wished to have made public or that might have affected public respect for government?

Questions for Further Thought

1. Compare and contrast President Johnson's Howard University Address (Document 28-16), to which Daniel Patrick Moynihan contributed, and Moynihan's memorandum to President Nixon (Document 30-1).
2. Does the recent impeachment and acquittal of President Bill Clinton affect your thinking about Watergate and the resignation of President Nixon? Does your understanding of the earlier crisis affect your understanding of the recent crisis?

The Economic Downturn

The national economy, which had flourished since the war years of the 1940s, began to reveal problems during the late 1960s. These intensified during the following decade to produce "stagflation," inflation *and* unemployment (see text p. 984). Many interacting factors contributed to the worsening economic situation. During the Johnson presidency, escalating expenditures on the war in Vietnam, combined with spending on domestic programs (from the space race to the Great Society), fueled budget deficits. IN 1971, the nation experienced its first trade deficit of the century, and international confidence in the dollar waned. President Nixon twice devalued the dollar to spur American exports and imposed temporary wage-price controls. Long accustomed to cheap energy but increasingly dependent on imported petroleum, the United States proved to be vulnerable to an oil embargo (1973–1974) and to price increases imposed by the Organization of Petroleum Exporting Countries (OPEC). The impact on economic developments was profound: overall economic growth slowed; workers' real income began to decline; "deindustrialization," the downsizing or closing of manufacturing plants and the laying off of workers, affected the nation's industrial heartland (the Northeast and Midwest); and optimism began to give way to pessimism (see text pp. 981–985).

Non-economic issues remained significant during the 1970s and beyond, of course, but the period cannot be understood without reference to America's changed economic fortunes. (See text pp. 981–985, including Figures 30-1 and 30-2; also Figures 26-1, 28-1, 28-5, 31-1, and 31-2; also Appendix A-10.) Document 30-3 provides periodic Gallup poll findings for 1950 to 1999. Document 30-4 reports on Homestead, Pennsylvania, and its residents during the deindustrialization of the 1970s and 1980s.

30-3   National Problems, 1950–1999

Gallup Polls

Polls reveal respondents' thinking at particular points in time. A series of such polls sheds light on change and continuity in public opinion, albeit not annually in this case. The nationwide Gallup polls reported here asked interviewees, "What do you think is the most important problem facing the country today?"

Source: Gallup polls reported in the *New York Times,* August 1, 1999. Copyright © 1999 by The New York Times Company. Reprinted by permission.

Questions

1. What most strikes you about the 1975 Gallup poll responses? How do you explain the differences between the 1970 and 1975 poll responses?
2. What most strikes you about the 1980 Gallup poll responses? How do you explain the differences between 1975 and 1980?

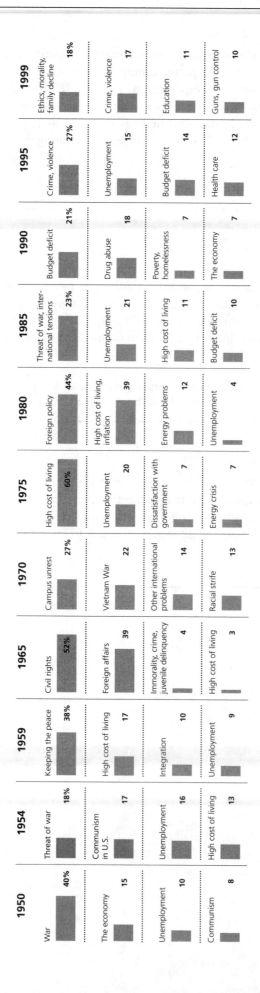

30-4   Homestead (1970s)

William Serrin

Homestead, Pennsylvania, was an industrial community dependent on the production of steel. It had been the scene of one of the most famous labor-management confrontations of the late nineteenth century (see text p. 569). The deindustrialization of the 1970s, which continued during the following decade, profoundly affected Homestead, its economic base, and its people (see text pp. 984–985). William Serrin left the *New York Times* to write about this story.

Source: William Serrin, *Homestead: The Glory and Tragedy of an American Steel Town* (New York: Times Books, 1992), 392–398. Copyright © 1992 by William Serrin. Reprinted by permission of Times Books, a Division of Random House, Inc.

Eighth Avenue continued to run down, and now the once-bustling street was a tatterdemalion thoroughfare made up of the few old stores that were hanging on and the Goodwill, Salvation Army, and Saint Vincent de Paul thrift shops. One of Chief Kelly's last fights had been to attempt to persuade the managers of the thrift shops to stop putting their collections of junk—worn-out toys, skates, sleds, books, kitchenware, clothes, shoes—on the sidewalk. He was not successful. But there was little market for such items. In the end, even Goodwill closed, and the windows were boarded up with plywood.

The borough building, constructed in 1909, the place where Mother Jones had been jailed and Frances Perkins had been refused permission by Burgess Cavanaugh to speak in Frick Park, was also closed. The building had not been maintained and was getting run-down. One day Chief Kelly was going down to the basement. A rotten step gave way, and he fell and wrenched his ankle. He was on crutches for several days. A half-dozen people who worked there came down with cancer, and it was thought that the building contained some carcinogen—asbestos perhaps—although this was never proven. Council meetings were moved to the old high school. The fire department was moved to a garage across the street, and the police department was moved into the old post office, which the country [sic] remodeled for the borough in exchange for the borough's agreeing to house a number of work-release prisoners in the building.

In June 1990, Saint Mary Magdalene's School closed. It was the last Roman Catholic school in Homestead. In the fall, it would have begun its one hundredth year. The students knew that they would miss their school enormously. "Everybody cares about you," Jackie Piskor said. "If you have a problem, you can go to any of the teachers, and they will help you, or to your friends, and they will help you." The students, even at their young age, knew that hard times had fastened on Homestead. They could not go across the street to play in Frick Park because they feared they would be bullied. There were often drugs being sold there, they said. Even Saint Mary Magdalene's Roman Catholic Church was locked, day and night.

Most of the students were enrolling in public schools. They said that they would especially miss their prayers. "How many times a day do you pray?" I asked. They counted the prayers, some using their fingers. "Seven," they said. The last day, the children came for half a day, and there was much crying in the halls and on the asphalt playground. A second-grade teacher, Nancy Stanich, tearfully embraced her students. Dave Lasos, a seventh grader, sat disconsolately in the hall, his head buried in his arms. Sister Marie Margaret, the principal, said "We have met our Waterloo."

The town government continued to face enormous problems. The borough's deficit increased from $30,000 in 1989 to $300,000 in 1990, and the population continued to fall. It was 4,179 in the 1990 census, down 17.9 percent from 5,092 in 1980. In 1988, the corporation sold the Homestead Works to the Park Corporation for $14 million—$2.5 million for the land and $11.5 million for the equipment and machinery. Soon, demolition crews arrived, and one by one the old mills came down. For a time, Mayor Simko continued to believe that the Valley Machine Shop would be purchased from Park and reopened, but the letter of intent that he had been expecting the day we had toured the works had not come through. The investors said that reopening the mill would not be feasible, in view of the depressed condition of the steel industry.

In 1990, Allegheny County reduced the assessed value of the mill site from $30 million to $14 million. In November, Homestead, Munhall, West Homestead, and the Steel Valley School District reached an agreement with Park to reduce the assessed value of the site from $14 million to $9.5 million. The agreement entitled Park to a refund on 1989 real estate taxes of $67,000 from the boroughs and $45,500 from the school district, which Park agreed to apply to future tax bills.

The town had become a place for small-time speculators. Wayne Laux, a man whom almost no one in Homestead knew anything about, began to buy buildings near the mill site—including the one that had housed Rufus "Sonnyman" Jackson's Skyrocket Lounge and Manhattan

Music Club—and then sold them to Park. Many were de-molished. Half a century after the demolition that had pre-ceded the wartime expansion of the works, lower Home-stead was again being razed.

The corporation and the union continued the missteps that had helped to bring about their downfall. In June 1990, the corporation agreed to pay $34 million in costs and penalties for the cleanup of waste water that had been illegally dumped into the Calumet River, in Indiana, by its Gary plant. In September 1990, a federal district court judge in Birmingham, Alabama, fined the corporation $4.1 million and gave prison terms to two union officials, Ther-mon Phillips and E. B. Rich, found guilty of conspiring with the corporation to obtain lucrative pensions for them-selves in exchange for agreeing to concessions during con-tract negotiations in December 1983. This was the agree-ment that the corporation had used to persuade local unions across the country to grant similar concessions. In December 1990, the corporation agreed to pay a $3.2 mil-lion fine levied by the Occupational Safety and Health Ad-ministration for hundreds of violations the administration said had occurred at its Pennsylvania plants.

The corporation's interest in steel continued to shrink. In early 1991, its steel operations became an independent subsidiary. In May, its stock was split into two—one for energy, one for steel—and the steel stock was dropped from the Dow Jones Industrial Average and replaced by the stock of the Walt Disney Company.

By this time, the national union's membership had dropped to 490,000, one-third of the 1.4 million who had belonged in 1979. In 1991, a plan to organize white-collar workers was announced, and a woman organizer with substantial experience in the field was hired. But the effort failed.

The local union meetings continued until the summer of 1987, and the union hall remained open after that to assist laid-off workers. No dues had come in from Homestead since the mill had been closed, and the national union had been helping the local with its bills. But the bad blood be-tween the national union leaders and Weisen had contin-ued, and finally the union saw an opportunity to close the hall. In December, Weisen had gone to the Soviet Union with his wife and their son Bobby for an operation on the broken vertebra in Bobby's neck. A drive to raise money for the trip had been started by Weisen's old supporters, but everyone wanted Bobby to get well, and Lynn Williams, the new president of the national union, stopped by the Weisens' home to give them a thousand dollars.

In February 1988, while Weisen was still in the Soviet Union, the national union ordered the Homestead union hall closed. Mike Stout, the grievance man, was furious, and to keep him quiet the union reluctantly allowed him to set up a local headquarters in an empty, ramshackle orange building, once a restaurant, on McClure Street, at the top of the hill. He put a sign on the door of the old hall

that said: "The international has shut our union hall down and moved us to a storefront on the corner of Sev-enteenth Street and McClure Street (orange building). We should have the same number, but if you have any prob-lems with TRA or SUB [Training and Relocation Allow-ance and Supplemental Unemployment Benefits], call me at home."

The orange building was run-down and hot and stuffy. There was no longer much spirit among the men who sat there in front of fans at desks trucked up from the old union hall. The place smelled like old hamburgers and french fries. Occasionally, unemployed workers came by for assistance, but soon they stopped coming. Not even Weisen came by much anymore. He was unemployed, like most others, and was looking for work. In November 1988 the orange building was closed. There had been eight union lodges in Homestead at the time of the 1892 strike. An Amalgamated Association lodge, the Spirit of Ninety-two, had been established in Homestead with the passage of the National Industrial Recovery Act, in June 1933. The steelworkers' union had had a local in Homestead since 1936, for more than half a century. Now there was no union in Homestead.

Most of the men who lost their jobs when the mill went down accepted their fate and settled in, living on part-time work or on pensions. Many had trouble sleeping and find-ing things to do with the time on their hands. They dropped children or grandchildren off at school, helped around the house, worked on the lawn. After a time, their wives and children got used to having them around. Some-times the men drove down by the works and watched the demolition crews taking it down. The men would have re-unions at one of the firehouses or social clubs, but those were not much fun. One by one they stopped going, and soon no one planned reunions anymore.

"I still think about that damn place," Bob Krovocheck said. He had worked in the mill for thirty-eight years and was fifty-six years old when he lost his job. His highest pay was twenty-seven thousand dollars in 1985. He tried working as a janitor for four dollars an hour, but he was overweight and had bad knees, and the work was too de-manding, so he had to quit. His wife had been seriously in-jured in an automobile accident on the Pennsylvania Turn-pike in 1981, and he spent much of his time taking care of her. They lived on his pension of $1,100 a month, $876 after taxes and medical deductions.

Krovocheck missed the mill enormously. "I dream about it every once in a while," he said. "I miss going to work, being around the guys, the eight-hour turn, the rou-tine. I miss the money, too. It was a good living. I wasn't living from payday to payday. It's funny. I remember that every once in a while one of us in the mill would say, 'Let's get our pension and get out of here.' But pensioneering ain't all that great, especially if you've got somebody sick you're taking care of."

"During the day, I take care of the wife, get the meals, keep the house halfway decent. It ain't like she would keep it. I do the cooking and laundry. I read quite a bit. I go up the street and have a couple of beers. I go to the store and get the groceries. I come home and make supper. I watch TV. I go to bed. I get rather depressed, especially when I drive up past where we worked, the structural mill. I'm okay, if you want to call me okay."

Richard Holoman, a craneman, had worked in the mill for thirty-two years and was fifty-one when he lost his job. His highest pay was $22,500 a year. After the mill went down, he had a job as a security guard for three months and worked for a short time cleaning an industrial garage, three and a half hours a night, for fourteen dollars a night. Then he got a job as a janitor at Saint Agnes's Roman Catholic Church, in West Mifflin. He changed light bulbs, mopped floors, cut the grass, fixed the sisters' car. It wasn't bad, as work goes. He could set his own hours, but mostly he worked 6:00 A.M. to 2:00 P.M., five days a week—good hours for an old steelworker, steady daylight.

Denny Wilcox, a roller, got a part-time job as a bank courier, twenty-five hours a week at $6.10 an hour. He received a pension of $1,100 a month. "We're not living high off the hog, but we're making it," he said. "It's hard. You start looking down on yourself. You'd think, if you put on an application that you have thirty five years of service, an employer would know that you are dedicated. You'd think they'd grab you in a minute. But they discriminate against you because of age. They all do. I think that's why I'm not full-time now, because they discriminate because of age. They know I get a pension."

Ray McGuire, a repairman, had worked in the mill for thirty-six years and had taken only two sick days. He got a pension of $1,000 a month and caught on as an electrician, going from one shop to another, wherever he was needed. Sometimes a temporary agency found him work, or else he would hear of something himself. He worked for a while at the machine company that now occupied part of the old Mesta Machine plant. One day he had to go to the Homestead Works to pick up some tools. "I went to the exact place where I worked, and I got so nauseated I thought I was going to throw up," he said. "I thought: 'I worked here. What are you people doing to this place? What are you doing to my cranes?' And then I thought: 'Wait a minute. This wasn't my place. These weren't my cranes.' But that's the way I thought—that it was my place." He lived in Pleasant Hills, not far from Homestead, but he no longer went to Homestead at night. He was afraid of crime there, and besides, he got despondent when he went to Homestead, even when he just drove through the town. "The place looks like a morgue," he said.

Bob Todd, a craneman and grievance man, was unemployed for a year. Then he was called to the Edgar Thomson Works, where he got a job as a safety man in the slab mill, making seventeen thousand dollars a year. It was not as much as he had been making at Homestead, but it was a job. About two hundred Homestead workers were given jobs there, and another few dozen were hired by the Irvin Works.

Bill Brennan, a millwright, had worked in the mill for thirty-nine years and was sixty-four when he retired on his pension of $775 a month after deductions. He also got Social Security, and his house was paid for. His father had worked at the Homestead Works, and so had his three brothers. In 1984, when he had a heart-bypass operation, he was on sickleave for six months. His heart was now okay, though he had to take three pills a day. When he went back into the mill after his bypass, the other millwrights carried him, hid him out, for six months—they did the heavy work that he had done and did not tell the supervisors. He would pick up a sledgehammer or a big crescent wrench, and the others would take it from him and tell him to go somewhere, get lost, and they would do the job. "I miss guys like that, good working people," he said.

Bobby Schneider, a roller, got a part-time job tending bar at the Slovak Club in Munhall. He had worked in the mill for thirty-one years and had earned $35,000 in his best year. The bartender's job wasn't much, though it got him out of the house and gave him something to do. He lived on a pension check of $1,077 a month after deductions. His wife worked as a secretary in a real-estate company. His section of the last beam rolled at the Homestead Works was still in the trunk of his car, four years after the mill went down. He had intended to shine it up and put it in the house, but he never got around to it. His two pals, Red Hrabic and Jimmie Sherlock, both lived on pensions of about $900 a month and were doing okay. The three of them met at Hess's Bar in Hunkie Hollow almost every afternoon at about four, or maybe at the Slovak Club, in Munhall, if Schneider was tending bar there.

There was much crying in Homestead. Men and women often went to wakes and funerals, for there were many deaths among the men from the works. I knew or heard of three dozen men who died or committed suicide. That's a lot of men gone, and at an early age, too. I think that many of them died because the mill closed, though I can't prove it. But it's a lot of dead guys, isn't it?

There was one man I never got out of my mind—Rich Locher, the hooker from Number Two Structural who had denounced the government's retraining programs at the meeting with the two men in the pinstripe suits from Senator Heinz's staff. I had planned to meet with Locher, but time passed, and I was busy. One winter day, preparing for a trip to Homestead, I wrote down his telephone number, thinking I would go see him. When I got to Homestead, I ran into Mike Stout, the former grievance man. When I told him that I was going to call Locher, he said: "Don't bother. Locher is dead. He finished the retraining program but couldn't get a nursing job, so he took a gun and killed himself—shot half his head away, in his garage." Stout continued with his paperwork and did not look up. One more death was not much to him. He knew too many stories like this.

I liked Locher. He was a good man. He had a temper and often used profane language, but don't many of us? He was an excellent father and husband, and he probably deserved more out of life than to take two brief vacations at hot trailer parks in Virginia and go out to eat once a month at McDonald's or Long John Silver's, to lose his job as a craneman and not get a job as a nurse. One more thing. Locher was right about the training programs. They were bullshit.

Questions

1. How does the plant's closing affect community institutions?
2. Why does the mill exert such a strong influence on its former workers?
3. What program is supposed to help unemployed steelworkers get back into the economy? Why is Serrin so critical of it?

Questions for Further Thought

1. Reflecting on the 1950s and 1960s, what most strikes you about the Gallup polls of 1950 to 1970?
2. How do the polls of 1985 to 1999 compare and contrast with those of 1950 to 1970 and 1975 to 1980?
3. After reviewing the text description of the Homestead strike of 1892 (p. 569) and reflecting on the text discussion of deindustrialization (pp. 984–985) and Document 30-4, compare and contrast the two chapters in the history of Homestead, its industry, and its people.

Reform and Reaction in the 1970s

Reform often triggers reaction: just as the civil rights movement of the 1950s and 1960s generated opposition even as it mobilized support, so did social movements of the 1960s and 1970s. Diverse groups contested a broad range of issues during the period—and beyond. Controversies raged within communities and in political arenas from local to national. The courts, legislative bodies, executive departments and agencies, and the electorate (in referenda)—all were involved. The environmental and consumer movements met with significant successes, including federal laws enacted during the Nixon administration. Race-related issues, especially affirmative action and school busing, were fought out in the courts and, in the case of busing, in communities, most bitterly in Boston. The gay liberation movement and its foes fought over local measures, attacking discrimination on the basis of sexual orientation. Among the most public debates were those between feminists and anti-feminists over the proposed Equal Rights Amendment (ERA) to the U.S. Constitution and over abortion rights, especially after the 7-2 decision of the Supreme Court in *Roe v. Wade* (1973), which declared women's constitutional right to abortions (see text pp. 985–987).

On these issues, see, in addition to the text, *Instructor's Resource Manual,* vol. 2, *Since 1865,* 4th ed., Document 14, D100–101, Equal Rights Amendments (1923, 1950, 1953, 1972); Document 11, D102, Title VII of the Civil Rights Act of 1964; and Document 9, D212–215, Reproductive Rights: *Roe v. Wade* (1973). See also text, D-22, Equal Rights Amendment (1972).

Document 30-5 provides Gloria Steinem's testimony in support of the ERA; Documents 30-6 is an excerpt from Phyllis Schlafly's anti-feminist *Power of the Positive Woman*. Document 30-7 offers relevant planks from the national political party platforms of the period.

30-5   Statement in Support of the Equal Rights Amendment (1970)

Gloria Steinem

Gloria Steinem (b. 1934), a graduate of Smith College, became a journalist, gaining a measure of fame for an exposé based on her experiences as an undercover reporter posing as a Playboy Bunny. She edited *Ms.,* the most successful mass-circulation feminist publication, (see text pp. 987, 990), which made her a major figure in the feminist movement. Even before this, however, she was prominent enough to testify before a Senate subcommittee on behalf of the ERA. Mentioned in her essay are Friedrich Engels (1820–1895), a German Socialist and a collaborator of Karl Marx, and Gunnar Myrdal (1898–1987), the Swedish author of the classic *An American Dilemma: The Negro Problem and American Democracy* (1944). Myrdal was also the co-winner of the Nobel Prize for Economics in 1974.

Source: The "Equal Rights" Amendment: Hearings before the Subcommittee on Constitutional Amendments of the Committee on the Judiciary, United States Senate, Ninety-First Congress, Second Session, on S. J. Res. 61, To Amend the Constitution so as to Provide Equal Rights for Men and Women, May 5, 6, and 7, 1970 (Washington D.C.: U.S. Government Printing Office, 1970), 331–335 (May 6, 1970).

During 12 years of working for a living, I have experienced much of the legal and social discrimination reserved for women in this country. I have been refused service in public restaurants, ordered out of public gathering places, and turned away from apartment rentals; all for the clearly-stated, sole reason that I am a woman. And all without the legal remedies available to blacks and other minorities. I have been excluded from professional groups, writing assignments on so-called "unfeminine" subjects such as politics, full participation in the Democratic Party, jury duty, and even from such small male privileges as discounts on airline fares. Most important to me, I have been denied a society in which women are encouraged, or even allowed to think of themselves as first-class citizens and responsible human beings.

However, after 2 years of researching the status of American women, I have discovered that in reality, I am very, very lucky. Most women, both wage-earners and housewives, routinely suffer more humiliation and injustice than I do.

As a freelance writer, I don't work in the male-dominated hierarchy of an office. (Women, like blacks and other visibly different minorities, do better in individual professions such as the arts, sports, or domestic work; anything in which they don't have authority over white males.) I am not one of the millions of women who must support a family. Therefore, I haven't had to go on welfare because there are no day-care centers for my children while I work, and I haven't had to submit to the humiliating welfare inquiries about my private and sexual life, inquiries from which men are exempt. I haven't had to brave the sex bias of labor unions and employers, only to see my family subsist on a median salary 40 percent less than the male median salary.

I hope this committee will hear the personal, daily injustices suffered by many women—professionals and day laborers, women house-bound by welfare as well as by suburbia. We have all been silent for too long. But we won't be silent anymore.

The truth is that all our problems stem from the same sex based myths. We may appear before you as white radicals or the middle-aged middle class or black soul sisters, but we are all sisters in fighting against these outdated myths. Like racial myths, they have been reflected in our laws. Let me list a few.

That women are biologically inferior to men. In fact, an equally good case can be made for the reverse. Women live longer than men, even when the men are not subject to business pressures. Women survived Nazi concentration camps better, keep cooler heads in emergencies currently studied by disaster-researchers, are protected against heart attacks by their female sex hormones, and are so much more durable at every stage of life that nature must conceive 20 to 50 percent more males in order to keep the balance going.

Man's hunting activities are forever being pointed to as tribal proof of superiority. But while he was hunting, women built houses, tilled the fields, developed animal husbandry, and perfected language. Men, being all alone in the bush, often developed into a creature as strong as women, fleeter of foot, but not very bright.

However, I don't want to prove the superiority of one sex to another. That would only be repeating a male mistake. English scientists once definitively proved, after all, that the English were descended from the angels, while the Irish were descended from the apes; it was the rationale for England's domination of Ireland for more than a century. The point is that science is used to support current myth and economics almost as much as the church was.

What we do know is that the difference between two races or two sexes is much smaller than the differences to be found within each group. Therefore, in spite of the slide show on female inferiorities that I understand was shown to you yesterday, the law makes much more sense when it treats individuals, not groups bundled together by some condition of birth. . . .

Another myth, that women are already treated equally in this society. I am sure there has been ample testimony to prove that equal pay for equal work, equal chance for advancement, and equal training or encouragement is obscenely scarce in every field, even those—like food and fashion industries—that are supposedly "feminine."

A deeper result of social and legal injustice, however, is what sociologists refer to as "Internalized Aggression." Victims of aggression absorb the myth of their own inferiority, and come to believe that their group is in fact second class. Even when they themselves realize they are not second class, they may still think their group is, thus the tendency to be the only Jew in the club, the only black woman on the block, the only woman in the office.

Women suffer this second class treatment from the moment they are born. They are expected to be, rather than achieve, to function biologically rather than learn. A brother, whatever his intellect, is more likely to get the family's encouragement and education money, while girls are often pressured to conceal ambition and intelligence, to "Uncle Tom."

I interviewed a New York public school teacher who told me about a black teenager's desire to be a doctor. With all the barriers in mind, she suggested kindly that he be a veterinarian instead.

The same day, a high school teacher mentioned a girl who wanted to be a doctor. The teacher said, "How about a nurse?"

Teachers, parents, and the Supreme Court may exude a protective, well-meaning rationale, but limiting the individual's ambition is doing no one a favor. Certainly not this country; it needs all the talent it can get.

Another myth, that American women hold great economic power. Fifty-one percent of all shareholders in this country are women. That is a favorite male-chauvinist statistic. However, the number of shares they hold is so small that the total is only 18 percent of all the shares. Even those holdings are often controlled by men.

Similarly, only 5 percent of all the people in the country who receive $10,000 a year or more, earned or otherwise, are women. And that includes the famous rich widows.

The constantly repeated myth of our economic power seems less testimony to our real power than to the resentment of what little power we do have.

Another myth, that children must have full-time mothers. American mothers spend more time with their homes and children than those of any other society we know about. In the past, joint families, servants, a prevalent system in which grandparents raised the children, or family field work in the agrarian systems—all these factors contributed more to child care than the labor-saving devices of which we are so proud.

The truth is that most American children seem to be suffering from too much mother, and too little father. Part of the program of Women's Liberation is a return of fathers to their children. If laws permit women equal work and pay opportunities, men will then be relieved of their role as sole breadwinner. Fewer ulcers, fewer hours of meaningless work, equal responsibility for his own children: these are a few of the reasons that Women's Liberation is Men's Liberation too.

As for psychic health of the children, studies show that the quality of time spent by parents is more important than the quantity. The most damaged children were not those whose mothers worked, but those whose mothers preferred to work but stayed home out of the role-playing desire to be a "good mother."

Another myth, that the women's movement is not political, won't last, or is somehow not "serious."

When black people leave their 19th century roles, they are feared. When women dare to leave theirs, they are ridiculed. We understand this; we accept the burden of ridicule. It won't keep us quiet anymore.

Similarly, it shouldn't deceive male observers into thinking that this is somehow a joke. We are 51 percent of the population; we are essentially united on these issues across boundaries of class or race or age; and we may well end by changing this society more than the civil rights movement. That is an apt parallel. We, too, have our right wing and left wing, our separatists, gradualists, and Uncle Toms. But we are changing our own consciousness, and that of the country. Engels noted the relationship of the authoritarian, nuclear family to capitalism; the father as capitalist, the mother as means of production, and the children as labor. He said the family would change as the economic system did, and that seems to have happened, whether we want to admit it or not.

Women's bodies will no longer be owned by the state for the production of workers and soldiers; birth control and abortion are facts of everyday life. The new family is an egalitarian family.

Gunnar Myrdal noted 30 years ago the parallel between women and Negroes in this country. Both suffered from such restricting social myths as: smaller brains, passive natures, inability to govern themselves (and certainly not white men), sex objects only, childlike natures, special skills, and the like. When evaluating a general statement about women, it might be valuable to substitute "black people" for "women"—just to test the prejudice at work.

And it might be valuable to do this constitutionally as well. Neither group is going to be content as a cheap labor pool anymore. And neither is going to be content without full constitutional rights.

Finally, I would like to say one thing about this time in which I am testifying.

I had deep misgivings about discussing this topic when National Guardsmen are occupying our campuses, the country is being turned against itself in a terrible polarization, and America is enlarging an already inhuman and unjustifiable war. But it seems to me that much of the trouble in this country has to do with the "masculine mystique;" with the myth that masculinity somehow depends on the subjugation of other people. It is a bipartisan problem; both our past and current Presidents seem to be victims of this myth, and to behave accordingly.

Women are not more moral than men. We are only uncorrupted by power. But we do not want to imitate men, to join this country as it is, and I think our very participation will change it. Perhaps women elected leaders—and there will be many of them—will not be so likely to dominate black people or yellow people or men; anybody who looks different from us.

After all, we won't have our masculinity to prove.

Questions

1. What comparisons does Steinem make between women and African Americans?
2. What arguments involving the family does Steinem indicate were used by ERA opponents? What is Steinem's response to those arguments?
3. According to Steinem, in what ways are women different from men? Why is this significant?

30-6   The Power of the Positive Woman (1977)

Phyllis Schlafly

Phyllis Schlafly (b. 1924) worked her way (at night, in a wartime munitions factory) through Washington University, earned an M.A. at Radcliffe College, married, and raised six children. Involved in the Republican Party for some years, she contributed a polemical book, *A Choice, Not an Echo*, to Barry Goldwater's drive for nomination in 1964. She regained prominence in the 1970s when she founded the National Committee to Stop ERA and played an important part in defeating the amendment (while simultaneously earning her J. D. from Washington University). An excerpt from her antifeminist book of this period follows (see text pp. 990–992).

Source: Phyllis Schlafly, *The Power of the Positive Woman* (New Rochelle, N.Y.: Arlington House, 1977), 16–19. Reprinted by permission of Phyllis Schlafly.

The women's liberationists and their dupes who try to tell each other that the sexual drive of men and women is really the same, and that it is only societal restraints that inhibit women from an equal desire, an equal enjoyment, and an equal freedom from the consequences, are doomed to frustration forever. It just isn't so, and pretending cannot make it so. The differences are not a woman's weakness but her strength. . . .

The new generation can brag all it wants about the new liberation or the new morality, but it is still the woman who is hurt the most. The new morality isn't just a "fad"—it is a cheat and a thief. It robs the woman of her virtue, her youth, her beauty, and her love—for nothing, just nothing. It has produced a generation of young women searching for their identity, bored with sexual freedom, and despondent from the loneliness of living a life without commitment. They have abandoned the old commandments, but they can't find any new rules that work.

The Positive Woman recognizes the fact that, when it comes to sex, women are simply not the equal of men. The sexual drive of men is much stronger than that of women. That is how the human race was designed in order that it might perpetuate itself. The other side of the coin is that it is easier for women to control their sexual appetites. A Positive Woman cannot defeat a man in a wrestling or boxing match, but she can motivate him, inspire him, encourage him, teach him, restrain him, reward him, and have power over him that he can never achieve over her with all his muscle. How or whether a Positive Woman uses her power is determined solely by the way she alone defines her goals and develops her skills.

The differences between men and women are also emotional and psychological. Without woman's innate maternal instinct, the human race would have died out centuries ago. There is nothing so helpless in all earthly life as the newborn infant. It will die within hours if not cared for. Even in the most primitive, uneducated societies, women have always cared for their newborn babies. They didn't need any schooling to teach them how. They didn't need any welfare workers to tell them it is their social obligation. Even in societies to whom such concepts as "ought," "social responsibility," and "compassion for the helpless" were unknown, mothers cared for their new babies.

Why? Because caring for a baby serves the natural maternal need of a woman. Although not nearly so total as the baby's need, the woman's need is nonetheless real.

The overriding psychological need of a woman is to love something alive. A baby fulfills this need in the lives of most women. If a baby is not available to fill that need, women search for a baby-substitute. This is the reason why women have traditionally gone into teaching and nursing careers. They are doing what comes naturally to the female psyche. The schoolchild or the patient of any age provides an outlet for a woman to express her natural maternal need.

This maternal need in women is the reason why mothers whose children have grown up and flown from the nest are sometimes cut loose from their psychological moorings. The maternal need in women can show itself in love for grandchildren, nieces, nephews, or even neighbors' children. The maternal need in some women has even manifested itself in an extraordinary affection lavished on a dog, cat, or a parakeet.

This is not to say that every woman must have a baby in order to be fulfilled. But it is to say that fulfillment for most women involves expressing their natural maternal urge by loving and caring for someone.

The women's liberation movement complains that traditional stereotyped roles assume that women are "passive" and that men are "aggressive." The anomaly is that a woman's most fundamental emotional need is not passive at all, but active. A woman naturally seeks to love affirmatively and to show that love in an active way by caring for the object of her affections.

The Positive Woman finds somebody on whom she can lavish her maternal love so that it doesn't well up inside her and cause psychological frustrations. Surely no woman is so isolated by geography or insulated by spirit that she cannot find someone worthy of her maternal love. All persons, men and women, gain by sharing something of themselves with their fellow humans, but women profit most of all because it is part of their very nature. . . .

Most women's organizations, recognizing the preference of most women to avoid hard-driving competition, handle the matter of succession of officers by the device of a nominating committee. This eliminates the unpleasantness and the tension of a competitive confrontation every year or two. Many women's organizations customarily use a prayer attributed to Mary, Queen of Scots, which is an excellent analysis by a woman of women's faults:

Keep us, O God, from pettiness; let us be large in thought, in word, in deed. Let us be done with faultfinding and leave off self-seeking. . . . Grant that we may realize it is the little things that create differences, that in the big things of life we are at one. . . .

Finally, women are different from men in dealing with the fundamentals of life itself. Men are philosophers, women are practical and 'twas ever thus. Men may philosophize about how life began and where we are heading; women are concerned about feeding the kids today. No woman would ever, as Karl Marx did, spend years reading political philosophy in the British Museum while her child starved to death. Women don't take naturally to a search for the intangible and the abstract. The Positive Woman knows who she is and where she is going, and she will reach her goal because the longest journey starts with a very practical first step.

Questions

1. Why does Schlafly refer to psychology in three instances?
2. How does Schlafly compare to reformers such as Frances Willard (Document 18-7) and Jane Addams (Document 20-5)?
3. Does Schlafly see men and women as true equals? Why or why not?

30-7   Democratic and Republican National Platform Planks on the Equal Rights Amendment and Abortion (1976, 1980)

As seen earlier, conflicts over social and other issues often find expression in the national platforms of political parties. The following planks were included in the Democratic and Republican platforms of 1976 and 1980 (see text pp. 987–1001).

Sources: Donald Bruce Johnson, comp., *National Party Platforms,* rev. ed., 2 vols. (Urbana: University of Illinois Press, 1978), vol. 2, *1960–1976,* 925–926, 976; Donald Bruce Johnson, comp., *National Party Platforms of 1980: Supplement to National Party Platforms, 1840–1976* (Urbana: University of Illinois Press, 1982), 60, 62, 181, 183.

DEMOCRATIC PARTY (1976)

Civil and Political Rights

To achieve a just and healthy society and enhance respect and trust in our institutions, we must insure that all citizens are treated equally before the law and given the opportunity, regardless of race, color, sex, religion, age, language or national origin, to participate fully in the economic, social and political processes and to vindicate their legal and constitutional rights.

In reaffirmation of this principle, an historic commitment of the Democratic Party, we pledge vigorous federal programs and policies of compensatory opportunity to remedy for many Americans the generations of injustice and deprivation; and full funding of programs to secure the implementation and enforcement of civil rights.

We seek ratification of the Equal Rights Amendment, to insure that sex discrimination in all its forms will be ended, implementation of Title IX and elimination of discrimination against women in all federal programs. . . .

We fully recognize the religious and ethical nature of the concerns which many Americans have on the subject of abortion. We feel, however, that it is undesirable to attempt to amend the U.S. Constitution to overturn the Supreme Court decision in this area. . . .

REPUBLICAN PARTY (1976)

Equal Rights and Ending Discrimination

Women

Women, who comprise a numerical majority of the population, have been denied a just portion of our nation's rights and opportunities. We reaffirm our pledge to work to eliminate discrimination in all areas for reasons of race, color, national origin, age, creed or sex and to enforce vigorously laws guaranteeing women equal rights.

The Republican Party reaffirms its support for ratification of the Equal Rights Amendment. Our Party was the first national party to endorse the E.R.A. in 1940. We continue to believe its ratification is essential to insure equal rights for all Americans. In our 1972 Platform, the Repub-

lican Party recognized the great contributions women have made to society as homemakers and mothers, as contributors to the community through volunteer work, and as members of the labor force in careers. The Platform stated then, and repeats now, that the Republican Party "fully endorses the principle of equal rights, equal opportunities and equal responsibilities for women." The Equal Rights Amendment is the embodiment of this principle and therefore we support its ratification.

The question of abortion is one of the most difficult and controversial of our time. It is undoubtedly a moral and personal issue but it also involves complex questions relating to medical science and criminal justice. There are those in our Party who favor complete support for the Supreme Court decision which permits abortion on demand. There are others who share sincere convictions that the Supreme Court's decision must be changed by a constitutional amendment prohibiting all abortions. Others have yet to take a position, or they have assumed a stance somewhere in between polar positions.

We protest the Supreme Court's intrusion into the family structure through its denial of the parents' obligation and right to guide their minor children. The Republican Party favors a continuance of the public dialogue on abortion and supports the efforts of those who seek enactment of a constitutional amendment to restore protection of the right to life for unborn children. . . .

DEMOCRATIC PARTY (1980)

Ensuring Basic Rights and Liberties

Equal Rights Amendment

The Democratic Party recognizes that every issue of importance to this nation and its future concerns women as well as men. As workers and consumers, as parents and heads of households, women are vitally concerned with the economy, energy, foreign policy, and every other issue addressed in this platform. The concerns of women cannot be limited to a portion of the platform; they must be reflected in every section of our Party's policy.

There is, however, a particular concern of women which deserves special emphasis—their entitlement to full equality in our society.

Women are a majority of the population. Yet their equality is not recognized in the Constitution or enforced as the law of the land. The choices faced by women—such as whether to seek employment or work at home, what career or profession to enter, and how to combine employment and family responsibilities—continue to be circumscribed by stereotypes and prejudices. Minority women face the dual discrimination of racism and sexism.

In the 1980s, the Democratic Party commits itself to a Constitution, economy, and society open to women on an equal basis with men.

The primary route to that new horizon is ratification of the Equal Rights Amendment. A Democratic Congress, working with women's leaders, labor, civil and religious organizations, first enacted ERA in Congress and later extended the deadline for ratification. Now, the Democratic Party must ensure that ERA at last becomes the 27th Amendment to the Constitution. We oppose efforts to rescind ERA in states which have already ratified the amendment, and we shall insist that past rescissions are invalid.

In view of the high priority which the Democratic Party places on ratification of the ERA, the Democratic National Committee renews its commitment not to hold national or multi-state meetings, conferences, or conventions in states which have not yet ratified the ERA. The Democratic Party shall withhold financial support and technical campaign assistance from candidates who do not support the ERA. The Democratic Party further urges all national organizations to support the boycott of the unratified states by not holding national meetings, conferences, or conventions in those states. . . .

The Democratic Party recognizes reproductive freedom as a fundamental human right. We therefore oppose government interference in the reproductive decisions of Americans, especially those government programs or legislative restrictions that deny poor Americans their right to privacy by funding or advocating one or a limited number of reproductive choices only.

Specifically, the Democratic Party opposes involuntary or uninformed sterilization for women and men, and opposes restrictions on funding for health services for the poor that deny poor women especially the right to exercise a constitutionally-guaranteed right to privacy. . . .

REPUBLICAN PARTY (1980)

Women's Rights

We acknowledge the legitimate efforts of those who support or oppose ratification of the Equal Rights Amendment.

We reaffirm our Party's historic commitment to equal rights and equality for women.

We support equal rights and equal opportunities for women, without taking away traditional rights of women such as exemption from the military draft. We support the enforcement of all equal opportunity laws and urge the elimination of discrimination against women. We oppose any move which would give the federal government more power over families.

Ratification of the Equal Rights Amendment is now in the hands of state legislatures, and the issues of the time extension and rescission are in the courts. The states have a constitutional right to accept or reject a constitutional amendment without federal interference or pressure. At the direction of the White House, federal departments launched pressure against states which refused to ratify ERA. Regardless of one's position on ERA, we demand that this practice cease. . . .

Abortion

There can be no doubt that the question of abortion, despite the complex nature of its various issues, is ultimately concerned with equality of rights under the law. While we recognize differing views on this question among Americans in general—and in our own Party—we affirm our support of a constitutional amendment to restore protection of the right to life for unborn children. We also support the Congressional efforts to restrict the use of taxpayers' dollars for abortion.

We protest the Supreme Court's intrusion into the family structure through its denial of the parents' obligation and right to guide their minor children. . . .

Questions

1. Compare and contrast the 1976 Democratic and Republican national platform planks dealing with the Equal Rights Amendment (ERA) and abortion. Compare and contrast the parties' 1980 platforms regarding the same issues.

2. How did the 1980 platform planks of each party echo those of four years earlier? How did they strike different notes?

3. How do you account for change and continuity, between 1976 and 1980, in the opposing parties' positions relative to the ERA and abortion?

Questions for Further Thought

1. How do you account for the emergence during the 1960s and 1970s of controversies over issues relating to women?
2. How do Documents 30-5, 30-6, and 30-7 fit into an overview of these controversies?
3. Compare and contrast geographic patterns of support for and opposition to woman suffrage with support for and opposition to the Equal Rights Amendment. (See text p. 650, Map 20-1, and p. 991, Map 30-1.)

From Ford to Reagan

The presidencies of Gerald Ford and Jimmy Carter were embattled. President Ford beat off the challenge of Ronald Reagan for his party's nomination in 1976 but lost to Carter in that year's general election. Although Carter received 50 percent of the popular vote (the only Democrat from 1968 through 1996 to do so), he failed to be reelected four years later, losing to Ronald Reagan. The mood of the electorate also revealed itself in reduced voter turnout rates, from a mean of 62 percent during the 1960s to a mean of 54 percent from 1972 to 1980. The nationwide enfranchisement of eighteen-year-olds in 1972 contributed to the sharp decline that year—young adults typically have low turnout rate—but long-term trends were also at work: the turnout rate declined in every presidential election from 1964 through 1988.

President Ford labored under heavy burdens. Undistinguished as a long-time congressman, he had not been elected to national office. Having pardoned Richard Nixon shortly after becoming president, he soon faced Democratic congressional majorities swollen in the 1974 elections held in the wake of Nixon's resignation and pardon. Economic problems, already discussed, beset the nation, whose chief executive was widely liked, but not necessarily respected.

President Carter likewise struggled in office. A former governor of Georgia, Carter had no national political experience. Being an outsider may have stood him in good stead as a post-Watergate presidential candidate, but it handicapped him as president. Carter did score successes in both diplomacy (brokering the Camp David Accords between Israel and Egypt and securing, at political cost to himself, the Panama Canal Treaties) and domestic policy (beginning the deregulation of industries). However, he failed to articulate a politically persuasive vision of America's future as the United States struggled with stagflation, the energy crisis, and the humiliating hostage crisis in Iran.

It would fall to Ronald Reagan to formulate a vision of America. Reagan, a former governor of California and a presidential aspirant since 1968, was a better actor than Carter. He would also prove to be a more successful president.

Document 30-8 provides a key section from an address by President Carter during July 1979, and Document 30-9 excerpts Reagan's acceptance speech at the Republican National Convention one year later.

30-8   The National Crisis of Confidence (1979)

Jimmy Carter

During the first half of 1979, various indicators pointed to economic problems for the United States—including spiraling inflation and unemployment and, as a consequence, political problems for the Carter administration. Unpleasant shocks added to widespread uneasiness. In March, an accident at the nuclear power station at Three Mile Island, Pennsylvania, reminded Americans that atomic energy carried serious risks. An energy crisis originating overseas brought gasoline shortages and higher prices, angering many, especially motorists in long lines at service stations (see text pp. 987, 998).

President Carter (b. 1924), who during April had proposed to Congress measures to deal with future energy needs, planned to address the nation regarding energy at the beginning of July. Instead, he retired to the Camp David presidential retreat, where for several days he consulted with public and private figures about problems confronting the nation. Carter then spoke to the nation on July 15. His address, "Energy and National Goals," dealt not only with America's energy crisis, but also with its "crisis of confidence." For Carter, worse was still to come, of course, in Iran and Afghanistan (see text pp. 999–1000).

Source: Public Papers of the Presidents of the United States: Jimmy Carter, 1979, Book 2, June 23 to December 31, 1979 (Washington D.C.: U.S. Government Printing Office, 1980), 1236–1241.

. . . I want to speak to you first tonight about a subject even more serious than energy or inflation. I want to talk to you right now about a fundamental threat to American democracy.

I do not mean our political and civil liberties. They will endure. And I do not refer to the outward strength of America, a nation that is at peace tonight everywhere in the world, with unmatched economic power and military might.

The threat is nearly invisible in ordinary ways. It is a crisis of confidence. It is a crisis that strikes at the very heart and soul and spirit of our national will. We can see this crisis in the growing doubt about the meaning of our own lives and in the loss of a unity of purpose of our Nation.

The erosion of our confidence in the future is threatening to destroy the social and the political fabric of America.

The confidence that we have always had as a people is not simply some romantic dream or a proverb in a dusty book that we read just on the Fourth of July. It is the idea which founded our Nation and has guided our development as a people. Confidence in the future has supported everything else—public institutions and private enterprise, our own families, and the very Constitution of the United States. Confidence has defined our course and has served as a link between generations. We've always believed in something called progress. We've always had a faith that the days of our children would be better than our own.

Our people are losing that faith, not only in government itself but in the ability as citizens to serve as the ultimate rulers and shapers of our democracy. As a people we know our past and we are proud of it. Our progress has been part of the living history of America, even the world. We always believed that we were part of a great movement of humanity itself called democracy, involved in the search for freedom, and that belief has always strengthened us in our purpose. But just as we are losing our confidence in the future, we are also beginning to close the door on our past.

In a nation that was proud of hard work, strong families, close-knit communities, and our faith in God, too many of us now tend to worship self-indulgence and consumption. Human identity is no longer defined by what one does, but by what one owns. But we've discovered that owning things and consuming things does not satisfy our longing for meaning. We've learned that piling up material goods cannot fill the emptiness of lives which have no confidence or purpose.

The symptoms of this crisis of the American spirit are all around us. For the first time in the history of our country a majority of our people believe that the next 5 years will be worse than the past 5 years. Two-thirds of our people do not even vote. The productivity of American workers is actually dropping, and the willingness of Americans to save for the future has fallen below that of all other people in the Western world.

As you know, there is a growing disrespect for government and for churches and for schools, the news media, and other institutions. This is not a message of happiness or reassurance, but it is the truth and it is a warning.

These changes did not happen overnight. They've come upon us gradually over the last generation, years that were filled with shock and tragedy. We were sure that ours was a nation of the ballot not of the bullet, until the murders of John Kennedy and Robert Kennedy and Martin Luther King, Jr. We were taught that our armies were always invincible and our causes were always just only to suffer the agony of Vietnam. We respected the presidency as a place of honor until the shock of Watergate. . . .

Energy will be the immediate test of our ability to unite this Nation, and it can also be the standard around which we rally. On the battlefield of energy we can win for our Nation a new confidence, and we can seize control again of our common destiny.

In little more than two decades we've gone from a position of energy independence to one in which almost half the oil we use comes from foreign countries, at prices that are going through the roof. Our excessive dependence on OPEC has already taken a tremendous toll on our economy and our people. This is the direct cause of the long lines which have made millions of you spend aggravating hours waiting for gasoline. It's a cause of the increased inflation and unemployment that we now face. This intolerable dependence on foreign oil threatens our economic independence and the very security of our Nation.

The energy crisis is real. It is worldwide. It is a clear and present danger to our Nation. These are facts and we simply must face them. . . .

In closing, let me say this: I will do my best, but I will not do it alone. Let your voice be heard. Whenever you have a chance, say something good about our country. With God's help and for the sake of our Nation, it is time for us to join hands in America. Let us commit ourselves together to a rebirth of the American spirit. Working together with our common faith we cannot fail. . . .

Questions

1. What evidence does Carter offer to support his argument that the American people are experiencing a "crisis of confidence"?

2. In his view, why is the crisis of confidence a much deeper problem than the shortage of energy, inflation, and the recession?

3. What does Carter propose to do to resolve the crisis of confidence? How do you think the American people—and American voters—responded to this speech?

30-9   Acceptance Speech, Republican National Convention (1980)

Ronald Reagan

Ronald Reagan (b. 1911), once a liberal Democratic supporter of Franklin Roosevelt and Harry Truman, moved into the conservative Republican camp during the 1950s. His support of Barry Goldwater in 1964 contributed to his own nomination for governor of California two years later. Elected, he won a second term in 1970. Twice unsuccessful in bids for the Republican presidential nomination (1968, 1976), Reagan triumphed in 1980 and went on to trounce Jimmy Carter in the election (see text pp. 1000–1001).

Source: Excerpted with the express permission of the Republican National Committee from Ronald Reagan, Acceptance Address, Republican National Convention, Detroit, Michigan, July 17, 1980, in *Vital Speeches of the Day*, vol. 46 (August 15, 1980), 642–646.

. . . This convention has shown to all America a party united, with positive programs for solving the nation's problems; a party ready to build a new consensus with all those across the land who share a community of values embodied in these words: family, work, neighborhood, peace and freedom.

Now I know we've had a quarrel or two but only as to the method of attaining a goal. There was no argument here about the goal. As President, I will establish a liaison with the 50 Governors to encourage them to eliminate, wherever it exists, discrimination against women. I will monitor Federal laws to insure their implementation and to add statutes if they are needed.

More than anything else, I want my candidacy to unify our country; to renew the American spirit and sense of purpose. I want to carry our message to every American, regardless of party affiliation, who is a member of this community of shared values.

Never before in our history have Americans been called upon to face three grave threats to our very existence, any one of which could destroy us. We face a disintegrating economy, a weakened defense and an energy policy based on the sharing of scarcity.

The major issue of this campaign is the direct political, personal, and moral responsibility of Democratic Party leadership—in the White House and in the Congress—for this unprecedented calamity which has befallen us. They tell us they've done the most that humanly could be done. They say that the United States has had its day in the sun, that our nation has passed its zenith. They expect you to tell your children that the American people no longer have the will to cope with their problems; that the future will be one of sacrifice and few opportunities.

My fellow citizens, I utterly reject that view. The American people, the most generous on earth, who created the highest standard of living, are not going to accept the notion that we can only make a better world for others by moving backward ourselves. And those who believe we can have no business leading this nation. . . .

Isn't it once again time to renew our compact of freedom; to pledge to each other all that is best in our lives; all that gives meaning to them—for the sake of this, our beloved and blessed land?

Together, let us make this a new beginning. Let us make a commitment to care for the needy; to teach our children the virtues handed down to us by our families; to have the courage to defend those values and virtues and the willingness to sacrifice for them.

Let us pledge to restore, in our time, the American spirit of voluntary service, of cooperation, of private and community initiative; a spirit that flows like a deep and mighty river through the history of our nation.

As your nominee, I pledge to you to restore to the Federal Government the capacity to do the people's work without dominating their lives. I pledge to you a Government that will not only work well but wisely, its ability to act tempered by prudence, and its willingness to do good balanced by the knowledge that government is never more dangerous than when our desire to have it help us blinds us to its great power to harm us. . . .

The head of a Government which has utterly refused to live within its means and which has, in the last few days, told us that this coming year's deficit will be $60 billion, dares to point the finger of blame at business and labor, both of which have been engaged in a losing struggle just trying to stay even.

High taxes, we are told, are somehow good for us, as if, when government spends our money it isn't inflationary, but when we spend it, it is.

Those who preside over the worst energy shortage in our history tell us to use less, so that we will run out of oil, gasoline and natural gas a little more slowly. Well, now,

conservation is desirable, of course. We must not waste energy. But conservation is not the sole answer to our energy needs.

America must get to work producing more energy. The Republican program for solving economic problems is based on growth and productivity.

Large amounts of oil and natural gas lay beneath our land and off our shores, untouched because the present Administration seems to believe the American people would rather see more regulation, more taxes and more controls than more energy.

Coal offers a great potential. So does nuclear energy produced under rigorous safety standards. It could supply electricity for thousands of industries and millions of jobs and homes. It must not be thwarted by a tiny minority opposed to economic growth which often finds friendly ears in regulatory agencies for its obstructionist campaigns.

Now make no mistake. We will not permit the safety of our people or our environmental heritage to be jeopardized, but we are going to reaffirm that the economic prosperity of our people is a fundamental part of our environment. . . .

It is essential that we maintain both the forward momentum of economic growth and the strength of the safety net between those in our society who need help. We also believe it is essential that the integrity of all aspects of Social Security be preserved.

Beyond these essentials, I believe it is clear our Federal Government is overgrown and overweight. Indeed, it is time our Government should go on a diet. Therefore, my first act as chief executive will be to impose an immediate and thorough freeze on Federal hiring. Then, we are going to enlist the very best minds from business, labor and whatever quarter to conduct a detailed review of every department, bureau and agency that lives by Federal appropriation. . . .

Our instructions to the groups we enlist will be simple and direct. We will remind them that Government programs exist at the sufferance of the American taxpayer and are paid for with money earned by working men and women and programs that represent a waste of their money—a theft from their pocketbooks—must have that waste eliminated or that program must go. . . .

Everything that can be run more effectively by state and local government we shall turn over to state and local government, along with the funding sources to pay for it. We are going to put an end to the money merry-go-round where our money becomes Washington's money, to be spent by states and cities exactly the way the Federal bureaucrats tell us it has to be spent.

I will not accept the excuse that the Federal Government has grown so big and powerful that it is beyond the control of any President, any administration or Congress. We are going to put an end to the notion that the American taxpayer exists to fund the Federal Government. The Federal Government exists to serve the American people and to be accountable to the American people. On January 20, we are going to reestablish that truth.

Also on that date we are going to initiate action to get substantial relief for our taxpaying citizens and action to put people back to work. None of this will be based on any new form of monetary tinkering or fiscal sleight-of-hand. We will simply apply to government the common sense that we all use in our daily lives.

Work and family are at the center of our lives, the foundation of our dignity as a free people. When we deprive people of what they have earned, or take away their jobs, we destroy their dignity and undermine their families. We can't support families unless there are jobs; and we can't have jobs unless the people have both money to invest and the faith to invest it. . . .

The American people are carrying the heaviest peacetime tax burden in our nation's history—and it will grow even heavier, under present law, next January. We are taxing ourselves into economic exhaustion and stagnation, crushing our ability and incentive to save, invest and produce.

This must stop. We must halt this fiscal self-destruction and restore sanity to our economic system.

I've long advocated a 30 percent reduction in income tax rates over a period of three years. This phased tax reduction would begin with a 10 percent "down payment" tax cut in 1981, which the Republicans in Congress and I have already proposed.

A phased reduction of tax rates would go a long way toward easing the heavy burden on the American people. But we shouldn't stop there. . . .

For those without skills, we'll find a way to help them get new skills.

For those without job opportunities we'll stimulate new opportunities, particularly in the inner cities where they live.

For those who've abandoned hope, we'll restore hope and we'll welcome them into a great national crusade to make America great again.

When we move from domestic affairs, and cast our eyes abroad, we see an equally sorry chapter in the record of the present Administration. . . .

—A Soviet combat brigade trains in Cuba, just 90 miles from our shores.

—A Soviet army of invasion occupies Afghanistan, further threatening our vital interests in the Middle East.

—America's defense strength is at its lowest ebb in a generation, while the Soviet Union is vastly outspending us in both strategic and conventional arms.

—Our European allies, looking nervously at the growing menace from the East, turn to us for leadership and fail to find it.

—And incredibly, more than 50, as you've been told from this platform so eloquently already, more than 50 of our fellow Americans have been held captive [in Tehran] for over eight years—eight months—by a dictatorial

foreign power that holds us up to ridicule before the world. . . . [In this sentence Reagan misspoke (8 years) and corrected himself (8 months).]

Who does not feel a growing sense of unease as our allies, facing repeated instances of an amateurish and confused Administration, reluctantly conclude that America is unwilling or unable to fulfill its obligations as leader of the free world?

Who does not feel rising alarm when the question in any discussion of foreign policy is no longer, "Should we do something?" but "Do we have the capacity to do anything?"

The Administration which has brought us to this state is seeking your endorsement for four more years of weakness, indecision, mediocrity and incompetence. No. No. No American should vote until he or she has asked: Is the United States stronger and more respected now than it was three-and-a-half years ago? Is the world safer, a safer place in which to live?

It is the responsibility of the President of the United States, in working for peace, to insure that the safety of our people cannot successfully be threatened by a hostile foreign power. As President, fulfilling that responsibility will be my No. 1 priority. . . .

Of all the objectives we seek, first and foremost is the establishment of lasting world peace. We must always stand ready to negotiate in good faith, ready to pursue any reasonable avenue that holds forth the promise of lessening tensions and furthering the prospects of peace. But let our friends and those who may wish us ill take note: the United States has an obligation to its citizens and to the people of the world never to let those who would destroy freedom dictate our future course of life on this planet. I would regard my election as proof that we have renewed our resolve to preserve world peace and freedom. That this nation will once again be strong enough to do that. . . .

[A]n American President told the generation of the Great Depression that it had a "rendezvous with destiny." I believe this generation of Americans today also has a rendezvous with destiny.

Tonight, let us dedicate ourselves to renewing the American compact. I ask you not simply to "trust me," but to trust your values—our values—and to hold me responsible for living up to them. I ask you to trust that American spirit which knows no ethnic, religious, social, political, regional or economic boundaries; the spirit that burned with zeal in the hearts of millions of immigrants from every corner of the earth who came here in search of freedom. . . .

I have thought of something that's not a part of my speech and worried over whether I should do it. Can we doubt that only a Divine Providence placed this land, this island of freedom, here as a refuge for all those people in the world who yearn to breathe free? Jews and Christians enduring persecution behind the Iron Curtain; the boat people of Southeast Asia, Cuba and of Haiti; the victims of drought and famine in Africa, the freedom fighters in Afghanistan, and our own countrymen held in savage captivity.

I'll confess that I've been a little afraid to suggest what I'm going to suggest. I'm more afraid not to. Can we begin our crusade joined together in a moment of silent prayer?

God bless America.

Thank you.

Questions

1. As outlined in this speech, what is Ronald Reagan's view of the proper relationship between the federal government and the American people?
2. What is Reagan's prescription for curing the ills of the American economy?
3. Candidate Reagan charged the Democratic administration with "weakness, indecision, mediocrity and incompetence." He also spoke positively of the need for a revival of the "American spirit." Do you think Reagan's appeal to the voters had more to do with the perceived failings of the Democrats or the Republican Party's conservative agenda?

Questions for Further Thought

1. Compare and contrast the speeches of President Jimmy Carter (Document 30-8) and Ronald Reagan (Document 30-9). What strikes you most about them? Do they shed light on the two speakers? How does the context influence different types of speeches (for example, campaign speeches, inaugural addresses, and presidential addresses—examples of all of which you have read)?
2. Compare and contrast the factors that contributed during the 1930s to the triumphs of the Democrats and liberalism with those that contributed during the 1960s and 1970s to the triumphs of the Republicans and conservatism.

CHAPTER *31*

A New Domestic and World Order, 1981–1996

★ ★ ★

The Reagan–Bush Years, 1981–1993

Ronald Reagan was easily elected president in 1980 and was even more decisively reelected four years later. Reagan's election victories and presidency (especially his first term) defined the 1980s much as Franklin Roosevelt's election victories (1932, 1936) and presidency had defined the 1930s. Each made effective use of his era's most direct and seemingly personal means of mass communication: radio in Roosevelt's case, television in Reagan's. Although the periods in which FDR and Reagan led the nation differed, as did the priorities of the two presidents, each sought to reorient government—to the extent that the term *revolutionary* was applied to both administrations.

For his part, President Reagan sought to cut taxes, reduce government's domestic spending, sharply increase military expenditures (beyond Carter's buildup), and (again outdoing Carter) curtail government's regulatory functions. In the end, taxing and spending policies combined to produce budget deficits and a mounting national debt. Domestic spending restraints and reductions primarily affected smaller programs that benefited the poor rather than larger ones that benefited the broader public. Reagan, like Roosevelt, fell short of effecting revolutionary change in America, but both presidents achieved much and reoriented the national debate over public policy for years to come.

Franklin Roosevelt died in office, to be succeeded by his vice-president, Harry Truman, who went on to win a presidential term in his own right. Ronald Reagan, who left the presidency after two terms, was followed by George Bush, who by winning handily in 1988 became the first serving vice-president since Martin Van Buren (in 1836) to become president. Bush failed to win reelection in 1992. Reagan's presidency proved to be a difficult act to follow (see text pp. 1000–1011).

In part, President Bush found Reagan's presidency difficult to follow because he had to deal with problems inherited from his predecessor, especially chronic budget deficits and the financial crisis of the nation's savings and loans associations (S&Ls). Bush addressed the budget crisis by negotiating a major tax increase and a freeze on

441

discretionary spending with congressional Democrats. Conservative Republicans were angered by Bush's acceptance of a tax increase, which violated his politic but unwise 1988 pledge of "no new taxes." Bush's administration cleaned up the S&L situation, but doing so proved to be expensive. In the final analysis, however, a short-lived economic recession, not as serious as the one that had buffeted the nation during Reagan's first term, likely hurt Bush most of all. Unlike Reagan, Bush lacked the political skills and the public support to survive the rocky spell.

In Document 31-1, Ronald Reagan recalls his formative years in an Illinois town. Donald T. Regan then recalls President Reagan, in whose administration he served (Document 31-2).

31-1   An American Life (1990)

Ronald Reagan

In his autobiography, Ronald Reagan (b. 1911) recalled growing up in Dixon, Illinois, where, at twenty-one, he cast his first vote for Franklin Roosevelt in 1932 and witnessed the Great Depression and the New Deal.

Source: Ronald Reagan, *An American Life* (New York: Simon & Schuster, 1990), 27–29, 66–69. Reprinted with the permission of Simon & Schuster. Copyright 1990 by Ronald W. Reagan.

With nearly ten thousand people, Dixon was more than ten times larger than Tampico. We arrived there in 1920 when I was nine years old, and to me it was heaven.

Dixon had a busy main street lined with shops, several churches, an elementary and a high school, a public library, a post office, a wire screen factory, a shoe factory, and a cement plant. At the outskirts of town, dairy farms stretched as far as you could see. It was a small universe where I learned standards and values that would guide me for the rest of my life.

Almost everybody knew one another, and because they knew one another, they tended to care about each other. If a family down the street had a crisis—a death or serious illness—a neighbor brought them dinner that night. If a farmer lost his barn to a fire, his friends would pitch in and help him rebuild it. At church, you prayed side by side with your neighbors, and if things were going wrong for them, you prayed for them—and know they'd pray for you if things went wrong for you.

I grew up observing how the love and common sense of purpose that unites families is one of the most powerful glues on earth and that it can help them overcome the greatest of adversities. I learned that hard work is an essential part of life—that by and large, you don't get something for nothing—and that America was a place that offered unlimited opportunity to those who did work hard. I learned to admire risk takers and entrepreneurs, be they farmers or small merchants, who went to work and took risks to build

something for themselves and their children, pushing at the boundaries of their lives to make them better.

I have always wondered at this American marvel, the great energy of the human soul that drives people to better themselves and improve the fortunes of their families and communities. Indeed, I know of no greater force on earth.

I think growing up in a small town is a good foundation for anyone who decides to enter politics. You get to know people as individuals, not as blocs or members of special interest groups. You discover that, despite their differences, most people have a lot in common: Every individual is unique, but we all want freedom and liberty, peace, love and security, a good home, and a chance to worship God in our own way; we all want the chance to get ahead and make our children's lives better than our own. We all want the chance to work at a job of our own choosing and to be fairly rewarded for it and the opportunity to control our own destiny. . . .

Later in life I learned that, compared with some of the folks who lived in Dixon, our family was "poor." But I didn't know that when I was growing up. And I never thought of our family as disadvantaged. Only later did the government decide that it had to tell people they were poor.

We always rented our home and never had enough money for luxuries. But I don't remember suffering because of that. Although my mother sometimes took in sewing to supplement my dad's wages and I grew up wearing my brother's clothes and shoes after he'd outgrown them, we always had enough to eat and Nelle was forever finding people who were worse off then we were and going out of her way to help them.

In those days, our main meal—dinner—was at noon and frequently consisted of a dish my mother called "oatmeal meat." She'd cook a batch of oatmeal and mix it with hamburger (I suspect the relative portions of each may have varied according to our current economic status), then serve it with some gravy she'd made while cooking the hamburger.

I remember the first time she brought a plate of oatmeal meat to the table. There was a thick, round patty buried in gravy that I'd never seen before. I bit into it. It was moist and meaty, the most wonderful thing I'd ever eaten. Of course, I didn't realize oatmeal meat was born of poverty.

Nowadays, I bet doctors would say it was healthy for us, too.

Dixon straddles the Rock River, a stretch of blue-green water flanked by wooded hills and limestone cliffs that meanders through the farmland of northwestern Illinois on its way to the Mississippi.

The river, which was often called the "Hudson of the West," was my playground during some of the happiest moments of my life. During the winter, it froze and became a skating rink as wide as two football fields and as long as I wanted to make it. In the summer, I swam and fished in the river and ventured as far as I dared on overnight canoe trips through the Rock River Valley, pretending with playmates to be a nineteenth-century explorer.

In my hand-me-down overalls, I hiked the hills and cliffs above the river, tried (unsuccessfully) to trap muskrats at the river's edge, and played "Cowboys and Indians" on hillsides above the river.

When we first moved to Dixon, we lived on the south side of the river. When we could afford it, we moved across the river to a larger house on the north side. As I look back on those days in Dixon, I think my life was as sweet and idyllic as it could be, as close as I could imagine for a young boy to the world created by Mark Twain in *The Adventures of Tom Sawyer....*

For a twenty-one-year-old fresh out of college, broadcasting the Big Ten games was like a dream, and as the end of the season approached, I prayed the people at WOC would offer me a permanent job. But after the final game, Pete told me the station didn't have an opening. He said if something came up, he'd call me, but with the Depression growing worse daily, he sounded as if there wasn't much hope.

Once again, disappointed and frustrated, I headed for home.

Back in Dixon, Jack [Reagan's father] reminded me that while I'd been talking about forward passes and quar-

terback sneaks, events a lot more important than football games had been occurring: Franklin D. Roosevelt had been elected the thirty-second president of the United States by a landslide and Jack predicted he would pull America out of its tailspin.

There weren't many Democrats in Dixon and Jack was probably the most outspoken of them, never missing a chance to speak up for the working man or sing the praises of Roosevelt.

I had become a Democrat, by birth, I suppose, and a few months after my twenty-first birthday, I cast my first vote for Roosevelt and the full Democratic ticket. And, like Jack—and millions of other Americans—I soon idolized FDR. He'd entered the White House facing a national emergency as grim as any the country has ever faced and, acting quickly, he had implemented a plan of action to deal with the crisis.

During his Fireside Chats, his strong, gentle, confident voice resonated across the nation with an eloquence that brought comfort and resilience to a nation caught up in a storm and reassured us that we could lick any problem. I will never forget him for that.

With his alphabet soup of federal agencies, FDR in many ways set in motion the forces that later sought to create big government and bring a form of veiled socialism to America. But I think that many people forget Roosevelt ran for president on a platform dedicated to reducing waste and fat in government. He called for cutting federal spending by twenty-five percent, eliminating useless boards and commissions and returning to states and communities powers that had been wrongfully seized by the federal government. If he had not been distracted by war, I think he would have resisted the relentless expansion of the federal government that followed him. One of his sons, Franklin Roosevelt, Jr., often told me that his father had said many times his welfare and relief programs during the Depression were meant only as emergency, stopgap measures to cope with a crisis, not the seeds of what others later tried to turn into a permanent welfare state. Government giveaway programs, FDR said, "destroy the human spirit," and he was right. As smart as he was, though, I suspect even FDR didn't realize that once you created a bureaucracy, it took on a life of its own. It was almost impossible to close down a bureaucracy once it had been created.

After FDR's election, Jack, as one of the few Democrats in town, was appointed to implement some of the new federal relief programs in Dixon. It removed him from the ranks of the unemployed and also gave me my first opportunity to watch government in action.

As administrator of federal relief programs, Jack shared a small office in Dixon with the County Supervisor of Poor. Every week, people who had lost their jobs came to the office to pick up sacks of flour, potatoes, and other food and pieces of scrip they could exchange for groceries at stores in town.

Occasionally, I dropped into the office to wait for Jack before we walked home together. I was shocked to see the fathers of many of my schoolmates waiting in line for handouts—men I had known most of my life, who had had jobs I'd thought were as permanent as the city itself.

Jack knew that accepting handouts was tough on the dignity of the men and came up with a plan to help them recover some of it. He began leaving home early in the morning and making rounds of the county, asking if anyone had odd jobs available, then, if they did, persuaded the people to let him find somebody to do the work. The next week when the men came in for their handouts, Jack offered the work he'd found to those who'd been out of work the longest.

I'll never forget the faces of these men when Jack told them their turn had come up for a job: They brightened like a burst of neon, and when they left Dad's office, I swear the men were standing a little taller. They wanted *work*, not handouts.

Not long after that, Jack told several men he had found a week's work for them. They responded to this news with a rustling of feet. Eventually, one broke the silence and said: "Jack, the last time you got me some work, the people at the relief office took my family off welfare; they said I had a job and even though it was temporary, I wasn't eligible for relief anymore. I just can't afford to take another job."

Later on, thanks again to his party connections, Jack was placed in charge of the Works Progress Administration office in Dixon. The WPA was one of the most productive elements of FDR's alphabet soup of agencies because it put people to work building roads, bridges, and other projects. Like Jack's informal program, it gave men and women a chance to make some money along with the satisfaction of knowing they *earned* it. But just as Jack got the program up and running, there was a decline in the number of people applying for work on the projects. Since he knew there hadn't been a cure for unemployment in Dixon, he began asking questions and discovered the federal welfare workers were telling able-bodied men in Dixon that they shouldn't take the WPA jobs because they were being taken care of and didn't need help from the WPA.

After a while, Jack couldn't get any of his projects going; he couldn't get enough men sprung from the welfare giveaway program. I wasn't sophisticated enough to realize what I learned later: The first rule of a bureaucracy is to protect the bureaucracy. If the people running the welfare program had let their clientele find other ways of making a living, that would have reduced their importance and their budget.

Questions

1. What experiences in Dixon does Reagan recall in this passage from his autobiography? What values does he claim were characteristic of Dixon?
2. What does Reagan say about the New Deal in Dixon? Do his recollections surprise you? Why or why not?

31-2 For the Record (1988)

Donald T. Regan

Donald T. Regan (b. 1918) served President Reagan first as secretary of the treasury, then as chief of staff. Here, in a book written while Reagan was still in office, Regan discusses the president.

Source: Excerpted from Donald T. Regan, *For the Record: From Wall Street to Washington,* 246–250, 266–268. Copyright © 1988 by Donald T. Regan. Reprinted by permission.

Ronald Reagan seemed to be regarded by certain members of his inner circle not as the powerful and utterly original leader that he was, but as a sort of supreme anchorman whose public persona was the most important element of the Presidency. According to the rules of this school of political management, controversy was to be avoided at nearly any cost: every Presidential action must produce a positive public effect. In practice, this meant stimulating a positive effect in the media, with the result that the press, not the people, became the President's primary constituency. . . .

It was [deputy chief of staff Michael] Deaver's job to advise the President on image, and image was what he talked about nearly all the time. It was Deaver who identified the story of the day at the eight o'clock staff meeting and coordinated the plans for dealing with it, Deaver who created and approved photo opportunities, Deaver who alerted the President to the snares being laid by the press that day. Deaver was a master of his craft. He saw—designed—each Presidential action as a one-minute or two-minute spot on the evening network news, or a picture on page one of the *Washington Post* or the *New York Times,* and conceived every Presidential appearance in terms of camera angles. . . .

Every moment of every public appearance was scheduled, every word was scripted, every place where Reagan was expected to stand was chalked with toe marks. The President was always being prepared for a performance, and this had the inevitable effect of preserving him from confrontation and the genuine interplay of opinion, question, and argument that form the basis of decision. . . .

The President is possessed of a philosophical agenda based on a lifetime of experience and thought. He is a formidable reader and a talented conversationalist with a gift for listening. It was precisely this gift that led to many of his gaffes and misstatements in encounters with the press: Ronald Reagan remembered nearly everything that was said to him. If someone told him (to use a wholly fictitious example) that there had been 35,987 hairs in Stalin's mustache, this fact would go into the Presidential memory bank, possibly to emerge weeks or months later in the middle of a press conference. It never seemed to occur to him that anyone would give him incorrect information. His mind was a trove of facts and anecdotes, something like the morgue of one of his favorite magazines, *Reader's Digest,* and it was impossible to guess when or why he might access any one of these millions of bytes of data. . . .

Reagan shunned the abstract, the theoretical, the cold and impersonal approach to problems. His love of stories was connected to this same tendency to see everything in human terms. Although even some of his intimates scoffed (ever so discreetly) at his bottomless fund of anecdotes about it, Reagan's experience as governor of California constituted a unique body of executive and political experience. He had a formidable gift for debate when he was allowed to debate in a spontaneous way. His problems in these matters, as in the first debate with Walter Mondale in 1984, nearly always resulted from his being overprogrammed. His briefers, forgetting that a President has a cast of thousands to remember facts for him, had crammed his mind with so many bits of information that he tried to rely on data instead of explaining the issue and defending his policy. I had seen him defend his ideas and critique the proposals of other heads of state with the best of them at six international economic summits, and it was not uncommon for him to render courageous decisions on domestic economic questions in the face of nearly unanimous advice and pressure to do the opposite. . . .

[Regan describes giving the president a working paper in August 1985 outlining what he thought the White House's priorities should be for the following year.]

Ronald Reagan read the paper while he was at the ranch and handed it back to me on his return without spoken or written comment.

"What did you think of it?" I asked.

It's good, the President replied, nodding in approval. It's really good, Don.

I waited for him to say more. He did not. He had no questions to ask, no objections to raise, no instructions to issue. I realized that the policy that would determine the course of the world's most powerful nation for the next two years and deeply influence the fate of the Republican party in the 1986 midterm elections had been adopted without amendment. It seemed, also, that I had been authorized as Chief of Staff to make the necessary arrangements to carry out the policy. It was taken for granted that the President would do whatever was asked of him to make the effort a success. We went on to the next item on the agenda.

I confess that I was surprised that this weighty matter was decided so quickly and with so little ceremony. In a way, of course, it was flattering; it is always gratifying to anticipate the boss's wishes with acceptable accuracy. Still, I was uneasy. Did the President really want us to do all these things with no more discussion than this? I decided that this must be the case, since always in the past, if he did not say no, the answer was yes. By now I understood that the President did not share my love of detail and my enthusiasm for planning. I knew that he was not an aggressive manager. Perhaps I should have quizzed him on tax policy or Central America or our approach to trade negotiations; certainly my instincts and the practice of a lifetime nudged me in that direction. But I held my tongue. It is one thing brashly to speak your mind to an ordinary mortal and another to say, "Wait a minute!" to the President of the United States. The mystery of the office is a potent inhibitor. The President, you feel, has his reasons.

Another President would almost certainly have had his own ideas on the mechanics of policy, but Reagan did not trouble himself with such minutiae. His preoccupation was with what might be called "the outer Presidency." He was content to let others cope with the inner details of running the Administration. . . . Reagan chose his aides and then followed their advice almost without question. He trusted his lieutenants to act on his intentions, rather than on his spoken instructions, and though he sometimes asked what some of his less visible Cabinet officers were doing with their departments, he seldom spontaneously called for a detailed status report. The degree of trust involved in this method of leadership must be unprecedented in modern American history. Sometimes—as was inevitable given that many of his closest aides, including almost all of the Cabinet, were virtual strangers to him—this trust was betrayed in shocking fashion. When that happened Reagan seldom criticized, seldom complained, never scolded. Not even the Iran-Contra debacle could provoke him into harsh words, much less subordinates who had let him down.

Never—absolutely never in my experience—did President Reagan really lose his temper or utter a rude or unkind word. Never did he issue a direct order, although I, at least, sometimes devoutly wished that he would. He listened, acquiesced, played his role, and waited for the next act to be written. From the point of view of my own experience and nature, this was an altogether baffling way of doing things. But my own style was not the case in point.

Reagan's method had worked well enough to make him President of the United States, and well enough for the nation under his leadership to transform its mood from pessimism to optimism, its economy from stagnation to steady growth, and its position in the world from weakness to strength. Common sense suggested that the President knew something that the rest of us did not know. It was my clear duty to do things his way.

Questions

1. What does Regan see as Ronald Reagan's strengths and weaknesses as president?
2. What relation, if any, do you see between the president's strengths and weaknesses, as viewed by Regan?

Questions for Further Thought

1. How would you compare and contrast the Ronald Reagan of the autobiography (Document 31-1) and the Ronald Reagan portrayed by Donald Regan (Document 31-2)?
2. How would you compare the rhetoric of Franklin Roosevelt (Documents 25-1, 26-1, 26-2, and 26-13) with that of Ronald Reagan (Documents 30-9 and 31-1)?

Foreign Relations under Reagan and Bush

Ronald Reagan became president at a difficult juncture for American foreign policy. Relations with the Soviet Union had turned sour following the Soviet invasion of Afghanistan late in 1979. The Carter administration had responded by curtailing key exports to the Soviet Union, boycotting the 1980 summer Olympic Games in Moscow, and calling for increased military spending and registration for the draft. The president had also enunciated the Carter Doctrine, warning that any "outside" effort to dominate the Persian Gulf would be resisted, by "military force" if need be. Meanwhile, developments in Iran during 1979 and 1980—the ouster of the shah, the militants' later seizure of the American embassy and diplomatic personnel in Teheran, and the failure of a mission to rescue the hostages—created another crisis, this one both serious (especially in its effect on petroleum prices) and humiliating.

President Reagan's first term was marked by further escalation of the renewed Cold War. Reagan not only employed strident anti-Soviet rhetoric, he accelerated the military buildup initiated by Carter and increased support for Afghan and other Islamic forces fighting the Soviet Army and the Soviet-backed regime in Afghanistan. Elsewhere, Reagan ordered air strikes against Libya's leader, Muammar Khadafy, to punish him for his sponsorship of terrorism, and dispatched marines to Lebanon, which was reeling under Muslim-Christian civil strife and the presence of the Palestine Liberation Organization (PLO) and Syrian and Israeli military forces. Muslim terrorists blew up the American embassy in Beirut and later a military barracks, killing more than two hundred marines, more than had died during any day of the war in Vietnam. In the Western Hemisphere, the United States took sides in internal conflicts in

Guatemala, Nicaragua, and El Salvador and militarily overthrew a Cuban-backed leftist government on Grenada, in the Caribbean.

During Reagan's second term, his administration was bruised by the Iran-Contra Affair, but it also played a role in defusing Soviet-American tensions. Iran-Contra, first exposed during 1986, involved clandestine dealings with the militant regime of Iran, then at war with Iraq, including weapons sales, in the hope that Iran would persuade its allies in Lebanon to release American hostages there. Proceeds from the arms sales were channeled to the Contras, who were fighting Nicaragua's Sandinista Communist government. At the same time, Reagan established a working relationship with Mikhail Gorbachev, who came to power in the Soviet Union during 1985 and sought to modernize his nation's weakening economy. Arms control talks resumed, and the two leaders met at four summit conferences between 1985 and 1988.

President George Bush, who succeeded Reagan, was standing watch when most Communist regimes (including that of the Soviet Union) collapsed, the Soviet Union itself fell apart, the Warsaw Pact was terminated, and Germany was reunified. The Cold War had ended in victory for the United States and its allies, but diplomatic-military crises still existed, leading to United Nations peace-keeping missions involving U.S. troops (as in Somalia, 1992–1993) or American intervention (as in Panama, 1989). Above all, large American and allied forces were deployed in the Persian Gulf area to pressure—and ultimately force—Saddam Hussein's Iraqis out of Kuwait (1900–1991) (see text pp. 1011–1015).

Document 31-3 offers the address of President George Bush to the United Nations General Assembly on the implications of the crisis in the Persian Gulf. Document 31-4 presents the reflections of university students who would not be called to serve in the military.

31-3   Iraqi Aggression in Kuwait (1990)

George Bush

Speaking before the United Nations General Assembly as communism was collapsing in Eastern Europe and the Soviet Union, President George Bush (b. 1924) spoke of the promise of "a new international order" and the threat posed to that new world order by Iraqi aggression.

Source: George Bush, "Aggression in the Gulf: A Partnership of Nations," October 1, 1990, in *Vital Speeches of the Day*, vol. 57 (October 15, 1990), 2–4.

. . . The founding of the United Nations embodied our deepest hopes for a peaceful world. And during the past year, we've come closer than ever before to realizing those hopes. We've seen a century sundered by barbed threats and barbed wire, give way to a new era of peace and competition and freedom. . . .

Not since 1945 have we seen the real possibility of using the United Nations as it was designed, as a center for international collective security. . . .

. . . Can we work together in a new partnership of nations? Can the collective strength of the world community expressed by the United Nations unite to deter and defeat aggression? Because the cold war's battle of ideas is not the last epic battle of this century.

Two months ago, in the waning weeks of one of history's most hopeful summers, the vast, still beauty of the peaceful Kuwaiti desert was fouled by the stench of diesel and the roar of steel tanks. And once again, the sound of distant thunder echoed across a cloudless sky. And once again, the world awoke to face the guns of August.

But this time, the world was ready. The United Nations Security Council's resolute response to Iraq's unprovoked aggression has been without precedent. Since the invasion on August 2, the Council has passed eight major resolutions setting the terms for a solution to the crisis. The Iraqi regime has yet to face the facts. But as I said last month, the annexation of Kuwait will not be permitted to stand. And this is not simply the view of the United States. It is the view of every Kuwaiti, the Arab League, the United Nations. Iraq's leaders should listen. It is Iraq against the world.

Let me take this opportunity to make the policy of my Government clear. The United States supports the use of sanctions to compel Iraq's leaders to withdraw immediately and without condition from Kuwait. We also support the provision of medicine and food for humanitarian purposes, so long as distribution can be properly monitored. Our quarrel is not with the people of Iraq. We do not wish for them to suffer. The world's quarrel is with the dictator who ordered that invasion.

Along with others, we have dispatched military forces to the region to enforce sanctions, to deter and if need be defend against further aggression. And we seek no advantage for ourselves, nor do we seek to maintain our military forces in Saudi Arabia for one day longer than is necessary. U.S. forces were sent at the request of the Saudi Government.

The American people and this President want every single American soldier brought home as soon as this mission is completed.

Let me also emphasize that all of us here at the U.N. hope that military force will never be used. We seek a peaceful outcome, a diplomatic outcome. And one more thing: in the aftermath of Iraq's unconditional departure from Kuwait, I truly believe there may be opportunities for Iraq and Kuwait to settle their differences permanently, for the states of the gulf themselves to build new arrangements for stability and for all the states and the peoples of the region to settle the conflicts that divide the Arabs from Israel.

But the world's key task, now, first and always, must be to demonstrate that aggression will not be tolerated or rewarded. . . .

The United Nations can help bring about a new day— a day when these kinds of terrible weapons and the terrible despots who would use them, or both, were a thing of the past. It is in our hands to leave these dark machines behind, in the dark ages where they belong, and to press forward to cap a historic movement towards a new world order, and a long era of peace.

We have a vision of a new partnership of nations that transcends the cold war; a partnership based on consultation, cooperation and collective action, especially through international and regional organizations; a partnership united by principle and the rule of law and supported by an equitable sharing of both cost and commitment; a partnership whose goals are to increase democracy, increase prosperity, increase the peace and reduce arms. . . .

I see a world of open borders, open trade and, most importantly, open minds, a world that celebrates the common heritage that belongs to all the world's people, taking pride not just in hometown or homeland but in humanity itself. I see a world touched by a spirit like that of the Olympics, based not on competition that's driven by fear, but sought out of joy and exhilaration and a true quest for excellence.

And I see a world where democracy continues to win new friends and convert old foes, and where the Americas—North, Central and South—can provide a model for the future of all humankind, the world's first completely democratic hemisphere. And I see a world building on the emerging new model of European unity, not just Europe, but the whole world whole and free.

This is precisely why the present aggression in the gulf is a menace not only to . . . one region's security, but to the entire world's vision of our future. It threatens to turn the dream of a new international order into a grim nightmare of anarchy in which the law of the jungle supplants the law of nations. And that's why the United Nations reacted with such historic unity and resolve. And that's why this challenge is a test that we cannot afford to fail. . . .

Questions

1. What role does Bush see the United Nations playing in the "new international order"?

2. Why, according to Bush, is Iraq's invasion of Kuwait a "menace" to "the dream of a new international order"?

31-4   University Students Reflect on the Gulf War (1991)

David Maraniss

The American military that fought and won the war against Iraq was an all-volunteer force. (Not since the 1970s had the United States resorted to the draft.) The students whose discussion is reported here by David Maraniss of the *Washington Post* talked during the aerial phase of Operation Desert Storm, before the mounting of the ground offensive against Iraq.

Source: David Maraniss, "It's Their War, Too," *Washington Post,* February 11, 1991. © 1991, *The Washington Post.* Reprinted with permission.

Seven buddies sit in the living room of their dormitory suite 12 floors above the classical orderliness of Vanderbilt University. They are the same age as many of the young men fighting in the Persian Gulf War: 20 and 21, on the cusp of adulthood. As privileged sons of professional America, their lives are not on the line, yet this is their war, too, and they sense that somehow it has changed them forever.

Perhaps the effect is not immediately obvious as they spend the day. They watch basketball at Memorial Gym. They eat pizza from Mazzio's and junk food from the Munchi Mart. They play baseball and racetrack Nintendo computer games. They retreat into their rooms to study English and political science. They listen to "Living Colour" and "Public Enemy" on their compact-disc players. They go to a dance or a movie.

But the change is occurring inside as they struggle with tough questions about who they are and what they are doing while so many of their chronological peers—so alike, yet different—sleep in trenches and drive light armored vehicles in the Saudi Arabian desert.

Here are the questions for these students: Should you fight in this war? Would you? Should there be a draft? Is it fair that you, white and middle class, are here while a disproportionate number of blacks and Hispanics are over there? Would you die if you went? Didn't your life seem so safe and comfortable for so many years? What happened? Does this war open up the possibility of one military conflict after another for the course of your life? Is that what you expected?

"No, this is not something we expected to face in our lives," said Mark Dusek, 20, a junior from Houston majoring in math and biology. On that point, all seven agreed. War was far from their minds as they entered college. They thought the world was becoming safer, especially as tension eased with the Soviet Union. Grenada and Panama did not seem like war to them. They could not remember Vietnam.

During the first semester, the television was used mostly to watch sports; now they tune in the war on CNN. From September to December, the only part of the newspaper read in their suite was the sports section, said Greg An-glum, 20, a junior economics major from Walt Whitman High School in Bethesda, Md. "Now we all read the front page."

This semester has been different from the day they returned in the second week of January. Mike Penn, 21, a senior communications major from Indianapolis, remembers driving back to school down Interstate 65 and seeing three big trucks hauling coffins from the Batesville Casket Co. "That's when it hit me that this was really happening and all our lives were changing," Penn said. "People were going to die."

Five of the seven agree with President Bush that the war is just or at least necessary. But not one wants to fight in it. All are opposed to a draft, though a few said one might be necessary as a last resort. They said they would gladly serve in non-military public service jobs.

"This might sound selfish, but I think it would be a shame to put America's best young minds on the front line," said Jason Bell, 20, a junior English major from Elizabethtown, Ky. "If we have to go, we have to go, but I think it would be a shame."

In one sense, these young men seem superfluous when considered within the war's urgent context. Yet they loom as potentially key players if war drags on and a draft—despite Bush's pledge to the contrary—is suddenly resurrected. Fair or not, it is then that the nation's support of the war might face its stiffest test, when the educated sons of influential white professionals are part of the equation. These seven understand that.

"If we get to the point where we need a draft, we should pull out," said Matt Pender, 21, a junior political science major from Ayer, Mass. Pender, editor of the campus newspaper, opposes the war. He and Penn hold the minority view among those in the suite, but that might change.

"If the ground war starts and they need more troops, who knows how the tide could turn?" said Bill Pierros, 21, a junior English major from Elgin, Ill.

Anglum, who worked last summer in Vice President Quayle's office, said he hopes there will not be a draft but would totally support one if needed. While he said he considers the war necessary, largely to protect U.S. energy needs, this is not a war he wants to fight. "I guess if I was trained to fight maybe I'd have a little different attitude," he said. "But I can't see myself shooting a gun. . . . I don't feel I could be an effective soldier."

None of the seven has relatives in the war. Only two have close high school friends in the conflict—Pierros and Chad Sanchez, 20, a junior chemical engineering major from Gonzales, La., a working-class town west of New Orleans where the military is a routine part of life. "A lot of guys from home signed up with the Marine reserves or National Guard right out of high school," Sanchez said. "None of them, I don't think, ever thought about going to war, but that's where they are now. Back home at Christmas, a friend and I spent a whole night with another friend who was about to go. He was scared. He's a gunner on the front line."

If these seven were on the front line, would they come home alive? Sanchez said he has thought about that many times since war started. He has decided that he would get killed trying to help a buddy in trouble. Perhaps he will never know. The students also have pondered the question of color and fairness in the volunteer military. Yes, they said, blacks and Hispanics seem to be in the war disproportionately. But the only short-range way to even things out would be a draft, an unacceptable solution to them.

"What do they say? White man's war, black man's fight," Bell said.

"We're talking about the injustices of a whole system," Penn said.

As late afternoon shadows fell across their living room, the seven came to grips with how their insular lives had changed. Pender said the United States has started something that will be hard to stop. Anglum said he is afraid that there will be more conflicts. Sanchez said he has been thinking more about what it means to bring children into the world. Pierros said he fears for his relatives in Greece, scene of terrorist activity. Penn said he would not feel as safe flying from Nashville to Chicago.

They were safe, a world away. They did not want to fight. They would rather eat cold pizza or write a term paper on dictators. "War is something you played in the backyard," Penn said. "None of us knew what it really was." They still do not, but they are thinking about it for the first time.

Questions

1. With which student statements do you most agree? Most disagree?
2. What light does the conversation shed on class and race in the United States?

Questions for Further Thought

1. Compare and contrast the crisis in the Persian Gulf with the crises of the Cold War.
2. What implications, if any, do you see in the present reliance on all-volunteer armed forces in the United States? Which earlier American wars were wholly or largely fought by volunteer forces? Which involved drafts? How did earlier American peacetime armed forces resemble or differ from those of our own time?

Uncertain Times

Americans faced a range of problems during the 1990s that left them concerned about the present and apprehensive about the future. Some, though by no means all, of those problems have diminished, but they have not disappeared.

Although the economy was showing a remarkable capacity for sustained growth as the decade drew to a close, with unemployment rates at their lowest in recent memory and inflation not banging at the door, inequality in income and (thanks to the booming stock market) wealth continued to grow. Although immigrants' share of the nation's population is smaller today than during various earlier periods, it is higher than at any other time since the Second World War. Large-scale immigration from Asia and Latin America is changing the composition of the nation's population. Resentment against immigration has again become apparent, including that of some immigrant groups against others. Thus California voters, including Hispanics, enacted Proposition 187 to deny undocumented aliens a range of publicly funded services. Californians subsequently terminated affirmative action in admissions to the University of California. This controversy has flared in other states, as well. When South Central Los Angeles exploded in rioting, looting, and arson in 1992, Korean businesses were a target, and those arrested for one offense or another included Latinos, African Americans, and whites.

Battles over feminism (including abortion rights) and gay rights have been prominent in America's culture wars since the 1960s and 1970s, with AIDS (acquired immunodeficiency syndrome), first identified in 1981, now figuring in the latter. As was to be expected, deeply felt conflicting beliefs have found expression in vigorous, often emotional, public debate. Again, a frightening amount of violence has been involved, with abortion providers and gays the targets.

Indeed, terrorism has reemerged as a threat. Foreign terrorists have attacked Americans abroad (as in the 1988 bombing of Pan Am Flight 103 over Scotland, which killed 270 people) and once at home (the 1993 bombing of the World Trade Center in New York City, which killed six and injured more than a thousand). However, it was Americans who perpetrated the bloodiest terrorist act within the United States in history: the killing of 168 people in the 1995 bombing of a federal building in Oklahoma City, Oklahoma (see text pp. 1015–1029, 1045–1047, 1050).

Document 31-5 provides George Gilder's analysis of wealth and poverty. Document 31-6 excerpts Jonathan Kozol's account of mothers and their children on welfare. Document 31-7 is California's Proposition 187, and Document 31-8 offers the experiences of a volunteer counselor who served in San Francisco General Hospital during the AIDS epidemic. The relationship between violence during the 1990s and violence during an earlier era is discussed in Document 31-9.

31-5   Wealth and Poverty (1981)

George Gilder

In *Wealth and Poverty*, a book that strongly influenced the Reagan administration, conservative theorist George Gilder argued that it was the immoral and irresponsible behavior of the poor themselves rather than any structural defects in the economy that perpetuated poverty in the United States.

Source: From George Gilder, *Wealth and Poverty* (New York: Basic Books, 1981), 68–71. Copyright © 1981 by George Gilder. Reprinted by permission of Georges Borchardt, Inc., on behalf of the author.

The only dependable route from poverty is always work, family, and faith. The first principle is that in order to move up, the poor must not only work, they must work harder than the classes above them. Every previous generation of the lower class has made such efforts. But the current poor, white even more than black, are refusing to work hard. Irwin Garfinkel and Robert Haveman, authors of the ingenious and sophisticated study of what they call *Earnings Capacity Utilization Rates,* have calculated the degree to which various income groups use their opportunities—how hard they work outside the home. This study shows that, for several understandable reasons, the current poor work substantially less, for fewer hours and weeks a year, and earn less in proportion to their age, education, and other credentials (even *after* correcting the figures for unemployment, disability, and presumed discrimination) than either their predecessors in American cities or those now above them on the income scale. (The study was made at the federally funded Institute for Research on Poverty at the University of Wisconsin and used data from the census and the Michigan longitudinal survey.) The findings lend important confirmation to the growing body of evidence that work effort is the crucial unmeasured variable in American productivity and income distribution, and that current welfare and other subsidy programs substantially reduce work. The poor choose leisure not because of moral weakness, but because they are paid to do so.

A program to lift by transfers and preferences the incomes of less diligent groups is politically divisive—and very unlikely—because it incurs the bitter resistance of the real working class. In addition, such an effort breaks the psychological link between effort and reward, which is crucial to long-run upward mobility. Because effective work consists not in merely fulfilling the requirements of labor contracts, but in "putting out" with alertness and emotional commitment, workers have to understand and feel deeply that what they are given depends on what they give—that they must supply work in order to demand goods. Parents and schools must inculcate this idea in their children both by instruction and example. Nothing is more deadly to achievement than the belief that effort will not be rewarded, that the world is a bleak and discriminatory place in which only the predatory and the specially preferred can get ahead. Such a view in the home discourages the work effort in school that shapes earnings capacity afterward. As with so many aspects of human performance, work effort begins in family experiences, and its sources can be best explored through an examination of family structure.

Indeed, after work the second principle of upward mobility is the maintenance of monogamous marriage and family. Adjusting for discrimination against women and for child-care responsibilities, the Wisconsin study indicates that married men work between two and one-third and four times harder than married women, and more than twice as hard as female family heads. The work effort of married men increases with their age, credentials, education, job experience, and birth of children, while the work effort of married women steadily declines. Most important in judging the impact of marriage, husbands work 50 percent harder than bachelors of comparable age, education, and skills.

The effect of marriage, thus, is to increase the work effort of men by about half. Since men have higher earnings capacity to begin with, and since the female capacity-utilization figures would be even lower without an adjustment for discrimination, it is manifest that the maintenance of families is the key factor in reducing poverty.

Once a family is headed by a woman, it is almost impossible for it to greatly raise its income even if the woman is highly educated and trained and she hires day-care or domestic help. Her family responsibilities and distractions tend to prevent her from the kind of all-out commitment that is necessary for the full use of earning power. Few women with children make earning money the top priority in their lives.

A married man, on the other hand, is spurred by the claims of family to channel his otherwise disruptive male aggressions into his performance as a provider for a wife and children. These sexual differences alone, which manifest themselves in all societies known to anthropology, dictate that the first priority of any serious program against poverty is to strengthen the male role in poor families.

These narrow measures of work effort touch on just part of the manifold interplay between family and poverty. Edward Banfield's *The Unheavenly City* defines the lower class largely by its lack of an orientation to the future. Living from day to day and from hand to mouth, lower class individuals are unable to plan or save or keep a job. Banfield gives the impression that short-time horizons are a deep-seated psychological defect afflicting hundreds of thousands of the poor.

There is no question that Banfield puts his finger on a crucial problem of the poor and that he develops and documents his theme in an unrivaled classic of disciplined social science. But he fails to show how millions of men, equally present oriented, equally buffeted by impulse and blind to the future, have managed to become far-seeing members of the middle classes. He also fails to explain how millions of apparently future-oriented men can become dissolute followers of the sensuous moment, neglecting their jobs, dissipating their income and wealth, pursuing a horizon no longer than the most time-bound of the poor.

What Banfield is in fact describing in his lower-class category is largely the temperament of single, divorced, and separated men. The key to lower-class life in contemporary America is that unrelated individuals, as the census calls them, are so numerous and conspicuous that they set the tone for the entire community. Their congregation in ghettos, moreover, magnifies greatly their impact on the black poor, male and female (though, as Banfield rightly observes, this style of instant gratification is chiefly a male trait).

The short-sighted outlook of poverty stems largely from the breakdown of family responsibilities among fathers. The lives of the poor, all too often, are governed by the rhythms of tension and release that characterize the sexual experience of young single men. Because female sexuality, as it evolved over the millennia, is psychologically rooted in the bearing and nurturing of children, women have long horizons within their very bodies, glimpses of eternity within their wombs. Civilized society is dependent upon the submission of the short-term sexuality of young men to the extended maternal horizons of women. This is what happens in monogamous marriage; the man disciplines his sexuality and extends it into the future through the womb of a woman. The woman gives him access to his children, otherwise forever denied him; and he gives her the product of his labor, otherwise dissipated on temporary pleasures. The woman gives him a unique link to the future and a vision of it; he gives her faithfulness and a commitment to a lifetime of hard work. If work effort is the first principle of overcoming poverty, marriage is the prime source of upwardly mobile work.

It is love that changes the short horizons of youth and poverty into the long horizons of marriage and career. When marriages fail, the man often returns to the more primitive rhythms of singleness. On the average, his income drops by one-third and he shows a far higher propensity for drink, drugs, and crime. But when marriages in general hold firm and men in general love and support their children, Banfield's lower-class style changes into middle-class futurity.

The key to the intractable poverty of the hardcore American poor is the dominance of single and separated men in poor communities. Black "unrelated individuals" are not much more likely to be in poverty than white ones. The problem is neither race nor matriarchy in any meaningful sense. It is familial anarchy among the concentrated poor of the inner city, in which flamboyant and impulsive youths rather than responsible men provide the themes of aspiration. The result is that male sexual rhythms tend to prevail, and boys are brought up without authoritative fathers in the home to instill in them the values of responsible paternity: the discipline and love of children and the dependable performance of the provider role. "If she wants me, *she*'ll pay," one young stud assured me in prison, and perhaps, in the welfare culture, she can and will. Thus the pattern is extended into future generations.

Questions

1. What does Gilder see as the major causes of poverty? What is his solution to poverty?
2. What is Gilder's analysis of the roles of women and men? What are the implications of this analysis?
3. Would Gilder's argument have appealed to President Reagan? Why or why not?

31-6   Rachel and Her Children (1988)

Jonathan Kozol

Social critic Jonathan Kozol described the world of the "welfare hotel" in his 1988 study *Rachel and Her Children*. Such institutions were the only shelter available for many homeless families in New York City in the 1980s.

Source: From *Rachel and Her Children* by Jonathan Kozol, 51–55. Copyright © 1988 by Jonathan Kozol. Reprinted by permission of Crown Publishers, a division of Random House, Inc.

There are families in this building whose existence, difficult though it may be, still represents an island of serenity and peace. Annie Harrington's family has a kind of pained serenity. Gwen and her children live with the peace of resignation. I think of these families like refugees who, in the midst of war, cling to each other and establish a small zone of safety. Most people here do not have resources to create a zone of safety. Terrorized already on arrival, they are quickly caught up in a vortex of accelerating threats and are tossed about like bits of wood and broken furniture and shattered houses in an Arkansas tornado. Chaos and disorder alternate with lethargy and nearly absolute bewilderment in face of regulations they cannot observe or do not understand.

Two women whom I meet in the same evening after Christmas, Wanda and Terry, frighten me by their entire inability to fathom or to govern what is going on inside and all around them.

Terry is pregnant, in her ninth month. She's afraid that, when she gives birth, she may not be able to bring home her baby from the hospital because she is not legally residing here.

Wanda, curled up like a newborn in a room no larger than a closet, is three months pregnant, planning an abortion.

Would doctors say these women are emotionally unwell? They might have no choice. Were these women sick before they came here? I don't see how we could possibly find out. What startles me is not that they have difficulty coping but that neither yet has given up entirely.

Terry: twenty-eight years old. She has three kids. She graduated from a school in Flushing and has worked for eight years as a lab assistant. Burnt out of her home, she stayed for two years with her sister's family: three adults, eight children, crowded into four unheated rooms. Evicted by her sister when the pressure on her sister's husband and their kids began to damage their own marriage, she had to take her children to the EAU at Church Street in Manhattan. Refusing to accept a placement at a barracks shelter, she's been sleeping here illegally for several nights in a small room rented to her cousin.

When we meet, she's in the corridor outside the crisis center, crying and perspiring heavily. She sits on a broken chair to talk to me. She's not on Medicaid and has been removed from AFDC. "My card's being reprocessed," she explains, although this explanation explains nothing. She's not on WIC. "I've got to file an application." Her back is aching. She is due to have her child any day.

This is the reason for her panic: "If I can't be placed before the baby's born, the hospital won't let me take the baby. They don't let you take a newborn if you haven't got a home." As we will see, this is not always so, but the possibility of this occurrence is quite real. Where are her kids? "They're here. I've got them hidden in the room."

She takes me to her cousin Wanda's room. I measure it: nine feet by twelve, a little smaller than the room in which I store my files on the homeless. Wanda's been here fifteen months, has four kids, no hot plate, and no food in the refrigerator. She's had no food stamps and no restaurant allowance for two months. I ask her why. (You ask these questions even though you know the answer will be vague, confused, because so many of these women have no possible idea of why they do or don't receive the benefits they do or don't deserve.) She's curled up in a tattered slip and a torn sweater on a mattress with no sheet. Her case was closed, she says. Faintly, I hear something about "an application." Her words are hard to understand. I ask her whether she was here for Christmas. The very few words she speaks come out in small reluctant phrases: "Where else would I go?" She says her children got some presents from the fire department. There's a painting of Jesus and Mary on the wall above the bed. "My mother gave it to me."

A week later I stop by to visit. She's in the same position: drowsy and withdrawn. I ask her if she celebrated New Year's Eve. "Stayed by my lonesome" is all that I understand. She rouses herself enough to ask me if I have a cigarette. In the vacuum of emotion I ask if she ever gets to do something for fun. "Go to a movie . . ." But when I ask the last time she's been to a movie she says: "1984." What was the movie? *Dawn of the Living Dead.*

When she says she's pregnant and is planning an abortion I don't care to ask her why, but she sits up halfway, props herself against a pillow, looks at Terry, shrugs, and mumbles this: "What you want to bring another baby into this place for? There ain't nothin' waitin' for them here but dirty rooms and dyin'."

Her children, scattered like wilted weeds around her on the floor, don't talk or play or move around or interrupt. Outside in the corridor I ask her cousin if the kids are sick. Terry says: "They're okay. They just didn't have no food to eat today." So I ask: "Did you?" She shakes her head. I go down to Herald Square, buy french fries and chicken at a fast-food store, milk and cookies at a delicatessen, and return. The minute I walk in Wanda sits up, clearheaded and alert. Her kids wake from their stupor. Fifteen minutes later, every bit of chicken, all the french fries, cookies, milk have been consumed. There is a rush of energy and talking in the room. The kids are pestering the adults, as they ought to.

"I have a problem," Wanda says. "My blood sugar goes down. It is called [pronounced very precisely] hypoglycemia."

I meet Terry one year later by sheer chance outside Grand Central Station. She's in a food line for the sandwiches distributed by a charitable group at 10:00 P.M. Her kids are with her. She's holding a baby in her arms. She tells me she's in another hotel near the Martinique. "Don't have no refrigerators there . . ."

I lose her in the crowd of people waiting for a meal.

In the subway station under Herald Square a woman who has seen me coming from the Martinique follows me and stops me by the stairs. Her hair is disheveled. Words spill from her mouth. She says that she was thrown out of the Martinique. Her children were sick with diarrhea. Someone "reported" her; for what I do not ask. After the Martinique she says that she was in a place I've never heard of called the Brooklyn Arms. Her youngest child, one year old, became much sicker there. City workers finally persuaded her to give up all three kids to foster care. She's living now in a crowded women's shelter where, she says, there are twelve women in a room. She shrieks this information at me on the platform not far from the shrieking trains.

"There's no soap, no hygiene. You go to the desk and ask for toilet paper. You get a single sheet. If you need another sheet you go back down and ask them for some more. I sleep on an army cot. The bathroom's flooded."

Is she telling me the truth? Is she on drugs? Is she unwell? Why did she elect to tell me this? Why do the words come out so fast? I feel unkind to cut her off, but I am frightened by her desperation. I leave her there, pouring out her words into the night.

The nurse in the Martinique says this: "A mother gave birth last week to a baby that weighed just over a pound. She was in her seventh month. Her children rubbed her belly while she cried. I called an ambulance."

The nurse is kind, compassionate, and overwhelmed. "People are fractured by this system. I'm responsible for 500 families, here and in another building. Custody cases. Pregnant women. Newborn children. I can get them into

WIC. I'm snowed . . ." She's on the telephone, buried in papers, talking with women, hearing their questions, trying to come up with answers. There are others like her in the crisis center who create a tiny zone of safety in the larger zone of fear. But twenty-five hardworking nurses like this woman would be scarcely equal to the miseries that flood across her desk out of this factory of pain and tears. . . .

Questions

1. How does Kozol challenge the belief that a "safety net" is in place to protect the welfare of the neediest?
2. Why does Kozol, an opponent of current governmental social welfare policies, focus on the experiences of families?
3. Why do the families depicted in Kozol's account seem incapable of improving their lot in life?

31-7   Proposition 187 (1994)

Anxiety about immigration often occurs during periods of economic stress, and California in the mid-1990s was no exception. As a bulwark of the military-industrial complex, the state might have suffered more than any other from the end of the Cold War. The "peace dividend" seemed to be a combination of high unemployment and taxes. Such was the environment in 1994, when Californians passed Proposition 187. The referendum sought to deny government services to illegal immigrants.

Source: California Secretary of State's Office, *1994 California Voter Information: Proposition 187, Text of Proposed Law.*

SECTION 1. Findings and Declaration.

The People of California find and declare as follows:

That they have suffered and are suffering economic hardship caused by the presence of illegal aliens in this state.

That they have suffered and are suffering personal injury and damage caused by the criminal conduct of illegal aliens in this state.

That they have a right to the protection of their government from any person or persons entering this country unlawfully.

Therefore, the People of California declare their intention to provide for cooperation between their agencies of state and local government with the federal government, and to establish a system of required notification by and between such agencies to prevent illegal aliens in the United States from receiving benefits or public services in the State of California.

SECTION 2. Manufacture, Distribution or Sale of False Citizenship or Resident Alien Documents: Crime and Punishment.

Section 113 is added to the Penal Code, to read:

113. Any person who manufactures, distributes or sells false documents to conceal the true citizenship or resident alien status of another person is guilty of a felony, and shall be punished by imprisonment in the state prison for five years or by a fine of seventy-five thousand dollars ($75,000).

SECTION 3. Use of False Citizenship or Resident Alien Documents: Crime and Punishment.

Section 114 is added to the Penal Code, to read:

114. Any person who uses false documents to conceal his or her true citizenship or resident alien status is guilty of a felony, and shall be punished by imprisonment in the state prison for five years or by a fine of twenty-five thousand dollars ($25,000).

SECTION 4. Law Enforcement Cooperation with INS.

Section 834b is added to the Penal Code, to read:

834b. (a) Every law enforcement agency in California shall fully cooperate with the United States Immigration and

Naturalization Service regarding any person who is arrested if he or she is suspected of being present in the United States in violation of federal immigration laws. . . .

SECTION 5. Exclusion of Illegal Aliens from Public Social Services.

Section 10001.5 is added to the Welfare and Institutions Code, to read:

10001.5. (a) In order to carry out the intention of the People of California that only citizens of the United States and aliens lawfully admitted to the United States may receive the benefits of public social services and to ensure that all persons employed in the providing of those services shall diligently protect public funds from misuse, the provisions of this section are adopted.

(b) A Person shall not receive any public social services to which he or she may be otherwise entitled until the legal status of that person has been verified as one of the following:

(1) A citizen of the United States.

(2) An alien lawfully admitted as a permanent resident.

(3) An alien lawfully admitted for a temporary period of time.

(c) If any public entity in this state to whom a person has applied for public social services determines or reasonably suspects, based upon the information provided to it, that the person is an alien in the United States in violation of federal law, the following procedures shall be followed by the public entity:

(1) The entity shall not provide the person with benefits or services.

(2) The entity shall, in writing, notify the person of his or her apparent illegal immigration status, and that the person must either obtain legal status or leave the United States.

(3) The entity shall also notify the State Director of Social Services, the Attorney General of California, and the United States Immigration and Naturalization Service of the apparent illegal status, and shall provide any additional information that may be requested by any other public entity.

SECTION 6. Exclusion of Illegal Aliens from Publicly Funded Health Care.

Chapter 1.3 (commencing with Section 130) is added to Part 1 of Division 1 of the Health and Safety Code, to read:

Chapter 1.3. Publicly-Funded Health Care Services

130. (a) In order to carry out the intention of the People of California that, excepting emergency medical care as required by federal law, only citizens of the United States

and aliens lawfully admitted to the United States may receive the benefits of publicly-funded health care, and to ensure that all persons employed in the providing of those services shall diligently protect public funds from misuse, the provisions of this section are adopted.

(b) A person shall not receive any health care services from a publicly-funded health care facility, to which he or she is otherwise entitled until the legal status of that person has been verified as one of the following:

(1) A citizen of the United States.

(2) An alien lawfully admitted as a permanent resident.

(3) An alien lawfully admitted for a temporary period of time.

(c) If any publicly-funded health care facility in this state from whom a person seeks health care services, other than emergency medical care as required by federal law, determines or reasonably suspects, based upon the information provided to it, that the person is an alien in the United States in violation of federal law, the following procedures shall be followed by the facility:

(1) The facility shall not provide the person with services.

(2) The facility shall, in writing, notify the person of his or her apparent illegal immigration status, and that the person must either obtain legal status or leave the United States.

(3) The facility shall also notify the State Director of Health Services, the Attorney General of California, and the United States Immigration and Naturalization Service of the apparent illegal status, and shall provide any additional information that may be requested by any other public entity. . . .

SECTION 7. Exclusion of Illegal Aliens from Public Elementary and Secondary Schools.

Section 48215 is added to the Education Code, to read:

48215. (a) No public elementary or secondary school shall admit, or permit the attendance of, any child who is not a citizen of the United States, an alien lawfully admitted as a permanent resident, or a person who is otherwise authorized under federal law to be present in the United States. . . .

SECTION 8. Exclusion of Illegal Aliens from Public Post-secondary Educational Institutions.

Section 66010.8 is added to the Education Code, to read:

66010.8. (a) No public institution of postsecondary education shall admit, enroll, or permit the attendance of any person who is not a citizen of the United States, an alien lawfully admitted as a permanent resident in the United States, or a person who is otherwise authorized under federal law to be present in the United States. . . .

SECTION 9. Attorney General Cooperation with the INS.

Section 53069.65 is added to the Government Code, to read:

53069.65. Whenever the state or a city, or a county, or any other legally authorized local governmental entity with jurisdictional boundaries reports the presence of a person who is suspected of being present in the United States in vi- *olation of federal immigration laws to the Attorney General of California, that report shall be transmitted to the United States Immigration and Naturalization Service. The Attorney General shall be responsible for maintaining ongoing and accurate records of such reports, and shall provide any additional information that may be requested by any other government entity. . . .*

Questions

1. To what extent are these findings and declarations convincing? What, if any, facts are missing?
2. Which provisions seem reasonable, and which seem unfair? Why?

31-8   A Week on Ward 5A (1989)

Ed Wolf

Ed Wolf was a volunteer counselor in a privately funded support group for AIDS patients and their families and friends known as the Shanti Project. His matter-of-fact description of a typical week in San Francisco General Hospital conveys some of the human cost of the AIDS epidemic. (Some terms in this account may be unfamiliar: *PWA* stands for People with AIDS; *ARC* stands for AIDS-Related Complex, a condition in which a patient tests HIV-positive and displays some of the symptoms of AIDS without having the full-blown symptoms of the disease; and *PWARC* stands for people with AIDS-related complex.)

Source: Ed Wolf, "A Week on Ward 5A," *Eclipse,* the Shanti Project, Spring 1989. In Nancy F. McKenzie, ed., *The AIDS Reader: Social, Political, and Ethical Issues* (New York: Penguin, 1991), 528–533. Reprinted by permission of the Shanti Project, San Francisco, CA 94102.

(All client names have been changed to maintain confidentiality.)

Seven days a week, every day of the year, there are Shanti counselors on Ward 5A to offer support to all who come here—patient, visitor and staff alike. We are counselor, advocate, educator, hand-holder, masseur, facilitator, and mediator all rolled into one.

There are currently seven of us, offering our services throughout the hospital. Together we are gay and straight, male and female, HIV-positive and HIV-negative, black, brown, and white. As a team we speak Spanish, French, Greek, and English. Some of us are raising kids, one is a grandparent, some take dance classes, some go kayaking and camping. Some have their own private practice, some are planning to go back to school. We keep journals, we cook, and some of us do volunteer work for other organizations.

Together we work as a team. Two, three, or four of us on the ward at any one time. We know we can lean on each other, learn from each other, and rely on each other. The days here can be very intense, and we use each other to unload, to enliven, to comfort.

SUNDAY

Ann spoke to me this evening about her brother, who is dying of AIDS. Ken was able to speak to her several days ago, but is now incoherent. Ann is from out of town and is filled with feelings of grief and loss. The doctors told her last week that Ken wouldn't live past Friday, and now, two days later, he's still alive. We spoke about the dying process and why it might be taking him so long to die. Is he ready yet? Has he said his goodbyes? Has she said hers?

She spoke tenderly, of how her brother's impending death has reopened for her an old wound, the death of her infant daughter several years ago.

We discussed together her ability to deal, and to cope, and to find ways to carry the immeasurable sadness she is experiencing.

Earlier this evening I spoke with a young man who had recently been diagnosed with pneumocystis. He described how his "journey" with AIDS was progressing, of his KS [Karposi's sarcoma] diagnosis last year, of the day he was first told he was HIV-positive. He asked me if I had taken the HIV-antibody test. I told him that I had, and that I had tested negative. I told him one of my first reactions had been "why me?" He told me he had the same reaction to his test results. Together we explored the randomness of things and the importance of separating judgment from the events that come into our lives. Before I left his room, he said he had recently stopped asking "why me?" "Nowadays," he said, "I ask 'what's next'"?

MONDAY

This morning, as I get ready to go to work, I wonder if Ken and his sister will still be at the hospital. Has he died during the night?

As Shanti counselors at San Francisco General Hospital, we are privileged to come into people's lives while they are experiencing extraordinary circumstances. We may become involved with a patient and his or her loved ones for several days or several weeks; often there's only enough time for a single visit. We are constantly opening up to new people and letting go of familiar faces. During my two days off-duty this past week, half of the ward was discharged and an equal number of patients were admitted. We often have feelings of incompleteness, of unfinishedness, with the rapid comings and goings of the patients and the visitors with whom we work. I am always reminded that life on the ward magnifies the larger picture—how we are all constantly walking in and out of each other's lives.

Every morning at 11 o'clock the Shanti counselors, social workers, and the charge nurse come together for report. Together we go over every patient with AIDS or ARC in the hospital and assess their varying needs. These patients are going home today; someone's being transferred to 5A from the Intensive Care unit. Someone's mom has come to see him for the first time since his diagnosis—can one of the Shanti counselors be sure to check in on them later today? Ken is still alive; his sister needs help finding a chaplain.

There are three Shanti counselors on duty today and we divide and prioritize the patients to be seen. I will follow up on Ken and his sister, but first there's someone a nurse wants me to talk with.

He's not a patient here. He's sitting in a chair in the corridor, a young black man who has just recently arrived in San Francisco. Jim tells me he has little money and needs a place to stay, says that he is HIV-positive, feels weak and tired all the time, and is having trouble keeping his food

down. He has not been diagnosed with either AIDS or ARC—can I help him?

I explain how without an actual AIDS/ARC diagnosis he cannot receive the services he's requesting through Shanti. I suggest some of the emergency shelters in San Francisco, some of the food lines, where to go for food stamps and general assistance. I encourage him to make an appointment at Ward 86, the outpatient clinic here at SFGH. Jim tells me the horrific story of his past year, of his enlistment in the military, of the standard blood tests they now require, and the shock he felt when he was rejected by the local board because he was HIV-positive.

Shunned by family and friends, he has come to San Francisco because "I heard how they help people here." As we part in the hallway, I am filled with a sense of helplessness and concern.

As I go in to see Ken, I am struck by the sound of his breathing. It is loud and labored, and the oxygen coming from the wall fills the room with a harsh hissing. He lies on his side; he cannot speak. His sister is not in the room, but his lover, Bill, is at his bedside, looking very tired and very sad. We talk about the death of his father and the similarity of the pain of losing a dad and a lover, the pain of losing anyone we love, of being left behind. I gently touch Ken's arm as Bill tells me a little about their seven years together; a special trip one summer, a mountain they had climbed. He has been wondering if Ken can still hear. As we talk he decides he probably can, and that these bittersweet sharings of their life together are like a memorial service. We wonder what it would be like to hear one's own memorial service, and decide it would be okay to know that you are missed, that you had left many loving memories behind. The sadness in the room swells up and as Bill cries, I gently move my hand and place it on the heart of the man in the bed.

As the day draws to a close, I check in with one of my coworkers. He listens as I describe the sadness that I felt in Ken's room, and how difficult it was for me to let the young HIV-positive man walk away down the hall, unable to do more for him. He tells me of an especially good connection he made with one of his patients, and how happy he is that another went home today.

TUESDAY

As I enter through the main lobby of the hospital this morning, I find myself wondering if Ken is still alive.

The day began in a rush as I encounter Ken's sister in the hallway. Ann has already extended her stay here in San Francisco for two days—she must get to the bus station and return home to her children and other responsibilities. But Ken is still alive. How can she leave him? We move into an empty room on 5A and sit together. Her eyes are swollen from all the crying she has done in the last few days. She says to me, "I must go and I can't go."

At first I am struck with the seeming impossibility of this dilemma. I experience a growing sense of my own inadequacies in trying to help in some way. I also know that this woman has her own answers and that she doesn't need me to tell her what to do. She sought me out to be a supportive presence, to be a sounding board perhaps, to discuss and explore her own options. As she tells me of her situation at home, it becomes increasingly clear that she must return to her children as soon as possible.

I ask her if she can tell Ken what she is telling me, how much it hurts to be leaving him now. We begin to talk about permission and the startling similarities between her need for permission to go home and Ken's need for permission to die in his own time, on his own terms.

She decides that she can do this. I ask her if she'd like me to come with her to Ken's room, and she softly says, "Thank you, no." As we return to the hallway, I give her a parting hug and know that I will not be seeing her again.

The tone of this interaction seems to reverberate through the rest of the day. I have lunch in the hospital cafeteria with one of the chaplains, and as he tells me about a recent weekend retreat he attended, I know that several floors above us Ken and his sister are gently parting.

Later in the day I meet with Alfredo, who is here visiting his brother Ramon. Ramon has pneumocystis, is from Mexico, and is far from his family. I listen as Alfredo speaks of life in Mexico City and the AIDS epidemic there, and for just a moment I see Ann looking out a bus window, heading home.

WEDNESDAY

The first half of every Wednesday is devoted to getting together with the other counselors. We alternate, from week to week, between support group and case presentation. This morning one of the counselors discussed an especially difficult series of interactions he had with a patient who was having problems with the nursing staff. We then had a business meeting and a short support group. Through these first four hours of the day, I repeatedly thought of Ken.

Wednesday is also discharge planning day, when many outside AIDS service agencies come together with the in-house staff to discuss the discharge plans for all PWAs and PWARCs currently in the hospital. It is here that I find out that Ken is still alive. The medical team reports that his "deep pain reflex" is gone and he is now comatose.

When the meeting ends, I go to see Ken. There is no one visiting. The room is filled with balloons, flowers, and get-well cards. Someone has placed a small teddy bear on the pillow near his head. Ken seems peaceful. His breaths are very short and far between as I place my hand on his chest and breathe with him for a while. I tell of some of my interactions with his sister and his lover, and that they have

told me they will be all right. I tell him it's okay to let go. I become aware of my own wish that his suffering will end soon, today, now. I am aware then of the necessity of my having to let go, of respecting the mystery of how and when any of us die.

The day is quickly coming to a close as I leave Ken's room and go to see one more patient. He was here a year ago and I remember him well. I have pulled our old chart on him and read through some of the previous conversations we had.

As I enter his room, I perceive how much Marvin has changed since we last met. His body is extremely thin; he is too weak to stand on his own. But the biggest change is in his mental status. He has been diagnosed with HIV dementia and is here awaiting placement.

Five of the sixteen patients on 5A this week are here because of dementia and the placement problems it creates. Because of the level of difficulty experienced in trying to connect with someone who is demented and the anguish it can cause the visitor, demented patients often spend a lot of time alone.

Today as I sit with Marvin, I find myself working hard to connect in any possible way. I ask about the television show he is watching; the lunch he has just been fed. I read all his get-well cards out loud and ask him about each of the senders.

Because his responses are minimal, I feel I have not connected. As I begin to leave his vacant eyes follow me and he asks, "You're not leaving yet, are you?"

I sit down and tell him I can stay a little longer. I am touched and moved by his question. I sit with him in silence now as he gazes blankly at the television, and I hold his hand. I assumed that my presence had not been felt and, in doing so, had almost missed the connection we were so clearly sharing.

THURSDAY

Today is my last day on the ward before a three-day weekend, my birthday weekend as a matter of fact, and I have made plans to go to the mountains. After 2 1/2 years on 5A, I have found it very important to take care of myself, especially on my days off. As I get ready for work, I think of the full week I've already had.

When I get to the hospital I see that Ken is still alive.

Morning report runs longer than usual because the census is very large.

All 16 beds on 5A are full and another 16 patients are on other wards. There are 14 patients with pneumocystis, many newly diagnosed. There will be a lot for the weekend counselors to do.

I go and say good-bye to Ken. A friend is visiting, and so is Ken's Shanti volunteer. Ken's breathing seems very faint, too delicate and weak to be keeping him alive. As I leave, I know I will not see him again. . . .

Questions

1. How does Wolf react to the pain he describes in Ward 5A? Does he seem involved with or detached from it?
2. What is the significance of his repeated thoughts of the patient named Ken?
3. What does the scrapbook reveal about the scale of the epidemic?

31-9   Anger of the 60s Takes Root in the Violent Right (1995)

Peter Applebome

The bombing of the Alfred P. Murrah Federal Building in Oklahoma City, Oklahoma, on April 19, 1995, brought to the fore concerns over anger with government, terrorism, armed private militias, and the like. The bombing occurred on the second anniversary of the controversial Federal Bureau of Investigation assault on the Branch Davidian Compound, near Waco, Texas. Peter Applebome, writing soon after the Oklahoma City bombing, provided perspective on the anger and violence of the 1960s and the 1990s.

Source: Peter Applebome, "Anger of the 60's Takes Root in the Violent Right," *New York Times*, May 7, 1995.

On the surface, few eras would seem to have less in common than the tie-dyed turmoil of the 1960's and the edgy, armed-to-the-teeth anger of the 1990's.

But many historians who track the nation's mood swings say they detect an odd and striking inversion in which the anger, discontent and distrust of authority that erupted on the left in the 60's have become the signatures of the right 30 years later.

The notion is not that the rumblings of the old left have been transformed into today's right-wing agenda or that the sporadic and largely inept violence of the 60's is mirrored in the horror of Oklahoma City. Instead, there is a sense that Vietnam War–era turmoil tore a hole in the post–World War II social fabric, and that although it was the left that opened the rift, it is the right that has driven a truck through it.

Indeed, many experts say that to understand today's right-wing anger it is necessary first to make sense of the tumult three decades ago.

"What happened in the 1960's was that the Government was successfully 'delegitimated,'" said Gerald Marwell, a sociologist at the University of Wisconsin who studies American political movements. "We had a period from World War II through the 1950's where the Government was seen as having rescued the nation from the Depression and successfully prosecuted the war, and then we were told in the 1960's that the emperor has no clothes and people shouldn't accept what they're told."

Historians acknowledge the limitations of comparing different eras. Many say any understanding of the passions and paranoias of the 90's must begin with the recognition that the nation's history is rife with bitter rifts and conspiratorial vapors. Indeed many historians find the relative, though hardly universal, degree of national consensus that marked the 1940's and 1950's to be the exception in American life rather than the norm.

"This is the most anti-state country in the Western world, probably on earth," said Michael Kazin, a historian at the American University in Washington and the author of "The Populist Persuasion: An American History" (Basic Books, 1994). "Throughout American history groups on the right and the left have seen the Federal Government as an alien force inimical to their interests, so you see this sort of thing over and over again."

What happened in the 60's, he wrote, is that the left "only discredited the old order without laying the political foundation for a new one."

Many scholars of American history have long acknowledged what the historian Richard Hofstadter called "the paranoid style in American politics," a tendency to view the world in terms of dense conspiracies that in various eras have centered on groups as diverse as Masons, Catholics, Jews, international bankers, Mormons, foreign gold traders, and the Bavarian illuminati.

To cite a more recent example, Senator Joseph McCarthy, during his campaign against Communist infiltration in 1951, described "a great conspiracy, a conspiracy on a scale so immense as to dwarf any previous such venture in the history of man," to undermine the United States Government from within.

The Soviet threat is gone, but conspiracy theories spring up with numbing frequency, exemplified most recently by the claim that the attack on the Federal Building in Oklahoma City was a Government plot to discredit the paramilitary groups that call themselves militias.

Even the details of the supposed conspiracies faxed and E-mailed among right-wing groups from Montana to Michigan are eerily similar to those alleged by the John Birch Society and other right-wing groups of the late 50's and early 60's.

Today there are claims that United Nations troops have taken over Yellowstone National Park and that sinister military vehicles identified with an inverted V are prowling rural Michigan. Three decades ago allegations included reports that 35,000 Chinese Communist troops were poised on the Mexico border ready to invade California, that the Army had been turned over to a Russian colonel in the United Nations and that an Army guerrilla warfare exercise in Georgia called Water Moccasin III was actually a United Nations operation prepared to take over the United States.

Still, the suspicions of today are hardly limited to the right.

Not far from Professor Marwell's office, Karlton Armstrong runs an outdoor juice stand on the University of Wisconsin Library Mall. Twenty-five years ago, Mr. Armstrong, then an antiwar activist, was one of the campus radicals who planted a fertilizer and fuel oil bomb at Sterling Hall, home of the university's Physics Department and of the oil bomb's target, the Army-Math Research Center. The explosion killed a graduate student, in one of the most infamous episodes of the era.

Mr. Armstrong, who served 7 years of his 14-year sentence for murder and arson in the bombing, is now 48 and has no sympathy for today's far-right fringe groups. He now views the Sterling Hall bombing as a betrayal of his own beliefs, even though the bomb was detonated with the intention that the building would be unoccupied.

But when asked about the sense of frustration and alienation abroad in the land, he said: "These people are rapidly becoming dispossessed, like they are losing what little power they had. I totally empathize with that sense of alienation."

And just as it was alienated hippies who preceded ring-wing groups in retreating to the woods to create communes free from the corrupting influences of the Government and urban life, the sensibilities of the 60's have left many with the same kind of distrust of Government now so endemic on the right.

"I don't consider myself a paranoid by any means, but I've been given plenty of reasons to fear my Government," said Susan Spangenberg of Madison, who is active in the

Wisconsin Alliance for the Medicalization of Cannabis, which seeks to make marijuana more readily available for medical uses. "The militias have the same civil rights as I do, as we all do, and if the Government can intrude on civil rights on the right, it could just as easily do it for someone who gets labeled a left-wing liberal."

To many on the left, there is something utterly perverse in any effort to link their philosophy with the armed extremist right of the 1990's. Many say the incessant anti-Government rhetoric of the right says more about the present than the turmoil of the 60's.

"Don't insult me," said Paul Soglin, the former antiwar activist who is now Mayor of Madison. "That's the thinking of very stupid people who need an elementary education in civics and political science."

He and others said the left of the 1960's was rooted in nonviolence and sought to prod the Government toward what it saw as appropriate action in ending the war in Vietnam and enforcing civil rights laws, while the extremist right is steeped in weapons and violence and opposed to almost all Government activism. Those on the right say a more telling difference is that the 1960's were also steeped in a contempt for traditional values.

But many experts see important points of convergence. Professor Marwell of Wisconsin and Professor Kazin of the American University see a libertarian strain from the 1960's that, intentionally or not, became more of a legacy than leftist politics. To the 60's left it might have meant the right to smoke pot, while to the 90's right it might mean the right to own guns, but the instinct is similar.

"My favorite button from the anti-draft S.D.S. was, 'Not With My Life You Don't,'" Mr. Kazin, a former antiwar activist himself, said, referring to the radical group Students for a Democratic Society. "It could be the slogan of the right wing today, a don't-tread-on-me, get-off-my-back kind of statement."

Others say that rather than the politics of the student movement of the 1960's and early 70's, it was the various upheavals and shocks of the era—from the Kennedy assassination to the Vietnam War to Watergate to unresolved issues of racial and sexual equality—that produced fault lines in American life that have never been bridged.

"There's a culture war, particularly the part of it that has to do with gender, that's still playing out today, whether it's overtly talked about or not," said Emily Rosenberg, a history professor at Macalester College in St. Paul, Minn.

Professors Kazin and Rosenberg both said a more compelling historical parallel than the 1960's may be the 1890's, when structural changes in the economy, anger at immigrants and the widespread sense that communities and individuals were losing economic control produced an angry populist movement and widespread social turmoil. Ms. Rosenberg noted that the last decade of a century has almost invariably produced a sense of momentous change, whether manifested as dread or as anticipation. She said she suspected the discord of the 90's could have further to run.

But the ripples of the 1890's are merely historical. The reverberations of the 1960's are still very real. Professor Marwell said one to watch would be whether the violence of Oklahoma City would discredit the right in the 1990's

in the way that the Sterling Hall bombing short-circuited the left in the 1960's. He said he thought it would.

"The bombing here in Madison almost ended the antiwar movement all by itself," he said. "The whole right may not be at fault for Oklahoma City, but I think they're underestimating the price they're going to pay."

Questions

1. What fundamental questions about the recent and contemporary United States does the article address?
2. Which statements cited in the article most impress you? Which least impress you?

Questions for Further Thought

1. Do the public opinion polls of 1990, 1995, and 1999 (Document 30-3) shed light on the "uncertain times" of the 1990s?
2. Compare and contrast the essays of George Gilder (Document 31-5) and Jonathan Kozol (Document 31-6).
3. How do the violence of the 1960s and early 1970s and the violence of the 1990s compare with one another—and with patterns of violence in earlier periods of American history?

Restructuring the Domestic Order: Public Life, 1992–1996

The presidential campaign of 1992 was marked by ironies. Earlier, the public standing of President George Bush during the crisis and war in the Persian Gulf led some Democrats to shy away from seeking their party's nomination to run against him. Not Bill Clinton, who went on to win that nomination. Then, the economic recession that contributed to Bush's vulnerability in 1992 gave way to an economic upswing by Election Day, too late to help Bush, but just in time to help Clinton.

The campaign also revealed the dissatisfaction of many with the two major parties and their nominees. Even though the mercurial H. Ross Perot, who ran for president as an independent, temporarily withdrew from the race during the summer, he ultimately polled 19 percent of the nationwide popular vote in this, his first try for any elective office. Perot's showing was the strongest of any third-party presidential candidate since Theodore Roosevelt (a former president and arguably the most popular public figure of his time) in 1912. Perhaps because Perot motivated some who otherwise would have abstained from voting, the voter turnout rate increased to its highest level since 1972.

President Clinton compiled a mixed record during his first term. He achieved limited victories and suffered one resounding defeat—on national health care reform—in Congress. Some of the president's appointments were noteworthy, but he backed away from other nominees when they ran into fire. During 1994, Kenneth Starr was named as independent counsel charged with investigating allegations regarding Bill and Hillary Clinton's prepresidential dealings in Arkansas and "related matters," soon to include alleged White House scandals, and, much later, the president's sexual affair with Monica Lewinsky. Also during 1994, the Republicans captured both houses of Congress. Divided control of government and highly "toxic politics" turned Washington, D.C., into a political cockpit. The Republicans' remarkable successes of 1994 did not translate into a presidential election victory two years later: Clinton easily beat back the challenge of Senate Majority Leader Bob Dole, while Ross Perot slid to 8 percent of the national vote and voter turnout fell to its lowest level since 1924. Republican strength in the House has ebbed slightly since 1994, but the GOP has now won majorities in three consecutive congresses for the first time since the 1920s (see text pp. 1030–1038, 1042–1045).

Document 31-10 offers the Republicans' "Contract with America." Document 31-11, a portion of President Clinton's State of the Union Address, includes his response.

31-10   The Contract with America (1994)

In 1994, the Republicans captured the House of Representatives (for the first time since 1952) and the Senate (control of which they had lost in 1986). *The Contract with America* had provided the Republicans with a single campaign tract for midterm House races across the nation. That representatives Newt Gingrich (Georgia) and Dick Armey (Texas) were prominent among the drafters of the contract reflected the southernization of the Republicans' congressional delegation. As late as 1960, Republicans held no Senate seats and only 7 of the 106 House seats from the eleven former Confederate states. In 1998, Republicans occupied 15 of the 22 seats in the Senate and 71 of the 125 in the House from these states. Indeed, the GOP now controls the House of Representatives *because* of its southern majority.

Gingrich and Armey, already prominent in the House, rose to power following the GOP victory—Gingrich as speaker, Armey as majority leader. Gingrich did not enjoy success for long. Early in 1999, he resigned from the House.

Source: Republican National Committee, *Contract with America: The Bold Plan by Representative Newt Gingrich, Representative Dick Armey, and the House Republicans to Change the Nation,* Ed Gillespie and Bob Schellhas, eds. (New York: Times Books, 1994), 1–11. Reprinted with the express permission of the Republican National Committee.

THE CONTRACT'S CORE PRINCIPLES

The Contract with America is rooted in 3 core principles:

Accountability

The government is too big and spends too much, and Congress and unelected bureaucrats have become so entrenched to be unresponsive to the public they are supposed to serve. The GOP contract restores accountability to government.

Responsibility

Bigger government and more federal programs usurp personal responsibility from families and individuals. The GOP contract restores a proper balance between government and personal responsibility.

Opportunity

The American Dream is out of the reach of too many families because of burdensome government regulations and harsh tax laws. The GOP contract restores the American dream.

THE CONTRACT

As Republican Members of the House of Representatives and as citizens seeking to join that body we propose not just to change its policies, but even more important, to restore the bonds of trust between the people and their elected representatives.

That is why, in this era of official evasion and posturing, we offer instead a detailed agenda for national renewal, a written commitment with no fine print.

This year's election offers the chance, after four decades of one-party control, to bring to the House a new majority that will transform the way Congress works. That historic change would be the end of government that is too big, too intrusive, and too easy with the public's money. It can be the beginning of a Congress that respects the values and shares the faith of the American family.

Like Lincoln, our first Republican president, we intend to act "with firmness in the right, as God gives us to see the right." To restore accountability to Congress. To end its cycle of scandal and disgrace. To make us all proud again of the way free people govern themselves.

On the first day of the 104th Congress, the new Republican majority will immediately pass the following major reforms, aimed at restoring the faith and trust of the American people in their government:

- FIRST, require all laws that apply to the rest of the country also apply equally to the Congress;

- SECOND, select a major, independent auditing firm to conduct a comprehensive audit of Congress for waste, fraud or abuse;

- THIRD, cut the number of House committees, and cut committee staff by one-third;

- FOURTH, limit the terms of all committee chairs;

- FIFTH, ban the casting of proxy votes in committee;

- SIXTH, require committee meetings to be open to the public;

- SEVENTH, require a three-fifths majority vote to pass a tax increase;

- EIGHTH, guarantee an honest accounting of our Federal Budget by implementing zero base-line budgeting.

Thereafter, within the first 100 days of the 104th Congress, we shall bring to the House Floor the following bills, each to be given full and open debate, each to be given a clear and fair vote and each to be immediately available this day for public inspection and scrutiny.

1. THE FISCAL RESPONSIBILITY ACT
A balanced budget/tax limitation amendment and a legislative line-item veto to restore fiscal responsibility to an out-of-control Congress, requiring them to live under the same budget constraints as families and businesses.

2. THE TAKING BACK OUR STREETS ACT
An anti-crime package including stronger truth-in-sentencing, "good faith" exclusionary rule exemptions, effective death penalty provisions, and cuts in social spending from this summer's "crime" bill to fund prison construction and additional law enforcement to keep people secure in their neighborhoods and kids safe in their schools.

3. THE PERSONAL RESPONSIBILITY ACT
Discourage illegitimacy and teen pregnancy by prohibiting welfare to minor mothers and denying increased AFDC for additional children while on welfare, cut spending for welfare programs, and enact a tough two-years-and-out provision with work requirements to promote individual responsibility.

4. THE FAMILY REINFORCEMENT ACT
Child support enforcement, tax incentives for adoption, strengthening rights of parents in their children's education, stronger child pornography laws, and an elderly dependent care tax credit to reinforce the central role of families in American society.

5. THE AMERICAN DREAM RESTORATION ACT
A $500 per child tax credit, begin repeal of the marriage tax penalty, and creation of American Dream Savings Accounts to provide middle class tax relief.

6. THE NATIONAL SECURITY RESTORATION ACT
No U. S. troops under U.N. command and restoration of the essential parts of our national security funding to strengthen our national defense and maintain our credibility around the world.

7. THE SENIOR CITIZENS FAIRNESS ACT
Raise the Social Security earnings limit which currently forces seniors out of the work force, repeal the 1993 tax hikes on Social Security benefits and provide tax incentives for private long-term care insurance to let Older Americans keep more of what they have earned over the years.

8. THE JOB CREATION AND WAGE ENHANCEMENT ACT
Small business incentives, capital gains cut and indexation, neutral cost recovery, risk assessment/cost-benefit analysis, strengthening the Regulatory Flexibility Act and unfunded mandate reform to create jobs and raise worker wages.

9. THE COMMON SENSE LEGAL REFORM ACT
"Loser pays" laws, reasonable limits on punitive damages and reform of product liability laws to stem the endless tide of litigation.

10. THE CITIZEN LEGISLATURE ACT
A first-ever vote on term limits to replace career politicians with citizen legislators.

Further, we will instruct the House Budget Committee to report to the floor and we will work to enact additional budget savings, beyond the budget cuts specifically included in the legislation described above, to ensure that the Federal budget deficit will be less than it would have been without the enactment of these bills.

Respecting the judgment of our fellow citizens as we seek their mandate for reform, we hereby pledge our names to this Contract with America.

Questions

1. How does *The Contract with America* demonize government?
2. What public sentiments does the contract capitalize on? How did those sentiments arise?
3. What are the advantages and dangers of using this kind of election strategy?

31-11   State of the Union Address (1996)

Bill Clinton

Congressional Republicans, in the majority in 1995 and 1996, soon provided President Clinton (b. 1946) with opportunities to counterattack. The temporary shutting down of the federal government during an impasse over the federal budget was blamed on the GOP. Meanwhile, Clinton moved toward the center on issues like reducing budget deficits and the national debt and reforming welfare. In doing so, he at once frustrated congressional Republicans, who felt that he was stealing their thunder, and unsettled congressional Democrats, who felt that he was abandoning their party's traditional positions. Less than ten months after delivering the State of the Union Address excerpted here, Clinton won reelection over Bob Dole (Kansas), the Senate Majority Leader

Source: Congressional Record–House of Representatives, 104th Congress, 2nd session, 142, no. 8 (January 23, 1996), H768–H769.

My duty tonight is to report on the State of the Union, not the state of our government but of our American community, and to set forth our responsibilities, in the words of our Founders, to "form a more perfect union."

The State of the Union is strong. Our economy is the healthiest it has been in three decades. We have the lowest combined rates of unemployment and inflation in 27 years. We have created nearly 8 million new jobs, over a million of them in basic industries like construction and automobiles. America is selling more cars than Japan for the first time since the 1970s, and for three years in a row we have had a record number of new businesses started in our country.

Our leadership in the world is also strong, bringing hope for new peace. And perhaps most important, we are gaining ground and restoring our fundamental values. The crime rate, the welfare and food stamp rolls, the poverty rate and the teem pregnancy rate are all down. And as they go down, prospects for America's future go up.

We must answer here three fundamental questions: First, how do we make the American dream of opportunity for all a reality for all Americans who are willing to work for it? Second, how do we preserve our old and enduring values as we move into the future? And third, how do we meet these challenges together as one America?

We know big government does not have all the answers. We know there's not a program for every problem.

We know and we have worked to give the American people a smaller, less bureaucratic government in Washington. And we have to give the American people one that lives within its means. The era of big government is over. But we cannot go back to the time when our citizens were left to fend for themselves. Instead, we must go forward as one America, one nation, working together to meet the challenges we face together. Self-reliance and teamwork are not opposing virtues. We must have both.

I believe our new, smaller government must work in an old-fashioned American way, together with all of our citizens through State and local governments, in the workplace, in religious, charitable and civic associations. Our goal must be to enable all our people to make the most of their own lives, with stronger families, more educational opportunities, economic security, safer streets, a cleaner environment and a safer world.

To improve the state of our union, we must ask more of ourselves. We must expect more of each other and we must face our challenges together.

Here in this place our responsibility begins with balancing the budget in a way that is fair to all Americans. There is now broad bipartisan agreement that permanent deficit spending must come to an end.

I compliment the Republican leadership and their membership for the energy and determination you have brought to this task of balancing the budget. And I thank the Democrats for passing the largest deficit reduction plan in history in 1993, which has already cut the deficit nearly in half in three years.

Since 1993, we have all begun to see the benefits of deficit reduction. Lower interest rates have made it easier for businesses to borrow and to invest and to create new jobs. Lower interest rates have brought down the cost of home mortgages, car payments and credit card rates to ordinary citizens. Now it is time to finish the job and balance the budget.

Though differences remain among us which are significant, the combined total of the proposed savings that are common to both plans is more than enough, using the numbers from your Congressional Budget Office, to balance the budget in 7 years and to provide a modest tax cut. These cuts are real. They will require sacrifice from everyone. But these cuts do not undermine our fundamental obligations to our parents, our children and our future by endangering Medicare or Medicaid or education or the environment or by raising taxes on working families.

I have said before, and let me say again, many good ideas have come out of our negotiations. I have learned a lot about the way both Republicans and Democrats view the debate before us. I have learned a lot about the good ideas that each side has that we could all embrace. We ought to resolve our remaining differences.

I am willing to work to resolve them. I am ready to meet tomorrow. But I ask you to consider that we should at least enact the savings that both plans have in common and give the American people their balanced budget, a tax cut, lower interest rates, and a brighter future. We should do that now and make permanent deficits yesterday's legacy.

Now it is time for us to look also to the challenges of today and tomorrow, beyond the burdens of yesterday. The challenges are significant. But our Nation was built on challenges. America was built on challenges, not promises. And when we work together to meet them we never fail. That is the key to a more perfect union. Our individual dreams must be realized by our common efforts.

Questions

1. How do Clinton's rhetoric and proposals suggest that he is seeking the political center?
2. In what ways does Clinton seek to establish that there are differences between even moderate Democrats and Republicans?

Questions for Further Thought

1. Compare and contrast the tone and proposals of congressional Republicans (Document 31-10) and President Clinton (Document 31-11).
2. Does the 1995 Gallup poll (Document 30-3) shed any light on the political landscape during Clinton's first term?